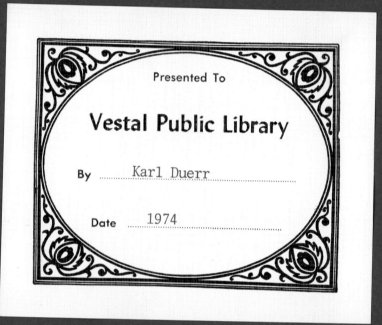

Grandma Moses

Grandma

OTTO KALLIR

HARRY N. ABRAMS, INC.
PUBLISHERS, NEW YORK

Moses

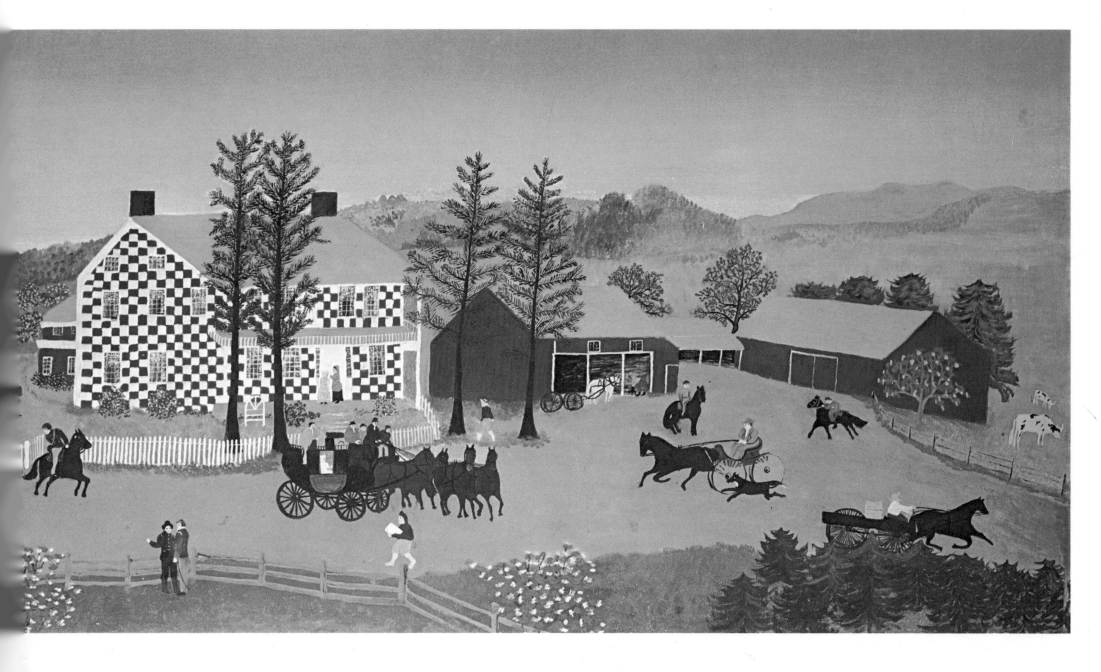

ON THE TITLE PAGE: *The Old Checkered House.* 1944 (Catalogue number 367)

Library of Congress Cataloging in Publication Data

Kallir, Otto
 Grandma Moses.

 Bibliography: p.
 1. Moses, Anna Mary (Robertson) 1860–1961.
 I. Moses, Anna Mary (Robertson) 1860–1961.
 ND237.M78K32   759.13   73–6930
 ISBN 0–8109–0166–8

PAUL ANBINDER, *Executive Editor*
MARGARET L. KAPLAN, *Editor*
NAI Y. CHANG, *Book Design*
ANN GOEDDE, *Index*

Library of Congress Catalogue Card Number: 73–6930
Text copyright © 1973 by Otto Kallir
Illustrations copyright © 1973 by Grandma Moses Properties, Inc.,
24 West 57th Street, New York, N.Y. 10019

The excerpts from Grandma Moses's *My Life's History,* 1952, edited
by Otto Kallir, are reprinted by permission of Harper & Row, New York.
The excerpts from Edward R. Murrow's interview with Grandma Moses
on "See It Now" are quoted by permission of CBS News

To

HILDEGARD BACHERT

*whose intimate acquaintance with Grandma Moses and
her art and whose longtime collaboration with me have
made this book possible*

Special thanks go to

NANCY GARNIEZ

*for her invaluable contribution, particularly in preparing
the Catalogue of the Works and the Index*

and to

MY WIFE

*for the great help and understanding she has
given me throughout*

CONTENTS

PART II *Growing Recognition*

PART III *Fame*

PART IV *The Range of Grandma Moses's Art*

Documentary Section

Author's Note

In this book an attempt is made to present and examine the art and personality of Anna Mary Robertson Moses. The author's close contact with the painter over a period of more than twenty years and his intimate knowledge of her work have made this undertaking possible. Since the first New York show all documentary material pertaining to the artist and her work has been preserved, thus forming the basis for a systematic study. Pertinent information previously published in books and articles has also been included. Nearly sixteen hundred pictures, created between the years 1918 and 1961, are catalogued, and most of them reproduced. The more awkward attempts, the sketchy small pictures, the incomplete works are shown along with the refined, finished paintings, for all are of interest in forming a valid impression of Grandma Moses's oeuvre.

It will be seen how the compelling urge of an old woman never to remain idle after having worked hard all her life, but to make something pretty and pleasing for her own enjoyment and the pleasure of those around her developed into an all-inclusive, consciously planned creative activity.

The art and personality of Grandma Moses are inseparable. Her paintings remain for everyone to see and judge for himself. Her personality, however, can best be evoked by her own writings—letters and autobiographical notes—and through first-hand reports of those who met her personally. Particular emphasis has therefore been laid upon the evidence of people who were able not only to describe her appearance and behavior, but also to find and uncover the roots of her vitality and strength.

I

BEGINNINGS

"I, Anna Mary Robertson…"

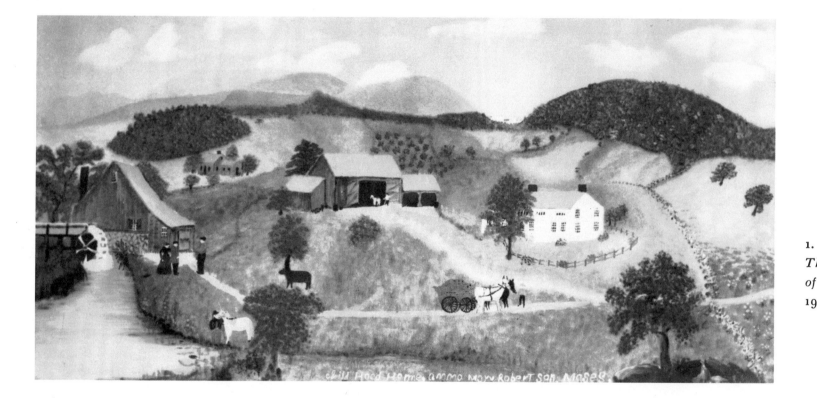

1.

*The Childhood Home
of Anna Mary Robertson Moses.
1942. 14 x 28". Cat. 160*

I anna Mary Robertson, was born
back in the green meadows and wild
woods, on a Farm in washington, Co.
In the year of 1860, Sept 7.
of Scotch Frish Paternal ancestry.
    Here I spent the first ten years
of my life with mother Father
and Sisters and Brothers,
those were my Happy days, free
from care or worry, helping

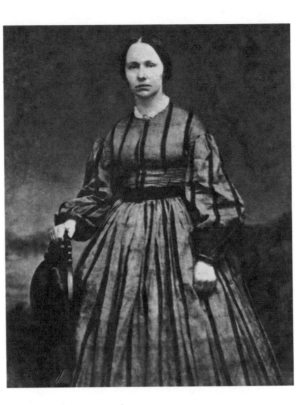

2.
Anna Mary's mother,
Mary Shannahan Robertson

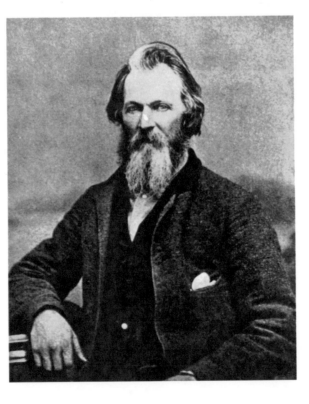

3.
Anna Mary's father,
Russell King Robertson

mother, rocking Sisters creadle
taking sewing lessons from
mother sporting with my Brothers.
making rafts to float over the
mill pond,
Roam the wild woods gathering
Flowers, and building air castles,
1870,
now came the hard years,
Schooling was in those days in
the country three months in
summer three in winter,
little girls did not go to school
much in winter, owing to the
cold, and not warm enough
clothing, there for my School days
were limited,
altho I was Kept busy helping at
Home, and the neighbors,
when twelve years of age I left
Home to earn my own living as
then was called a hired girl,
This was a grand education
for me, in cooking, House
Keeping, in moralizeing and
mingleing with the out side world,

I went to live with a Family by
the name of mrs & mr Thomas
whitesides, they were lovely
people, while well along in
years,
 I was cared for by them as a
child of thair one,
 Presbyterians by creed,
one of my duties was to drive the
Horse "old black joe" to church for
them on Sunday mornings; and
place boquets on the Pulpit in
the churish, always remember the
text,
living with the whitesides
for three years, caring for
mrs whiteside who was an invalid
and died,
 Then I kept house for mr white
side for a year till his nephue
and wife could come and take
care of the Farm, and Him,
 I was very proud in those days,
could get up such fine dinners,
for his Friends who came from far off
to see Him,

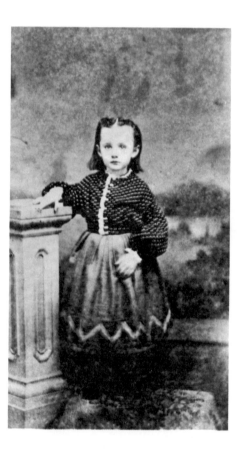

4. Anna Mary at the age
of four

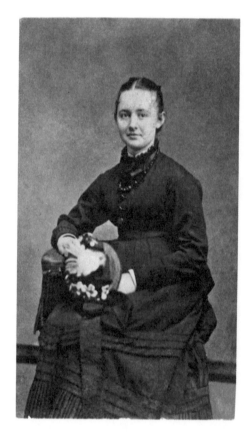

5. Anna Mary at the age
of fifteen

21

when the minster came and I
could bring out the fine linen and
the china tea set, and the heavy
Silver, then with hot bisqwits
home mad butter and Haney, with Home
cured dryed beef, I was proud,
    But I some times now, think they
came for eats more than to see Him,
    Then mr whiteside died,
    and I drifted away from that
neighborhood,

                    1880.
Still woorking as a hired girl, and
care ing for th sick
    Those were busy days,

In the Fall of 1887,
nov 9 I married Thomas Solmonmoses,
a Farmer by occupation,
we left on our wedding trip for
north carolina- to take charge of
of a Horse ranch in north carolina,
But we never reached thire,
we were Kidnaped at Staunton, v,a.

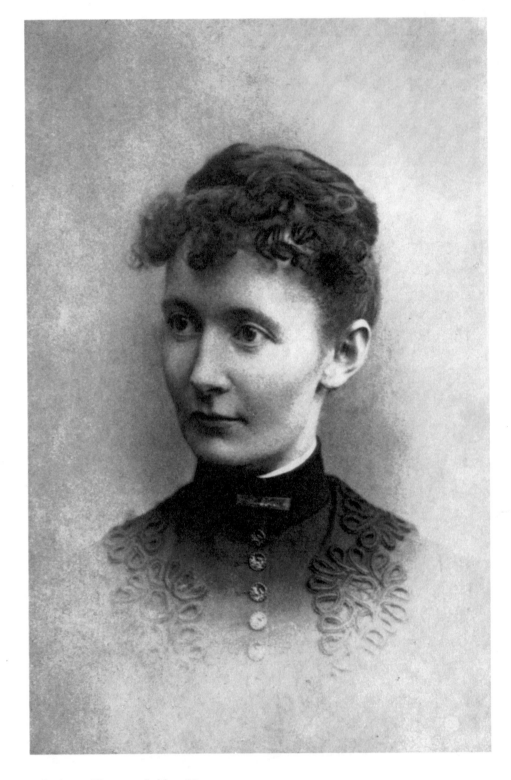

6. Anna Mary as a bride, 1887

22

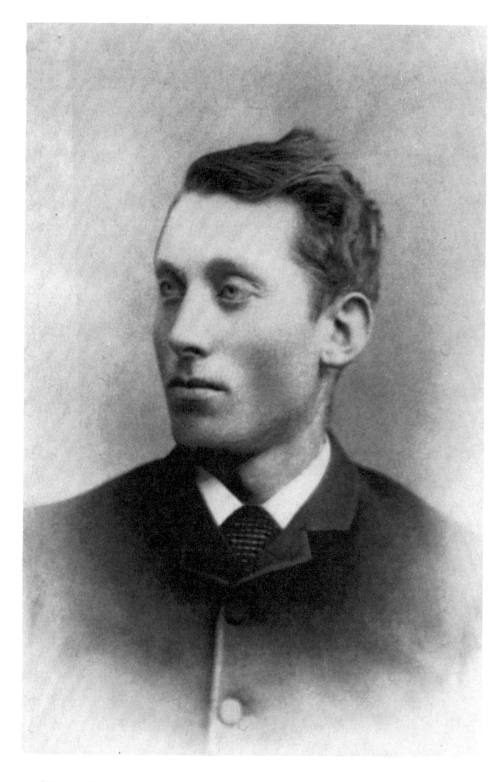

7. Thomas Salmon Moses, the bridegroom, 1887

or I should say over perswaded,
to go no father south
So we hired a Farm near Staunton
verginia for a year to see if we
would like the south,
and the people there were over
anxious for northeners or westners to
come in and build up the State,
They were in a way helpless
since the colared help had been
taking from them,
we remained on this Farm one
year, then moved farther down
the valley on to a Six hundred
acre dairy Farm,
Here I commenced to make Butter
in pound prints and ship it to
the white Sulphur Springs, W, va,
I also made potato chips, which was
a novelty in tho days,
this we continued for severel years.
Here our ten children were Born,
and there I left five little graves
in that beautifull Shenadoah valley,

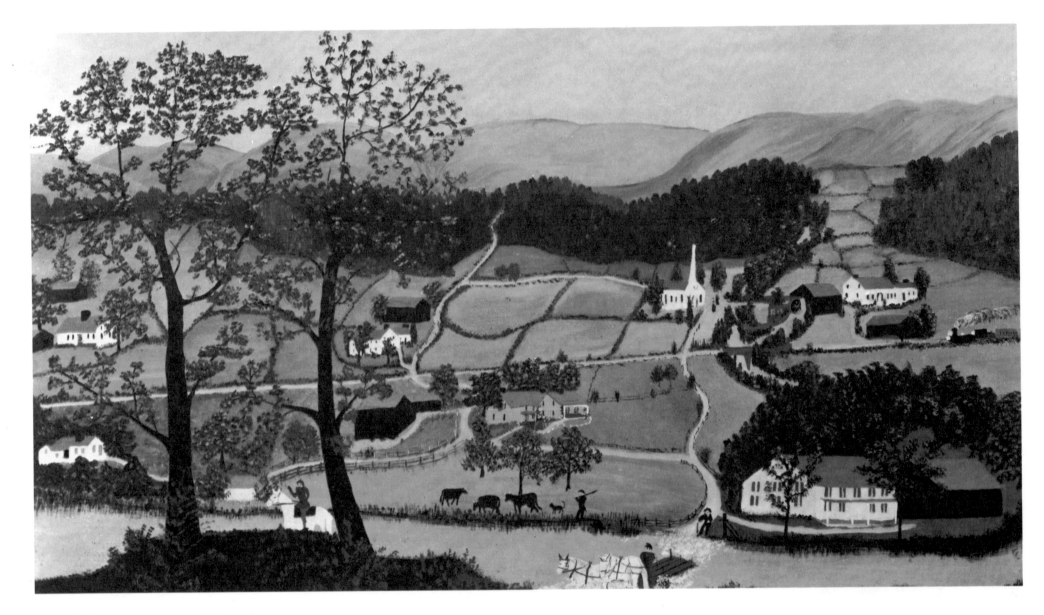

8. *Belvedere.* 1946. 16¾ x 27″. Cat. 646

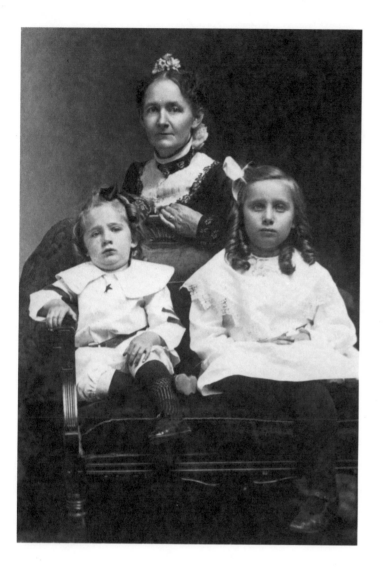

9. Anna Mary Moses with two of her youngest children, Hugh and Anna, c. 1904

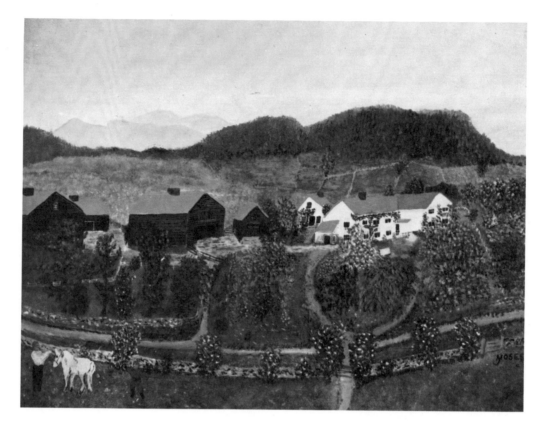

10.
Grandma Moses's Home, 1925. 1952.
18 x 24". Cat. 1022

Coming to new york State Dec 15, 1905, with our five children to educate and put on thire one footing,
we bought a Farm and went in to the dairy business selling milk, and doing genarel Farm woork,
Here my oldest daughter married and left Home, Here my two oldest sons bought a Farm and struck out for them selves,
Here Jan 15, 1927. my Husband died, my yongest son and wife taking over the Farm,
Leaving me unoccupied, I had to do somthing, so took up painting pictures in worsted, then in oil,

25

This autobiographical sketch was written by Anna Mary Robertson Moses in 1945. It is an outline of the years up to her husband's death in 1927, that is to say, the time preceding her career as a painter.

The astonishing story of Anna Mary Robertson Moses's development has aroused the interest of the American and the European public for more than three decades. As "Grandma Moses" she has become known all over the world. Wherever her pictures were shown, they met with exceptional response—in the United States, in Western Europe, and in Russia. People everywhere have been impressed by her paintings, which so vividly depict life in rural America, the changing seasons, the daily chores and pleasures of farm life, of which the artist was a part for close to a century.

Early Attempts

ALTHOUGH ANNA MARY MOSES STARTED PAINTING SERIOUSLY only in her old age, one cannot set an exact date for the beginning of her artistic activities, because, almost without being aware of it, she had from early childhood on done painting and decorating in her home. "When I was quite small," she once wrote,

> my father would get me and my brothers white paper by the sheet, it was used for newspapers. He liked to see us draw pictures, it was a penny a sheet and it lasted longer than candy. My oldest brother loved to draw steam engines, the next brother went in for animals, but as for myself I had to have pictures and the gayer the better. I would draw the picture, then color it with grape juice or berries, anything that was red and pretty in my way of thinking.

But the inclination for painting, shared also by her father (plate 11) and other members of the family, was always subordinated to the duties and obligations of everyday life. Anna Mary did not have the leisure to develop her talent, either in her early youth, as a young housewife in Virginia, or after the family returned to the State of New York in 1905. But her artistic urge often expressed itself in a desire to decorate objects of daily use around the house. Two examples have been preserved: a fireboard and a table (plates 12–17). She wrote about the fireboard:

> One time I was papering the parlor, and I ran short of paper for the fireboard. So I took a piece of paper and pasted it over the board, and I painted it a solid color first, then I painted two large trees on each side of it, like butternut trees. And back in it I did a little scene of a lake and painted it a yellow color, really bright, as though you were looking off into the sun light. In the front, to fill in that space, I brought in big bushes. I daubed it all on with the brush I painted the floor with. It run on three or four years, and we re-papered the parlor and papered over the picture. When

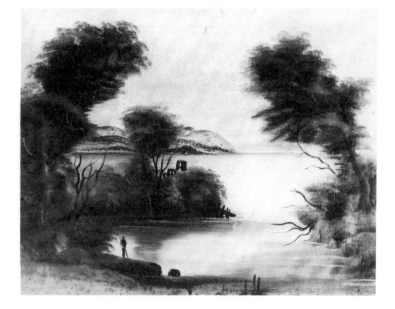

11. Painting by Russell King Robertson, Anna Mary's father

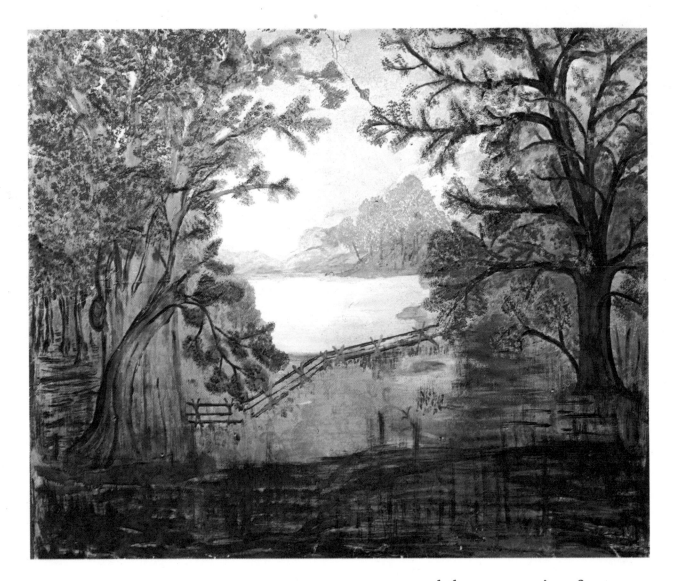

12. *Fireboard.* 1918. 32¼ x 38¾″. Cat. 1

we re-papered the room again a few years ago, we took the paper off the fireboard, but the colors had faded somewhat. That was my first large picture.

About the table she wrote:

> I have an old tip-up table, on which I paint. My aunt gave it to me thirty-five years ago, it was built for a log cabin. . . . The table was made of pine planks, under the top between the standards there was a box in which they kept their pewter dishes. . . . Then one day my aunt sent it to me for a flower stand; I have painted scenes on the standards and covered the top with postal cards, and now use it for my easel.

The painting on the fireboard is dated May 10, 1918, and those on the table were done about 1920. It is interesting to note that these first attempts already show a painterly technique rarely found in works of self-taught artists.

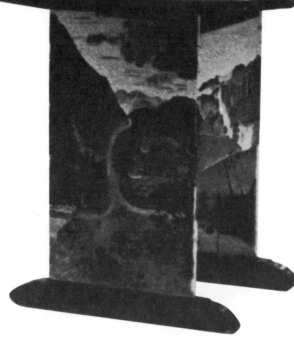

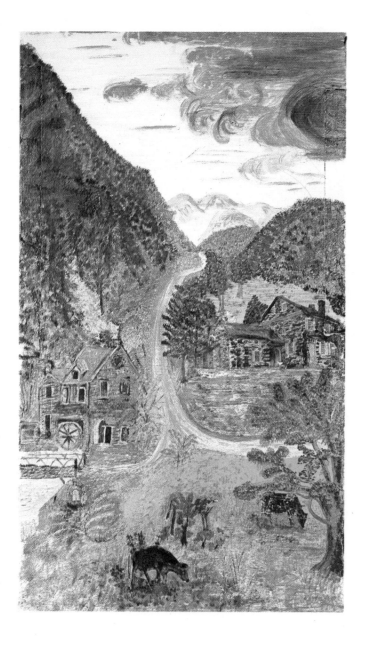

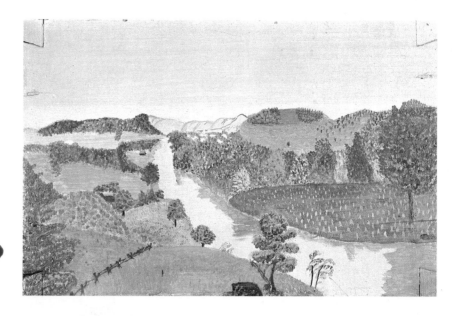

13—17. "Tip-up" table and details.
c. 1920. Cat. 2

THE OLD Mc. MURRY
DINING TABLE
MADE FOR THE
OLD LOG HOUSE
IN 1762.

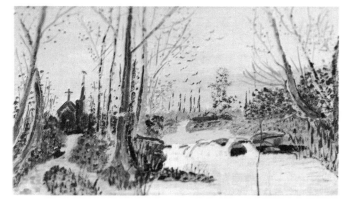

Louis Caldor Discovers Anna Mary Moses

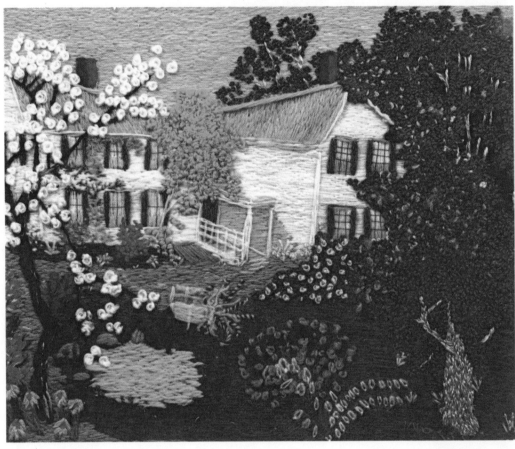

18.
My Old Homestead.
Worsted, 9¼ x 11".
Cat. 20W

ONLY IN HER LATE SEVENTIES, when housework became too strenuous for her, did Mrs. Moses start to make pictures that were meant to be framed and hung on the wall. Dorothy Moses, wife of her youngest son, Hugh, who shared the home with her, tells about her mother-in-law's artistic efforts:

> While she was at her daughter's [Anna Moses's] home in Bennington [in the 1930s] she started making yarn pictures, which were very beautiful—as she designed her own pictures and they were done in lovely bright colors. . . . She gave away many and also sold some. . . .
>
> When her sister Celestia called on us one day and saw these

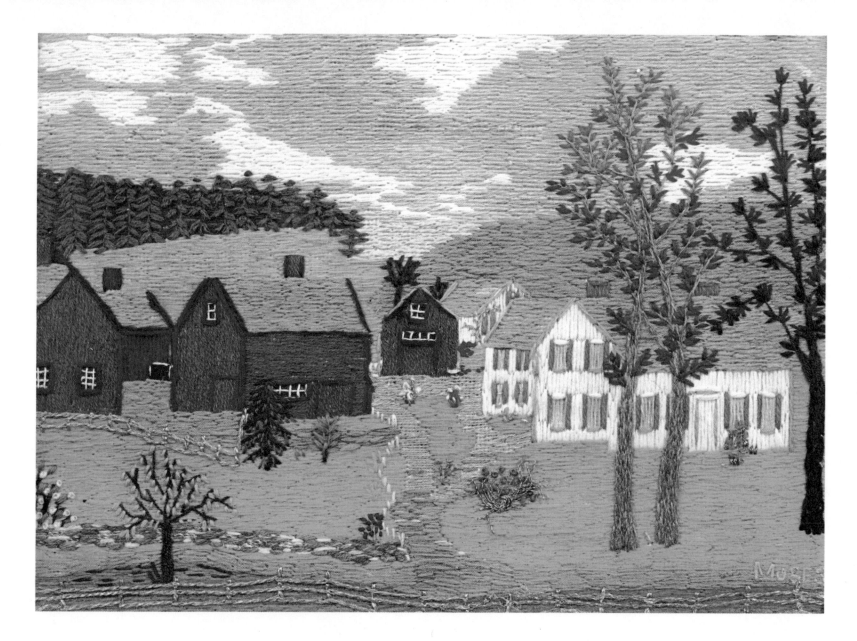

19.
Mt. Nebo on the Hill.
Worsted, 10 x 14".
Cat. 34W

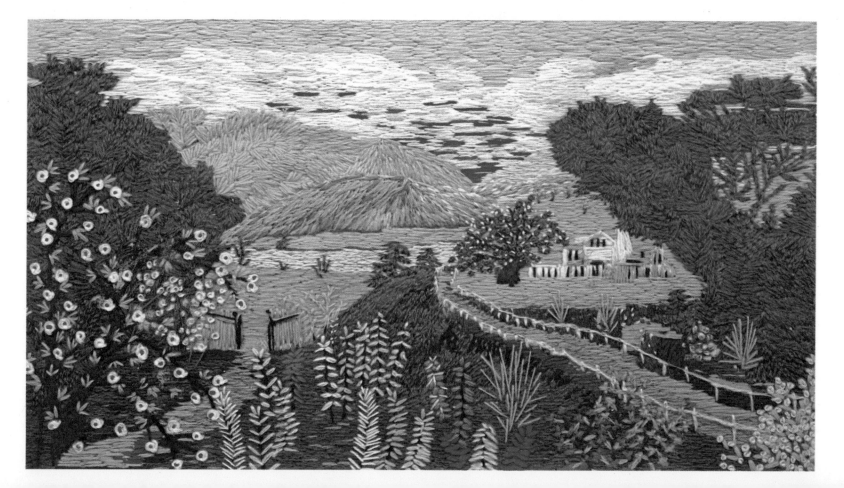

20.
The Roadside Garden.
Worsted, 9¼ x 16¼".
Cat. 17W

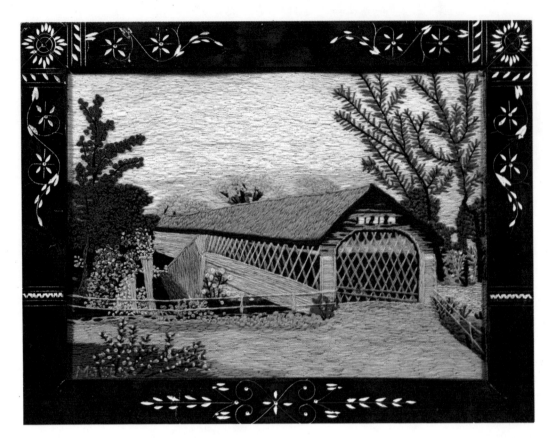

pictures, she told her she should try to paint some—she "knew" she could as long as she could make such beautiful ones in yarn. For her first picture Grandma used a piece of canvas which had been used for mending a threshing machine cover, and some old house paint. We told her it was very good and to try and paint more—which she did. . . .

Some of the first she painted, Hugh and I took along with some yarn pictures down to the Woman's Exchange in Thomas's Drugstore in Hoosick Falls where they were put on display in the window. This is where the ball started rolling for Grandma. One day [Easter 1938] Louis Caldor, an art collector from New York who was passing through Hoosick Falls, stopped at the drugstore and was very much amazed at the wonderful collection. He went in and asked all about the pictures and who the artist was and where she lived. Later he came here and met Grandma. He asked her to paint some pictures for him, which she did, and which he brought to New York. . . .

Louis Caldor made many efforts to interest people in these pictures. He was turned down everywhere. Now and then he was told that the works he showed were quite "nice" but unimportant, and not in line with contemporary art; above all, nobody wanted to waste time and money in promoting an unknown artist who was close to eighty. Caldor had almost given up trying when in 1939 he chanced to hear of plans for a show, "Contemporary Unknown American Painters," to be held in the Members' Rooms of the Museum of Modern Art in New York City. Its organizer was Sidney Janis, a member of the museum's Advisory Board. Caldor went to see Janis, who selected three paintings by Anna Mary Moses.

The exhibition took place from October 18 to November 18, 1939. The three paintings, listed as loans from Louis J. Caldor, were *Home, In the Maple Sugar Days* (plate 22), and *First Auto* (correct title: *The First*

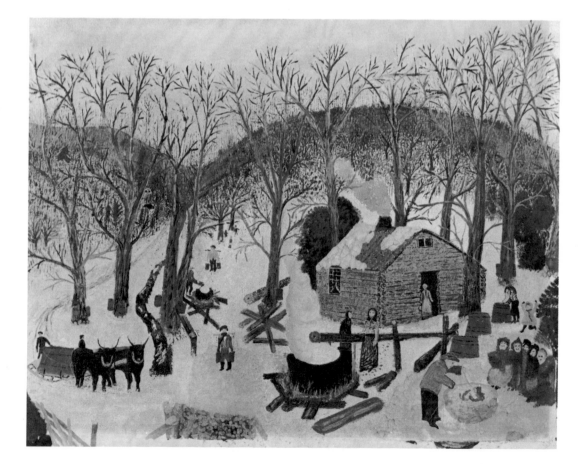

22.
In the Maple Sugar Days.
1939 or earlier. 15¼ x 19¼".
Cat. 43

Automobile; plate 41). Aside from the works by Mrs. Moses, the show contained pictures by seventeen other artists: Patsy Santo, Samuel Koch, Ella Southworth, Gregorio Valdes, Morris Hirshfield, Cleo Crawford, Byron Randall, R. J. Bump, Rev. W. S. Mulholland, Hazel Knapp, Fred Fredericks, W. Samet, Alex Fletcher, Bernard Frouchtben, Flora Lewis, Gene Frances, and Dorothy B. Leake.

When the exhibition closed, Louis Caldor's loans were returned to him. About half a year went by after this initial success without Caldor being able to achieve anything more for the artist. However, he remained in touch with her, encouraged her to continue painting, and sent her painting material of more professional quality than she had used in the beginning. He then heard of a new gallery that had recently opened, whose owner was said to be interested in folk art. So Mr. Caldor came to see me for the first time.

First One-Man Show

In the fall of the year 1939 I had opened a branch of my Paris Galerie St. Etienne on Fifty-seventh Street in New York City. In Paris, as well as previously in Vienna, I had mainly concentrated on twentieth-century Expressionist art, but I also had a special liking for folk art and "primitive" painting. I was therefore interested when Caldor offered to show me American folk art that he had collected on business trips through New York State.

Among other objects, he brought pictures which he said had been done by an old woman who lived on a farm in Eagle Bridge, New York, about thirty miles from Albany. These were small pictures, some of them painted, others embroidered in yarn. Their artistic quality varied greatly; some had doubtless been copied from prints and illustrations, but quite a few were very good.

One painting in particular commanded my attention. It was a sugaring-off scene (plate 23). In a snow-covered clearing, people were busy collecting sap from the trees and carrying it in large buckets to a kettle over a fire, children were running around or waiting for the maple candy being prepared by the figure at the left, a sleigh piled with wood for the fire was being unloaded, a team of oxen was approaching—it all added up to a well-balanced scene of animated activity. But what struck me more than this was the way in which the artist had handled the landscape. While the figures were done in a rather clumsy fashion, the landscape was painted with astonishing mastery. Though she had never heard of any rules of perspective, Mrs. Moses had achieved an impression of depth, passing from the tall bare trees in the foreground, the huts and large, clearly outlined groups, to hazy tones in the distance, where smoke rising from the chimney mingled with the bluish gray of an early morning in winter, creating an atmosphere of compelling truth and closeness to nature.

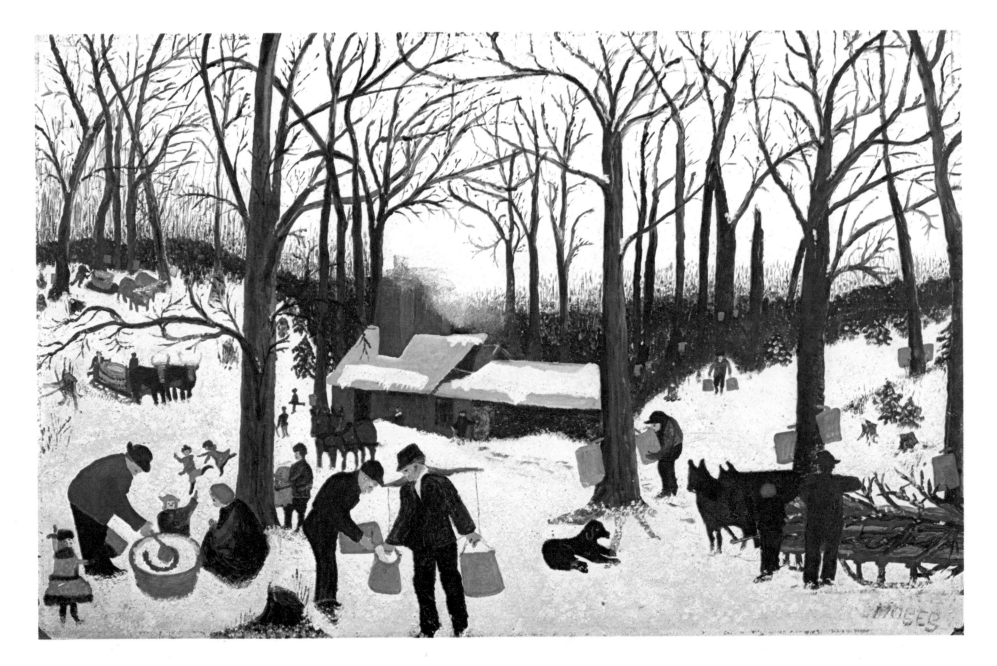

23. *Bringing in the Maple Sugar.* 1939 or earlier. 14 x 23". Cat. 42

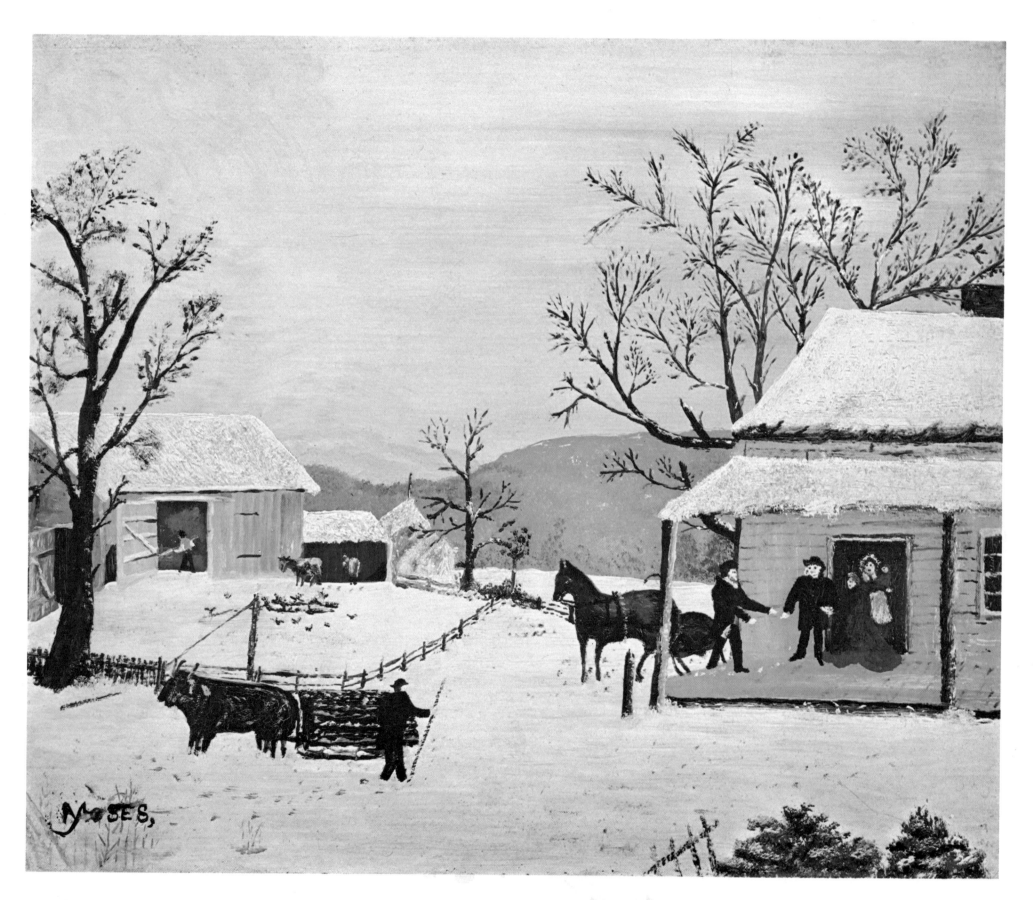

24. *Home for Thanksgiving.* 1940 or earlier. 10½ x 12½". Cat. 34

I asked to see more, and Caldor said that he kept a number of pictures in his car, which was parked in Riverdale, a half-hour's drive away. They could only be inspected after 8 P.M., since he worked all day. Eager to get a more definite impression, I agreed to this rather strange way of presenting an artist. We drove out and, the parking lot being unlit, Caldor showed me the pictures by the beam of a flashlight; they were piled up on the back seat of his car.

Some of the pictures had great artistic quality, others were uninteresting attempts or obvious copies. There were also more yarn pictures, which did not seem to fit in with the rest. Only later did I realize that Mrs. Moses, in her desire to create pictorial scenes, had at first embroidered pictures. The term "picture" meant the same to her whether the scene was embroidered or painted. Still, the positive impression of what I had seen predominated, and I told Mr. Caldor that I would be willing to give the artist a one-man show at my gallery, on condition that the choice of works be left to me.

After the pictures had been assembled at the gallery I was able to examine them at leisure. All were in old frames, either from the Moses attic or from those of neighbors. The size of a painting was determined by the available frame. Most were on cardboard or Masonite, a few on canvas. Grandma Moses later described her way of preparing a picture:

> well I like masonite tempered presd wood. the harder the better,
> I prefer it to canvas, as it will last longer,
> I go over this with linseed oil, then with three coats of flat white paint, now I saw it to fit the Frames.
> A picture with out a fraim is like a woman without a dress. In my way of thinking.

The artist had written a title on the back of almost every picture, usually in pencil. Some, like *Where the Muddy Missouri Rolls,* also bore lengthier inscriptions:

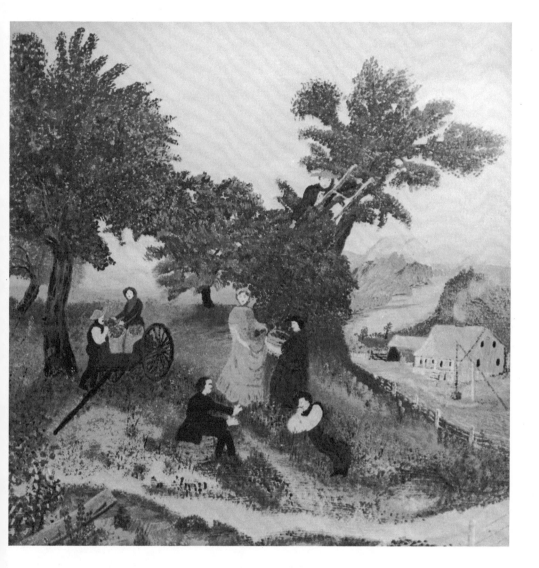

25. *Apple Pickers.* 1940 or earlier. 13 x 12½". Cat. 5

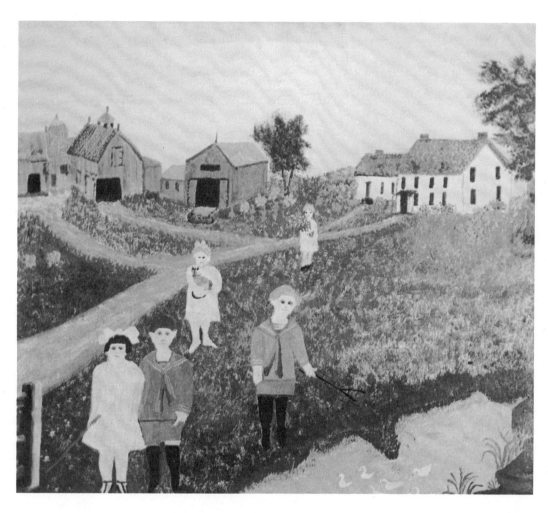

26. *All Dressed Up for Sunday.* 1940 or earlier. 11¼ x 13". Cat. 3

WHERE THE MUDDY MISSOURI ROLL[S] ON TO THE SEA

WHERE MAN IS A MAN, IF HE IS WILLING TO TOIL,

AND THE HUMBLE MAY GATHER THE FRUIT OF THE SOIL.

This was obviously quoted from a poem that had influenced her choice of subject.

Many of the titles Grandma Moses gave her pictures, then and later, indicate what she considered to be the essential content of a painting. In this first show there were such titles as *Apple Pickers, All Dressed Up for Sunday* (plates 25, 26), and *The Old Churchyard on Sunday Morning*. Each bespoke the artist's involvement with a given theme. One felt that what she tried to express was always a personal experience, what she depicted was always something she had been part of. Whether the picture was of a washday or a Sunday, it was *her* washday, *her* Sunday.

Even when she took material for a picture from a print, magazine, or newspaper, she strove not merely to produce a copy, but to transform the subject into something of her own. For example, she gave her personal touch to a Currier and Ives print, *Home for Thanksgiving;* in color and atmosphere her painting (plate 24, listed as *A Winter Visit* in the first exhibition) far surpasses the print. She had created something fresh and new.

The exhibition opened on October 9, 1940, under the unassuming title "What a Farm Wife Painted." It contained thirty-four small-size pictures, with the exception of two or three that exceeded twenty inches in width. There was no catalogue, but the visitors were given a mimeographed list of the paintings on exhibit.

The general reaction was surprisingly favorable. The simplicity and candor of the pictures, the artist's ability to express in a clear, uncomplicated way what she had to say, established immediate contact between work and beholder. This impression was strongly echoed by

40

THE GALERIE ST ETIENNE

REQUESTS THE HONOR OF YOUR COMPANY

AT THE PREVIEW OF THE EXHIBITION

WHAT A FARM WIFE PAINTED

WORKS BY MRS. ANNA MARY MOSES

BORN GREENWICH, N. Y., 1860

ON WEDNESDAY, OCTOBER 9TH, 1940

FROM NINE TO ELEVEN O'CLOCK IN THE EVENING

46 WEST 57TH STREET   NEW YORK CITY

27. Invitation to the first one-man show

PAINTINGS BY ANNA MARY (ROBERTSON) MOSES

Born Greenwich, N.Y., 1860

1. Down in the Glen
2. Where the Muddy Missouri Rolls
3. The Old Red Sleigh
4. Farm Along the River
5. Village in Winter
6. The Covered Wagon
* 7. Backyard at Home
8. Starry Eyes
* 9. All Dressed Up for Sunday
10. Guardian Angel
11. The Hills of New England
12. On the Bridge
13. The Burning at Troy, New York
14. Home from the Honeymoon
*15. Bringing in the Hay
16. The Old House at the Bend of the Road
17. A Fire in the Woods
18. The Old Sugar House Among the Trees
19. Bringing in the Sugar
20. Shenandoah Valley (South Branch)
*21. Home
22. In the Maple Sugar Days
23. The Old Automobile
24. Shenandoah Valley, 1861 (News of the Battle)
25. Cambridge in the Valley
26. Turkey in the Straw
27. A - On the Road to Greenwich
    B - The Waterfalls
28. A Winter Visit
29. The Old Churchyard on Sunday Morning
30. Apple Pickers
31. At the Old Well
32. The Village by the Brookside
33. September Hills (Loaned by Miss Ona Robertson)
*34. Mt. Nebo-on-the Hill (Loaned by Louis J. Caldor)

*Scenes from Mrs. Moses' own farm

GALERIE ST. ETIENNE
46 West 57th Street
New York City

28. List of the paintings exhibited

many newspaper notices; a leaflet containing some of the first reviews was printed at the time and distributed.

We had invited the artist to the opening of the show but she declined, saying she did not need to come since she knew all the pictures anyway.

The name "Grandma Moses" appeared for the first time in an article in the *New York Herald Tribune* of October 8, 1940, which read: "Mrs. Anna Mary Robertson Moses, known to the countryside around Greenwich, New York, as Grandma Moses, began painting three years ago, when she was approaching 80." From then on Anna Mary Robertson Moses became known as Grandma Moses.

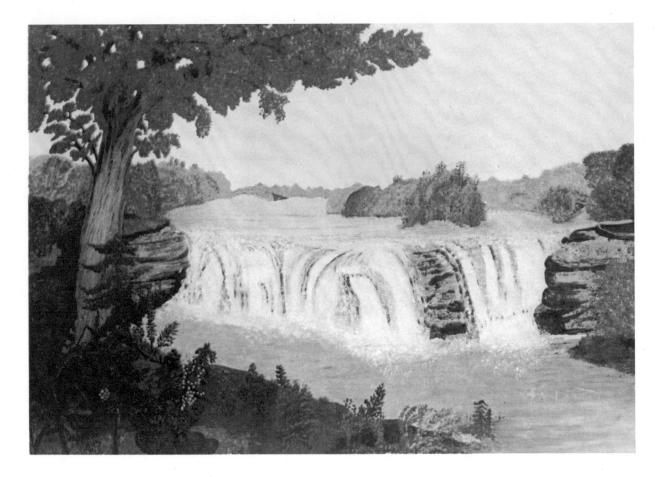

29.
The Waterfalls.
1940 or earlier. 14 x 22".
Cat. 72

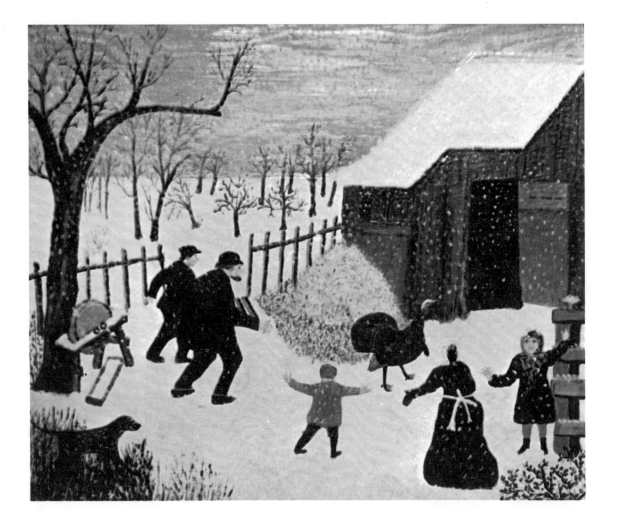

30.
Turkey in the Straw.
1940 or earlier. 11½ x 13½".
Cat. 63

42

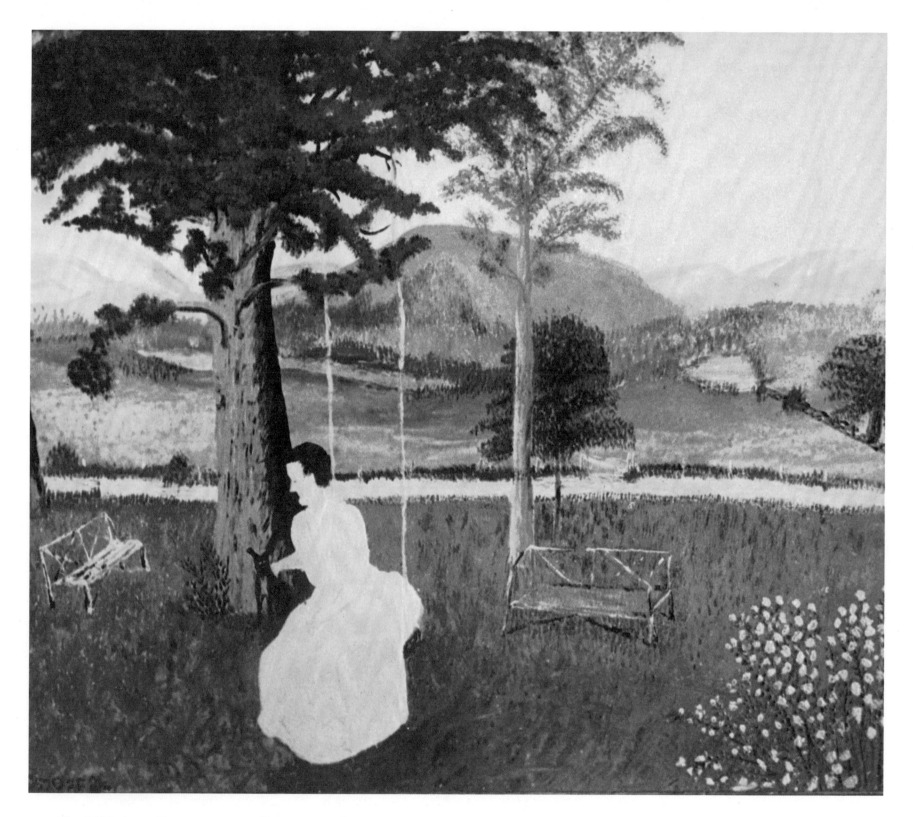

31. *The Old Swing at Home.* 1940 or earlier. 10 x 12″. Cat. 59

Grandma Moses Comes To New York

SHORTLY BEFORE THE END OF THE SHOW AT THE GALERIE ST. ETIENNE, Gimbels Department Store requested the pictures for an exhibition to be held in the store's auditorium for a Thanksgiving Festival on November 14. The exhibition hall was larger than my gallery, so a number of paintings not previously shown, as well as some "worsted" pictures, were added.

Grandma Moses was invited to the festivity, and this time she accepted. She arrived by train, accompanied by Mrs. Carolyn Thomas, the owner of the drugstore in Hoosick Falls where Louis Caldor had found her pictures.

Since 1905, when she had passed through on her way back from Virginia to her native village, she had been in New York only once or twice. The immense changes that had altered every facet of the city were bewildering. After having spent almost eighty years of her life in the country, seldom meeting anyone beyond the realm of her daily life and experience, Grandma Moses was suddenly confronted with several hundred strangers who had come to see her.

Louis Caldor had advised her to take along some homemade bread and preserves. She followed his suggestion and expected to talk about her products, remembering that only a few years earlier, when she had exhibited both her preserves and some paintings at the Cambridge Fair, she had won a prize for her jams while her pictures remained unnoticed.

But now people had come to Gimbels to see her pictures and to meet the artist. She later described her entrance into the hall:

> Someone handed me one of those little old ladies' bouquets and then someone pinned something on me, it felt just like a black bug, but I couldn't look down. It was a microphone, I was on the air. They took me by surprise, I was in from the back woods, and I

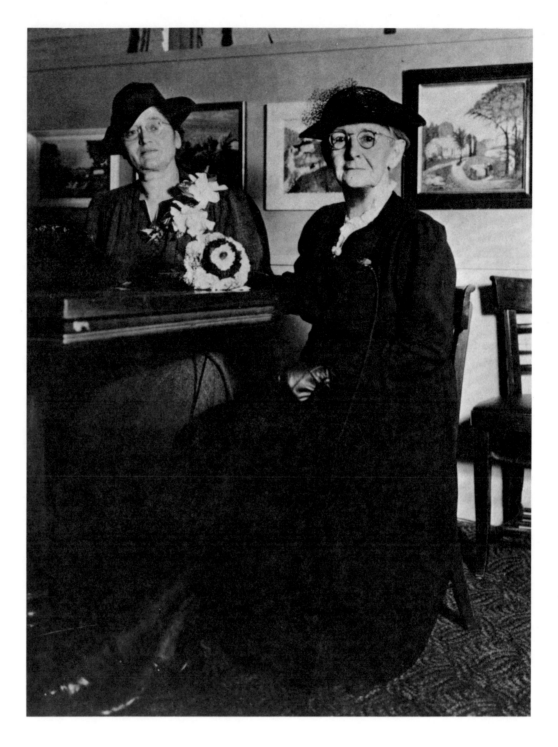

didn't know what they were up to. So while I thought I was talking to Mrs. Thomas, I spoke to four hundred people at the Thanksgiving Forum in Gimbels' auditorium.

Afterwards, oh it was shake hands, shake, shake, shake—and I wouldn't even know the people now. My, my, it was rush here, rush there, rush every other place—but I suppose I shouldn't say that, because those people did go to so much bother to make my visit pleasant.

The following day Grandma Moses, accompanied by Mrs. Thomas, came to see me at my gallery. It was our first meeting. As far as I remember, we talked about her trip and her impressions of the city, hardly at all about her painting. Shortly afterward she returned to Eagle Bridge. At that time I did not in the least expect that within a few years a close cooperation in all matters concerning her artistic work would develop between us, as well as a warm and enduring personal friendship.

The public's reaction to the larger display of Grandma Moses's pictures at Gimbels was an interesting indication of future trends. While many judged them with kindly condescension, there were also those who, even though favoring contemporary modern art forms, recognized her work as a valid artistic expression.

In January 1941, the exhibition was sent to the Whyte Gallery in Washington, D.C., where it was received with even more favorable comment than in New York. The artist had come to the attention of the public.

New York State Prize

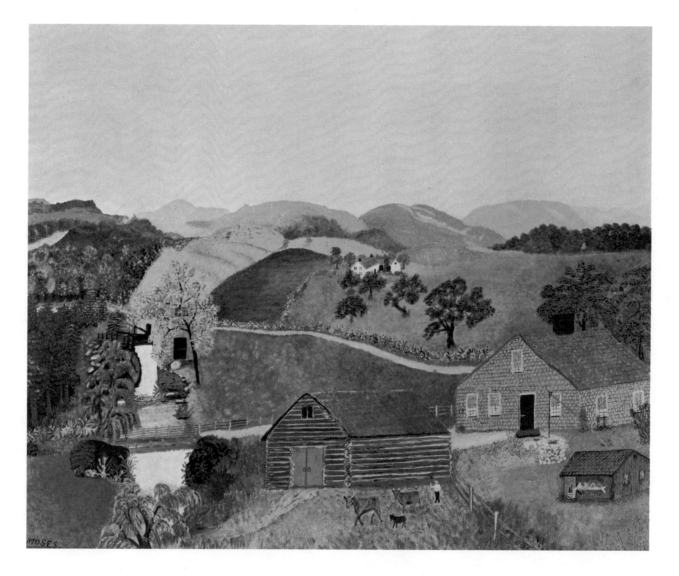

33.
Old Oaken Bucket.
1941. 25 x 31". Cat. 94

DURING THE INTERVAL BETWEEN HER FIRST SHOW IN NEW YORK in October 1940 and an exhibition at the Syracuse Museum of Fine Arts (now the Everson Museum of Art) in May 1941, Grandma Moses had gained considerable assurance. She now ventured into larger-size pictures, and their composition was on a broader, freer scale. One of these new paintings was *Old Oaken Bucket* (plate 33), which illustrates

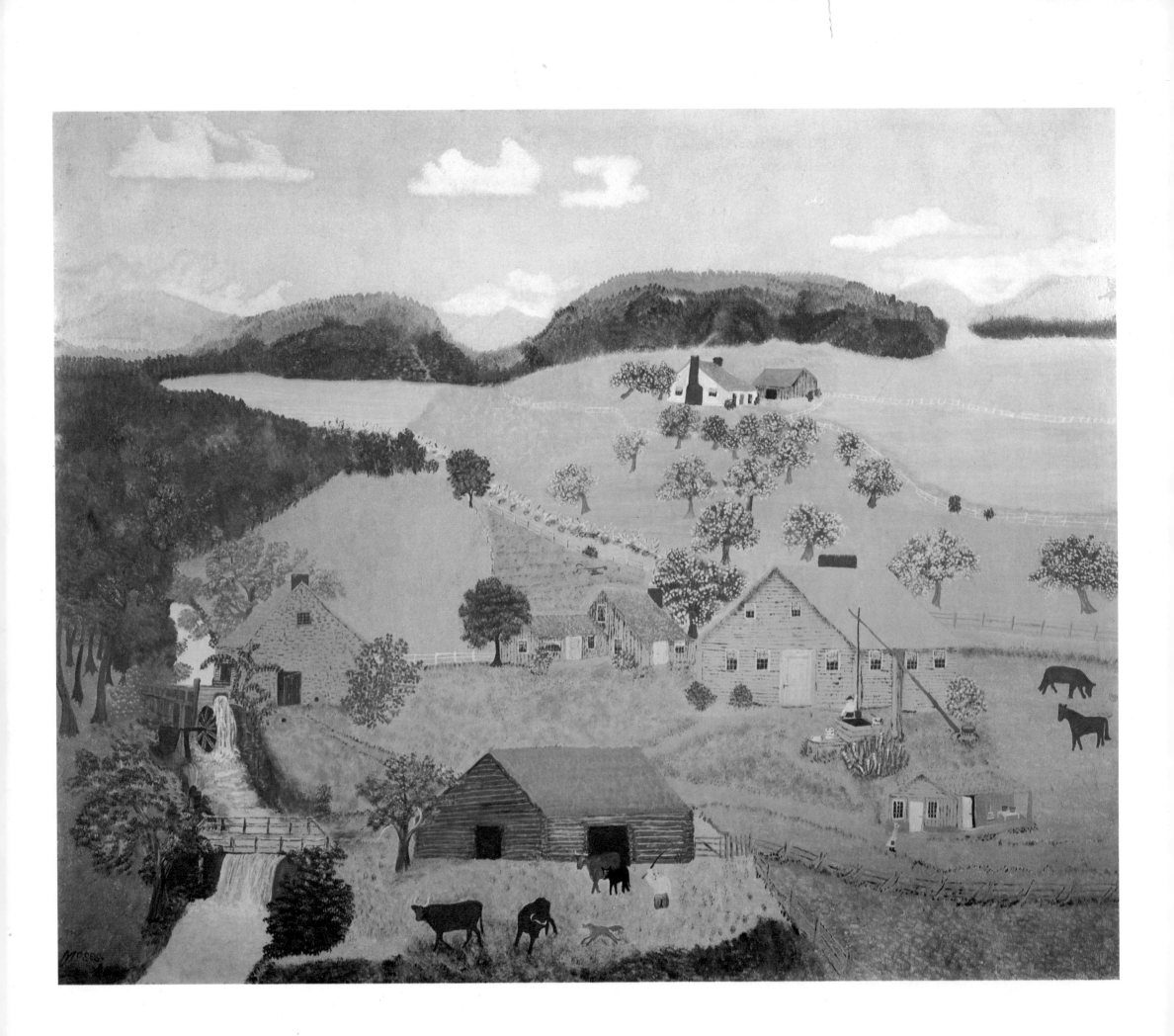

a popular song she had learned in her youth. Explaining how she came to paint it, she wrote:

> That winter I had the grippe, and they kept me in bed, and I planned mischief then. When I was lying there, I thought I was going to paint the story of the "Old Oaken Bucket," because I knew how it originated. I painted it when I got up, that was the first one I tried, but later I painted it again and could remember more of the details.
>
> Then I was requested to send several pictures out to the gallery in Syracuse, where they had an exhibition. I sent the "Old Oaken Bucket," the "Checkered House," and a picture with a young colt in it. Hugh and Dorothy persuaded me to attend the show, so we went to Syracuse. My picture, "The Old Oaken Bucket," took the New York State Prize, and Mr. Thomas J. Watson bought it.

In November of that year, Fred E. Robertson, the artist's youngest brother and a talented self-taught artist in his own right, gave his sister a book in which to record her paintings, as well as labels to be attached to the backs of the pictures. Book and labels represent the most important documents for identification of her work. They are described and analyzed in the Introduction to the Catalogue of the Works.

◀ 34.
The Old Oaken Bucket.
1943. 23½ x 30".
Cat. 238

Artistic Progress

A ONE-MAN SHOW THE FOLLOWING YEAR should be mentioned. It was held from December 8 to December 22, 1942, at the American-British Art Center in New York, whose director, Ala Story, had begun to take an interest in the artist. Thirty-two paintings were on display, among them one listed in the catalogue as *Black Horses* (plates 35, 36; Grandma Moses herself had titled this picture *Lower Cambridge Valley*). The quality of the painting so impressed me that I consider it the turning point in my evaluation of the artist.

If up to that time I had looked upon Grandma Moses's work as interesting and appealing folk art, I suddenly realized that here was an outstanding painter. Her progress within two short years was astonishing. Whereas the early pictures are for the most part small, the figures often cramped in little surrounding space and the colors of the landscapes without much range, in *Black Horses* a new conception seems to have emerged, as though the artist's eyes had been opened to broad vistas of nature.

There was the view of the Cambridge Valley and the panorama of the distant mountain range and, above all, there was the subtle blending of muted colors. Forests, meadows, hills, and fields planted with a variety of crops were all painted in their own appropriate tones, yet formed a harmoniously integrated whole. To keep the picture from being a mere landscape, Grandma Moses had "brought in" (as she would say) two cantering black horses in the lower right foreground which attract the beholder's attention. A brown horse, with two children astride, stands docilely on the left, counterbalancing the other group. The artist later noted that the black horses had belonged to her great-grandfather and that one of them was killed in the Battle of Walloomsac during the Revolutionary War.

In the following years Grandma Moses created many new paintings that confirmed the fact of her development. In most of her early work she had represented single objects, such as a covered bridge, an old mill, a waterfall, an ancient car. The subject itself was all-important and the artist used the landscape as a setting; she did not as yet possess the ability she was soon to acquire to create a landscape which would not merely serve as surrounding scenery.

This development can be traced by comparing early and later versions of the same theme. One of the pictures included in the first exhibition was *The Burning of Troy* (plate 38), done in about 1939. It shows a covered bridge on fire. The idea for this painting derived from an illustration and story (plate 37) Mrs. Moses had cut out of a Troy, New York, newspaper, which "77 years later" recalled the catastrophe of Saturday, May 10, 1862. By a few pencil lines on the clipping she had indicated how she intended to change the oval illustration into a rectangular painting. More important, her imagination transformed the black-and-white newspaper print into a dramatic scene of flaming reds and dark billowing clouds of smoke, harsher and cruder colors than she would use in later years but forcefully evocative of the terrible event. This first version makes use of most of the elements shown in the newspaper illustration: the horse and cart looming very large in the foreground, the figures of running men carrying buckets darkly outlined against the flaming interior of the bridge, the brick structure supporting the bridge, and even a small boat tied to a post at the river's edge. The representation of the subject is all that matters, the bridge itself filling the entire width of the picture, flames and smoke reaching up to the top, leaving just enough space at the sides to indicate the approaches to the bridge and the river it spans.

In 1943 the artist used the same theme for a large painting titled *The Burning of Troy in 1862* (plate 39). But it shows an entirely different mood, less dramatic, more picturesque. It is now a wide landscape, serene in spite of the burning bridge that dominates the center of the painting. The hurrying figures and the horse and buggy have become less prominent. There is a cluster of charming houses and trees on the

51

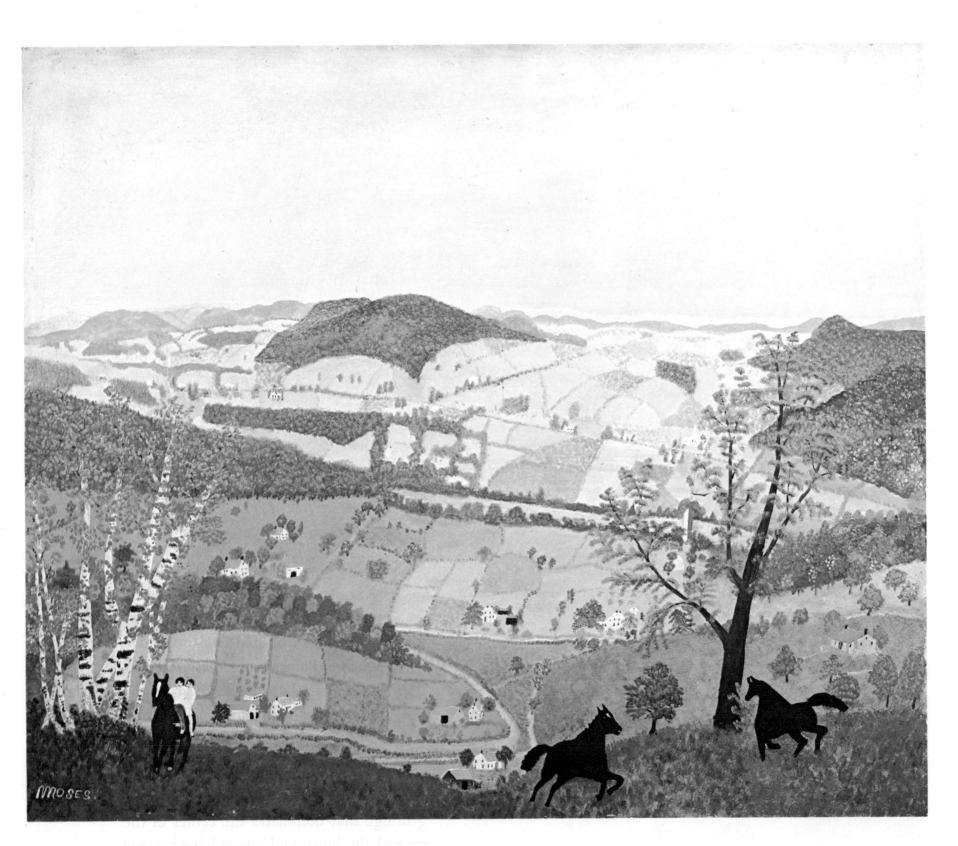

35. *Black Horses*. 1942. 20 x 24". Cat. 181

36. *Black Horses* (detail) ▶

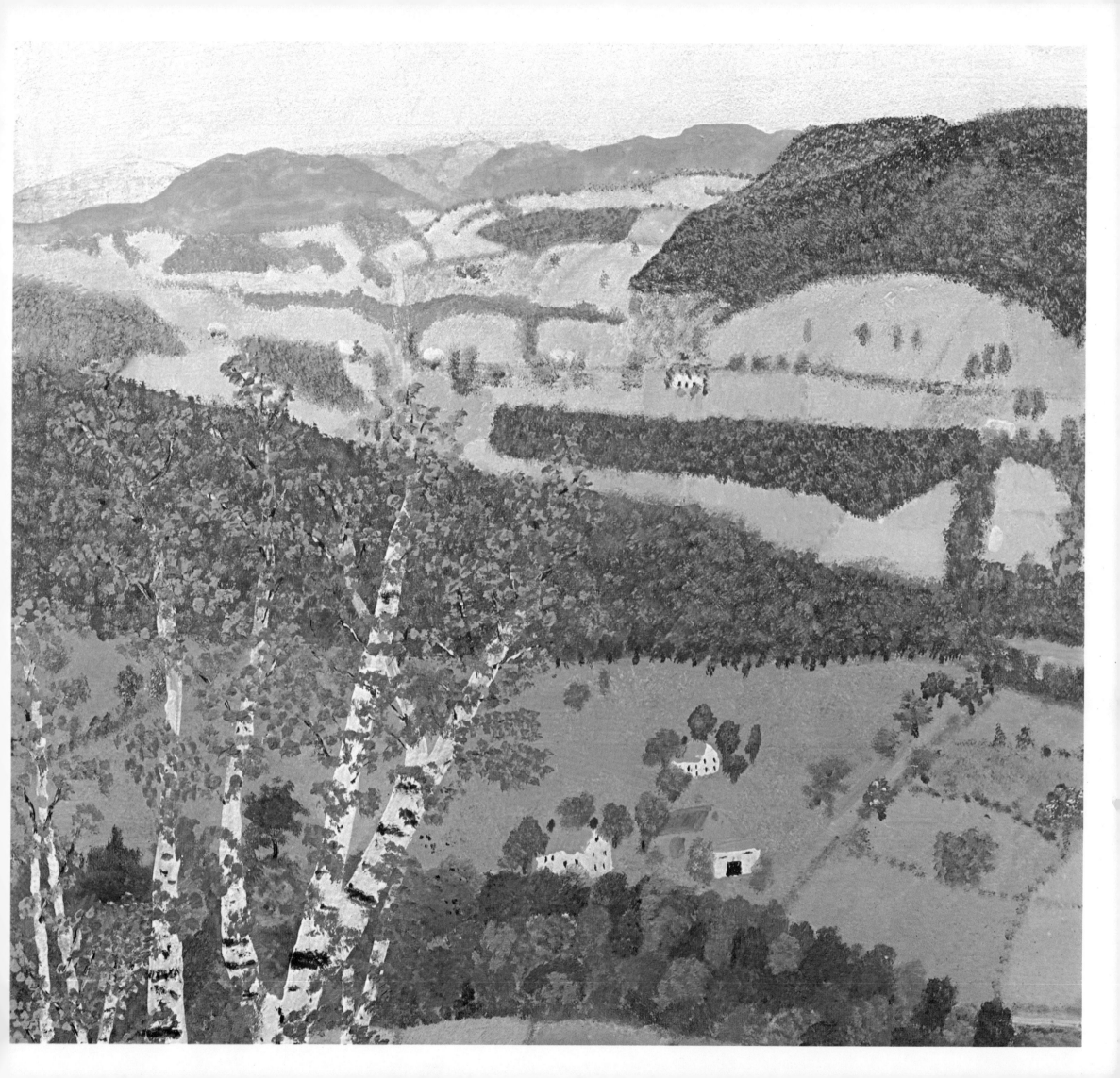

37.
Newspaper clipping of 1939
about the Great Fire of 1862

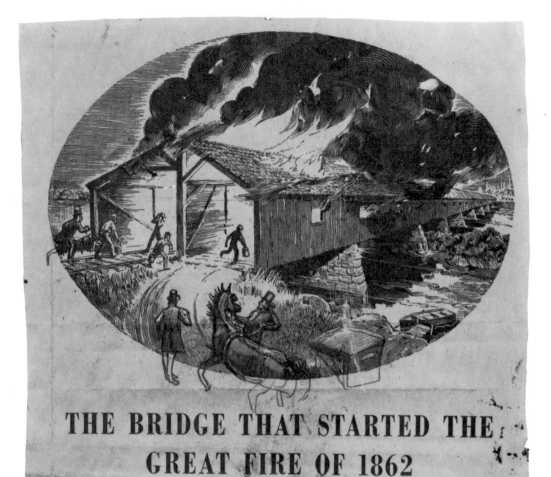

THE BRIDGE THAT STARTED THE GREAT FIRE OF 1862

A COW started the great fire of Chicago. An earthquake started the great fire of San Francisco. But Troy's Great Fire was started by an old covered bridge.

From New York Bay to the head of navigation at Waterford, it was the first bridge ever built across the Hudson. Nearly a third of a mile long, it was wide enough to accommodate a railroad track, a carriage road, and a footway.

On Saturday, May 10, 1862, it nearly destroyed the city of Troy. A gale was blowing from the northwest, when a spark from a locomotive lodged in the shingles on the roof. In a twinkling, the entire bridge was in flames and the wind had carried burning embers to all parts of the city.

The fire started at noon. By six o'clock in the evening, seventy-five acres in the heart of Troy had been "swept over as by the hand of a destroying fiend."

"Tears and despondency," says a historian, "could not recall the burned property which had been slowly accumulated by the incessant industry of many years." But by the latter part of July, 181 buildings had been rebuilt, and by November, all but a few of the burned lots were covered with new and superior structures.

Once again, the famous "enterprise of the Trojans" had not failed. And this bank is proud to have played a part in rebuilding the stricken city. Today, 77 years later, the Manufacturers National joins with other Troy banks in looking forward to a great industrial and commercial future.

far river bank, apparently removed from danger. To the left of the bridge the river flows quietly through a hilly countryside painted in soft hues, the sky is high and clear above the burning bridge, and on the right a willow tree is delicately outlined against the river. Distant hills melt into the pale blue of the horizon.

There are several more versions of this subject, the last one—a small

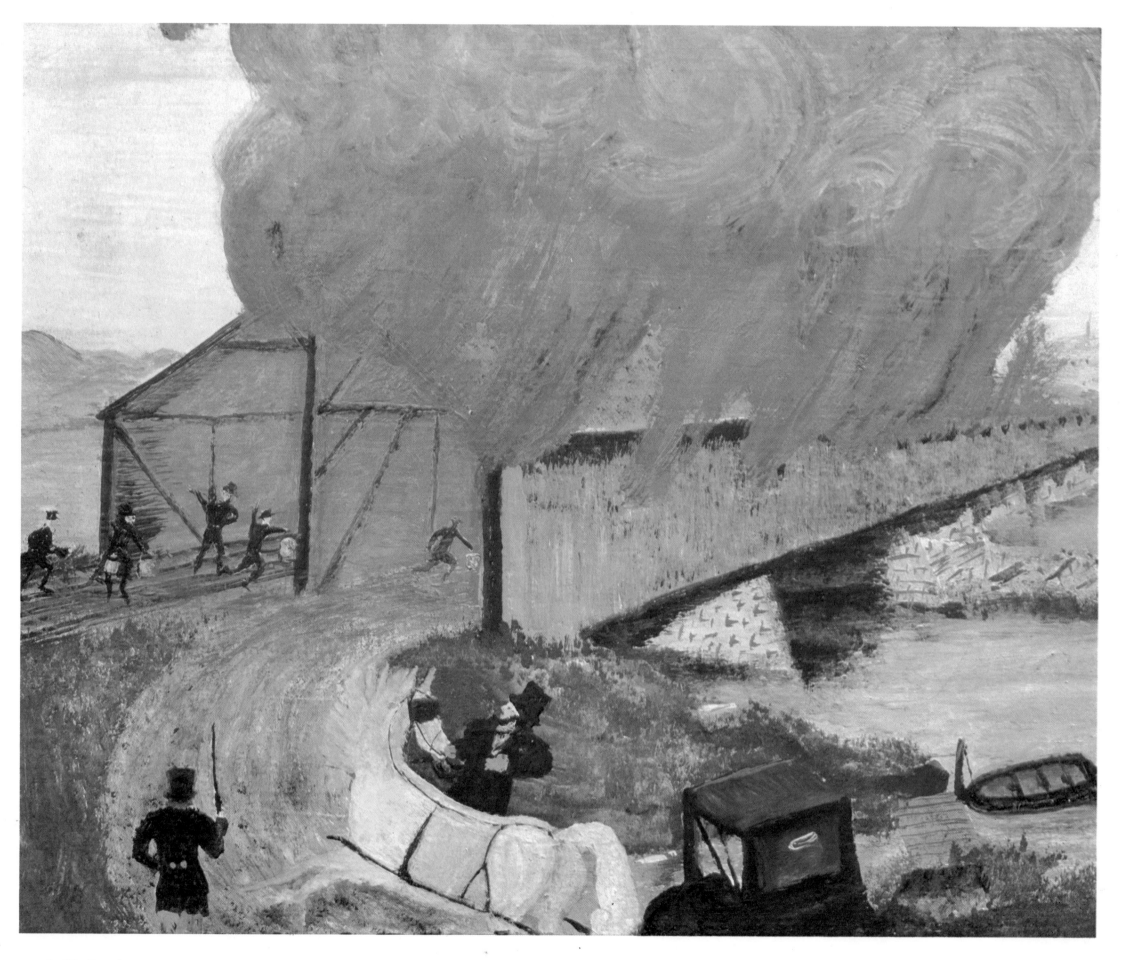

38. *The Burning of Troy.* c. 1939. 9 x 11¼". Cat. 62

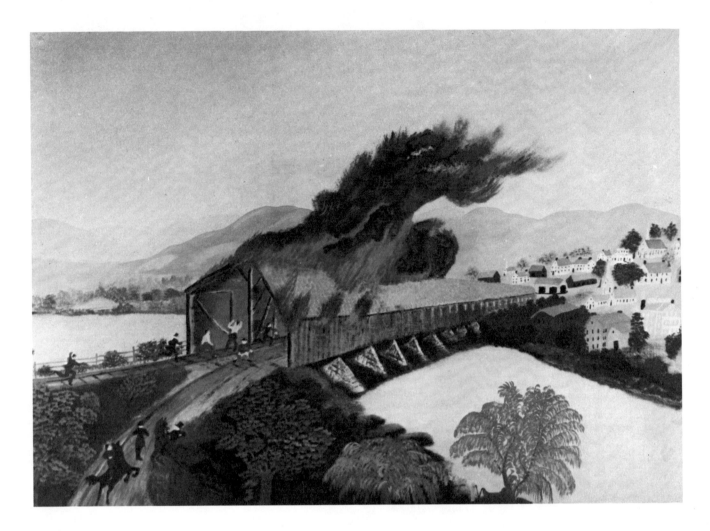

picture—painted in 1959 (plate 40). Grandma Moses had kept the clipping from the Troy newspaper all that time.

Three other paintings, each to my knowledge an original composition, also demonstrate the artist's progress: *The First Automobile* (1939 or earlier), *Automobile 1913* (1943), and *The Old Automobile* (1944) (plates 41–43). In the earliest, the clumsy car takes up the greater part of the foreground, framed by a sketchy landscape dominated by two trees in bloom. In the second version, *Automobile 1913,* the landscape predominates. In the center foreground there is again an open car with four people in it, as clumsy as the previous one. It evidently had been put in after the landscape was completed. Its motion and noise are indicated by two shying horses. Three children watch the unfamiliar

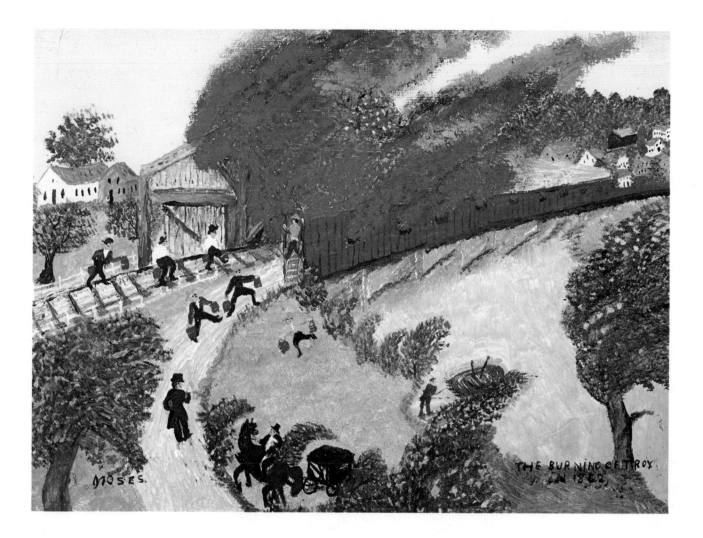

40.
Great Fire. 1959.
12 x 16". Cat. 1407

sight, a farmer plows his field, a tree-shaded house with barn and small cottages are scattered in the valley. A dark sky over distant hills gives the picture a somewhat somber aspect.

One year later Grandma Moses took up the subject for a third time. Now the old car, though again placed in the center of the foreground, has become incidental in a delicately painted landscape; the hues of the forests fade into ever softer greens toward the background, and the coloring of the hills conveys an impression of great distance. Everything is quiet and at peace; it could be a scene of a hundred years ago, were it not for the newfangled contraption before whose rattling and speed, filling the air with visible dust clouds, the horse in front of a buggy rears in terror.

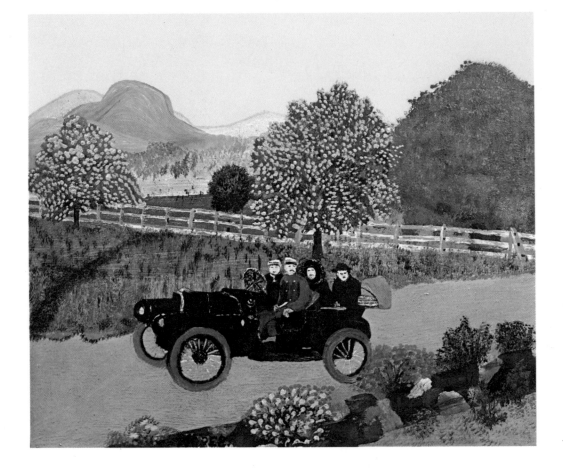

41. *The First Automobile.* 1939 or earlier. 9¾ x 11½″. Cat. 6

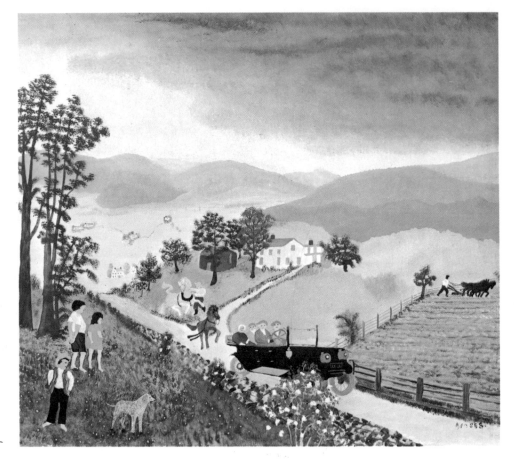

42. *Automobile, 1913.* 1943. 17¾ x 21¼″. Cat. 271

43. ▶
The Old Automobile. 1944.
18¾ x 21½″. Cat. 442

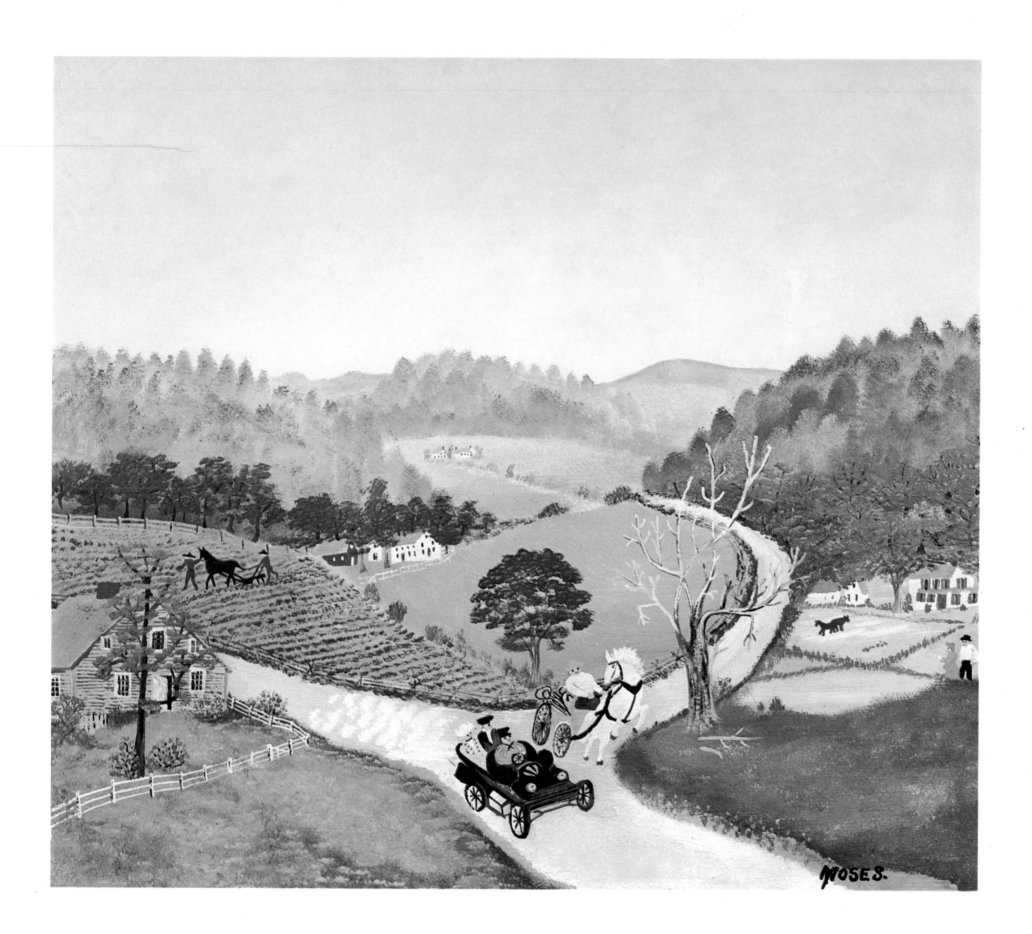

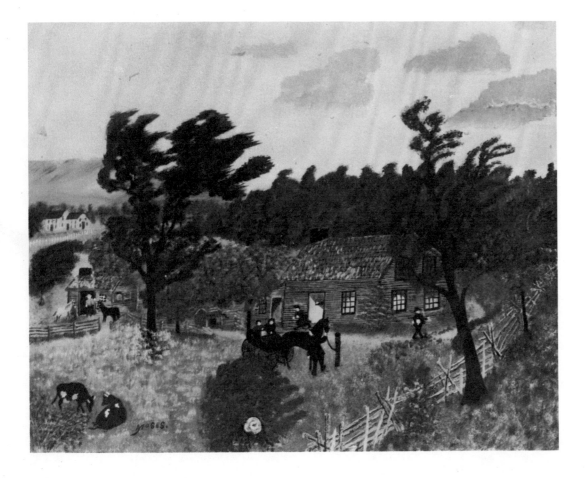

44.
The Hitching Post.
1948. 15 x 19¼".
Cat. 785

45.
The Doctor.
1950. 20 x 24".
Cat. 957

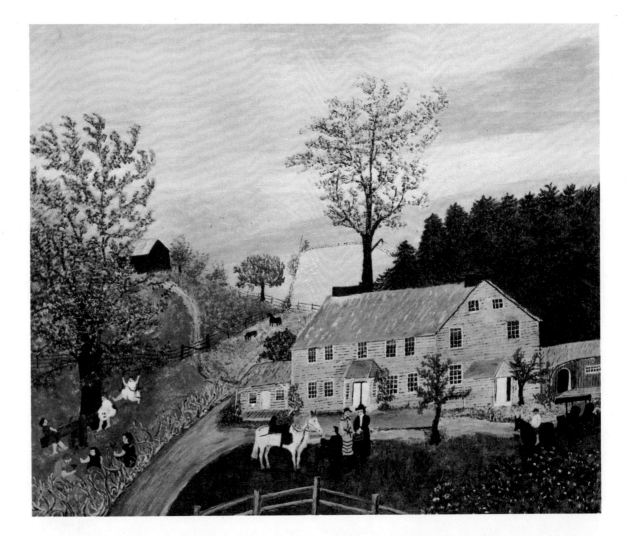

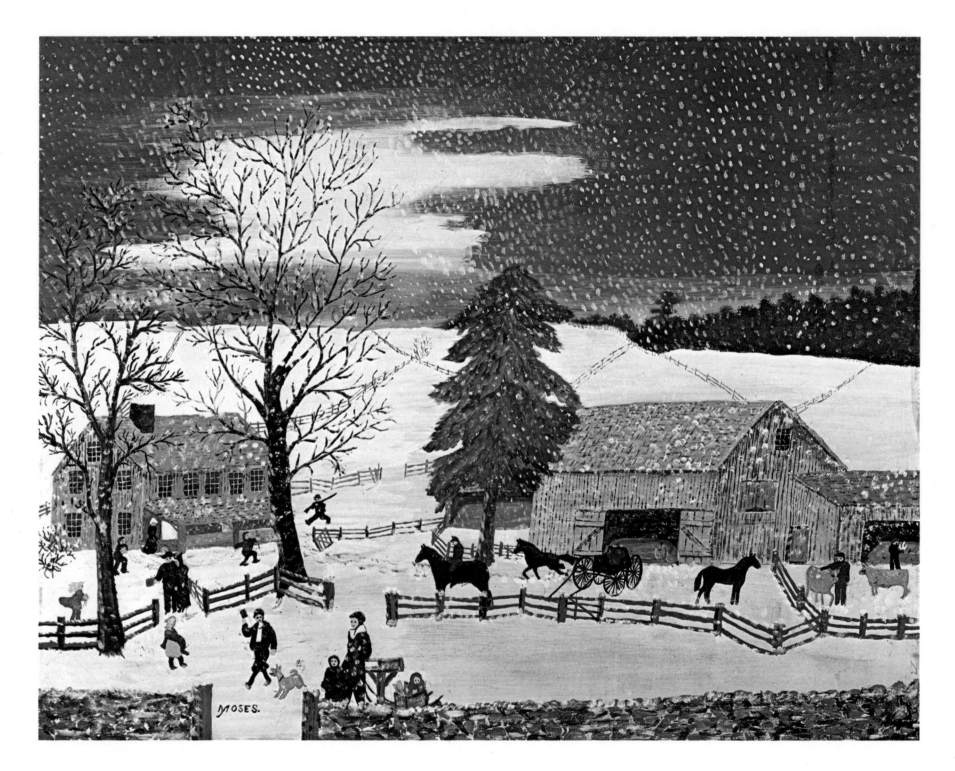

46. *The Mailman Has Gone.* 1949. 16¾ x 21½". Cat. 818

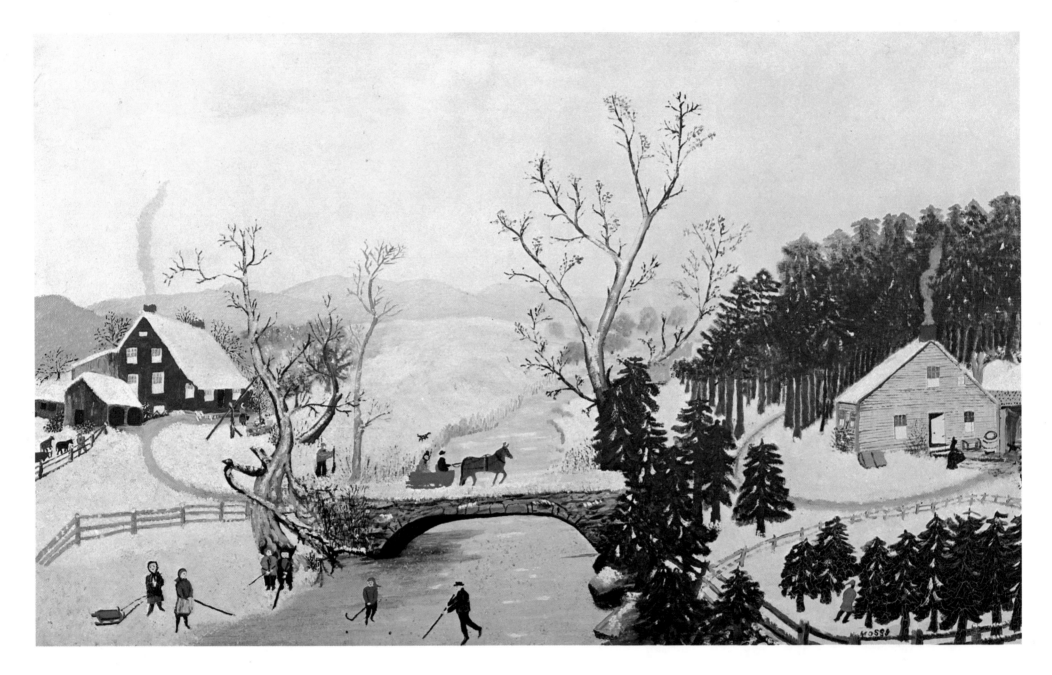

47. *Over the River to Grandma's House.* c. 1941. 18 x 30". Cat. 87

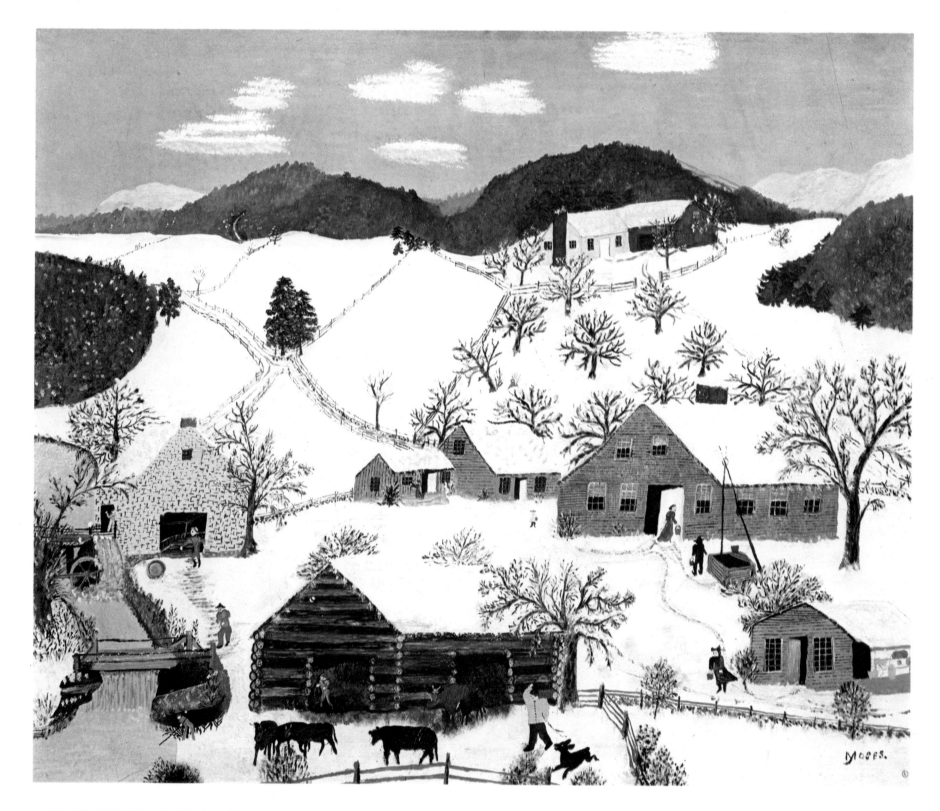

48. *The Old Oaken Bucket in Winter.* 1950. 20 x 24". Cat. 912

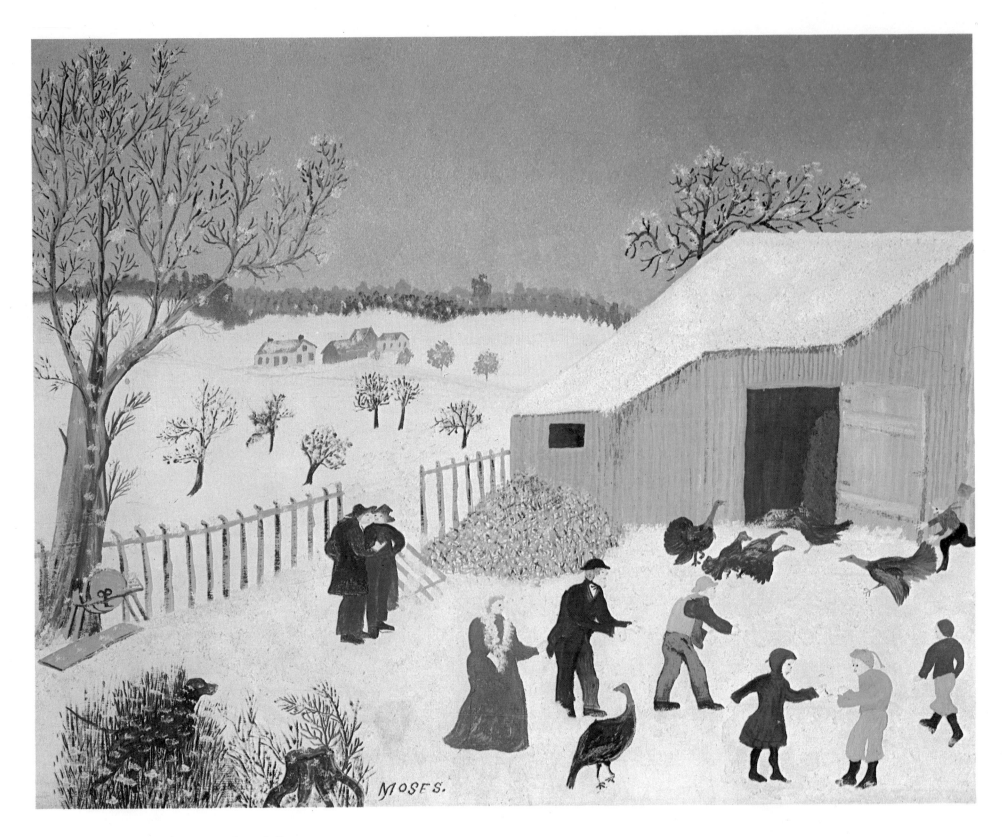

49. *Thanksgiving Turkey.* 1943. 16 x 20". Cat. 293

Grandma Moses often chose to title a picture for a detail quite subordinate to the general composition. In *The Hitching Post* (plate 44), for instance, two windblown trees dominate the scene, rather than the horse-and-buggy being tied to the hitching post that gives the picture its name.

The title of a charming summer landscape with trees and meadows and children playing out of doors is *The Doctor* (plate 45). A man and a woman are standing in front of a large house; evidently the doctor has just arrived on horseback and is talking to the lady of the house who has come out to meet him.

A very dramatic landscape with falling snow and a dark, stormy sky bears the title *The Mailman Has Gone* (plate 46). There is a roadside mailbox, and among a number of people a man is proudly holding up a perhaps long awaited letter.

The narrative content has become part of an all-over visual impression. The fluid technique, far removed from that of a "primitive," can be traced even in Grandma Moses's earliest pictures; she rapidly gained assurance and mastery as her work progressed.

After the 1942 exhibition at the American British Art Center and others at various galleries in the following years, the work of Grandma Moses became widely known. As a result, she received many letters from people who wrote that they liked a certain painting they had seen and wanted her to "paint just such a picture" for them. Among the themes most in demand were Over the River to Grandma's House, The Old Oaken Bucket, Catching the Turkey, The Checkered House, and Sugaring Off. Although Grandma Moses did not enjoy these "orders," she obliged, because, as she said, she did not want to disappoint her friends. This explains the frequent recurrence of these titles.

It is interesting to note, however, that the artist hardly ever copied her paintings exactly. She found ways to vary the composition of a given

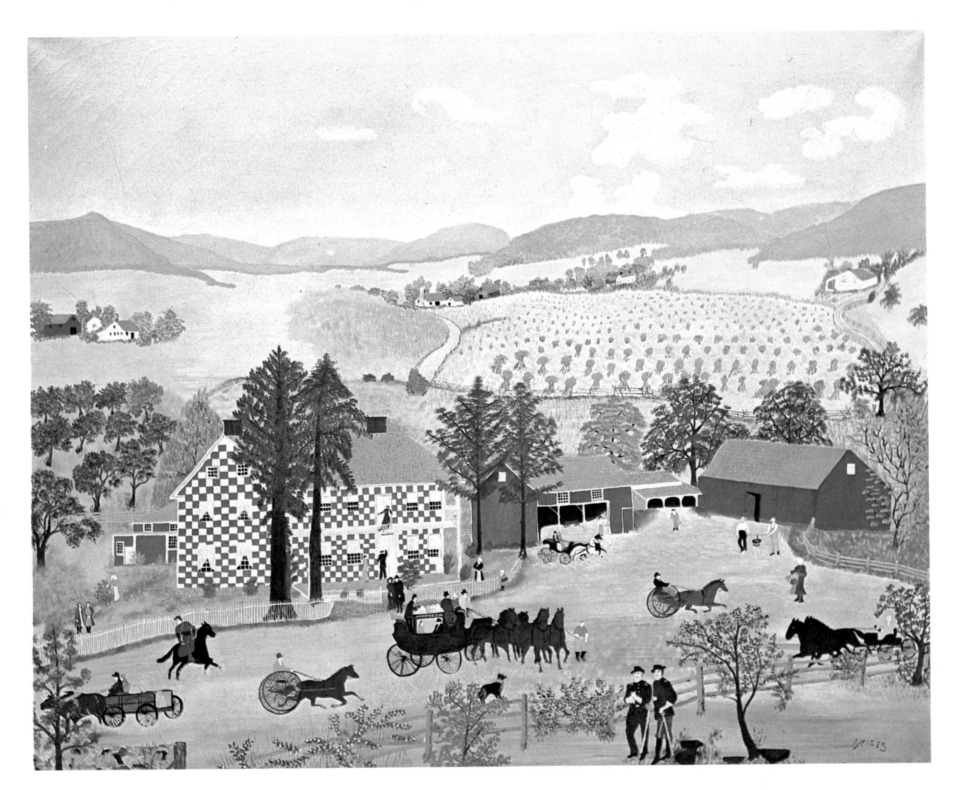

50. *Checkered House.* 1943. 36 x 45". Cat. 317

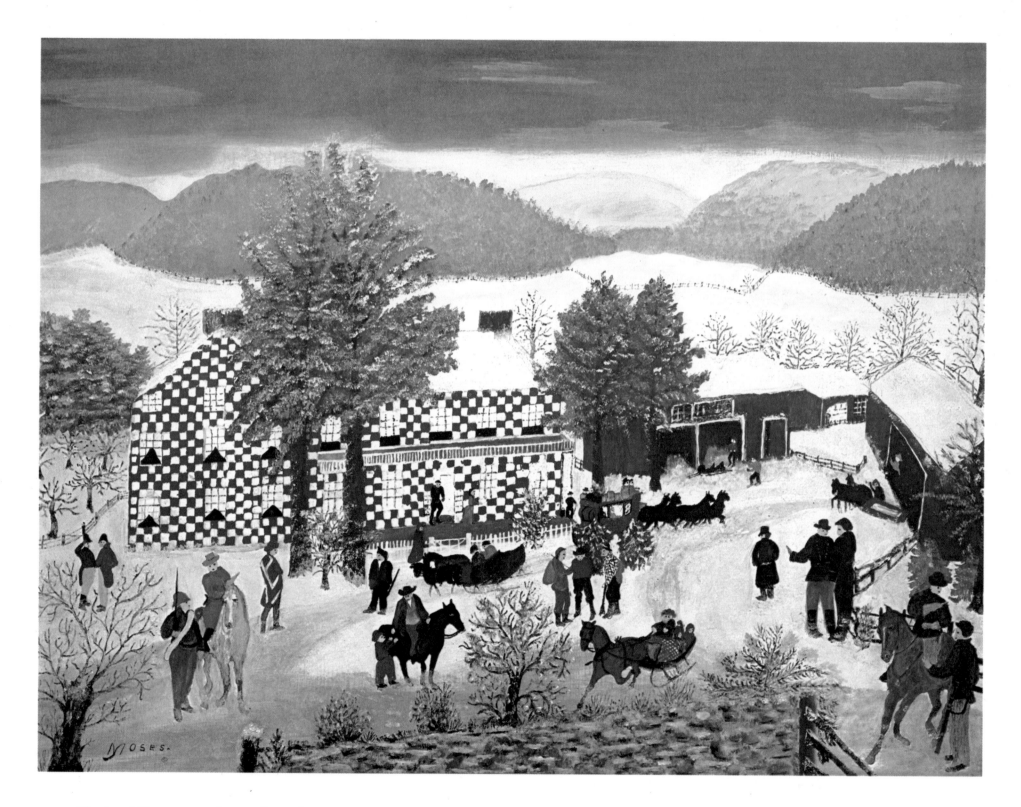

51. *Checkered House.* 1955. 18 x 24". Cat. 1165

theme, now as a winter scene, now as a spring, summer, or fall landscape. This gave her the means to change the atmosphere and tone of a painting.

If one calls to mind how many artists have simply copied their successful paintings upon order, one can only admire how this untaught woman avoided repeating her own work. What she did retain in each variant were the characteristics of any specific theme.

The *Checkered House* (plates 50, 51), for example, always shows a large building with a red-and-white checkerboard design, barns and sheds, a wide road in the foreground alive with horses pulling carriages, riders on horseback, and men in uniform. In her youth she had seen this building, which was a landmark near Cambridge, New York. Later she wrote about it: "The Checkered House is old. . . . It was the Headquarters of General Baum in the revolution war, and afterwards he used it as a Hospital, then it was a stopping place for the stage, where they changed horses every two miles, oh we traveled *fast* in those days."

Looking at two variations of the *Checkered House,* I once asked her how she managed to represent the same motif in a fresh form. She said that she visualized the picture she was about to paint as though framed in her window and that she had only to imagine she was looking out on the scene either from the right or from the left and that accordingly all parts of a composition would shift into place.

The figures that populate her landscapes are for the most part "types" who perform certain standard chores: the men carrying wooden buckets in "sugaring off" pictures, for instance (plates 52, 55, 63), or the ones catching the turkey (plates 49, 62, 64). Sometimes there are soldiers in old uniforms, indicating a historical setting (plates 50, 51, 60).

Such figures were often taken from books or old prints, or from the newspaper clippings which she kept in a box. This helps to explain their recurrence in Grandma Moses's paintings, whereas the landscape

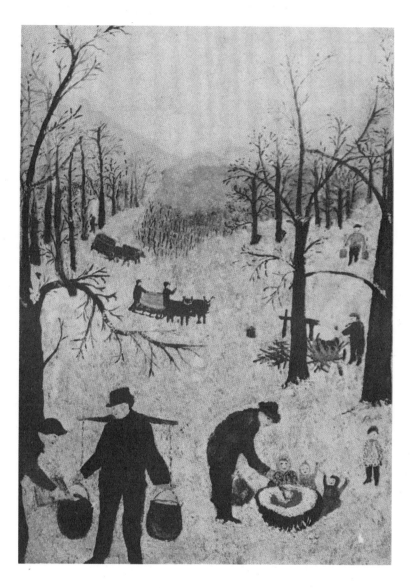

52. *Sugaring Off in Maple Orchard* (detail). See plate 63

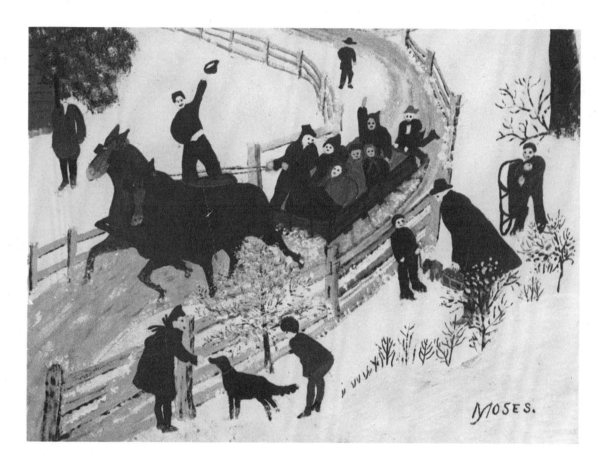

53. *Joy Ride* (detail). See plate 188

is always the original artistic expression of her own vision. Remarkably enough, the animals in her pictures are seldom stereotyped in the way that her human figures are. Rarely did she copy them; they are painted with natural ease and abandon, with the emphasis not on details of their appearance but on their movements, which are astonishingly well observed. One need only study the horses in her paintings (plates 53, 54): in the winter pictures some of them trot heavily through the snow, straining to draw a laden sleigh; others are unburdened and light in their movements or even try to break out. This seemingly effortless

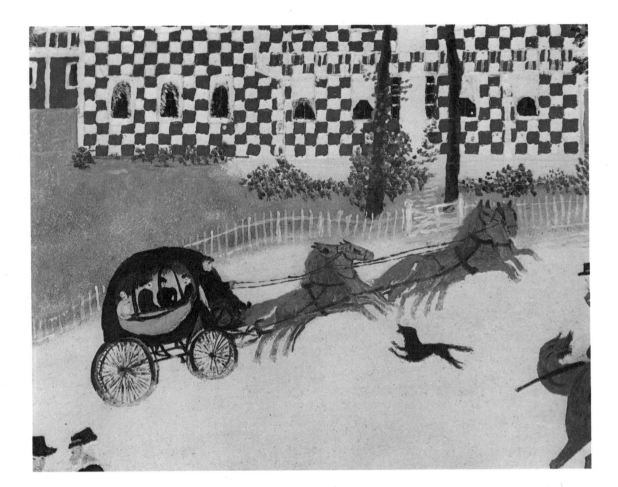

54. *The Old Checkered House in 1860* (detail). See plate 60

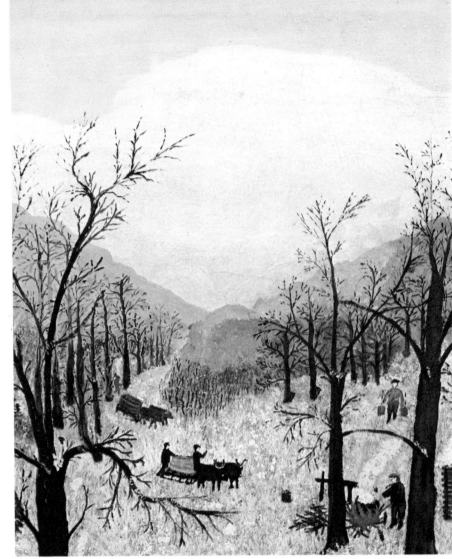

55. *Sugaring Off in Maple Orchard* (detail). See plate 63

touch, achieved also in the landscapes, was not at her disposal in the human figure.

The blending of two distinct components—sensitively felt and beautifully represented nature scenes, painted in an almost Impressionist manner, with primitive though often colorful human figures—into artistic harmony constitutes what has become known and recognized the world over as the Grandma Moses style.

The Early Years to 1946

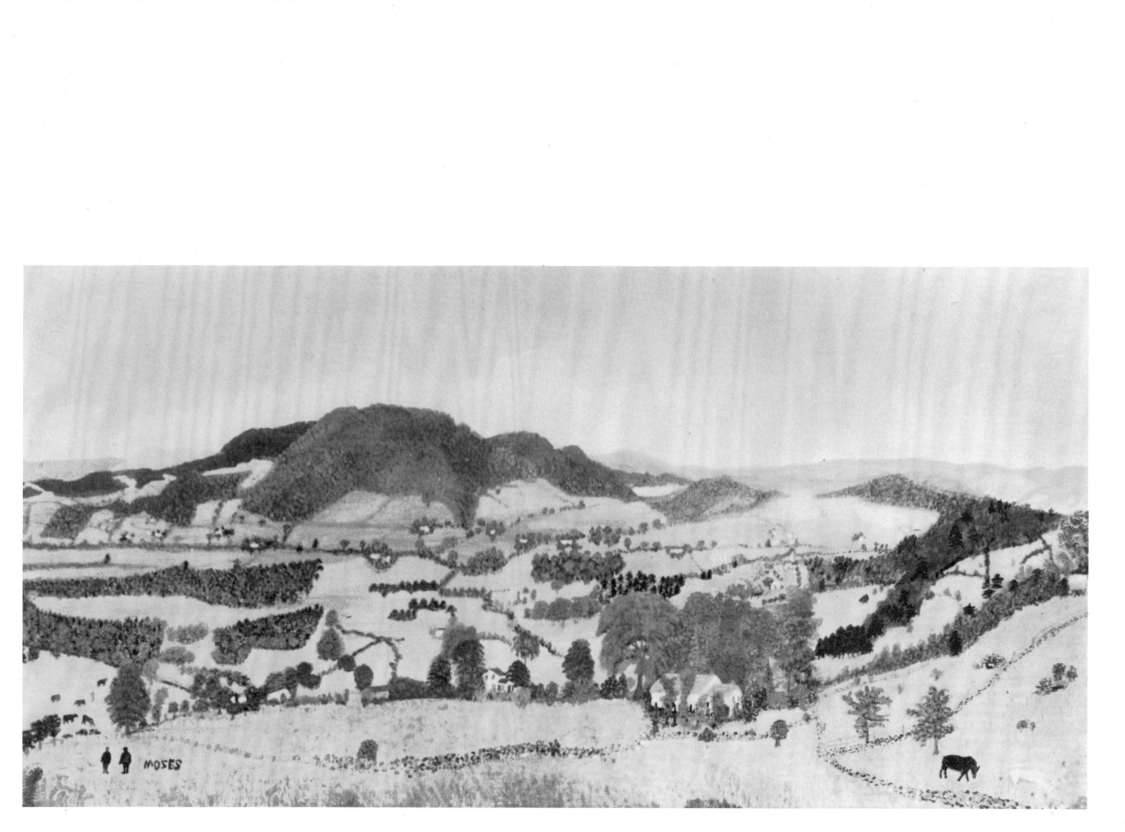

56. *My Hills of Home.* 1941. 17¾ x 36″. Cat. 99

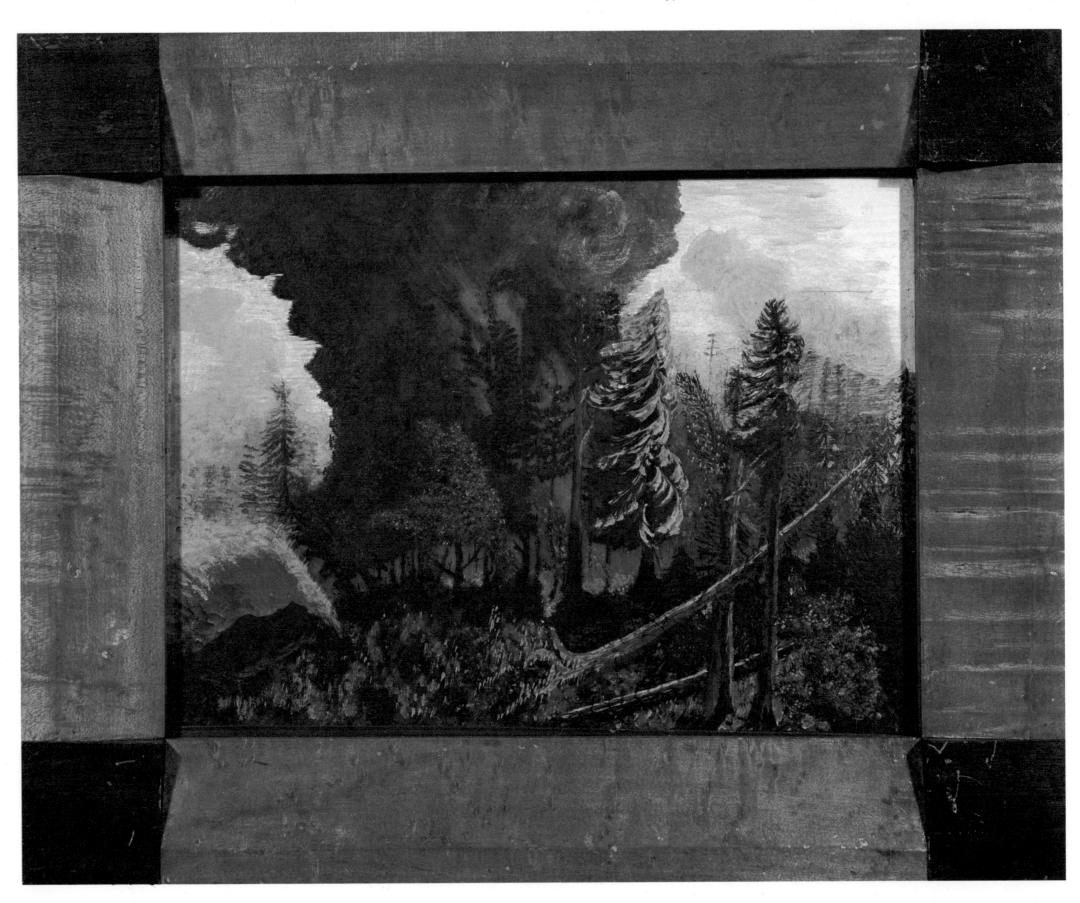

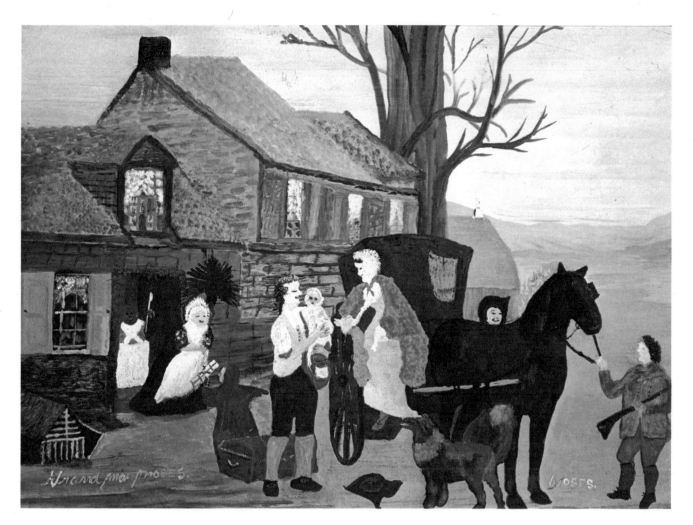

58.
Home for Thanksgiving.
c. 1932. 10 x 14". Cat. 33

59. *Home in Winter.* c. 1938. 6 x 16". Cat. 38

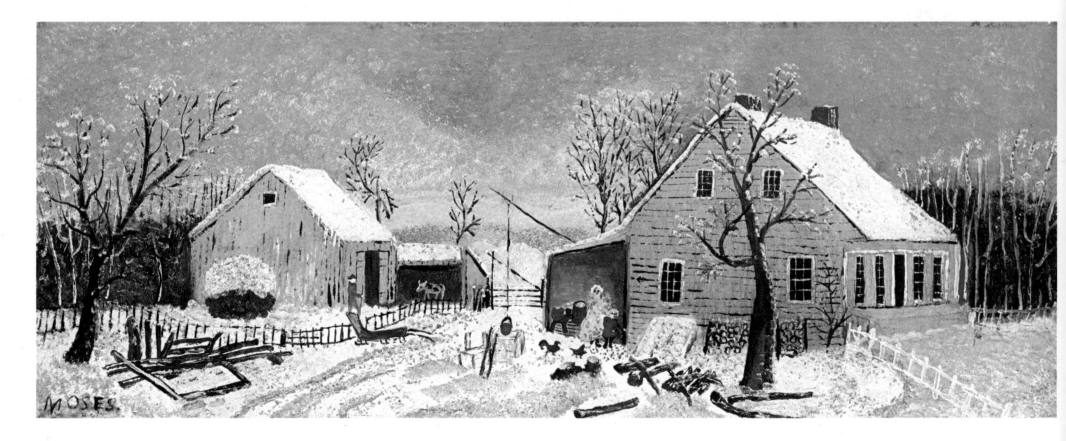

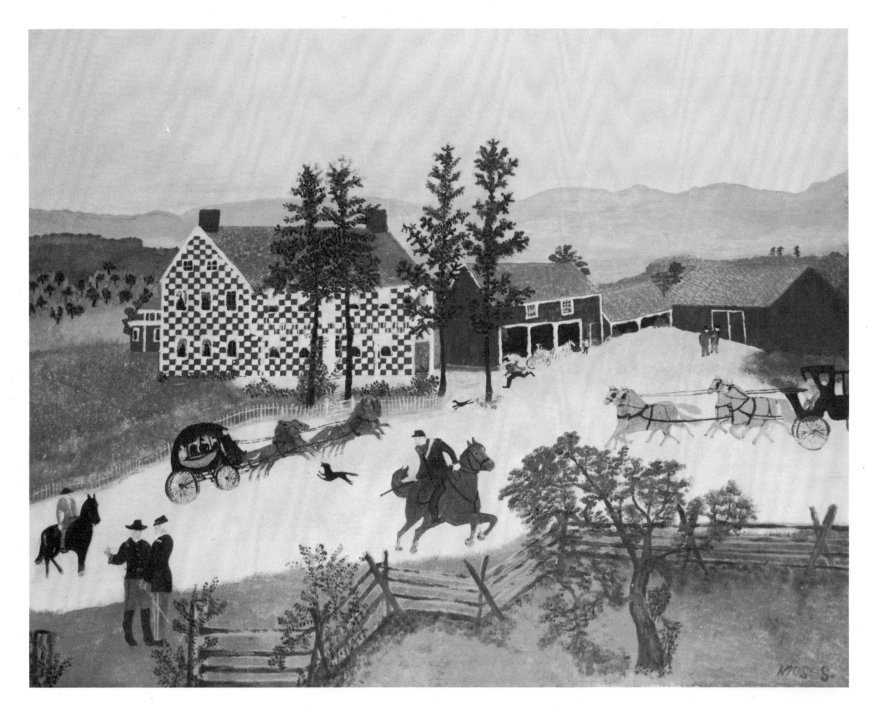

60. *The Old Checkered House in 1860.* 1942. 16 x 20". Cat. 144

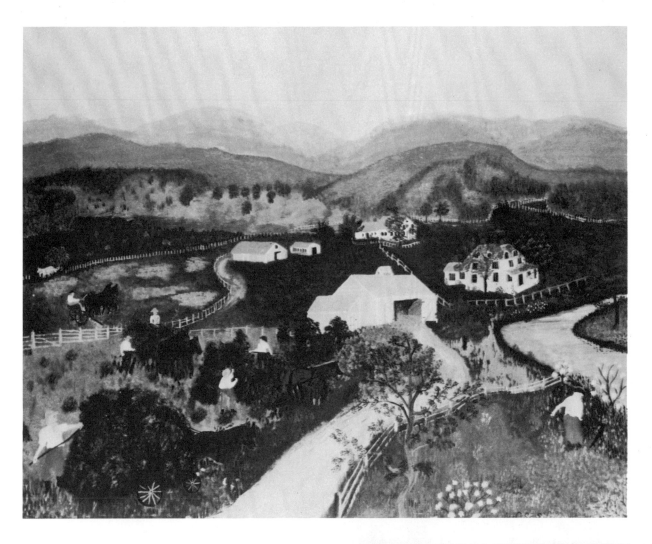

61.
It's Haying Time.
1942. 21½ x 26″. Cat. 158

62.
Catching the Thanksgiving Turkey.
1943. 18½ x 24¼″. Cat. 260

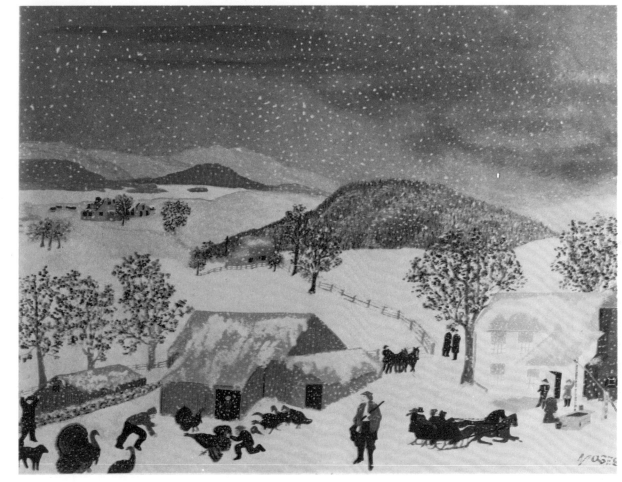

77

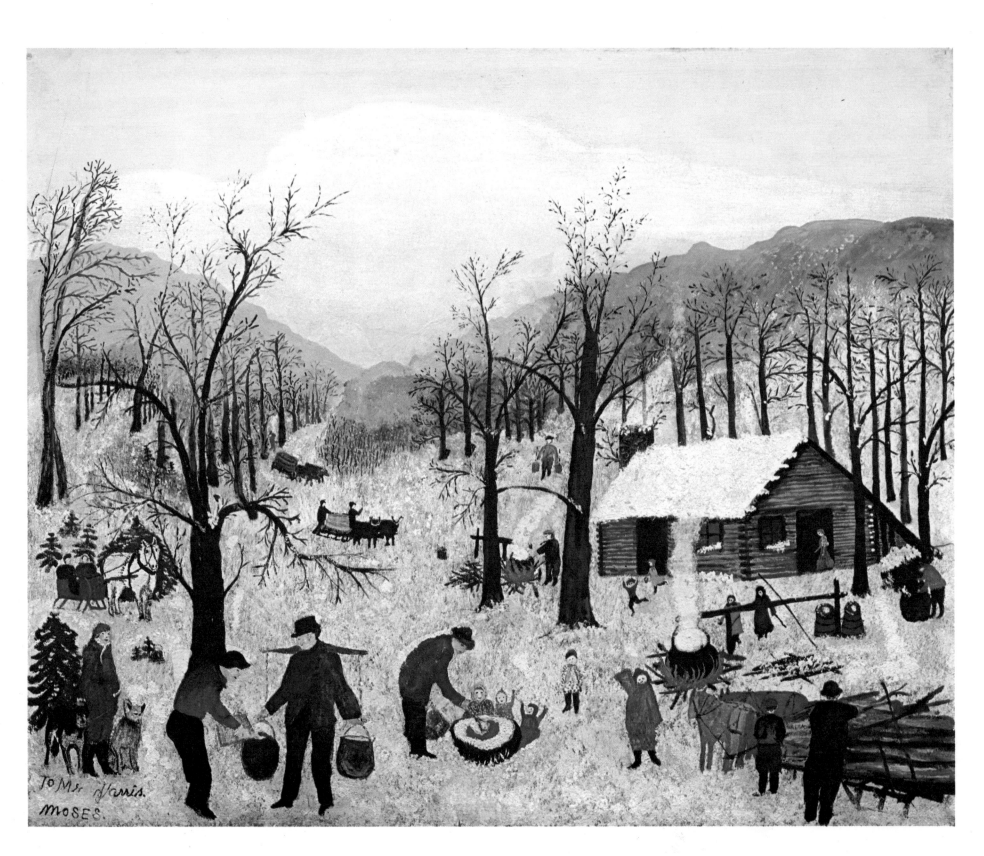

63. *Sugaring Off in Maple Orchard.* 1940. 18⅛ x 24⅛". Cat. 56

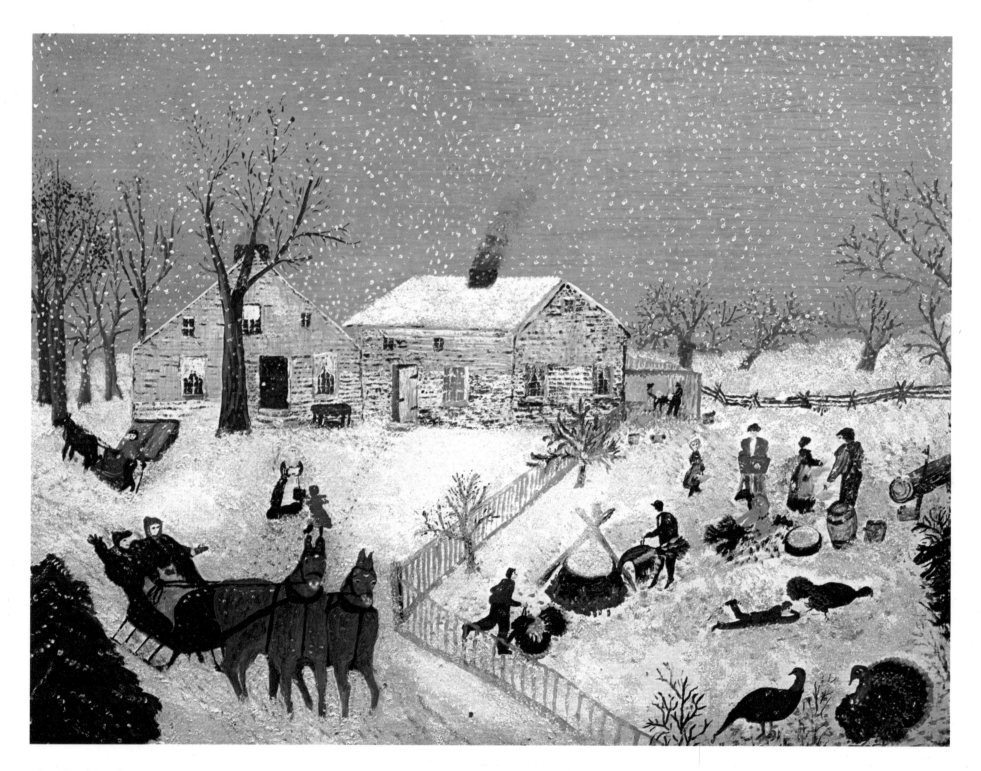

64. *Catching the Turkey.* 1940. 12 x 16″. Cat. 64

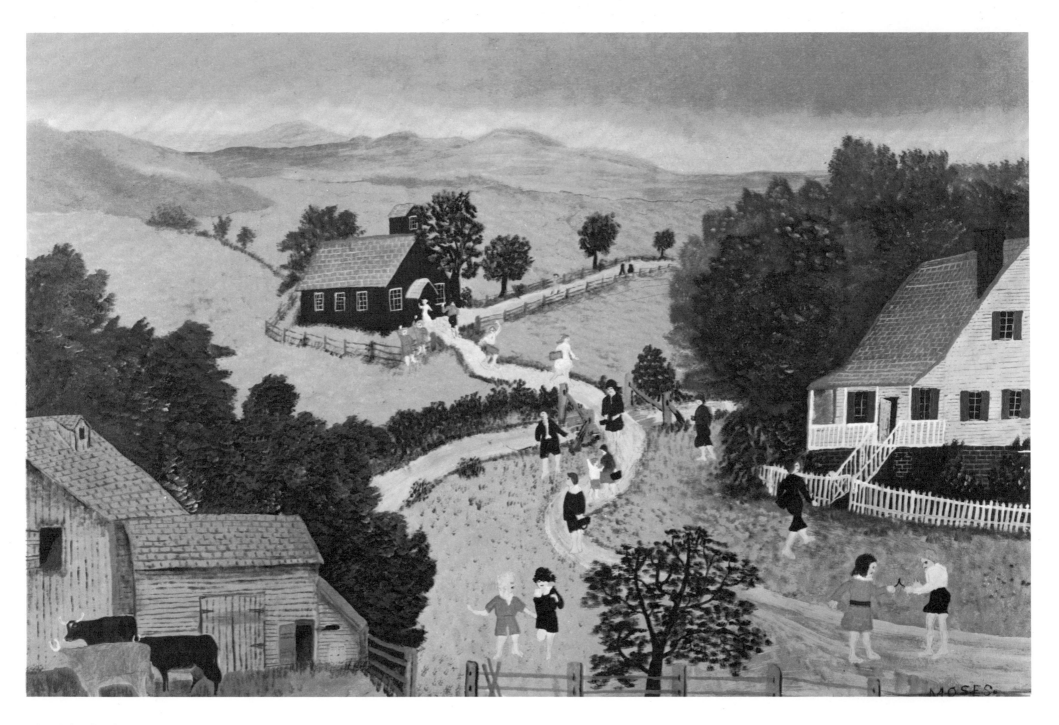

65. *School Is Out.* 1943. 17¼ x 26¾". Cat. 273

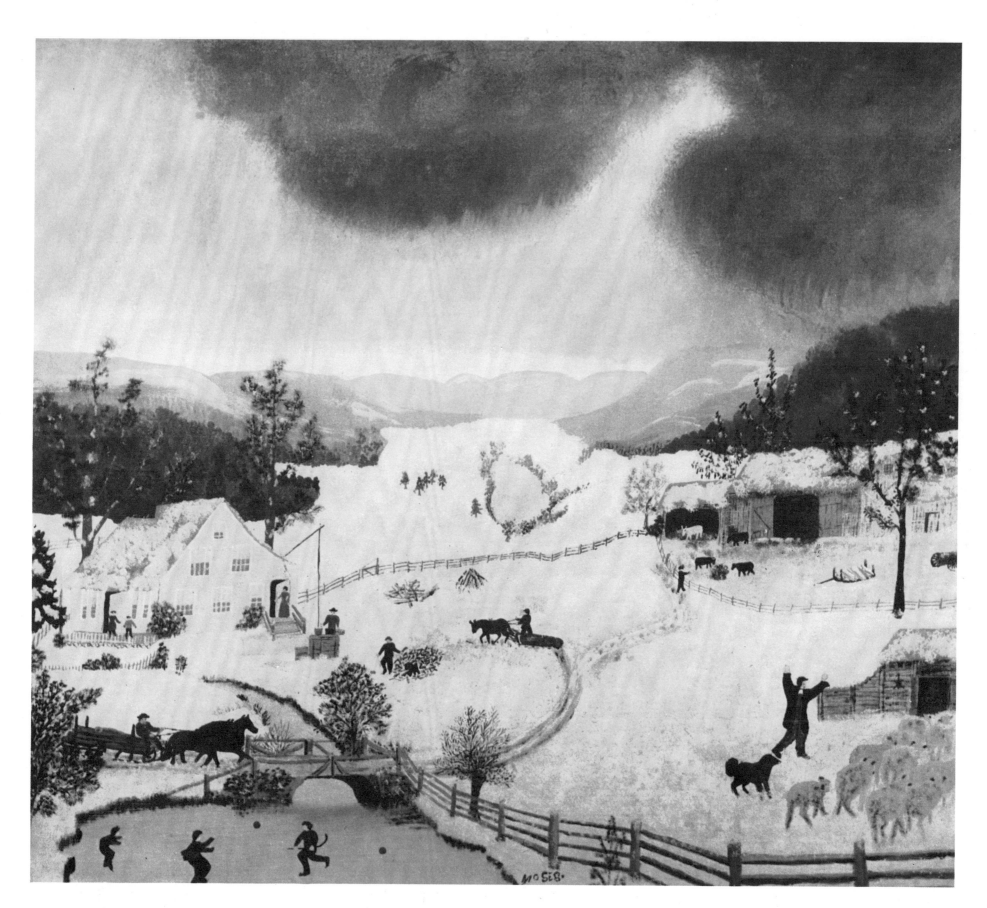

66. *December.* 1943. 18½ x 21¾". Cat. 287

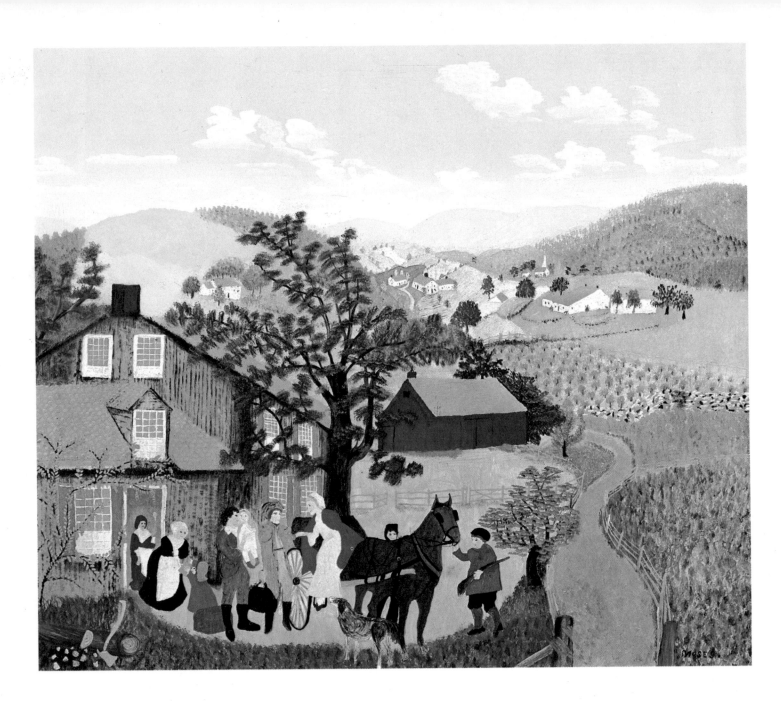

67.
The Daughter's Homecoming.
1943. 19¾ x 23½". Cat. 216

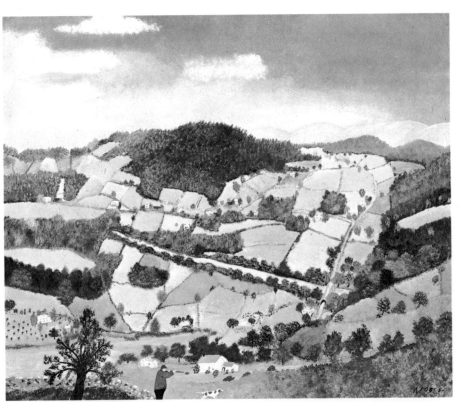

68.
Lower Cambridge Valley. 1943.
19¾ x 23¾". Cat. 244

82

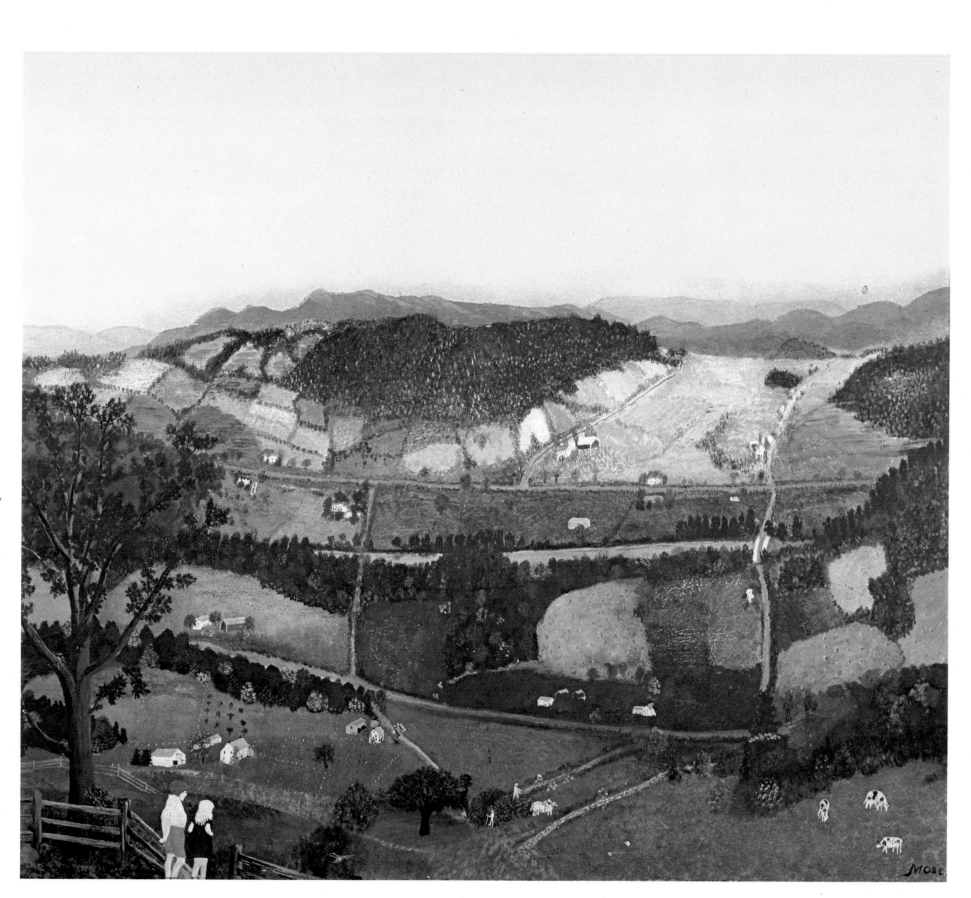

69. *Cambridge Valley.* 1942. 23½ x 27". Cat 164

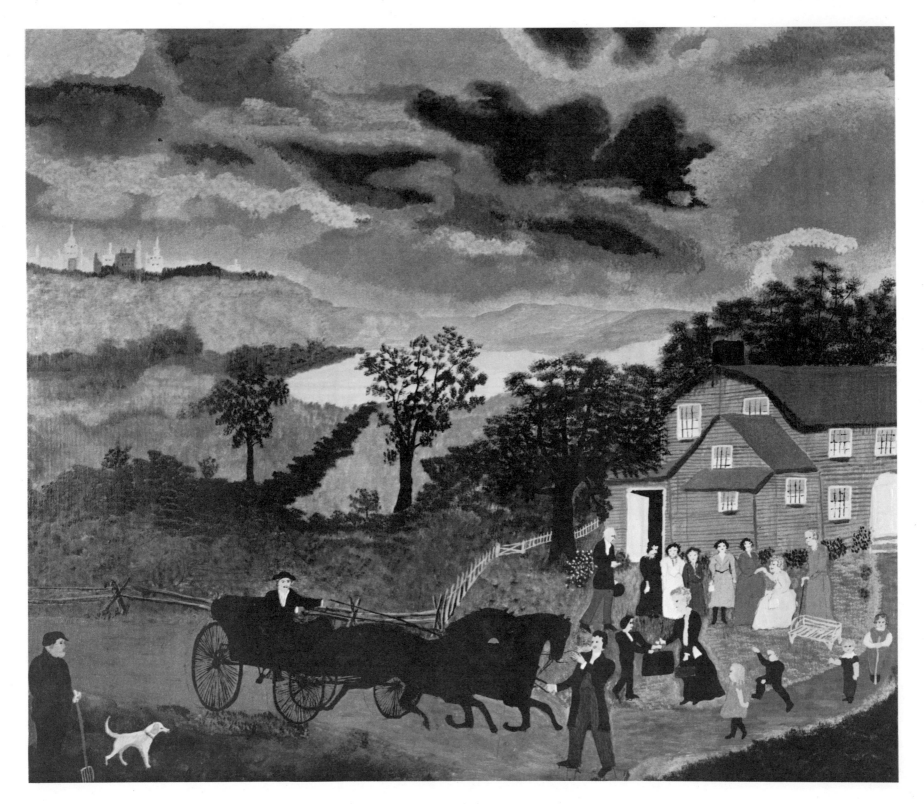

70. *Grandma Going to the Big City.* 1943. 21 x 24". Cat. 278

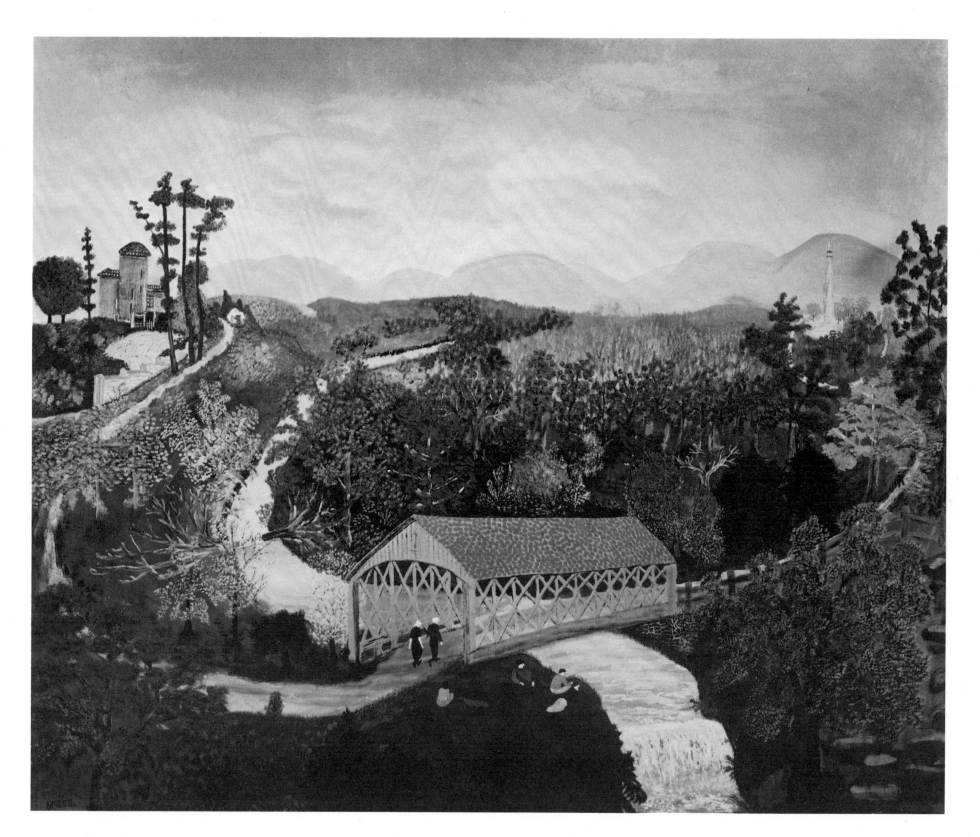

71. *In the Park*. 1944. 36 x 45". Cat. 343

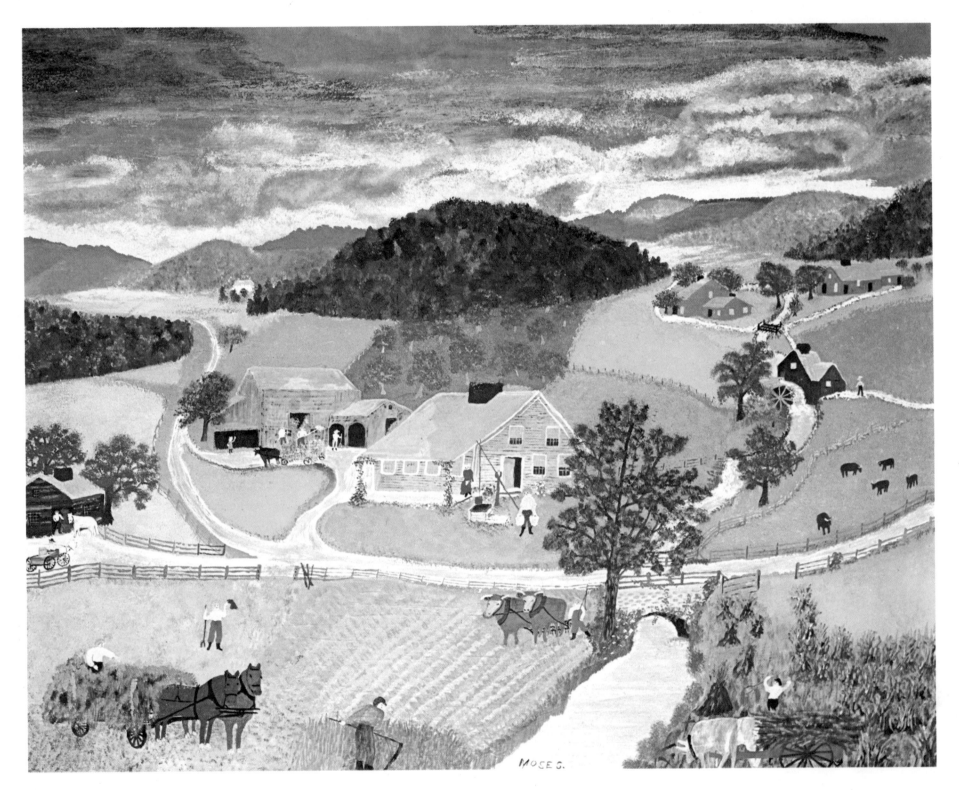

72. *Home of Hezekiah King in 1800, No. 4*. 1943. 23 x 29". Cat. 265

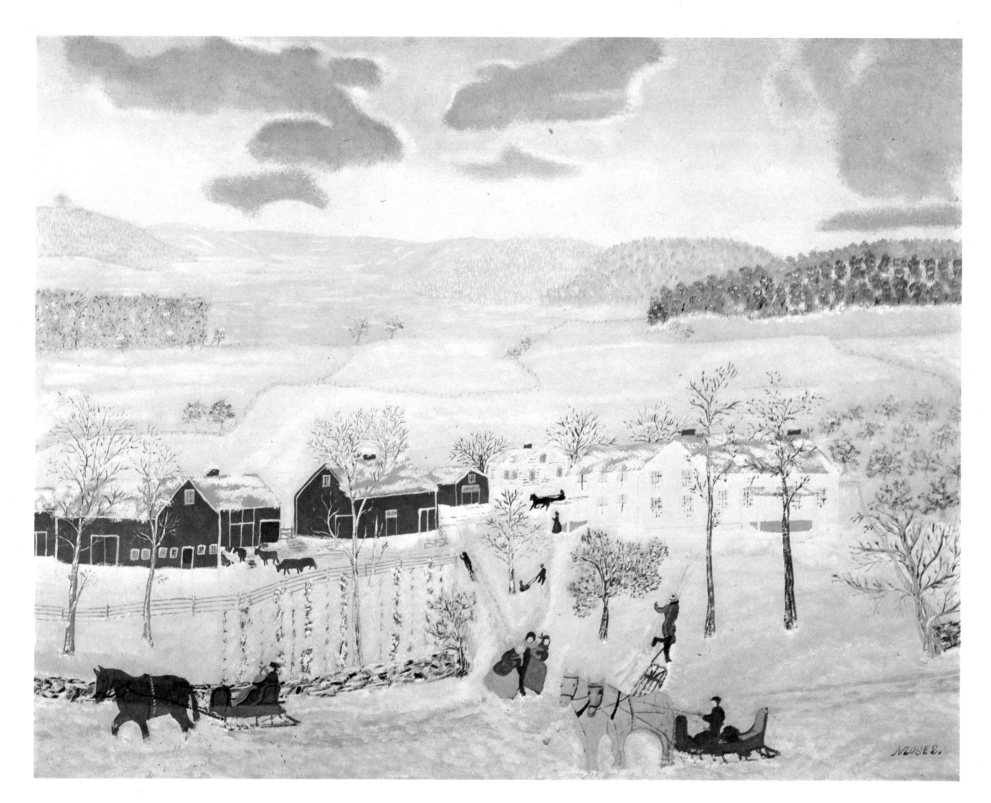

73. *Mt. Nebo in Winter.* 1943. 20½ x 26½". Cat. 275

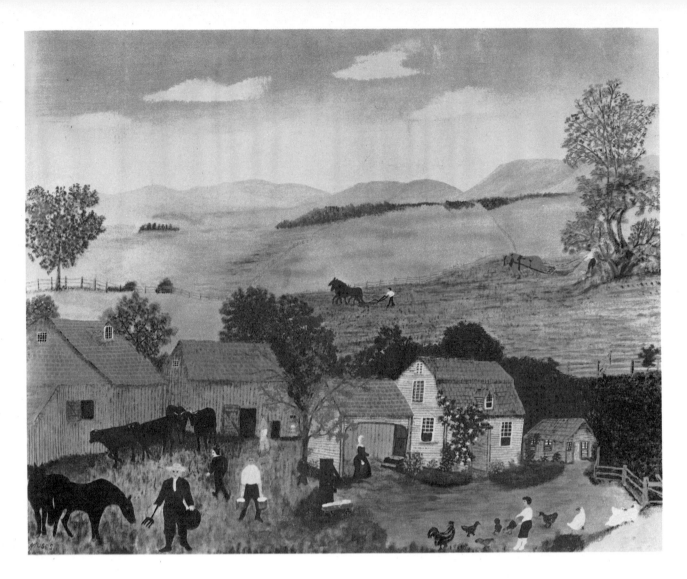

74.
In the Springtime.
1944. 24 x 30". Cat. 331

75.
Cambridge.
1944. 19 x 23". Cat. 353

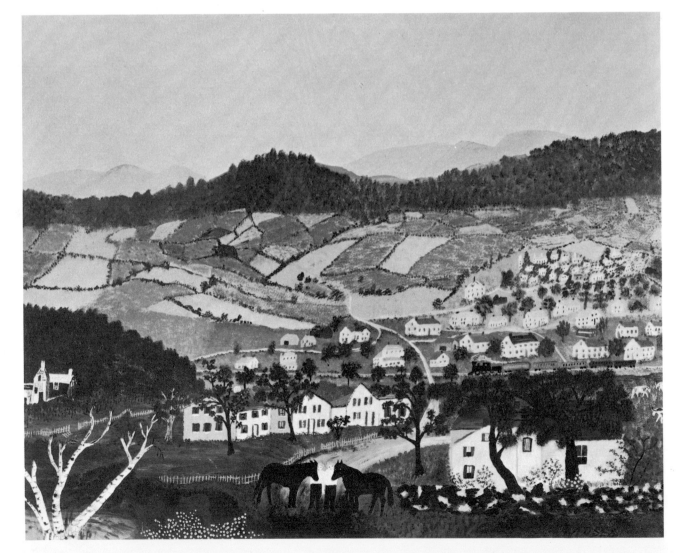

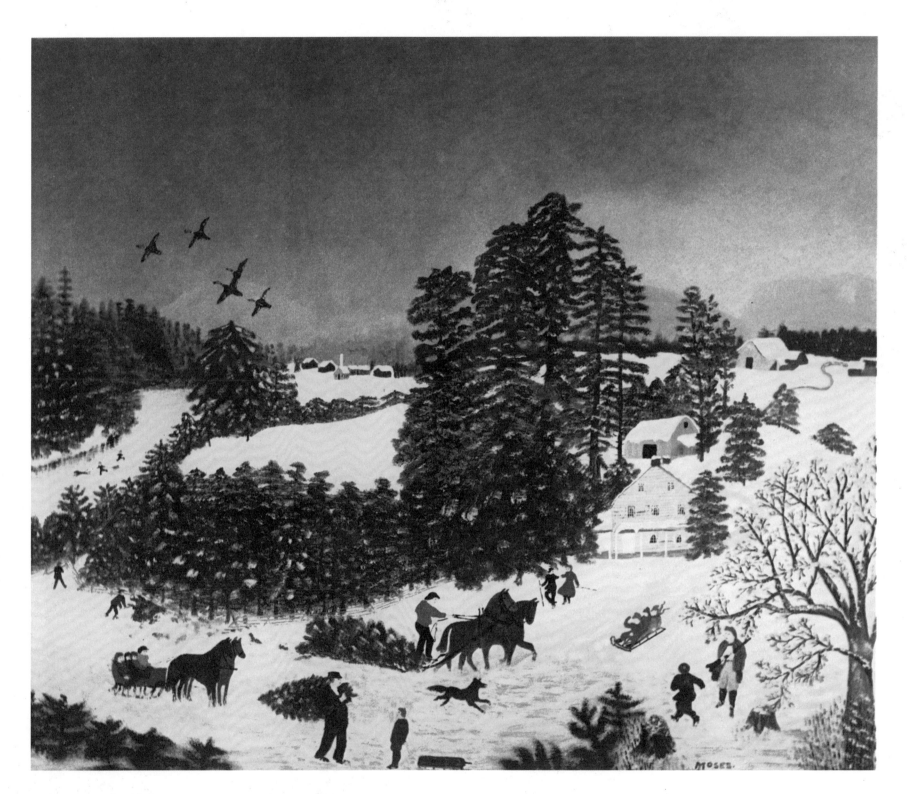

76. *Out for the Christmas Trees.* 1944. 24 x 29½". Cat. 444

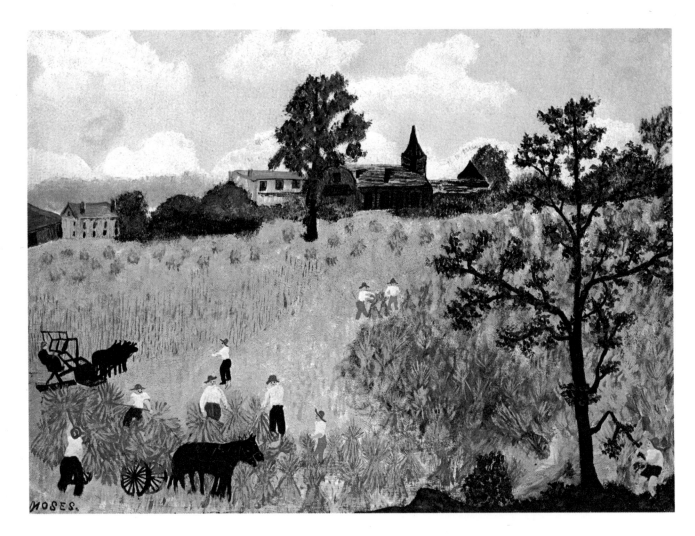

77.
In Harvest Time.
1944. 12 x 17". Cat. 379

78.
The Sun Has Gone Down.
1944. 6 x 9". Cat. 397

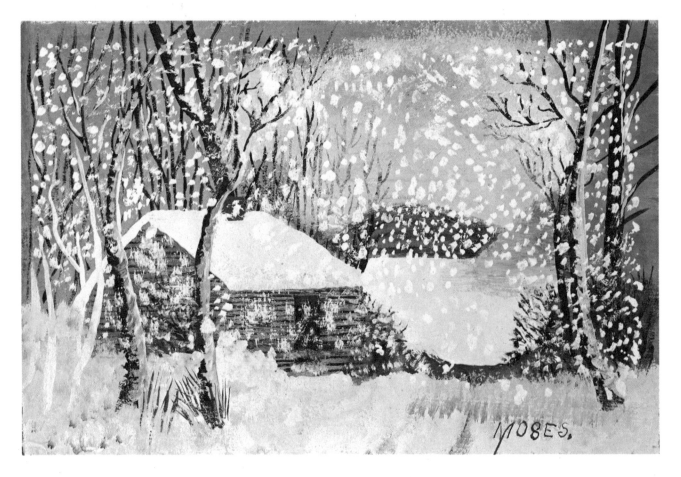

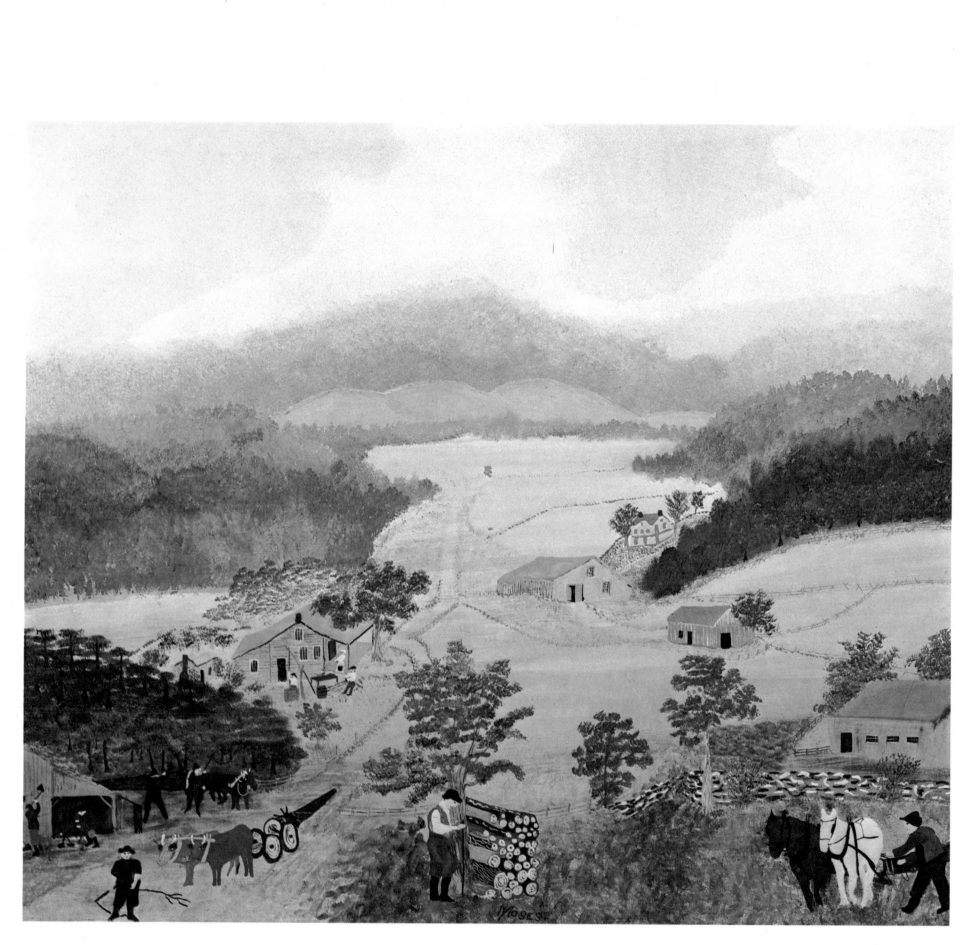

79. *First Wagon on Cambridge Pike.* 1944. 20 x 24". Cat. 415

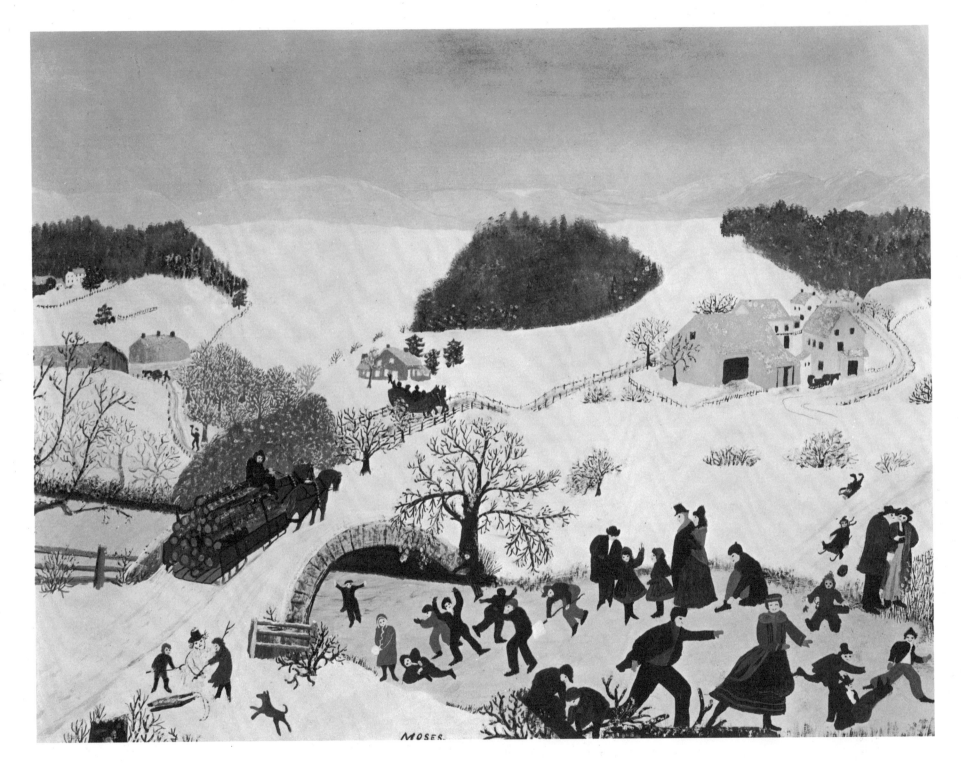

80. *The First Skating*. 1945. 17¾ x 23". Cat. 486

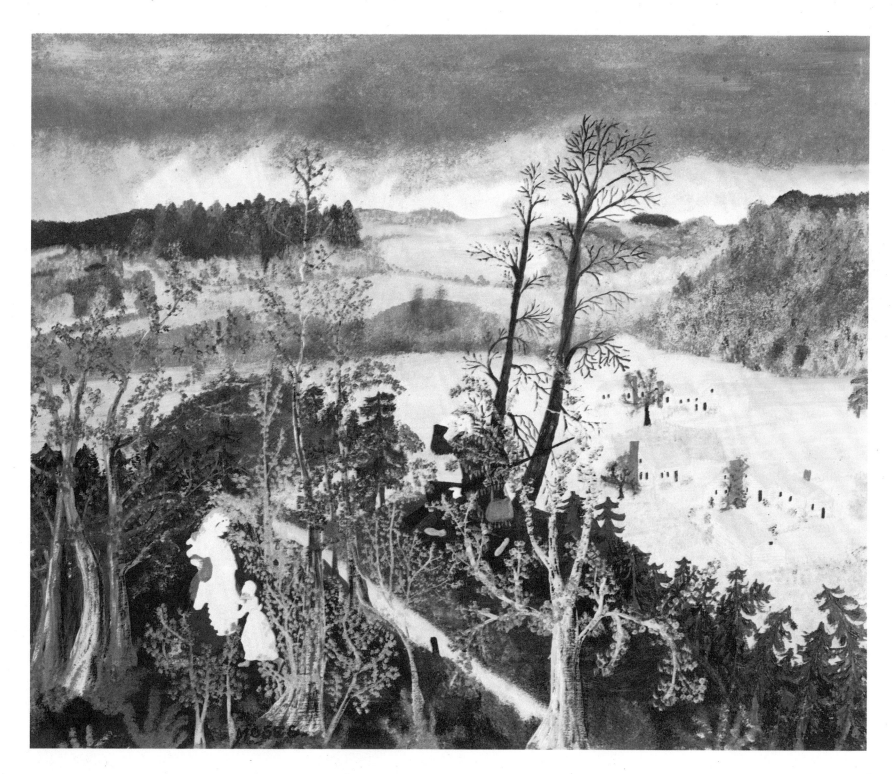

81. *The Lookout, 1777, Vermont.* 1945. 17 x 21". Cat. 508

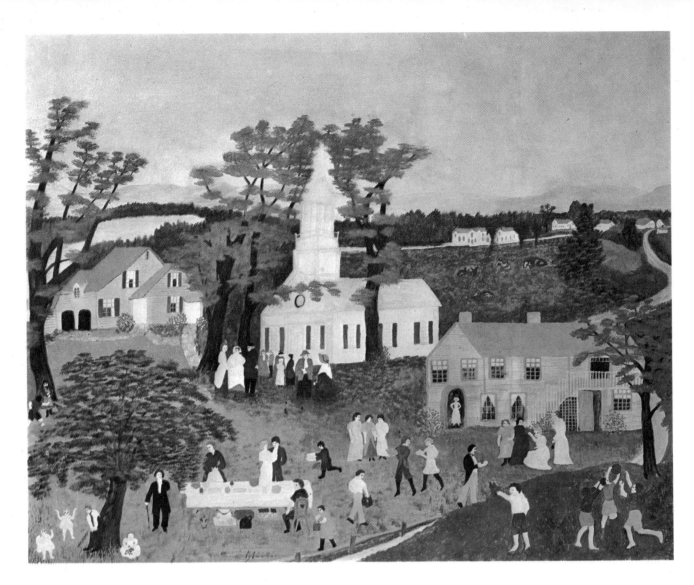

82.
Picnic. 1945.
24 x 30". Cat. 484

RIGHT:
83.
Wild Roses. 1945.
10¾ x 9¼". Cat. 495

FAR RIGHT:
84.
Wild Daisies. 1945.
11¾ x 7¾". Cat. 496

94

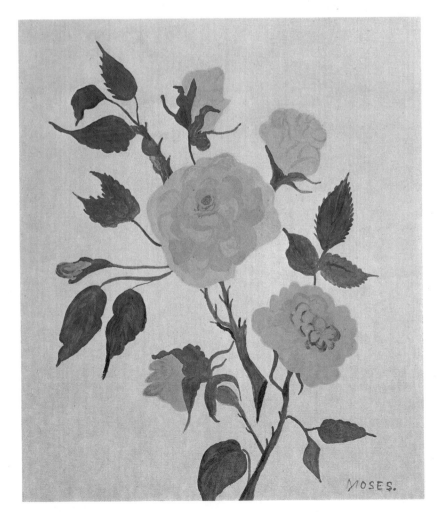

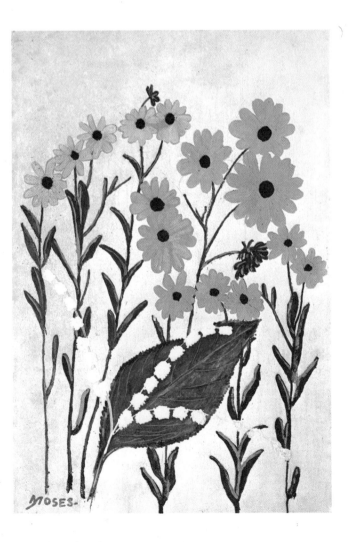

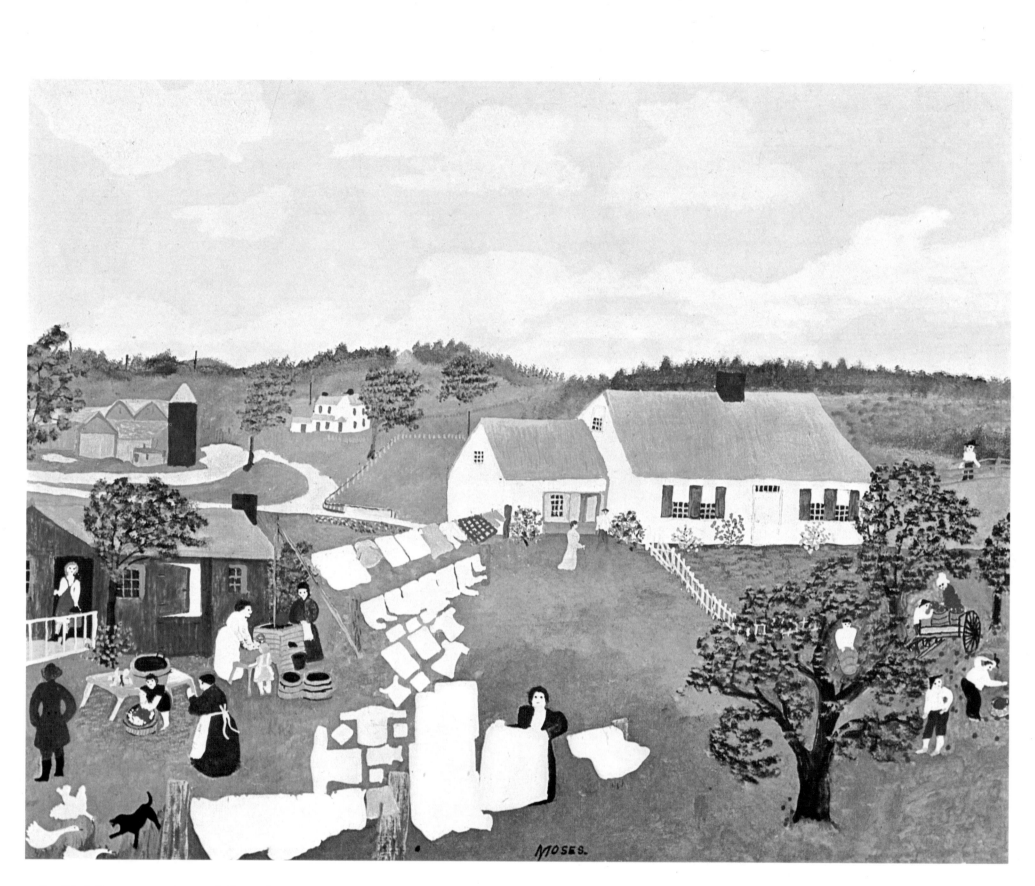

85. *Wash Day.* 1945. 17¾ x 23½". Cat. 498

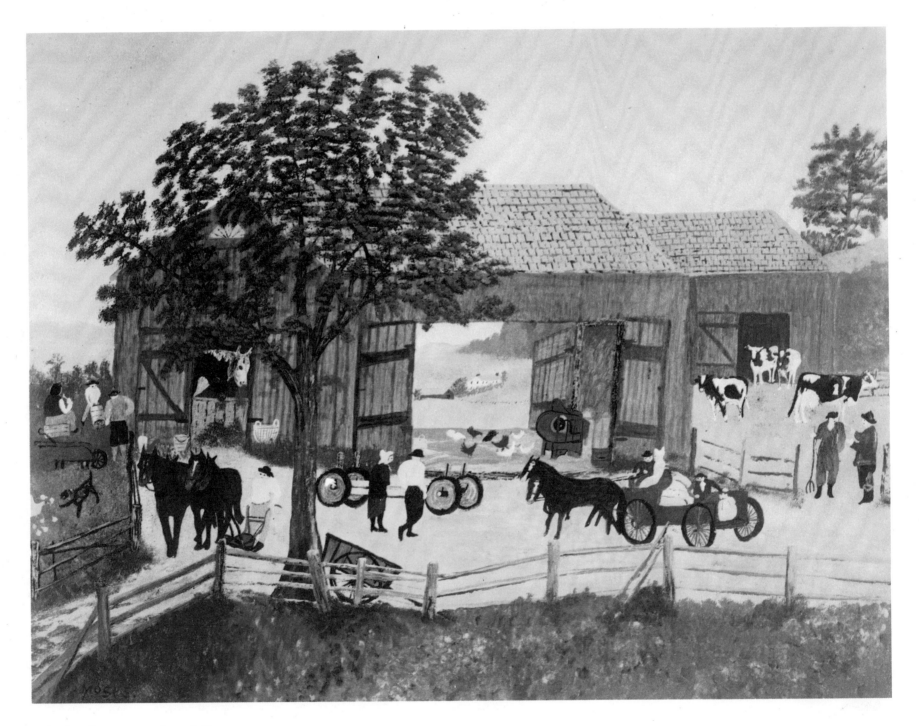

86. *Our Barn*. 1945. 18 x 24". Cat. 541

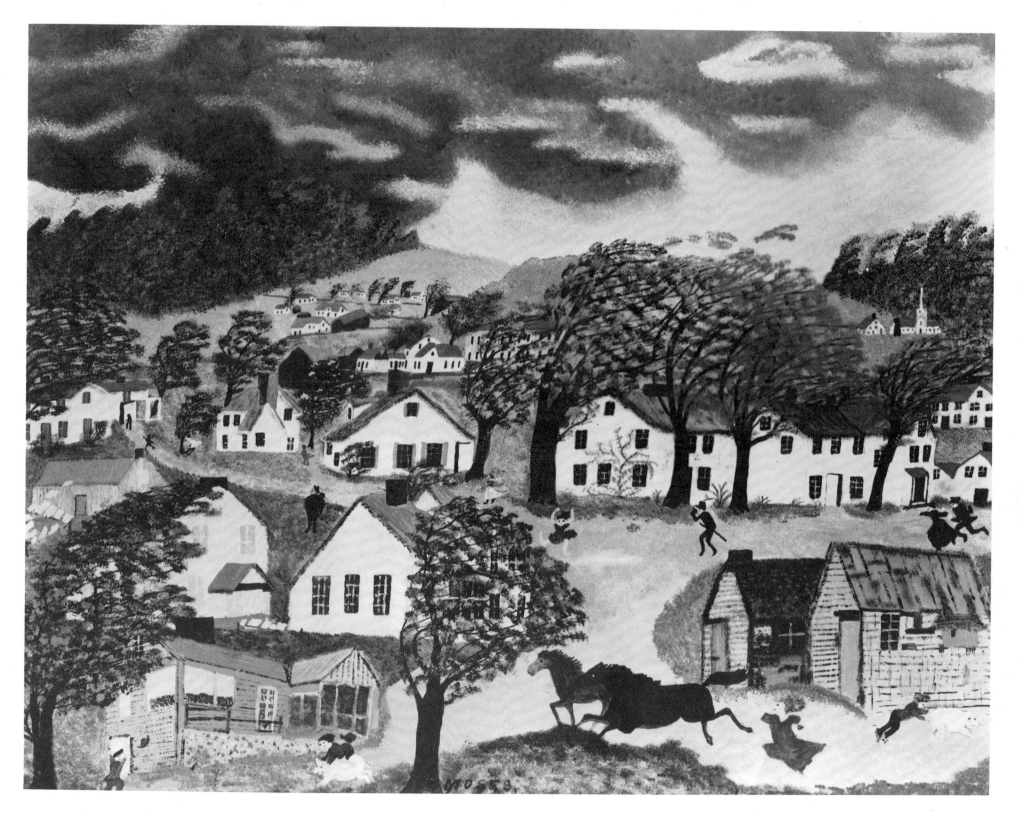

87. *Hurricane in Hoosick Falls.* 1945. 15¾ x 20". Cat. 566

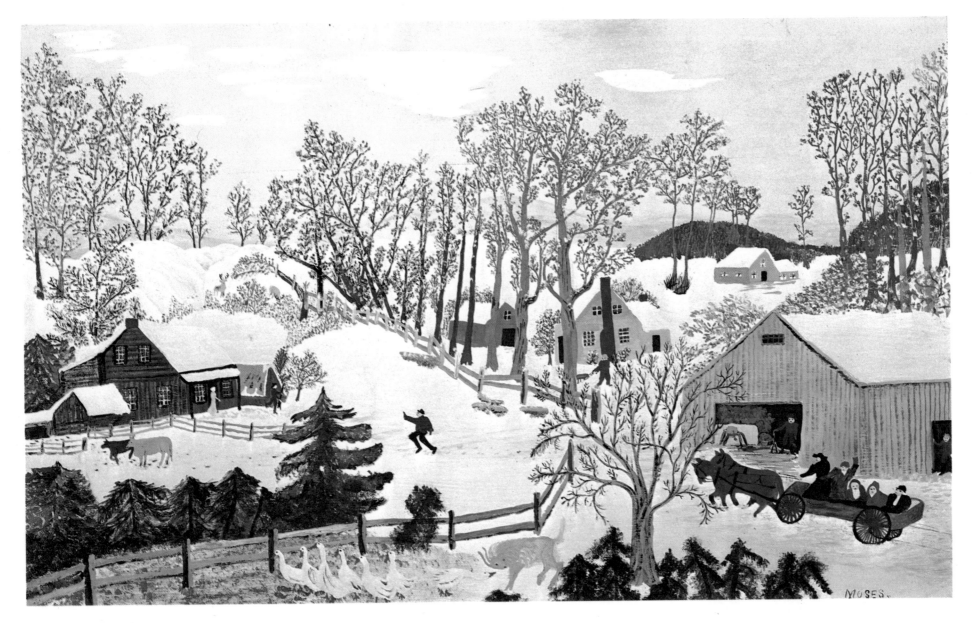

88. *Early Springtime on the Farm*. 1945. 16 x 25¾". Cat. 500

II
GROWING RECOGNITION

"Grandma Moses: American Primitive"

Having realized her importance as an artist and witnessed the public's growing interest, I decided, in 1945, to write a book on Grandma Moses. I had often visited her at her home in Eagle Bridge and we naturally discussed the project. From our many conversations and even more from her letters, I found, to my delight, that her ability to express herself was not limited to painting. She had a most vivid and personal style, as well as a spelling all her own. It was fascinating to listen when she told stories of her family and of events she had witnessed or been told about in her youth, some of historical interest, others just local anecdotes.

Feeling that here was a rich source of first-hand information about rural life in nineteenth-century America, I encouraged Grandma to write down what came to her mind whenever she felt like doing so. In the course of a year she sent me three autobiographical sketches, one of which is reproduced in facsimile at the beginning of the present volume. She sent along a letter, saying in her modest way: "Here is my life's history, can you make anything out of it? . . . You see, I don't know how to go about such things."

She also agreed to write comments on the forty paintings to be reproduced in the book. They were not only descriptions of the pictures, but also stories about the depicted events. Everything was written in her own clear and meticulous hand and was so charming and original that I decided to have the comments reproduced in facsimile opposite each illustration.

The book was published in 1946 (Dryden Press) under the title *Grandma Moses: American Primitive*. Louis Bromfield, who had been interested in the artist for a number of years, wrote the introduction. The book proved an immediate success, and was republished in 1947 (Doubleday)

101

with additional colorplates. Widely reviewed in the American press and in some European papers, it drew increased attention to Grandma Moses. Museums and art centers the country over asked to present her work.

89.
Sugaring Off. 1943.
23 x 27". First color reproduction, 1948.
Cat. 276

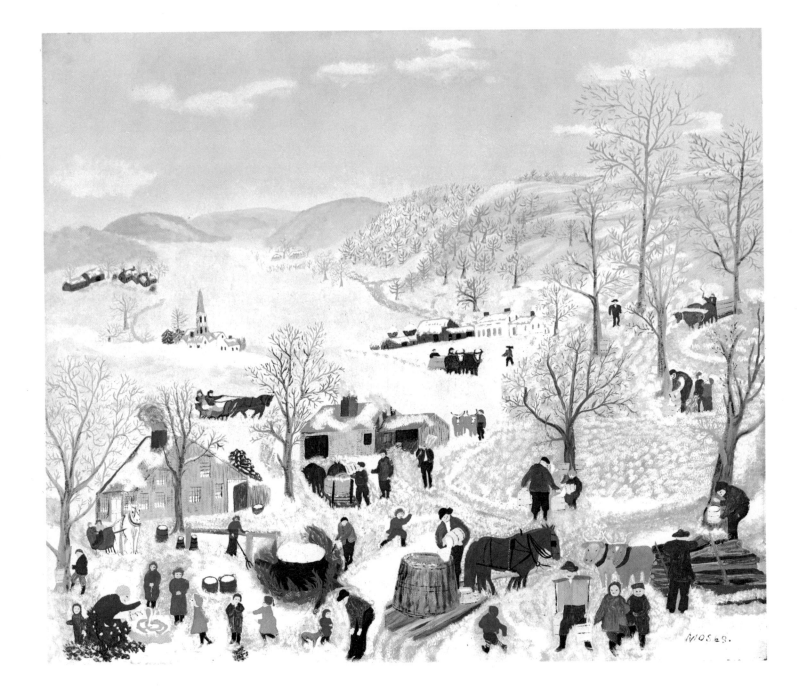

Reproductions and Christmas Cards

GRANDMA MOSES HAD NEVER HAD THE IDEA of selling her paintings for high prices; still less would the thought have entered her mind that she might receive money from reproductions of her pictures. She had always been a conscientious and thrifty housekeeper and she could not understand why she should get more for a painting than she had asked; it seemed to her almost an offense. I had already become familiar with this attitude in the course of the first exhibition. Two or three of her works had been sold for a substantially higher sum than what Louis Caldor had paid her. Not having met Mrs. Moses personally at the time, I suggested to Caldor that she be sent an additional amount. No sooner had the check been mailed than it was returned by Mrs. Moses with the remark that everything had been paid for, she was not owed anything, and she did not want the money.

Later on I once sent her twenty dollars above the price she had indicated for a picture. She kept it this time but wrote: "In regard to paying for paintings you do not have to pay more then I ask." (October 3, 1945) On a previous occasion she had written: "Don't pay me in advance as it puts me under obligation, and that I don't want now. Ive got to that age where I want to keep my House in order." (September 15, 1943)

Soon after the first exhibitions, requests came to reproduce Moses paintings. In order to protect them from unauthorized use, all her pictures were registered at the Copyright Office in Washington. Large, excellent-quality color reproductions of her important pictures were printed (see plate 89) which could be afforded by wide circles and contribute to making the artist's work known.

Christmas and greeting cards also helped to spread her popularity. The firm of Brundage Greeting Cards published the first set of sixteen Grandma Moses Christmas cards in 1946. Then, in 1947, Hallmark

103

acquired the right to reproduce the artist's paintings on Christmas and greeting cards and published them for many years.

When Grandma Moses received a large sum of money in royalties from the first Christmas card venture in 1946, she was at a loss to understand how she came to get it, and she did not cash the check. Visiting her some time later, I inquired why she had not done so, whereupon she produced it and seemed puzzled. I tried to explain that some of the paintings she had sold were earning all this money for her by being reproduced on Christmas cards and that she was participating in what they brought. She shook her head but promised to follow my suggestion and take the check to the bank in Hoosick Falls. The next day, the cash was lying in bundles on the table, and she said she had kept her word.

Seeing that Grandma Moses was not able to cope with such business matters, it was decided to have a lawyer take care of her financial affairs. Starting in 1947, all receipts from the sale of paintings and all royalties derived from copyrights went to Sylvester Scott of Hoosick Falls; he was a longtime friend, personally interested in the artist's work, and he administered her income almost up to the time of her death.

Documentary Film

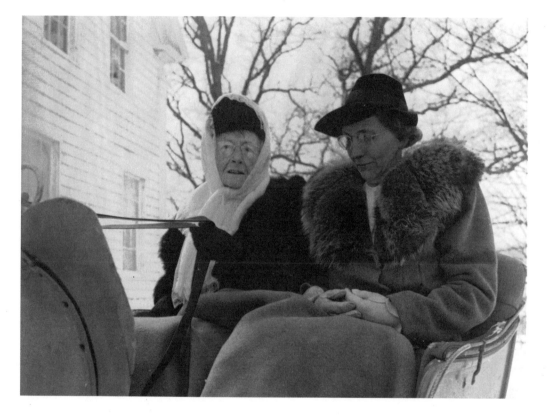

90.
Grandma Moses with her
daughter-in-law, Dorothy,
during making of documentary film.
Photo by Erica Anderson

ALA STORY, WHO SHARED MY CONVICTION of the artist's importance, had been working closely with me since 1945—our association lasted many years. In 1946 we began making plans for a film on Grandma Moses. Erica Anderson, who was to gain fame with her movie on Albert Schweitzer, went up to Eagle Bridge from time to time and took color pictures of the artist, her home, her family, the setting of her daily life, and the surrounding countryside. They were as yet disconnected color shots with no guiding script. The motion picture producer Jerome Hill then arranged the material to form a documentary, which was completed in 1950. Archibald MacLeish wrote and narrated the text; the music was composed by Hugh Martin and arranged by Alec Wilder. The film received the "Certificate of Nomination for Award" from the Academy of Motion Picture Arts and Sciences.

105

Visit to Washington

In May 1949, Grandma Moses was invited to go to Washington, D.C., to receive the Women's National Press Club Award. The President of the United States was to present "certificates of achievement" to six women who were being honored "for their outstanding contributions to their respective fields for the year 1948."

Grandma Moses left her home in Eagle Bridge on May 12 in the company of her daughter-in-law Dorothy. They arrived in New York by train. A wheelchair had been prepared at the station to take Grandma to a taxi. "That was humiliating to me, but I couldn't have walked it," she later wrote. She and Dorothy spent two nights at our home in New York.

The press wished to meet her, so I arranged a small exhibition of the artist's paintings at my gallery.

The next day the *New York Herald Tribune* wrote:

> There was a host of reporters, photographers and radio people in the room when Grandma walked in. . . . After surviving the ordeal by flash bulbs she moved over to a sofa, where she faced a solid ring of reporters with a devil-may-care attitude. . . . The questions came thick and fast and mixed up. She not only displayed the utter independence of the elderly but it was evident that she was having the reporters on a bit. . . . When asked if she was excited at the prospect of seeing President Truman and Mrs. Franklin D. Roosevelt, who also is receiving the award, she said, "No. Not at all." . . . Somebody asked if she wanted to paint the New York City scene.
>
> "It doesn't appeal to me," she said.
>
> "You mean it doesn't appeal to you as painting material?" someone asked.
>
> "As any material," said Grandma crisply.

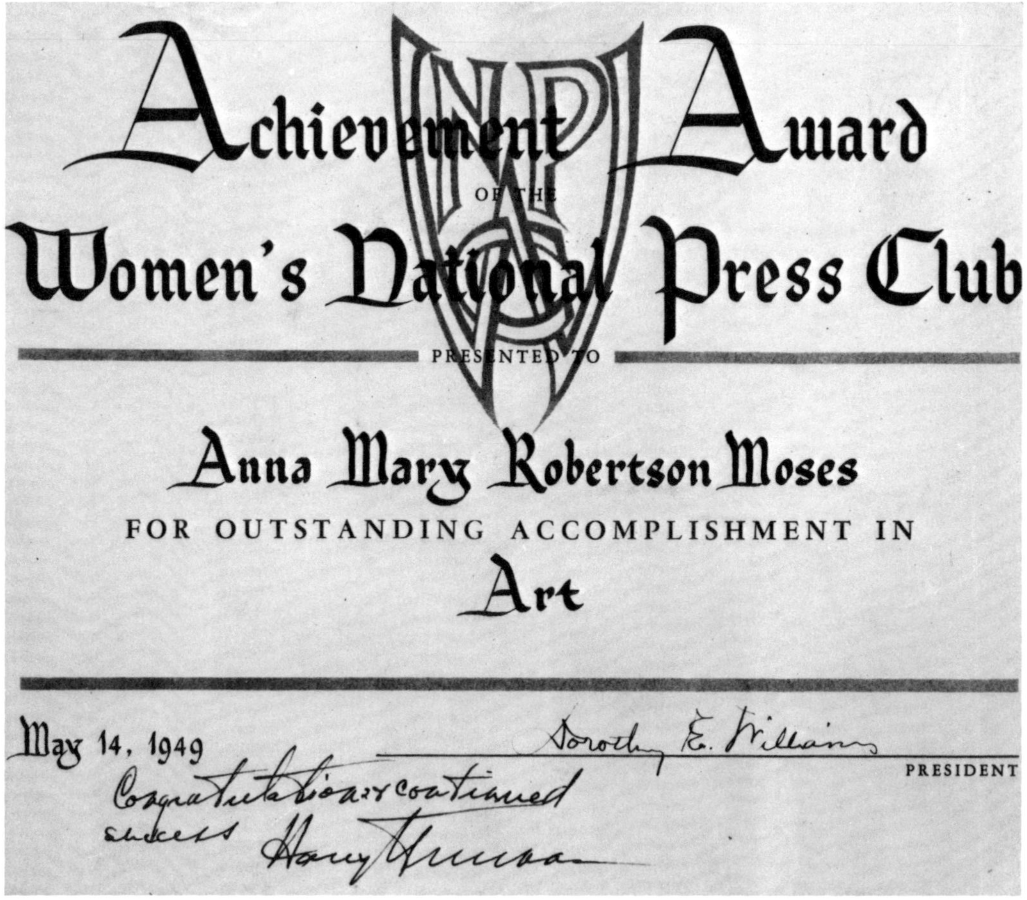

91. Achievement Award

With characteristic understatement she called her painting a pleasant occupation. "As I finish each picture, I think I've done my last, but I go right on," she said.

On the evening of May 14 the official dinner took place in the Presidential Room of the Statler Hotel in Washington. Seven hundred guests attended, among them the diplomatic corps, the Supreme Court Justices, and the members of the President's Cabinet with their wives. When Grandma Moses entered the hall, she received a big ovation, which she smilingly acknowledged without interrupting her progress toward the dais, where she was seated next to Mrs. Truman. The President handed her the award "for outstanding accomplishment in Art," which he had inscribed for her.

The other recipients were: Mrs. Franklin D. Roosevelt for her work as Chairman of the United Nations Human Rights Commission; Mary

107

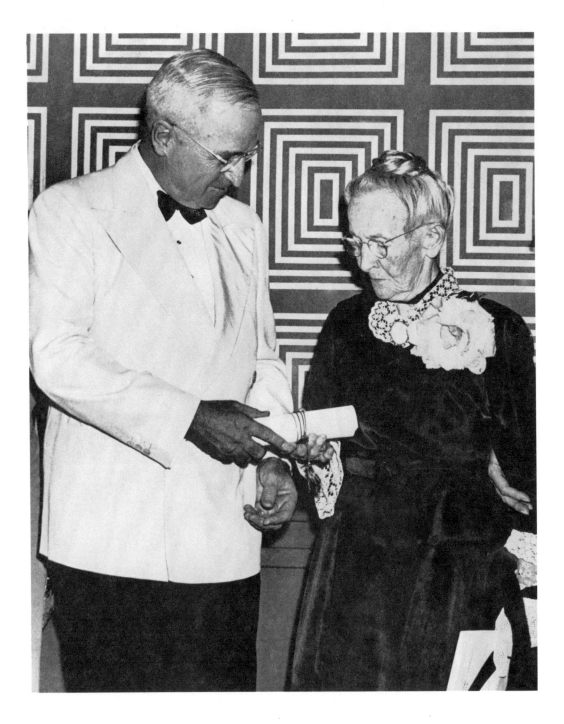

Jane Ward, author of *The Snake Pit,* a novel which focused attention on the need for improving mental institutions; Madeleine Carroll for outstanding achievement in the theater; Dorothy McCullough Lee, the first woman to be elected mayor of a city exceeding 500,000 (Portland, Oregon); and Marjorie Child Husted, of General Mills, Inc., for achievement in business.

During the dinner Grandma Moses carried on a lively conversation with the President and his wife. He told me afterward how charmed and impressed he was by her and added that he would very much like to see her again and that therefore, if at all possible, he would attend a tea

THE WHITE HOUSE
WASHINGTON

May 26, 1949

Dear Grandma Moses:

I certainly appreciated your good letter of May
twenty-third. I am glad you enjoyed your visit
to Washington.

Mrs. Truman and I were delighted to see you
at the dinner and to have you at the Blair House
for tea. My piano playing doesn't amount to
much but I am glad you enjoyed it.

I hope you have many, many happy years ahead
of you.

Sincerely yours,

Harry Truman

Mrs. Anna Mary Robertson Moses
Eagle Bridge
New York

93. Letter from President Truman to
Grandma Moses, May 26, 1949

to which the award recipients had been invited by Mrs. Truman the following day.

When we arrived at Blair House, where the Trumans were living while the White House was being remodeled, the President was already there and he again chatted with Mrs. Moses. "After the tea," Grandma recalled, "we had a terrific thunderstorm, so we sat down on a couch to wait till the shower was over. President Truman sat beside me and said, 'Don't be afraid, as this is a large building with many lightning rods on it.' Maybe he thought Grandma might be afraid. I talked with him, and I could not think but that he was one of my own boys. I even asked him to play something on the piano." At first he was reluctant and suggested he would turn on the radio instead, but Mrs. Moses insisted, so he smilingly went to the piano and played a minuet by Paderewsky. "That was a delight," she wrote. "Then the shower was over, and he ordered his own car to take us to the Hotel Statler, that was an honor."

Next day Grandma Moses visited the Phillips Gallery, where a large loan exhibition of her paintings had been arranged. In 1941 Mr. and Mrs. Duncan Phillips had been the first to acquire a Grandma Moses picture for an American museum; they subsequently added several more to their collection (see plates 94, 216).

When Grandma Moses and Dorothy returned home on May 20, "her many friends, neighbors and relatives in Eagle Bridge were joined by folks from all over Rensselaer County who came to welcome Mrs. Moses. . . . Several hundred automobiles jammed the village's only street, as an estimated 800 persons—almost twice the population of Eagle Bridge—assembled at the World War II Honor Roll in the center of the little community. . . . She was back home again after receiving the largest welcome the small village could give. . . ." (*Troy Record,* May 21, 1949) School children sang and presented her

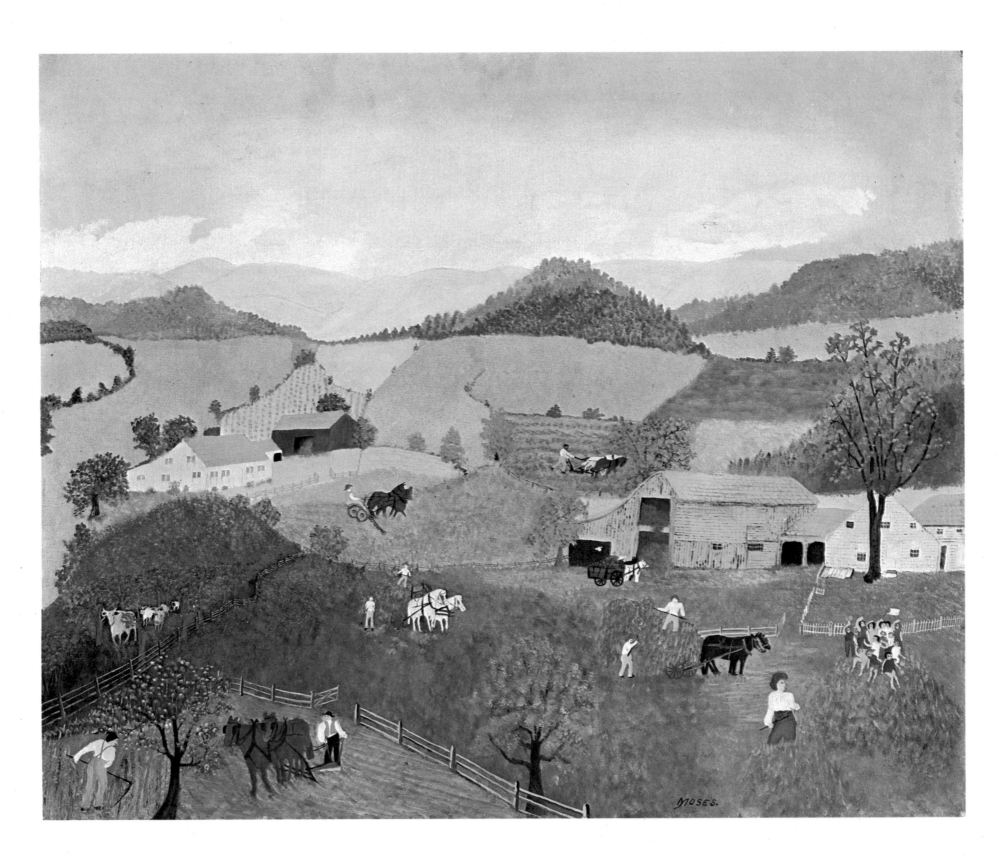

110   94. *The McDonnell Farm.* 1943. 24 x 30". Cat. 313

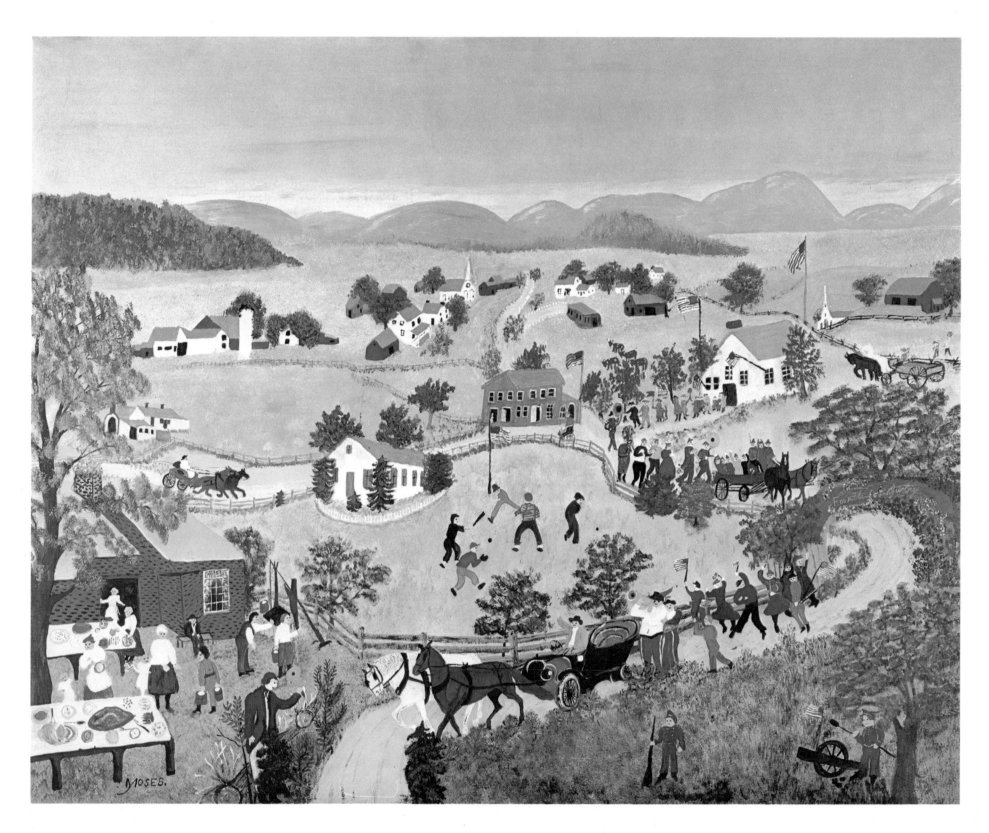

95. *July Fourth*. 1951. 23⅞ x 30". Cat. 999

with flowers. The Hoosick Falls High School band played and escorted her all the way home.

Perhaps of the honors she had received, she enjoyed most the welcome she got in Eagle Bridge. "In a way I was glad to get back and go to bed that night," she wrote later.

When President and Mrs. Truman moved into the remodeled White House, I wrote to Mrs. Truman on March 21, 1952: "As I have seen in the papers, the White House will be reopened on April lst. It would be a great pleasure to me to dedicate on this occasion an original painting by Grandma Moses to the White House and to the American people, if the President and you would approve of my intention, and if there is a place for it." My suggestion was accepted, and *July Fourth* (plate 95), which the artist had painted in August 1951, has been hanging at the White House ever since.

Moving to a New House

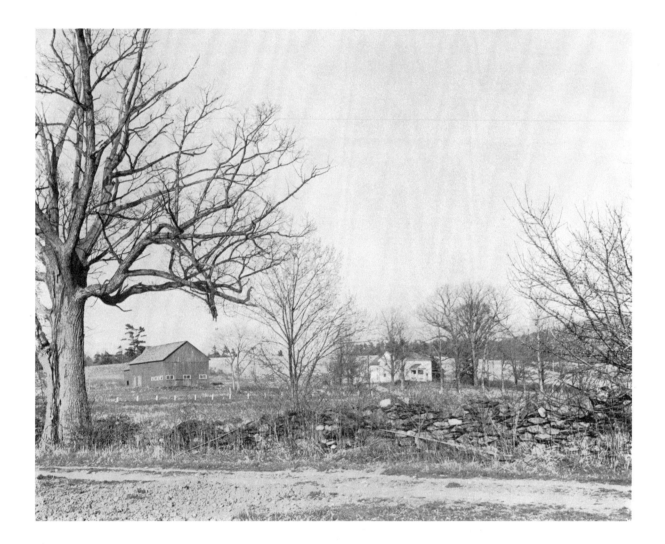

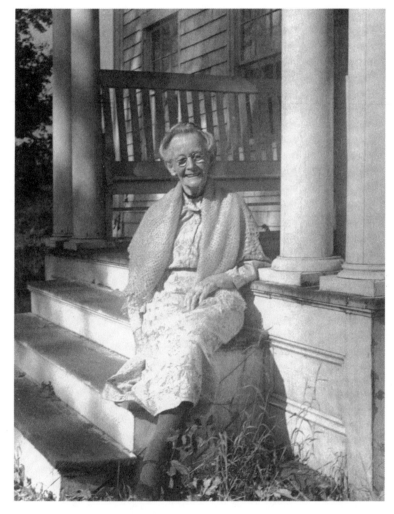

96. Grandma Moses's old house, Eagle Bridge, N.Y.

97. Grandma Moses on the front-porch steps of the old house, c. 1946

GRANDMA MOSES WAS NOT TO STAY MUCH LONGER in the old farmhouse, although she referred to it as "home" for the rest of her life. Her youngest son, Hugh, who had taken care of the Moses farm, had died suddenly in February 1949. Grandma stayed on with her daughter-in-law Dorothy, but her two surviving sons, Forrest and Loyd, were building a more comfortable ranch-style house for her across the road. She moved

113

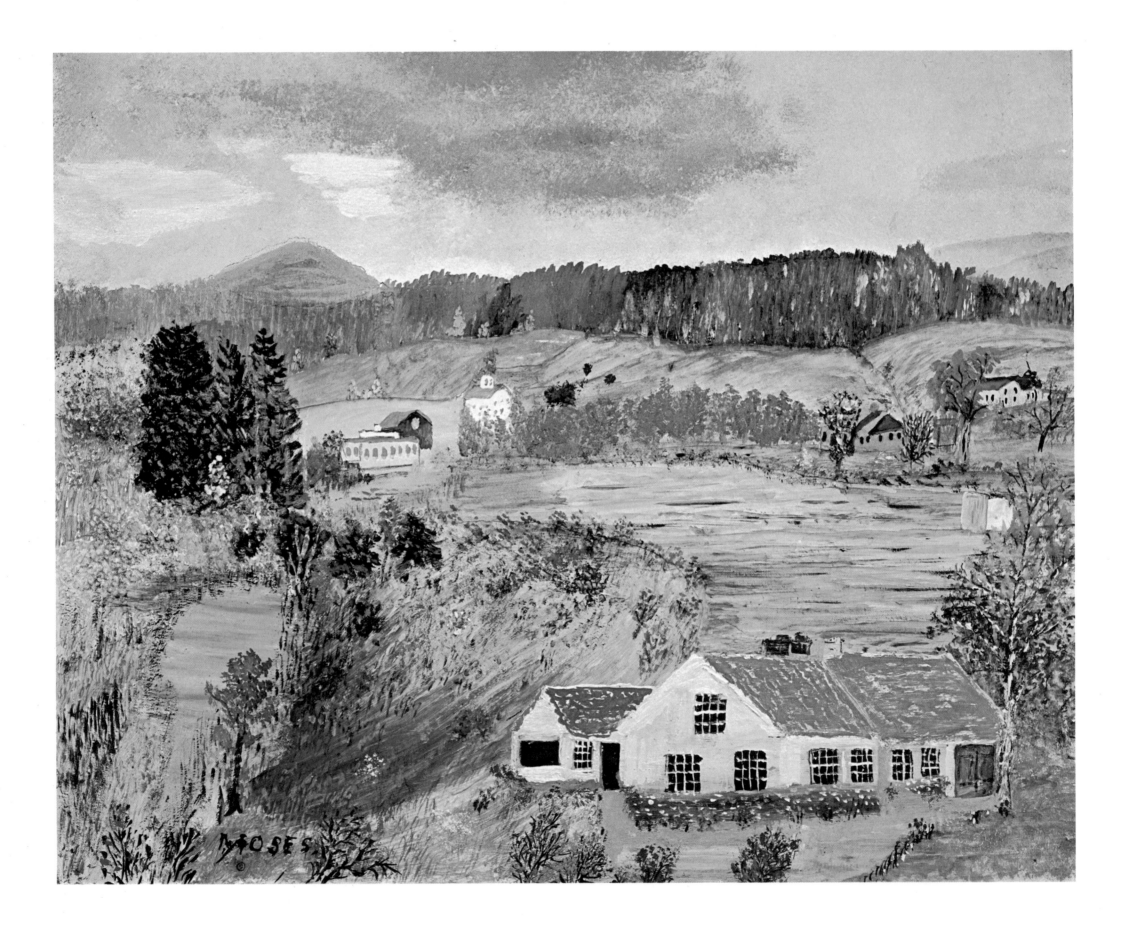

99.
Grandma Moses in front of
the new house, 1952

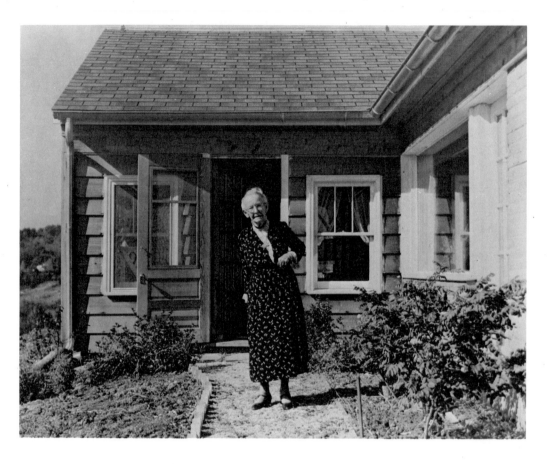

 98.
Grandpa's House. 1951.
9¼ x 12″. Cat. 995.
In spite of its title, this picture
shows the house to which the artist
moved in April 1951

into it in April 1951. Her daughter, Winona Fisher, came from California to care for her and eventually took over more and more of the tasks that Grandma had been doing herself, such as letter writing, making entries in the Record Book, and sometimes writing labels for pictures. Aside from seeing to it that her mother was comfortable, Mrs. Fisher had a keen understanding of her significance as an artist and as a personality. After Mrs. Fisher's death in 1958, Forrest Moses and his wife Mary moved in with Grandma and took care of her.

First European Exhibitions

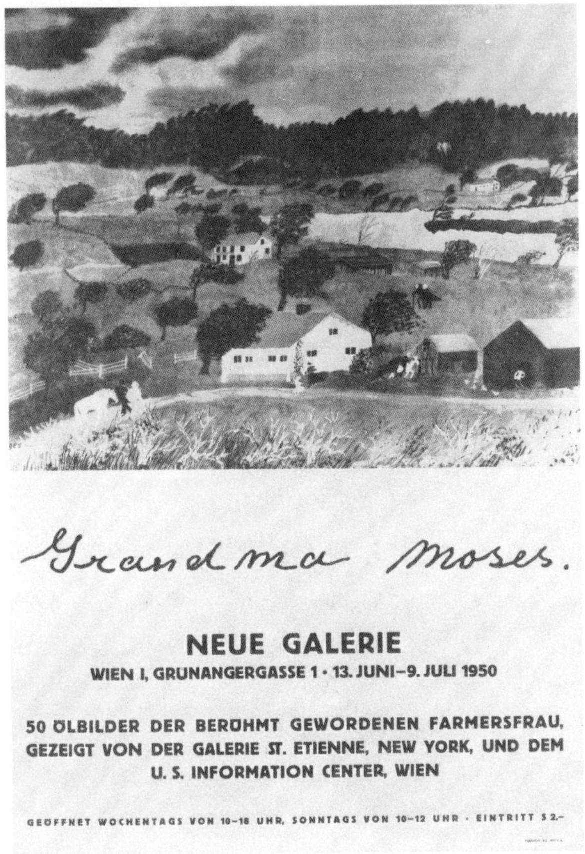

100. Poster of the first
Moses exhibition to travel
in Europe

SHORTLY AFTER WORLD WAR II, European papers and magazines had begun to take notice of Grandma Moses. Many articles, frequently accompanied by illustrations, were published on the story of Anna Mary Robertson Moses and on the attention her work was receiving in the United States. A desire to see the original paintings was repeatedly expressed, and in 1950 a collection of fifty pictures was assembled and sent to Europe under the sponsorship of United States Information Centers or embassies. The exhibition was shown in Vienna, Munich, Salzburg, Berne, The Hague, and Paris. While the initial reaction to the "Grandma Moses phenomenon" had been one of skepticism, a first-hand acquaintance with the artist's work brought about a complete change of attitude. The enthusiastic response to the shows surpassed all expectations. Great numbers of visitors and many favorable reviews and comments bore witness to the surprise and pleasure the originality of her art had evoked. "Grandma Moses is one of the key symbols of our time. . . . She is clearly an artist, whose paintings reveal a quality identical with genius. . . ." wrote a critic for the noted London magazine *Art News and Review*.

These European exhibitions and some lectures on American folk art I had given met with such interest that in 1954 the Smithsonian Institution organized the show "American Painting: Peintres Naïfs from 1700 to the Present." It was circulated in Europe by the United States Information Agency. The collection, which included works by Grandma Moses, presented a cross-section of American folk painting. The confrontation of European art circles with what had been until then a totally unfamiliar form of American painting proved most instructive.

In contrast to Europe, no art schools had existed in America until well into the nineteenth century. People who painted had to find their own

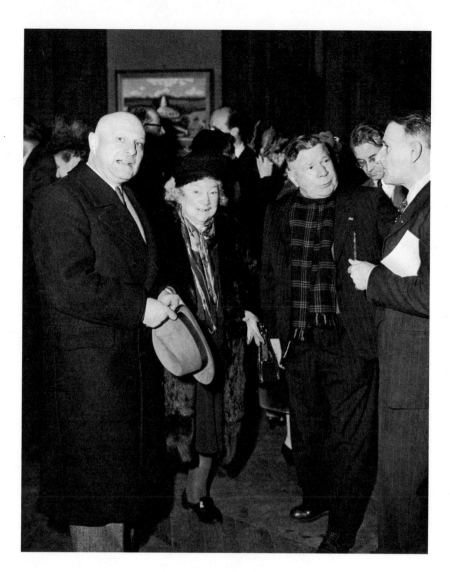

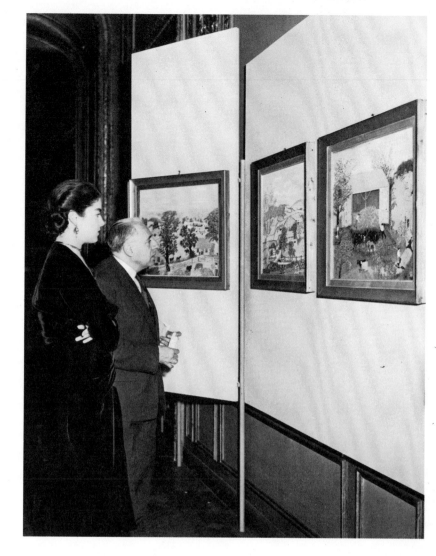

101. Opening, Grandma Moses exhibition, Paris,
December 1950: M. Bizardel, Director of
Fine Arts, Musées et Bibliothèque de la
Ville de Paris, with the French Primitive
painter Camille Bombois and Mme Bombois

102. At the opening of the Grandma Moses
exhibition in Paris, December 1950:
Darthea Speyer, Assistant Cultural Officer
of the U.S. Embassy, Paris, with Jean
Cassou, art historian, then chief curator
of the Musée National d'Art Moderne, Paris

technical and artistic means of expression. The importance of this art
had not been recognized until fairly recently. Within the framework
of the show, Grandma Moses proved to be not so much an isolated
figure as a link in a long chain. Each of these untaught artists had found
his individual way of expressing ideas of his time and experiences of
his daily life. Like all "peintres naïfs," they painted for pleasure in
their spare time. Edward Hicks (1780–1849), the painter of the *Peaceable
Kingdom*, was a Quaker preacher; John Kane (1860–1934), a manual

117

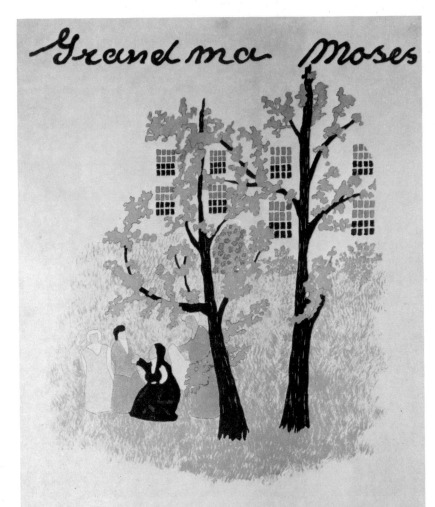

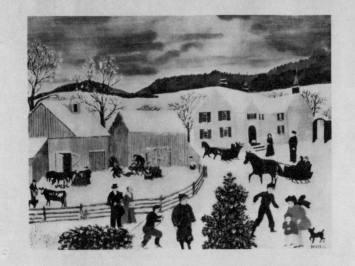

103—4. Posters of the first Moses exhibition to travel in Europe

laborer, mainly depicted the industrial landscape of Pittsburgh; Horace Pippin (1888–1946) took his inspiration from a Negro cultural background. Grandma Moses was a farmwife and her work re-creates the American rural scene.

"My Life's History"

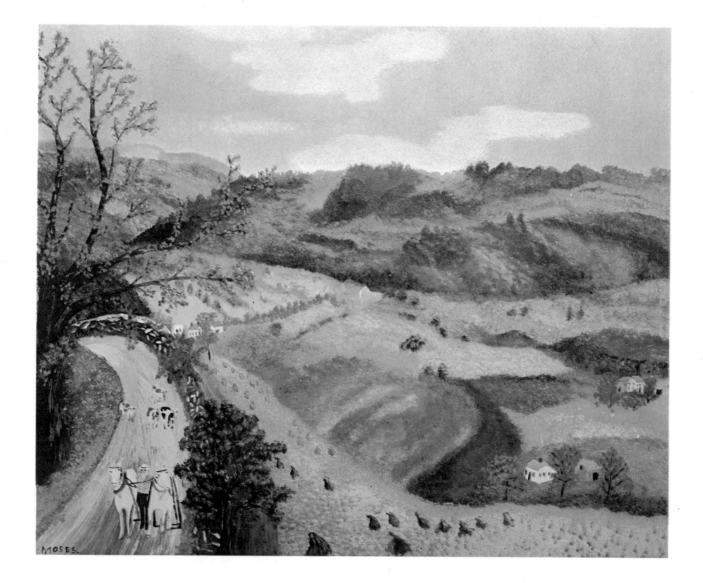

105.
My Homeland. 1945.
16 x 20". Cat. 510

GRANDMA MOSES'S AUTOBIOGRAPHY, *My Life's History,* is the most important source of first-hand information about the artist.

The ability to express herself in a highly personal and original way has already been mentioned. I was convinced that what had appeared in print in 1946–47 was but a small part of what she had to say. Therefore, I urged her to write more about her life. She wrote a short piece titled "I Remember," which was published in the *New York Times Magazine* in 1948. It began:

What a strange thing is memory, and Hope, one looks backward, the other forward, The one is of to day, the other is the tomorrow, memory is History recorded in our brain, memory is a painter it paints pictures of the past and of the day,

Her autobiography was to open with these words. In the course of the next few years she jotted down little stories and sketches, sending in all 169 handwritten pages; of these only 37 deal with the years in which she had become a world-famous artist, an indication of how little importance she attached to her success as a painter, as compared to the vivid recollections of the full life she had led before as farmwife and head of a large family.

When Grandma Moses came to New York in 1949 I tried using a tape recorder to spare her the trouble of writing down her memories. But she disliked microphones; she preferred, she said, to write everything herself. After the principal content of the book had been written and its general plan had emerged, she dictated connecting passages at her home in Eagle Bridge. Some corrections in spelling were made at her insistence, although the editor was reluctant to alter what he regarded as part of her characteristic way of expressing herself.

Descriptions of everyday life on the farm alternate with recollections of historical events, such as the death of President Lincoln and the still strained relations between North and South long after the Civil War. Many of these memories form a lively commentary to the paintings that illustrate them.

120

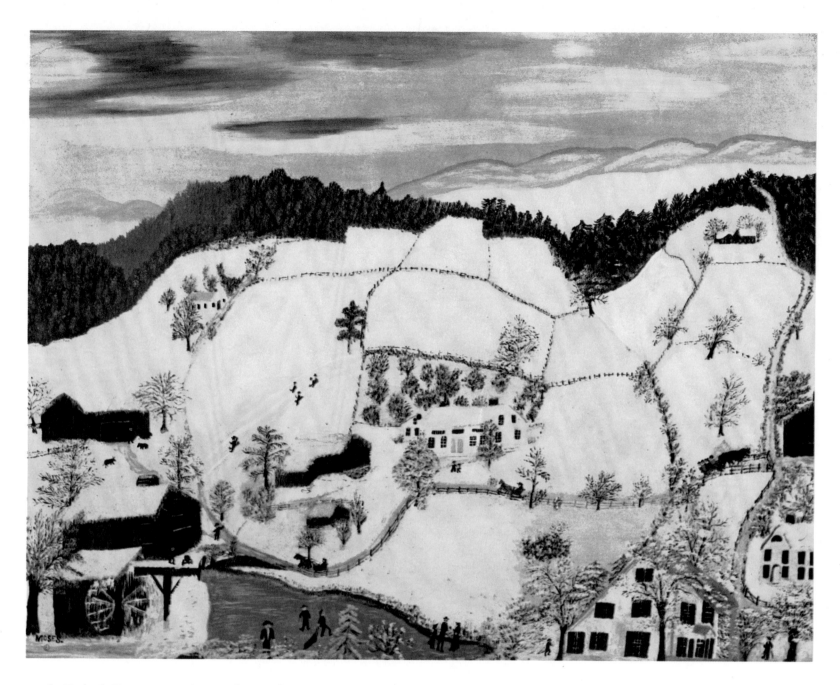

106. *Father's Home.* 1952. 18 x 24". Cat. 1056

At the end of the book Grandma Moses summarizes:

> In the foregoing chapters I have tried to tell you many true facts
> as they were in my days. It is hard in this age for one to realize
> how we grew up at all. I felt older when I was 16 than I ever did
> since. . . .
>
> Things have changed greatly and still are changing, can they
> change much more? . . .
>
> And yet I wonder sometimes whether we are progressing. In

121

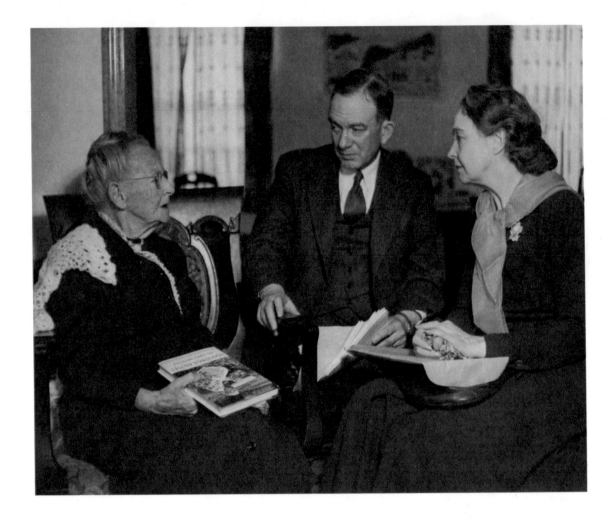

107. Grandma Moses, Otto Kallir, and Lillian Gish in Eagle Bridge, 1952

my childhood days life was different, in many ways, we were slower, still we had a good and happy life, I think, people enjoyed life more in their way, at least they seemed to be happier, they don't take time to be happy nowadays. . . .

I have written my life in small sketches, a little today, a little yesterday, as I thought of it, as I remembered all the things from childhood on through the years, good ones, and unpleasant ones, that is how they come, and that is how we have to take them. I look back on my life like a good day's work, it was done and I feel satisfied with it. I was happy and contented, I knew nothing better and made the best out of what life offered. And life is what we make it, always has been, always will be.

The book was published in 1952 (Harper); it subsequently appeared in England and, in translation, in Germany and Holland.

108.
"Let home be made happy,"
written by Anna Mary in 1874

Let home be made happy.

Industry is a homely virtue yet worthy of all praise. even nature herself reads us a lecture upon it. Let us go for a moment from the homes of men to the quiet forest. here we shall find no discord or tumult of worldly traffic. it is silent. but look around and see what has been done by the busy hand of nature. will you look at nature and see her with industrious fingers weaving flowers and plants and grasses and trees and shrubs to ornament every part of the earth. and will you go home no wiser for this hint? Will you go home to that dear spot upon which the heart should shine as the sun in spring-time shines upon the flowers. and permit it to be the scene of idleness negligence and waste.

Will you permit it to be a naked shelter from the weather. like the den of a wild beast. will not adorn it by your industry as nature adorns the fields and the forest.

If you say that this is somewhat fanciful and should be regarded rather as an illustration then let it be so. still are not the works of nature designed to have an influence of this kind upon us. then let man be happy in adorning his home. in making his home the dwelling of happiness and comfort. let him as far as circumstances will permit be industrious in surrounding it with pleasing objects in decorating it within and without with things that tend to make it agreeable and attractive. let industry and taste make home the abode of neatness and order a place which brings satisfaction to every inmate and which in absence draws back the heart by the fond memories of comfort and contents. let this be done and this dear spot will become more surely the home of cheerfulness. kindness and peace. The parents who would have their children happy must be persevering in bringing them up in the midst of a pleasant. a cheerful. a happy home.

there are many happy homes scattered all over our land some are princely abods in the city. others beautiful suburban residences. but among them all there are none more homelike and peaceful than those quiet farmhouses we find among the green hills and fields of the country. and none seem more deserving to be called dear home. in them we find freedom from the weary rounds of fashion. The wife and mother finds time to devote herself to her children. and her examples and influence impress on their minds those principles which will govern their whole after life.

Waste not your time in geathering unnecessary wealth for them but fill their minds and souls with seeds of virtue.

Let children join with their parents in trying to make home a happy place they can at least practice obedience to parents and kindness to all around. For if you do not when you come to leave it!h! how much you will think of home. but leave it you must soon. the lapse of years will bring around the time when you are to go from home you are to leave that dear old place to go out in the world & meet its temptations and to contend with its storms The day will come in which you are to leave the fireside of so many enjoyments the friends endeared to you by so many acts of kindness. you are to say "GoodBye" to your Mother you are to leave a Fathers protection to go forth and act without an adviser. and rely upon your one unaided judgment you are to bid Farewell to Brother and Sister no more to see them but on occasional visits at your home.

Oh! how cold and desolate will the world appear. how your heart will shrink from launching forth to meet its tempest and its storms. Then you will think of your happy home and say.

'Mid pleasure and palaces though we may roam
Be it ever so humble ther's no place like home.

Farewell peaceful cottage farewell happy home
Forever I'm doomed a poor exile to roam
This poor aching heart must be laid in the tomb
Ere its cease to regret the endearments of home.

123

David Shaw wrote a dramatization which was televised in March 1952, with Lillian Gish playing the role of Grandma Moses.

Several years later, on one of my visits, Grandma Moses gave me a composition written in her own hand in the year 1874. She had later added a penciled line: "This was last day of school." I seem to remember her telling me that she had given this speech in class at the end of her last school year. It is titled "Let Home Be Made Happy." Anna Mary was fourteen at the time, yet her handwriting already resembles that of the mature woman.

Even though the teacher must have helped formulate the text, the ideas it expresses give insight into the young girl's mental capacity. The guidelines for "good and happy living" she set down at that time are no different from those she practiced throughout her life. She must have treasured this paper, for she kept it from youth on into her old age.

The artistic inclination that showed itself so early is revealed by her remarks on the importance of bringing happiness and harmony to a home by decorating it and making it ever more beautiful: ". . . then let man be happy in adorning his home. in making his home the dwelling of happiness and comfort. let him as far as circumstances will permit be industrious in surrounding it with pleasing objects in decorating it within and without with things that tend to make it agreeable and attractive. . . ."

Ceramic Tiles

ANNA MARY'S DESIRE TO MAKE HER SURROUNDINGS PLEASING TO THE eye remained with her throughout her life. There exist a number of objects decorated by her own hand, such as the case of an old clock and those tree mushrooms known popularly as "the Artist's Fungus," which become hard as wood when dried. On these she painted small landscapes. When Mrs. Helen C. Beers, a friend who lived in a neighboring town, suggested in 1951 that she try making sketches on ceramic tiles, she took up the idea with great pleasure. The comparatively easy technique and the playful, noncommital way she could jot down "what the mind may produce," as she once wrote, appealed to her. Mrs. Beers, who worked in ceramics as a hobby, provided six-inch-square tiles and ceramic paints, and instructed the ninety-one-year-old artist in their use.

Over a period of about a year, Mrs. Moses did eighty-five tiles. Some are simple designs, almost drawings, with spare use of color; others are little paintings whose flowing colors make interesting effects on the ceramic background. Mrs. Beers glazed and fired the completed tiles (see plates 110–15).

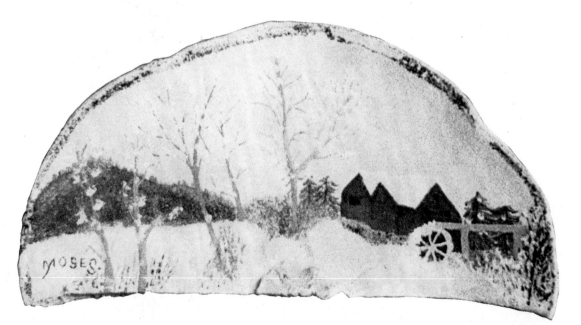

109.
Painting made on
a tree mushroom

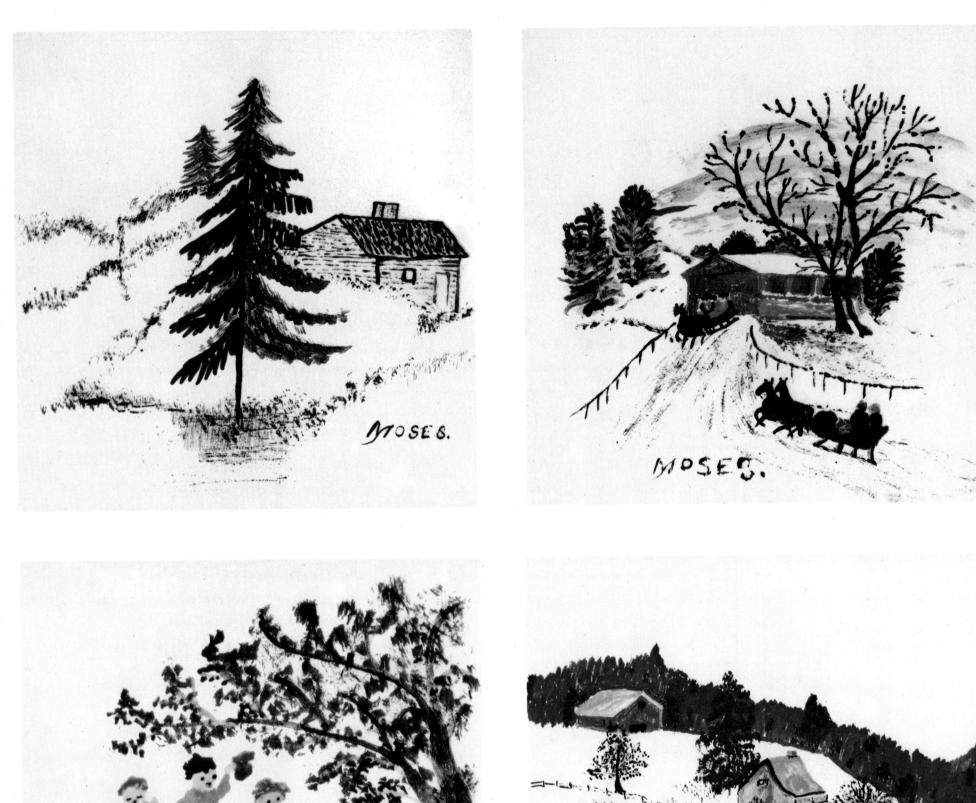

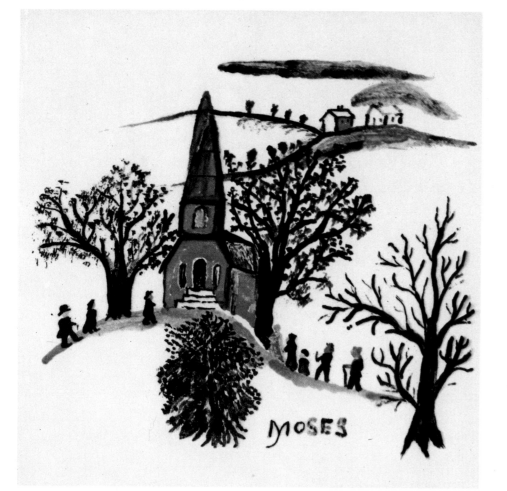

110—15.
Ceramic tiles. 1951—52. Each 6 x 6″.
Numbered and titled on the reverse by
the artist.

Left to right, top row:

No. 2: *A House*
No. 16: *Narrow Road*
No. 26: *Church Goers*

Left to right, bottom row:

No. 35: *Playing*
No. 42: *Hilltop*
No. 51: *The Marsh*

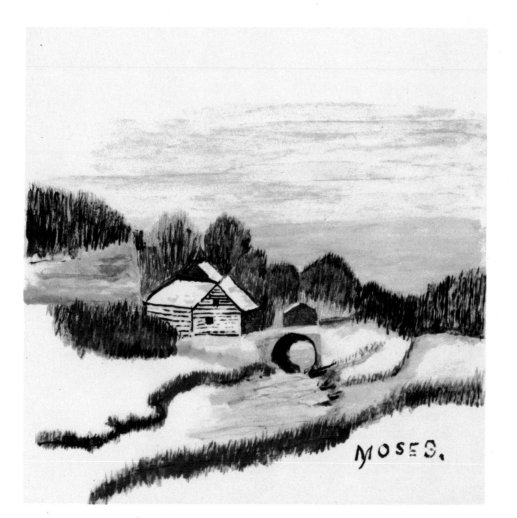

1946 to 1953

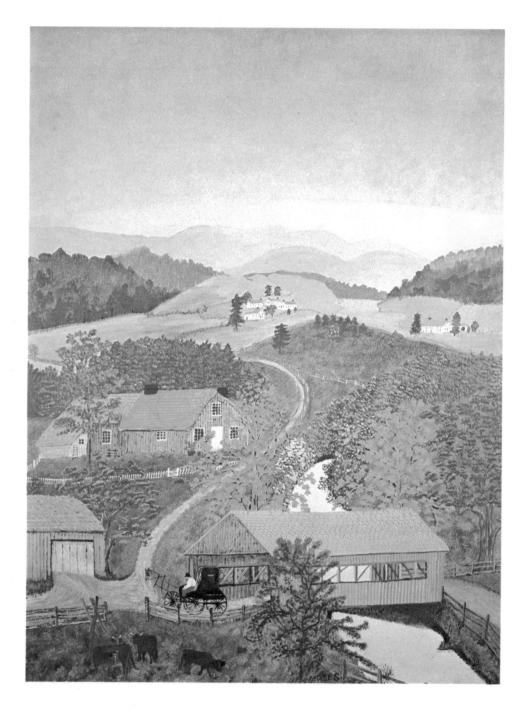

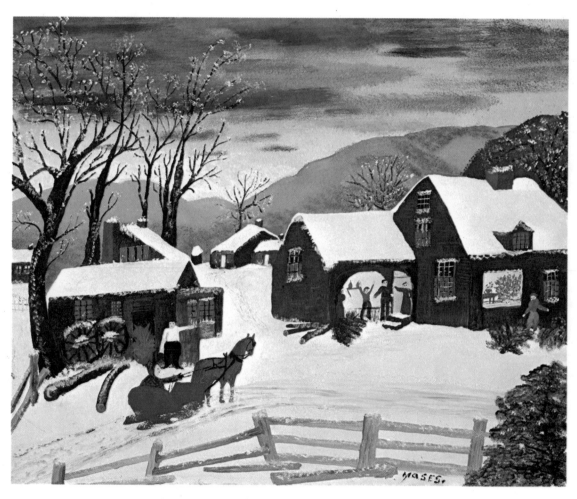

116. *Covered Bridge with Carriage.* 1946. 27½ x 21½". Cat. 645

117. *The Lone Traveler.* 1946. 16 x 19¾". Cat. 594

131

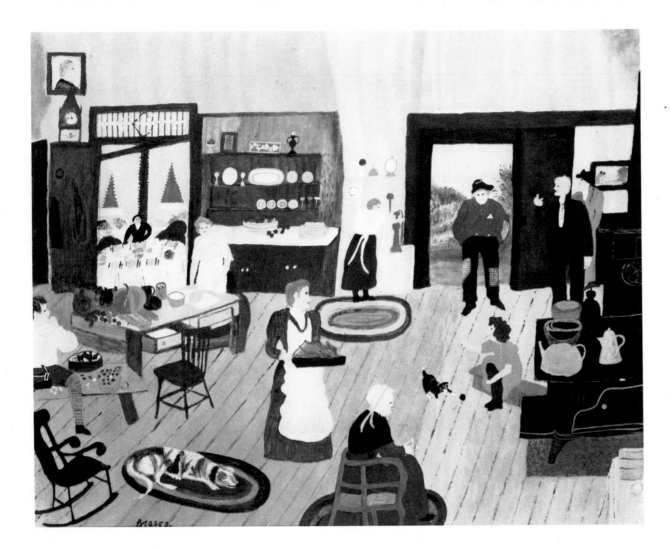

118.
A Tramp on Christmas Day.
1946. 16 x 19⅞". Cat. 595

119.
Miss Helen Frick's Residence, Bedford, N.Y. 1946.
21¼ x 25¼". Cat. 603

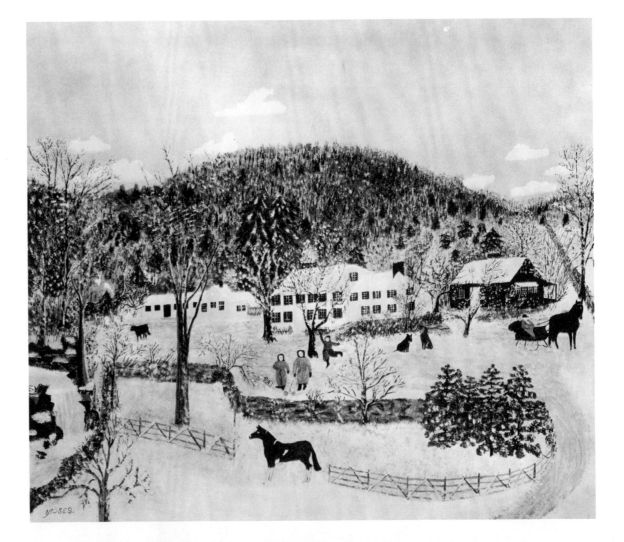

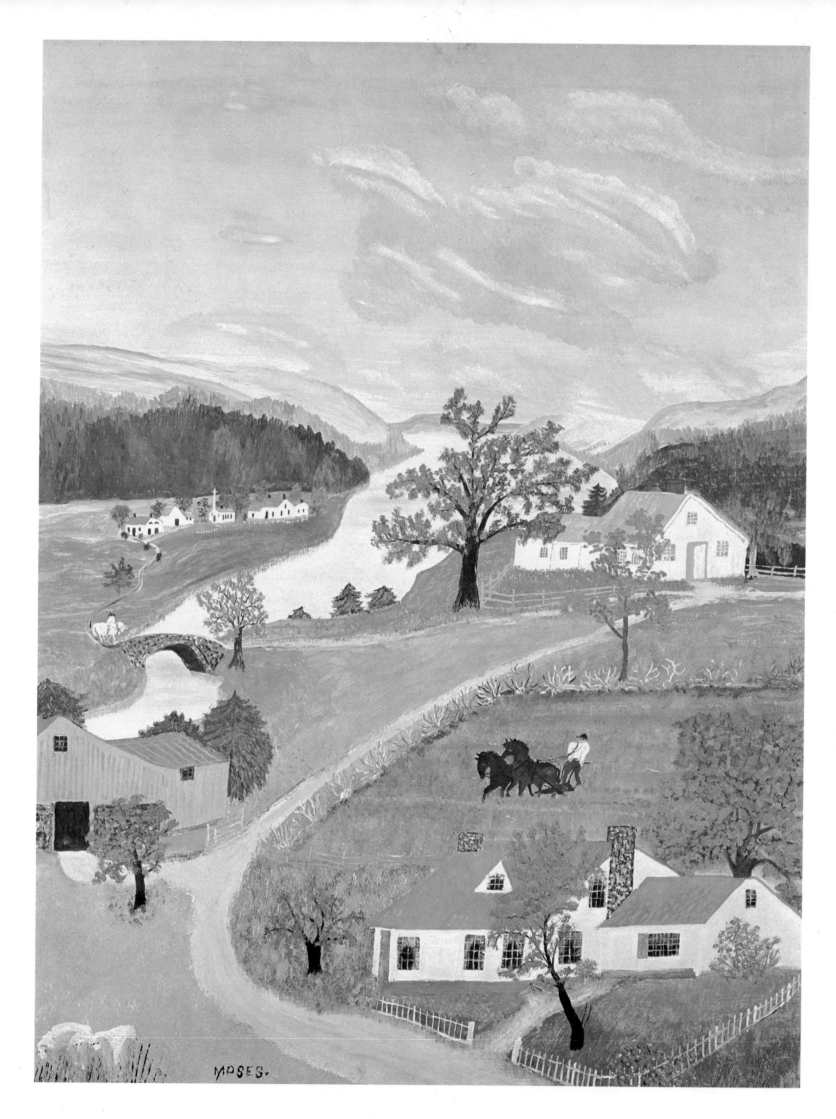

120.
The Spring in Evening.
1947. 27 x 21". Cat. 706

133

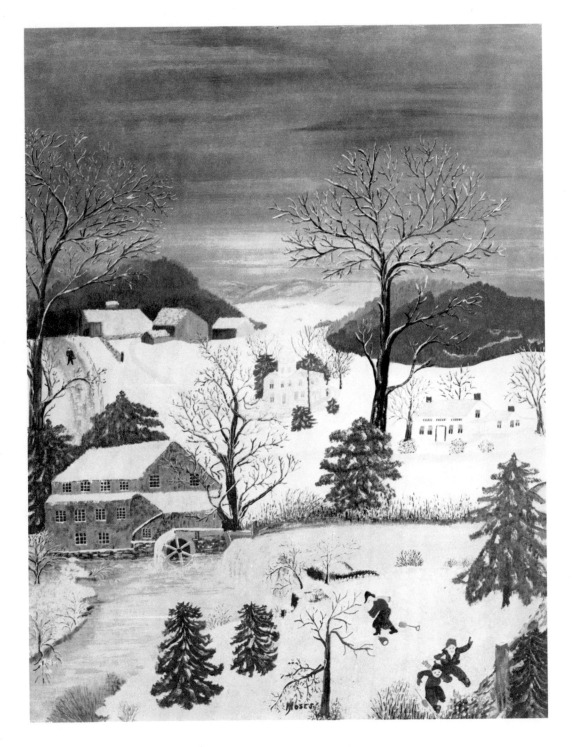

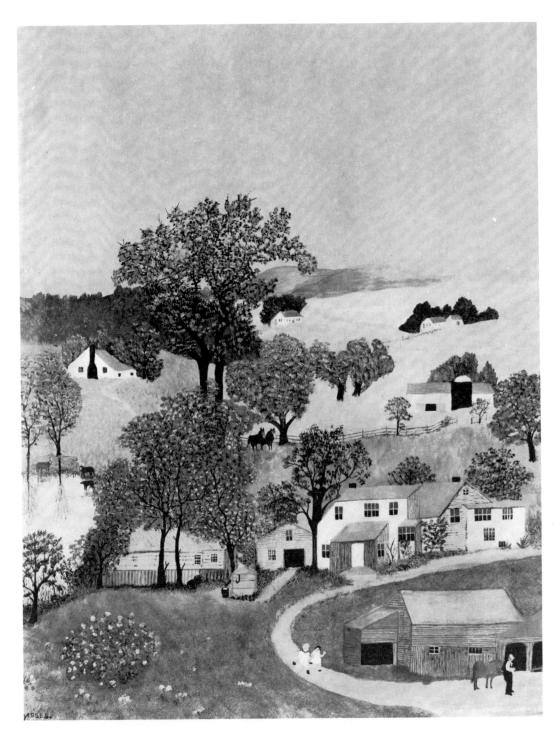

121. *Taking Leg Bale for Security.* 1946. 27 x 20¾". Cat. 642

122. *Home in the Springtime.* 1946. 27¼ x 21½". Cat. 643

134

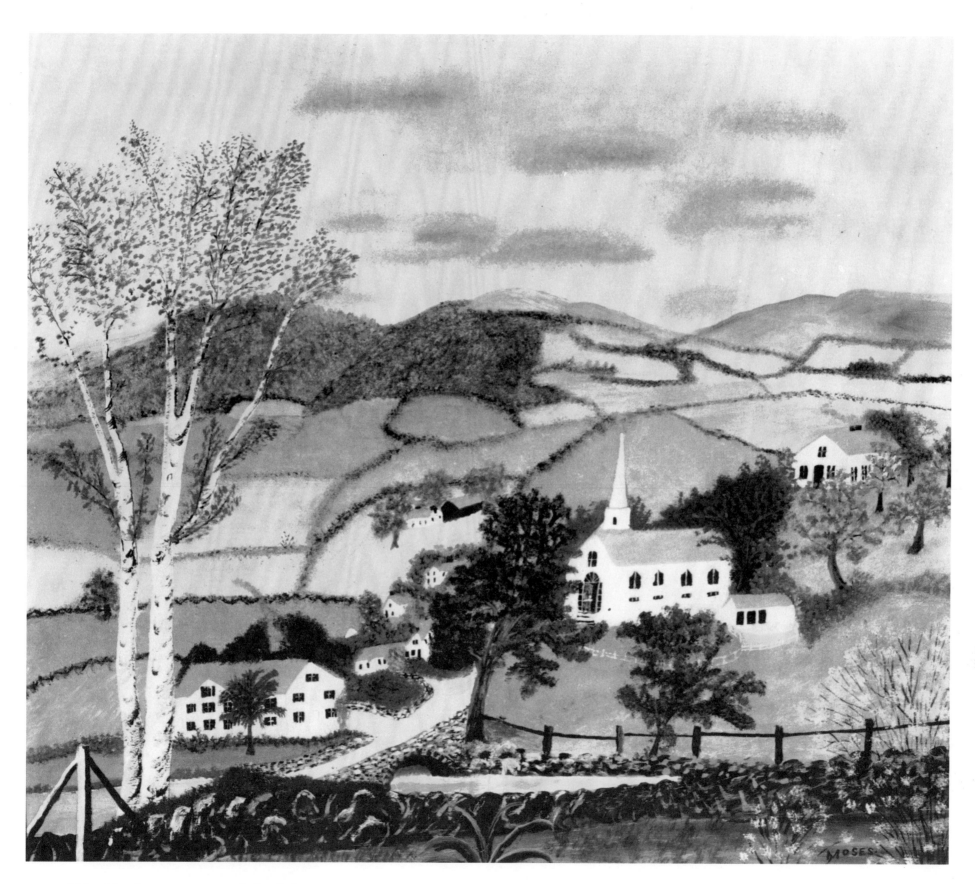

123. *A May Morning.* 1947. 19½ x 22″. Cat. 676

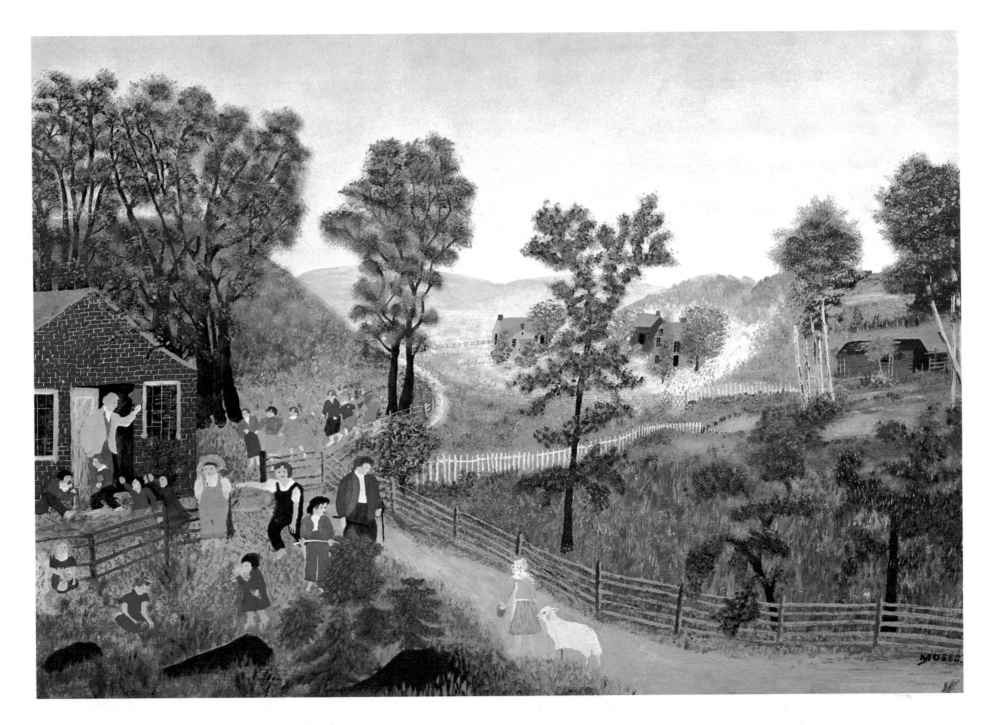

124. *Mary and Little Lamb.* 1947. 24 x 34½". Cat. 650

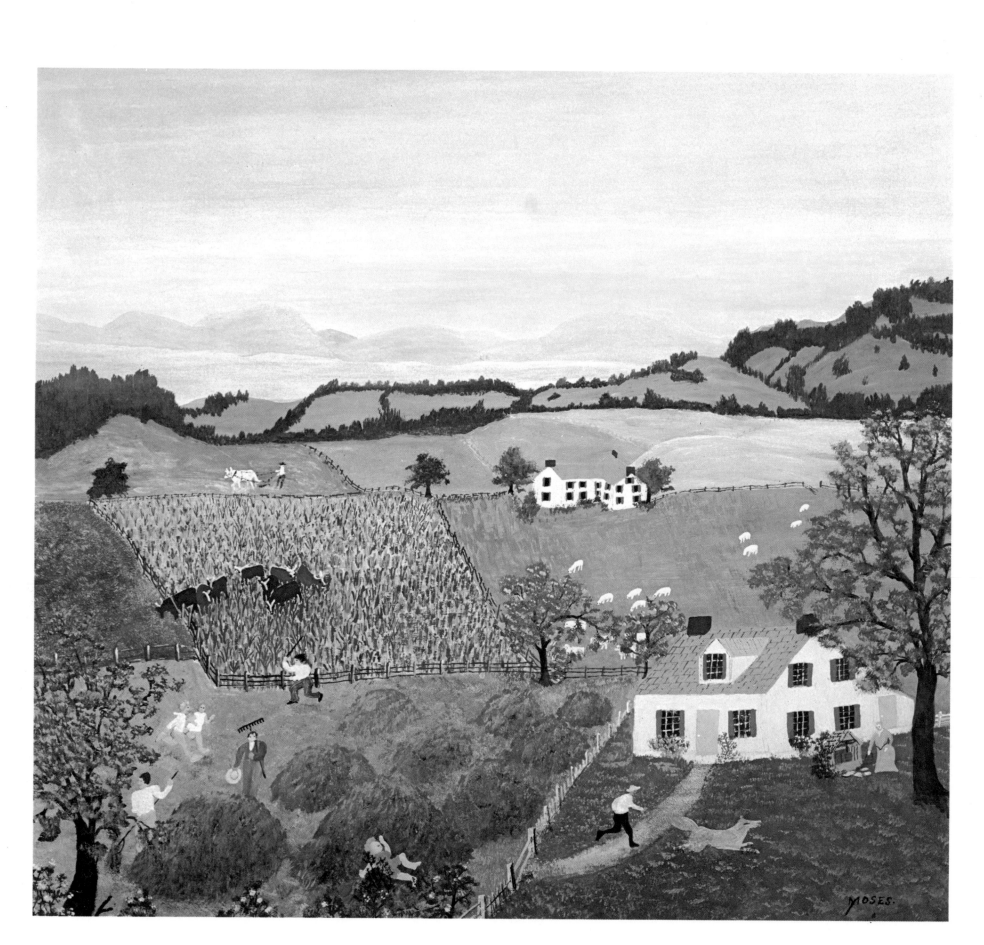

125. *Little Boy Blue.* 1947. 20½ x 23". Cat. 660

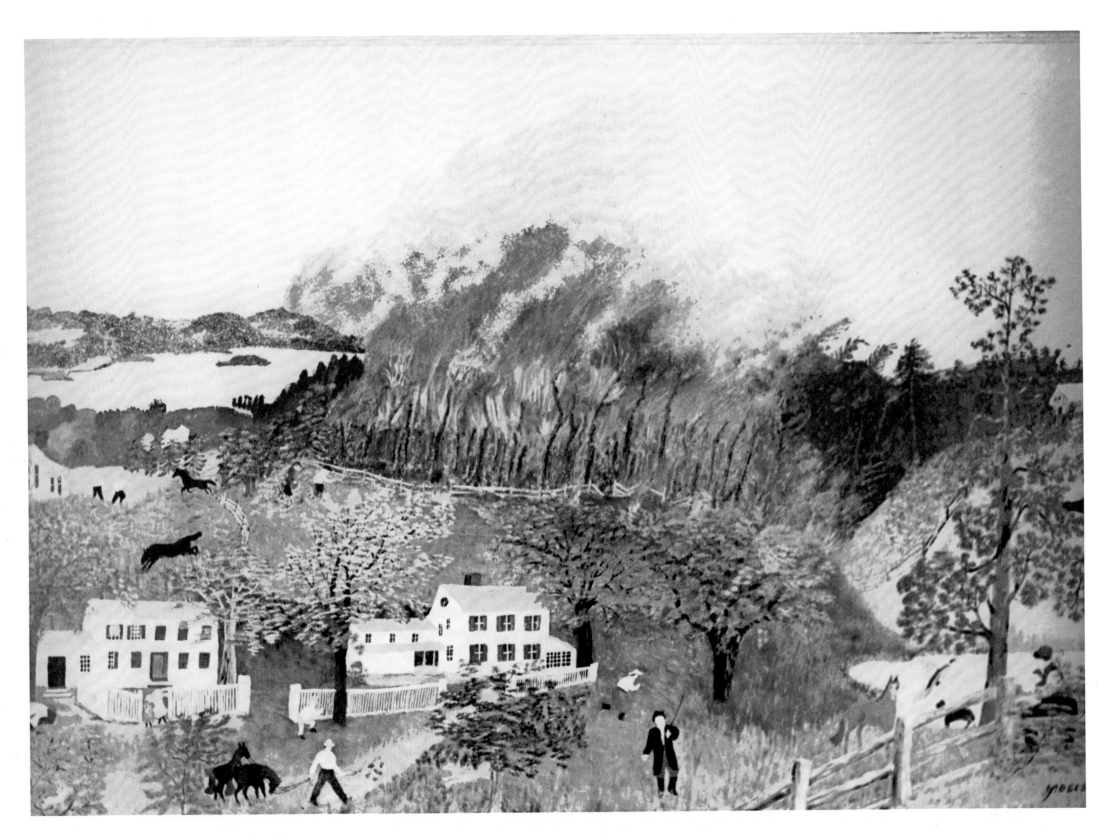

126. *A Fire in the Woods.* 1947. 24 x 36¼". Cat. 694

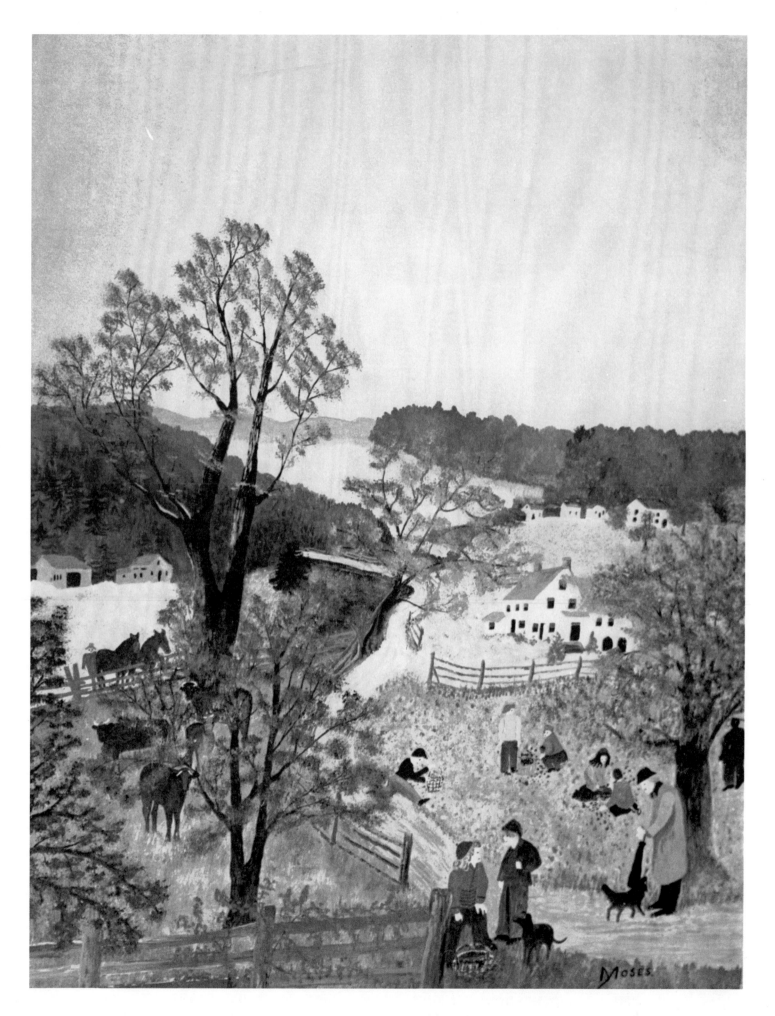

127.
Under the Butternut Tree.
1947. 27 x 21". Cat. 704

139

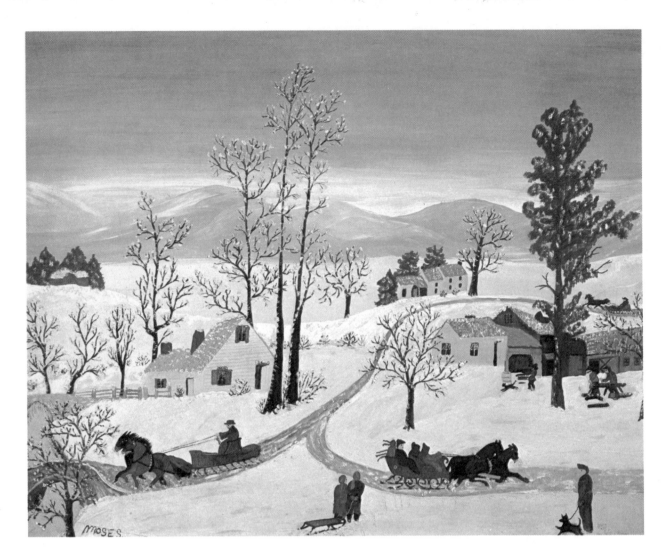

128.
The Dividing of the Ways.
1947. 16 x 20". Cat. 701

129.
Through the Bridge by the Mill.
1948. 20 x 30". Cat. 769

140

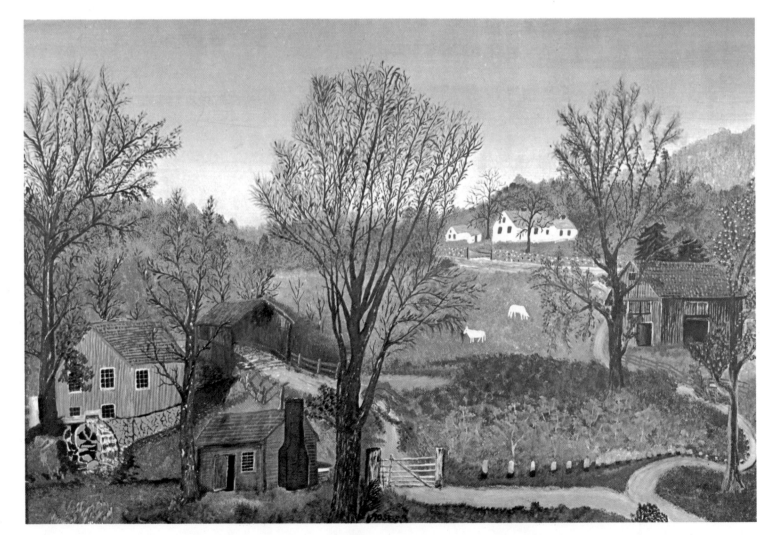

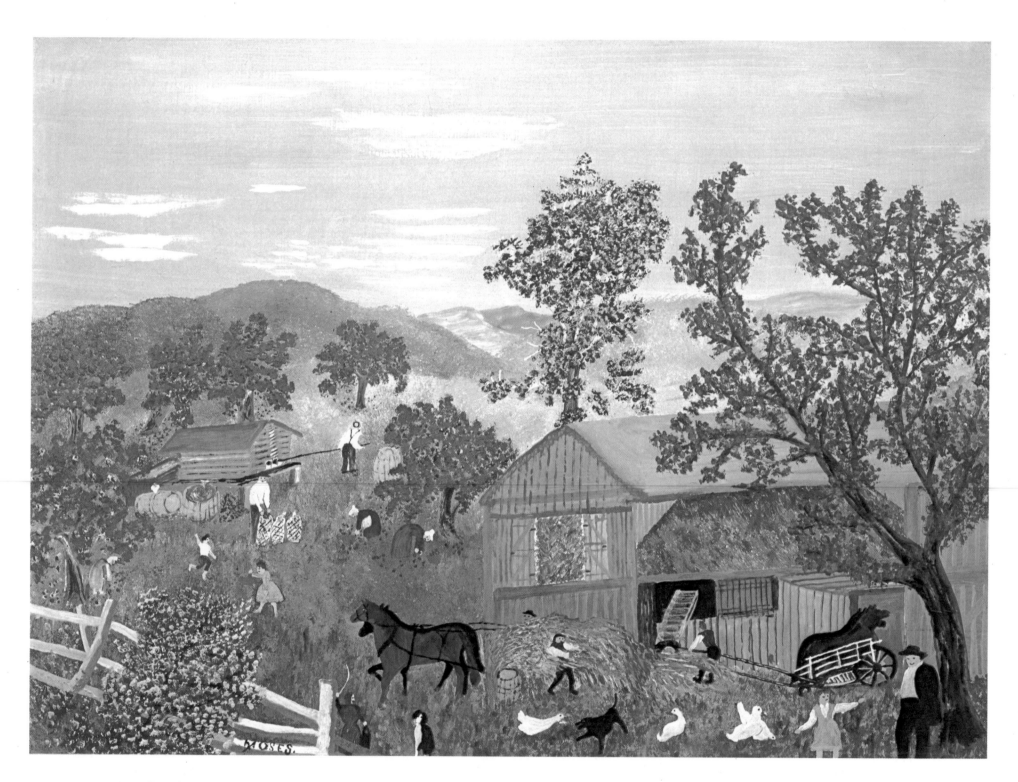

130. *For This Is the Fall of the Year.* 1947. 16 x 21¾". Cat. 711

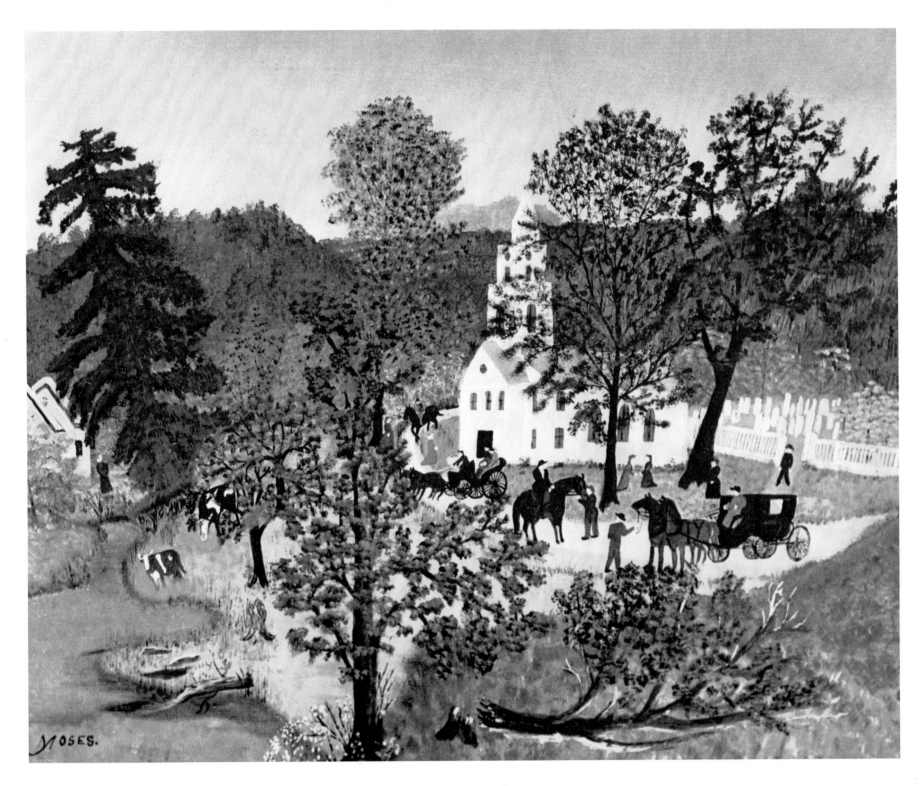

131. *The Church in the Wild Wood.* 1948. 16¼ x 20". Cat. 788

142

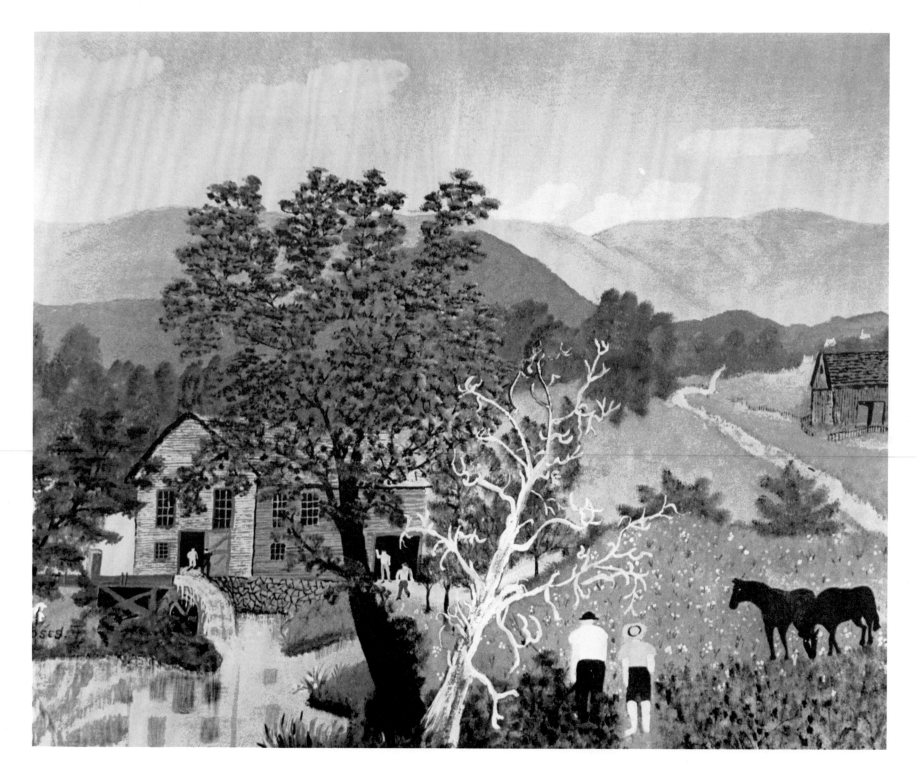

132. *The Dead Tree.* 1948. 16 x 20". Cat. 792

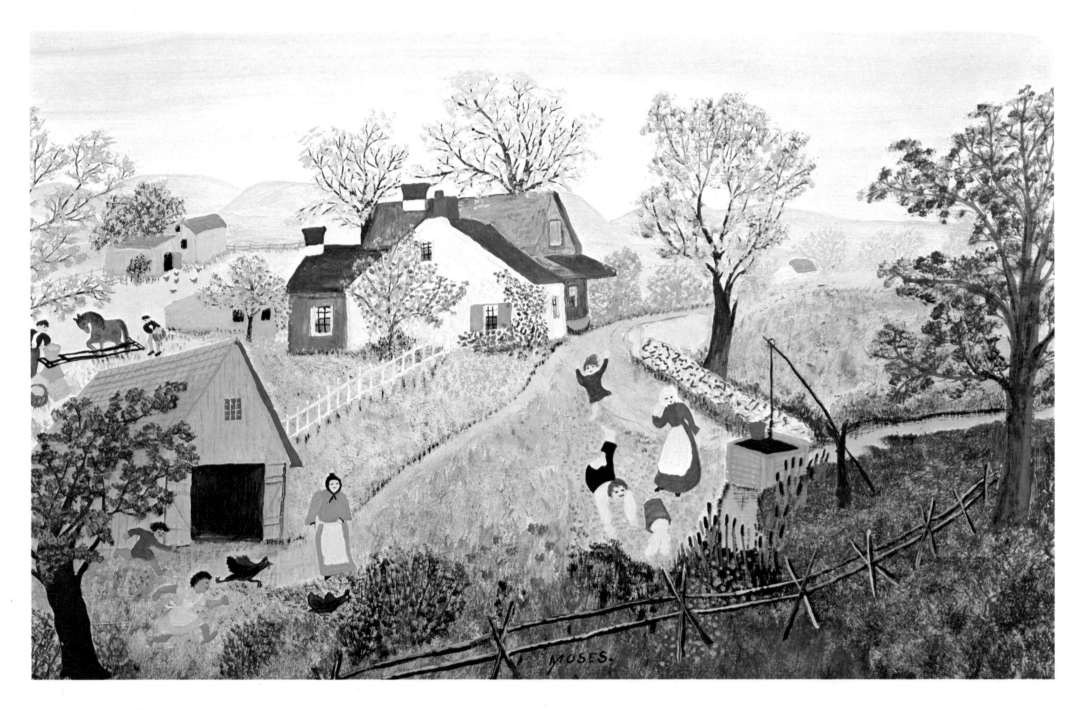

133. *Jack and Jill.* 1947. 12½ x 19¾". Cat. 718

144

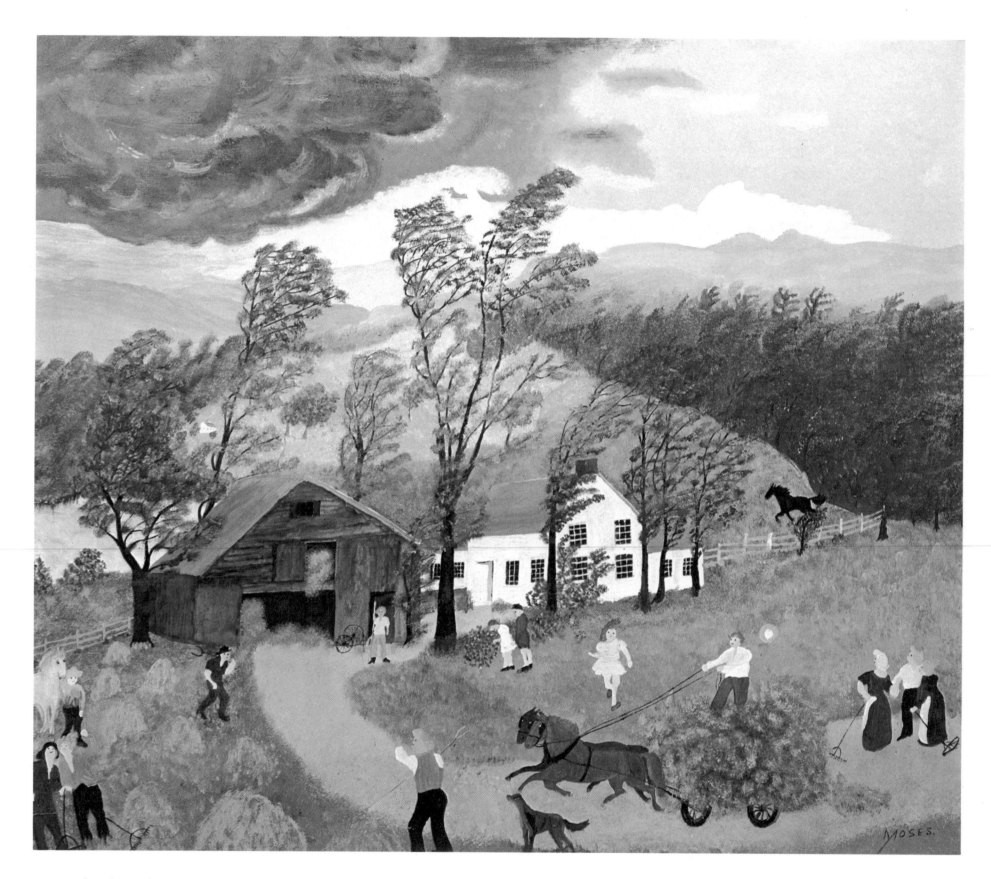

134. *The Thunderstorm*. 1948. 20¾ x 23¾". Cat. 729

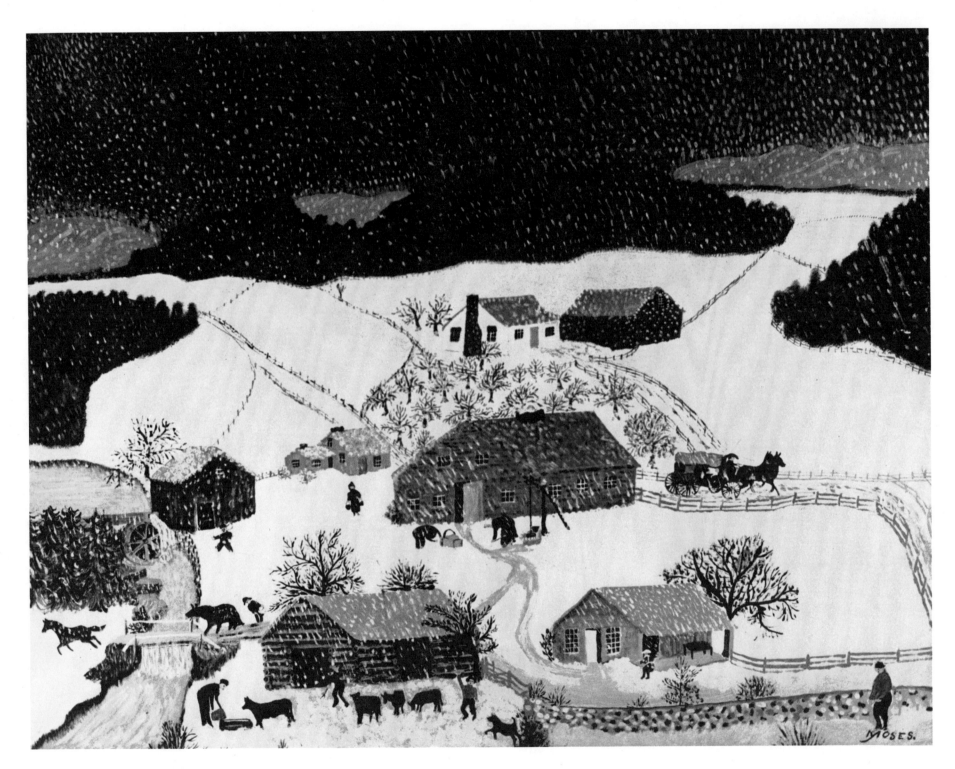

135. *The Old Oaken Bucket.* 1949. 16¾ x 21½". Cat. 821

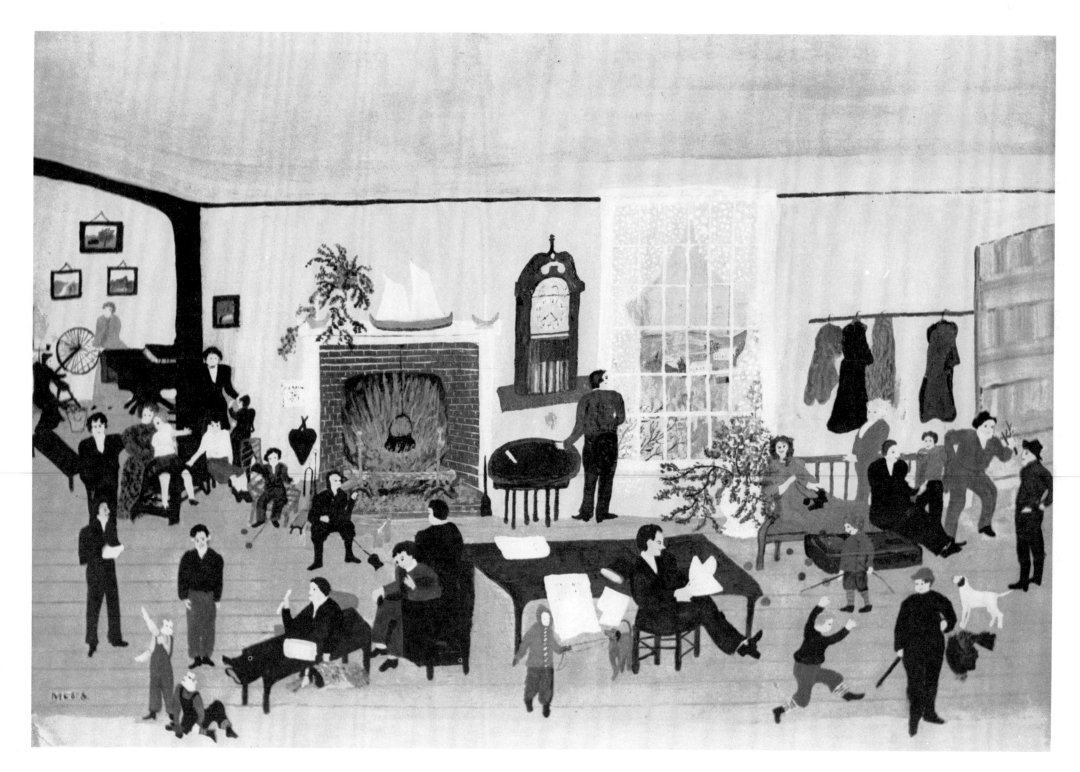

136. *The Meeting House.* 1949. 18¾ x 26¼". Cat. 878

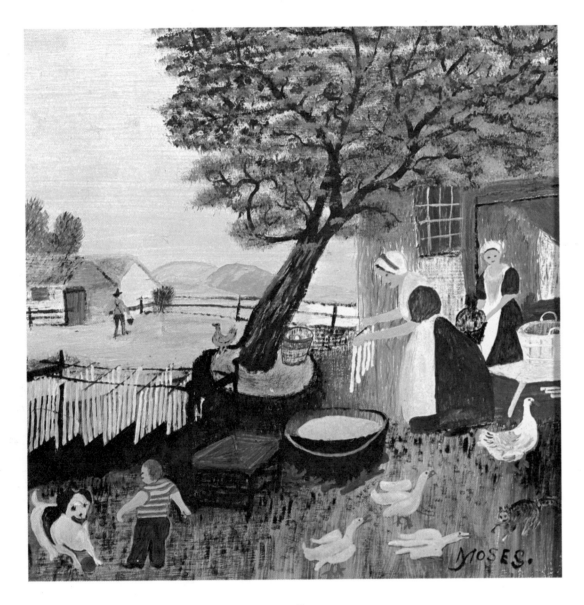

137. *Candle Dip Day in 1800.* 1950. 9 x 9¼". Cat. 941

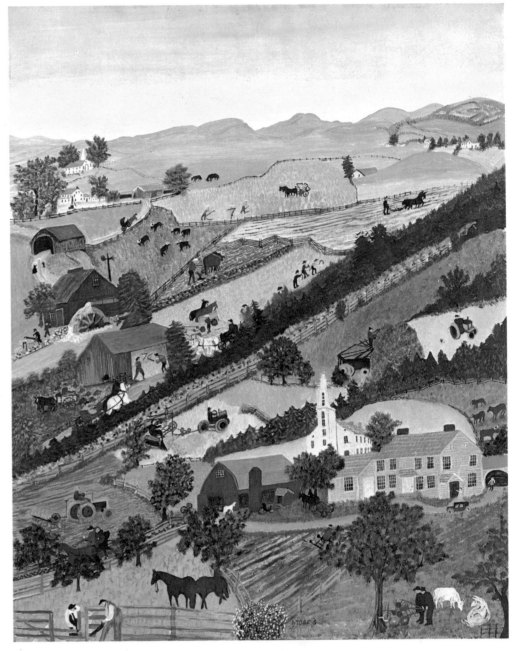

138. *Year 1860, Year 1940.* 1949. 26 x 21". Cat. 847

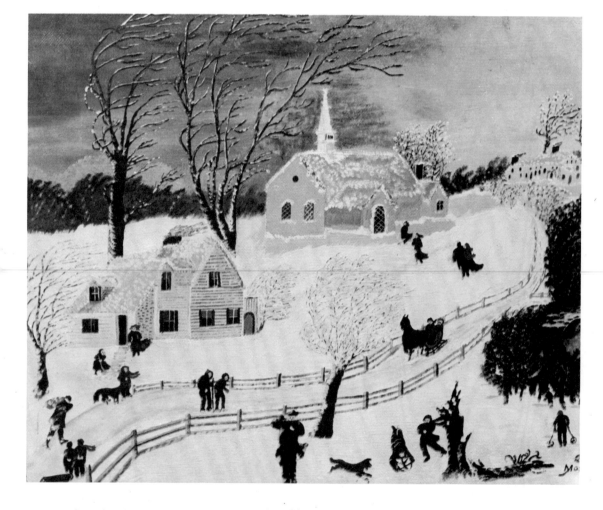

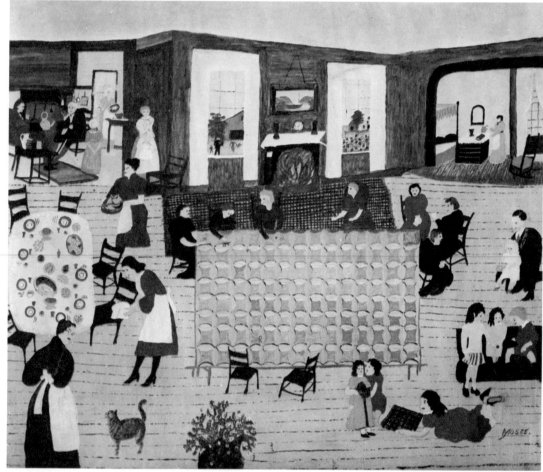

139. *The Wind in Winter.* 1950. 20 x 24". Cat. 887

140. *A Quilting Bee.* 1950. 20 x 24". Cat. 911

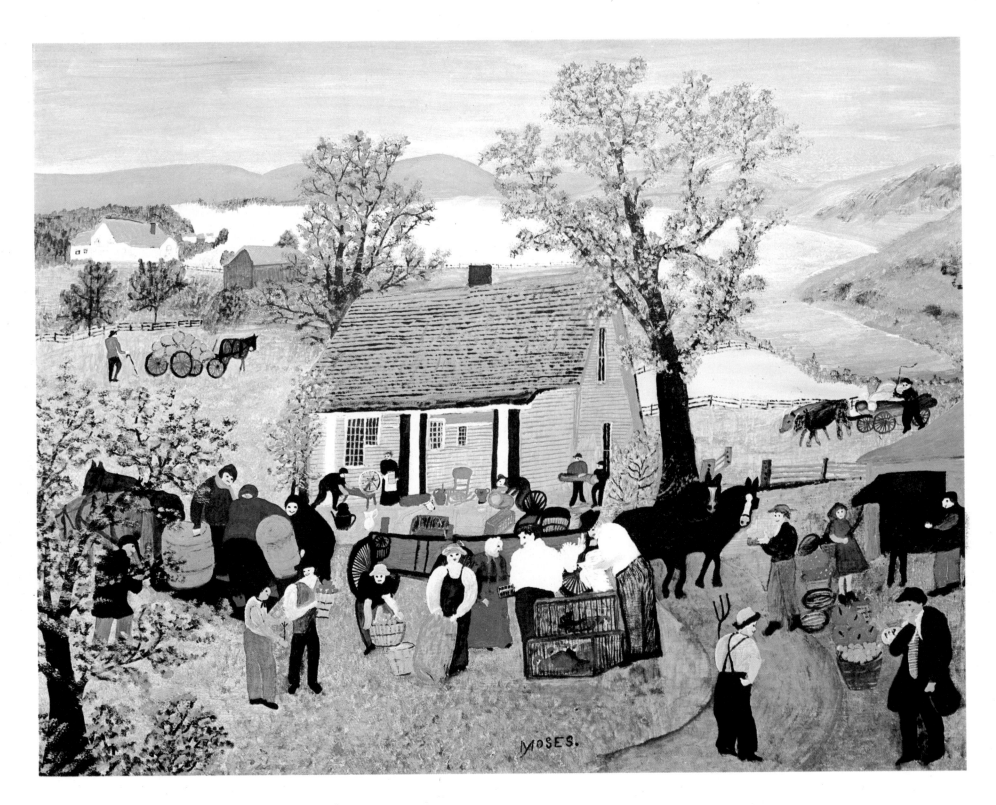

141. *Moving Day on the Farm*. 1951. 17 x 22". Cat. 965

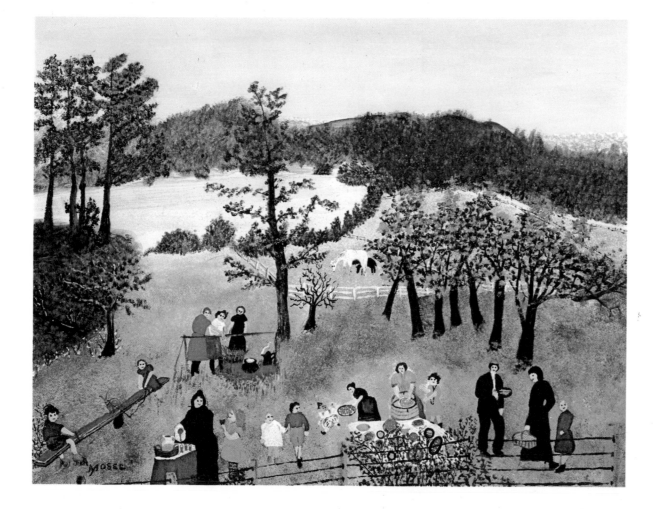

142.
The Family Picnic.
1951. 16¾ x 22".
Cat. 966

143.
A Country Wedding. 1951.
17 x 22". Cat. 968

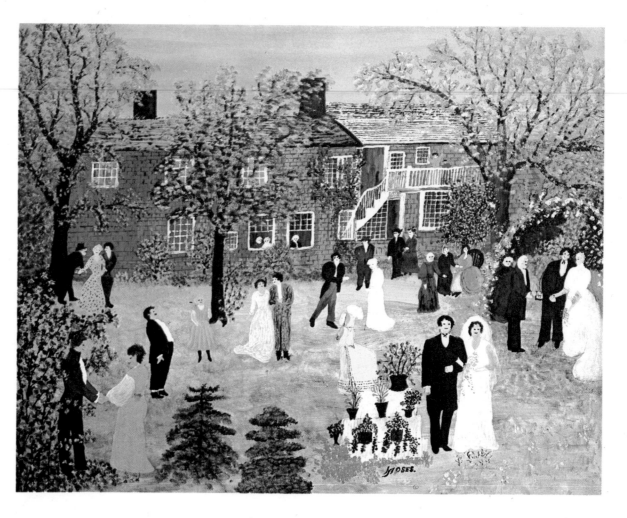

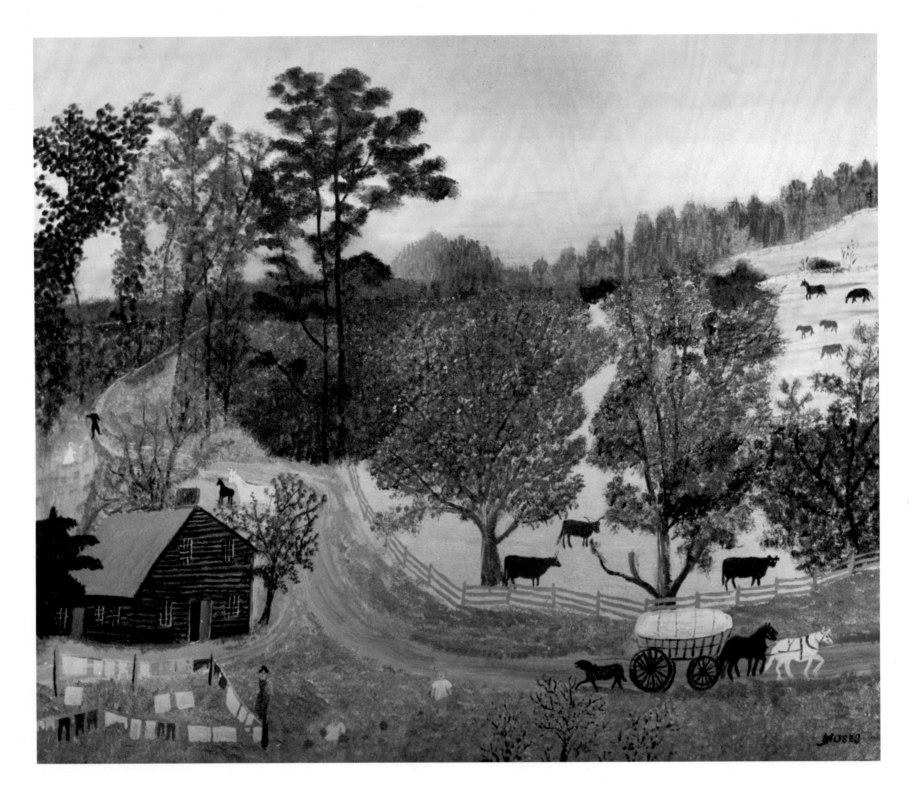

144. *Laundry Day*. 1950. 20 x 24". Cat. 916

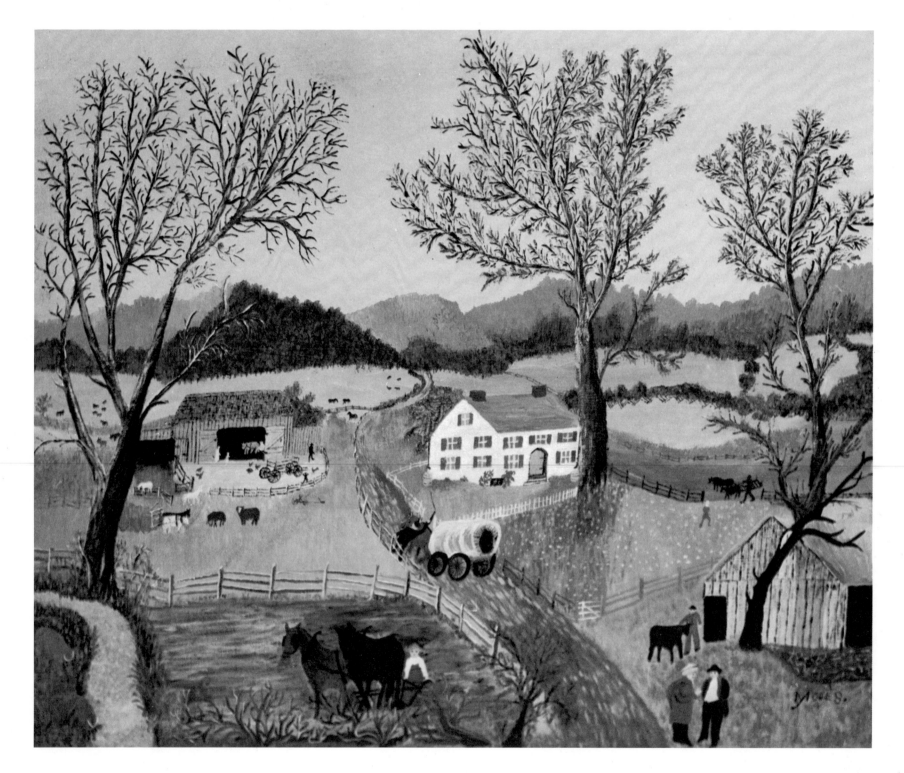

145. *Over Land.* 1950. 20 x 24". Cat. 924

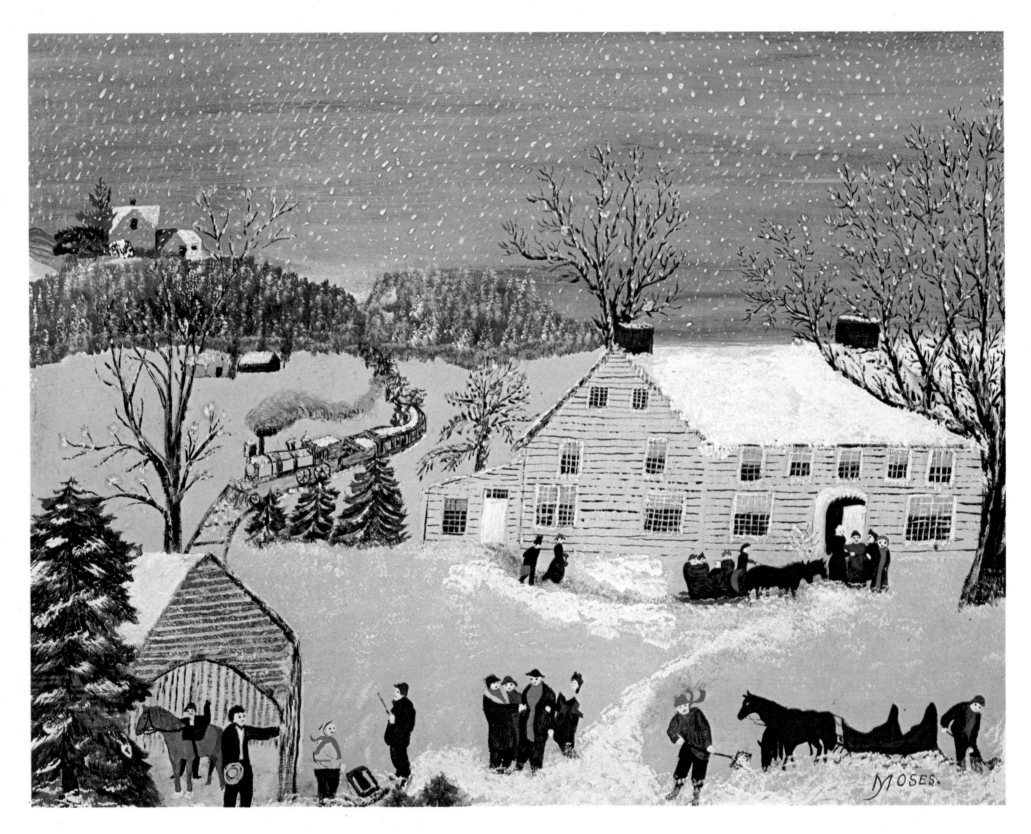

146. *The Departure.* 1951. 17 x 22". Cat. 969

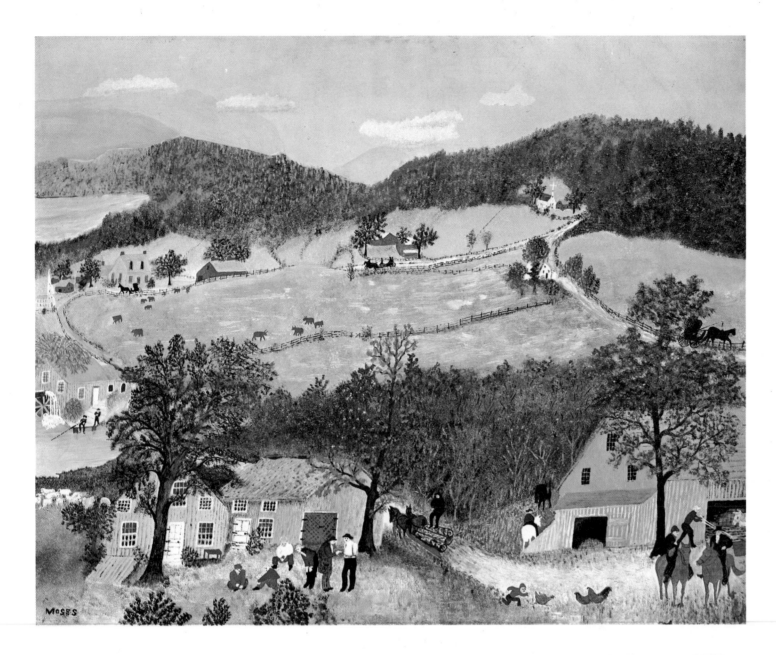

147. *We Are Resting.* 1951. 24 x 30". Cat. 970

148.
Barn Roofing. 1951.
18 x 24". Cat. 986

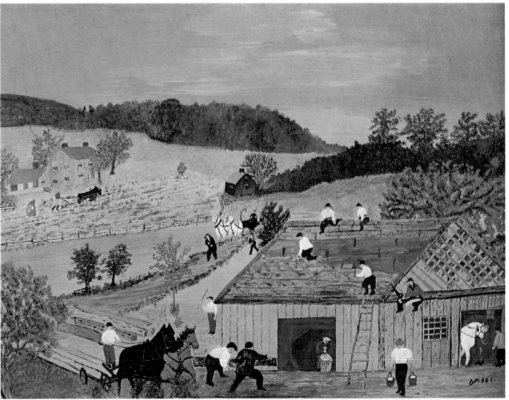

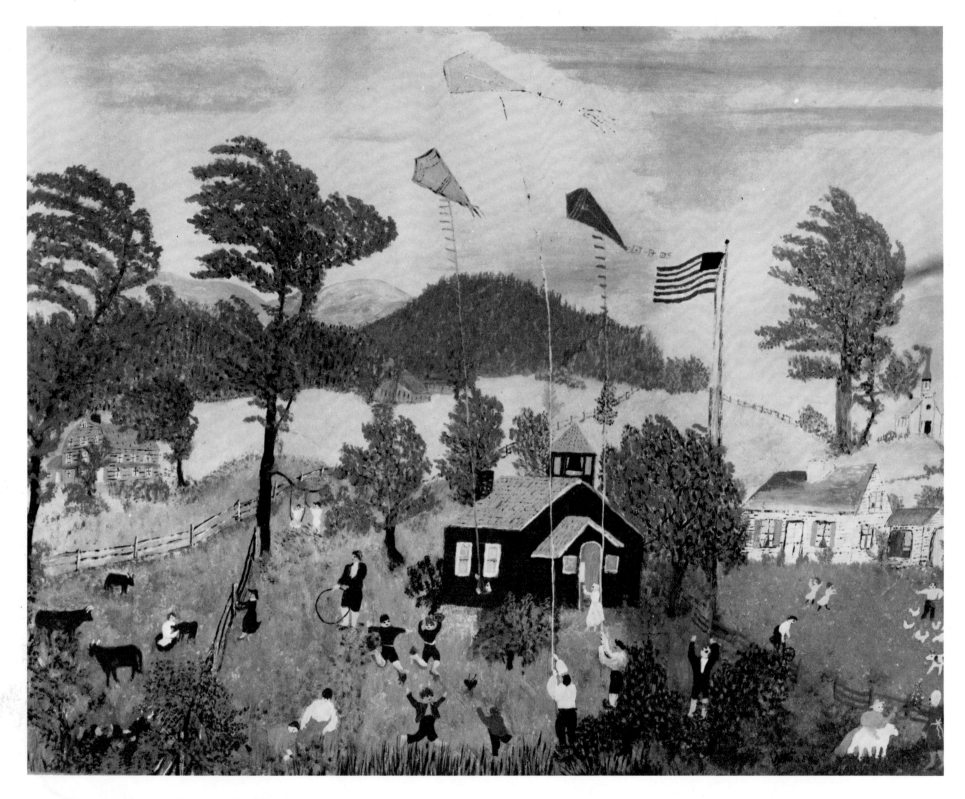

149. *Flying Kites*. 1951. 18¼ x 24". Cat. 981

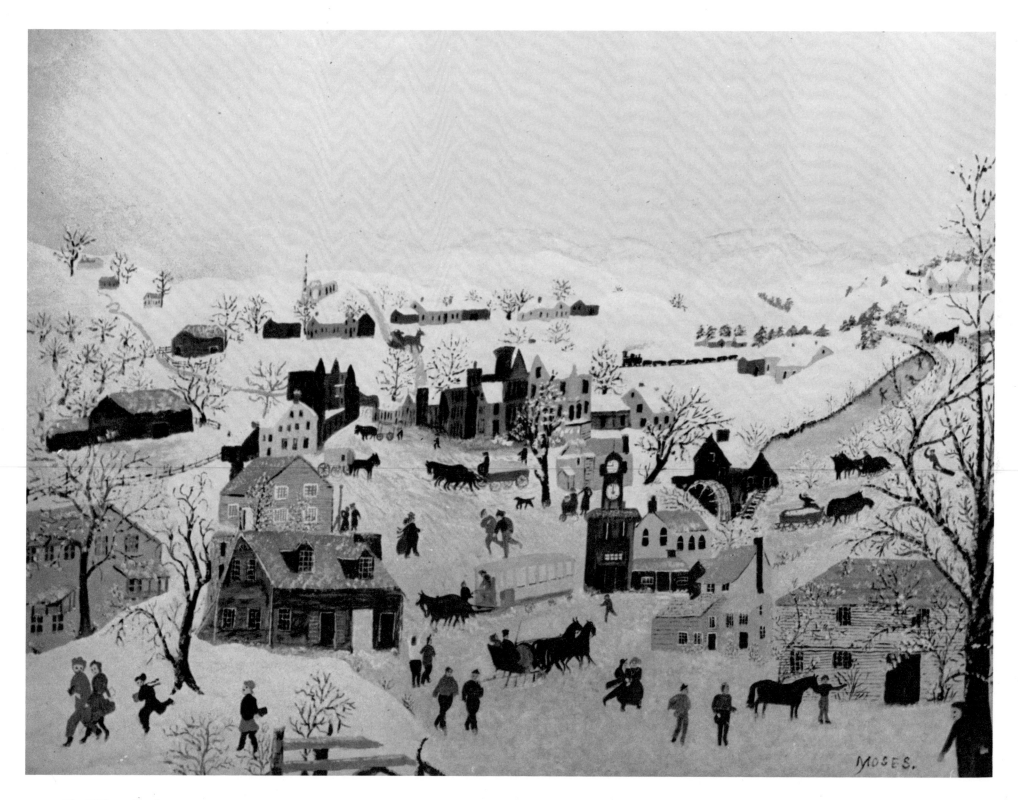

150. *The Village Clock.* 1951. 18 x 24". Cat. 1001

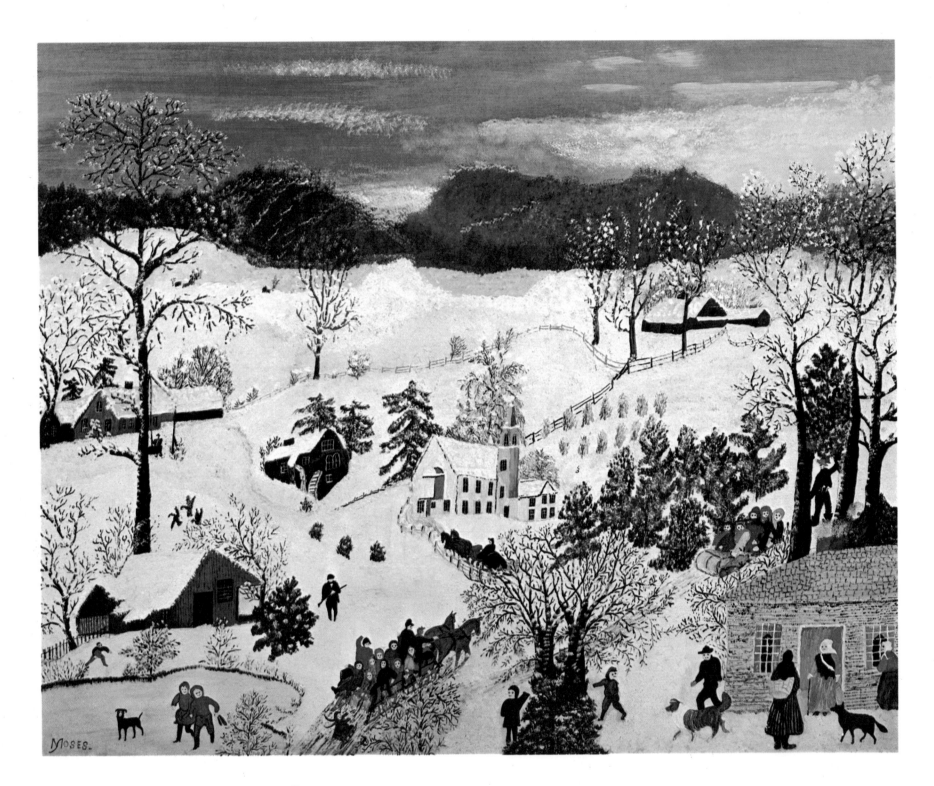

151. *It Snows, Oh It Snows.* 1951. 24 x 30". Cat. 971

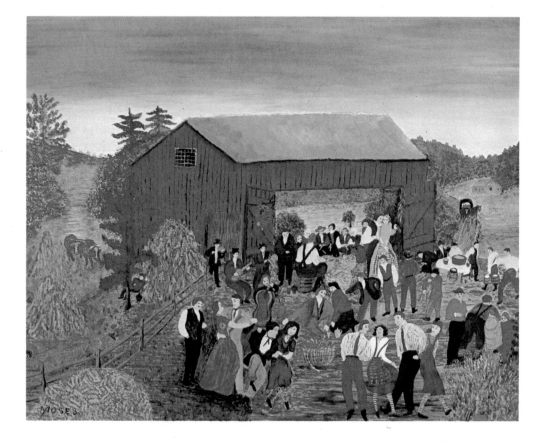

152. *Husking Bee.* 1951. 19 x 24". Cat. 987

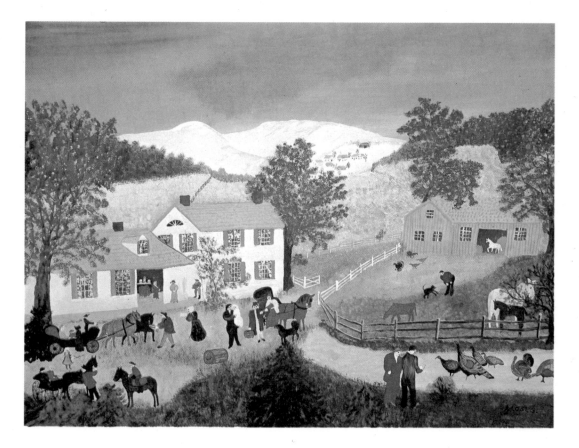

154. *Home for Thanksgiving.* 1952. 18 x 24". Cat. 1062

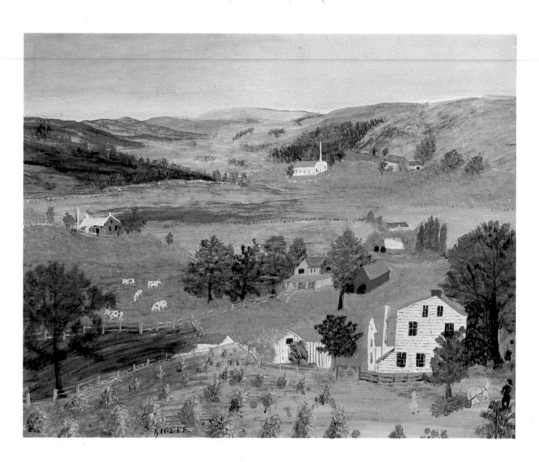

153. *Ripe Pumpkins.* 1951. 13 x 16". Cat. 990

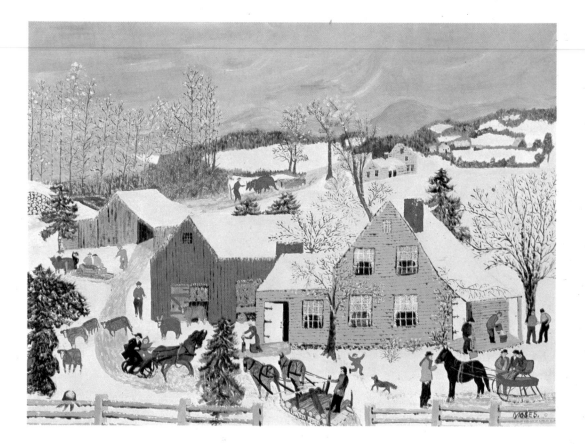

155. *Busy Day.* 1952. 18 x 24". Cat. 1033

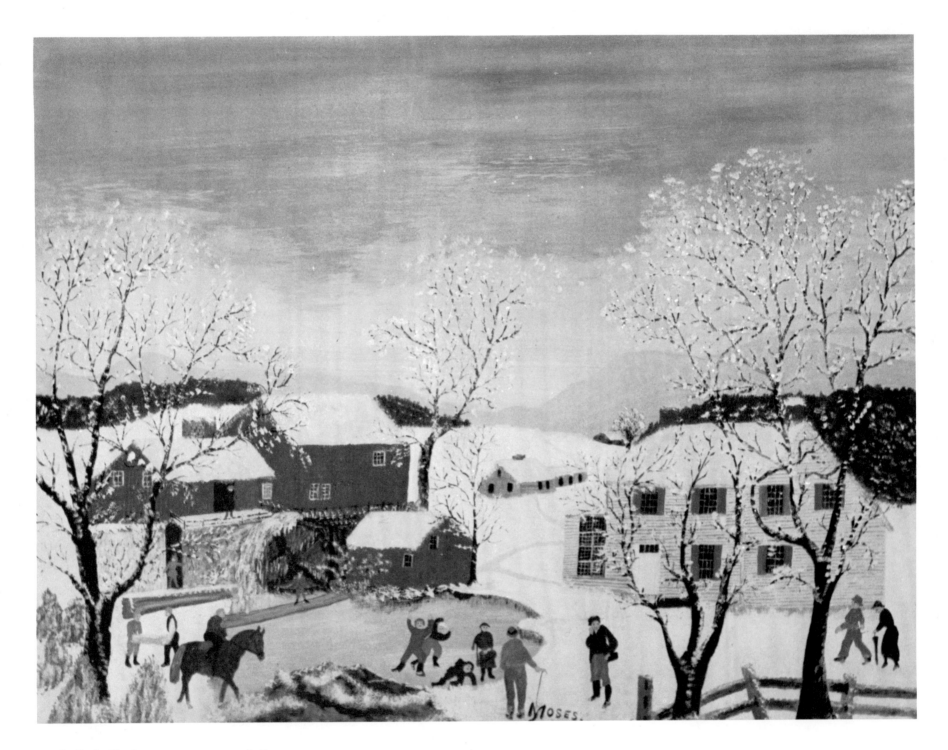

156. *Early Skating.* 1951. 17⅞ x 23⅞". Cat. 1002

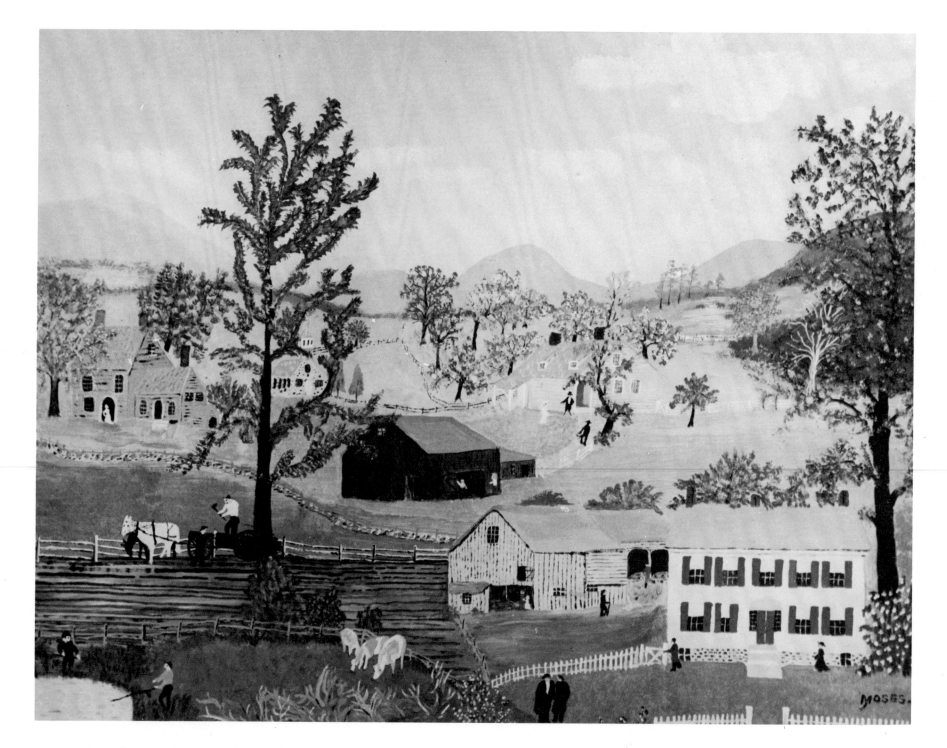

157. *A Beautiful Morning.* 1951. 18 x 24". Cat. 1010

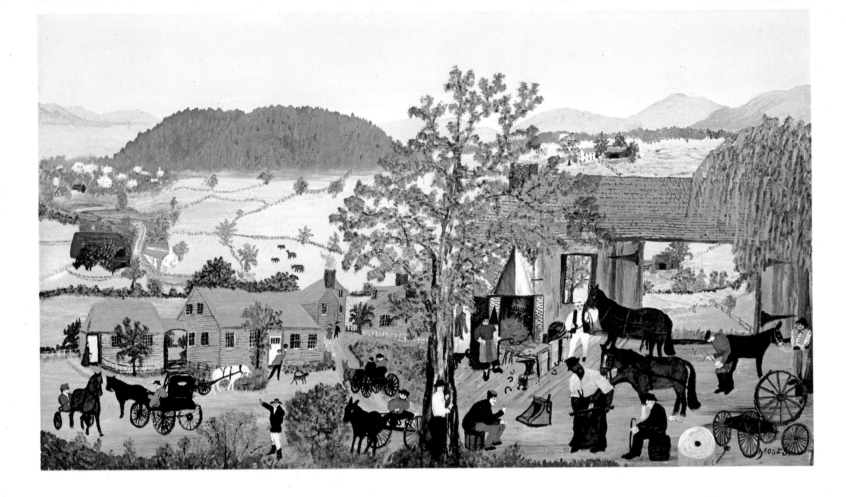

158.
Blacksmith Shop. 1951.
16 x 28". Cat. 996

159.
Busy Street. 1952.
18 x 24". Cat. 1054

162

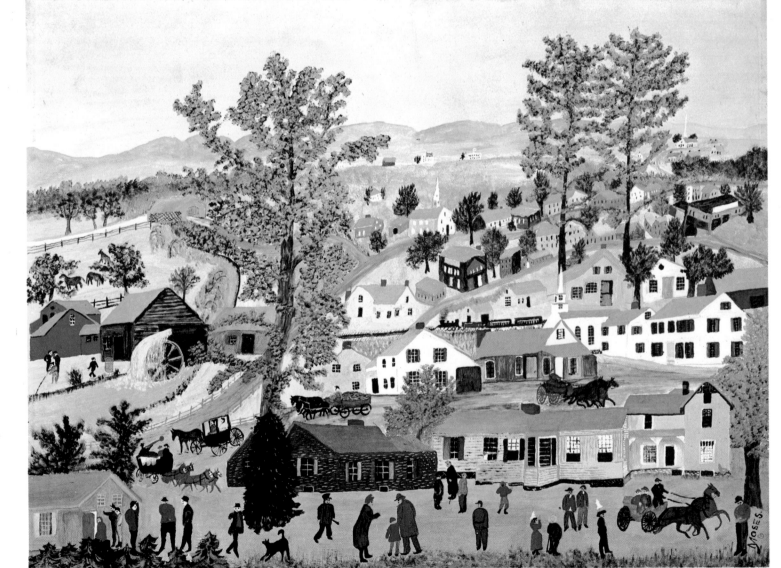

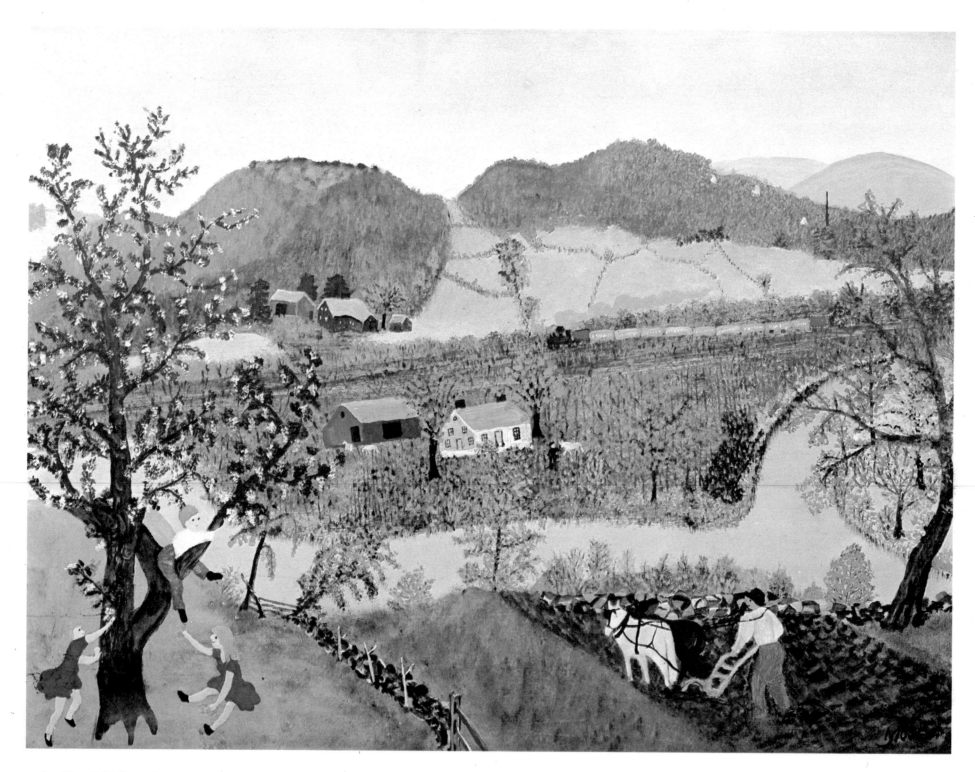

160. *Hoosick River, Summer*. 1952. 18 x 24". Cat. 1032

III

FAME

New York Herald Tribune Forum, 1953

NEW YORK
Herald Tribune

ANNUAL FORUM

•

SPEAKER'S TICKET

TUESDAY, OCTOBER 20, 1953   1:45 P.M.

WALDORF-ASTORIA HOTEL

*Please take the Park Avenue Elevators
to the third floor West Foyer.*

Grandma Moses

161. Grandma Moses's ticket

AMONG THE EVENTS IN WHICH GRANDMA MOSES took part during the last decade of her life was the 22nd Annual Forum arranged by the *New York Herald Tribune* in October 1953. The theme chosen for that year was "New Patterns for Mid-Century Living." The symposium took place in the Grand Ballroom of the Waldorf-Astoria Hotel and was attended by two thousand delegates. The opening address was to have been delivered by Dag Hammarskjold; it was read in his absence by Dr. Ralph Bunche. Among other prominent speakers were John Foster Dulles, Secretary of State, and Francis Henry Taylor, Director of the Metropolitan Museum of Art in New York.

Grandma Moses came to New York with her daughter, Mrs. Fisher. Her appearance was scheduled for the third session, on October 20. The subject for that day was "Time on Our Hands," and the discussion centered on "how the extra hours, the leisure time created by technical advances could best be put to use." After I had given a brief address on "Amateur Painters in America," I introduced the artist and we had an informal conversation—we had discussed it in general terms, but it was not rehearsed.

When she came onto the stage, a little bent but walking with firm steps toward her chair, she was given a standing ovation. Smiling, she faced the crowd, took her seat, and, producing a handkerchief, waved to the audience. This gesture of gracious and spontaneous response brought renewed cheers and applause. It was characteristic of her complete lack of self-consciousness and immediately created an atmosphere of warmth between her and the audience. In the following dialogue she answered all my questions without a moment's hesitation, sometimes interspersing her answers with joking remarks, to the great delight of her listeners. The way in which she spoke about the subject closest to her heart—her painting—and the great modesty with which

167

she regarded her artistic achievement were received by the audience with increasing admiration. The impression Grandma Moses made was expressed by an editorial published in the *New York Herald Tribune* of October 22, 1953:

> For all who suffer from what might be called living strain—and many do complain about the malady—a few minutes' exposure to the presence of Grandma Moses is powerful therapy. On Tuesday this ninety-three-year-old lady made one of her rare trips to the city from her up-state home in Eagle Bridge, N.Y., to appear at the annual *Herald Tribune* Forum. Some said that she stole the show. Others were impressed with her astonishing vitality, her mental alertness, her humor, simplicity, graciousness, enjoyment of the occasion, and so on. The plain fact is, everybody felt reinvigorated while in her presence. . . .
>
> She holds within herself, in utter unawareness, the wisest secrets of life, secrets composed of many elements, yet as natural and immediate in their expression as a child's smile. While many distinguished persons were appearing before the Forum, a little old lady of ninety-three stepped into their midst and endeared herself to all by her simple aliveness. . . .

Grandma Moses and Edward R. Murrow, 1955

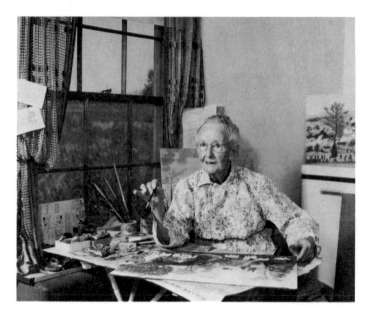

162. Grandma Moses painting in
the room behind the kitchen.
Photo by Ifor Thomas

IT HAD LONG BEEN MY WISH to observe Grandma Moses while painting, but she seemed reluctant to let me watch, so I did not insist. It turned out that she did not consider it proper for a gentleman to enter her bedroom, which she used as a studio. Situated on the second floor of the old house, it was reached by a steep staircase which she climbed countless times a day. After she moved into the new house, she painted in a small room behind the kitchen, and there I could sometimes watch her at work for a few minutes.

Then, in 1953, Edward R. Murrow, the radio and television commentator, wrote to Grandma Moses about interviewing her for television. This seemed to me a good opportunity to film the step-by-step creation of a painting. I knew from experience that she could face any unfamiliar situation or person with complete self-assurance, yet I felt a little uneasy at the thought of a meeting between two such entirely different personalities. However, the importance of the project prompted me to persuade Grandma Moses to go through with this rather strenuous task. Mr. Murrow and his associate, Fred Friendly, agreed to the idea wholeheartedly. The project remained in the planning stage for two years; it was finally realized for Mr. Murrow's television program "See It Now."

The crew of CBS technicians stayed in Eagle Bridge not only for the interview itself, which took place on June 29, 1955, but until the artist had completed an entire painting in front of the cameras. We were in the midst of a heat wave, not exactly the best time to spend many hours under hot floodlights. Everyone was a little tense and uncomfortable, everyone except Grandma Moses, who remained cool and unruffled throughout. The crew had brought along two large movie cameras; one

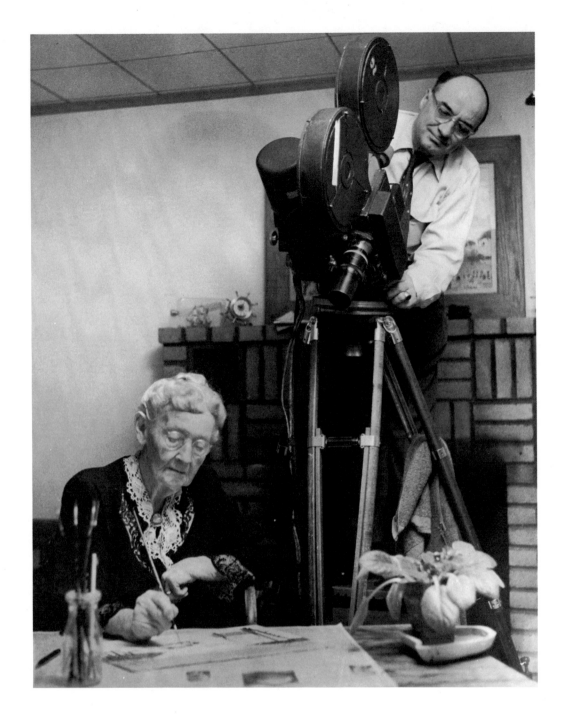

163.
Preparations for
Edward R. Murrow's interview
with Grandma Moses,
June-July 1955

was mounted high above the table on which the artist worked, the other faced her at a distance of about fifteen feet. It was thus possible to take pictures of Grandma Moses as she painted and at the same time to follow the progress of her work in every detail. The artist, who was close to ninety-five, worked for several days under the hot lamps.

She had chosen one of her favorite subjects, a sugaring-off scene. After grounding a Masonite board with flat white paint that she applied with a broad housepainter's brush, she took a pencil and drew a fine line across the upper part of the board to mark how far the sky would go. She then took a narrower brush and began to paint the sky, starting at the left. While working, she explained that it was going to be an overcast winter's day; otherwise she would have painted the sky a light blue or a blackish gray, according to whether she wanted to represent a sunny day or perhaps an oncoming snowstorm. After completing the sky, she again took the pencil and indicated with a few delicate lines the contours of mountains and hills. She then proceeded to paint these, either squeezing the various colors directly onto a fine brush or mixing them in small bowls and thinning them with turpentine; for this purpose she often used the lids of preserve jars. She now painted the distant mountains in shades of blue and the closer hills in brown and greenish tones. Without finishing the upper part of her painting, she again took up her pencil and began drawing objects in the foreground, trees and houses, all in scarcely visible outlines, as if only to reserve a certain place for each. After doing this, she began to work on the whole picture, now in this, now in another part, here a tree that reached over the entire surface up to the top, there some small shrubs and trees to form a border in the foreground. Once in a while she would interrupt her work for a moment, close her eyes, and then quickly fill in an empty space with the outline of a house, because "something had been missing here." But there was never any prolonged pause that might indicate that the artist was uncertain how to proceed. She always appeared to be following a plan and to know exactly what was to come next and what the final result was to be.

She painted the figures directly into the picture without first sketching them. It was interesting to see how she repeated certain types from previous versions of that specific subject. She seemed to know their exact functions so well that she could easily put them in their proper places. While working on a house or a tree, she sometimes interrupted herself to dab a few spots of brown, blue, or red here and there; these would become dresses, shoes, or the hat of a man who could soon be recognized. After she had taken up a fine brush and indicated face and

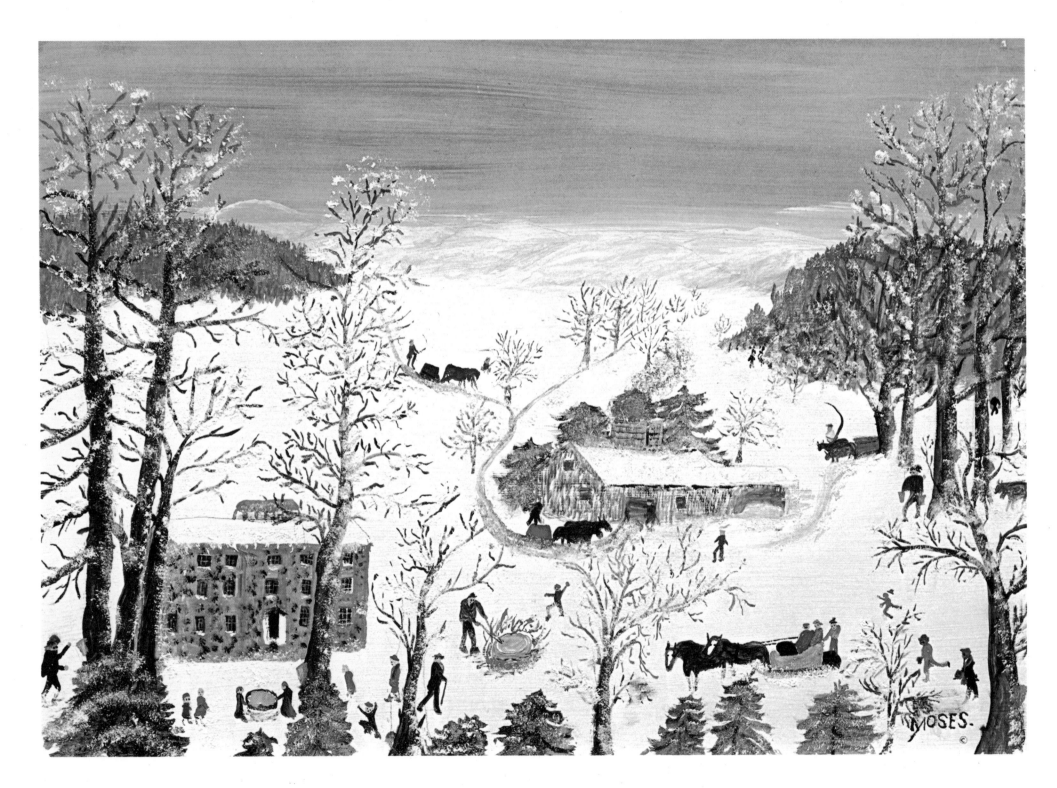

164. *Sugaring*. 1955. 11⅛ x 16". Cat. 1190

hands by little pink spots, she sometimes used a match or even a pin to put in the eyes and the mouth, "because the brushes are not fine enough." One could observe her imagination at work and see how each figure she painted meant something to her. After completing the painting (plate 164), she took "glitter" from a box and sprinkled it on the snow that covered the ground and the branches. A friend had in previous years tried to dissuade her from this "treatment" of her pictures, but she could not understand his objection. She said that if he had ever seen the snow on a sunny day, he would realize that it glitters.

The interview with Edward R. Murrow began after the painting was grounded and sketched. Grandma Moses did not share the general excitement; she had watched the complicated preparations with amusement and a trace of irony.

The "tip-up" table, which she had decorated with landscapes long before, had been brought into the living room for her to work on. After a few opening questions by Ed Murrow, Grandma pushed aside her painting and began interviewing her interviewer. She put a piece of paper before him and told him to draw something. When he protested, saying he could not draw, she replied with her usual remark that anybody could and that there was nothing to it. After that, the interview developed into a lively conversation touching upon many subjects, no longer a matter of questions and answers but an animated give-and-take that did not lag for a moment. Those present were somewhat taken aback by Murrow's last question: "What are you going to do for the next twenty years, Grandma Moses?" Without faltering for a second, seriously and calmly, she raised her hand and said: "I am going up yonder. Naturally—naturally, I should. After you get to be about so old you can't expect to go on much farther."

> MURROW: But you don't spend much time thinking about it or worrying about it. Do you?
> GRANDMA MOSES: Oh, no. No. No. You don't worry because

173

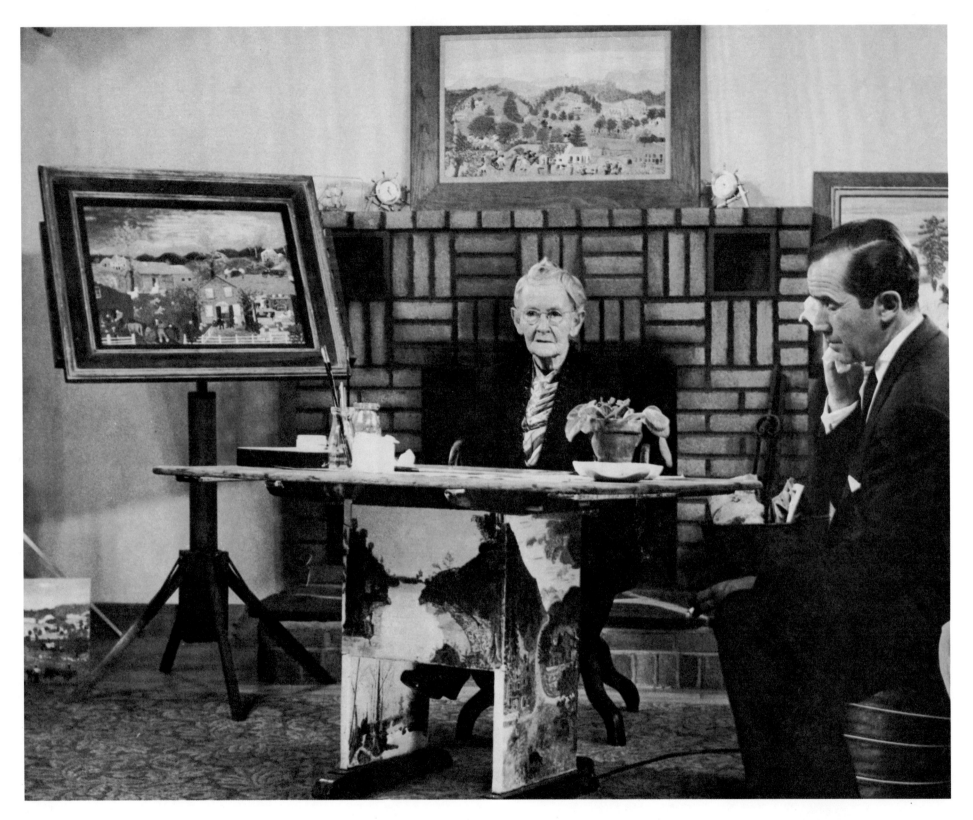

165. Grandma Moses and Edward R. Murrow, June 29, 1955.   Interview for "See It Now." Grandma Moses painted *Sugaring* during and after the show

you think, well, what a blessing it will be to be all united again. I'm the last one left of my sisters and brothers. . . .

MURROW: So this is something that in a sense you have no fear about or no apprehension?

GRANDMA: Oh, no. Go to sleep and wake up in the next world. I think that's the way. Did you ever know when you went to sleep?

MURROW: No, I don't think so.

GRANDMA: When the last thought came—you didn't know.

MURROW: No. That's true.

GRANDMA: You might wake up the next morning and think, well, that's what I was thinking about, but you didn't know when that last thought came. Well, that's the way you'll go to sleep.

Murrow, so poised and aloof, was visibly taken off guard by the turn of the conversation and closed the interview with the words: "Well, you will leave more behind you than most of us will, when you go to sleep."

Ed Murrow and all who had witnessed the interview felt that it had been an unforgettable experience. When CBS arranged a program on April 30, 1965, in commemoration of Edward Murrow's death, the last part of his interview with Grandma Moses was included among the most memorable moments of his broadcasting career.

Painting the Eisenhower Farm

166. Card from General Dwight D. Eisenhower

GRANDMA MOSES HAD ALWAYS ADMIRED GENERAL EISENHOWER, and he in turn had long shown interest in her art. Himself an amateur painter, he had devoted much time to this hobby before becoming president.

In 1952, while still in France, he sent Mrs. Moses a reproduction of one of his paintings with a hand-written inscription. She treasured this tribute to her art, and had it framed and hung in her living room.

Toward the end of 1955, President Eisenhower's Cabinet decided to mark the third anniversary of his inauguration by giving him a Grandma Moses painting. It was agreed that she would paint a picture of the Eisenhower Farm at Gettysburg, Pennsylvania.

She had never been there, and was uncertain how to comply with this unusual request, but she felt greatly honored by the "order" and was ready to try her best. She was sent about twenty black-and-white and color photographs showing house and grounds from all sides. Using

176

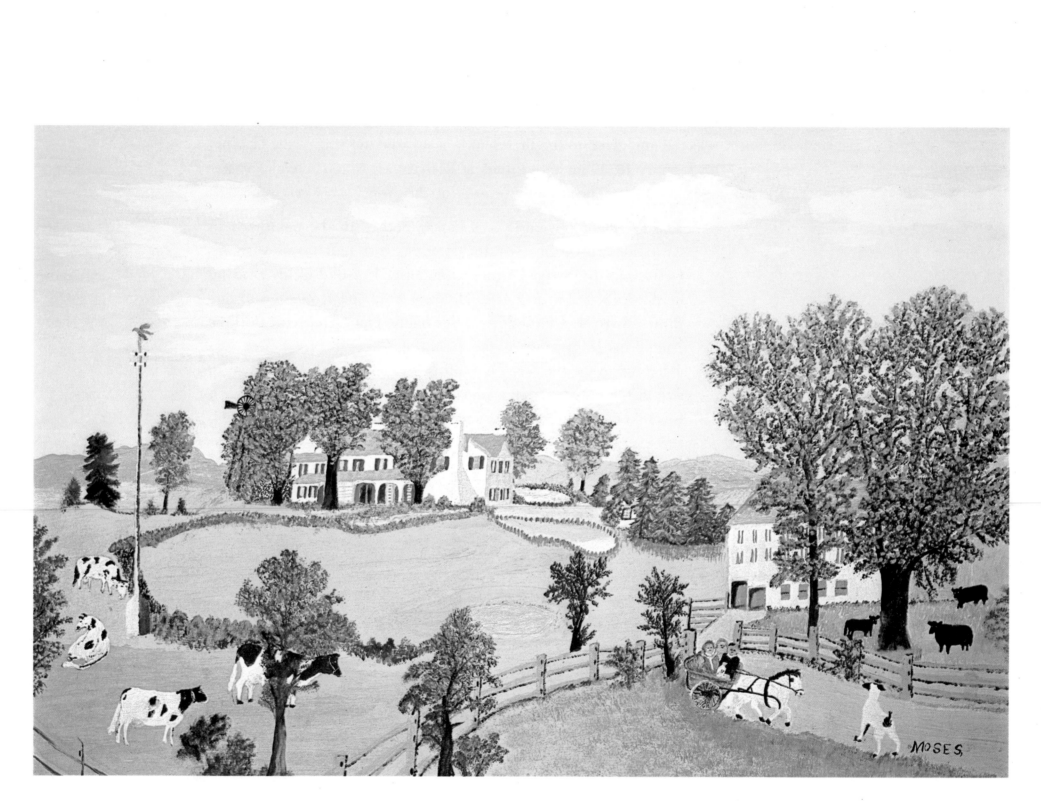

167. *The Eisenhower Farm.* 1956. 16 x 24". Cat. 1205

this material as a guide, she created two paintings each giving a different view of the farm. The more representative one (plate 167) was selected and given to the President in a surprise meeting of the Cabinet on January 18, 1956. Vice President Richard M. Nixon acted as master of ceremonies. The next day's issue of the *New York Times* reported:

> The President obviously was happy both with the painting and with the artistic liberties the famous artist had taken with his Gettysburg property. Farmer Eisenhower is proud of his growing herd of Black Angus cattle. He owns only one Holstein and one Brown Swiss. But Grandma Moses painted four Holsteins to three Angus cattle grazing in the pastures. General Eisenhower was delighted to see the recently built golf green, which had grown in size in the transfer from a photograph to an oil canvas. "I wish it was that big," said the President to Mrs. Eisenhower. He spotted his three grandchildren—David, Susan and Barbara Eisenhower— riding in the pony cart. The Great Dane that usually precedes them looked more like a wire fox-terrier.

168. A letter to President Eisenhower

Historical Themes

GRANDMA MOSES REPEATEDLY USED HISTORICAL EVENTS she had been told about or which occurred in her lifetime as subjects for her paintings.

When President Lincoln was assassinated in 1865, Anna Mary was not quite five years old, but the event remained vivid in her mind throughout her life. In 1957 she painted a small picture (plate 169) showing a village street, with the doors of the church and the houses draped in black bunting. In recollecting this very early experience, she wrote:

> One day, mother, aunt Lib and I, we left Greenwich to come down to grandma's, just above Eagle Bridge where she lived. Mother was driving the buggy, an old fan horse, a gentle horse. . . . I don't remember the trip so much until we got down into Coila. . . .
>
> Mother noticed that everything was trimmed in black. I remember her saying, "Oh, what has happened?" It was war times. . . . She went into the store and asked what had happened. The pillars on the store were all wrapped in black bunting. And this man told her that President Lincoln was shot the night before. And I remember her coming back to the buggy and she said to aunt Lib, "Oh, what will become of us now?" And if she hadn't used those words, I don't suppose I would have ever remembered it.

Grandma Moses was especially interested in the history of her neighborhood and knew a great deal about it. The Revolutionary War, in which some of her ancestors had taken part, particularly fascinated her. In 1953 she painted three pictures of the Battle of Bennington (plates 170–72), which had taken place close by—the site is marked by a monument. In preparation for her work she looked up many historical details in reference books. In the first two versions she painted the monument in the background; when it was pointed out to her that this was an amusing error, since naturally no monument existed at that time, she made a third painting without it.

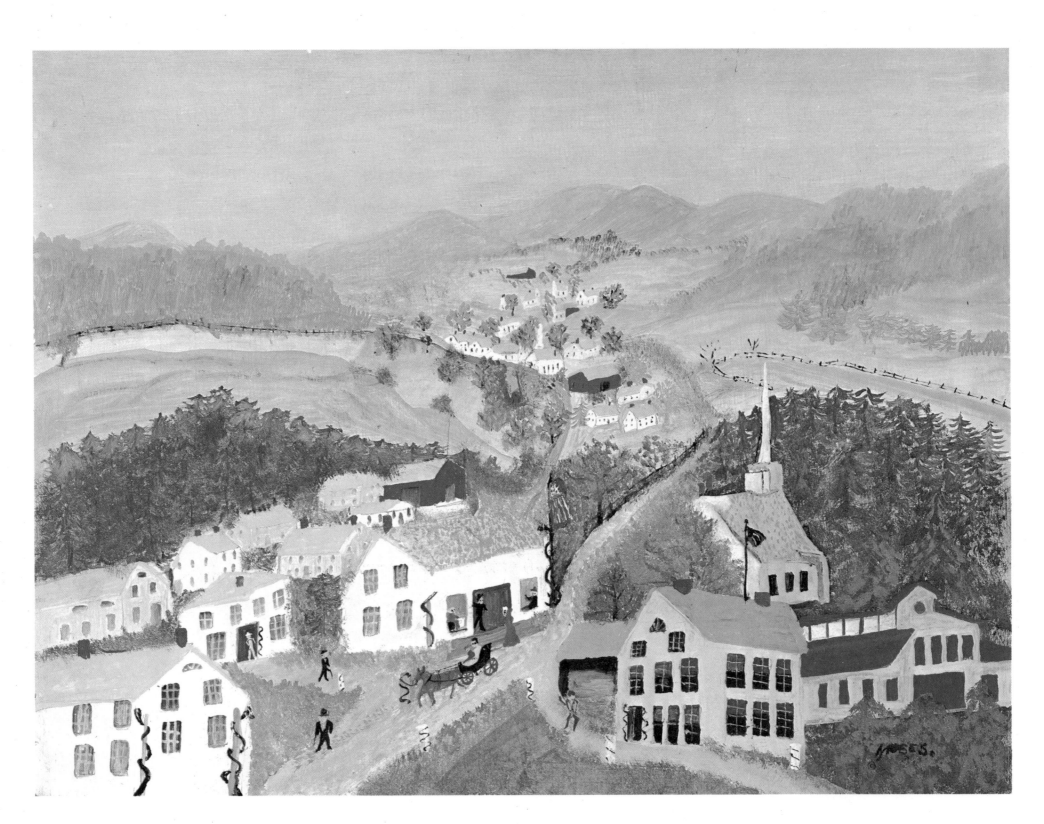

169. *Lincoln.* 1957. 12 x 16⅛". Cat. 1305

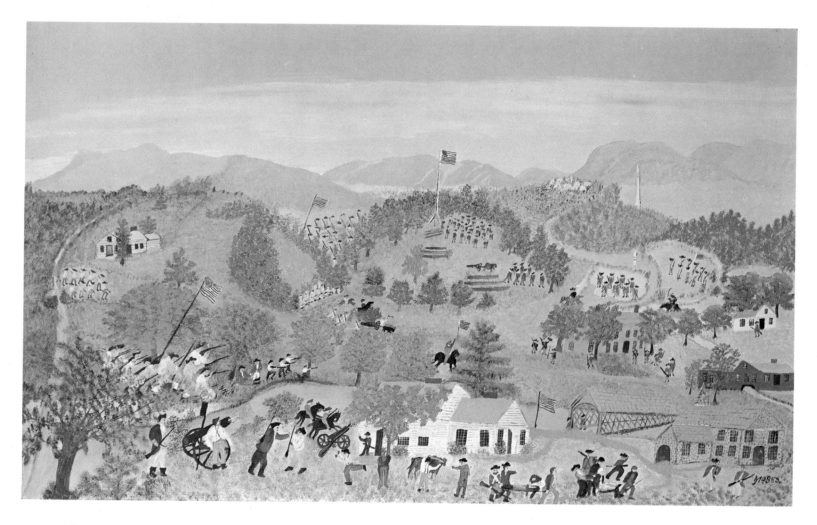

170. *The Battle of Bennington.* 1953. 18 x 30½". Cat. 1100

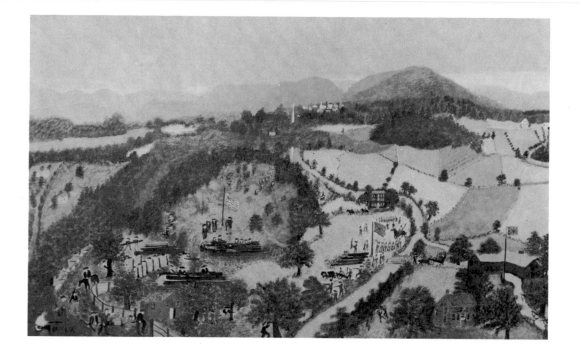

171. *Before the Battle of Bennington.* 1953. 18 x 30". Cat. 1099

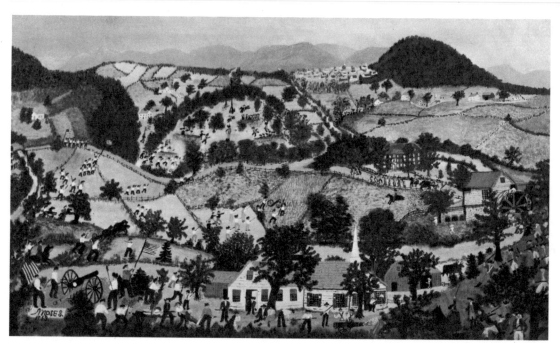

172. *Battle of Bennington.* 1953. 17½ x 29¾". Cat. 1113

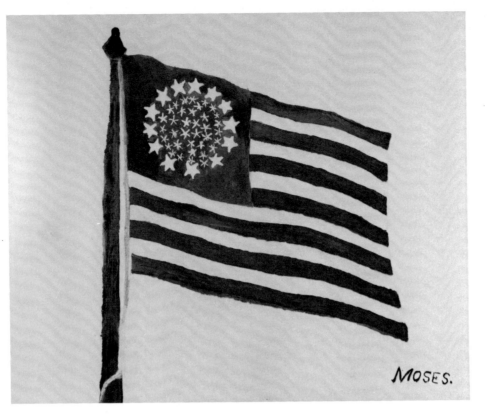

173.
Old Glory. 1958.
12 x 16″. Cat. 1368

Grandma Moses never ceased to follow current events with lively interest and understanding. In 1959 Alaska became the forty-ninth state of the Union. During the preceding year there had been much discussion about how the new flag should look with one star added to forty-eight. The idea stimulated Grandma's recollections, for she had many times witnessed the growth of the United States and the changing of the flag.

She made a design for the new American flag, basing it on "the first flag with stars and stripes [which] was that of Ticonderoga. It had a circle of thirteen. Why not fill the others in?" she wrote. It was a sketch of just the flag without background, on a 12-by-16-inch board. She called it *Old Glory* (plate 173). On a second small oil painting dated the same day, December 6, 1958, Grandma Moses showed this new flag being hoisted to the accompaniment of salvos from two cannons at the foot of the flagpole.

Hundredth Birthday, September 7, 1960

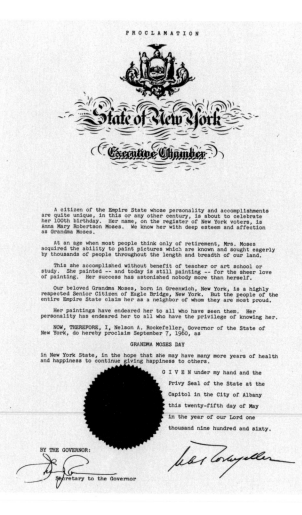

174.
Proclamation by Governor
Nelson A. Rockefeller, 1960

PROCLAMATION

State of New York
Executive Chamber

A citizen of the Empire State whose personality and accomplishments are quite unique, in this or any other century, is about to celebrate her 100th birthday. Her name, on the register of New York voters, is Anna Mary Robertson Moses. We know her with deep esteem and affection as Grandma Moses.

At an age when most people think only of retirement, Mrs. Moses acquired the ability to paint pictures which are known and sought eagerly by thousands of people throughout the length and breadth of our land.

This she accomplished without benefit of teacher or art school or study. She painted -- and today is still painting -- for the sheer love of painting. Her success has astonished nobody more than herself.

Our beloved Grandma Moses, born in Greenwich, New York, is a highly respected Senior Citizen of Eagle Bridge, New York. But the people of the entire Empire State claim her as a neighbor of whom they are most proud.

Her paintings have endeared her to all who have seen them. Her personality has endeared her to all who have the privilege of knowing her.

NOW, THEREFORE, I, Nelson A. Rockefeller, Governor of the State of New York, do hereby proclaim September 7, 1960, as

GRANDMA MOSES DAY

in New York State, in the hope that she may have many more years of health and happiness to continue giving happiness to others.

G I V E N under my hand and the
Privy Seal of the State at the
Capitol in the City of Albany
this twenty-fifth day of May
in the year of our Lord one
thousand nine hundred and sixty.

BY THE GOVERNOR:

Secretary to the Governor

PREPARATIONS FOR THE HUNDREDTH BIRTHDAY of Grandma Moses began early. In May 1960, Governor Nelson A. Rockefeller issued a proclamation declaring September 7 "Grandma Moses Day" in New York State.

As the day approached, many newspapers requested personal interviews. Fearing that it would be too strenuous for the centenarian to have dozens of reporters descend on her home in Eagle Bridge, her family allowed only a very few to see her. One of the most sensitive reports was written by Joy Miller of the Associated Press, whose article was published nationwide on September 4:

Your impression of Grandma Moses is that she is very fragile and very old. She's sitting in the living room, looking small at one end of a big sofa, wearing a blue print dress and pink sweater, with a black ribbon around her throat. Her arthritic fingers are curled together in her lap. You advance hesitantly. How do you address America's best known primitive painter? . . . Is it too forward to call her "Grandma"? . . . Do you have to shout?

But she has sighted company. Her face lights up in a gamin grin, her hazel eyes sparkle behind their spectacles. Her welcoming hand grasps yours with startling vigor.

As she chats about this and that, the character of a remarkable woman emerges: kindly, humorous, unaffected, indomitable, with sight and hearing in admirable repair. You become aware that her seemingly frail 100-pound frame supports a spirit that's at once robust and ageless.

From the beginning of September, mailbags full of cards and letters swamped the Eagle Bridge Post Office. Hundreds of telegrams arrived, piles of gifts were stowed away in the sunporch of the farmhouse, where Grandma Moses took loving care of her geraniums, African violets, and coleus. President and Mrs. Eisenhower, Vice President and Mrs. Nixon, and former President and Mrs. Truman sent birthday tributes. President Truman had never failed to remember Grandma's birthday since their meeting in 1949.

For the benefit of friends and neighbors who could not come on the 7th, which was a working day, Grandma Moses's family gave a birthday party at her home on Sunday the 4th. After this, Forrest and Mary Moses had to hold open house for more than a week to accommodate the steady stream of visitors. In the midst of all this excitement Grandma Moses was cheerful and serene and seemed to enjoy everything. When she had realized that her efforts to discourage an elaborate celebration would fail, she said: "I'm going to sit right here, just so, and the others

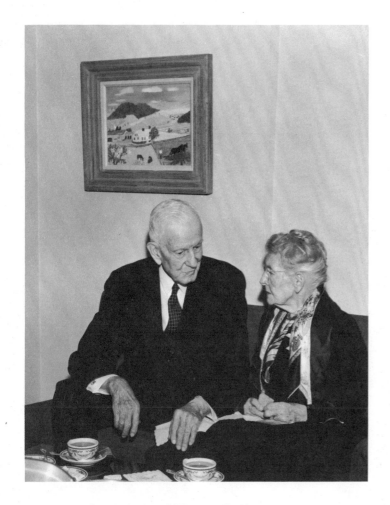

175. Grandma Moses and Thomas J. Watson, 1955

can do the work. I wish they wouldn't fuss, but it's a nice excuse for the young people to get together."

Several weeks went by before the excitement subsided and she could go back to the quiet life she had been leading of late.

In honor of Grandma Moses's hundredth birthday, the IBM Gallery of Arts and Sciences arranged a loan exhibition, "My Life's History," which ran from September 12 to October 6, 1960. The gallery had been inaugurated five years earlier with a comprehensive Moses show. Although Thomas J. Watson, the artist's longtime friend and active supporter, had died in 1956, his family remained interested in her work, as did the art department of IBM.

The pictures for the birthday exhibition were selected to depict events from the life of the artist as she remembered them. Most of the captions that accompanied the paintings were taken from her autobiography, but a few quotations from the previous book, *Grandma Moses: American Primitive*, were also included.

Prominent personalities who had taken a personal interest in the artist and in her work formed the honorary committee. Among them were former President and Mrs. Truman, Eleanor Roosevelt, Irving Berlin, Jean Cassou, Walt Disney, Lillian Gish, and Thornton Wilder.

"*The Night Before Christmas*"

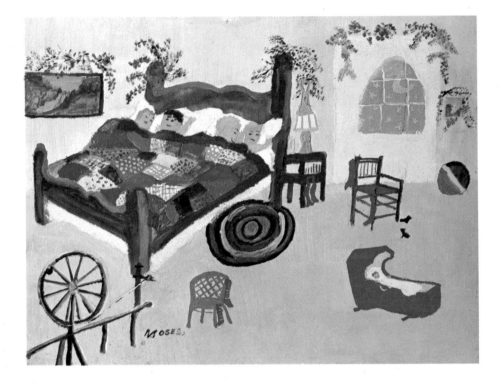

176. *Waiting for Santa Claus.* 1960. 12 x 16". Cat. 1463

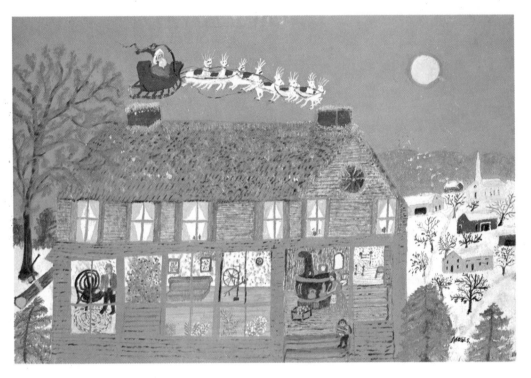

177. *Santa Claus II.* 1960. 16 x 24". Cat. 1456

EARLY IN 1960 GRANDMA MOSES'S STRENGTH HAD BEGUN TO FAIL. She could no longer walk around very much and was more and more confined to the house; painting lifted her spirits and gave her a fresh incentive every day. At that time a proposal was made by Bennett Cerf and Robert Bernstein of Random House that she illustrate Clement C. Moore's famous poem, *The Night Before Christmas*. The idea of creating pictures for a Christmas story did not appeal to her. She had declared time and again that she only wanted to paint scenes and situations she knew from her own experience. She once wrote to me (March 4, 1944): "Some one has asked me to paint Biblical pictures, and I say *no* I'll not paint something that we know nothing about, might just as well paint something that will happen 2 thousand years hence."

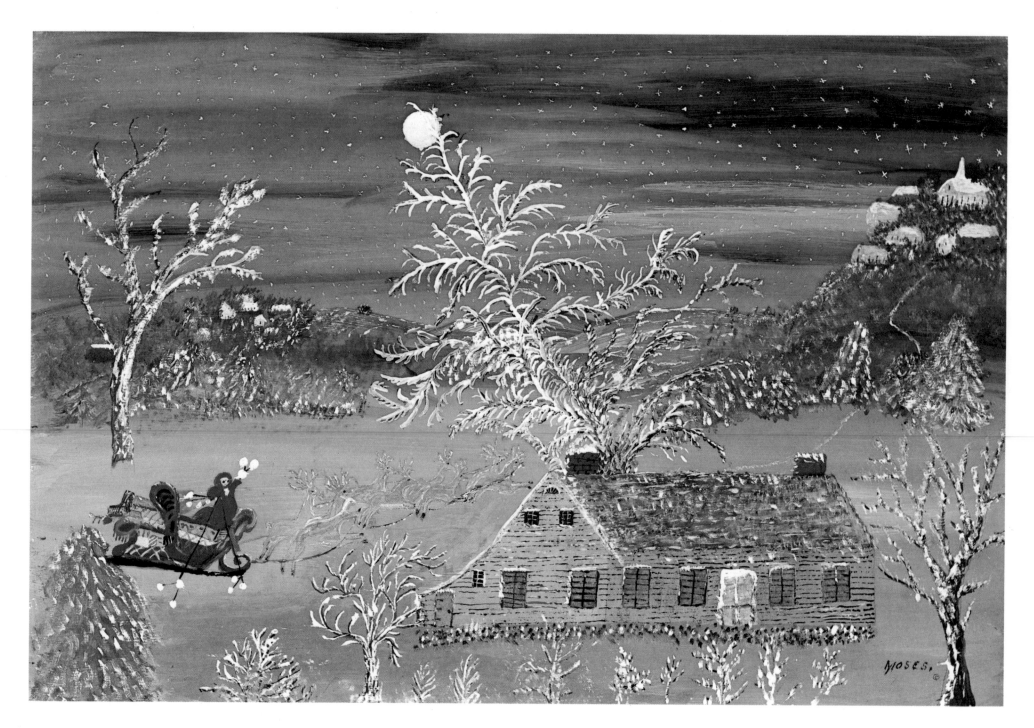

178. *So Long till Next Year.* 1960. 16 x 24". Cat. 1461

Still, she took up the project, for she liked the poem and knew it by heart. At first she dutifully tried to follow the text and painted scenes and objects familiar to a child's conception of Christmas—stockings hanging by the fireplace, candy canes, and toys (plates 176, 177). As her work progressed, her imagination unfolded. *So Long till Next Year* (plate 178), one of the many paintings done for the book (though finally not published in it), was obviously meant to conclude the series. This work far transcends any factual illustration.

It is a pure artistic expression of almost dreamlike quality and is also remarkable in that this effect is achieved entirely by means of color. The intense blue of a deep, clear winter night is illumined by an almost white moon that bathes the unrealistic feathery branches of the trees in a silvery light; stars are scattered across the dark sky. There are only these two colors, blue and white, except for a few beautifully distributed patches of red—Santa's coat and the red chimneys. The reindeer, quite substantial and lifelike in the other illustrations, are, as they should be, otherworldly apparitions receding into the beyond. One can imagine a child, still half asleep yet expecting the miraculous, stepping to the window in the middle of the night and experiencing this vision of a transformed world.

Grandma Moses's work on the book, begun in March 1960, was interrupted by the commotion caused by her hundredth birthday. She completed the pictures in November of 1960, but did not live to see the book's publication in 1962. It has since become very popular and is read and shown every year on the December 24th telecast of the CBS-TV children's program "Captain Kangaroo."

The Last Months

On July 18, 1961, Forrest and Mary Moses took Grandma to the Health Center at Hoosick Falls. Forrest wrote me: "Grandma feels good, only for her legs, they are so weak; her hearing is good again and her voice is strong." She had fallen several times, and it was decided that she would be better off under professional care. Grandma Moses was quite unhappy at the nursing home, and hoped her stay there would be only temporary.

As long as she had been at home she had continued to paint, completing more than twenty-five pictures after her hundredth birthday. At the nursing home, however, she was not allowed to do what had become her most important activity. Her physician, Dr. Clayton Shaw, who had been the family's doctor for fifty years, felt that she "would not rest if she had her paints."

During one of his visits she hid the doctor's stethoscope. When he asked, "Where's my stethoscope?" Grandma Moses replied: "That's what I won't tell you. I hid it. It's a forfeit. You take me back to Eagle Bridge and you'll get back your stethoscope."

Just before her 101st birthday I visited her and found her in good spirits. She was mentally alert and full of plans. "As soon as I get back home, I will start painting again," she said. Asked how she would celebrate her birthday this year, she said: "Much as I enjoy visiting with my friends and neighbors, I have come to see that *one* hundred-year celebration is enough for anybody, and I would like to spend my 101st birthday the same as my first day, very quiet."

Again Governor Rockefeller proclaimed September 7 as Grandma Moses Day in New York State. On that day the Health Center at Hoosick Falls was described as resembling "one huge bowl of flowers," for at Grandma's request the bouquets were shared by the other

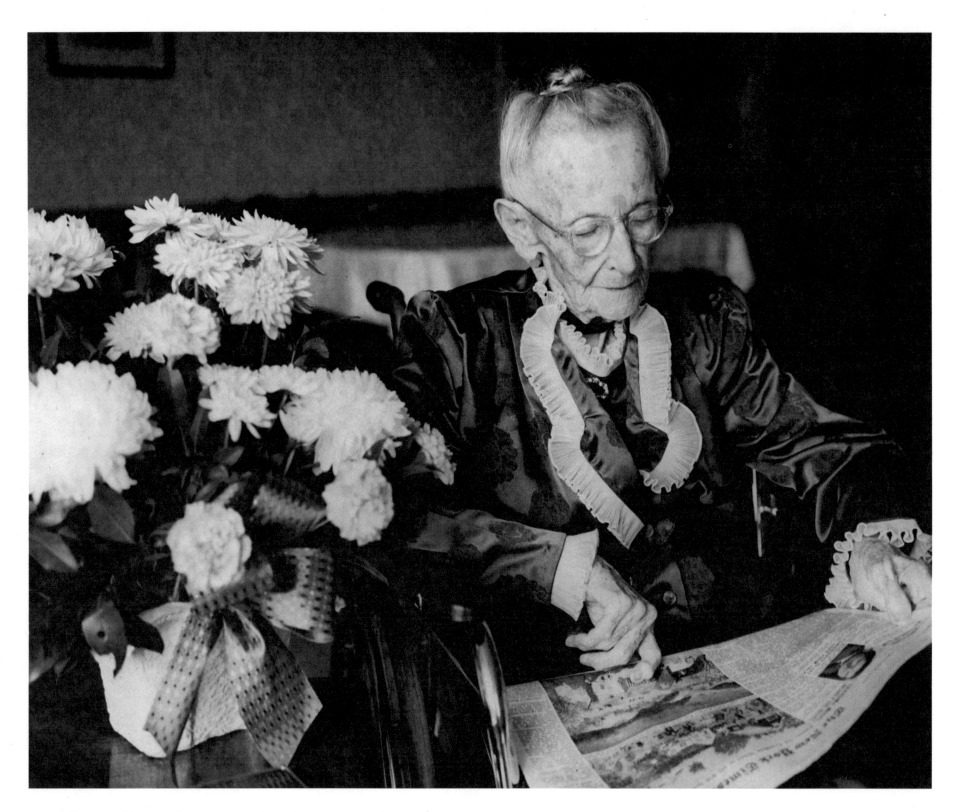

179. Grandma Moses on her 101st birthday, September 7, 1961

190

THE WHITE HOUSE

WASHINGTON

September 5, 1961

Dear Grandma Moses:

I want again to send you my warmest best wishes
as you reach another milestone in your long and
celebrated career.

Your painting and your personal influence continue
to play a large and valuable role in our national
life.

Both Mrs. Kennedy and I want to wish you best
health and happiness in the years ahead.

Sincerely,

Grandma Moses
Eagle Bridge, New York

180.
Letter from President John F. Kennedy

patients at the home. Among the tributes she received was a letter from President John F. Kennedy.

In October 1961, Random House published *The Grandma Moses Story Book*, a collection of stories for children by various authors, illustrated with her paintings. This was the last of her books the artist saw published.

The Death of Grandma Moses

EARLY IN THE AFTERNOON OF DECEMBER 13, 1961, Dr. Shaw called from Hoosick Falls to tell me that Grandma Moses had passed away a short while before. "She just wore out," he said. Her death had been expected for some weeks; she had grown steadily weaker, her mind had begun to wander, and she slept for long hours. Her daughter-in-law Dorothy had been at Grandma Moses's bedside every day during these last weeks and months.

News of the artist's death was broadcast over all radio networks and published nationwide on the front pages of newspapers. Her passing brought words of sympathy from all over the country.

President Kennedy issued the following statement:

> The death of Grandma Moses removes a beloved figure from American life. The directness and vividness of her paintings restored a primitive freshness to our perception of the American scene. All Americans mourn her loss. Both her work and her life helped our nation renew its pioneer heritage and recalled its roots in the countryside and on the frontier.

Governor Nelson A. Rockefeller said the death of Grandma Moses "is a loss to all of us in New York State and to those everywhere who loved simplicity and beauty. She painted for the sheer love of painting, and throughout her 101 years, she was endeared to all who had the privilege of knowing her."

Of the numerous editorials on her life, her artistic achievement and its meaning for our time, one tribute is reprinted here from *The New Yorker* of December 23, 1961:

> The death of a very old person seems no more natural, no less an untoward incursion, than the death of a young one. Perhaps death seems natural only to Nature herself—and even she may have some

doubts. Yet we cannot think of the life, now concluded, of Anna Mary Robertson Moses without cheerfulness. To live one allotted span as a farm wife and the mother of ten children, and then, at the age of seventy-six, to begin another, as an artist, as Grandma Moses, and to extend this second life into twenty-five years of unembarrassed productiveness—such a triumph over the normal course of things offers small cause for mourning. If we do mourn, it is for ourselves; she had become by her hundredth year one of those old people who, as old buildings civilize a city or spindly church spires bind up a landscape, make the world seem safer. Shaw and Brancusi were examples; Churchill and Schweitzer still are. They pay the world the great compliment of being reluctant to leave it, and their reluctance becomes a benediction.

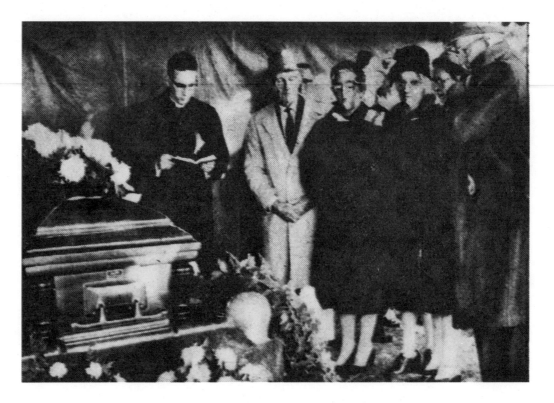

181.
The Reverend Joel B. Miller conducting graveside rites for Grandma Moses, December 16, 1961. UPI photo

193

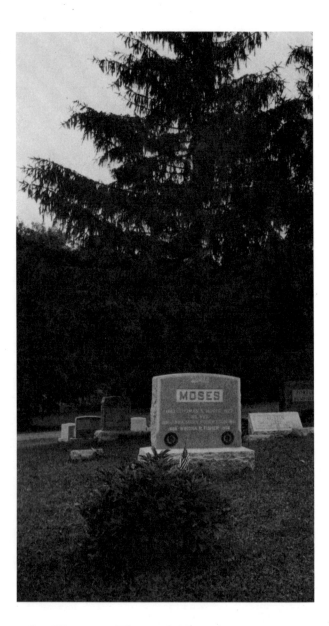

182. The grave: Thomas S. Moses /
his wife / Anna Mary Robertson /
Winona R. Fisher. Maple Grove
Cemetery, Hoosick Falls, N.Y.
Photo by John Woodruff

Grandma Moses was buried on December 16 in a hilltop grave in Maple Grove Cemetery, Hoosick Falls, overlooking the Hoosick Valley. About a hundred friends and neighbors joined with the family in a fifteen-minute Episcopal service conducted at her Eagle Bridge house by the Reverend Joel B. Miller, Rector of St. Mark's Episcopal Church in Hoosick Falls, of which she had been a member. The house was so crowded that mourners stood in the hall and in the kitchen. The priest interpolated into the service phrases of his own which had reference to Grandma's special gifts as an artist, but there were no eulogies.

A thirty-five-car cortege proceeded from the house to the cemetery some five miles distant, with Washington County sheriff's deputies as escort to the county line and Rensselaer County deputies taking over at that point. The day was clear and bright and bitter cold, with temperatures in the low teens, but almost all those at the house continued to the cemetery. Along the route, groups of people waited in front of their homes to pay their last respects.

At the graveside, Father Miller read briefly from the burial service of the Book of Common Prayer. Anna Mary Robertson Moses was buried next to her husband, Thomas Salmon Moses, her son Hugh, and her daughter Winona. The services were marked by the simplicity that was the keynote of Grandma Moses's life. Father Miller said: "It was exactly what she would have wanted—a simple, farmhouse, family funeral."

Exhibitions, 1962—1972

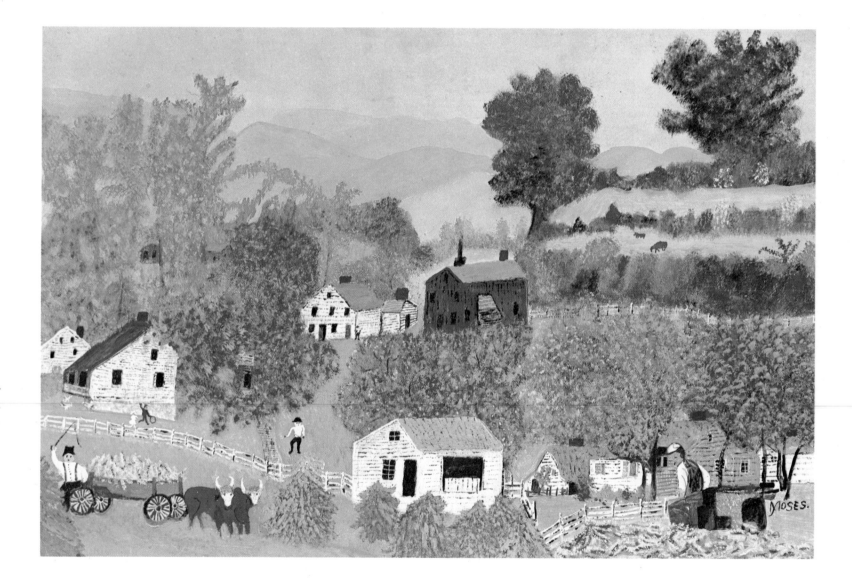

183.
Corn. 1958.
16 x 23⅞". Cat. 1362

A PHENOMENON OFTEN OBSERVED is that the public's interest slackens after an artist's death; his fame becomes dimmed, his name no longer appears in the news. Then, sometimes, he is rediscovered. Finally the pendulum that has swung far out in both directions levels off to an objective and lasting evaluation.

Such a development seemed very likely in the case of Grandma Moses.

195

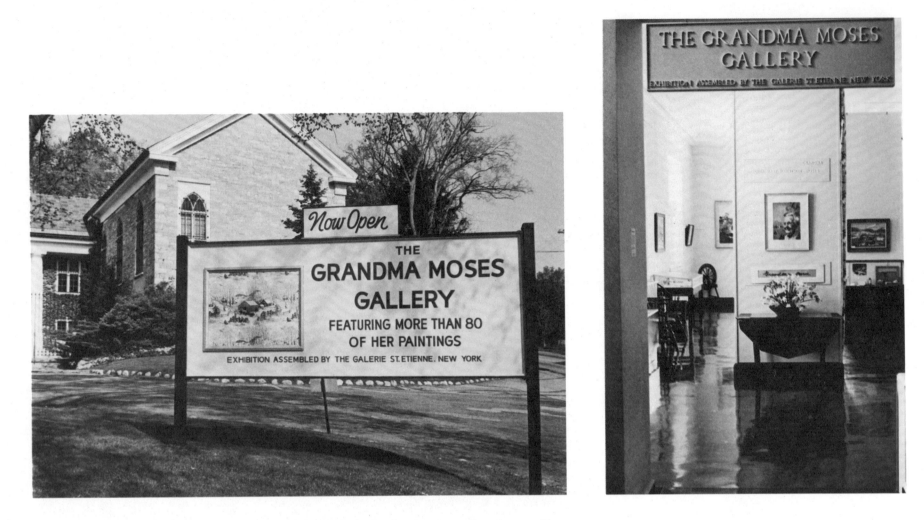

184–85. The Grandma Moses Gallery, 1968–72, at the Bennington Museum, Bennington, Vt.

So much had been written about her exceptional rise to fame in old age, and now the appealing aura surrounding her person faded with her passing. But the public's interest, far from diminishing, has steadily grown as her art, stripped of anecdotal embellishments, emerges and speaks for itself.

One-man shows and museum exhibitions that took place in the decade following the artist's death were received with great interest. In November 1962, a memorial show was held at the Galerie St. Etienne, New York. The catalogue reproduced details of pictures to draw attention to various characteristics of the artist's painting technique.

A traveling show, sponsored and circulated by the Smithsonian Insti-·tution (1962–64) found the greatest response. The collection was presented at museums in nine American cities and thereafter in eight

196

European countries, finally going to Russia at the invitation of the Soviet Ministry for Culture. It was exhibited at the Pushkin Museum in Moscow in December of 1964. "The show was very well received by the public, once they had overcome their initial surprise," wrote the Counselor for Cultural Affairs of the United States Embassy in Moscow. "Judging by the comments we heard . . . the evident delight that Grandma Moses took in the execution of all her work was the most impressive aspect for the Soviets. They were surprised, and quite pleased, to find a total absence of 'social message'. . . . I would judge that 100,000 viewers would not be too generous an estimate. . . . There were lines of people waiting to see the show. . . . The Embassy regards the Moses exhibit as a successful and very valid effort . . . to increase Soviet understanding of the United States and its people."

From 1964 on, the Hammer Galleries, New York, in cooperation with the Galerie St. Etienne, has been presenting Moses exhibitions at Christmas time.

In 1963, 1965, and 1967 the Bennington Museum in Vermont arranged Grandma Moses shows that met with such lively response that the idea of establishing a more permanent exhibition arose. The Grandma Moses Gallery was opened in a wing of the museum on May 10, 1968. Beginning with her first known picture, the *Fireboard*, "worsted" pictures, and small early paintings, the collection contained prominent works from the artist's two productive decades. In addition, photographs, exhibition posters, and documents conveyed a vivid impression of her life and the development of her fame as an artist. The Grandma Moses Gallery was closed after the 1972 season.

The most comprehensive Moses exhibition ever assembled, titled "Art and Life of Grandma Moses," was presented at the Gallery of Modern Art in New York in 1969. A total of 141 paintings lent by museums and collectors all over the country showed a cross-section of the artist's entire oeuvre.

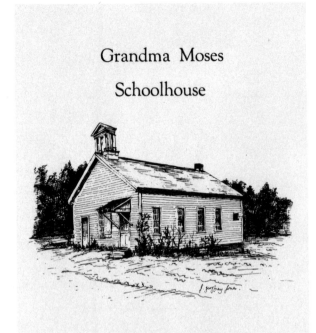

Grandma Moses

Schoolhouse

An Exhibition of Mementos

Eagle Bridge, New York

186.
The Grandma Moses Schoolhouse.
From a drawing by J. Geoffrey Jones

Shortly after Grandma Moses's death the little one-room schoolhouse in Eagle Bridge, where Anna Mary had gone to school, was up for sale. Her son Forrest and daughter-in-law Mary acquired it and had it moved to a site next to the old Moses farm. Leaving the original structure untouched, they filled it with countless memorabilia, including the old shop sign of Thomas's Drugstore in Hoosick Falls, where Louis Caldor had first seen her pictures, as well as objects and souvenirs she had assembled from childhood on. The schoolhouse was opened to the public in 1966. It has recently been acquired with its entire contents by the Bennington Museum and set up adjacent to it.

The Grandma Moses Stamp

In 1969, THE UNITED STATES GOVERNMENT paid tribute to the memory of Grandma Moses by issuing a six-cent stamp, an honor accorded to but a few American artists.

Senator Kenneth B. Keating first brought up the idea on the Senate floor in 1960, on the occasion of the artist's forthcoming hundredth birthday. The *Congressional Record* of June 20, 1960 (vol. 106, no. 113), includes the following statement:

> Mr. President, one of the leading citizens of my State is, in the fullest sense of the word, a citizen who belongs to all the world. She is Anna Mary Robertson Moses of Eagle Bridge, N.Y., better known everywhere as Grandma Moses.
>
> This great lady and artist has brought an inspiring message to people all over the world. Not only has Grandma Moses become a legend in her time; she has also demonstrated to elderly people everywhere that the opportunity for achievement and satisfaction really knows no age. By her example and through her paintings she has projected a wonderful and indelible image of America to the four corners of the globe.
>
> In my view, the message of Grandma Moses and all she stands for could be communicated ideally through the issuance of a commemorative stamp bearing one of her paintings. It would be a fitting tribute on the occasion of her 100th birthday on September 7 of this year. I have made this suggestion to the Postmaster General and I am hopeful an affirmative response will be forthcoming.

It took nine years for Senator Keating's idea to be realized. When the decision to issue the stamp was finally reached, J. Carter Brown, Director of the National Gallery of Art in Washington, D.C., was asked to suggest a painting. He recommended *July Fourth* (plate 95), owned

199

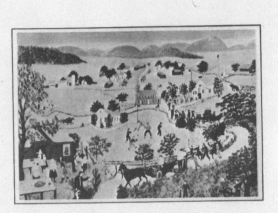

On the First Day of Senior Citizens Month
Honoring All Older Americans

GRANDMA MOSES

Commemorative Stamp Ceremony May 1, 1969

AUDITORIUM
U.S. Department of Health, Education, and Welfare

Washington, D.C.

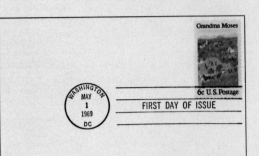

PROGRAM

WELCOME
The Honorable Patricia Reilly Hitt
Assistant Secretary
United States Department of
Health, Education, and Welfare

INTRODUCTION OF SPECIAL GUESTS
The Honorable John D. Twiname
Deputy Administrator
Social and Rehabilitation Service

READING: PRESIDENTIAL PROCLAMATION
SENIOR CITIZENS MONTH

REMARKS
The Honorable John B. Martin, Jr.
Commissioner-Designate
Administration on Aging

ADDRESS AND PRESENTATION OF ALBUMS
The Honorable James W. Hargrove
Assistant Postmaster General
of the United States

Six inks and three passes through the press were required to print the Grandma Moses stamp. Yellow, red, green, and blue were applied in two offset passes. Blue and black were printed on the Giori press. Robert J. Jones of the Bureau of Engraving and Printing designed the stamp. It will be issued in panes of 50, with an initial printing of 120 million.

Grandma Moses painted "July Fourth" in 1951 at the age of 91. It hangs in the White House. A detail of that painting today becomes this year's edition in the American Folklore series of postage stamps, which have re-awakened memories of Johnny Appleseed, Davy Crockett, and Daniel Boone. The painting, her son Forrest Moses says, represents a composite of Fourths, rather than a particular one, and includes all the remembered "good times" — the flag, the playing children, and the reliable horse pulling the new-fangled automobile.

Mrs. Anna Mary Moses of Eagle Bridge, New York, took up painting at the age of 76 and continued almost to the time of her death at 101. She completed more than 1200 paintings and they are now avidly sought by collectors and museums. Her first efforts sold for $3 to $5. Her theme was the bygone aspects of farm life, and her primitive art has enchanted millions. She is a most fitting representative of the creativity older Americans offer their country and communities. Issuance of her stamp on the first day of Senior Citizens Month gives greater meaning to both.

187. Folder distributed to the guests attending the Grandma Moses
Commemorative Stamp Ceremony, May 1, 1969

by the White House, as a suitable subject. The design for the stamp is a detail from that painting. Printed on a two-plate Giori press in six colors, in an edition of 166,630,400, the stamp was released in a ceremony in Washington on May 1, 1969, marking the beginning of Senior Citizens' Month.

1953 to 1961

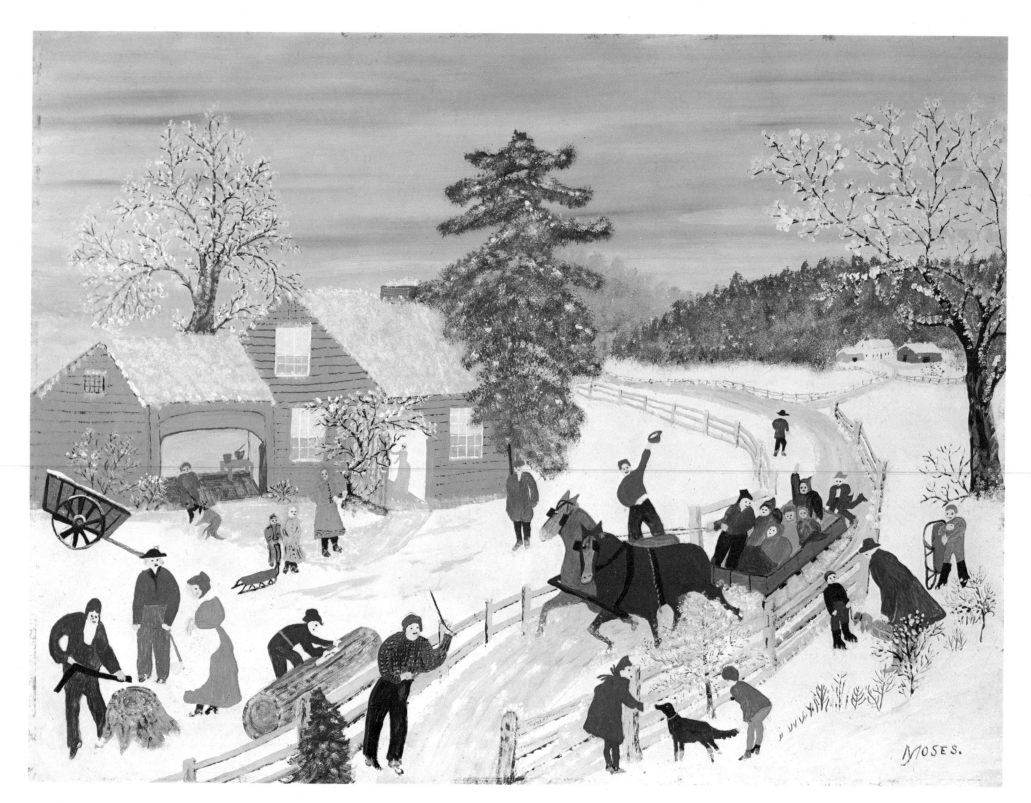

188. *Joy Ride*. 1953. 18 x 24". Cat. 1079

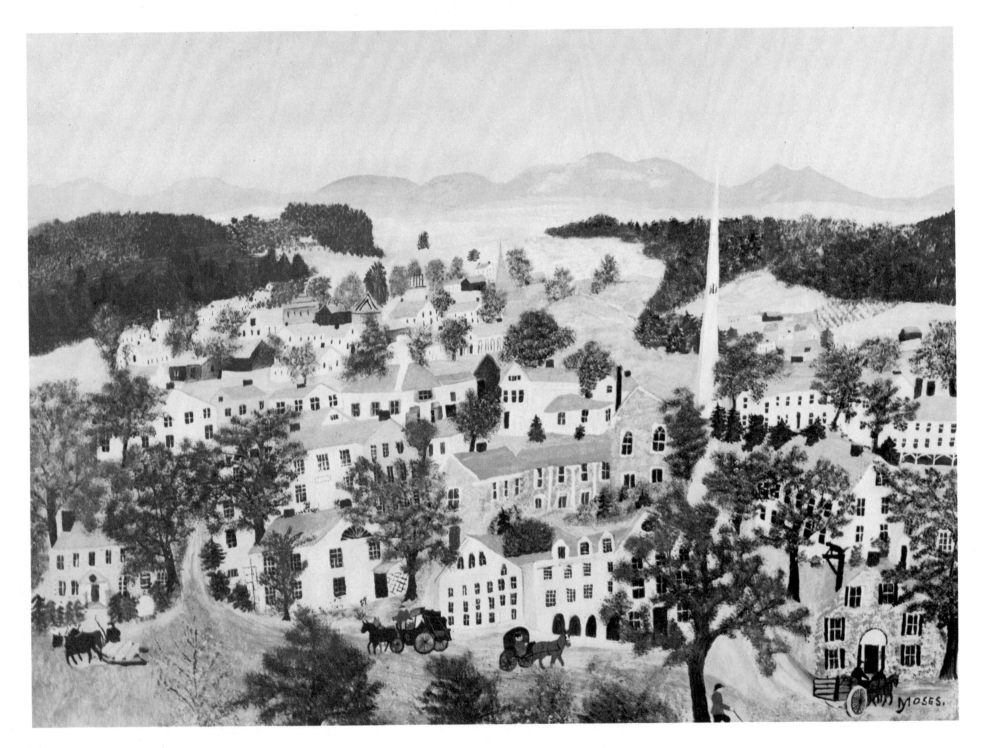

189. *Bennington*. 1953. 18 x 24″. Cat. 1070

204

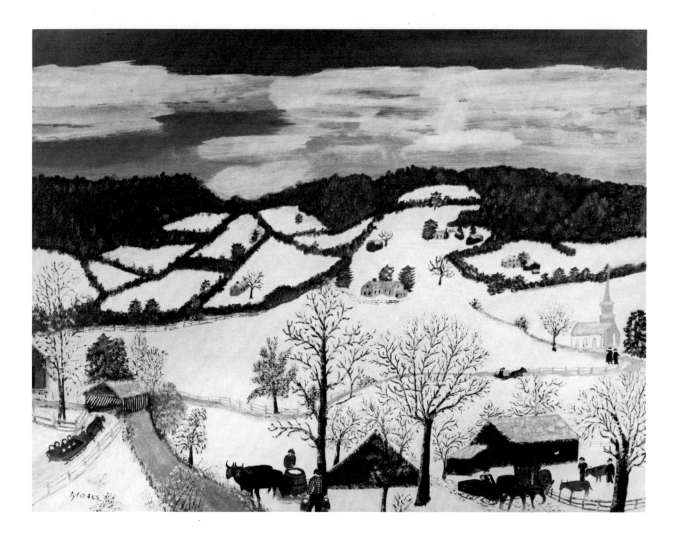

190.
Dark Sky. 1953.
18¼ x 24". Cat. 1072

191.
Springtime. 1953.
18 x 24". Cat. 1080

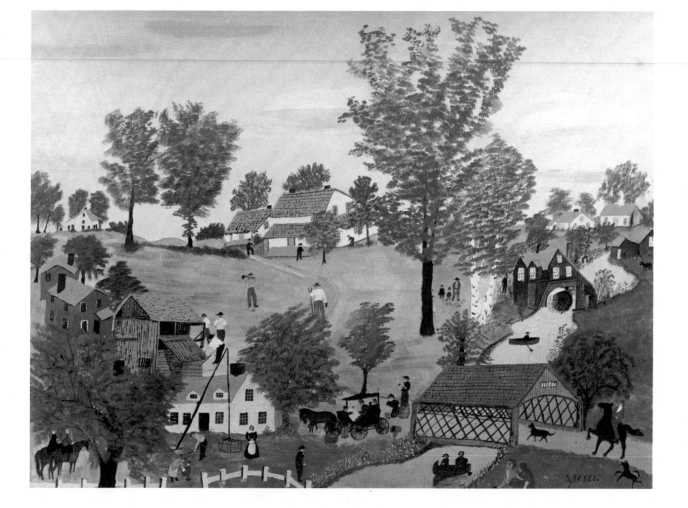

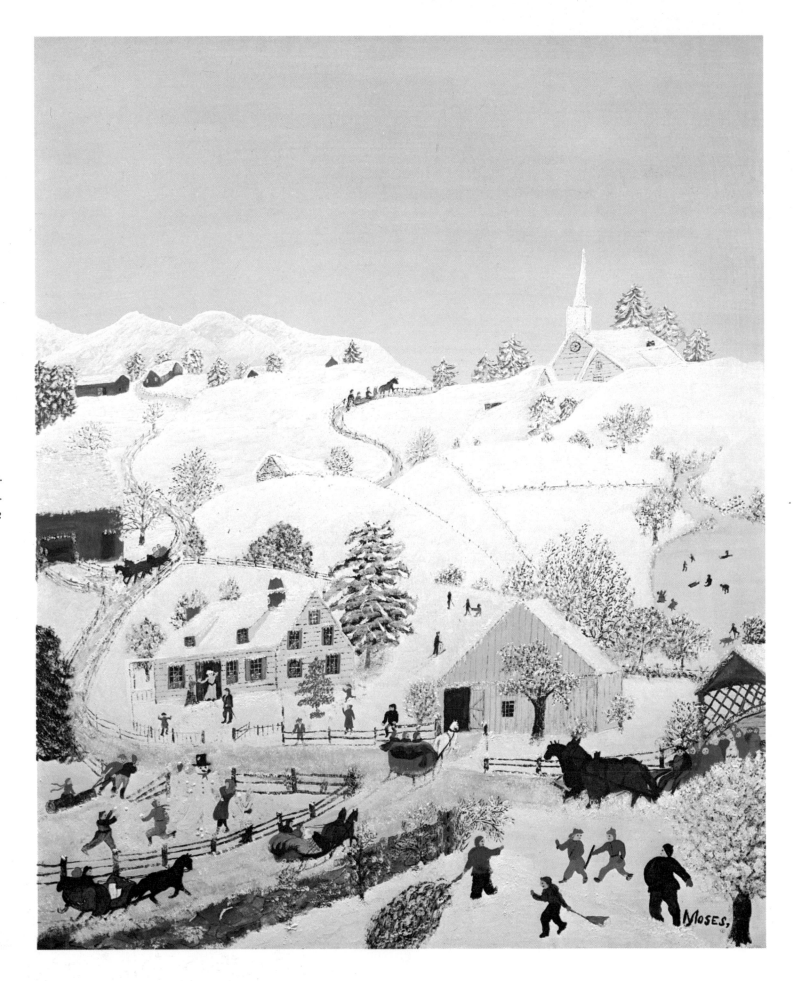

192.
White Christmas. 1954.
23¾ x 19¾". Cat. 1162

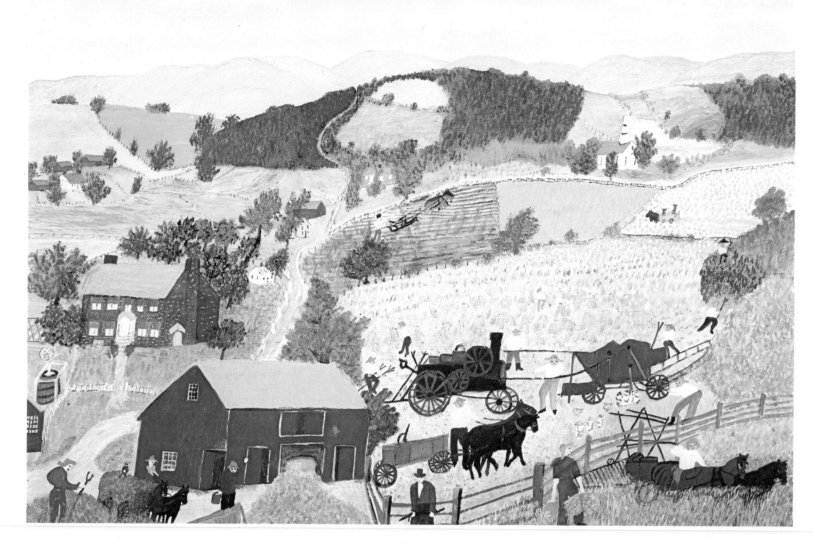

193. *The Thrashers.* 1954. 18 x 24½". Cat. 1148

194.
An Artist. 1954.
12 x 18". Cat. 1121

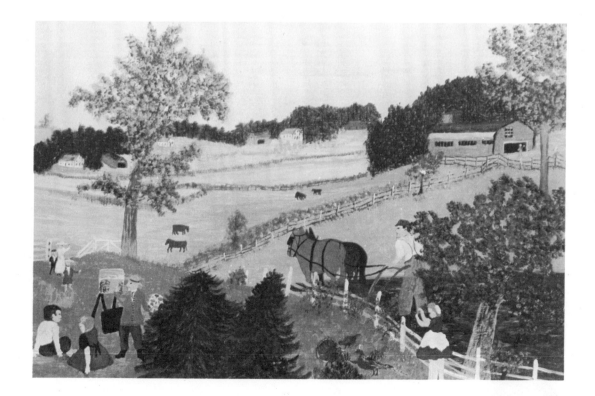

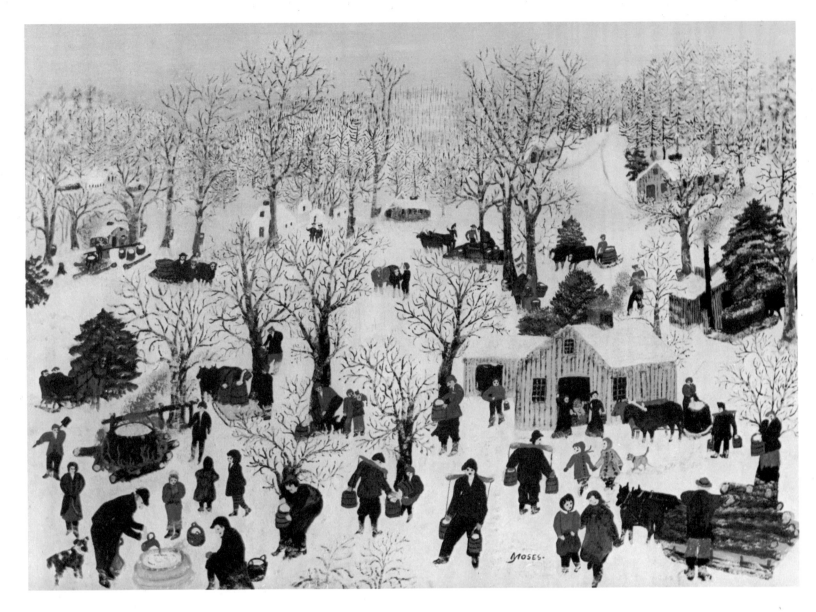

195. *Sugaring Off.* 1955. 18 x 24". Cat. 1166

196.
Horseshoeing. 1955.
12 x 16". Cat. 1181

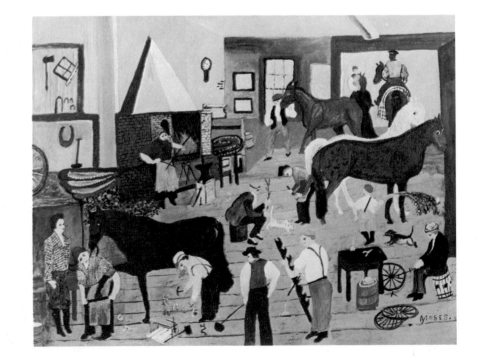

208

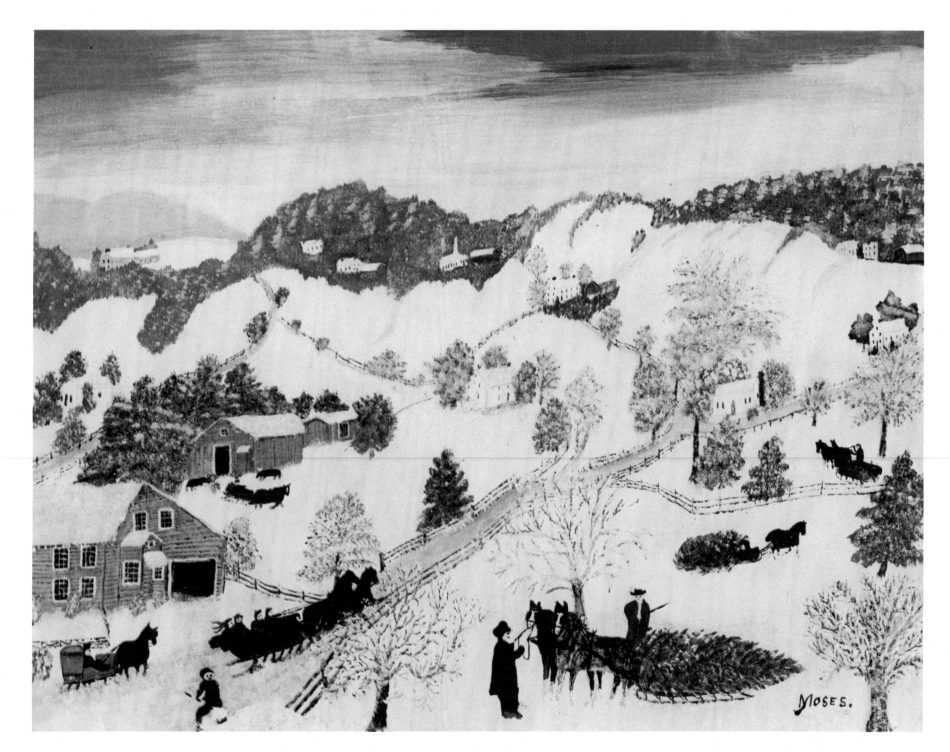

197. *Christmas Trees.* 1955. 18 x 24". Cat. 1189

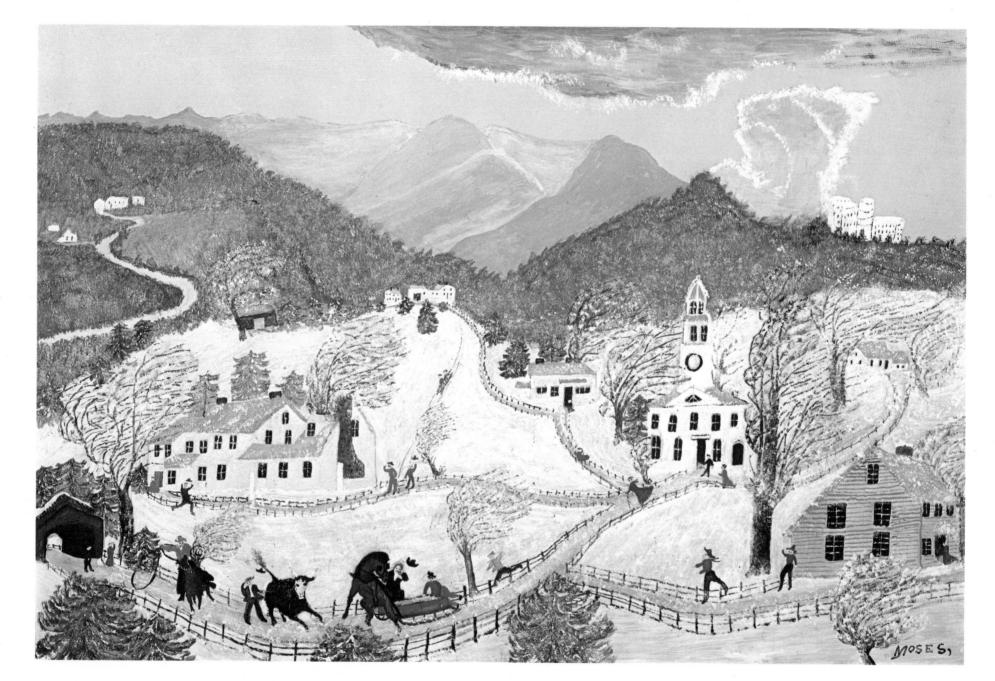

198. *A Blizzard.* 1956. 15⅞ x 24". Cat. 1249

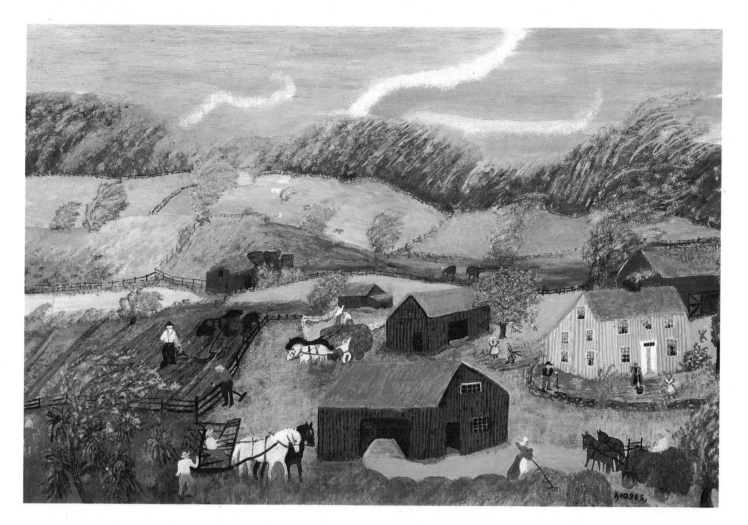

199.
Wind Storm. 1956.
16 x 24". Cat. 1250

200.
Snowed In. 1957.
12 x 16". Cat. 1273

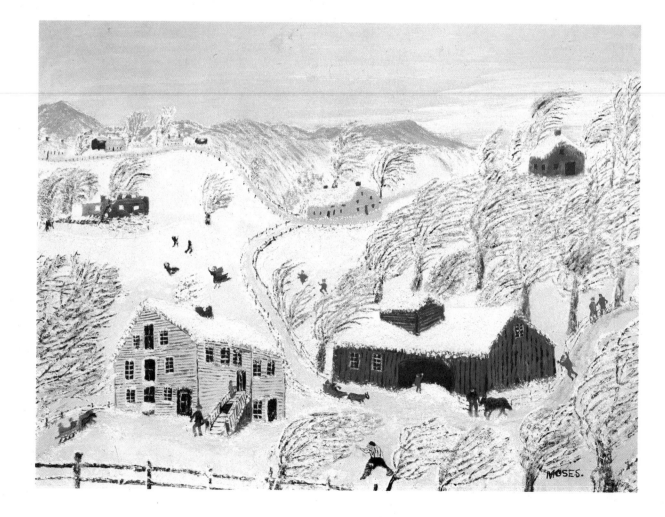

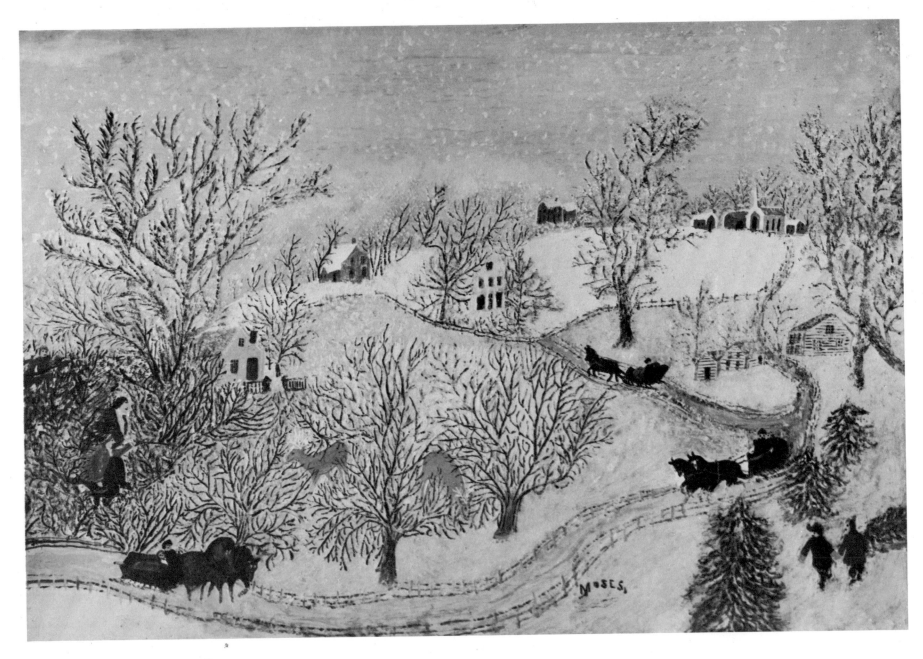

201. *The Deer.* 1958. 16 x 24". Cat. 1323

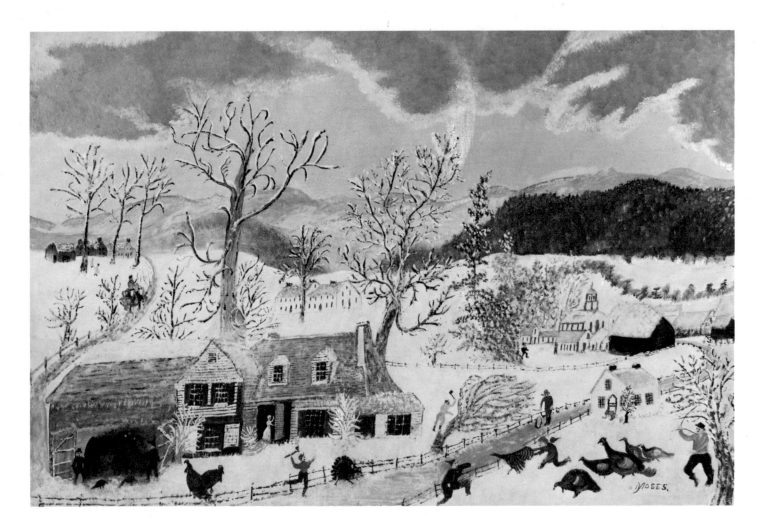

202.
Turkeys. 1958.
16 x 24". Cat. 1325

203.
A Blizzard. 1958.
16 x 24⅛". Cat. 1343

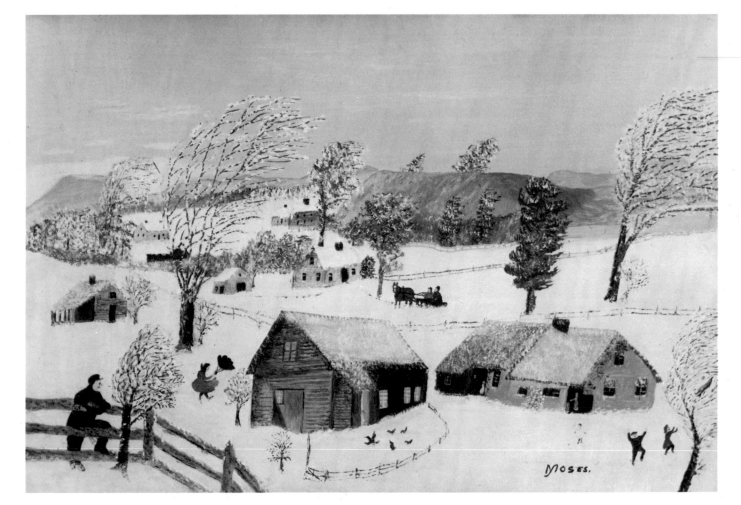

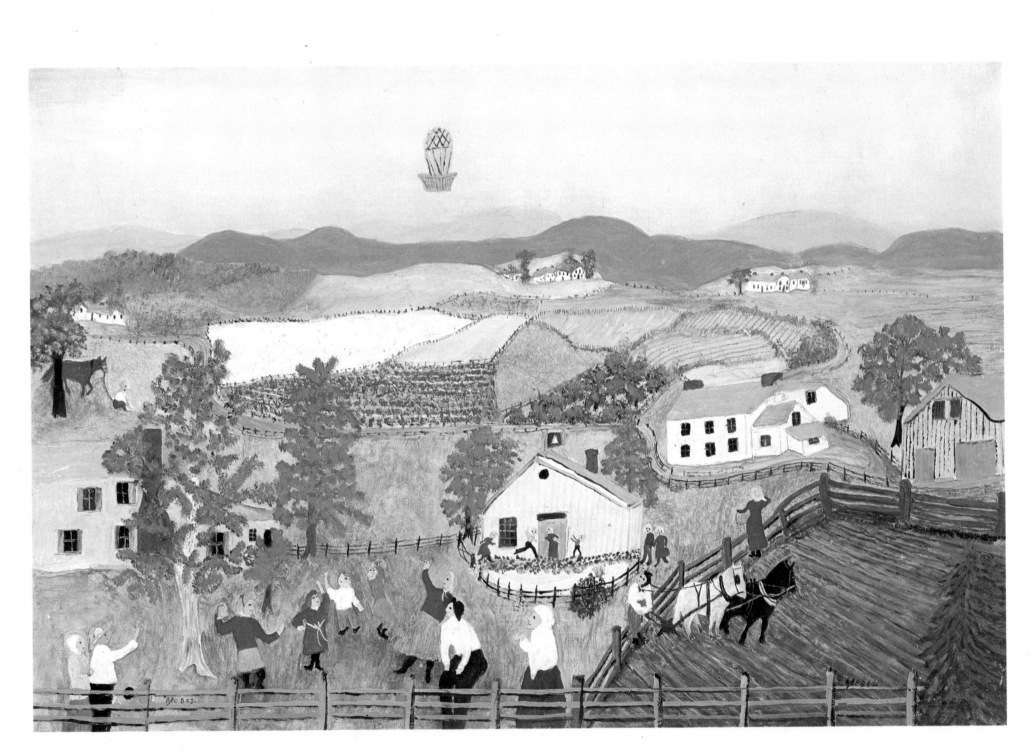

204. *Balloon.* 1957. 15⅞ x 24". Cat. 1289

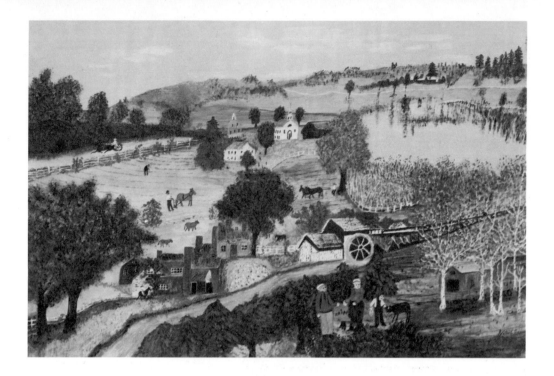

205.
Come Bossy. 1958.
16⅛ x 24⅛". Cat. 1365

206.
The Last Snow. 1959.
16 x 24". Cat. 1389

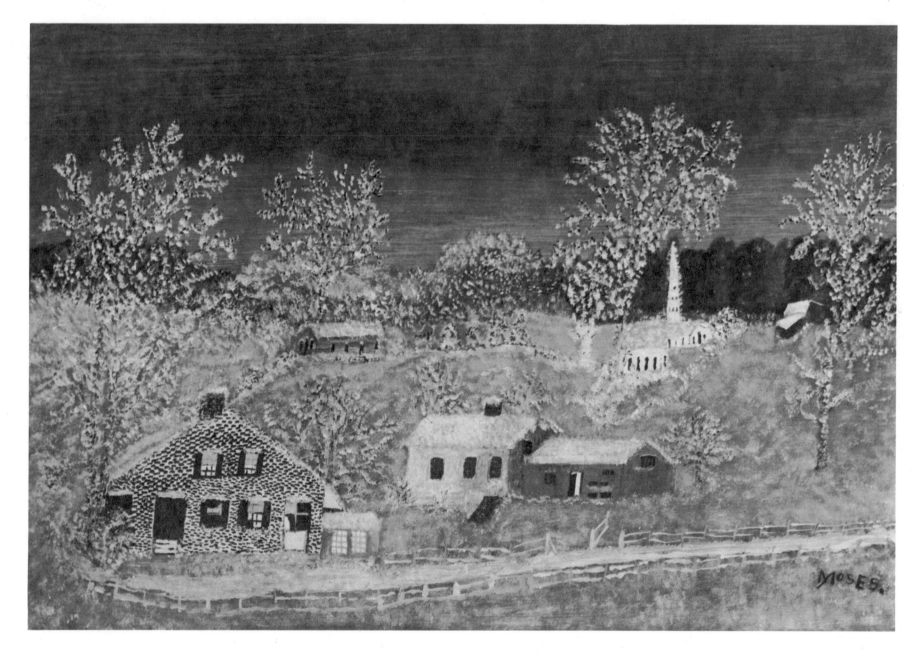

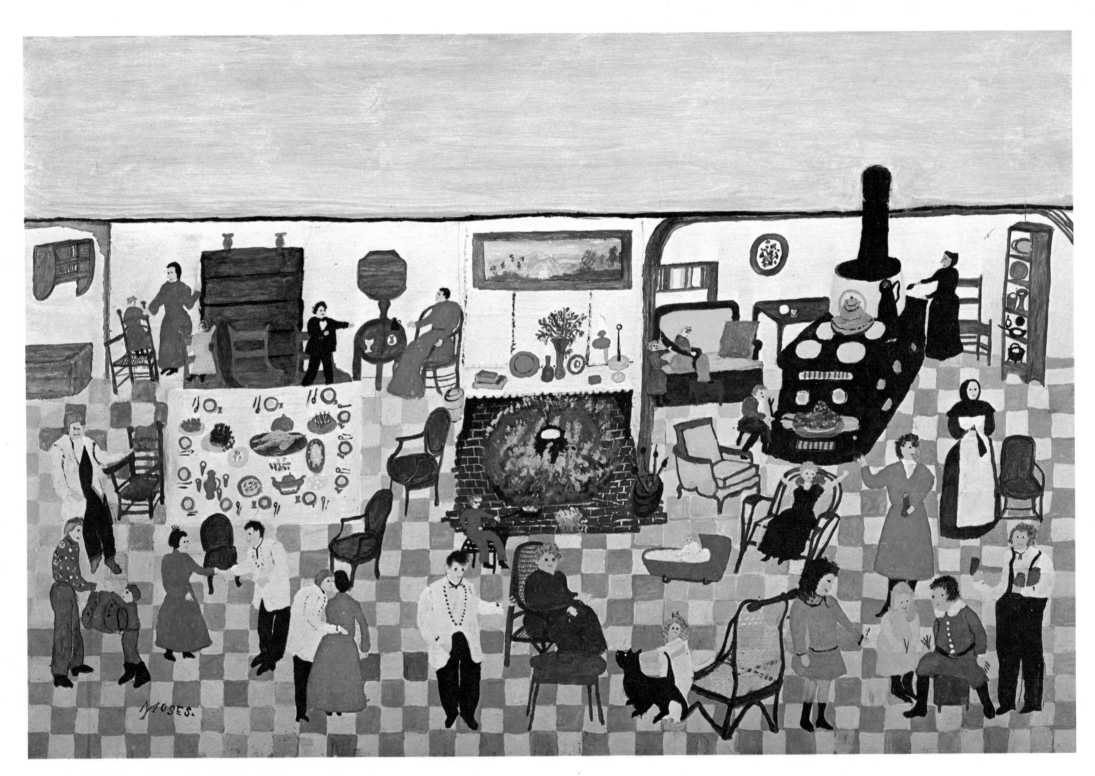

207. *Old Times.* 1957. 16 x 24". Cat. 1296

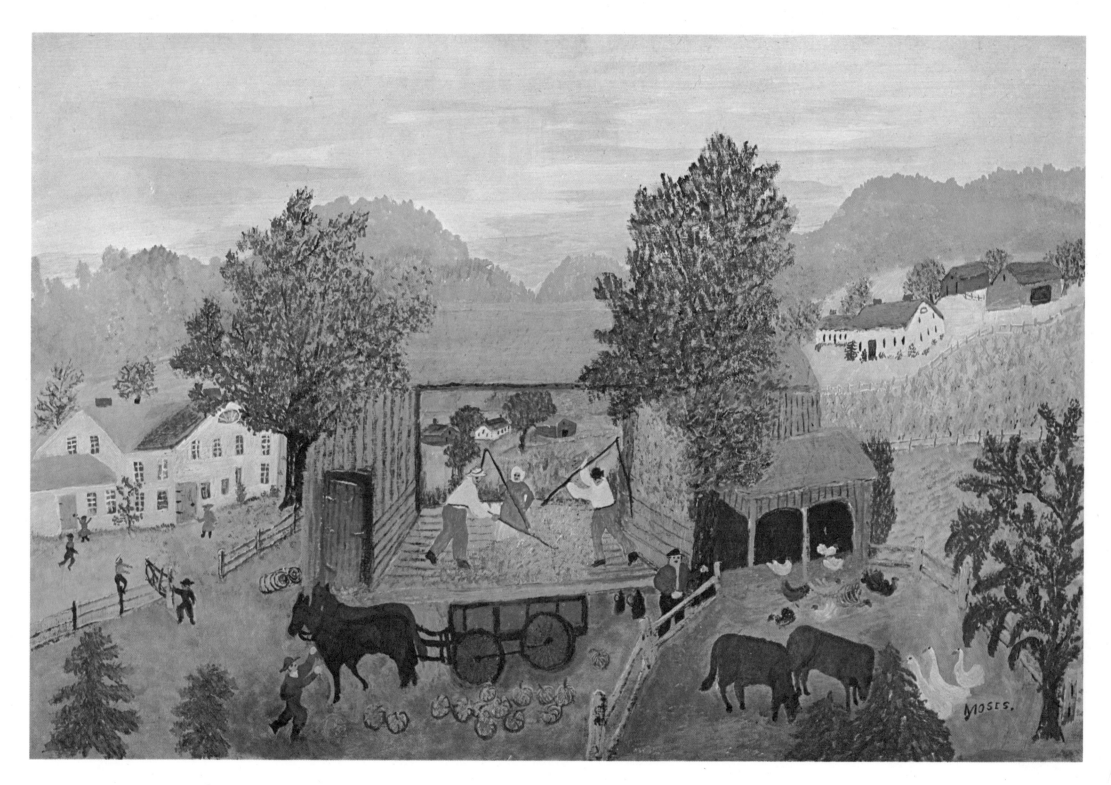

208. *Pumpkins.* 1959. 16 x 24". Cat. 1380

217

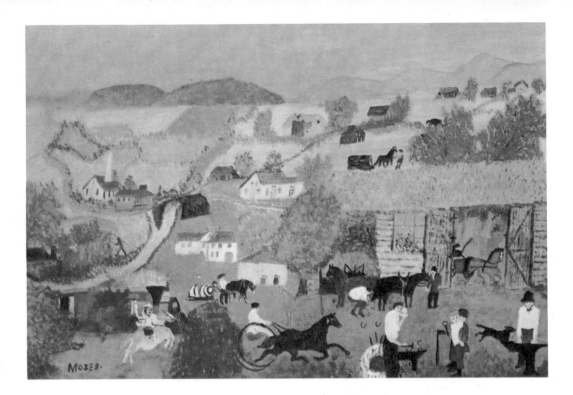

209.
Horseshoeing. 1960.
16 x 24". Cat. 1471

210. *Witches.* 1960. 16 x 24". Cat. 1477

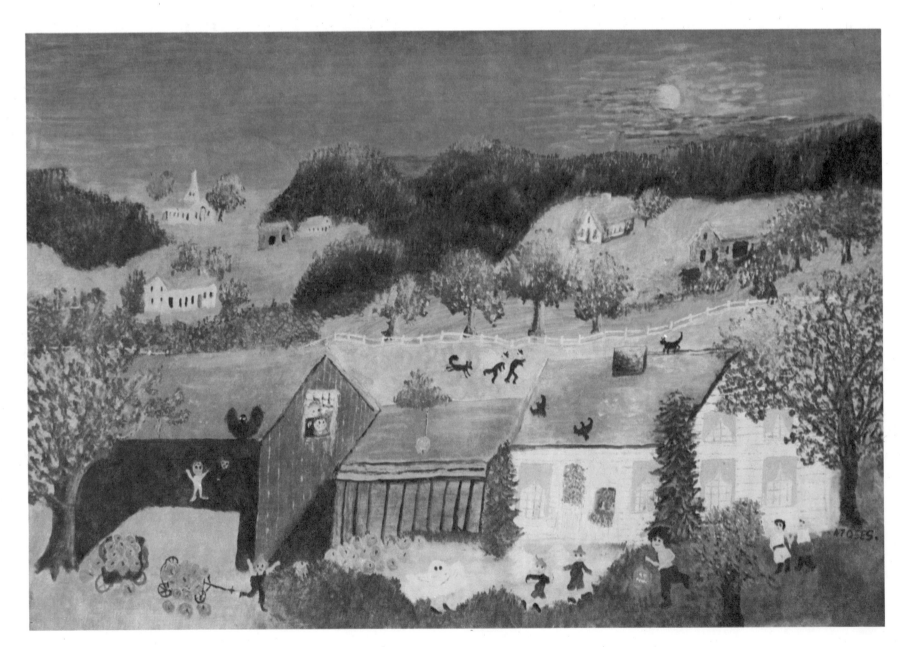

218

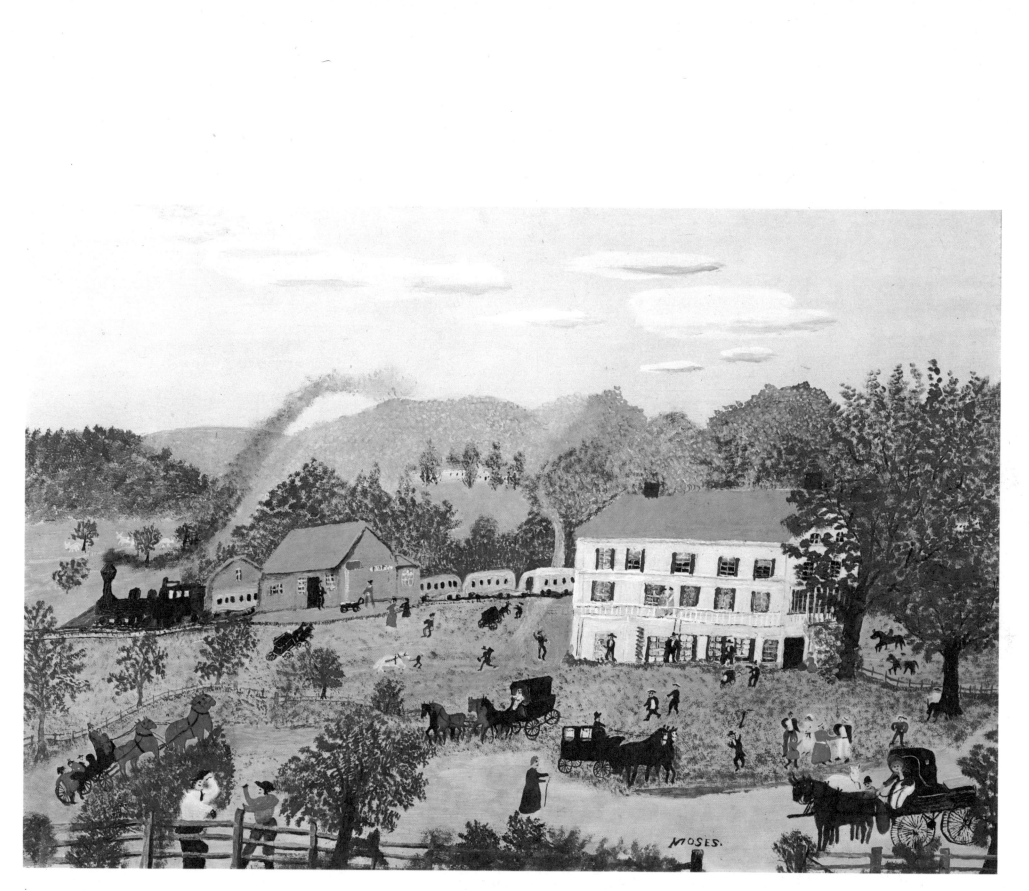

211. *Eagle Bridge Hotel.* 1959. 16 x 24". Cat. 1387

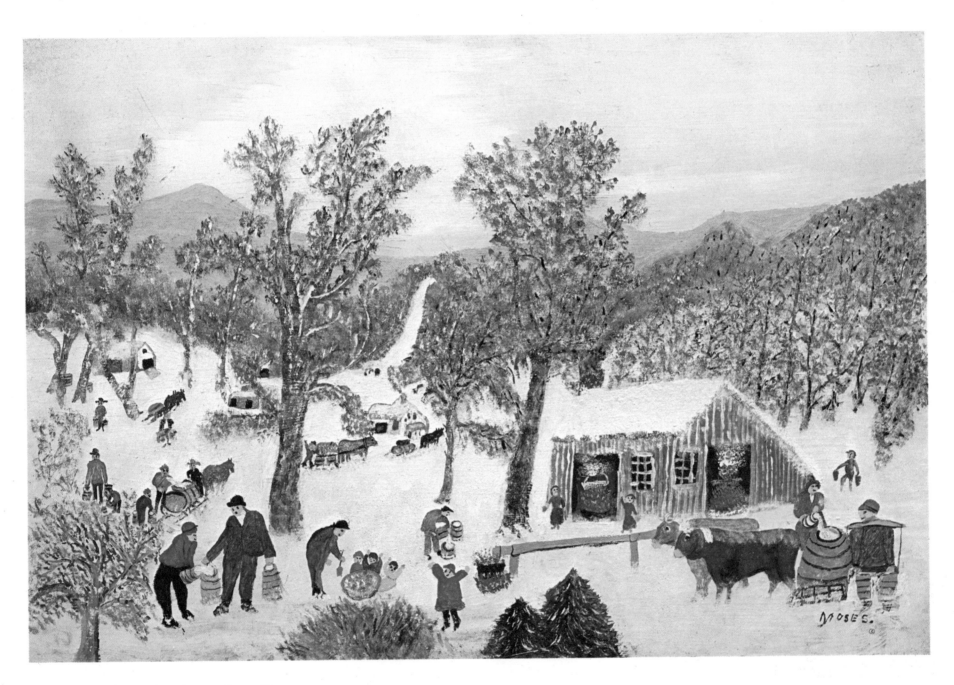

212. *Sugar Time*. 1960. 16 x 24″. Cat. 1468

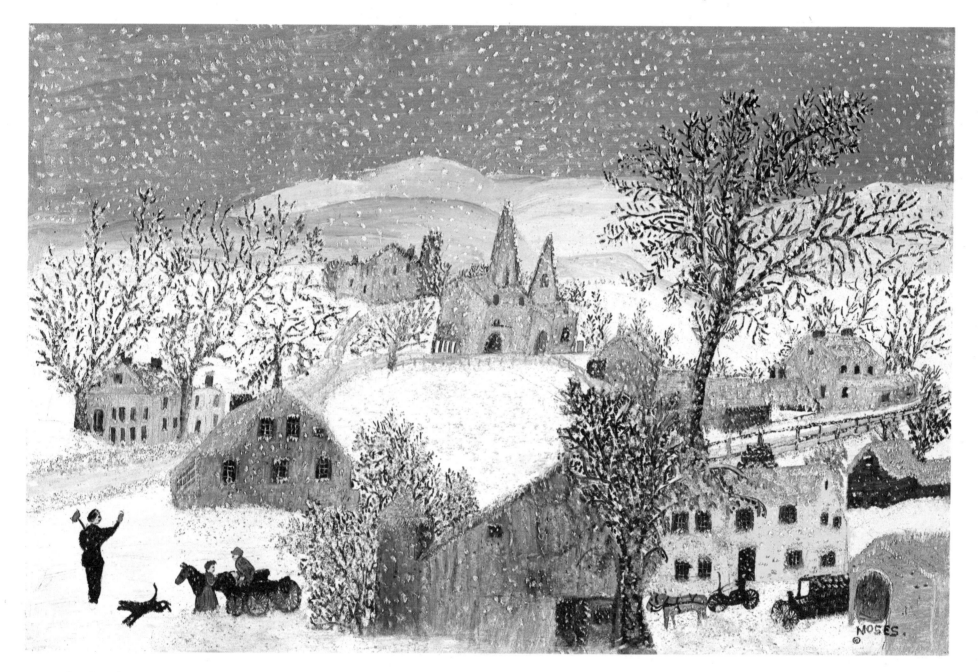

213. *Get Out the Sleigh.* 1960. 16 x 24". Cat. 1474

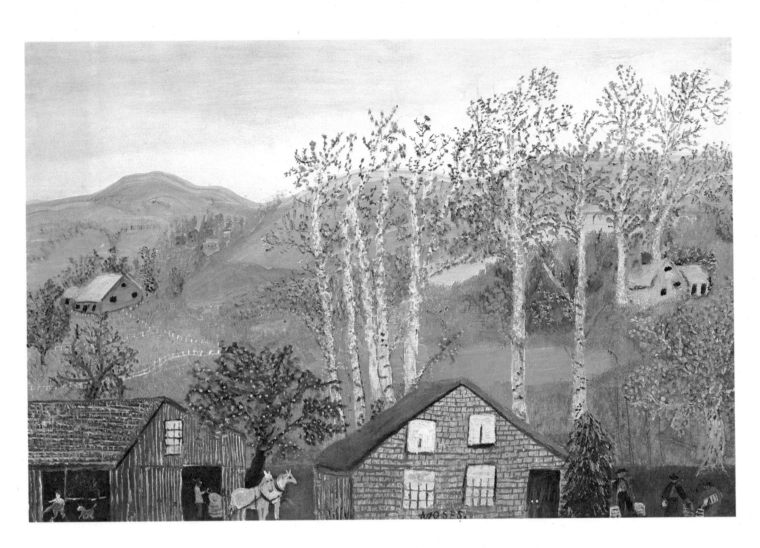

214.
White Birches. 1961.
16 x 24″. Cat. 1489

215.
Sugar Candy. 1961.
16 x 24″. Cat. 1495

222

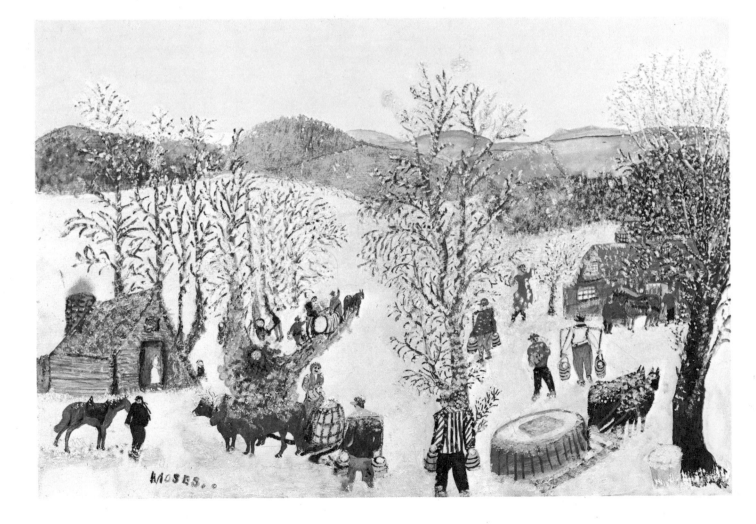

IV

THE RANGE OF GRANDMA MOSES'S ART

Evolving Her Own Style

Grandma moses has been called a "primitive" painter, a term generally applied to artists who have had no professional training. She shared with other so-called "primitives" a naive and almost childlike approach to her subject, not worrying whether she would be able to solve a problem with the artistic means at her disposal. However, as her technical ability progressed and developed, so did her gifts as a painter, and she achieved works which far outrank what one is wont to label "primitive." It cannot be said of many artists—whether professional or self-taught— that they have created a distinctive style of their own, as has Grandma Moses.

The artist's work is basically concerned with one theme: life on the farm and in the country. But on closer study, it reveals an astonishing variety of treatment and subject matter.

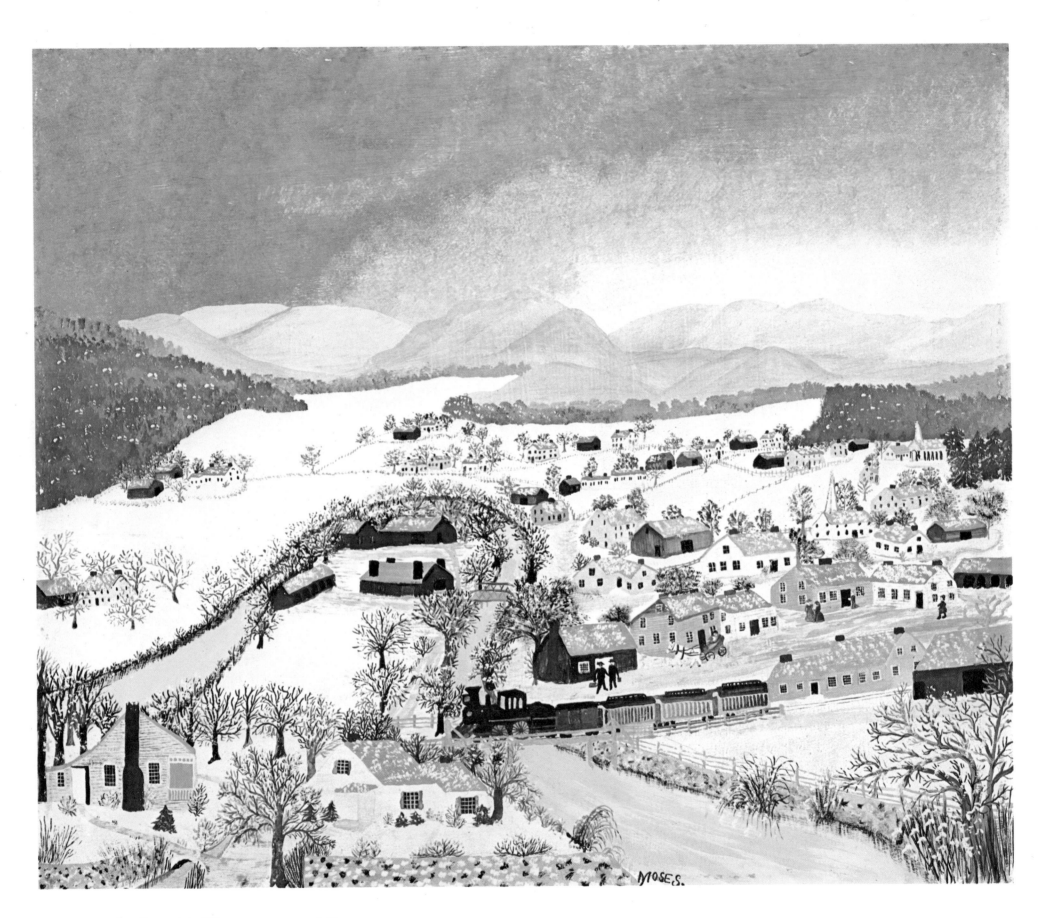

216. *Hoosick Falls, N.Y., in Winter.* 1944. 20 x 24". Cat. 425

Landscapes

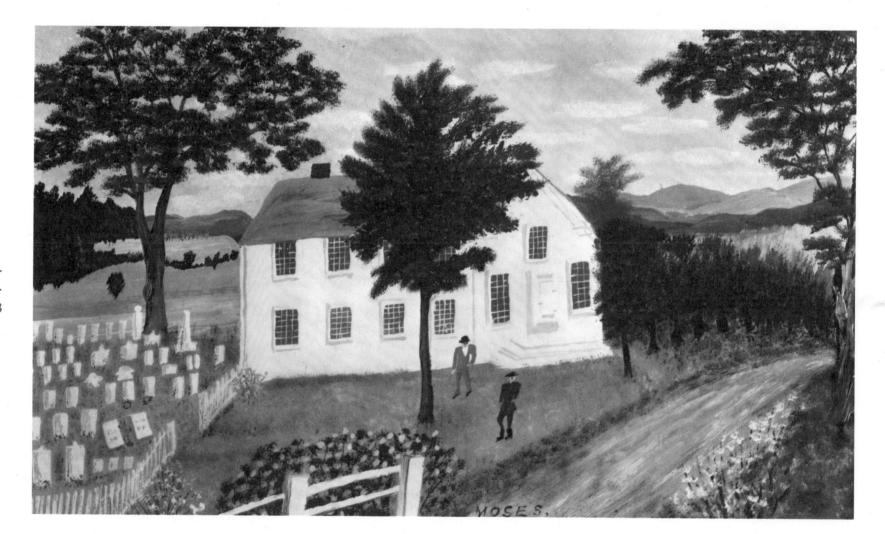

217.
The Whiteside Church. 1945.
9¾ x 17". Cat. 543

MOST OF HER PAINTINGS ARE LANDSCAPES, often depicting the countryside where New York borders Vermont. This is "Grandma Moses Country," the region she knew and loved for a lifetime, where year after year she watched the passing of the seasons. This landscape often forms the setting for the specific events and activities she pictured. Towns, villages, and particular buildings in the area that had played a role in her life—

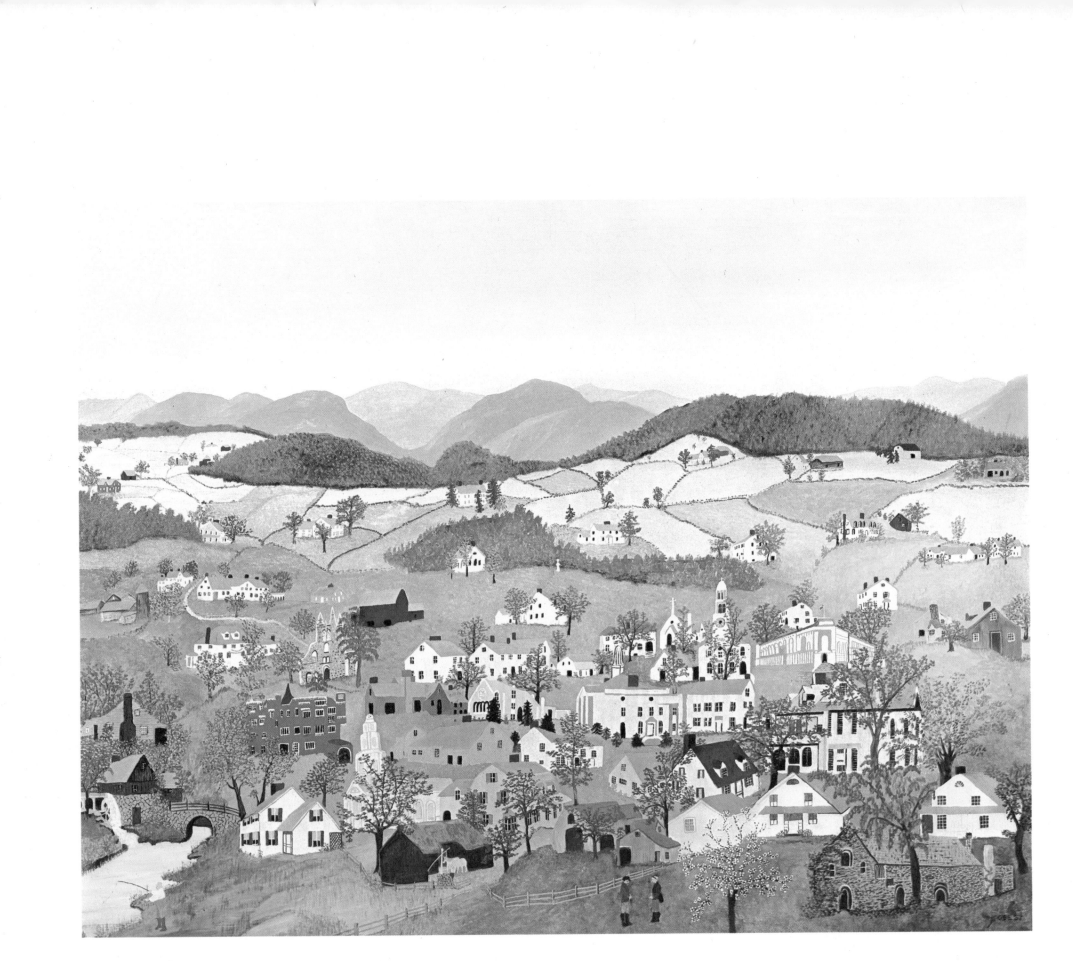

218. *Williamstown.* 1946. 36 x 48". Cat. 617

Bennington, Hoosick Falls, Williamstown, the schoolhouse in Eagle Bridge, the Whiteside Church—became her subjects.

She attained the highest artistry in some of the pure landscapes, such as two works that represent the countryside as she saw it from her house: *Hoosick Valley (from the Window)* and *Hoosick River, Winter* (plates 220, 221). The one depicts a spring day, with fruit trees in bloom. There is no "action," the barely indicated figures of grazing cattle only serving to emphasize the tranquillity of the scene framed by the window and its white-dotted net curtains. In *Hoosick River, Winter* the cold starkness of a winter's day is simply and beautifully rendered; the frozen river is seen between snow-covered fields and bare trees; the distant hills are gray. The hunters in the foreground underscore the mood. The stillness of winter is upon the land.

The landscape of Virginia, where the artist lived in her early married years, was equally dear to her. She frequently painted "that beautiful Shenandoah Valley" and the various places where she and her husband had lived and raised their children.

Apple Butter Making (plate 222) evokes a recollection from this time. It is set in the orchard and meadows of the "Dudley Place" near Staunton, Virginia, where the family lived for eight years. "Just a common farm," she later described it. The large house in the foreground at the right can be identified as the family's actual abode; a photograph that Grandma Moses kept shows a house almost identical with the one in the picture. This work is interesting both in its well-planned and tidily executed composition—the many people, each busy with a particular chore, are in correct proportion to their surroundings—and in its color scheme of predominating greens and reds. The chief color accent is provided by the meticulously painted red-brick house with green shutters and a white portico. A kettle for boiling down the cider and apples hangs over an open fire in the orchard. In spite of the importance of the house, the circular spot of fire is, so to speak, the heart of the painting, because of

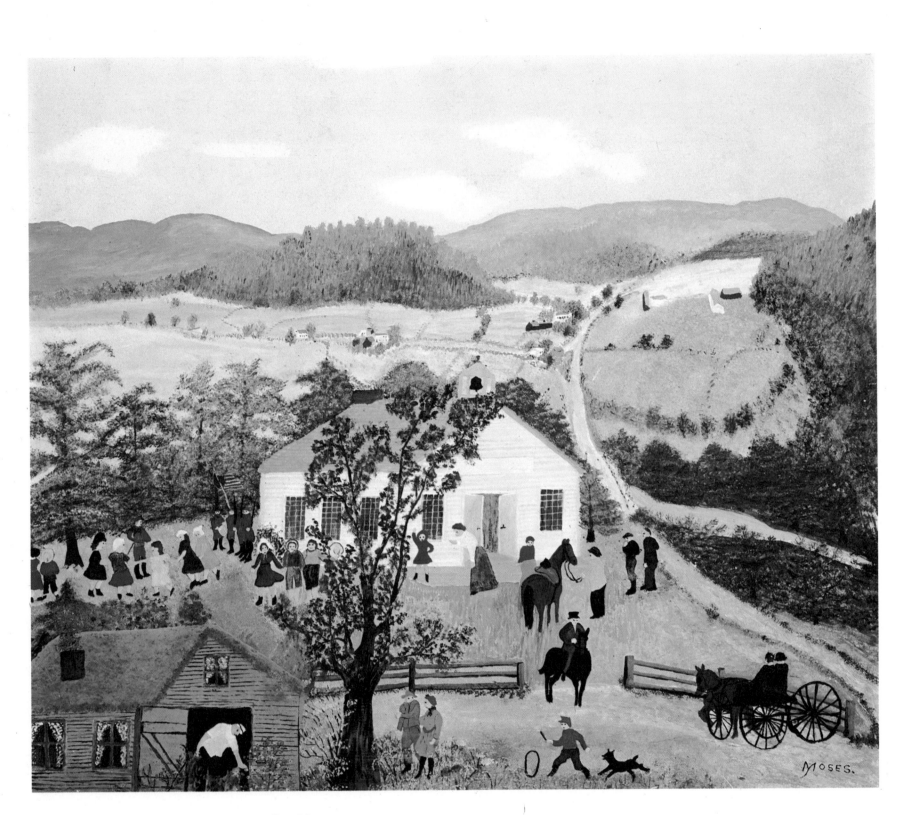

219. *The Schoolhouse.* 1949. 21 x 25". Cat. 864

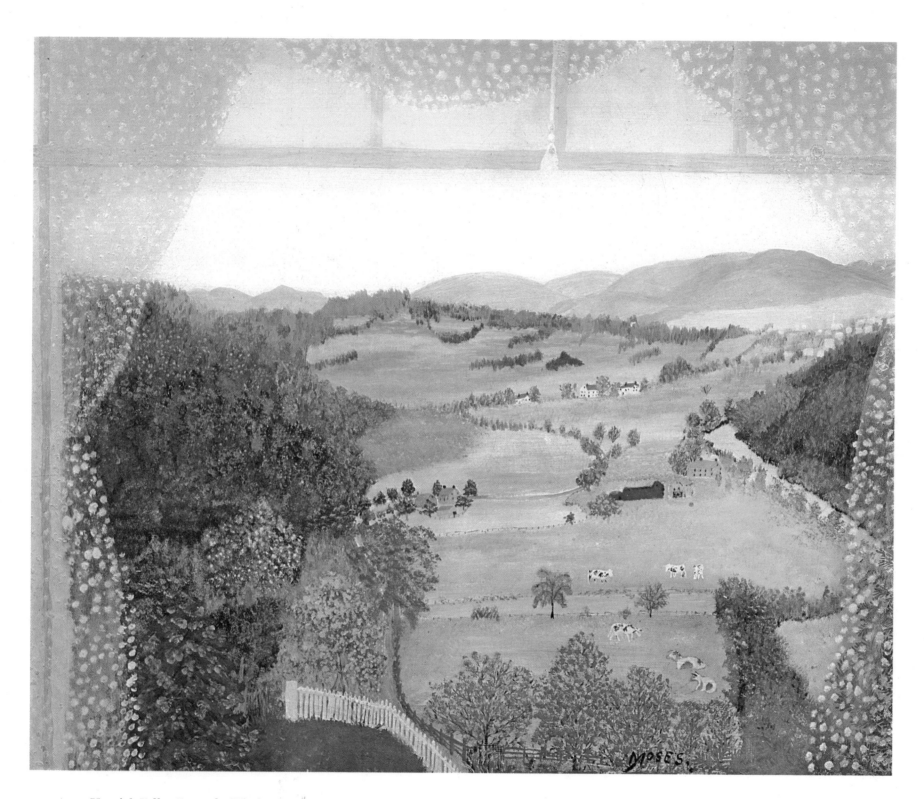

220. *Hoosick Valley (from the Window).* 1946. 19½ x 22″. Cat. 611

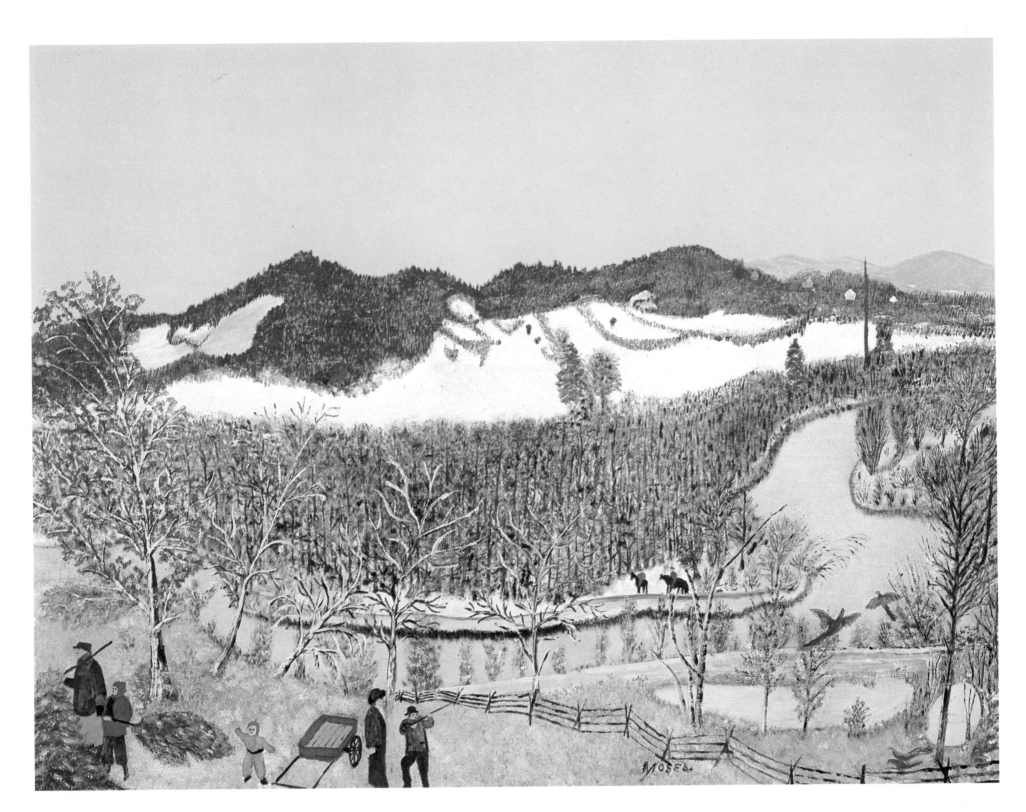

221. *Hoosick River, Winter.* 1952. 18 x 24". Cat. 1031

its concentration of color and its decisive part in the process of the work. Beyond a faintly visible white fence in the background is the river bank. Here, as in so many of the artist's pictures, trees play an important role; she loved them especially and observed their various shapes and tones. In this summer painting they are bushy with abundant deep-green foliage. There is an interesting detail in the left foreground: the figure of a woman dressed in a gown of pale mauve, a color that does not otherwise appear in the painting. It is said that Grandma Moses sometimes used this color when she put herself into a picture.

Between 1943 and 1950, Grandma Moses created about twenty very large paintings measuring up to 36 by 48 inches. She was first encouraged to venture into this format by Ala Story, who sent her two large canvases in the summer of 1943 and suggested that she paint two winter scenes. The bedroom in which Grandma worked in the "old home" was far too small to accommodate a large table or easel; she therefore had to lay the canvases on her bed while painting—a strenuous procedure for a woman in her eighties. She first did a winter landscape, *Over the River* (plate 224), and then, instead of another snow picture, *Checkered House* (plate 50). During the following years, Mrs. Story sent her more large canvases. In between, the artist also did several paintings of similar size on Masonite board, her favorite material ("it will last longer").

Considering that only a few years earlier Grandma Moses's first timid attempts had been small paintings in which she depicted specific objects and narrowly defined scenes, one cannot but be amazed at the daring and confidence with which this very old woman undertook the task of painting such large pictures. They are freely and harmoniously composed, giving full scope to her imagination, and they rank among her very best.

A number of them deal with themes the artist had taken up formerly

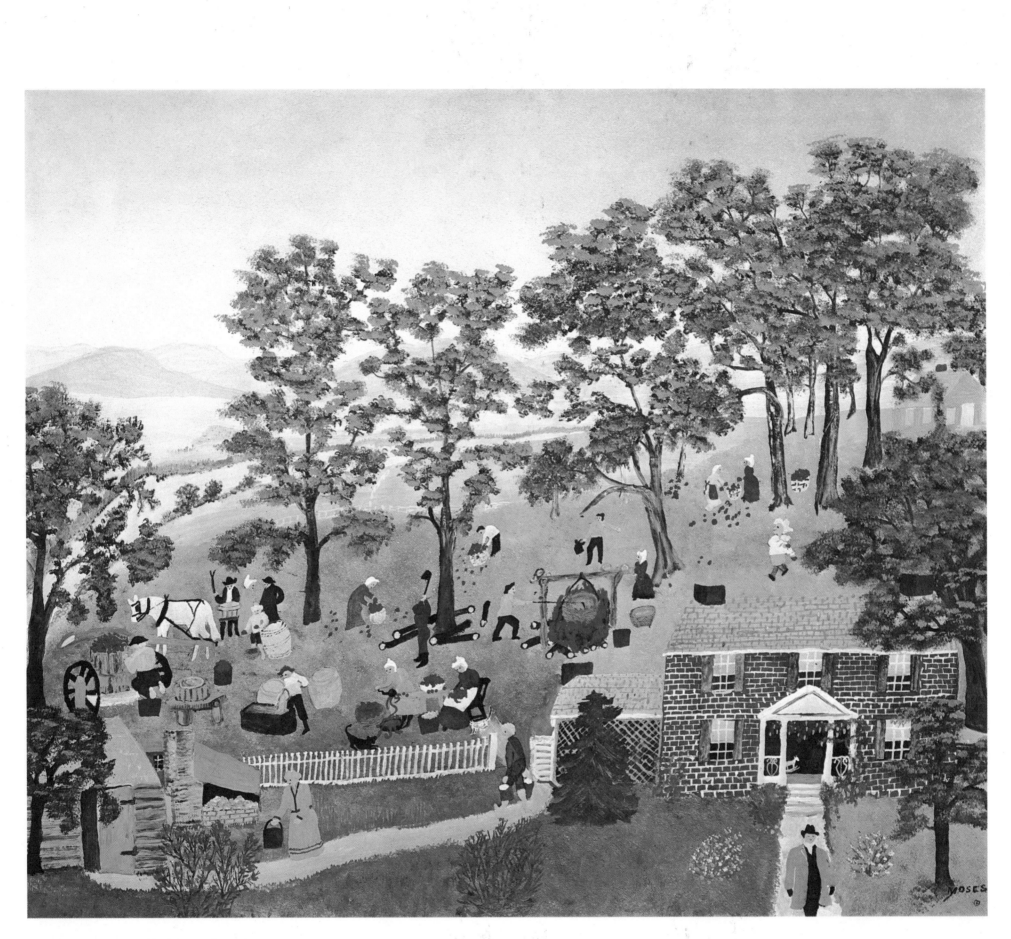

222. *Apple Butter Making.* 1947. 19¼ x 23¼". Cat. 654

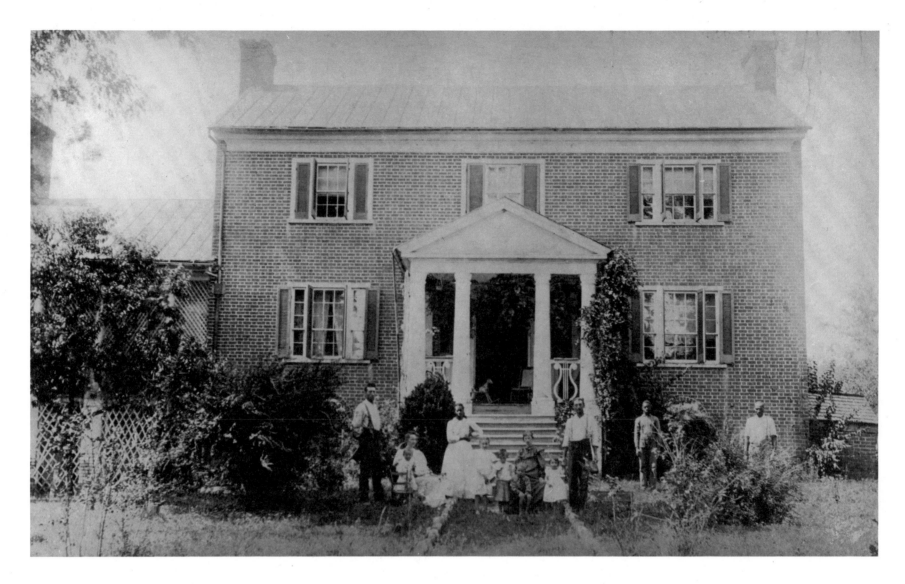

223. The Moses family in front of the Dudley Place in Virginia, c. 1892

in smaller pictures, but the large versions never give an impression of being empty, artificially enlarged, or "filled in" to make use of the greater space. Sometimes the large canvas is a summing up of many previous artistic experiments and achievements, as for instance *Grandma Moses Going to Big City* and *Grandma Moses's Childhood Home* (plates 225, 226). These two works are especially interesting for the sense of rhythm they convey.

In *Grandma Moses Going to Big City*, the very accurately rendered compound of the Moses farm is circled by a country road leading from in front of the buildings into the background. A driveway goes up to the house and on it there is the old car that will take Grandma to the railroad station. This beautifully composed painting, in which everything is in perfect proportion, is, by the way, another example of an incidental scene that gives a picture its title.

In *Grandma Moses's Childhood Home* the rhythm is especially marked. Two wide circles formed by roads surround buildings, meadows, and orchard; they are linked by a large barn in the center.

Out for Christmas Trees (plate 227), painted on Masonite, is one of the artist's most popular and frequently reproduced pictures. It is the ideal example of a "Grandma Moses" if one has come to think of her mainly as an artist of the winter scene. Strong and simple, it is painted in tones of white and deep green. Among the clusters of fir trees a few tall trees that have shed their foliage stand out, their bare, snow-covered branches silhouetted against a gray sky. Horse-drawn sleighs are arriving or leaving; the movement of the animals is masterfully observed. The figures are comparatively small and do not detract from the overall atmosphere of a winter landscape. There is a typical tiny "aside": a small boy stands beside a little fir tree, no taller than himself, probably intending to chop it down and carry it home for his own.

The Barn Dance and *Country Fair* (plates 228, 229), which show a wealth of charming detail integrated into the surrounding landscape, are the last large paintings Grandma Moses created. She was nearly ninety at the time, and conceded that the physical strain was getting to be too much for her. From then on she returned to smaller pictures.

While the majority of Grandma Moses's landscapes are static and show nature in a mood of undisturbed peace, she also did a number in which it is in a state of turmoil. A disturbance in the atmosphere is generally represented by windblown trees bending under a gale and, as in her blizzard and thunderstorm pictures, by a sky dark with menacing

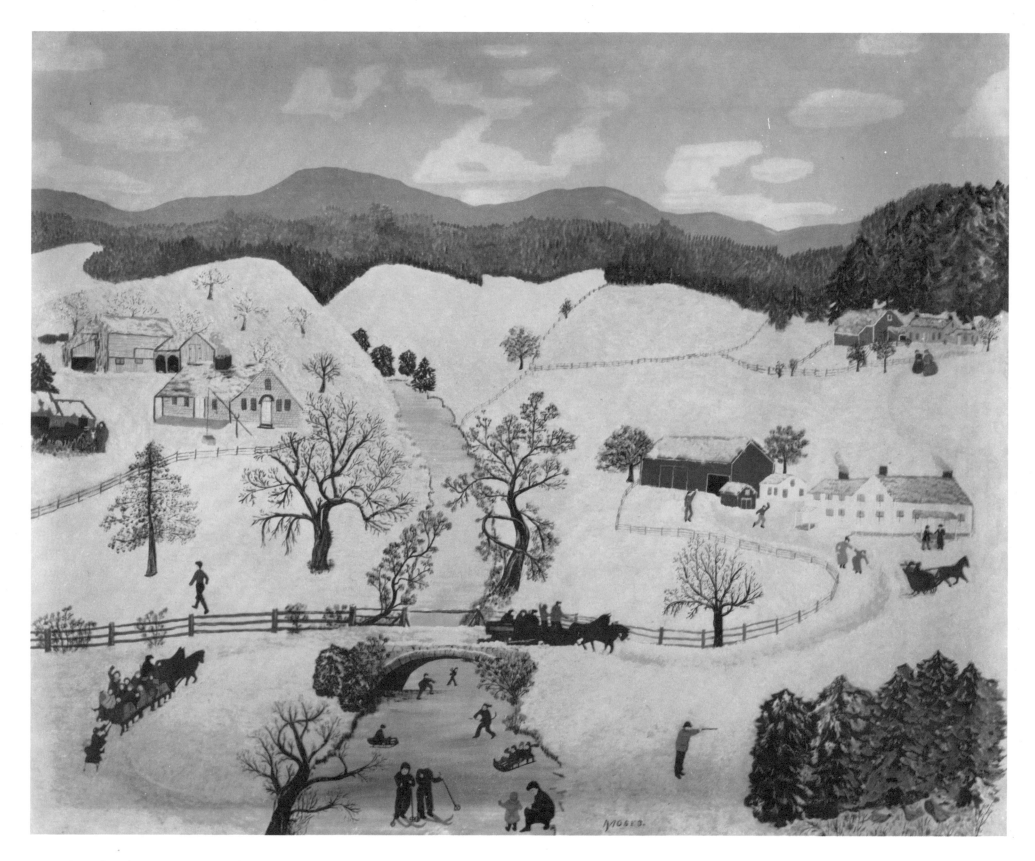

224. *Over the River*. 1943. 34 x 45". Cat. 277

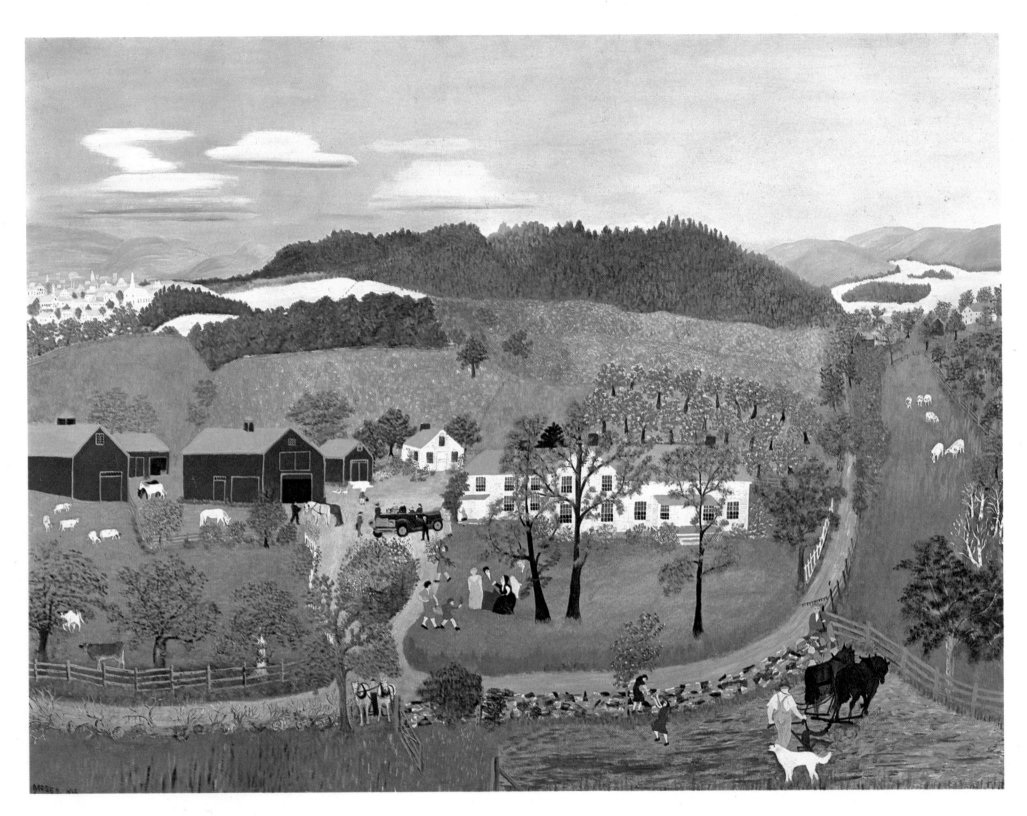

225. *Grandma Moses Going to Big City*. 1946. 36 x 48". Cat. 577

238

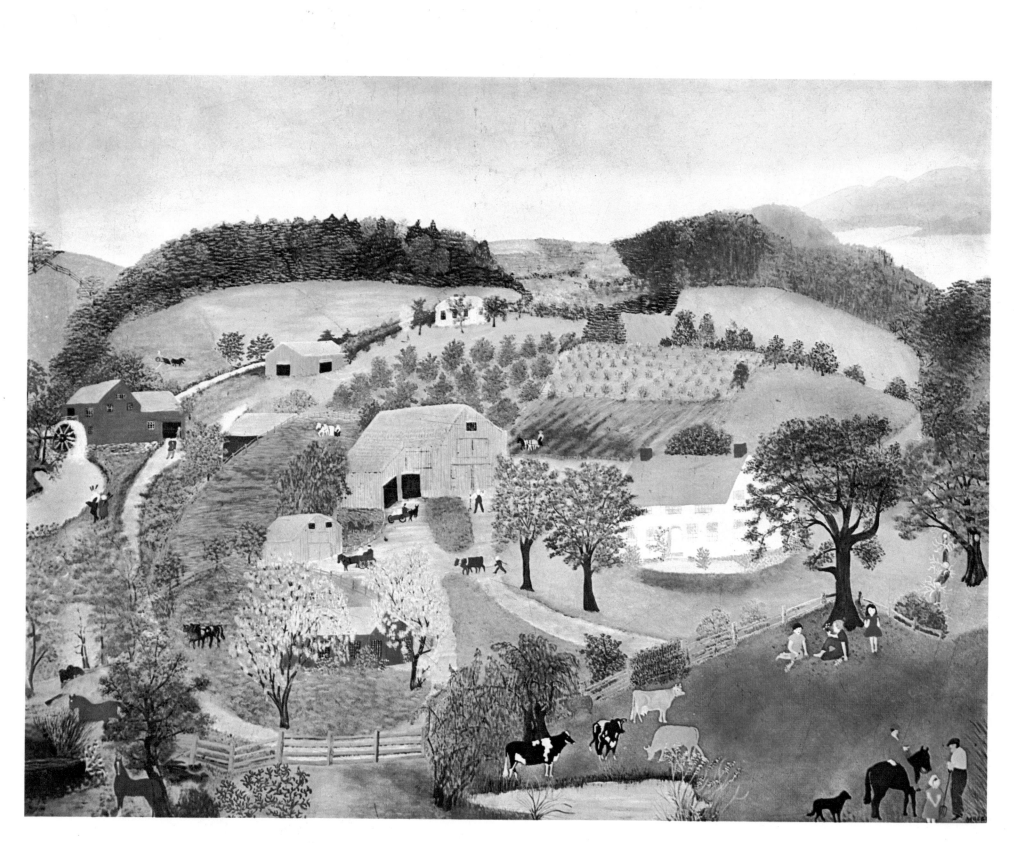

226. *Grandma Moses's Childhood Home.* 1946. 36 x 48". Cat. 575

clouds. People and animals hurry for shelter, frightened and helpless before the forces of nature.

A Storm Is on the Waters Now (plate 230) is a powerful, almost eerie evocation of impending danger. Under a black sky and past dark, storm-tossed trees, two white horses gallop in terror toward a white house, conveying a mood of inescapable violence in an almost Surrealist fashion.

Taking in Laundry (plates 231, 232) is not quite so dramatic. It shows people busy salvaging their day's work before the oncoming storm, but still able to cope with nature.

Another painting that depicts commotion, though not in a threatening way, and that stands out for its subject matter, composition, and imagination is *Halloween* (plates 233–35), painted in 1955. It records the many activities characteristic of that particular October night. Barrels of cider and buckets of harvested apples are being prepared for the customary apple dunking, which has already begun inside the house. Jack O'Lantern pumpkins glow in the dark—for it is evening, with a pale moon beginning to shine. There seem to be goblins everywhere, or just boys playing all kinds of tricks. The children are running around, either to admire the pumpkins or because they are scared. Little white faces pop up, it is not clear whether of ghosts or real people. The wildest pranks are going on on the roof, where a cart is being rolled back and forth to make uncanny noises in the house below. Two tiny yet very conspicuous "witches" seem almost to float in mid air, little white phantoms quite other-worldly in the midst of robust country folk. The colors of the painting are strong and warm, especially in the foreground: rich tones of red, brown, and dark green; a view into the house shows a blazing fire in a red brick fireplace. This vivid detail is counterbalanced by a group of men unloading barrels from a horse-drawn cart; the simplicity and strength with which the artist has shown them is reminiscent of Bruegel. A white fence in the very foreground closes in the manifold lively scenes. Gradually, as they fade into the background, the

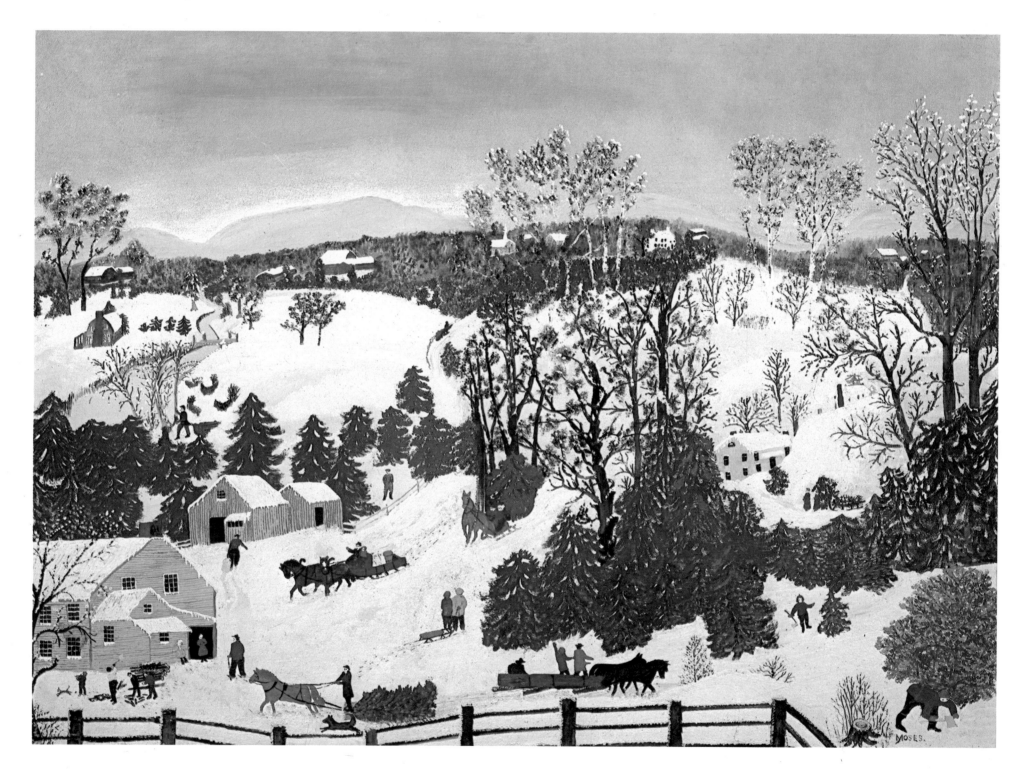

227. *Out for Christmas Trees.* 1946. 26 x 36″. Cat. 606

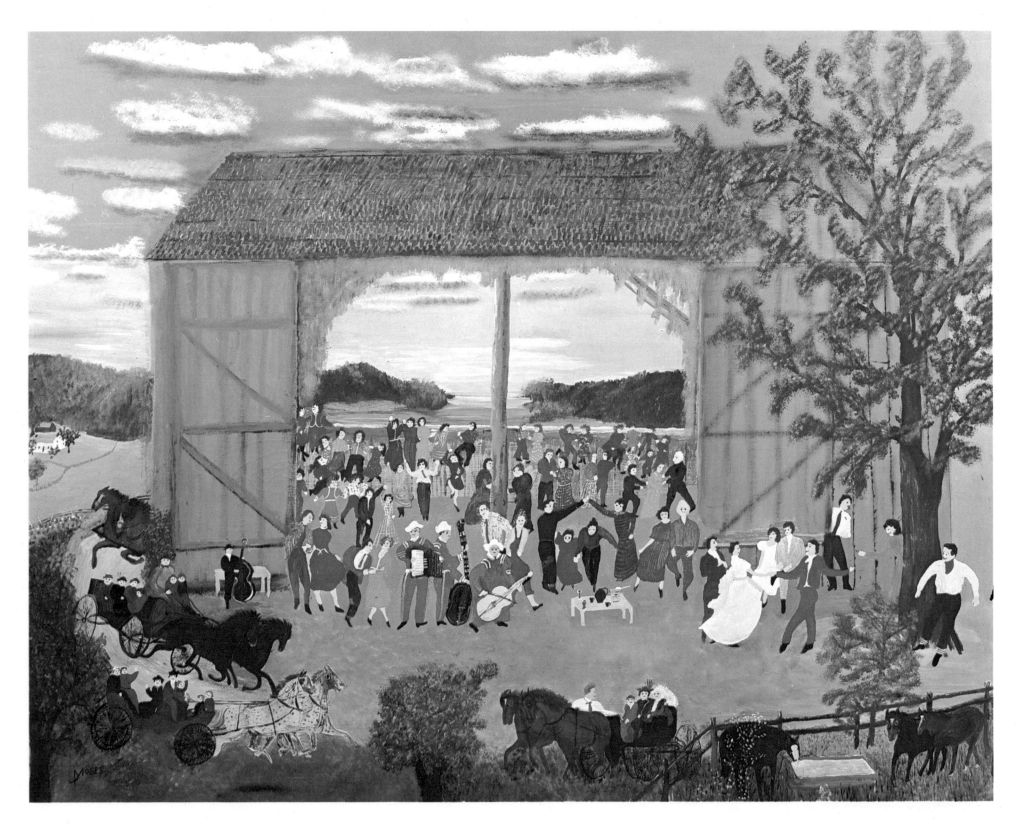

228. *The Barn Dance.* 1950. 35 x 45". Cat. 920

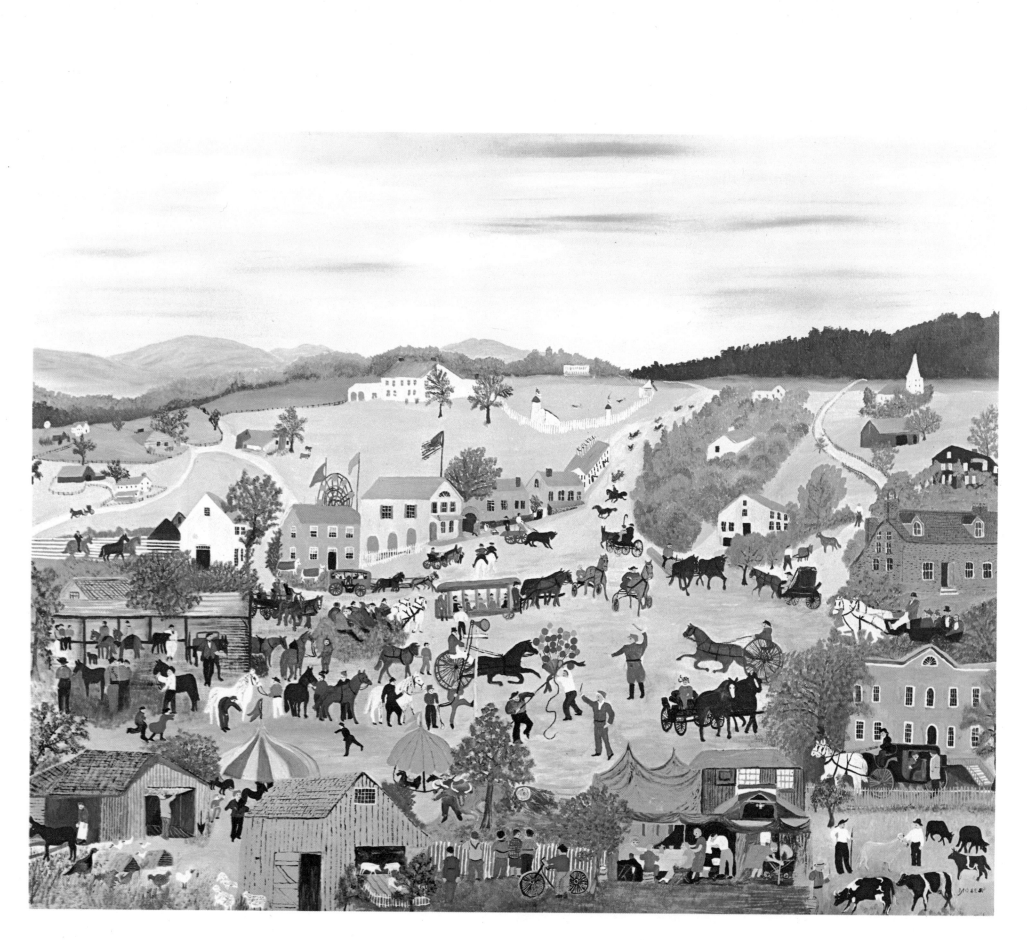

229. *Country Fair.* 1950. 35 x 45". Cat. 921

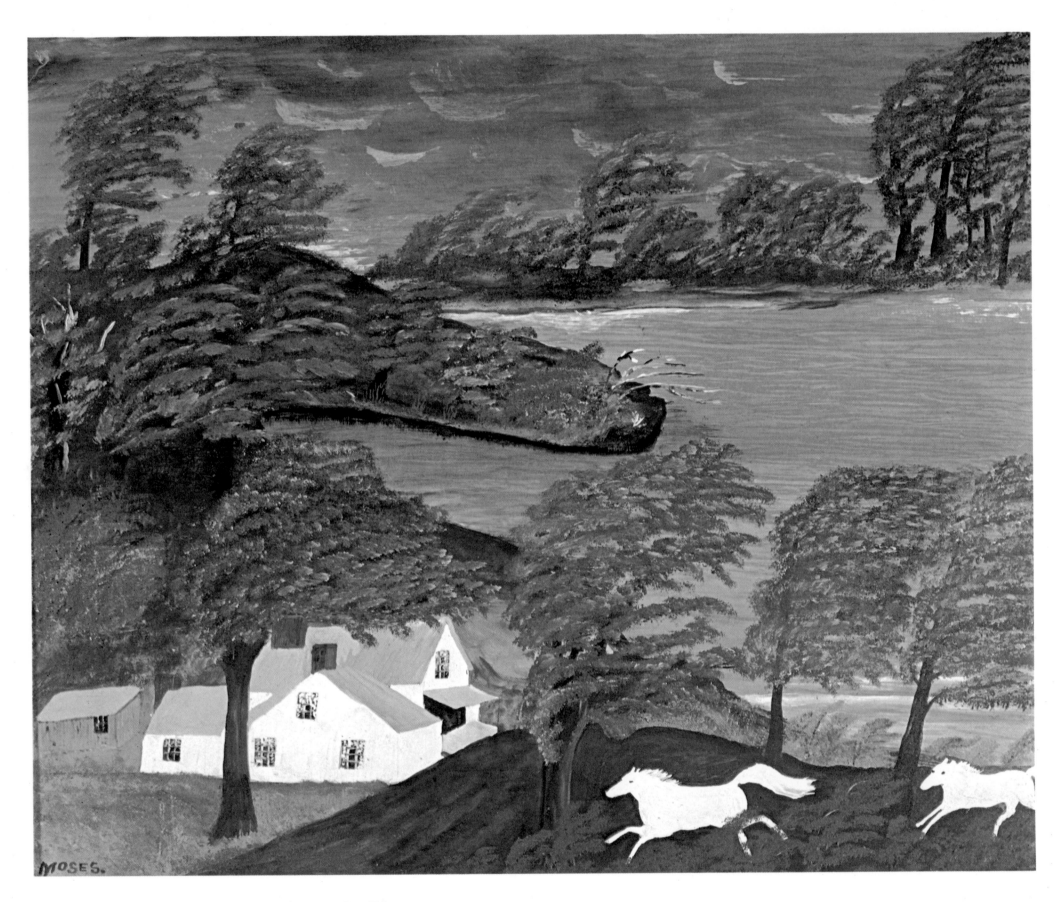

230. *A Storm Is on the Waters Now.* 1947. 16 x 20¼". Cat. 666

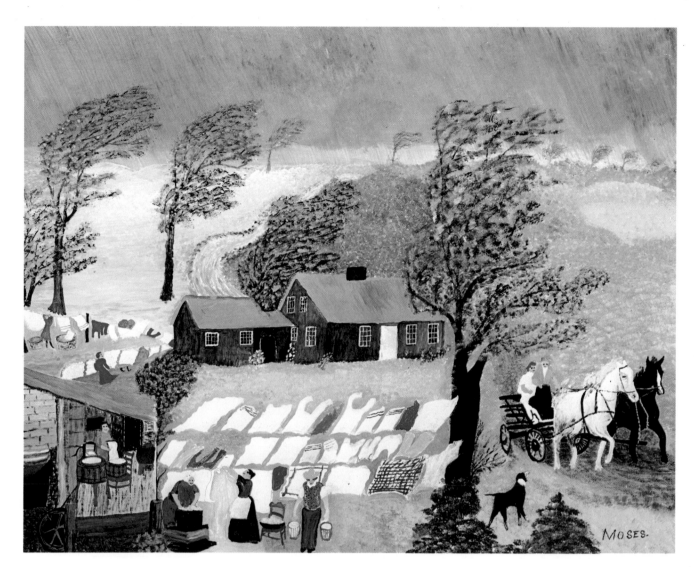

231. *Taking in Laundry.* 1951. 17 x 21¾". Cat. 967

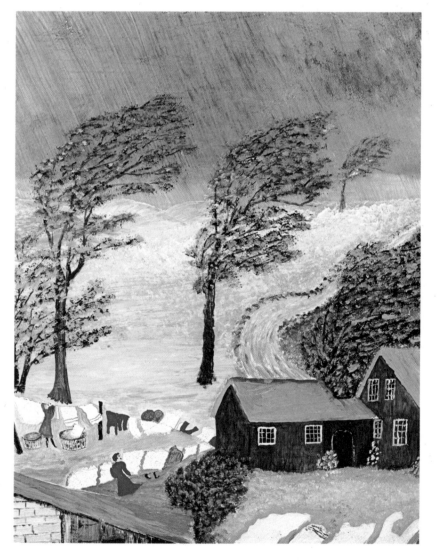

232.
Taking in Laundry
(detail)

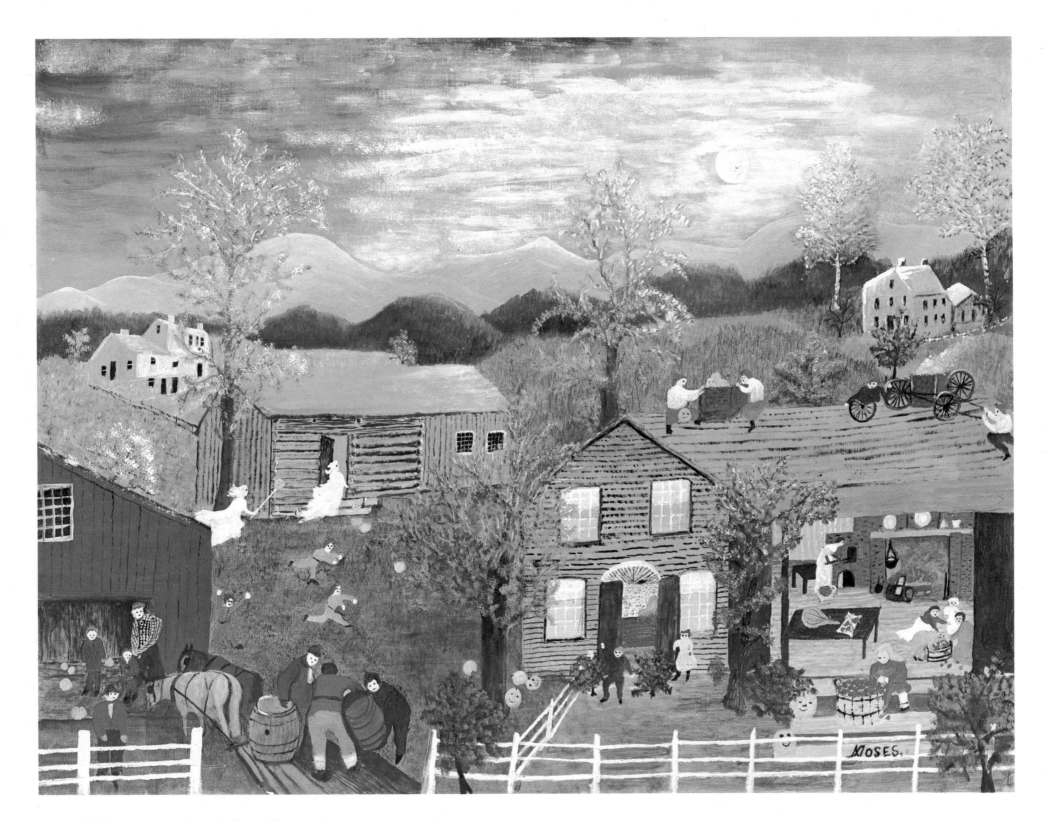

233. *Halloween.* 1955. 18 x 24". Cat. 1188

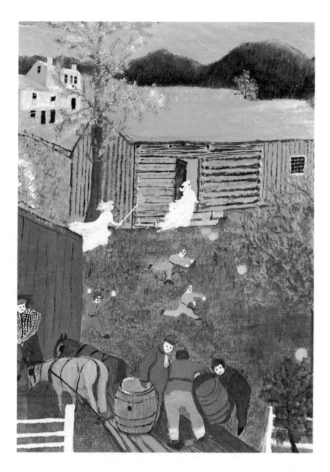
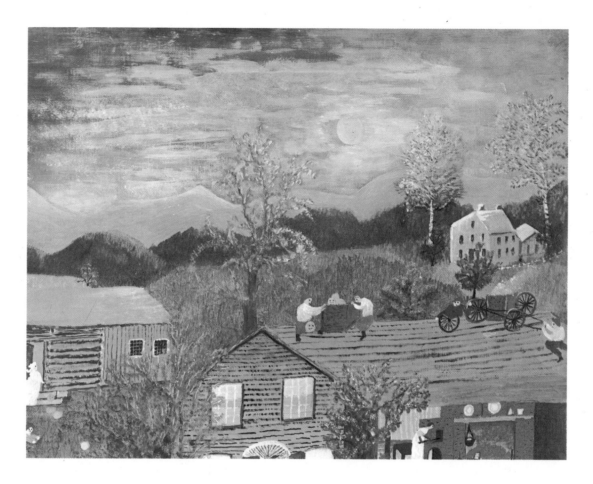

234–35. *Halloween* (details)

colors become more subdued: gray houses and dark, distant hills, and finally, above all the commotion, a quiet, cold wintry sky. The composition of this remarkable painting is unified and softened by the tall trees, their yellow autumn foliage spreading, as it were, a delicate veil over the bustling life below.

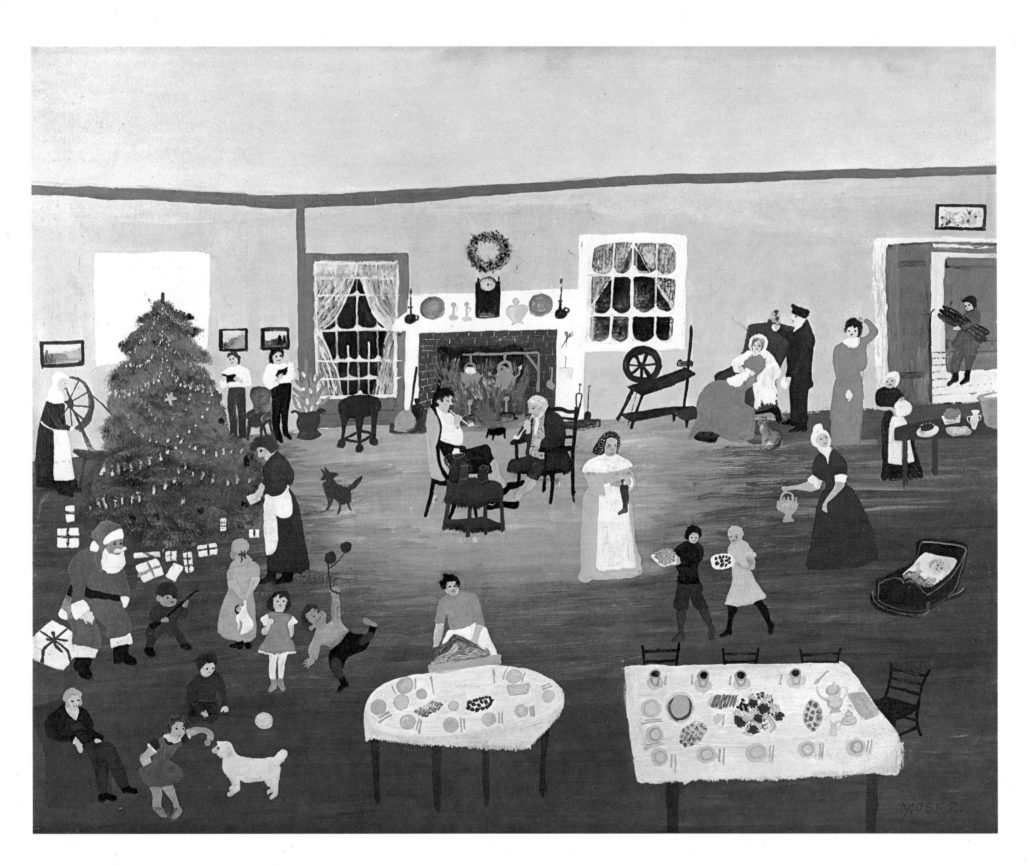

236. *Christmas at Home.* 1946. 18 x 23". Cat. 586

Interiors

SOMETIMES THE ARTIST WOULD DEVIATE from her familiar path. She was not satisfied with painting only what the public had come to expect. Time and again she tried to tackle problems that posed a challenge, as though to prove to herself that she could still learn and progress. Such experiments often resulted in extraordinary achievements. She continued to the very last her earnest endeavors at "improving" instead of just making it easy for herself. This seems all the more remarkable since people did everything they could to make her repeat what had led her to fame.

One of the problems she tried to cope with was interiors. Some customs and festivities that she remembered demanded an indoor setting. The artist was aware that her scant knowledge of perspective and her inadequacy in depicting human figures were more evident in such paintings than in her landscapes. She wrote in a letter to a friend: "I tryed that interior but did not like it so I erased it, that dont seem to be in my line. . . . Well maybe I try again." In spite of these difficulties she actually did more than twenty interiors in the course of the years.

One of the earliest was *Christmas at Home* (plate 236), painted in 1946. In order not to omit anything that goes into the celebration of a joyful family Christmas, Grandma Moses made the room far larger than it would be in an average farmhouse. It easily accommodates a huge Christmas tree, two tables in the foreground festively decked in white and laden with refreshments, a fireplace flanked by two windows in the center of the back wall with two elderly men seated in front of it. There are some two dozen figures in this lively and cheerful picture, old and young, besides a baby in a cradle, two dogs, a cat, and Santa Claus himself bringing in packages. Even the doorway is not deserted—a boy is about to enter with logs for the fire. This painting, eminently naive, is filled with the joy of storytelling, every detail a beloved experience and memory.

249

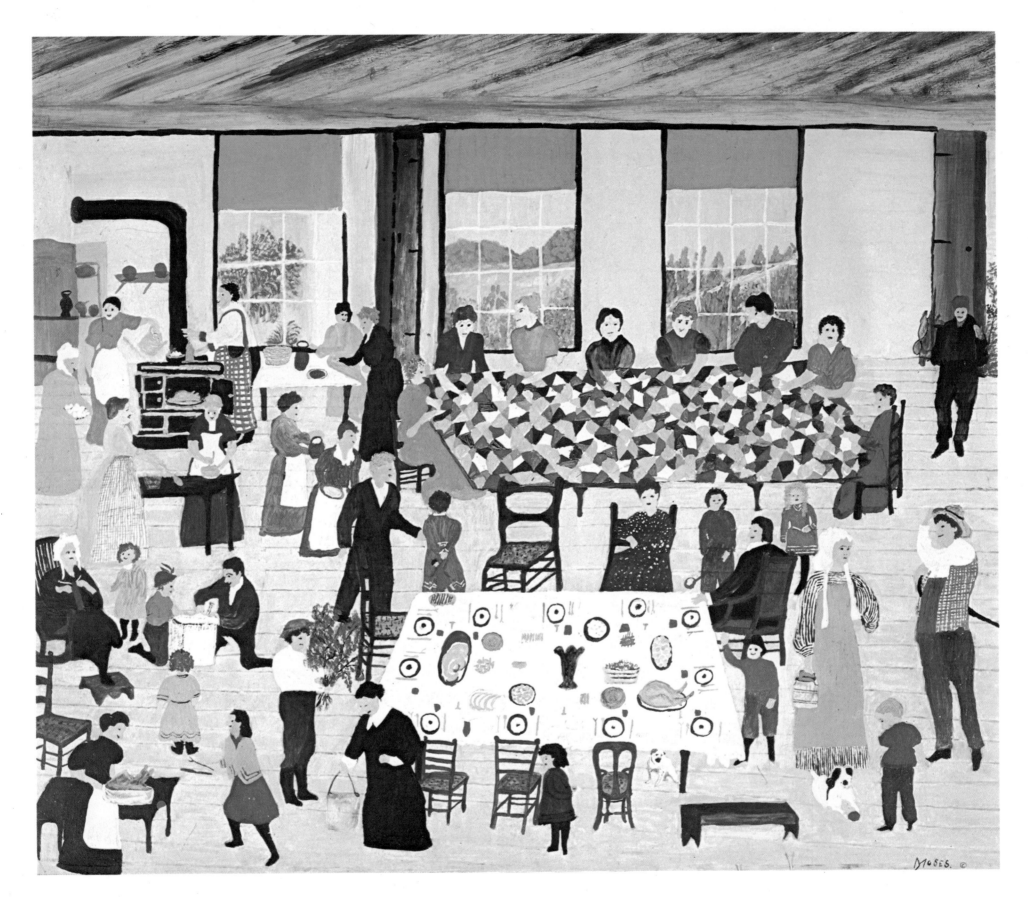

237. *The Quilting Bee.* 1950. 20 x 24". Cat. 883

Another interior, *The Quilting Bee* (plate 237), painted in 1950, is remarkable both for its folkloristic content and its composition. Here is Grandma Moses's description of the custom:

> Back in Revolutionary War times quilting bees were a necessity as well as a thing of art. The women took great pride in their needle work. Every well regulated house had one room set aside which was called the quilting room; the quilting frames were set up on the backs of chairs or stands. The women of the neighborhood would gather to sew, sometimes at night, but candle light was very poor for fine stitches, which the women of those days prided themselves in. Some of the designs were beautifully done, such as the Sunflower, Rising Sun and Friendship, where each one wrote her name in the center of the block. There are a few of those old quilts scattered through the country, highly cherished by their owners.

This interior is composed in a somewhat more sophisticated way than *Christmas at Home*, yet the overall appearance is that of a "primitive" painting. Whereas in the earlier work the figures and objects seem scattered around to fill in any space, *Quilting Bee* is clearly divided into three planes—background, middle ground, and foreground. Here, too, the room is very large, almost a hall, with three windows and the indication of a beamed ceiling. The windows look out onto a landscape of delicate hues—the ones in *Christmas at Home* are dark, indicating that it is night. The main activity takes place in the upper center of the picture, where a large frame bears a many-colored quilt on which eight women are working. To the left stands an old-fashioned iron cooking stove with busy women around it. In the foreground a table with a white cloth is set for the meal. The composition of a picture with two almost equally large areas placed parallel to each other might have become clumsy, but the artist has successfully solved the problem by loosening up the composition with many incidental figures and by showing a fairly wide amount of floor space between the furnishings of the room. The

251

general impression is one of almost stylized order with the colorful quilt forming the focal point.

Views out of windows, as seen in this painting, were themes occasionally taken up by the artist. They might show a sunny landscape, or indicate the night outside, or be "blind," giving a shut-in impression. Once in a while she would combine the view into a house with the surrounding landscape or give glimpses into rooms as though the fourth wall had been opened up, like a doll's house. Examples can be found in the paintings for *The Night Before Christmas*.

Perhaps Grandma Moses's two most unusual interiors are the pictures *In the Studio* (plate 253), done in 1944, and *Rockabye* (plate 238), painted thirteen years later, in 1957. In both of them she attempted self-portraits, to my knowledge the only ones she ever did. Though she quite often included herself among the figures populating a scene—carrying a milk pail, standing in a doorway, or about to enter a carriage— these are always featureless representations.

Since the subject had not appeared in her work before, it is very likely that she painted the first picture at the suggestion of a friend, coping with the theme as best she could. The artist was certainly too modest and not introspective enough to consider doing a self-portrait for its own sake. She is therefore surrounded by many objects of her daily life—her own small paintings decorate the walls, a huge and colorful flower arrangement stands on the table to her right, a vase with tall black-eyed susans in a corner on the floor. Two large, partly curtained windows in the rear are like pictures in themselves, one giving a view of the garden with a girl beneath a tree, the other of a path leading up to one of the familiar red barns. Grandma occupies the center of the scene, seated in a wide rocking chair, yet she seems to have lavished more care on the objects in the room than on herself. Her dress is plain and unadorned, while even the upholstery of the chair shows a design. The pale gray of the dress contrasts with the strong tones of flowers and dark heavy furniture. It is interesting that she is not wearing

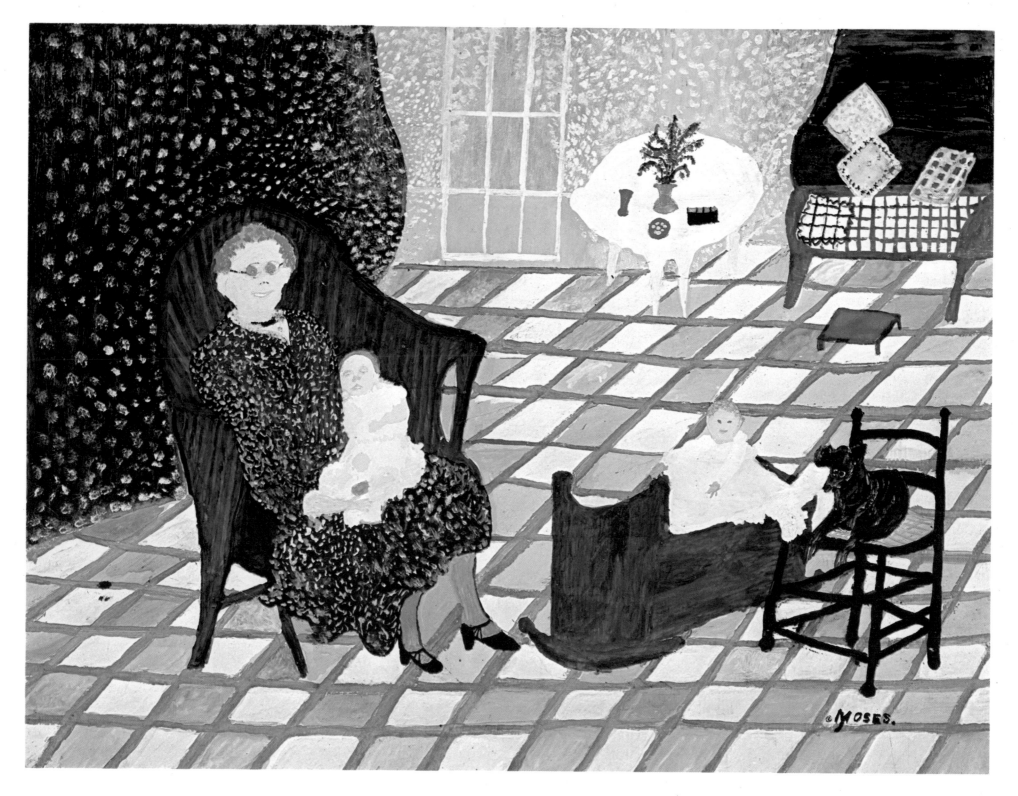

238. *Rockabye.* 1957. 11⅞ x 16". Cat. 1303

the glasses to which she was accustomed at that time—her eyes, two dark dots, look out at the beholder in an almost uneasy way.

Rockabye, the later, far smaller painting, reveals more of the artist's personality. In contrast to the almost cluttered appearance of the earlier picture, here the setting is a rather bare living room. Grandma, seated to the left in a wicker chair, dominates the composition. A dark-green curtain with white dots provides a lopsided but very effective background. It is touching to note the accuracy and detachment with which Grandma Moses saw herself. There she is, the little frail old lady, as others may have seen her, with no embellishment, no softening light. She is wearing her familiar black-and-white print dress, there is a narrow black ribbon around her neck, and her gray-stockinged feet and very characteristic shoes are side by side, a bit apart, in a not too graceful but most realistic way.

The features of Grandma's face here, too, are not very marked and her glasses, clear and sparkling in real life, are strangely dim and opaque. She is holding a baby on her lap, but in an unconcerned manner which perhaps reflects her matter-of-fact and totally unsentimental attitude. There is a second child in a cradle to the right; nearby, a chair with a dog; toward the back, a table with trinkets and a settee with cushions. More striking than these is the carefully drawn linoleum that covers the floor in a pattern of dark and light squares outlined in green.

There is a window in the back, but it, like Grandma's glasses, is "blind" and permits no view to the outside. If one were tempted to interpret this work psychologically, one might say that it conveys a sense of both calm and resignation. The very old woman and the tiny new human being—a circle of life that has come full way around.

Last Paintings

239.
239.
The hands of
Grandma Moses

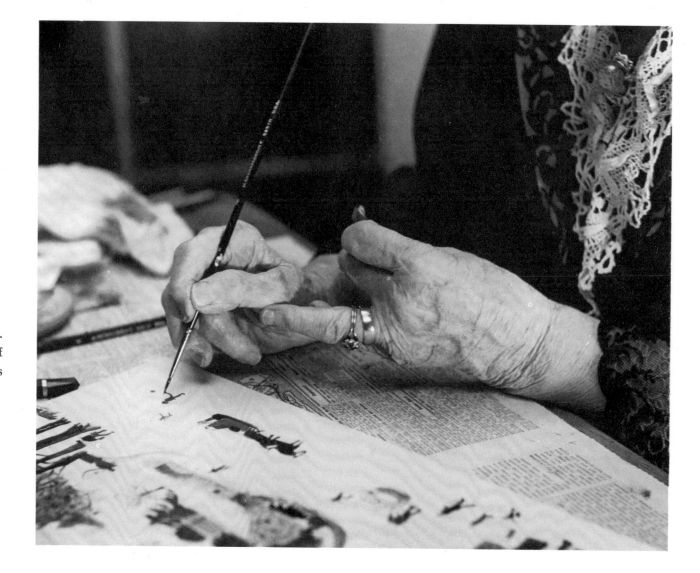

THE ARTIST RETAINED THE STEADINESS OF HER HAND into her very old age. Supporting her right hand with the left, she would fill in with absolute accuracy the finest details, such as window slits in distant small buildings or the eyes in human faces. Then gradually, toward the end of 1959, some of her pictures show a changed way of painting whereby the subject matter is almost dissolved into color. This can be observed in

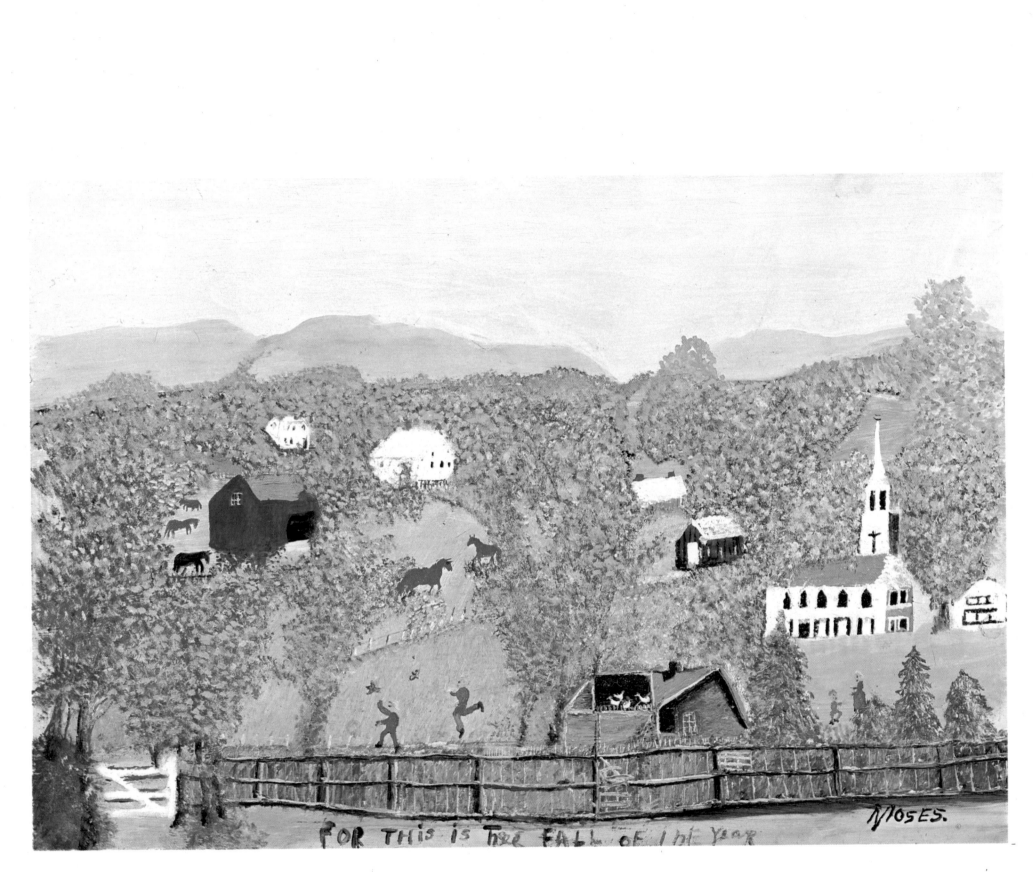

240. *Falling Leaves.* 1961. 16 x 24". Cat. 1490

256

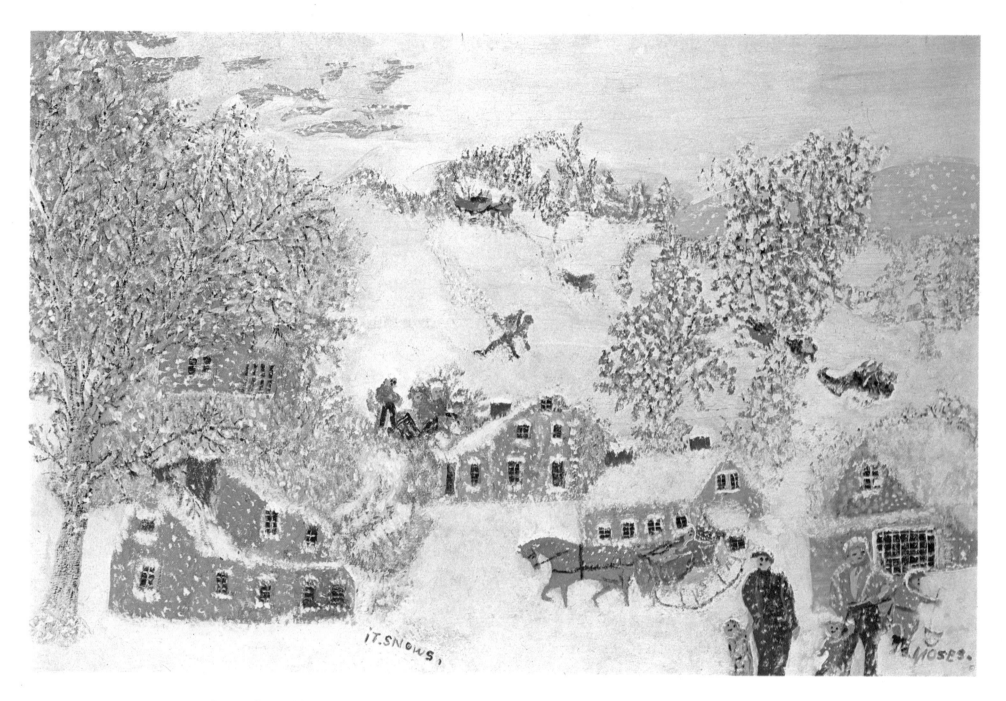

241. *The Deep Snow.* 1961. 16 x 24". Cat. 1486

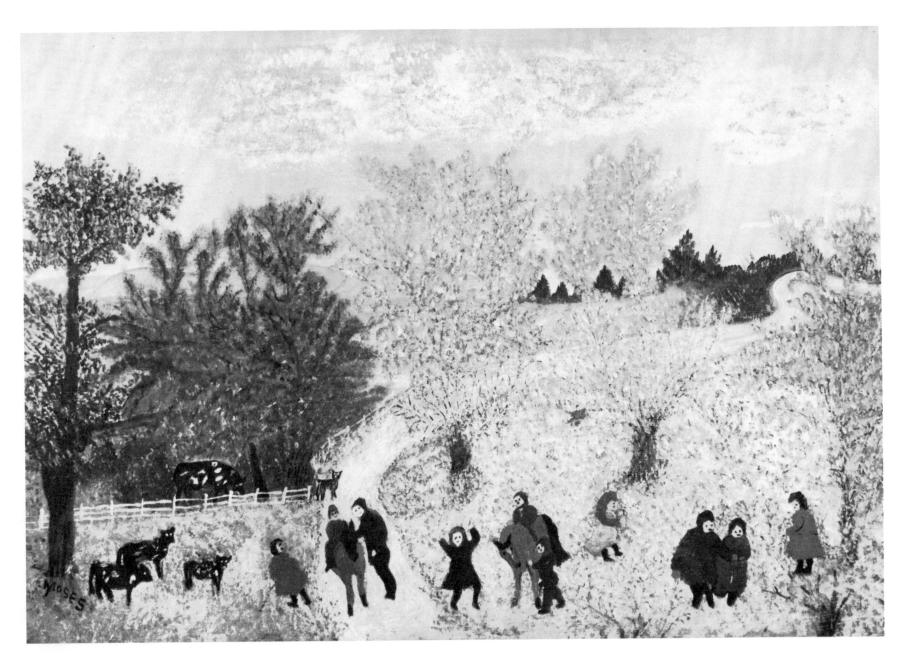

242. *Autumn Leaves.* 1959. 16 x 24". Cat. 1432

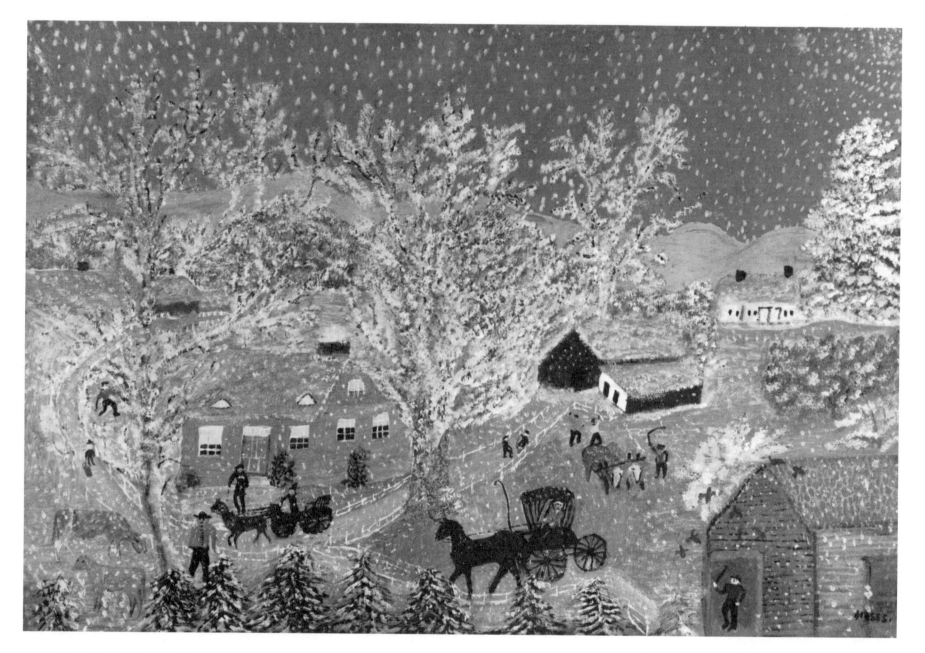

243. *Last Snowfall.* 1959. 16 x 24". Cat. 1438

259

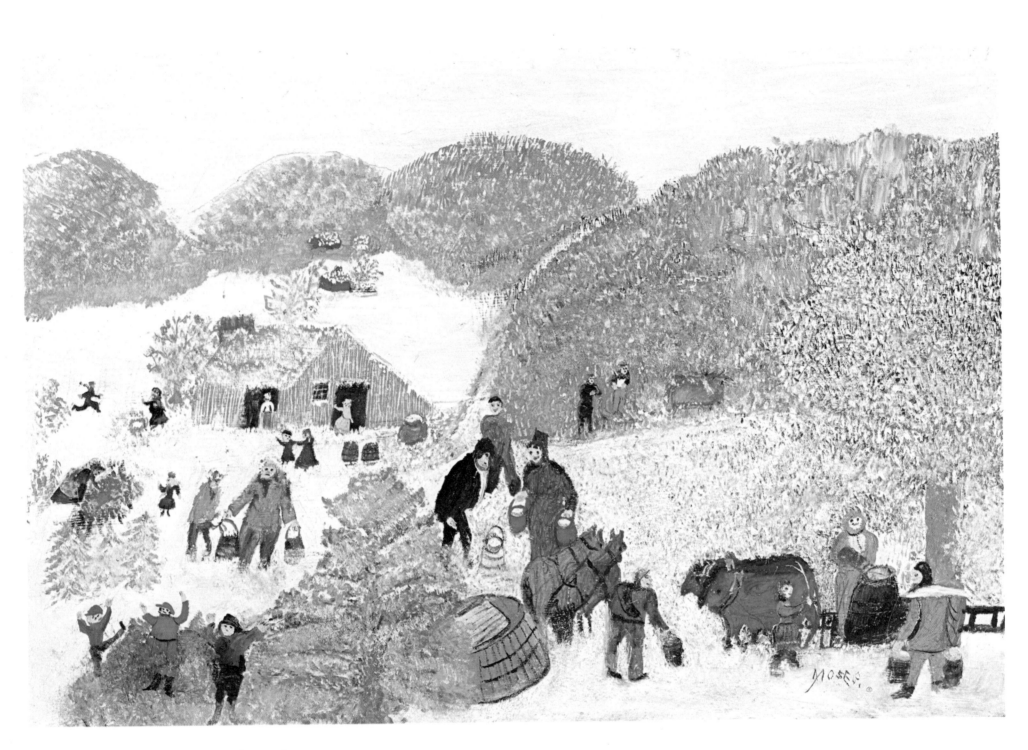

244. *Vermont Sugar.* 1961. 16 x 24". Cat. 1496

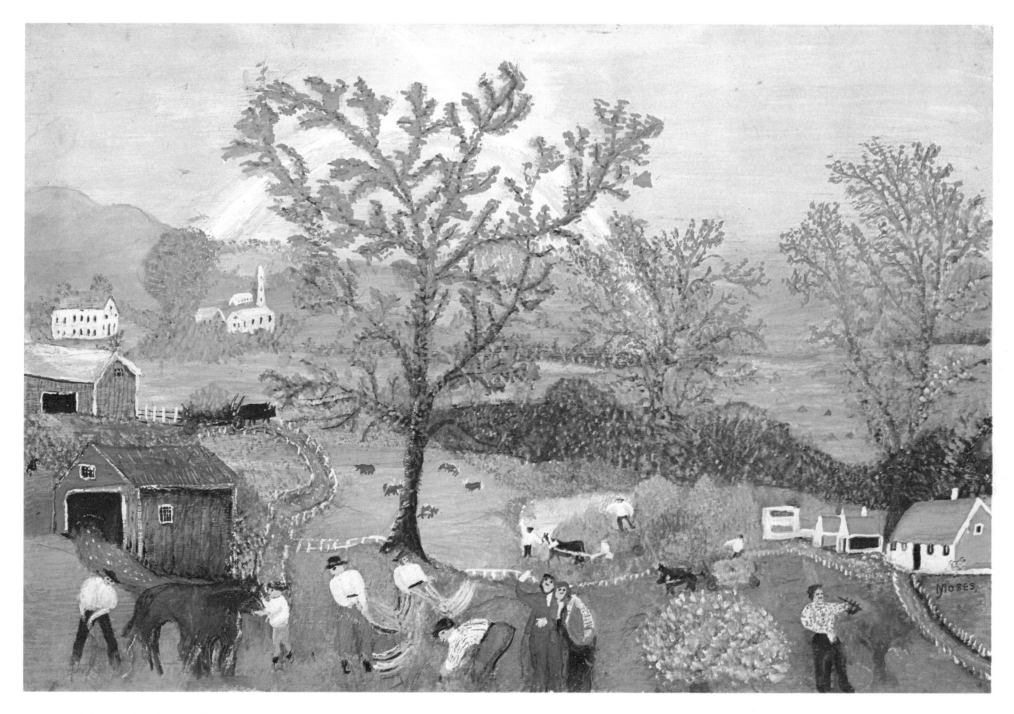

245. *Rainbow.* 1961. 16 x 24". Cat. 1511

Autumn Leaves and *Last Snowfall* (plates 242, 243), painted when she was ninety-nine, and in *Falling Leaves, The Deep Snow*, and *Vermont Sugar* (plates 240, 241, 244), painted in the last year of her life. There are, of course, human figures, barns, fences, and even a cart or two in these pictures, but they are more roughly daubed in, as though—which may well have been the case—the artist had become impatient with detail and mainly wanted to bring out the general impression of a nature scene, whether the yellow leaves of autumn or the softly falling snow.

Grandma Moses gave the title *Rainbow* to the very last picture she completed (plate 245). Its label bears the number 1997 and the date June 1961. After Grandma Moses's death, Emily Genauer wrote about this painting in the *New York Herald Tribune* of December 14, 1961:

> The pale rainbow she lightly sketched in that picture, arching over a lush summer landscape of her beloved Cambridge Valley . . . will never be strengthened now, as she had planned to strengthen it. No matter. It will remain a strong enough span for those looking at it—or, indeed, at any of her pictures—to be able to reach her simple, peaceful, idyllic nineteenth-century world from their own frantic world of today.
>
> A span leading only to escape need not be strong. Nostalgia and dreams are stout enough materials for its fashioning. But Grandma Moses' span was made of faith. So strong was her own, so certain her conviction that the earth and all growing things . . . are proof that there *is* a meaning to life, that somehow, looking at her pictures we are reassured.

Epilogue

THE WORLD OF GRANDMA MOSES is bright and serene; man is in perfect harmony with nature, the tasks he performs are dictated by the daily necessities of farm and country life, as unquestionable as rain or sunshine. Nowhere is there a sign of overwhelming toil; nothing is either good or bad, everything is natural. If Grandma Moses permits herself any personal slant, it is expressed by her strong and charming sense of humor. Mischief of any kind is always good-natured fun—the *Halloween* picture is full of it.

When the artist, departing from the serenity that emanates from most of her paintings, does represent a disturbance, it is not man-made but springs powerfully from nature, as in her representations of stormy and windswept landscapes.

Never could she have re-created the beauty of a landscape, the changing seasons, the activities that they entail—plowing, haying, harvesting, sugaring—had she not deeply felt and loved nature in all its aspects and varying moods. But it would not have occurred to her to represent them for their pure aesthetic value or to "romanticize" a scene. She painted what she saw and intimately knew, and the beauty which radiates from her work is the natural result of her vision.

No doubt some present-day critics find the world of Grandma Moses too simple, too unproblematic, lacking in the awareness of the strife and grief that overshadow our lives. Although she certainly had experienced them, what she expressed in her art are the everlasting sources of vitality from which man draws his strength, courage, and hope. She has shown an image of her country far different from what has come to be regarded as "typically American," and the image is truer and more enduring.

Jean Cassou, the former director of the Musée National d'Art Moderne

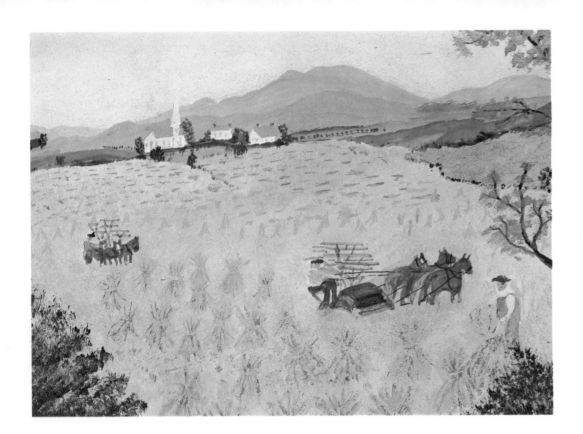

246. *In Harvest Time* (detail)

247. *In Harvest Time*. 1945. 18 x 28". Cat. 537

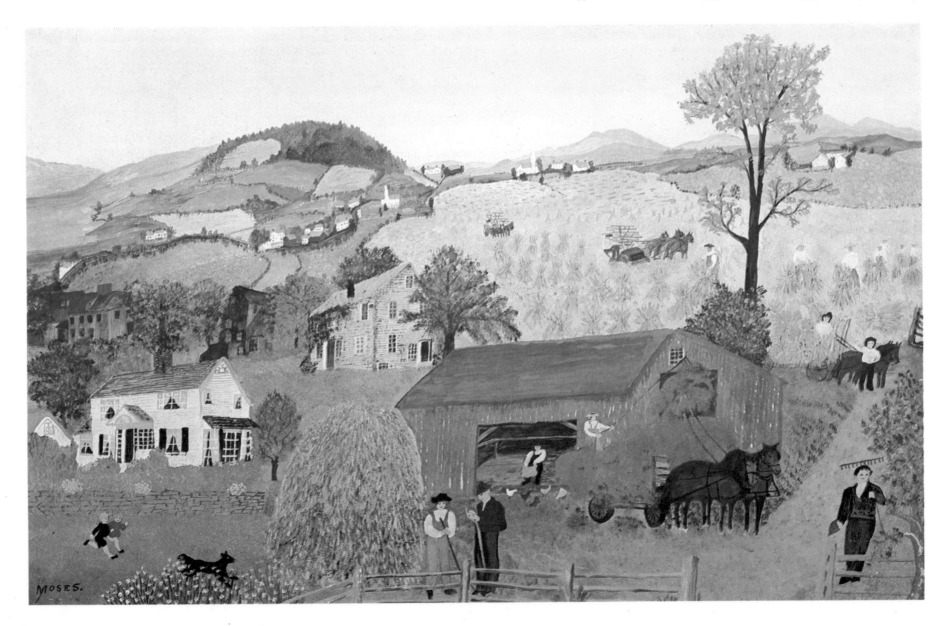

264

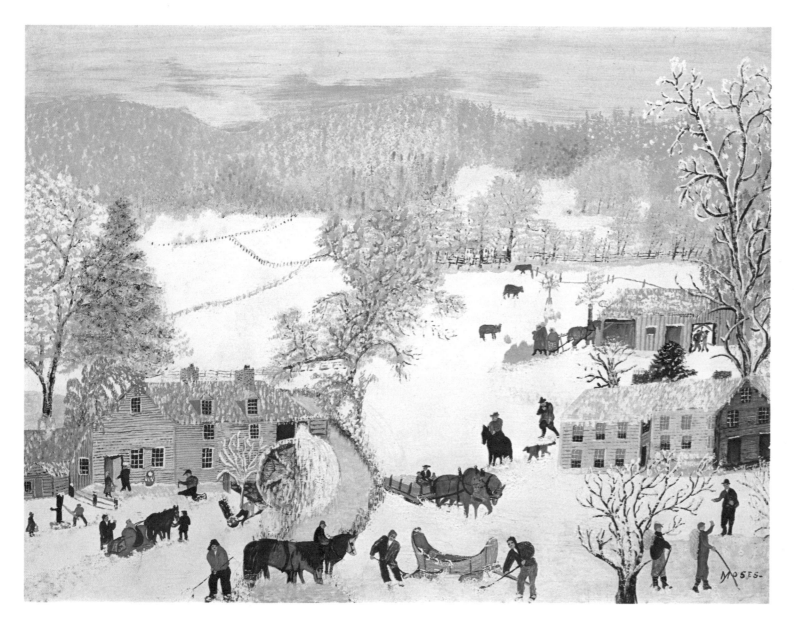

248. *A Frosty Day.* 1951. 18 x 24″. Cat. 985

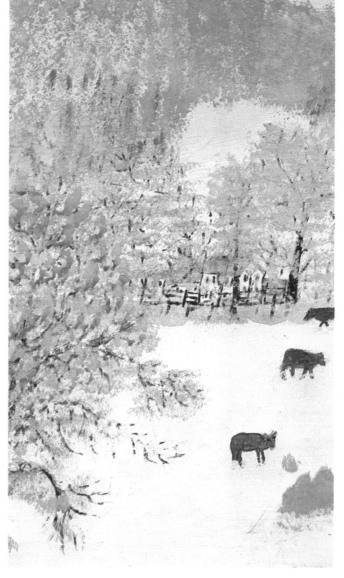

249. *A Frosty Day* (detail)

265

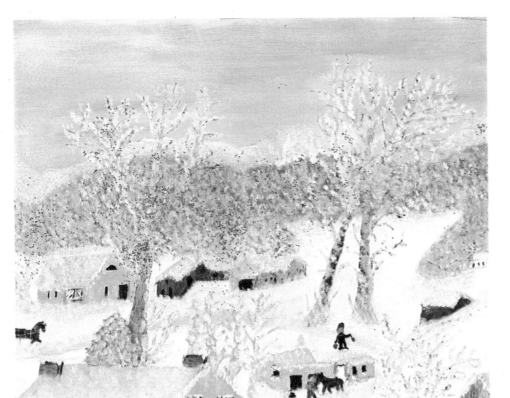

250. *Green Sleigh* (detail)

251. *Green Sleigh*. 1960. 16 x 24". Cat. 1449

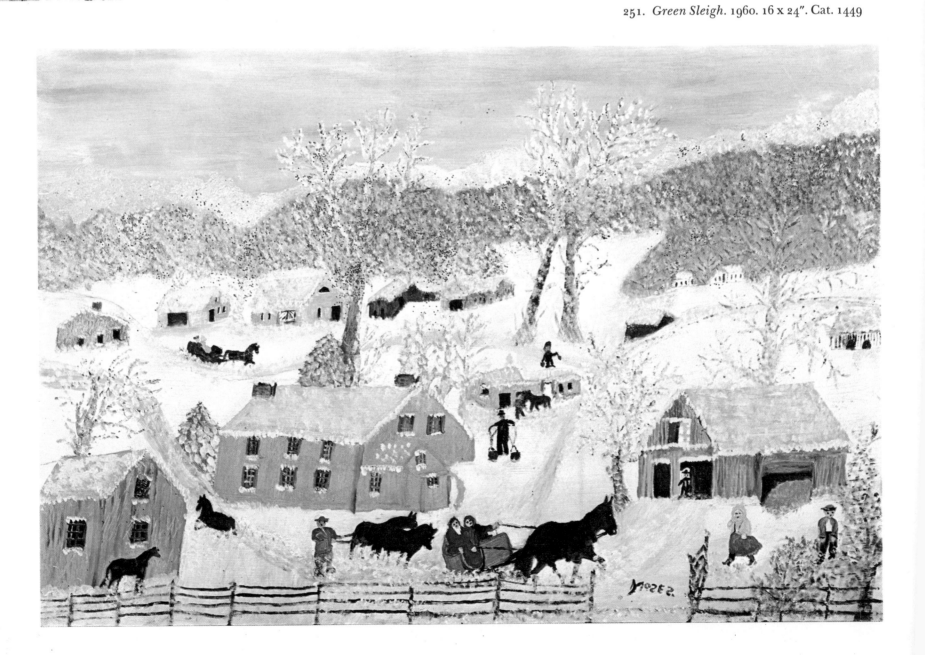

266

in Paris, one of the foremost European authorities on modern art, has expressed most concisely and beautifully what Anna Mary Robertson Moses's work means to the world of art and to our time. He wrote on the occasion of the artist's hundredth birthday:

> The Primitives are the salt of the earth. Through their existence alone does contemporary art, so knowing, so sophisticated and daring, preserve in its depth sources of freshness and life. Thus the Cubists had at their side the Douanier Rousseau, and their marvelous intellectual speculations were counterbalanced by the companionship of this pure heart, inspired by the genius of the people and of nature. The United States through its "avant-garde" is making the most daring aesthetic experiments, but also has its primeval forces, its springs of fresh water. From her small-town vantage point, the adorable Grandma Moses comes to the defense of the countryside, the empire of foliage and birds, and upholds the rights of nature. She would have us know that there is still a bit of paradise left on this earth and that art may reach out as far as it will with its most advanced branches, because it is deeply rooted in the rich soil of Grandma Moses's garden.

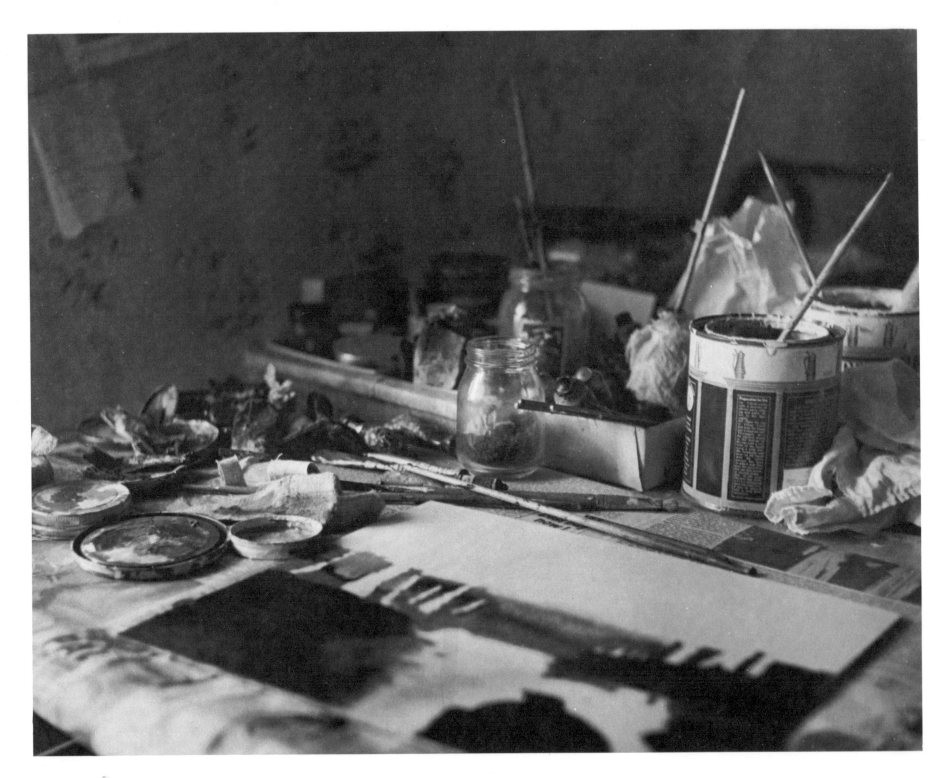

252. Grandma Moses's painting table

"How Do I Paint?"

1

EagleBridge April 7th 1947.

How do I Paint?
well first I get a frame, then I saw my masonite board to fit the frame.

Then I go over the board with Oil,
Then give the board three coats of flat white paint,

Now it is ready for the scene, what ever the mind may produce,

A land scape picture, an Old Bridge A Dream, or a summer or winter scene,

Child hoods memory, what ever one fancys,

But always somthings pleasing and cheerful and I like bright colors and activity,

Why do I use masonite or hard wood to paint on?

Becaus it will last many years longer than canvas,

Some times the frames are hard to obtain, they may be pretty frames but in a delapidated condistion,

2

Then I must use hammer and nails with plastico, the frames should allwise blend with the painting for best affect,

why did I start to paint in my old age?

well to tell the truth, I had neuritus and artheritus so bad that I could do but little work, but had to keep busy to pass the time away, I tryed worsted pictures, then tryed oil,

and now I paint a great deal of the time,

It is a very pleasant Hobby if one does not have to hurry,

I love to take my time and finish things up right,

At first I painted for pleasure,
Then I was called upon to do more than I could, to live up to my promises,

when I first commenced to paint with oil, I thought every painting would be my last one,

So I was not so interrested,

269

3

Then the reyuerts commenced to come,
from this one and that one,
"Paint me one yust like that one "
So I have painted on and on till now,
    Those that I have keept track of are "177",
But that is not all of them,
I think I'm dowing better work then at
first,
    But it is owing to better brushes and
paint,
I don't advise any one to take it up as
a buisness proprosition, unless they
really have talent, and are crippled
so as to deprive then of phyical labor,
    Then with kelp they might make
a living,
    But with taxes and income tax there
is little money in that kind of art
for the ordinary artis
But I will say that I have did remarkalle
for one of my years. and experience,
thanks to mr Louis Coldor, mr Otto Kallir and
alla Story, through those, life has been a
    Success,

4 As for publicity, that I'm too Old to care
care for now,
    Some times it makes me think
of a dream that my Father once told at
the breakfast table one morning many
years ago,
    He said, "I had a dream about you last
night anna mary"
        was it good or bad Pa, ?
And he said that depends on the future,
Dreams cast their shadows before us,
    He dreamed, I was in a large Hall
and there were many people there,
They were claping their hands and shouting,
and I wondered what it was all about, and
looking I saw you anna mary corning
my way, walking on the shoulders of
men, you came right on steping from
one shoulder to another waving to me,
    Of late years I have often thought
of that dream, sience all the publicty
about me, an of Mother saying, to Father,
"Now Russell anna Mary would look nice
walking on mens sloulders"!

5 She saw the folly of that dream,
Or did she? did that dream cast its
shadows before?
    I often wonder, now that I'm getting
letters from all most every country on the
Globe,
        and such kind wellwishing letters,
and they come to Grandma from faraway,
    I love to have visitors, they are awlwise
walcomed, and they bring in news of the
owter world, which is realy delightful.

    I have had the experience of being on
the radio twice,
    the first time was a year ago while
in new york attending my exhibition at
the American British art centre,
    Here, I met Bessie Beatty who has a radio
broadcast daily, who asked me to go on
the air at one of her broadcasts,
I dident think too much of this idea, but
was glad to help her so I excepted,

6 They had gone to a lot of trouble,
        Sending two men from new
york city,
    Carl Schutzman an Engineer who
came with a poratable transmiting
apparatus, was very patient listing
for the switchover to Eagle Bridge,
        then there were four men from the
Troy telephone company, to make
connections between Grandma moses and
new york city,
    I presume they were some nervous
moments for those men, who had gone
to all of that trouble and expense, for
fear all would not go right,
    we found that we had but three
minuts time alowed for the talk,
        now who can say much in three
minuts,?
    So we had to boil it down to the three
minuts, mr Gene Hurley and I went
over the program several times, so
as to time it to three minuts
    He was very nice and pactient

[The second time was in April 1946 on the program "We the People."]

271

with me,

For I am a dumm Dora, when it comes to such work, it is out of my line of business,

Erick C Anderson was with us that night one who represents motion Pictures Portraits of newyork,

which made it very pleasent for me, It was a delightful evening for me,

I enjoyed it, and I hope all the others did to

After the refreshments, they all departed for their Homes,

Leving the house so lonesom,

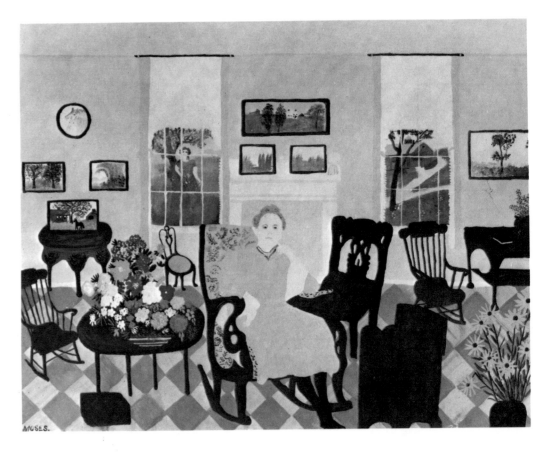

253. *In the Studio.* 1944. 18 x 23½". Cat. 461

Documentary Section

Biographical Outline

1860   September 7, Anna Mary Robertson is born in Greenwich, N.Y.

1872–87   Works as a hired girl on neighboring farms.

1887   November 9, marries Thomas Salmon Moses.

1887–1905   Lives and farms in Virginia. Ten children are born, of whom five die in infancy.

1905   Returns to New York State; purchases a farm in Eagle Bridge.

1909   Her mother dies in February, her father in June.

1918   Paints her first large picture, on the fireboard in her parlor.

c. 1920   Paints landscapes on the panels of her "tip-up" table and occasional pictures for relatives and friends.

1927   January 15, Thomas Salmon Moses dies.

1930s   Lives in Bennington from about 1930. After the death of her daughter Anna Moses in February 1932, she cares for two grandchildren. Embroiders "worsted" pictures. Returns to Eagle Bridge in 1935. Begins to paint in earnest. Exhibits pictures along with preserves at country fairs.

1938   Exhibits pictures in Thomas's Drugstore, Hoosick Falls, N.Y., where Louis J. Caldor discovers them.

1939   October 18 to November 18, three paintings are included in a show of "Contemporary Unknown American Painters" in the Members' Rooms of the Museum of Modern Art, New York.

1940   October 9, the opening of her first one-man show, titled "What a Farm Wife Painted," at the Galerie St. Etienne, New York. In November, visits New York to attend an exhibition of her work at Gimbels Thanksgiving Festival.

1941   New York State Prize is presented to her for *The Old Oaken Bucket* at the Syracuse Museum of Fine Arts (now the Everson Museum of Art).

1946   Publication of *Grandma Moses: American Primitive* by Otto Kallir, with an introduction by Louis Bromfield and autobiographical notes by Grandma Moses. The first Christmas cards reproducing her paintings are published.

1949   In February, her youngest son, Hugh, dies. In May, the Women's National Press Club Award, "for outstanding accomplishment in Art," is presented to Grandma Moses by President Harry S Truman in Washington, D.C. In June, she receives an Honorary Doctorate from Russell Sage College, Troy, N.Y.

1950   Erica Anderson creates a documentary color film, with narration by Archibald MacLeish.

1951   Grandma Moses receives an Honorary Doctorate from the Moore Institute of Art, Philadelphia.

1952   *My Life's History* is published.

1953   Grandma Moses is guest speaker at the *New York Herald Tribune* Forum in New York.

1955   Edward R. Murrow interviews Grandma Moses for a telecast in his "See It Now" series.

1958   October 14, her daughter Winona Fisher dies.

1960   Paints pictures illustrating *The Night Before Christmas*, by Clement C. Moore.

1960 and 1961   Governor Nelson A. Rockefeller proclaims the artist's birthday "Grandma Moses Day" in the State of New York.

1961   In June, paints her last picture, *Rainbow*. December 13, Grandma Moses dies at the Health Center, Hoosick Falls.

Catalogue of the Works

INTRODUCTION

Grandma Moses worked more or less casually, especially in the beginning, taking pleasure in painting as she had in doing needlework of different kinds throughout her life. A study of her paintings shows that she made repeated use of motifs borrowed from various sources, combining and recombining them in much the way an experienced housewife uses elements of different patterns in making clothing for her family and decorative objects for her home.

At first she often copied from reproductions. *Autumn in the Berkshires,* which is sometimes referred to as her "first painting," was copied from a reproduction that had hung in the Moses home since about 1893, according to the artist's son, Forrest Moses. She seems to have liked this subject, for she repeated it several times in wool and in oil.

It is not possible to trace all the pictures, mostly of small size, which Grandma Moses made in the period before her true development as a painter. A study of the early paintings will reveal the difficulty of putting them into accurate chronological order. Their style is very inconsistent, and their artistic quality depends more on the artist's feeling for the subject and, perhaps, for the intended recipient of the picture than on her concern with the painting as such. There are, however, a few pictures that were given to friends and relatives whose recollections permit the assignment of approximate dates.

Then there are the pictures which Louis J. Caldor assembled between 1938 and 1941. The first Moses works to appear at an exhibition were the three paintings displayed at the Museum of Modern Art in 1939 and those in her one-man show at the Galerie St. Etienne in 1940. Some of Caldor's purchases may have been painted years earlier, however, and we know about the exhibited pictures only that they were painted previous to the shows.

A number of works are known to have been made during 1941, most likely prior to the time late in that year when she began numbering and dating her work and keeping records.

In November 1941, when people had begun to be interested in Grandma Moses, her brother, Fred E. Robertson, presented the artist with a book in which to enter her paintings. The book is bound in black boards; it measures 7¾ by 10 inches and bears the word "Record" in gold lettering on the cover. The pages are numbered from 1 to 152, and the first one is inscribed in Fred Robertson's hand.

To make it easier for his sister to keep the records, he put headings on pages 4–5, 6–7, and 8–9: "Painting number / Year completed / Title of painting / Notes on disposition of same etc." In spite of this preparation, Grandma Moses was so eager to begin "bookkeeping" that she started the book by listing nine pictures on page 2 and twelve on page 3; it must be assumed that these were works she had completed recently. She also noted the prices she had received and the names of the buyers. Some of these entries are dated "Nov. 1941"; one is dated, probably in error, "Sept. 1941." They went to neighbors who bought them for $3 to $5 each, and to Louis Caldor, Sidney Janis, and Leon Salter. On page 4 she listed nine pictures with the date "1942, Feb" (some painted in 1941). Page 5 is blank.

Painting Number	Year Completed	Title of painting

1942, Feb   a long Road, sold for $4.00 to mr callor, n.y. city
"   "   Tolles pasture "   "   "   "   "   "
"   "   the Debate "   "   "   "   "   "
"   "   the Covared Bridge in winter, sold to mr callor, For $2,00
"   "   when the cows come Home, sold to mr callor, For $200
  porring wax, sold, For $2000 mr callor, n.y. city

Fishgard a welsh Farm, no 1 and 2,

Description and Disposition of

1941	the foot Bridge	84
1941	the Brook in the woods.	85
1941	the Dearest spot on earth, no 1,	86
1941	the first snow,	87
1941	a cottage by the sea, worsted no 2	88
1941	winter on the river worsted,	88
1941	summer on the Lake,	100
1941	a church in the sunshine,	101
1941	white Birches	102
1941	a snow covared Bridge,	103
1941	the old Home dreams, no 1,	104
1941	a sleigh ride in winter,	105
1941	Home in autumn.	106
1941	Home in the Lodge	107
1941	mt tom,	108
1941	south east view of cabrack	109
1941	the Farm,	110
1941	the Back door	111
1941	Kinloch Rannock pirthshir,	112
1941	Gathering up the fagots,	113
1941	down by the old mill stream	114
1941	sun set in fall,	115
1941	the old swiming pool	116
1941	over the Bridge, and Home	117
1941	connecticut	118
1941	catching the turkey, no 1	119
1941	over the river to grandma House no 1	120
1941	over the river to Grandma House, no 2	121

On pages 6–11 the artist listed pictures she remembered having painted and sold before receiving the notebook. The list of titles shows the numbers 1 through 173 and the dates 1939 through 1942, but actually the list comprises only 164 titles; Grandma Moses used the number 28 twice and jumped from 89 to 100. Quite a few known early paintings bear titles which may be found in this list; however, the numbers on the list do not refer to any numbers on the pictures. On pages 12–17 of the Record Book a new list appears, this one with prices. The pages are headed "the year of 1938," "the year 1939," and so on.

It is very likely that Grandma Moses made these lists not only from memory but also from notes. Many titles recur between pages 6 and 17; at times, entire groups of paintings appear on several pages in the same sequence and sometimes with the same prices. In such instances there is no doubt that she listed the same painting twice or even three times.

In general, Record Book entries for the years 1941–45 (pages 18–38) reflect a period of exuberant activity. She found herself suddenly popular, her work in great demand. Requests came in the mail and from travelers who made a detour through Eagle Bridge to buy a painting directly from the artist. Many pictures dating from this period were not recorded in her book; among those that were, slight variants appear in the titles in addition to the inconsistencies in numbering. Earlier listings in the Record Book are sometimes referred to in lists of pictures sold to particular clients.

At this time, Grandma Moses began noting more frequently the prices for which she sold her pictures. A comparison of prices with dimensions indicates that she priced them according to size. On page 18 (1943), for example, a picture measuring 6¼ by 8 inches is listed as having been sold for $2; one measuring 11½ by 13¾ inches brought $5; and one 23 by 26¾ inches brought $15.

It is not possible to establish at what point Grandma Moses began to put numbers on her paintings. The logic of her early system of numbering defies analysis. The first pictures on which numbers appear were painted in 1941 but bear such numbers as 2010, 202, 2211! A painting dated February 9, 1942, is numbered 9, while in January of that year she used 29 and 199. Such discrepancies also appear in the Record Book. On page 24 the number 469 is followed by 500; on pages 31–32 there is a jump from 808 to 1000; on page 35 Grandma Moses "progressed" from 1099 to 1010, but on page 39 from 1099 to 1100. The number the artist assigned to a picture is included in the Catalogue of the Works with the letter M preceding it: M. 1022, for example.

From page 39 (that is, following 1945) up to the last painting, entries were made in a quite systematic manner. After 1955 they were written by Mrs. Winona Fisher and, after Mrs. Fisher's death in 1958, by Forrest Moses.

At about the same time that Fred Robertson gave Grandma Moses the Record Book, he also presented her with labels to paste on the reverse side of her pictures. On these labels she was to enter date, number, and title. When the supply of labels ran out in 1950, new ones were printed. In later years the new type of label was filled in by Mrs. Fisher and by Forrest Moses.

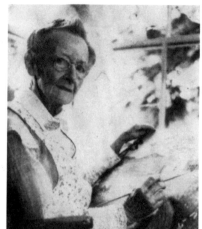

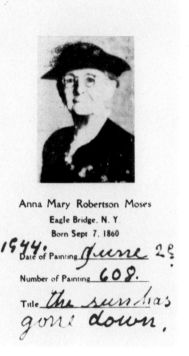

Anna Mary Robertson Moses
Eagle Bridge, N. Y.
Born Sept 7, 1860

1944:
Date of Painting *June 2?*
Number of Painting *608.*
Title *the sun has gone down.*

GRANDMA MOSES
Anna Mary Robertson Moses
Date of Painting *Oct 12, 1955,*
Number of Painting *16 95,*
Title *September,*
The copyright of this painting is the property of
GRANDMA MOSES PROPERTIES, Inc.
46 West 57th Street, N. Y. C.

When Grandma Moses had finished a number of pictures she would line them up, sometimes asking members of her family for their reactions, and then paste the labels on the backs of the pictures and make her entries in the Record Book. This procedure accounts for the appearance of the same date on several pictures; it also explains the confusion which sometimes occurred within and between groups.

In addition to the primary sources of documentation—the pictures themselves, their labels, and photographs of them—reference was made principally to the artist's Record Book and correspondence, and to records kept over the years, letters from owners, reproductions in catalogues, newspapers, and magazines. The Catalogue of the Works does not claim to be complete, and certain inaccuracies and inconsistencies in the recording of the vast amount of information are inevitable. But it is hoped that together with the Index, it will serve as a useful guide to the oeuvre of Grandma Moses.

HOW TO USE THE CATALOGUE

Organization

The Catalogue contains all the Moses pictures that could be identified, with the entries ordered chronologically and numbered consecutively.

It begins with the WORSTED pictures, which the artist embroidered, generally in wool. Most were done in the early years, and only a few are datable. These have therefore been listed alphabetically by place name or first noun, in that order; dates are indicated where known. Their numbers are followed by W to indicate WORSTED.

The listing of the oil paintings begins with the group headed EARLY PAINTINGS THROUGH 1940, also presented in alphabetical order as above. Under ABOUT 1941 are listed alphabetically the pictures *believed* to have been painted in that year; then, in chronological order, those *known* to have been painted early in that year. From late 1941 through 1961 the pictures are listed in chronological sequence, since after that time the artist's labels, her Record Book, and other sources make dating more reliable. A few paintings about which insufficient data exist are grouped at the conclusion of the dated listings under the heading PAINTINGS THAT CANNOT BE RELIABLY DATED.

Six photographs are reproduced of pictures about which no information is available. It is very possible that they correspond to unillustrated paintings included in the Catalogue or in the Index.

Finally, eighty-five original TILES are listed. These were numbered consecutively by the artist and have not been assigned Catalogue numbers.

Information Given in Catalogue Entries

Each work is identified by the title given it by Grandma Moses; if no title is known, it is listed as "Untitled" with a brief descriptive phrase to specify its subject. The title is followed by the number assigned by Grandma Moses, preceded by the letter M—if such a number exists. Then follows the date, which is usually not the day the artist completed the picture but the recording date for several works at a time.

All the paintings were done in oil and tempera, most of them on Masonite panels, some on cardboard. Therefore, no mention is made of medium, but the ground is described when it is different—for example, canvas or glass.

Grandma Moses signed almost all her pictures MOSES; when there is an unusual signature or an inscription, this is indicated.

When a particular work can be identified with a Record Book listing, the page number is given; for example: "RB p. 41."

Whenever possible, the last known owner of a painting is listed. Where this information was unavailable, the sale of a picture through an art gallery or auction house is given, if known, as an aid in tracing the work.

Bibliographical references in the Catalogue are restricted to illustrations in prominent publications and to reproductions. Exhibitions are listed only where useful as provenance or as source material for dating.

Every work for which a photograph was available is illustrated, either in the body of the text or in the Catalogue.

An INDEX TO THE WORKS begins on page 329.

281

NBC	*The Night Before Christmas.* Clement C. Moore. Illustrated by Grandma Moses (see Bibl. No. 6)
Oldenbourg	Greeting cards (see Bibl. No. 21)
RB	Followed by a number, refers to the artist's Record Book and the page on which a picture is listed
Six of My Favorite Paintings	Portfolio of six color reproductions (see Bibl. No. 22)

WORSTED PICTURES

(In alphabetical order)

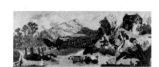

1W. *Autumn in the Berkshires*
9 x 21¾". Formerly collection Louis J. Caldor

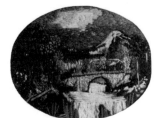

2W. *Bridge*
6½ x 8¼". Formerly collection Louis J. Caldor

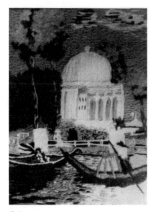

3W. *Cairo*
1933. 10 x 8". The Bennington Museum, Bennington, Vt.

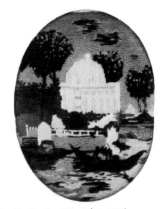

4W. *The Castle of Thrift* (M. 1223)
Nov. 6, 1947. 10¾ x 8¾" (oval). RB p. 43

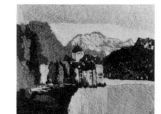

5W. *An Old Castle on a Lake*
9 x 12". Formerly collection Louis J. Caldor

6W. *Cottage by the Lakeside*
Formerly collection Louis J. Caldor

7W. *Cottage by the Sea*
1938. Inscribed on reverse: "with love & best wishes '38, Grandma" Collection Evalyn L. Herrington

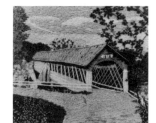

8W. *The Cottage by the Sea* (M. 219)
1941. 11 x 14¼". RB p. 3 "Home by Sea." Formerly collection Louis J. Caldor

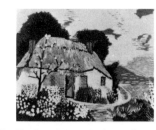

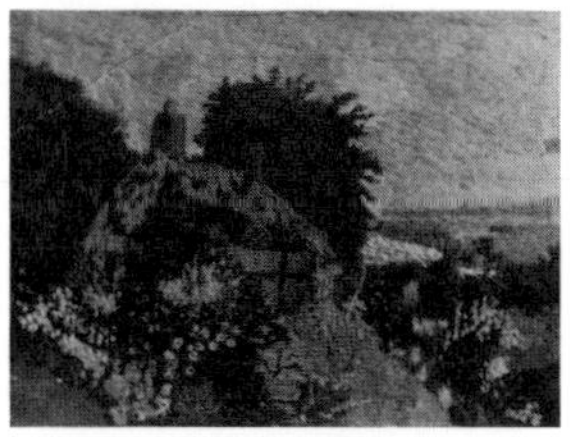

9W. *Cottage in Flower Garden*
About 1931. 9 x 12". Collection Mr. and Mrs. George O. Cook

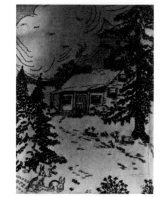

10W. *Cottage in Winter*
Embroidery on linen, 19¾ x 15½". Inscribed by the artist on reverse: "The linen in this picture was growen [sic] in Wash. Co., was spun and woven by one Ann Robertson Whiteside in the year of 1789." The Bennington Museum, Bennington, Vt.

11W. *Cottage in Winter*
Collection Mrs. Loyd R. Moses

12W. *Covered Bridge*
About 1939. Signed by the artist in embroidery in 1949. Collection Mrs. Louis Cassell

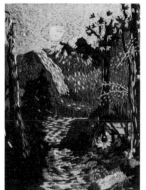

13W. *The Covered Bridge, 1818*
7½ x 9½". Galerie St. Etienne, New York

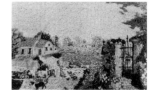

14W. *Evening Camping in the Woods*
10 x 8". Formerly collection Louis J. Caldor

15W. *Foot Bridge*
Formerly collection Louis J. Caldor

16W. *The Garden Gate*
7⅛ x 11⅝". Galerie St. Etienne, New York

17W. *The Roadside Garden*
9¼ x 16¼". Formerly collection Louis J. Caldor. (See plate 20)

18W. *Gates Ajar*
Collection Mrs. Earl Anderson

19W. *For in the Highlands My Home*
Collection Ernest W. Meuser

20W. *My Old Homestead*
9¼ x 11". Formerly collection Louis J. Caldor. (See plate 18)

21W. *Covered Bridge at Hoosick*
9¾ x 11¾". Collection Elizabeth Decker

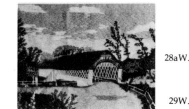

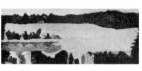

22W. *Hoosick Bridge, 1818*
10¼ x 14½". Formerly collection Louis J. Caldor

23W. *The Old Hoosick Bridge, 1818*
10 x 14". Formerly collection Louis J. Caldor. (See plate 21)

24W. *The Old White House Bridge, Hoosick, N.Y.*
Collection Lucy Mahar

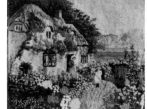

25W. *Along the Hoosick River*
8 x 19½". Unfinished. Formerly collection Louis J. Caldor

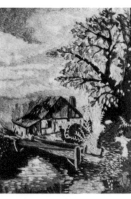

26W. *House and Flower Garden*
About 1931. 11 x 14". The name "Mother" is embroidered on the picture in floss. Collection Mr. and Mrs. George O. Cook

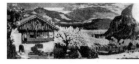

27W. *White House Between Trees* (M. 1139)
Aug. 16, 1946. 8 x 18½". RB p. 40. Collection Kathryn Lowry

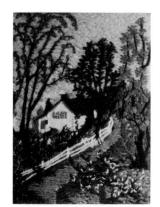

28W. *The Little White House on the Hill*
8¾ x 6¾". Formerly collection Louis J. Caldor

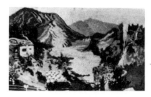

28aW. *Out on the Marsh*
4 x 12". Sidney Janis Gallery, New York

29W. *Mill*
Collection Marguerite F. McNally

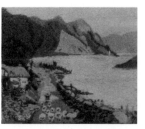

30W. *The Old Mill by the Brookside*
14¼ x 11". Formerly collection Louis J. Caldor

31W. *Miller in the Dell*
Formerly collection Louis J. Caldor

32W. *My Mountain Home*
Formerly collection Louis J. Caldor

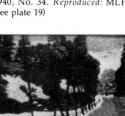

33W. *Mountain Landscape*
8½ x 21". Formerly collection Louis J. Caldor

34W. *Mt. Nebo on the Hill*
10 x 14". Formerly collection Louis J. Caldor. G. St. E. Exhibition 1940, No. 34. *Reproduced:* MLH. (See plate 19)

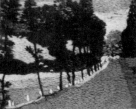

35W. *The River Road* (M. 1140)
Aug. 16, 1946. 7¾ x 10". RB p. 40. Private collection

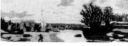

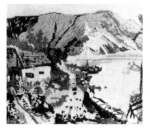

36W. *Shepherd Comes Home*
14 x 24". The Bennington Museum, Bennington, Vt.

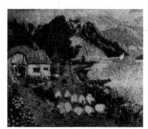

37W. *The Shepherd Comes Home from the Hills*
21½ x 27½". The Bennington Museum, Bennington, Vt.

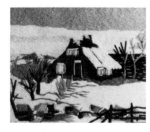

38W. *When the Shepherd Comes Home*
11½ x 14". Collection Sharon R. Curry and Carol R. Wakefield

39W. *When the Shepherd Comes Home*
8¼ x 10½". Formerly collection Louis J. Caldor

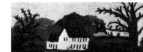

40W. *Snowbound*
8 x 10". Formerly collection Louis J. Caldor

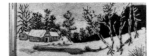

41W. *Down by the Swamp*
Sept. 2, 1947. 7½ x 17½''. Private collection

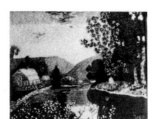

42W. *[Untitled] Cottage by a River*
5½ x 13''. Collection Sharon R. Curry and Carol R. Wakefield

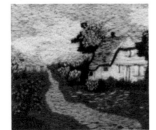

43W. *[Untitled] House*
6½ x 7½''. Collection Mrs. B. R. Robertson

44W. *[Untitled] White House with Winding Road*
1936 or earlier. 8 x 10½''. The artist's signature is pasted on the reverse. Collection Elizabeth Mosall

45W. *[Untitled] Landscape*
According to the owner, this picture was made while the artist was in Virginia. Collection Margaret Brooke

46W. *[Untitled] Winter Scene*
Collection Ernest W. Meuser

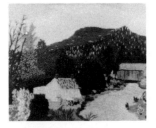

47W. *The Old Covered Bridge in Vermont*
11 x 14''. Title inscribed by the artist in pencil on reverse. Formerly collection Louis J. Caldor

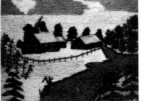

48W. *Sunset in Virginia*
11 x 14''. Formerly collection Louis J. Caldor

49W. *Winter Landscape*
9 x 12''. Collection Gordon Wright

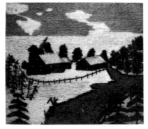

50W. *Winter on the Lake* (M. 218)
1941. 10 x 12''. Galerie St. Etienne, New York

51W. *Winter Scene*
1952. 9¼ x 21¾''. Collection Helen A. Sheldon

52W. *Winter Sunset*
Formerly collection Louis J. Caldor

THE PAINTINGS

1. *Fireboard*
May 10, 1918 (dated on the painting by the artist). Paper, 32¼ x 38¾". (See plate 12)

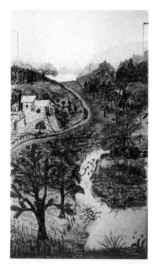

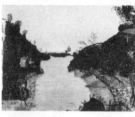

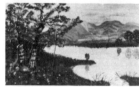

2. *"Tip-up" table*
About 1920. Landscapes painted on six wooden panels forming the standards of a table which is inscribed on the bottom:

THE OLD McMURRY DINING TABLE MADE FOR THE OLD LOG HOUSE IN 1762

Collection Mrs. Hugh W. Moses. (See plates 13-17)

EARLY PAINTINGS THROUGH 1940

(In alphabetical order)

3. *All Dressed Up for Sunday*
11¼ x 13". Pencil sketch of landscape on reverse. Formerly collection Louis J. Caldor. G.St.E. Exhibition 1940, No. 9. (See plate 26)

4. *Apple Orchard*
Collection Mary Bilodeau

5. *Apple Pickers*
13 x 12½". Formerly collection Louis J. Caldor. G.St.E. Exhibition 1940, No. 30. (See plate 25)

6. *The First Automobile*
9¾ x 11½". Formerly collection Louis J. Caldor. MOMA Exhibition 1939, No. 16; G.St.E. Exhibition 1940, No. 23. (See plate 41)

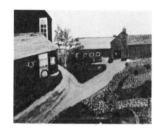

7. *Back Yard at Home*
12 x 16½". Formerly collection Louis J. Caldor. G.St.E. Exhibition 1940, No. 7

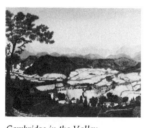

8. *Autumn in the Berkshires*
Before 1938. Threshing canvas, 8 x 14¼". Formerly collection Louis J. Caldor

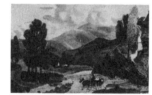

9. *Autumn in the Berkshires*
15¾ x 20½". Formerly collection Louis J. Caldor

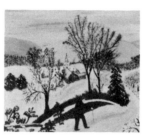

10. *Bridge*
10 x 12". Titled by the artist on reverse. Formerly collection Louis J. Caldor. G.St.E. Exhibition 1940, No. 12

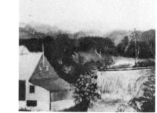

11. *Cambridge in the Valley*
14¾ x 21¾". Formerly collection Louis J. Caldor. G.St.E. Exhibition 1940, No. 25. *Reproduced:* GMAP ("Cambridge")

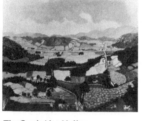

12. *The Cambridge Valley*
19 x 23". Title inscribed on face and description of the scene on reverse by the artist. Sidney Janis Gallery, New York. *Reproduced:* Janis

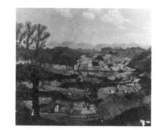

12a. *The Cambridge Valley*
19 x 23". Sidney Janis Gallery, New York

13. *Canoe on the River*
Formerly collection Louis J. Caldor

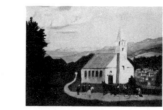

14. *Church*
About 1940. 10 x 14". Collection Leo Curtis

15. *The Old Churchyard on Sunday Morning*
14 x 17¾". Formerly collection Louis J. Caldor. G.St.E. Exhibition 1940, No. 29

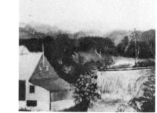

16. *Saw Mill at the Connecticut*
6¾ x 8½". Initialed lower right: "TSM." Formerly collection Louis J. Caldor

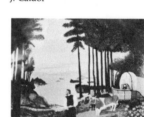

17. *The Covered Wagon*
11 x 14". Formerly collection Louis J. Caldor. G.St.E. Exhibition 1940, No. 6

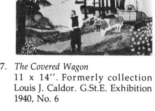

18. *The Dearest Spot on Earth*
1940. 7¾ x 9¾". Collection Mrs. Hugh W. Moses

19. *Dorset Road*
Formerly collection Louis J. Caldor

20. *Gathering Up the Fagots*
Formerly collection Louis J. Caldor

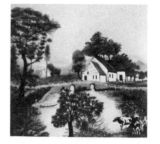

21. *Farm Along the River*
15 x 17¼". Formerly collection Louis J. Caldor. G.St.E. Exhibition 1940, No. 4

22. *A Fire in the Woods*
10¼ x 15". Formerly collection Louis J. Caldor. G.St.E. Exhibition 1940, No. 17. (See plate 57)

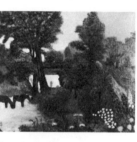

23. *Down in the Glen*
10¾ x 13¾". Formerly collection Louis J. Caldor. G.St.E. Exhibition 1940, No. 1

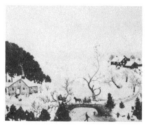

24. *To Grandmother's House We Go*
1940. 19 x 23". Collection Cmdr. and Mrs. Harold L. Crossman. *Reproduced:* Parke-Bernet Sale No. 2199, May 15, 1963, No. 59

25. *Down at Grandpa's House*
Formerly collection Louis J. Caldor

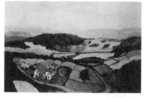

26. *On the Road to Greenwich*
14 x 22". Originally painted on reverse of *The Waterfalls* (Catalogue No. 72); the heavy cardboard was later separated. Formerly collection Louis J. Caldor. G.St.E. Exhibition 1940, No. 27A. *Reproduced:* GMAP ("Cambridge Valley")

27. *The Old Home at Greenwich Road*
8 x 10". Parke-Bernet Sale No. 1344, May 7, 1952, No. 24

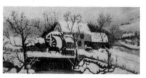

28. *The Old Grist Mill in Winter*
7¾ x 15¾". Collection Carolyn H. Thomas

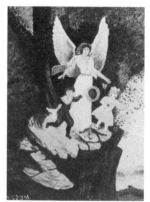

29. *The Guardian Angel*
9 x 7". Formerly collection Louis J. Caldor. G.St.E. Exhibition 1940, No. 10

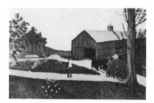

30. *Bringing in the Hay*
13½ x 22". Formerly collection Louis J. Caldor. G.St.E. Exhibition 1940, No. 15

31. *Home*
Formerly collection Louis J. Caldor. MOMA Exhibition 1939, No. 14; G.St.E. Exhibition 1940, No. 21

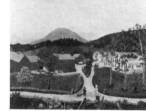

32. *Home*
1940. Canvas, 14 x 18". Sidney Janis Gallery, New York. *Reproduced:* Janis; *New York Times Magazine,* April 6, 1941

33. *Home for Thanksgiving*
Paper, 10 x 14". Inscribed, perhaps by first owner, on reverse: "Phyllis Wood 1932." Signed later twice: "Grandma Moses" and "Moses." (See plate 58)

34. *Home for Thanksgiving*
10½ x 12½". Formerly collection Louis J. Caldor. G.St.E. Exhibition 1940, No. 28 ("A Winter Visit"). (See plate 24)

35. *Home from the Honeymoon*
Formerly collection Louis J. Caldor. G.St.E. Exhibition 1940, No. 14. *Reproduced: The Washington Daily News*, Jan. 10, 1941

36. *Home in Autumn*
Formerly collection Louis J. Caldor

37. *Home in the Hills*
Formerly collection Louis J. Caldor

38. *Home in Winter*
c.1938. 6 x 16". Galerie St. Etienne, New York. (See plate 59)

39. *Going Home*
Formerly collection Louis J. Caldor

40. *The Old House at the Bend of the Road*
Formerly collection Louis J. Caldor. G.St.E. Exhibition 1940, No. 16

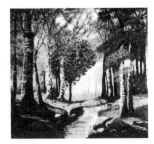

41. *The Huntsman's Dream*
11½ x 13½". Formerly collection Louis J. Caldor

42. *Bringing in the Maple Sugar*
14 x 23". Collection Otto Kallir. G.St.E. Exhibition 1940, No. 19. *Reproduced: GMAP.* (See plate 23)

43. *In the Maple Sugar Days*
Canvas, 15¼ x 19¼". Signed vertically. Collection Mr. and Mrs. Henry Matalene, Jr. MOMA Exhibition 1939, No. 15; G.St.E. Exhibition 1940, No. 22. (See plate 22)

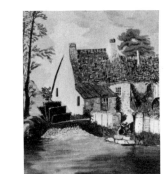

44. *My Forefather's Mill*
14 x 12". Inscribed by the artist on reverse: "My Forefathers." Formerly collection Louis J. Caldor

45. *The Old Red Mill*
Formerly collection Louis J. Caldor

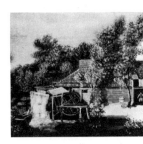

46. *The Miller in the Dell*
9½ x 11½". Formerly collection Louis J. Caldor

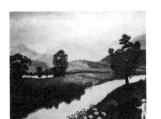

47. *Where the Muddy Missouri Rolls*
12 x 16". Inscribed by the artist on reverse, a long poem (quoted in text on p. 40) and "Missouri." Formerly collection Louis J. Caldor. G.St.E. Exhibition 1940, No. 2

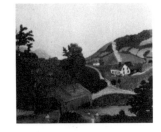

48. *Hills of New England*
14 x 16". Collection Mrs. Ian McDonald. G.St.E. Exhibition 1940, No. 11

49. *Owl Kill Bridge*
Formerly collection Fred E. Robertson

50. *September Hills*
G.St.E. Exhibition 1940, No. 33

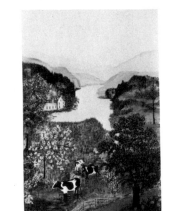

51. *Shenandoah Valley, South Branch*
About 1938. Oilcloth, 19¾ x 14". Left half of a painting cut in two by the artist in spring, 1938. Formerly collection Louis J. Caldor. G.St.E. Exhibition 1940, No. 20. *Reproduced: GMAP; GMSB*

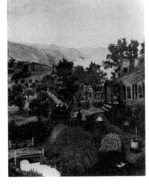

52. *Shenandoah Valley (1861 News of the Battle)*
About 1938. Oilcloth, 20½ x 16¼". Right half of a painting cut in two by the artist in spring, 1938. Collection David Le Boutillier. G.St.E. Exhibition 1940, No. 24

53. *Starry Eyes*
Tin. G.St.E. Exhibition 1940, No. 8

54. *Gypsy Hill Park, Staunton, Va.*
1924. 32 x 14". The Bennington Museum, Bennington, Vt.

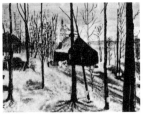

55. *Sugar House Among the Trees*
Collection Harold L. Downey. G.St.E. Exhibition 1940, No. 18

56. *Sugaring Off in Maple Orchard*
Sept. 1940. Canvas, 18⅛ x 24⅛". Inscribed by the artist: "To Mr. Janis." Private collection. *Reproduced: Brundage; GMAP; GMFP; GMSB; Janis; Six of My Favorite Paintings* portfolio. (See plates 52, 55, 63)

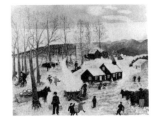

57. *Sugaring Off*
Sept. 1940. 18⅛ x 24⅛". Collection Mrs. Albert D. Lasker. *Reproduced: MLH*

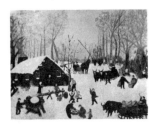

58. *Sugaring Off*
Canvas, 14 x 18¼". Collection Gerald Moses

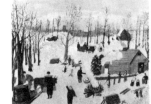

58a. *Sugaring Off*
12 x 16½". Sidney Janis Gallery, New York

59. *The Old Swing at Home*
10 x 12". Formerly collection Louis J. Caldor. (See plate 31)

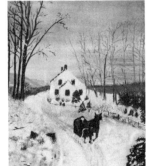

60. *Going to Town*
10¼ x 8¼". Formerly collection Louis J. Caldor

61a. *Trail of the Lonesome Pine*
About 1929. Title inscribed by the artist. Formerly collection James Vandenberg

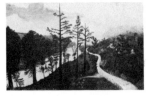

61b. *Trail of the Lonesome Pine*
Reverse of the above

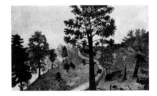

62. *The Burning of Troy*
About 1939. 9 x 11¼". Formerly collection Louis J. Caldor. G.St.E. Exhibition 1940, No. 13. (See plate 38)

63. *Turkey in the Straw*
11½ x 13½". Signed by the artist in 1955. Collection Mr. and Mrs. Joseph Kelly Vodrey. G.St.E. Exhibition 1940, No. 26. *Reproduced: GMFP.* (See plate 30)

64. *Catching the Turkey*
Nov. 1940. 12 x 16". Formerly collection Louis J. Caldor. (See plate 64)

65. *Turkeys in the Snow*
1940 or 1941. c. 9 x 11". Clare J. Hoffman, Inc., Toledo, Ohio

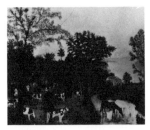

66a. *[Untitled] Grazing Cattle, Early Fall*
Early 1920s. Glass, 15¾ x 17½". The Bennington Museum, Bennington, Vt.

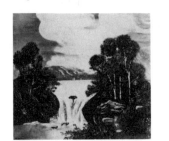

66b. *[Untitled] Waterfall*
Reverse of the above

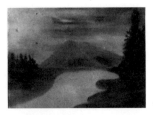

67. *[Untitled] Landscape*
About 1929. Glass, small. Signed later. Formerly collection James Vandenberg

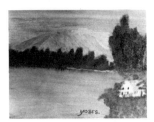

68. *[Untitled] Landscape*
About 1929. Glass, small. Signed later. Collection Mrs. Benjamin Harrison Namm

69. *[Untitled] Scottish Scene*
About 1940(?). Collection Mrs. M.R. Shook

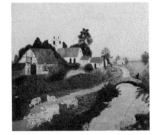

70. *The Village by the Brookside*
12 x 14". Formerly collection Louis J. Caldor. G.St.E. Exhibition 1940, No. 32

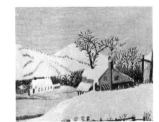

71. *Village in Winter*
8 x 10". Formerly collection Louis J. Caldor. G.St.E. Exhibition 1940, No. 5

72. *The Waterfalls*
14 x 22". Originally painted on reverse of *On the Road to Greenwich* (Catalogue No. 26); the heavy cardboard was later separated. Formerly collection Louis J. Caldor. G.St.E. Exhibition 1940, No. 27B. (See plate 29)

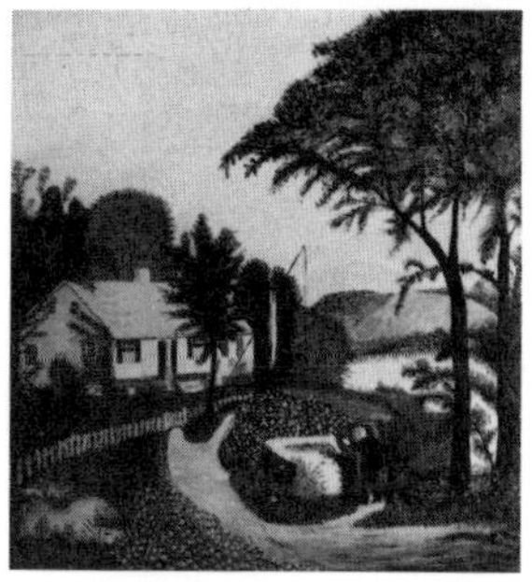

73. *At the Old Well*
14 x 14″. Formerly collection Louis J. Caldor. G.St.E. Exhibition 1940, No. 31

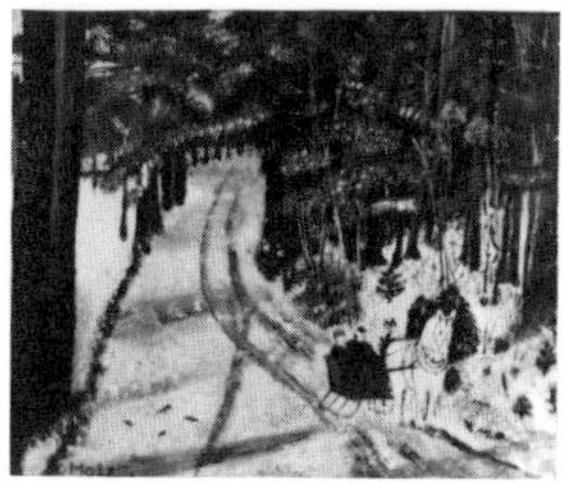

74. *A Winter Sleigh Ride*
8¼ x 10¼″. Title inscribed by the artist on reverse. Formerly collection Louis J. Caldor. G.St.E. Exhibition 1940, No. 3 ("The Old Red Sleigh")

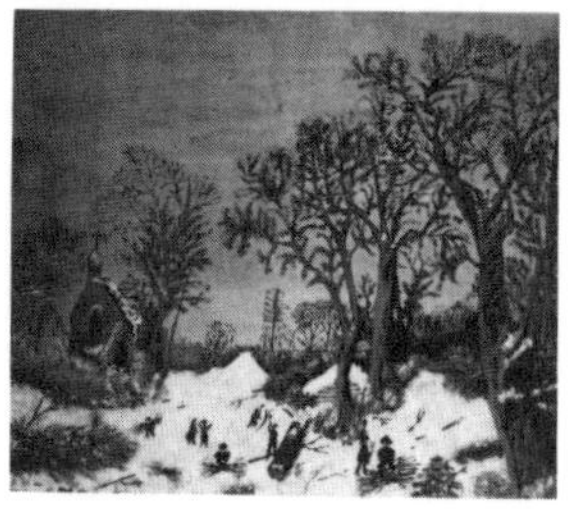

75. *Chopping Wood for the Minister*
10 x 11¾″. Formerly collection Louis J. Caldor

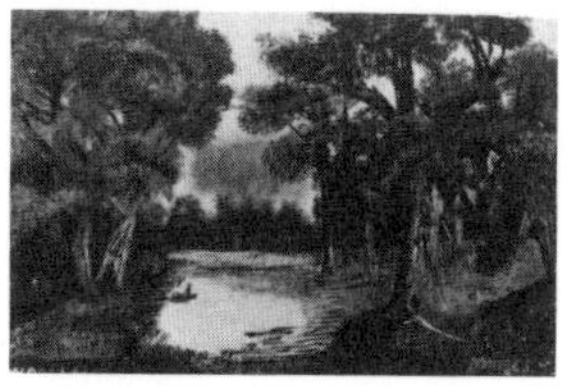

76. *Woodland*
Glass, 6⅞ x 9″. Title inscribed by the artist. Formerly collection Louis J. Caldor

ABOUT 1941

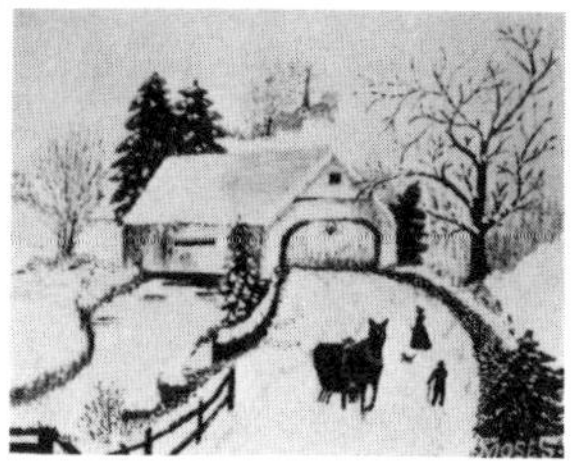

77. *The Old Covered Bridge*
8⅝ x 10⅝″. The Wadsworth Atheneum, Hartford, Conn. Gift of Mr. and Mrs. Andrew G. Carey

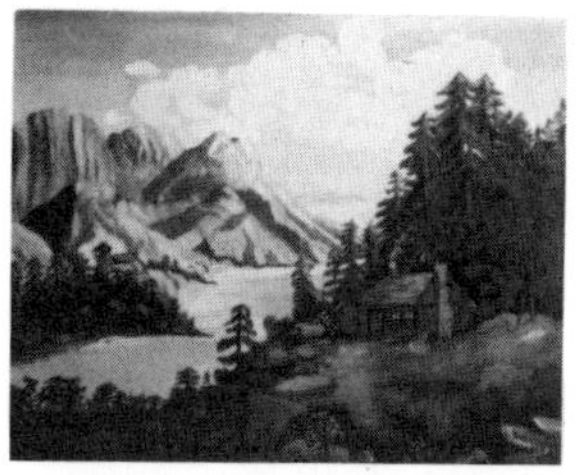

78. *Home in the Lodge*
1941 or earlier. 18¾ x 23¾″. Collection Mrs. Hugh W. Moses

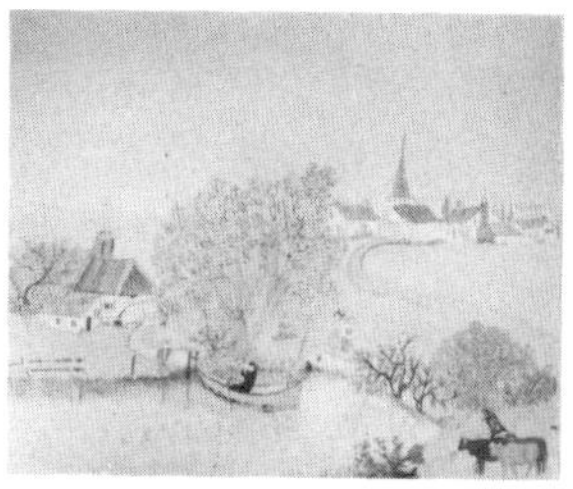

79. *Ireland*
16 x 20″. Collection Baron Frederick L. von Soosten

80. *Kinloch Rannoch, Perthshire, Scotland*
9½ x 11¼″

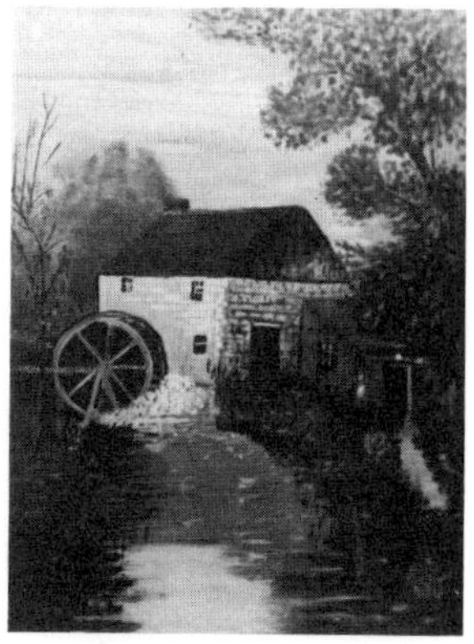

81. *The Old Blue Mill*
1941 or earlier. 10¼ x 8″. Collection Marguerite F. McNally

82. *The Old Brown Mill*
Collection Ernest W. Meuser

83. *Missouri*
Collection Mr. and Mrs. John Chemidlin

84. *Moonlight*
Collection Mr. and Mrs. John Chemidlin

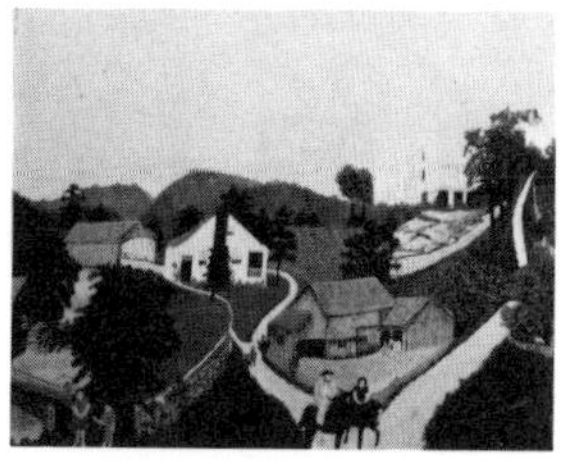

85. *Myer's Castle, Whitehall, N.Y.*
Collection Mrs. Martin M. Janis

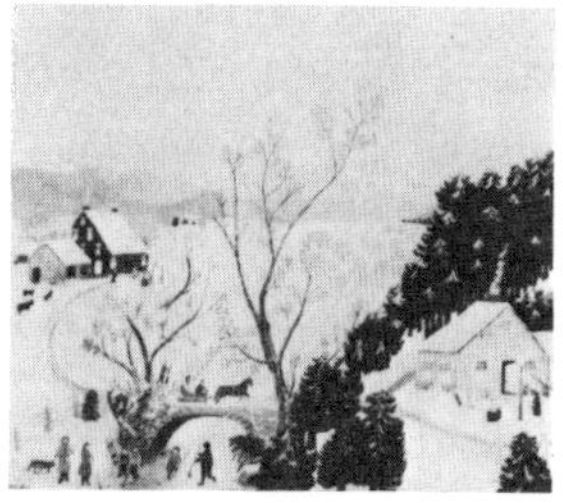

86. *Over the Bridge Through the Snow, to Grandmother's House We Go, on Thanksgiving Day in the Morning*
19 x 23″. Collection Cyrus L. Fulton

87. *Over the River to Grandma's House*
18 x 30″. *Reproduced:* GMSB. (See plate 47)

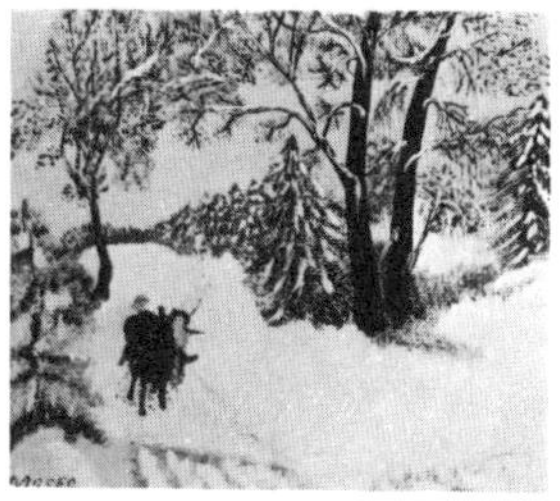

88. *Deep Snows*
8 x 10″. Collection Thomas McDermott

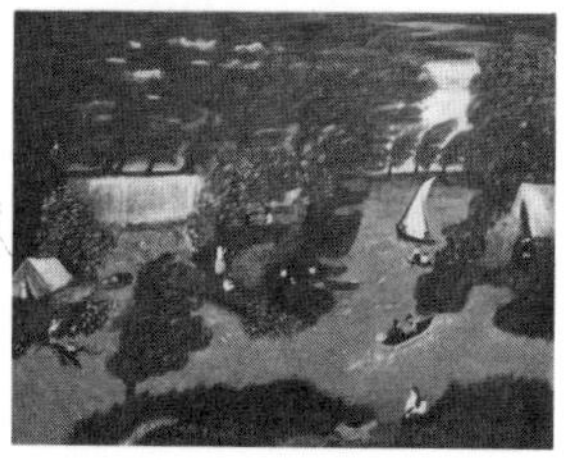

89. *Storm in Camp*
19 x 25″. Collection Eleanor Potter

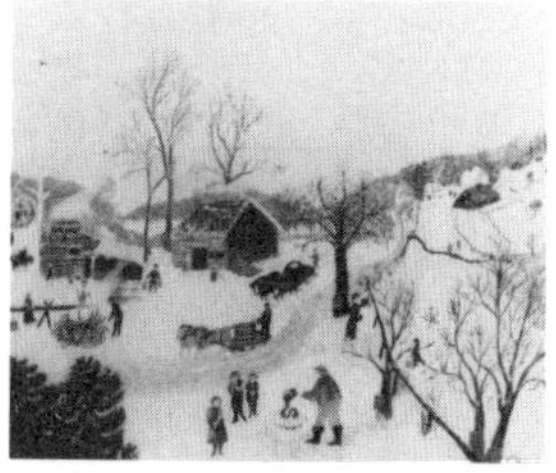

90. *Sugaring Off*
16 x 20″. Parke-Bernet Sale No. 2326, Jan. 27, 1965, No. 67

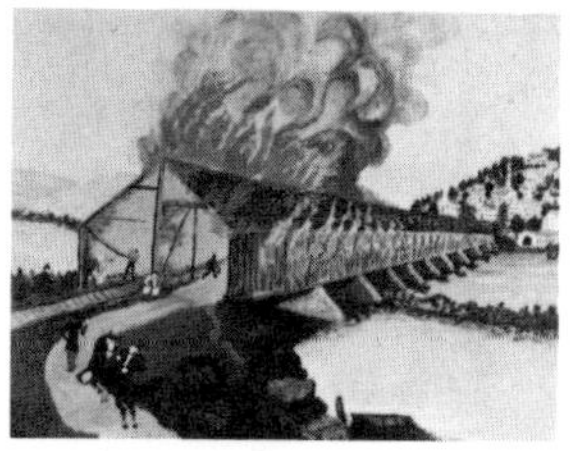

90a. *Burning of Troy Bridge*
Canvas, 12 x 16″. Sidney Janis Gallery, New York

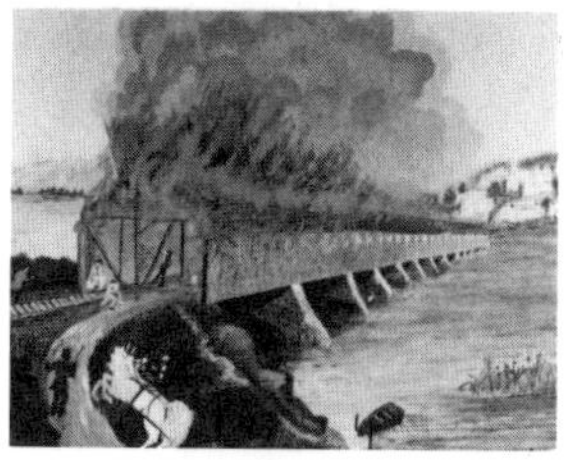

90b. *Burning of Troy Bridge*
12¼ x 16″. Sidney Janis Gallery, New York

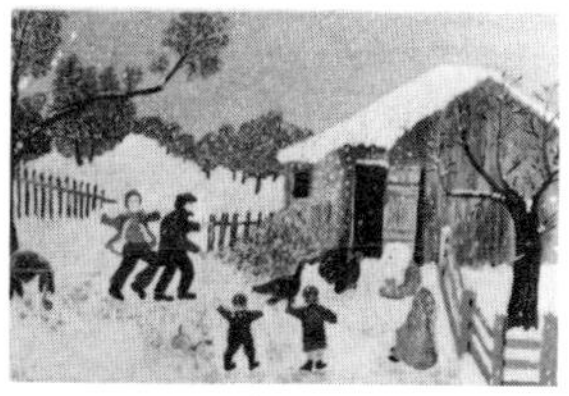

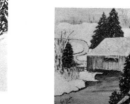

90c. *Thanksgiving Turkey*
8 x 12″. Sidney Janis Gallery, New York

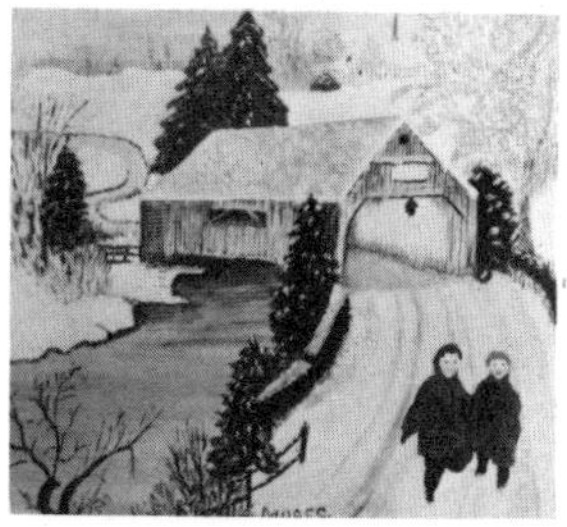

91. *[Untitled] Covered Bridge in Winter*
10¼ x 10½″. RB p. 4. Formerly collection Louis J. Caldor

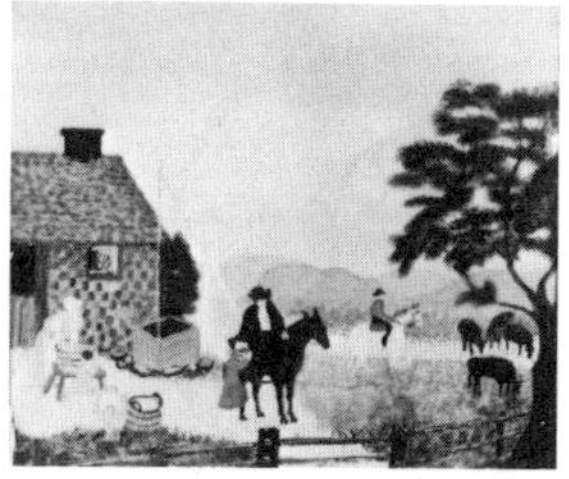

92. *[Untitled] Woman Washing*
9¼ x 11¼″. RB p. 3 listed as "Thirsty." Formerly collection Louis J. Caldor

1941

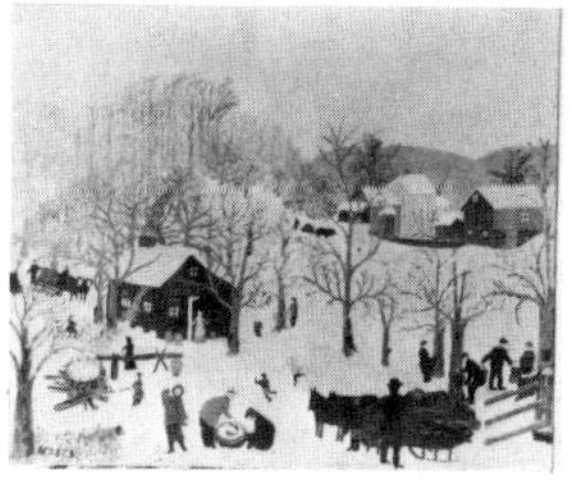

93. *Maple Sugar Orchard*
Formerly collection Thomas J. Watson

94. *Old Oaken Bucket*
25 x 31″. RB p. 10 "The Old Oaking Bucket." Collection John N. Irwin II. New York State Prize, Syracuse, 1941. (See plate 33)

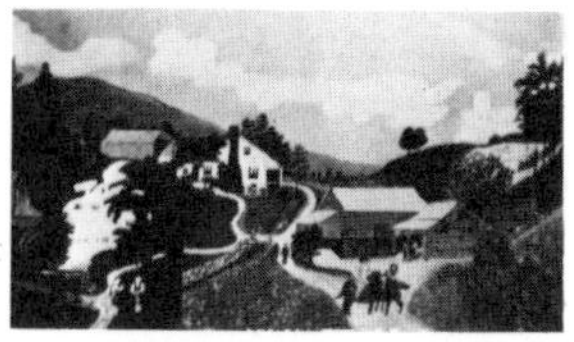

95. *Myer's Castle, Whitehall, N.Y.* (M. 115)
14½ x 26½″. RB p. 3. Collection Rose Gordon. Parke-Bernet Sale No. 2199, May 15, 1963, No. 44

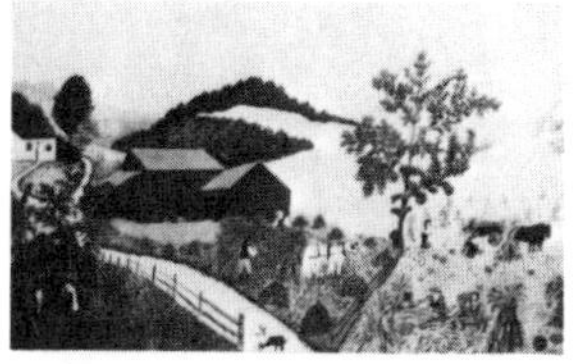

96. *Autumn in Canastota* (M. 116)
14½ x 26½″. RB p. 3. Collection Rose Gordon. Parke-Bernet Sale No. 2199, May 15, 1963, No. 43

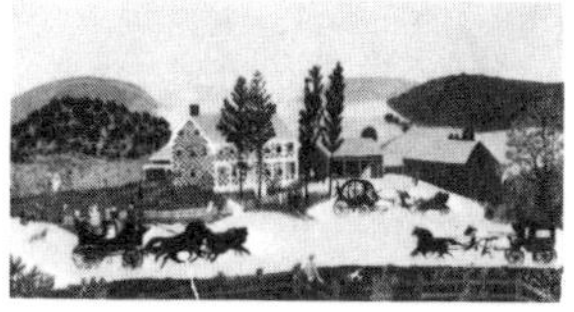

97. *After the Wedding* (M. 117)
17½ x 30″. RB p. 3 "The Old Checkered House." The Shelburne Museum, Shelburne, Vt. Sale of Hiram J. Halle Estate, Pound Ridge, N.Y., Oct. 12, 1961, No. 1716. O. Rundle Gilbert, auctioneer

98. *The Old Southern Home*
RB p. 3

99. *My Hills of Home*
17¾ x 36″. Memorial Art Gallery of the University of Rochester, N.Y. Marion Stratton Gould Fund. (See plate 56)

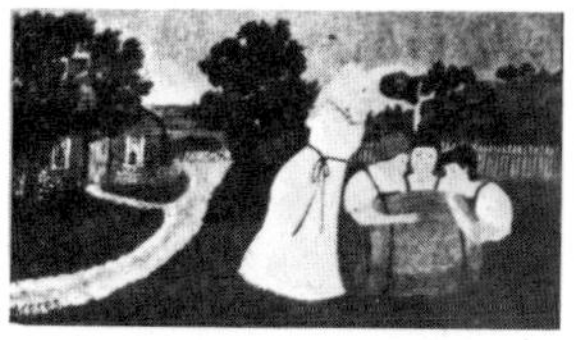

100. *The Spirit of the Cider Barrel*
Canvas, 7¼ x 12½″. RB p. 3

101. *Kinloch Rannoch*
RB p. 2. Collection the Reverend King

102. *The Old Brown Mill by Moonlight*
13 x 16″. RB p. 2. Collection Dr. Mildred Pine Harter

103. *Maple Sugar Orchard*
RB p. 2. Collection Mrs. Wallace

104. *The Old Old Mill*
RB p. 2. Collection Mrs. S. H. Rudd

105. *Over the Bridge and Home*
RB p. 2. Formerly collection Victoria Allen

106. *The Pheasants*
8 x 10″. RB p. 2. Collection Mrs. John T. Kelly

107. *The Rose Garden*
RB p. 2. Formerly collection Mrs. David Armstrong

108. *The Old Village Street*
RB p. 2. Collection Mrs. Schifer

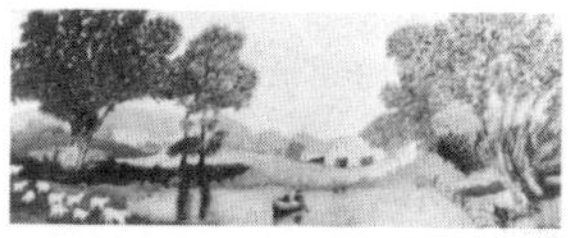

109. *Sheep Pasture* (M. 2010; *sic*)
8½ x 21½″. RB p. 3. Formerly collection Louis J. Caldor

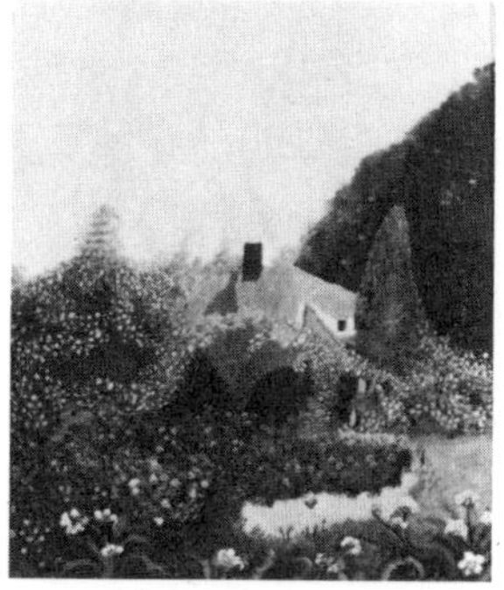

110. *Rose Garden* (M. 202)
11¼ x 9¾″. Collection Mrs. Kenneth F. Clark

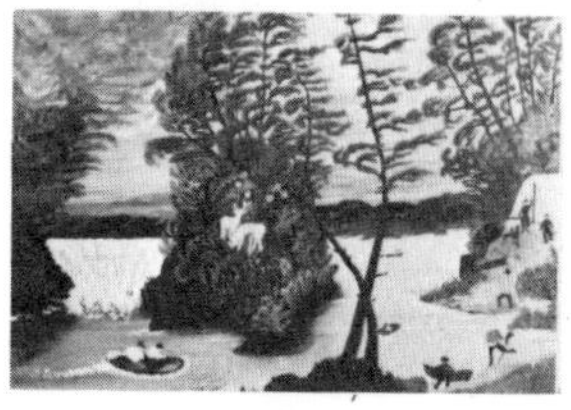

111. *The Coming Storm in Camp* (M. 204)
15 x 20″. RB p. 3 "Before the Storm on the Lake." Formerly collection Louis J. Caldor

112. *All Is Still* (M. 207)
14½ x 19½". Collection Marjorie Fitzgerald

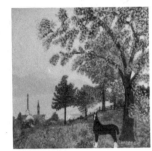

113. *Total* (M. 208)
11¾ x 12⅛". RB p. 4 "Totles Pasture." Formerly collection Louis J. Caldor

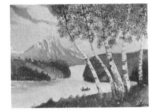

114. *The White Birches* (M. 212)
10½ x 14". Collection Mrs. John Wilson

115. *The Old Blue Mill* (M. 213)
9¾ x 14". Collection Mrs. Jay Williams

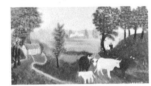

116. *When the Cows Come Home* (M. 214)
8¼ x 15¼". RB p. 4. Formerly collection Louis J. Caldor

117. *Cold Morning on the Lake* (M. 216)
Small. Collection Judge Ray Braswell

118. *A Cold Morning on the Pond* (M. 220)
8 x 10". Collection Timothy J. Cooney

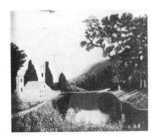

119. *The Church by the Pond* (M. 2211; *sic*)
12 x 14". Parke-Bernet Sale No. 1395, Jan. 7, 1953, No. 101 ("The Church by the Lake")

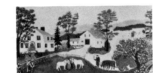
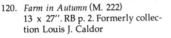

120. *Farm in Autumn* (M. 222)
13 x 27". RB p. 2. Formerly collection Louis J. Caldor

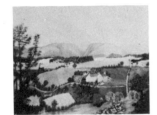
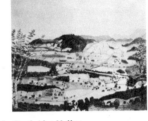

121. *Belvedere in the Shenandoah Valley* (M. 223)
c. 20 x 26". *Reproduced:* Parke-Bernet Sale No. 2185, April 11, 1963, No. 134

122. *Home Sweet Home* (M. 227)
Small. RB p. 3. Collection Florence Teets

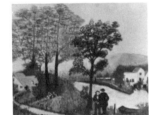

123. *A Debate* (M. 240)
12 x 15¾". Title inscribed by the artist. RB p. 4. Formerly collection Louis J. Caldor

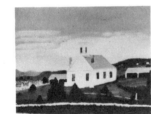

124. *King Church* (M. 240)
December. 10¼ x 12½". Collection Sharon R. Curry and Carol R. Wakefield

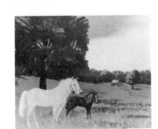

125. *Topsy* (M. about 240)
13 x 15¾". Collection Sharon R. Curry and Carol R. Wakefield

126. *Old Covered Bridge, Waite's Corners*
December. Canvas, 8 x 12". Collection Josephine Ferris

1942

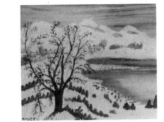

127. *Cambridge Valley*
Collection Mainbocher

128. *Covered Bridge*
Collection Mrs. Stuart Peabody

129. *Anna Mary Robertson Moses Birthplace, No. 1*
RB p. 3 "sold to Mr. Janis"

130. *Over the Bridge to Grandma's House*
17 x 26". *Reproduced:* GMAP; *Harper's Bazaar*, Dec. 1942

131. *Sugaring Off*
c. 23 x 27". Collection Mrs. Enoch Perkins

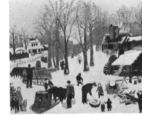

132. *Sugaring Off*
17 x 21". Collection H. Ralston

133. *A House by the Flat Wood* (M. 199)
Jan. 20. 8 x 10". Collection Dr. and Mrs. Willard H. Sweet, Jr.

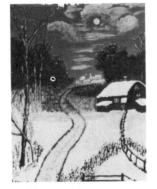

134. *On the Back Road* (M. 29)
Jan. 29. 10 x 8". Collection Mrs. Howard Harrington

135. *Home Among the Snow Hills* (M. 9)
Feb. 9. 8 x 10". Formerly collection Louis J. Caldor

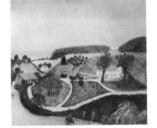

136. *Washington County*
Feb. 30. 16 x 20"

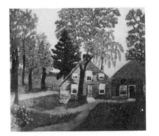

137. *The Old Kenyon Home*
March. 8½ x 10½". Collection George Cothran. Parke-Bernet Sale No. 2169, Feb. 20, 1963, No. 41

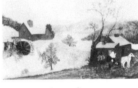

138. *Lake Senepp [Sunapee]*
March. 18½ x 22¾". Private collection

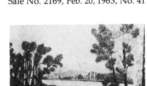
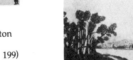
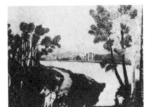

139. *The Checkered House of 1850, Cambridge, N.Y.*
March. 12 x 20". Parke-Bernet Sale No. 2185, April 11, 1963, No. 101 ("The Checkard of 1850, Cambridge, N.Y.")

140. *The Old Grist Mill in Shenandoah*
March. 18 x 18". Title on label: "The Old Grist Mill in Shandoah." Sold through Vigeveno, Los Angeles

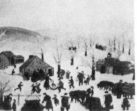

141. *Maple Orchard*
April. 18 x 23". Collection Ernst Kober. *Reproduced:* Parke-Bernet Sale No. 2326, Jan. 27, 1965, No. 105

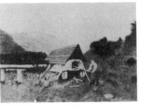

142. *Old Oven* (M. 248)
April 22. Small. Collection Martha Guy

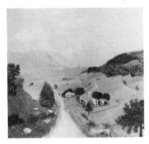

143. *Which Way* (M. 249)
April 23. 9¾ x 15". RB p. 20. Collection David H. Griffin

144. *The Old Checkered House in 1860*
May 20. 16 x 20". Private collection. (See plates 54, 60)

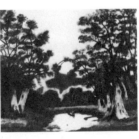

145. *Wood Lane* (M. 260)
May 26. 9½ x 11½". The Fine Arts Gallery of San Diego, Calif. Bequest of Mr. Earle W. Grant, 1971

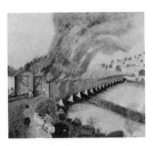

146. *Burning of Troy, 1862* (M. 200)
13 x 15". *Reproduced:* Parke-Bernet Sale No. 2251, Jan. 29, 1964, No. 36

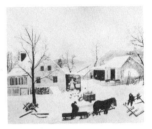

147. *November* (M. 203)
June 10. 18½ x 22¾". Collection John Crawford

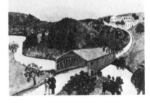

148. *Vermont* (M. 205)
June 12. 13½ x 13". Collection Mr. and Mrs. Thomas G. Vitez

149. *In Camp* (M. 208)
14 x 20". Parke-Bernet Sale No. 2751, Oct. 24, 1968

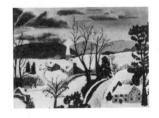

150. *An Old Covered Bridge* (M. 209)
17¾ x 21¾". Collection W.P. Hutchison. *Reproduced:* Parke-Bernet Sale No. 2382, Nov. 18, 1965, No. 102

151. *In Days Gone By* (M. 211)
June 23. 16 x 20". RB p. 20. Collection Mr. and Mrs. R. Yamin. *Reproduced:* Parke-Bernet Sale No. 2024, March 23, 1961, No. 120

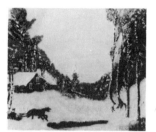

152. *Silvery Brook* (M. 224)
10½ x 12½''. The Joseph H. Hirshhorn Museum and Sculpture Garden, Smithsonian Institution, Washington, D.C. Parke-Bernet Sale No. 2017, Feb. 16, 1961, No. 93

153. *Thanksgiving Turkey* (M. 224)
20⅜ x 12¼''. Collection the late Allen Eaton

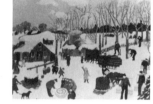

154. *Pouring the Wax* (M. 225)
20¼ x 26''. RB p. 4. Collection Arthur Temple

155. *In the Snow Hills*
June 30. 9½ x 11½''. Collection Dr. and Mrs. Willard H. Sweet, Jr.

155a. *Thanksgiving, Nov. 27* (M. 220)
July 4. 7½ x 9½''. Collection Mrs. Kenneth F. Clark

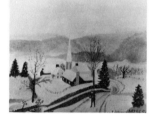

156. *It's Winter in the Valley* (M. 228)
July 12. 10¾ x 12¾''. Collection Jack S. Josey

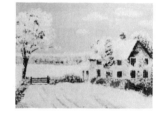

157. *Frosty Morning* (M. 225)
July 16. 10¼ x 13¼''. Collection Mrs. Hugh W. Moses

158. *It's Haying Time* (M. 226)
July 17. 21½ x 26''. Hammer Galleries, New York. *Reproduced:* Arthur Jaffe. (See plate 61)

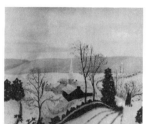

159. *Down the Valley* (M. 229)
July 25. 10 x 12''. Collection Mrs. Lawrence D. Stanley

160. *The Childhood Home of Anna Mary Robertson Moses* (M. 229)
14 x 28''. Title inscribed by the artist. RB p. 3: ''Anna Mary Robertson Moses Birthplace No. 2.'' Formerly collection Louis J. Caldor. (See plate 1)

161. *So Cold* (M. 230)
8¾ x 10¾''. Parke-Bernet Sale No. 2017, Feb. 16, 1961, No. 78

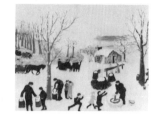

162. *Can a Duck Swim?* (M. 237)
July 22. 15¼ x 18½''. RB p. 17. Sold through Vigeveno, Los Angeles

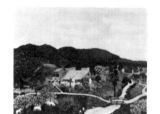

163. *Across the Lowlands* (M. 233)
July 25

164. *Cambridge Valley* (M. 234)
July 25. 23½ x 27''. (See plate 69)

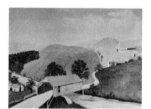

165. *Sugaring Off* (M. 238)
Aug. 8. 19¼ x 23¼''. Collection Jack S. Josey

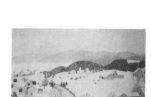

166. *Sugaring Off* (M. 239)
Aug. 8. 9 x 12''. Formerly collection Mrs. Kenneth F. Clark

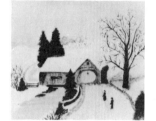

167. *An Old Covered Bridge* (M. 240)
Aug. 8. 9¾ x 12''. Collection Mrs. Kenneth F. Clark

168. *Cambridge Valley* (M. 246)
Aug. 17. 21 x 25''. Collection Carter Burden

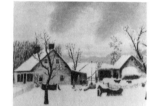

169. *The Home of Hezekiah King* (M. 248)
Aug. 20. 20 x 28''

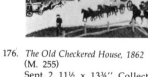

170. *The Old Covered Bridge* (M. 280)
Aug. 28. 14¼ x 20''. Parke-Bernet Sale No. 1330, March 27, 1952, No. 201; Sale No. 1466, Nov. 12, 1953, No. 64

171. *December* (M. 252)
Aug. 28. 8 x 10''. Collection Mrs. Richard B. Leake III

172. *December* (M. 251)
Aug. 29. 8 x 11''. Collection Henry P. Allen

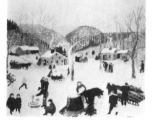

173. *To Grandma's House We Go on Thanksgiving Day* (M. 253)
Sept. 1. 16 x 22¾''. Collection R.J. Hatfield

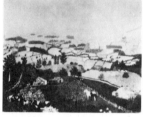

174. *Hoosick Valley* (M. 253)
Sept. 2. 15¼ x 20½''. Galerie St. Etienne, New York

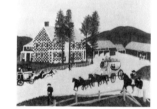

175. *December* (M. 254)
Sept. 2. 11¾ x 13½''. Collection Mrs. Kenneth F. Clark

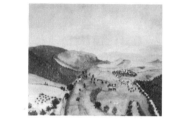

176. *The Old Checkered House, 1862* (M. 255)
Sept. 2. 11½ x 13¾''. Collection Mrs. Kenneth F. Clark

177. *Aunt Polly's Home* (M. 256)
Sept. 9. 11½ x 16''

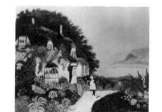

178. *By the Sea* (M. 257)
Sept. 9. 11½ x 15¾''. Sold through Vigeveno, Los Angeles

179. *In Maple Sugar Time* (M. 257)
September 14. 18 x 20¼''. Collection David H. Griffin

179a. *The Home of Mrs. Clark, Cambridge* (M. 267)
About September. Collection Mrs. Kenneth F. Clark

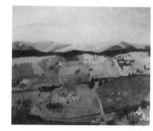

180. *Upper Cambridge Valley* (M. 268)
Oct. 7. 19½ x 23½''. RB p. 18. *Reproduced:* Parke-Bernet Sale No. 1976, May 18, 1960, No. 70; Sale of May 23, 1961, No. 86

181. *Black Horses*
Autumn, 1942. 20 x 24''. RB p. 18 ''Lower Cambridge Valley.'' Collection Otto Kallir. *Reproduced:* GMAP; Hallmark; MLH (German edition); Oldenbourg. (See plates 35, 36)

182. *Mt. Nebo* (M. 274)
Oct. 17. Sold through ABAC, New York

183. *When the Leaves Fall* (M. 278)
Oct. 21. RB p. 18. Sold through ABAC, New York

184. *Grand* (M. 271)
RB p. 18 ''Grand No. 2.'' Formerly collection Fred E. Robertson

185. *Roses* (M. 277)
9½ x 12''. RB p. 18. Collection Mrs. Serge Darmory

186. *December* (M. 300)
Oct. 28. Collection Mrs. Paul Green

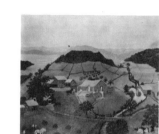

187. *Home of Hezekiah King, 1776* (M. 302)
Nov. 6. 25 x 29¼''. RB p. 18. *Reproduced:* GMAP; Hallmark; Parke-Bernet Sale No. 3285, Dec. 8, 1971, No. 81

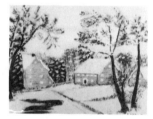

188. *Belvedere, 1890* (M. 303)
Nov. 6. 23 x 26¾''. Inscribed by the artist: ''In Remembrance of Belvidere.'' RB p. 18. Galerie St. Etienne, New York

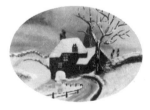

189. *Pennsylvania* (M. 304)
Nov. 7. 8 x 10''. RB p. 18. Parke-Bernet Sale No. 2245, Jan. 9, 1964, No. 79

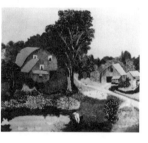

190. *Sunset Beyond Old Mill* (M. 305)
Nov. 8. 6½ x 8½'' (oval). RB p. 18. Collection Marguerite F. McNally

191. *Cold So Cold* (M. 305)
Nov. 14. 9 x 11''. RB p. 18. Collection Louis Held

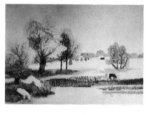
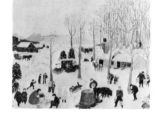

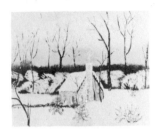

192. *Night Is Coming* (M. 306)
Nov. 17. 8 x 10". RB p. 18

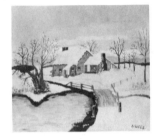

193. *Aunt Polly's Home* (M. 311)
Nov. 24. 11⅝ x 13¾". RB p. 18.
Collection Lee A. Doerr

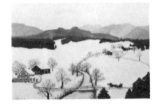

194. *Over the River to Grandma's House on Thanksgiving Day* (M. 315)
Dec. 1. 13¼ x 19¾". RB p. 18. Collection Mr. and Mrs. Robert Guy Williams

195. *A Dream*
Dec. 2. RB p. 18

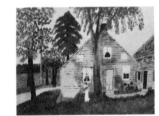

196. *Old Kenyon Home* (M. 316)
Dec. 3. 6¼ x 8". RB p. 18 "The Old Kynon House." Collection Margaret Foster

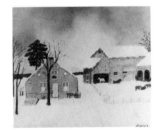

197. *A Home in the Country* (M. 319)
11 x 13". RB p. 19. The Bennington Museum, Bennington, Vt.

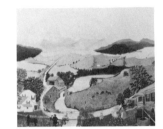

198. *Childhood Memories* (M. 320)
24 x 30". Collection H. Ralston

199. *To Grandmother's House We Go*
December. Collection Mrs. Malcolm MacGruer

200. *Bought with a Prize*
About December. c. 20 x 24". RB p. 19, listed in sequence between a known M. 318 and M. 321

200a. *Merry Christmas* (M. 321)
Dec. 14. 5 x 12". RB p. 19. Collection Mrs. Walter Shea

201. *The Blue Sledge* (M. 324)
Dec. 24. 10 x 12". RB p. 19. Collection Mrs. John T. Kelly

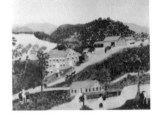

202. *Haunted House* (M. 325)
22 x 26". RB p. 19. Collection R.W. Meyer

203. *The Dear Deers*
December. 12 x 9½". RB p. 19 "My Dears Deers." Collection J.H. Smith, Jr.

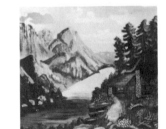

204. *Adirondacks*
About 1942. 14¼ x 17". Collection Bruce McCart

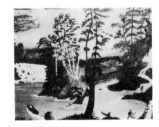

205. *Camping*
About 1942. 16 x 20". Private collection

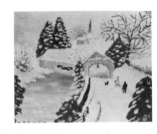

206. *Covered Bridge*
About 1942. 7 x 9". Collection Marguerite F. McNally

207. *Grazing*
About 1942. 10 x 12¼". Sold through ABAC, New York

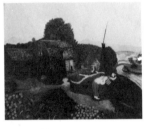

208. *In Olden Times*
About 1942. Collection Mrs. Martin M. Janis

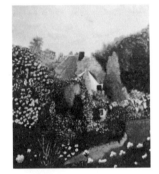

209. *The Rose Garden*
About 1942. 12 x 9". Collection Helen Woodruff

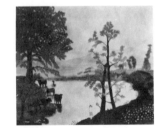

210. *Spring*
About 1942(?). 18½ x 22⅞". Collection Mrs. Cass Canfield

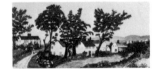

211. *Village Street*
About 1942. 9 x 21". Sold through Vigeveno, Los Angeles

212. *Grandma Moses's Birthplace*
About 1942 (?). Formerly collection Mary C. Canfield

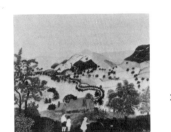

213. *Down in Shenandoah*
About 1942(?). Sold through Vigeveno, Los Angeles

1943

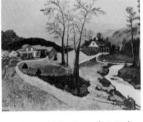

214. *Catching the Thanksgiving Turkey* (M. 327)
Jan. 25. 20 x 24". RB p. 19. Collection Dorothy Schiff

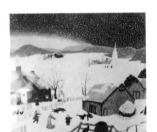

215. *Sycamore Farm* (M. 328)
Jan. 25. 18 x 24". RB p. 19. Collection Aline Barnsdale

216. *The Daughter's Homecoming* (M. 329)
Jan. 25. 19¾ x 23½". RB p. 19. *Reproduced:* Christie, Manson & Woods, London, Sale of Feb. 25, 1972, No. 195. (See plate 67)

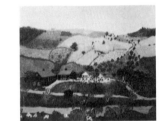

217. *Home of Hezekiah King, 1776* (M. 331)
Jan. 25. 19 x 23½". RB p. 19. Phoenix Art Museum, Ariz.

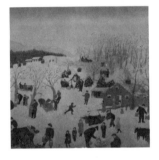

218. *The Home of John Brown* (M. 332)
Jan. 25. 16 x 20". RB p. 19. *Reproduced:* Parke-Bernet Sale No. 3285, Dec. 8, 1971, No. 80

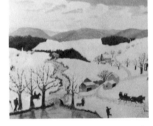

219. *Sugaring Off* (M. 334)
Feb. 12. 19 x 23". RB p. 19. Formerly collection Karl Nierendorf

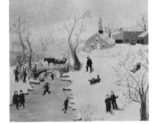

220. *The Trappers I* (M. 335)
Feb. 12. c. 20 x 24". RB p. 19. Sold through Vigeveno, Los Angeles

221. *The Trappers II* (M. 336)
Feb. 12. 19¾ x 24". RB p. 19. Collection Frank Jay Gould. *Reproduced:* Brundage; GMAP

222. *The Daughter's Homecoming* (M. 337)
Feb. 12. 20 x 24". RB p. 20. Collection Herbert Segerman

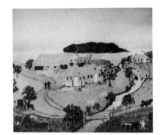

223. *Home of Hezekiah King* (M. 339)
Feb. 12. 19 x 23¾". RB p. 19 "Home of Hezekiah King 1800." Collection William L. Elkins

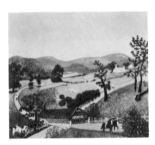

224. *Missouri* (M. 340)
Feb. 12. 20 x 23¾". RB p. 19. Galerie St. Etienne, New York. *Reproduced:* GMAP ("Sunday—The Covered Bridge")

225. *Thanksgiving Day* (M. 341)
Feb. 15. Small. RB p. 19. Collection Cleveland Dodge

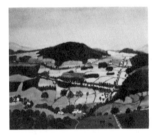

226. *Cambridge Valley in Summer* (M. 329)
Feb. 20. 19¾ x 23¾". RB p. 19. *Reproduced:* Parke-Bernet Sale No. 1711, Nov. 20, 1956, No. 65

227. *Cambridge Valley Looking North* (M. 330)
Collection Richard Mason

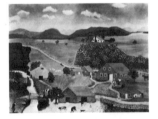

228. *The Old Oaken Bucket* (M. 333)
Feb. 20. 24 x 30". New York State Historical Association, Cooperstown

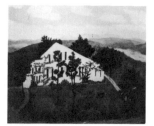

229. *Mt. Nebo* (M. 334)
20¼ x 24". *Reproduced:* Parke-Bernet Sale No. 2072, Dec. 13, 1961, No. 59

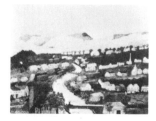

230. *Village of Hoosick Falls* (M. 336)
18 x 24". RB p. 20(?). *Reproduced:* Parke-Bernet Sale No. 1904, May 6, 1959, No. 81

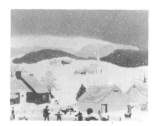

231. *Catching the Thanksgiving Turkey* (M. 338?)
About February. c. 20 x 24". Collection Geralda Pheatt-Hoffman

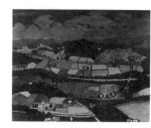

232. *Cambridge Valley* (M. 341 or 343?)
17 x 24". Collection Dr. Howard McKinney

233. *Mineyhaha [Minnehaha] Laughing Water*
February. Large. According to a letter by the artist, painted for her sister

234. *Thanksgiving*
February

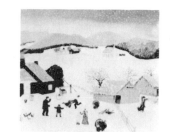

235. *Catching the Thanksgiving Turkey* (M. 342)
March 4. 19½ x 24". RB p. 19. Collection Charles J. Rosenbloom

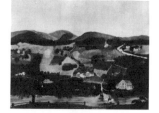

236. *Sunday* (M. 343)
March 4. 12 x 17¾". RB p. 19. Collection Hildegard Bachert

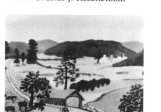

237. *Belvedere, Va.* (M. 344)
March 4. 20 x 26". Sold through Whyte Bookshop & Gallery, Inc., Washington, D.C.

238. *The Old Oaken Bucket* (M. 343)
March 8. 23½ x 30". Collection Hildegard Bachert. *Reproduced:* GMAP; GMSB; Arthur Jaffe; *Town and Country*, April 1, 1945. (See plate 34)

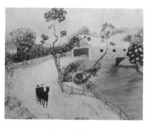

239. *Old Bridge* (M. 344)
March 19. 9½ x 11¾". RB p. 19 "The Old Pink Bridge." Collection Anna Thornton

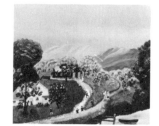

240. *In School Days* (M. 335)
March 22. 18¾ x 22½". RB p. 19. *Reproduced:* Parke-Bernet Sale No. 1466, Nov. 12, 1953, No. 57

241. *Belvedere* (M. 337)
March 24. 20 x 24". Sidney Janis Gallery, New York

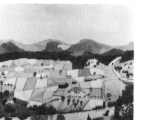

242. *Hezekiah King's Home in Winter* (M. 338)
March 25. 19½ x 23¾". Collection Kenneth L. Isaacs

243. *Over the River to Grandma's House on Thanksgiving* (M. 341)
March 28. 17¾ x 23". Collection Mrs. David Shelly

244. *Lower Cambridge Valley* (M. 344)
March 31. 19¾ x 23¾". Hammer Galleries, New York. (See plate 68)

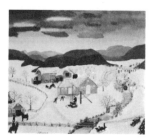

245. *Spring in the Valley* (M. 346)
March. 18 x 24". RB p. 19. Clare J. Hoffman, Inc., Toledo, Ohio. *Reproduced:* Ford

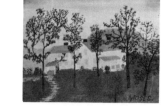

246. *Mt. Nebo* (M. 344 or 347?)
April 12. Small. Collection Mrs. Hugh Dorr

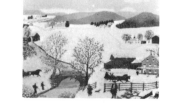

247. *Over the River Through the Snow, to Grandma's House We Go on Thanksgiving Day in the Morning* (M. 345)
April 12. 18¼ x 23¼". Collection Aline Barnsdale

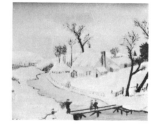

248. *A Day Before Christmas* (M. 350)
April 12. 10 x 12". Collection Mrs. Hugh Dorr

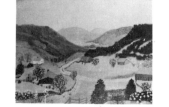

249. *Summer in the Valley* (M. 348)
April 12. 10¾ x 14½". Collection Mrs. Hugh Dorr

250. *[Untitled] A Winter Scene*
April 12. 5 x 6". Collection Mrs. Hugh Dorr

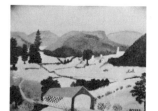

251. *Sunday* (M. 349)
April 13. c. 9 x 12". Collection Mrs. Hugh Dorr

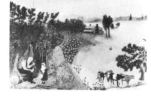

252. *In Days of Thrift* (M. 349)
April. c. 20 x 24". RB p. 20. Collection Mrs. Raymond B. Fosdick

253. *The Old Oaken Bucket* (M. 352)
April 27. 18 x 24". RB p. 20. Collection Fritz Henle

254. *The Old Oaken Bucket in Fall*
April 28. 18 x 24". Sold through Vigeveno, Los Angeles

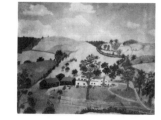

255. *Giving Thanks* (M. 347)
May 4. 18 x 24". RB p. 19

256. *The 15th [or Tenth] of April* (M. 352)
RB. p. 20 dated May 10, 1943

257. *In Klondike* (M. 350)
May 11. Picture of waterfall on reverse. Collection Lew Abramson

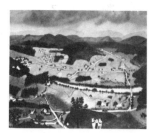

258. *Sycamore Farm* (M. 350)
May 20. 18 x 24". RB p. 20. Collection Ernest A. Gross

259. *Cambridge Valley in Fall* (M. 351)
RB p. 20 dated May 20, 1943

260. *Catching the Thanksgiving Turkey* (M. 353)
May 22. 18½ x 24¼". Private collection. *Reproduced:* Black and Lipman; Brundage; GMAP; MLH. (See plate 62)

261. *Sugaring Off* (M. 353)
RB p. 20 dated May 25, 1943

262. *Planting on Sycamore Farm* (M. 354)
RB p. 20 dated June 2, 1943

263. *Cambridge in May* (M. 355)

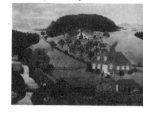

264. *The Old Oaken Bucket* (M. 357)
17 x 23". *Reproduced:* Parke-Bernet Sale No. 2251, Jan. 29, 1964, No. 43

265. *Home of Hezekiah King in 1800, No. 4* (M. 359)
June 26. 23 x 29". RB p. 20. (See plate 72)

266. *The Old Oaken Bucket in Winter* (M. 382)
18 x 24". Collection Mrs. D. Swann

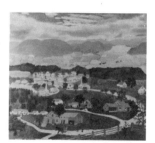

267. *Cambridge Village* (M. 430)
23 x 30". RB p. 21. Collection Professor and Mrs. Hollis Todd

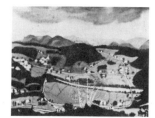

268. *Cambridge and Valley* (M. 430)
July 26. 21½ x 28½". RB p. 21 "Cambridge Valley." Collection Dr. and Mrs. Lawrence A. Funt

269. *First Wagon on Cambridge Pike* (M. 431)
July 26. 26 x 34". RB p. 21 "First Wagon on Cambridge Pike built by Archibald Elexander Robertson with ax saw." Sidney Janis Gallery, New York

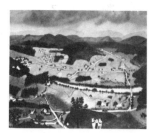

270. *Cambridge Valley* (M. 432)
July 26. 24 x 29¾". RB p. 21 "Cambridge and Valley." Galerie St. Etienne, New York. *Reproduced:* Oldenbourg

271. *Automobile, 1913* (M. 433)
July 26. 17¾ x 21¼". RB p. 21. Formerly collection Artur Schnabel. *Reproduced:* BG. (See plate 42)

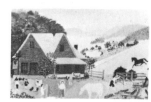

272. *Childhood Memories* (M. 434)
July 26. 17½ x 27". RB p. 21. Sidney Janis Gallery, New York

273. *School Is Out* (M. 435)
July 26. 17¼'' x 26¾''. RB p. 21.
Collection Mrs. J. N. Rosenberg.
(See plate 65)

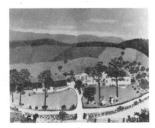

274. *Mt. Nebo in Summer* (M. 440?)
August. c. 20 x 26''. RB p. 21 "Mt.
Nebo in Spring 1920''; also p. 22
"Mt. Nebo in Summer.'' Collection
Mrs. Girdner Provost

275. *Mt. Nebo in Winter* (M. 441)
Aug. 6. 20½ x 26½''. RB p. 21 "Mt.
Nebo in Winter 1921.'' Private col-
lection. *Reproduced:* GMAP; MLH.
(See plate 73)

276. *Sugaring Off* (M. 442)
Aug. 6. 23 x 27''. RB p. 21. Private
collection. *Reproduced:* BG; Brun-
dage; *Christian Science Monitor
Magazine,* Jan. 5, 1946; GMAP;
GMSB; Hallmark; Arthur Jaffe.
(See plate 89)

277. *Over the River* (M. 443)
Aug. 20. Canvas, 34 x 45''. RB p.
21. Collection Mrs. Jack Kapp. (See
plate 224)

278. *Grandma Going to the Big City*
(M. 443)
Aug. 27. 21 x 24''. RB p. 22.
Sidney Janis Gallery, New York.
(See plate 70)

279. *Hoosick Falls* (M. 444)
Aug. 27. RB p. 22 "to Mr. Janis''

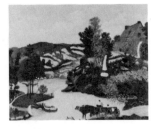

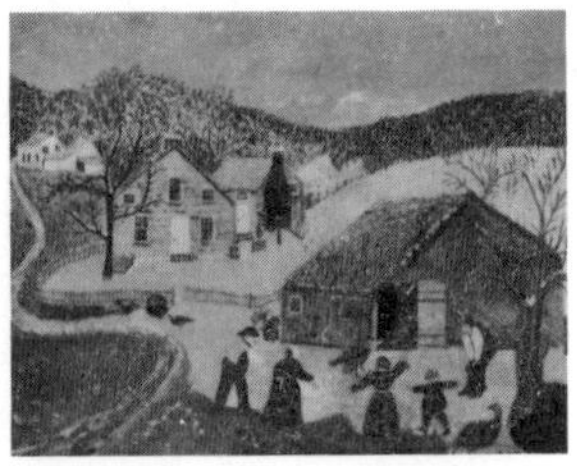

280. *Catching the Thanksgiving Turkey*
(M. 444)
Aug. 27. 14 x 20''. Sold through
Vigeveno, Los Angeles

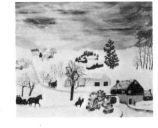

281. *When the Leaves Turn*
August. 18 x 23½''. Collection Mr.
and Mrs. R. Yamin. *Reproduced:*
Parke-Bernet Sale No. 2024, March
23, 1961, No. 122

282. *All Is Still* (M. 445)
Sept. 16. 10¾ x 14½''. RB p. 22.
Collection Mrs. Hugh Dorr

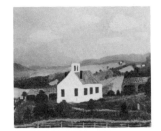

283. *Old King Church* (M. 446)
Sept. 16. 10 x 12''. RB p. 22. Collection Pearl King

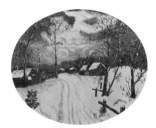

284. *February Moon* (M. 447)
Sept. 16. 7½ x 10'' (oval). RB p. 22.
Collection Mae R. Allen

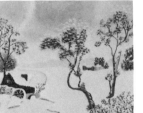

285. *Old Oaken Bucket* (M. 448)
Oct. 1. 25¾ x 29½''. RB p. 22

286. *The Old Oaken Bucket* (M. 451)
Oct. 2. RB p. 23. Formerly collection Mary C. Canfield

287. *December* (M. 449)
Oct. 4. 18½ x 21¾''. RB p. 22. Private collection. (See plate 66)

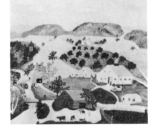

288. *Evening* (M. 453)
Oct. 8. 23¾ x 29¾''. RB p. 23. *Reproduced:* GMSB

289. *Morning* (M. 454)
Oct. 8. RB p. 23. Sold through
ABAC, New York

290. *It Will Snow* (M. 455)
Oct. 11. RB p. 23. Sold through
ABAC, New York

291. *The Truants* (M. 456)
Oct. 13. RB p. 23. Sold through
ABAC, New York

292. *Home of Brother Joe's* (M. 457)
Oct. 13. RB p. 23. Sold through
ABAC, New York

293. *Thanksgiving Turkey* (M. 458)
Oct. 13. 16 x 20''. RB p. 23. The
Metropolitan Museum of Art,
New York. Bequest of Mary Still-
man Harkness, 1950. (See plate 49)

294. *Beautiful Winter* (M. 460)
Oct. 30. RB p.23. Collection Jay
Slade

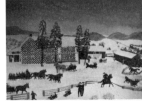

295. *A Mill in Winter* (M. 461)
Oct. 30. RB p. 23. Collection Jay
Slade

296. *Memories of My Girlhood* (M. 461)
Oct. 30. RB p. 23. Collection Jay
Slade

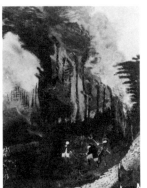

297. *A Fire in the Woods* (M. 462)
Nov. 1. 18¾ x 14½''. RB p. 24. Formerly collection Ala Story. *Reproduced:* GMAP

298. *The Burning of Troy in 1862* (M. 463)
Nov. 1. 19 x 30''. RB p. 24. Galerie
St. Etienne, New York. (See plate
39)

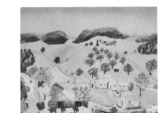

299. *The Old Oaken Bucket in 1800*
(M. 464)
Nov. 1. 22 x 30''. RB p. 24. Collection Mr. Shirley C. Burden. *Reproduced:* Parke-Bernet Sale No.
1330, March 27, 1952, No. 167

300. *Mowing the Swale* (M. 464)
Nov. 1. RB p. 24

301. *Over the River to Grandma's House*
(M. 465)
Nov. 1. RB p. 24

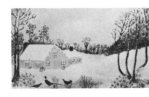

302. *The Old Checkered House in
Cambridge Valley* (M. 466)
Nov. 8. 22 x 30''. RB p. 24 with
"1862'' after title. Collection Mrs.
David Shelly

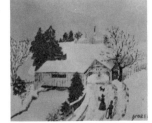

303. *The Old Pink Bridge* (M. 467)
Nov. 8. 8 x 10''. RB p. 24 "The Old
Pink Bridge in Winter.'' Collection
Helen Woodruff

303a. *Spring* (M. 501)
Nov. 8. 15 x 22''. RB p. 24 dated
Nov. 11

304. *Going to Church* (M. 469)
Nov. 9. 9¾ x 7¾''. RB p. 24. Collection Evalyn L. Herrington

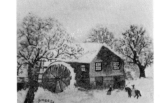

305. *An Old Mill in Winter* (M. 500)
Nov. 10. 8 x 10''. RB p. 24

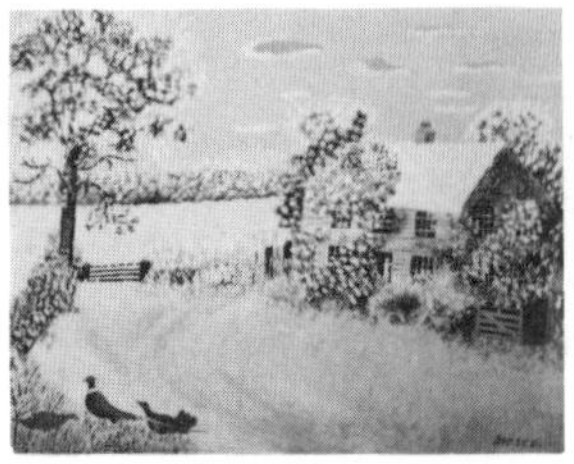

306. *So Cold* (M. 510)
Nov. 20. 11¾ x 14¾''. RB p. 25.
Collection Mr. and Mrs. Henry E.
Roberts

307. *The Sun Goes Down* (M. 513)
Nov. 20. c. 8 x 10'' (oval). RB p. 25.
Collection the Reverend Milton E.
Skiff

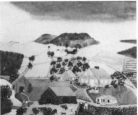

308. *The Pheasants* (M. 514)
Nov. 20. 9 x 16''. RB p. 25 num-
bered 516. Collection Marguerite
F. McNally

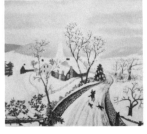

309. *There Is a Long Long Road* (M. 517)
Nov. 22. 11¾ x 13¾''. Collection
Maurice J. Perry

310. *Old Covered Bridge* (M. 518)
Dec. 6. Canvas, 36 x 45''. RB p. 26.
Collection Mrs. Barbara Johnson

311. *Sugaring Off* (M. 517?)
Dec. 6. Canvas, c. 36 x 45''. RB p.
26. Sold through ABAC, New York

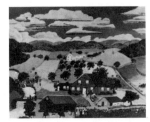

312. *The Hoosick Bridge* (M. 517)
December. 24 x 30''. RB p. 26. Collection Mr. and Mrs. Cyril Jalon

313. *The McDonnell Farm* (M. 518)
Dec. 12. 24 x 30''. RB p. 26. The
Phillips Collection, Washington,
D.C. *Reproduced:* GMAP. (See plate
94)

314. *The Old Blue Mill of 1843* (M. 522)
Dec. 16. 7 x 9''. RB p. 26. Collection Forrest S. White

315. *The Old Mill of 1843* (M. 524)
Dec. 16. 7 x 9''. RB p. 26. Collection Forrest S. White

316. *In Alaska* (M. 524)
Dec. 29. c. 8 x 9''. RB p. 26. Collection Mrs. R.W. Elliott

317. *Checkered House*
Canvas, 36 x 45''. IBM Corpora-
tion, Armonk, N.Y. (See plate 50)

318. *The Old Covered Bridge*
c. 8 x 10''. Formerly collection
Mrs. John C. Clark

319. *The Hoosick Bridge*
Formerly collection Lillian F. Herrington

320. *Over the River to Grandma's House*
Collection Bess C. Lambert

321. *[Untitled] Winter Scene*
7 x 9''. Collection the Reverend
Milton E. Skiff

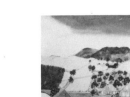

322. *Old Oaken Bucket*
About 1943. 24 x 29½''. Collection
Dr. Charles R. Moore. *Reproduced:*
Parke-Bernet Sale No. 2096, March
21, 1962, No. 53

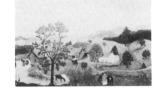

323. *Old Oaken Bucket*
1943. 22 x 28''. Private collection.
Reproduced: New York Graphic
Society silk screen with the title
"The Old Homestead''

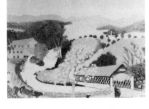

324. *Scenes of My Childhood*
About 1943. 22½ x 36¼''. Collection Mrs. Martin M. Janis

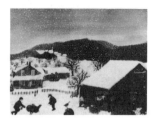

325. *Catching the Thanksgiving Turkey*
About 1943. 12¼ x 16¼''. RB p. 24(?). The Fine Arts Gallery of San Diego, Calif. Gift of Pliny F. Munger, 1958

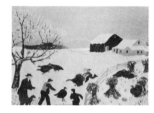

326. *Catching the Thanksgiving Turkey*
About 1943. c. 12 x 16''. Collection Walker Stuart

1944

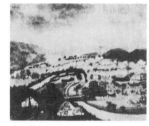

327. *The Village Hoosick Falls*
1943 or 1944. *Reproduced:* Catalogue, Vigeveno, Los Angeles, April 1944

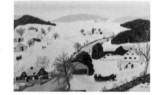

328. *Over the River to Grandma's House on Thanksgiving Day* (M. 525)
Jan. 10. 17 x 26''. RB p. 26

329. *Belvedere, Virginia* (M. 526?)
Jan. 10. RB p. 26. Formerly collection J.B. Neumann

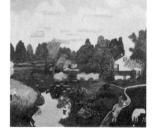

330. *Mowing of the Swamp* (M. 527)
Jan. 10. 18¾ x 21¾''. RB p. 26. *Reproduced:* Parke-Bernet Sale No. 2114, May 16, 1962, No. 63

331. *In the Springtime* (M. 528)
Jan. 10. 24 x 30''. RB p. 27. Formerly collection Mrs. Stephen C. Clark. *Reproduced:* GMAP; Hallmark. (See plate 74)

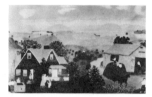

332. *In Summertime* (M. 529)
Jan. 10. 22½ x 36''. RB p. 27. Sold through Vigeveno, Los Angeles

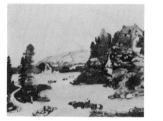

333. *In the Berkshires* (M. 530)
Jan. 12. 24 x 30''. RB p. 27. Collection Ross Peacock. *Reproduced:* Parke-Bernet Sale No. 1904, May 6, 1959, No. 75; Sale No. 2914, Oct. 22, 1969, No. 112; Sale No. 3090, Oct. 15, 1970, No. 98

334. *Early Sugaring Off*
Jan. 15. RB p. 27

335. *Going to Grandma's* (M. 531?)
Jan. 21. RB p. 27

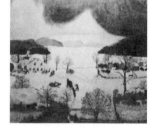

336. *December* (M. 532)
Jan. 21. 20 x 25''. RB p. 27. Private collection

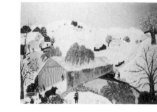

337. *The Old Bridge in the Valley* (M. 533)
Jan. 25. 21½ x 30''. RB p. 27. Collection Sherman Ewing

338. *Sunrise* (M. 534)
Feb. 1. RB p. 27

339. *Pharaoh's Daughter*
Feb. 1. RB p. 27

340. *Mt. Vesuvius* (M. 546)
Feb. 10. RB p. 27

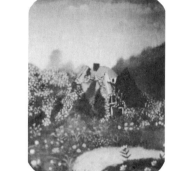

341. *Hoosick Valley* (M. 558)
Feb. 15. Canvas, 36 x 45''. RB p. 27 in a list dated Jan. 15, 1944. Private collection. *Reproduced:* Plaza Art Galleries Sale No. 2963, May 5, 1949, No. 165

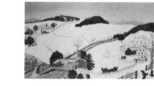

342. *The Last Covered Bridge* (M. 559)
Feb. 15. Canvas, 36 x 45''. RB p. 27 in a list dated Jan. 15, 1944. Private collection. *Reproduced:* Plaza Art Galleries Sale No. 2963, May 5, 1949, No. 164

343. *In the Park* (M. 600)
Feb. 15. Canvas, 36 x 45''. RB p. 27 "Deers in the Park" in a list dated Jan. 15, 1944. Galerie St. Etienne, New York. *Reproduced:* GMAP. (See plate 71)

344. *Brother's Water Wheel* (M. 542)
Feb. 22. RB p. 27. Collection R.M. Beck

345. *Storm in Camp* (M. 545)
Feb. 25. RB p. 27

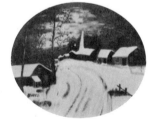

346. *A Winter's Night* (M. 547)
Feb. 25. 8 x 10'' (oval). RB p. 27. Collection W. Perry

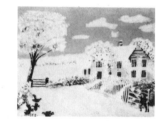

347. *In the Rose Garden* (M. 548)
Feb. 25. 10 x 8''. RB p. 27

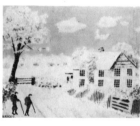

348. *Over the River to Grandma's House* (M. 550)
Feb. 28. c. 20 x 33''. RB p. 28. Clare J. Hoffman, Inc., Toledo, Ohio

349. *The Birthplace of John Brown*
February

350. *Hoosick Falls* (M. 553?)
March 2. RB p. 28

351. *The Old Oaken Bucket in Winter*
March 3. RB p. 28

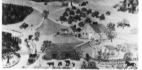

352. *The Old Oaken Bucket* (M. 553)
March 4. 22¼ x 36''. RB p. 28 dated March 1, 1944. Collection Mrs. Stanley Bergerman

353. *Cambridge* (M. 556)
March 4. 19 x 23''. RB p. 28 "Cambridge Washing Co." The Shelburne Museum, Shelburne, Vt. (See plate 75)

354. *Lake Eden, Vermont*
March 15. RB p. 28

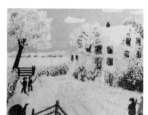

355. *A Frosty Morning* (M. 555)
March 18. 12 x 15¼''. RB p. 28. Parke-Bernet Sale No. 1757, May 8, 1957, No. 88

356. *The Falls of Mineyhaha [Minnehaha]* (M. 544)
March 19. c. 16 x 20''. RB p. 27. Collection Truman Jones

357. *A Frosty Morning*
March 20. RB p. 28 "Mr. Simmons"

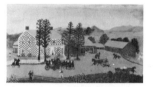

358. *A Frosty Morning, No. 5* (M. 557)
March 20. 11⅞ x 14½''. RB p. 28. Collection Lisa Meyers

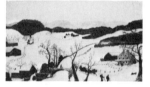

359. *Frosty Morning* (M. 560)
March 22. 12 x 15''. RB p. 28. Parke-Bernet Sale No. 2326, Jan. 27, 1965, No. 112

360. *Frosty Morning*
March 22. RB p. 28

361. *I Got Him*
April 6. Small. RB p. 28 "for Mrs. Slade"

362. *The Old Brown Mill* (M. 561)
April 6. Small. RB p. 28. Collection Jay Slade

363. *The Old Old Mill* (M. 562)
April 6. Small. RB p. 28. Collection Mrs. M.E. Albert

364. *The Old Red Mill in Springtime* (M. 567)
April 6. RB p. 28 "for Mrs. Slade"

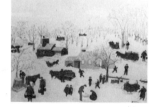

365. *The Old Checkered House in Winter* (M. 568)
April 28. 23 x 42''. RB p. 29. Collection Mr. and Mrs. Bob Hope

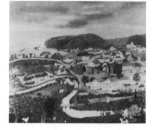

366. *Hoosick Falls* (M. 569)
April 29. 21 x 26''. Sold through Vigeveno, Los Angeles

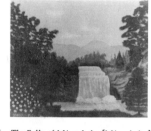

367. *The Old Checkered House*
April 29. 24 x 43''. RB p. 29 numbered 570. *Reproduced:* Christie, Manson & Woods, London, Sale of Feb. 25, 1972, No. 204

368. *Over the River to Grandma's* (M. 563)
April 29. 19¼ x 33¼''. Collection William Nichols. Parke-Bernet Sale No. 1302, Jan. 10, 1952, No. 106

369. *Over the River to Grandma's House on Thanksgiving Day* (M. 571)
April 29. 24 x 34''. RB p. 29 numbered 570. Sold through Vigeveno, Los Angeles

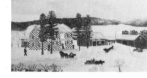

370. *Sugaring Off* (M. 572)
April 29. 24¼ x 33''. RB p. 29. *Reproduced:* Parke-Bernet Sale No. 1481, Jan. 6, 1954, No. 37

371. *The Old Oaken Bucket in Winter* (M. 572)
April 29. 24 x 32¼''. RB p. 29. Sold through ABAC, New York

372. *The Old Oaken Bucket* (M. 573)
April 29. 22½ x 33''. RB p. 29. Collection Dr. F. Norman Nagel

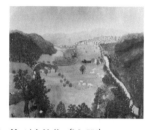
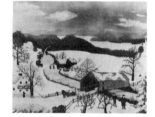

293

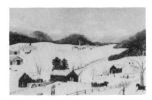

373. *Over the River to Grandma's House* (M. 576)
April 29. 20½ x 33¾". RB p. 29. Collection Arthur Stringari. *Reproduced:* Parke-Bernet Sale No. 2276, April 23, 1964, No. 50

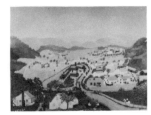

374. *Hoosick Falls, N.Y.* (M. 577)
April 29. 23 x 33". RB p. 29. Southern Vermont Art Center, Manchester

375. *Springtime* (M. 578)
April 29. 20 x 32¾". RB p. 29. Collection Louis Bromfield

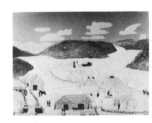

376. *The Old Oaken Bucket of 1760 in Winter* (M. 577)
May. 24 x 34". RB p. 29 dated May 3, 1944

377. *Cambridge* (M. 579?)
May 6. RB p. 29

378. *The Mill on the Lowlands*
May 11. Small. RB p. 29

379. *In Harvest Time* (M. 583)
May 21. 12 x 17". RB p. 29. *Reproduced:* GMAP. (See plate 77)

380. *The Hoosick Bridge* (M. 584)
May 21. 11¾ x 15". RB p. 29

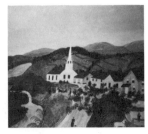

381. *The Village Mill* (M. 585)
May 21. 14 x 16". RB p. 29. Sold through Ferargil Galleries, New York

382. *Quiet* (M. 586)
May 21. 14 x 15½". RB p. 29. Sold through Whyte Bookshop & Gallery, Inc., Washington, D.C.

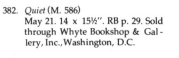

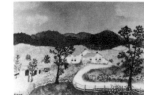

383. *Brother's Home* (M. 586)
May 21. 12¼ x 20". RB p. 29. Formerly collection Artur Schnabel

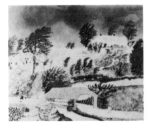

384. *It Will Rain* (M. 580)
May 31. 17½ x 21½". RB p. 29 numbered 590. Sold through Vigeveno, Los Angeles

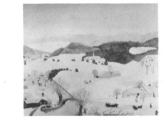

385. *Winter (Over the River to Grandma's House)* (M. 591)
June. Canvas, 35 x 45". RB p. 29. Sold through ABAC, New York

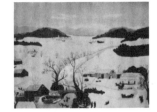

386. *Over the River to Grandma's House* (M. 591)
June 13. 32½ x 44½". The University of California at Los Angeles

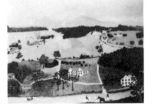

387. *The Old Checkered House in 1860* (M. 592)
June 13. 35½ x 44¾". RB p. 29. Formerly collection Ala Story. *Reproduced: Book of the Month Club News,* June 1953 (cover); GMAP; Arthur Jaffe

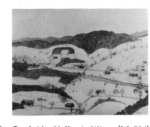

388. *Cambridge Valley in Winter* (M. 594)
June 15. 21¾ x 29¼". RB p. 30

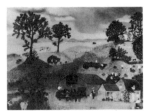

389. *Haymaking* (M. 595)
June 15. 24 x 33¾". RB p. 30. *Reproduced:* Christie, Manson & Woods, London, Sale of Feb. 25, 1972, No. 203

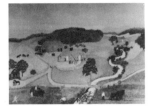

390. *Home of Hezekiah King* (M. 595)
June 23. 24 x 34". RB p. 30. Sold through Maxwell, San Francisco

391. *The Hoosick Bridge* (M. 598)
June 23. RB p. 30. Sold through ABAC, New York

392. *Rose Garden* (M. 600)
June 23. 10¼ x 11". RB p. 30. Sold through Vigeveno, Los Angeles

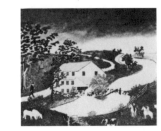

393. *The Old Mill in Shenandoah* (M. 601)
June 23. 23 x 29". RB p. 30. *Reproduced:* Parke-Bernet Sale No. 1622, Nov. 9, 1955, No. 63

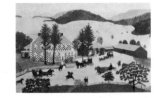

394. *Belvedere* (M. 602)
June 23. 23 x 30". RB p. 30

395. *Church Among the Hills* (M. 604)
June 25. 20½ x 23¾". RB p. 30. The Parrish Art Museum, Southampton, N.Y.

396. *A Home in the Woods* (M. 606)
June 29. 8 x 9¼". RB p. 30. Parke-Bernet Sale No. 1944, Jan. 22, 1960, No. 152

397. *The Sun Has Gone Down* (M. 608)
June 29. 6 x 9". RB p. 30. Private collection. *Reproduced:* GMSB. (See plate 78)

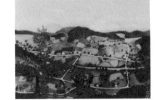

398. *Cambridge in Summer* (M. 669)
June 29. 24 x 34". RB p. 30 numbered 609. Formerly collection Ala Story

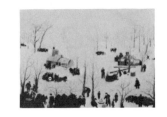

399. *Sugaring Off* (M. 700)
June 29. 23 x 33". RB p. 30. Private collection

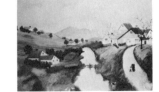

400. *In the Spring* (M. 702)
July 8. 12 x 17½". RB p. 30. Collection Mrs. Herbert Abraham

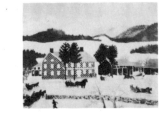

401. *The Checkered House in Winter, 1853* (M. 706)
July 14. 21 x 27½". RB p. 30. Zanesville Art Center, Ohio. Gift of Mr. and Mrs. A.D. Nast, Jr., in memory of Mr. and Mrs. Frank Ransbottom

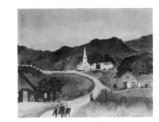

402. *Mountain Top* (M. 777)
July 18. 4½ x 6¼". RB p. 30. Sold through Vigeveno, Los Angeles

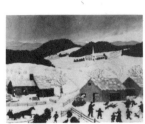

403. *Catching the Thanksgiving Turkey* (M. 778)
July 22. 22 x 28". RB p. 31 dated July 24, 1944. Collection Allan Bluestein

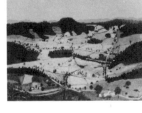

404. *The Cambridge Valley, N.Y.* (M. 781)
July 25. 19¾ x 26". RB p. 31. *Reproduced:* Parke-Bernet Sale No. 2251, Jan. 29, 1964, No. 44

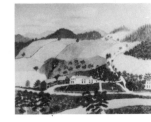

405. *The Sycamore Farm* (M. 782)
July 26. 19¾ x 26¼". RB p. 31

406. *The Church in the Hills*
July 27. 20 x 26". RB p. 31. Sold through ABAC, New York

407. *Over the River to Grandma's House*
Aug. 7. c. 24 x 30". RB p. 31. Also known as "Covered Bridge." Sold through ABAC, New York

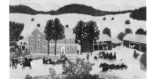

408. *The Checkered House in Summer* (M. 786)
Aug. 7. 24 x 31¾". RB p. 31. Private collection. *Reproduced:* Parke-Bernet Sale No. 1959, March 16, 1960, No. 88

409. *In Spring*
Aug. 7. Small. RB p. 31

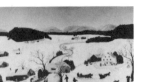

410. *Over the River to Grandmother's House*
Aug. 7. 20 x 36". Collection Sharon R. Curry and Carol R. Wakefield

411. *January*
Aug. 24. c. 10 x 12". RB p. 31. Sold through ABAC, New York

412. *February* (M. 789)
Aug. 24. c. 10 x 12". RB p. 31. Sold through ABAC, New York

413. *Hoosick Falls II* (M. 791)
Aug. 24. 19¾ x 25½". RB p. 31. Collection Lilli Palmer

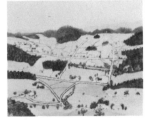

414. *Cambridge Valley* (M. 792)
Aug. 24. 19 x 24". RB p. 31. Sidney Janis Gallery, New York

415. *First Wagon on Cambridge Pike* (M. 793)
Aug. 24. 20 x 24". RB p. 31. (See plate 79)

416. *The Old Mill in June* (M. 704)
Sept. 4. RB p. 31 numbered 804. Sold through Whyte Bookshop & Gallery, Inc., Washington, D.C.

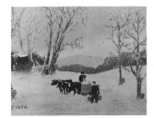

417. *Gathering Sap* (M. 788)
Sept. 4. 8¾ x 11½". RB p. 31 numbered 798. Private collection

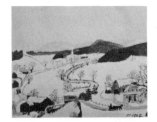

418. *Over the River to Grandma's* (M. 794)
Sept. 4. 8¾ x 11¾". RB p. 31. Private collection

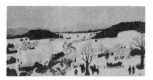

419. *Over the River to Grandma's House*
(M. 794)
Probably September 1944.
19¼ x 35¼". Not originally labeled
by the artist; the numbered label
was attached in 1959. Collection
David Sterns

420. *Sugaring Off* (M. 795)
Sept. 4. 9¾ x 13⅞". RB p. 31. Collection David Sterns

421. *Gathering March Sap* (M. 797)
Sept. 4. Small. RB p. 31. Sold
through ABAC, New York

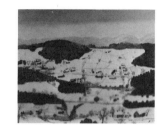

422. *March* (M. 799)
Sept. 4. 9¾ x 15". RB p. 31. Private collection

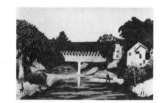

423. *Covered Bridge*
Sept. 4. 5¾ x 8". RB p. 31 "Old
Hoosick Bridge"

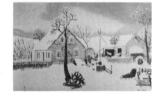

424. *The Old Red Mill in Winter* (M. 805)
Sept. 4. 19¾ x 23¾". RB p. 31. Collection Mrs. A.K. Sibley

425. *Hoosick Falls, N.Y., in Winter*
(M. 810)
Sept. 5. 20 x 24". RB p. 31. The
Phillips Collection, Washington,
D.C. *Reproduced:* Art in America
portfolio; Brundage; GMAP;
Hallmark; Jasmand and Kallir;
MLH (also German and Dutch edi-
tions). (See plate 216)

426. *January* (M. 1008)
Sept. 7. Small. RB p. 32

427. *Gathering Sap* (M. 1005)
Sept. 15. 7 x 8¼". RB p. 32. Sold
through ABAC, New York

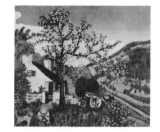

428. *Cambridge Valley in Winter*
(M. 1011)
Sept. 28. 23¾ x 29¾". RB p. 32.
Collection Dorothy C. Golden

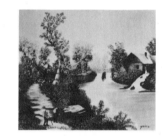

429. *Old Covered Bridge, Woodstock, Vt.*
(M. 1012)
Sept. 28. 16 x 24". RB p. 32. Col-
lection A.M. Adler

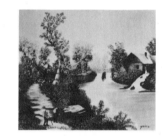

430. *All Is Quiet* (M. 1014)
Sept. 28. 15½ x 18½". RB p. 32.
Collection Fred R. Jaeckel

431. *The Duck Pond*
About September 1944. 7 x 8".
Collection Mrs. I.H. Van Gelder

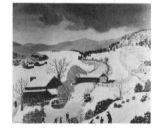

432. *Over the River to Grandma's* (M. 120;
sic)
Oct. 15. 13½ x 22¼". RB p. 32
numbered 120 instead of 1020. Collection Janet Mealy

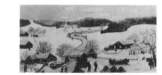

433. *Over the River* (M. 118; *sic*)
Oct. 16. 14 x 28". RB p. 32 numbered 118 instead of 1018. Collection Nancy Hamilton

434. *A Dream* (M. 1022)
Oct. 17. RB p. 32

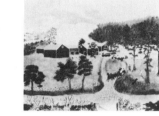

435. *May* (M. 1026)
Oct. 24. 10 x 12½". RB p. 32.
Parke-Bernet Sale No. 2326, Jan.
27, 1965, No. 85

436. *Over the Hills and Through the Snow*
(M. 1027)
Oct. 24. RB p. 32 numbered 1023.
Sold through Saidenberg, New
York

437. *Cambridge Valley in Summer*
About October 1944. Large. Formerly collection Cole Porter

438. *Spring* (M. 1033)
Nov. 14. c. 10 x 12". RB p. 32
dated Oct. 30, 1944, numbered
1032. Sold through Saidenberg,
New York

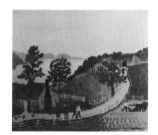

439. *April* (M. 1034)
Nov. 14. 11 x 13". RB p. 32. Collection Hildegard Bachert

440. *June* (M. 1035)
Nov. 14. 10½ x 17". RB p. 33. Sold
through Whyte Bookshop & Gallery, Inc., Washington, D.C.

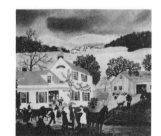

441. *Home for Thanksgiving* (M. 1036)
Nov. 14. 23¼ x 26¼". RB p. 33.
Collection Mrs. Raymond C.
Harper. *Reproduced:* GMAP

442. *The Old Automobile* (M. 1036)
Nov. 14. 18¾ x 21½". RB p. 33.
Private collection. *Reproduced:*
GMAP; GMSB; Hallmark; MLH
(also German and Dutch editions);
Oldenbourg. (See plate 43)

---

443. *Grandma Goes to the City* (M. 1037)
Nov. 14. 22¼ x 26¼". RB p. 33.
Reproduced: Parke-Bernet Sale No.
1497, Feb. 24, 1954, No. 80

444. *Out for the Christmas Trees* (M. 1038)
Nov. 14. 24 x 29½". RB p. 33. Col-
lection Anson Brooks. *Reproduced:*
Brundage; GMAP. (See plate 76)

445. *We Have Turkey* (M. 1039)
Nov. 20. RB p. 33

446. *Great Grandfather's Home*
Nov. 20. Small. RB p. 33

447. *Home to Grandpa's* (M. 1044)
Nov. 25. Small. RB p. 33. Sold
through ABAC, New York

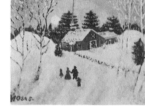

448. *Deep Snow* (M. 1045)
Nov. 25. 6½ x 8". RB p. 33. Collection Mrs. K. Gottry

449. *Summertime* (M. 1047)
Nov. 25. Small. RB p. 33. Sold
through ABAC, New York

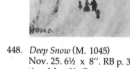

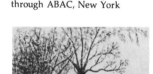

450. *By the Road* (M. 1048)
Nov. 25. 6½ x 8¼". RB p. 33. Private collection

451. *An Old Bridge* (M. 1049)
Small. RB p. 33 "The Bridge of
1881," dated Nov. 25, 1944. Sold
through ABAC, New York

452. *An Old Mill* (M. 1050)
Nov. 25. 7½ x 7¾". RB p. 33.
Parke-Bernet Sale No. 2751, Oct.
24, 1968, No. 86

453. *Mt. Anthony* (M. 1051)
Nov. 25. Small. RB p. 33. Sold
through ABAC, New York

---

454. *The Sun Has Gone Down* (M. 1052)
Nov. 25. 6 x 7¾". RB p. 33. Collection Mrs. K. Gottry

455. *The House in the Woods* (M. 1053)
Nov. 25. 6½ x 7½". RB p. 33. Collection Mrs. Willis E. Ruffner

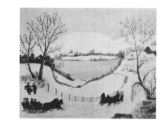

456. *Home* (M. 1060)
Nov. 25. 9⅛ x 11⅞". RB p. 33.
Collection Laraine Day

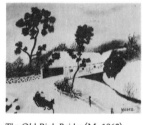

457. *Over the Bridge Through the Snow to
Grandma's House* (M. 1061)
Nov. 25. 10 x 22". Collection
Hazel Kearney Heber

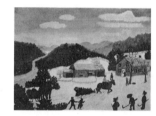

458. *The Old Pink Bridge* (M. 1062)
Nov. 25. 9¼ x 12". RB p. 34. Collection Rebekah Harkness

459. *The Beautiful* (M. 1063)
Nov. 25. RB p. 34. Collection
Joseph Ellis

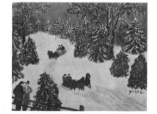

460. *Out of the Woods* (M. 1064)
Nov. 25. 9 x 12". RB p. 34. Collection Mrs. K. Gottry

---

461. *In the Studio* (M. 1062)
Nov. 27. 18 x 23½". RB p. 33.
Sidney Janis Gallery, New York.
(See plate 253)

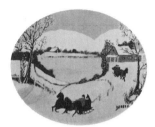

462. *Quiet* (M. 1066)
Dec. 1. 8 x 10" (oval). RB p. 34

462a. *Brotherhood Church* (M. 1067)
Dec. 1. 8 x 10". RB p. 34. Collection Mr. and Mrs. H.W. Hitchcock

463. *A-Hunting* (M. 1071)
Dec. 1. RB p. 34

464. *Vermont Snow Plow* (M. 1080)
Dec. 12. RB p. 34. Collection
William D. Crane

465. *Pull Hard*
Dec. 12. Small. RB p. 34

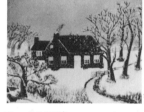

466. *Bringing in the Christmas Tree*
(M. 1082)
Dec. 12. 9 x 12½". RB p. 34. Pri-
vate collection

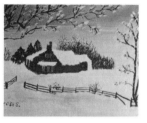 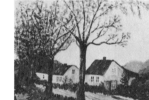

467. *All Is Quiet* (M. 1083)
Dec. 12. 11¾ x 15". RB p. 34. Collection Helen Woodruff

468. *A-Skating We Will Go* (M. 1084)
Dec. 14. Small. RB p. 34

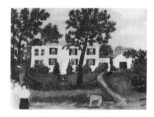

469. *Hitchcock Home, Cambridge*
(M. 1086)
Dec. 16. 8½ x 12". RB p. 34. Col-
lection Mrs. K. Gottry

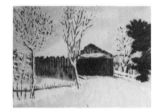
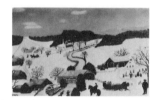
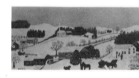

470. *Hitchcock Home, Cambridge [No. 2]* (M. 1087)
Dec. 16. 9 x 12''. RB p. 34. Collection Mr. and Mrs. H. W. Hitchcock

471. *Home of Hitchcock, Florida [No. 1]* (M. 1088)
Dec. 16. 9 x 12''. RB p. 34. Collection Mr. and Mrs. H.W. Hitchcock

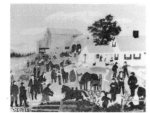

472. *Hitchcock Home, Florida* (M. 1090)
Dec. 16. 9 x 12''. RB p. 34. Collection Mrs. K. Gottry

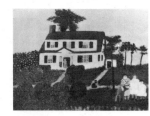

473. *Hoosick Falls in Winter* (M. 1091)
Dec. 21. 19½ x 24¾''. RB p. 34. Abby Aldrich Rockefeller Folk Art Collection, Williamsburg, Va.

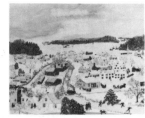

474. *The Sale* (M. 1091)
Dec. 21. 12 x 16''. RB p. 35. Collection Mr. and Mrs. H.W. Hitchcock

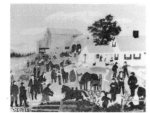

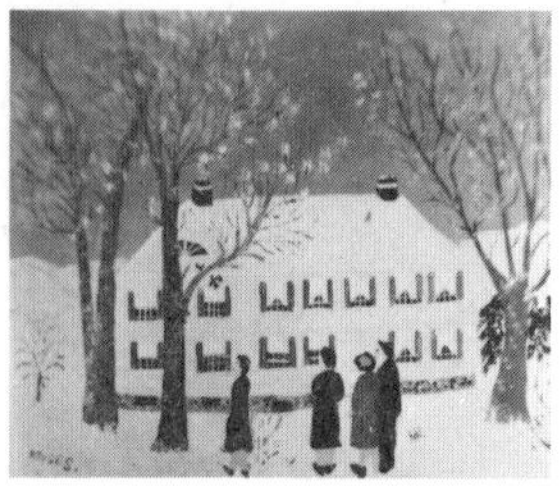

475. *Hitchcock in Winter* (M. 1093)
Dec. 21. 7¾ x 9⅜''. RB p. 35. Hallmark Cards, Inc., Kansas City, Mo.

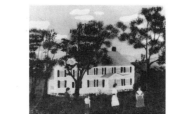

476. *Hitchcock in Summer* (M. 1094)
Dec. 21. 8½ x 11''. RB p. 35

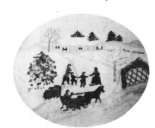

477. *Bringing in Tree* (M. 1097)
Dec. 21. 8 x 10'' (oval). RB p. 35. Collection Mrs. O.W. Leibiger

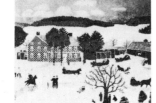

478. *Checkered House in Winter*
About 1944. 24 x 33¼''. *Reproduced:* Parke-Bernet Sale No. 1302, Jan. 10, 1952, No. 103

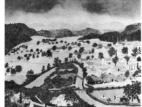

479. *The Village of Hoosick Falls*
About 1944. Canvas, 35 x 45''. Private collection

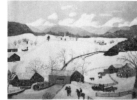

480. *Old Red Mill*
About 1944. 25 x 35''. Collection Mr. and Mrs. Freeman F. Gosden. *Reproduced:* GMAP

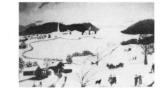

481. *Over the Bridge to Grandma's House*
About 1944. Collection Mrs. Lytle Hull

482. *So Cold*
9⅜ x 12''. Parke-Bernet Sale No. 2245, Jan. 9, 1964, No. 80

1945

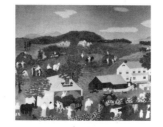

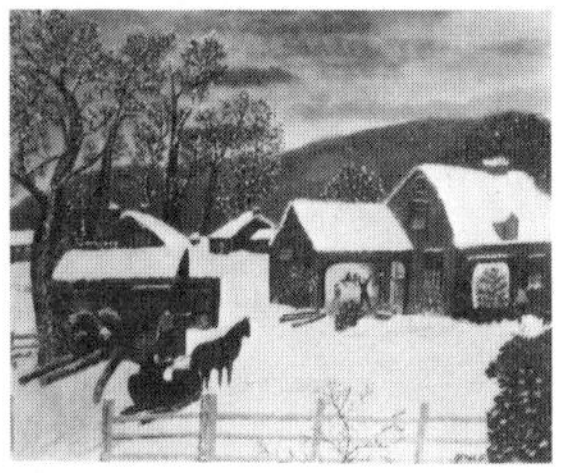

483. *The Lonely Tramp or Traveler* (M. 1003)
Jan. 3. 16 x 20''. RB p. 38(?). Private collection. *Reproduced:* Brundage; GMAP ("Christmas")

484. *Picnic* (M. 1010)
Feb. 1. 24 x 30''. RB p. 35. Collection Mr. and Mrs. A. Lerman. *Reproduced:* GMAP; Parke-Bernet Sale No. 2914, Oct. 22, 1969, No. 110. (See plate 82)

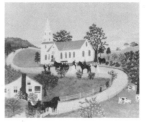

485. *Haying Time* (M. 1011)
Feb. 1. 24 x 30''. RB p. 35. *Reproduced:* BG; GMAP; GMSB

486. *The First Skating* (M. 1013)
Feb. 1. 17¾ x 23''. Collection Renée C. Amory. *Reproduced:* Brundage; GMAP. (See plate 80)

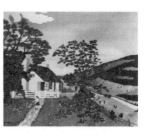

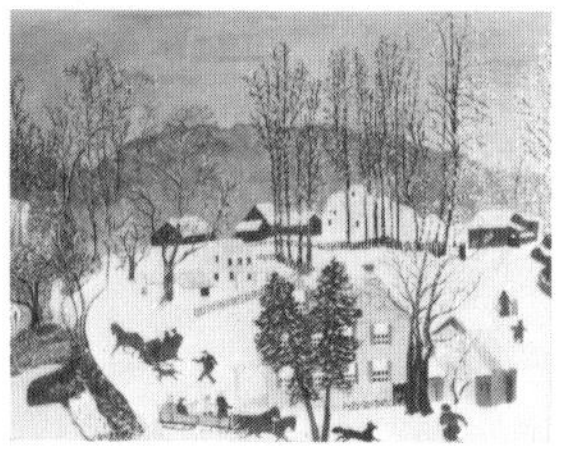

487. *The First Snow* (M. 1013)
Feb. 1. 17¾ x 23''. RB p. 35 numbered 1012. Collection Mrs. Lester D. Avnet

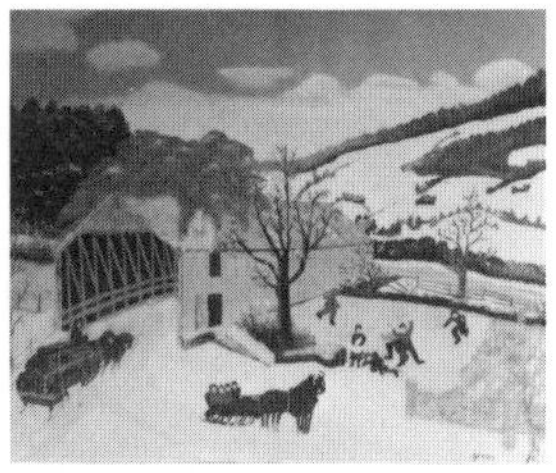

488. *The Old Covered Bridge* (M. 1014)
Feb. 1. 17½ x 24¼''. RB p. 35. Private collection

489. *The First Autumn Leaves* (M. 1015)
Feb. 1. RB p. 35

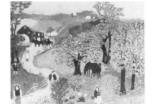

490. *In the Spring* (M. 1016)
Feb. 1. 16 x 20''. RB p. 35. Sold through Vigeveno, Los Angeles

491. *We Will Have Christmas* (M. 1017)
Feb. 1. 12½ x 15½''. RB p. 35. Collection Mrs. Ralph W. Zastrow

492. *The Sun Has Gone Down* (M. 1018)
Feb. 1. Small. RB p. 35

493. *Going Home* (M. 1019)
Feb. 1. Small. RB p. 35

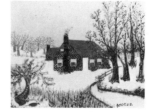

494. *Home in Winter* (M. 1020)
Feb. 1. 9⅛ x 12''. Collection the Reverend Wesley Gallup

495. *Wild Roses* (M. 1022)
Feb. 1. 10¾ x 9¼''. RB p. 35 numbered 1021. Private collection. (See plate 83)

496. *Wild Daisies* (M. 1022)
Feb. 1. 11¾ x 7¾''. RB p. 35. Private collection. (See plate 84)

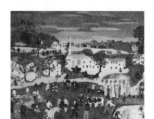

497. *Bondsville Fair* (M. 1023)
March 3. 18 x 23¼''. RB p. 35. *Reproduced:* GMAP

498. *Wash Day* (M. 1024)
March 3. 17¾ x 23½''. RB p. 35. Museum of Art, Rhode Island School of Design, Providence. *Reproduced:* GMAP. (See plate 85)

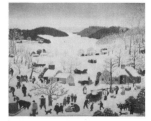

499. *After the Snow Storm* (M. 1025)
March 3. 18½ x 27½''. RB p. 35 numbered 1024.

500. *Early Springtime on the Farm* (M. 1026)
March 3. 16 x 25¾''. RB p. 35 numbered 1025. Private collection. *Reproduced:* Brundage; GMAP; GMSB; MLH (Dutch edition). (See plate 88)

501. *A Wreath of Roses* (M. 1026)
March 3. RB p. 35

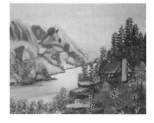

502. *Going to Church* (M. 1027)
March 3. 16 x 20''. RB p. 36. Collection Mrs. T. Baldwin. *Reproduced:* GMAP

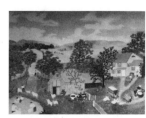

503. *Flowers of Spring* (M. 1028)
March 3. 16 x 20''. RB p. 36. Sold through Vose, Boston

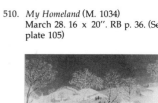

504. *Home Dear Home* (M. 1030)
March 3. 16 x 20''. RB p. 36 numbered 1029. Sold through Vigeveno, Los Angeles

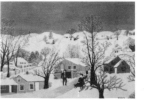

505. *Sugaring Off* (M. 1030)
March 3. 26¼ x 31''. RB p. 36. New York State Historical Association, Cooperstown

506. *The Bridge in the Cove* (M. 1031)
March 3. RB p. 36

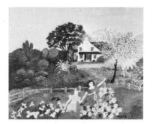

507. *In the Adirondacks* (M. 1036)
March 28. 16 x 20''. RB p. 36. The Bennington Museum, Bennington, Vt. *Reproduced:* Parke-Bernet Sale No. 3265, Nov. 12, 1971, No. 81

508. *The Lookout, 1777, Vermont* (M. 1032)
March 28. 17 x 21''. RB p. 36. Formerly collection Bernard M. Douglas. *Reproduced:* GMAP. (See plate 81)

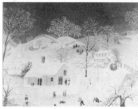

509. *May: Making Soap, Washing Sheep* (M. 1033)
March 28. 17¼ x 24¼''. RB p. 36. Collection Mrs. Raymond Evans. *Reproduced:* GMAP

510. *My Homeland* (M. 1034)
March 28. 16 x 20''. RB p. 36. (See plate 105)

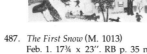

511. *A Winter's Day, 1870* (M. 1035)
March 28. 17¼ x 24''. RB p. 36. Collection Mrs. J. Winton Gottlieb. *Reproduced:* GMAP

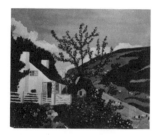

512. *Down in the Valley* (M. 1041)
April 5. 10 x 12". RB p. 36. Private collection

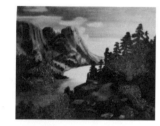

513. *In the Adirondacks* (M. 1043)
April 5. 16 x 21¼". RB p. 36. Collection Edward Moses

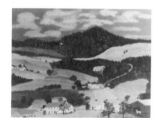

514. *Spruce Mountain, Vt.* (M. 1046)
April 6. 16 x 20". RB p. 36. Sold through Vigeveno, Los Angeles

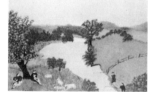

515. *In May* (M. 1043)
May 1. 9¾ x 14". RB p. 36. Sold through Vose, Boston

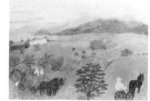

516. *June* (M. 1044)
May 1. 9¼ x 12¾". RB p. 36. Sold through Vigeveno, Los Angeles

517. *In June* (M. 1045)
May 1. 13 x 16½". RB p. 36 "June Haying Time," dated June 1, 1945. Collection Mr. and Mrs. Anthony Hope

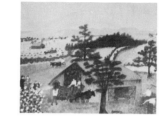

518. *Mt. Nebo* (M. 1052)
May 1. RB p. 36. Sold through Vigeveno, Los Angeles

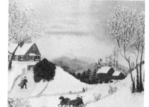

519. *Here We Go, High Oh* (M. 1051)
May 5. 11½ x 15". RB p. 36. Sold through Vigeveno, Los Angeles

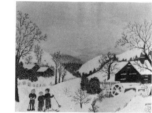

520. *The Young Skiers* (M. 1053)
May 15. 16 x 20". RB p. 36

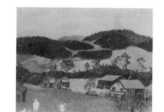

521. *Home of Childhood* (M. 1054)
May 15. c. 16 x 20". RB p. 36

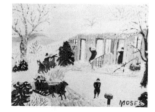

522. *There Goes the Bride* (M. 1058)
May 22. c. 8 x 10". RB p. 37. Private collection

523. *September* (M. 1048)
May 30. 10 x 13¼". RB p. 36. Sold through Vigeveno, Los Angeles

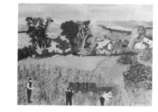

524. *October* (M. 1049)
May. c. 9 x 12". RB p. 36. Collection Dorothy R. DuMond

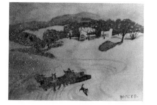

525. *A Heavy Snow* (M. 1050)
May 30. 10 x 12". RB p. 45 "A Heavy Snow Storm." Sold through Vigeveno, Los Angeles

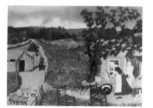

526. *A-Skating Let's Go* (M. 1002)
June 23. RB p. 37 numbered 1062, dated July 23, 1945. Collection Mr. and Mrs. Frank Stainton

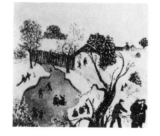

527. *July, Harvest Time* (M. 1046)
June 30. 9¾ x 14". RB p. 36 dated May 30, 1945. Sold through Vigeveno, Los Angeles

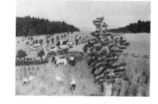

528. *Down on the Farm in Summer* (M. 1060)
July 23. 20½ x 27½". RB p. 37. Reproduced: GMSB

529. *Out on the Lake*
15¼ x 19¾". RB p. 37 numbered 1061, dated July 23, 1945

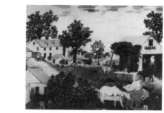

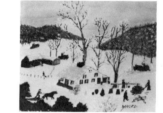

530. *Maple Sugar Time* (M. 1073)
Aug. 13. 10 x 12". RB p. 37. Collection Mrs. Milton Hepner. Reproduced: Brundage

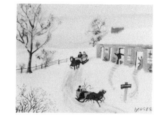

531. *There Goes the Bride* (M. 1075)
Aug. 13. 6¾ x 7¾". RB p. 37. Sold through ABAC, New York. Reproduced: Brundage

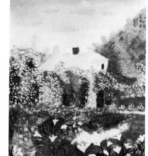

532. *The Rose Garden* (M. 1076)
Aug. 13. 9¾ x 8". RB p. 37. Collection Martin A. Smith

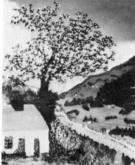

533. *Down in the Valley* (M. 1077)
Aug. 13. 9¾ x 8". RB p. 37. Collection Martin A. Smith

534. *Almost Home* (M. 1078)
Aug. 13. 10 x 12". RB p. 37. Formerly collection Cora P. Waite

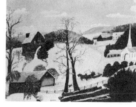

535. *Winter Is Here* (M. 1054)
Aug. 28. 20½ x 26½". RB p. 37. Collection Mr. and Mrs. Louis Holland. Reproduced: Brundage; Hallmark; Parke-Bernet Sale No. 1659, March 14, 1956, No. 91

536. *Jack O'Lantern* (M. 1055)
Aug. 28. RB p. 37. Sold through Marshall Field, Chicago

537. *In Harvest Time* (M. 1057)
Aug. 28. 18 x 28". RB p. 37 numbered 1056. Private collection. Reproduced: Art in America portfolio; Hallmark; MLH. (See plates 246, 247)

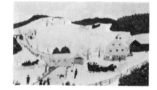

538. *Belvedere*
About August 1945. 18½ x 25½". Reproduced: Parke-Bernet Sale No. 1224, Feb. 14, 1951, No. 67

539. *A Blanket of Snow* (M. 1059)
Sept. 4. RB p. 37. Sold through Vigeveno, Los Angeles

540. *The Apple Tree* (M. 1060)
Sept. 4. RB p. 38. Sold through Vigeveno, Los Angeles

541. *Our Barn* (M. 1061)
Sept. 11. 18 x 24". RB p. 38. Reproduced: GMAP; Parke-Bernet Sale No. 1675, May 2, 1956, No. 71. (See plate 86)

542. *Berry Pickers* (M. 1062)
Sept. 11. RB p. 38. Sold through ABAC, New York

543. *The Whiteside Church* (M. 1063)
Sept. 11. 9¾ x 17". RB p. 38. Collection Mrs. Walter LeVine. Reproduced: GMAP; GMSB. (See plate 217)

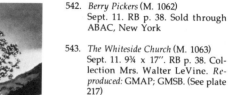

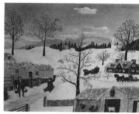

544. *Down on the Farm in Winter* (M. 1073)
Sept. 20. c. 20 x 26". RB p. 37 dated July 25, 1945. Formerly collection Ala Story. Reproduced: Hallmark

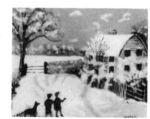

545. *Over the River to Grandma's* (M. 1065)
Oct. 12. 11¾ x 19½". Private collection. Reproduced: Brundage; Parke-Bernet Sale No. 2158, Jan. 24, 1963, No. 120

546. *The Old Oaken Bucket* (M. 1066)
Oct. 12. 9 x 21¾". RB p. 38 numbered 1065. Sold through Denver Art Galleries, Colo.

547. *The Tabor Home* (M. 1067)
Oct. 12. 10½ x 12½". RB p. 38

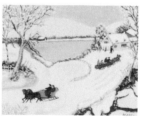

548. *A Frosty Morning* (M. 1068)
Oct. 12. 9 x 11¾". RB p. 38. Collection Mrs. William J. Donovan. Reproduced: Brundage

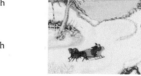

549. *Home from Church* (M. 1069)
Oct. 12. 10¾ x 13¾". RB p. 38. Collection Mrs. Richard Henning. Parke-Bernet Sale May 1965, No. 66. Reproduced: Brundage

550. *Winter Evening* (M. 1070)
Oct. 12. Small. RB p. 38

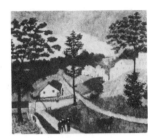

551. *Oh See the New Colty* (M. 1071)
Oct. 12. 11 x 13½". RB p. 38. *Reproduced:* Parke-Bernet Sale No. 2567, May 11, 1967, No. 31

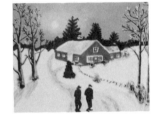

552. *Moonlight Evening* (M. 1073)
Oct. 15. 10 x 13". RB p. 38. Sold through Vigeveno, Los Angeles. *Reproduced:* Brundage

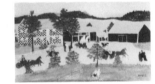

553. *The Checkered House in 1860* (M. 1074)
Oct. 15. 10½ x 17¾". RB p. 38

554. *Going to Vespers* (M. 1075)
Oct. 15. Small. RB p. 38

555. *After the Snow Storm* (M. 1076)
Oct. 15. 8 x 10". RB p. 38. Sold through ABAC, New York

556. *Mount Airy* (M. 1077)
Oct. 15. 8 x 9½". RB p. 38. Sold through Vigeveno, Los Angeles

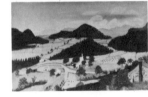

557. *Arlington Green* (M. 1078)
Oct. 18. 16 x 24". RB p. 38 the number corrected by the artist to read 1079. Formerly collection Ala Story

558. *Early Morning* (M. 1079)
Nov. 5. 9 x 11". RB p. 38. Sold through Vigeveno, Los Angeles

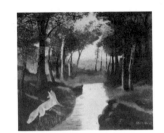

559. *The Fox Glen* (M. 1080)
Nov. 5. 11 x 13¼". RB p. 38. Collection Mr. and Mrs. George O. Cook

560. *The Spirit of the Cider Barrel* (M. 1081)
Nov. 5. 10¾ x 12½". RB p. 38. Collection Gerald Moses

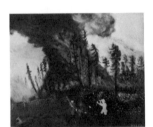

561. *Woodfire* (M. 1082)
Nov. 5. 11½ x 14¼". RB p. 38

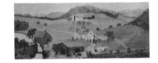

562. *The Old Oaken Bucket* (M. 1083)
Nov. 5. 8 x 18". RB p. 38. Private collection

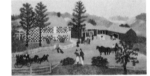

563. *The Checkered House in 1860* (M. 1084)
Nov. 5. 8½ x 15¾". RB p. 38. Private collection

564. *Down the Hill by Joshua's* (M. 1085)
Nov. 5. 8 x 9¾". RB p. 38. Sold through Marshall Field, Chicago

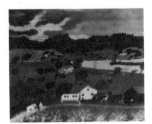

565. *Hurricane at Home* (M. 1086)
Dec. 5. 16 x 19¾". RB p. 38. Oesterreichische Staatsgalerie, Vienna

566. *Hurricane in Hoosick Falls* (M. 1087)
Dec. 5. 15¾" x 20". RB p. 39. Sold through ABAC, New York. (See plate 87)

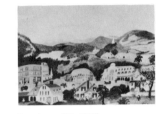

567. *Bennington* (M. 1088)
Dec. 6. 17¾ x 25¾". RB p. 39

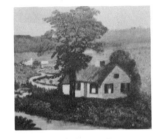

568. *Let Me Drive* (M. 1089)
Dec. 10. 10 x 13¾". RB p. 39. Sold through Vigeveno, Los Angeles

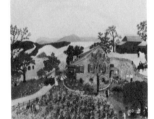

569. *In the Twilight* (M. 1090)
Dec. 10. 11 x 13". RB p. 39. Collection Sam Wood

570. *[Untitled] Winter Scene* (M. 1095)
Dec. 14. 6 x 14". Collection Mrs. John R. Austin

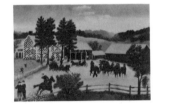

570a. *The Harvest*
About 1945. Canvas, 30 x 38". Sidney Janis Gallery, New York

1946

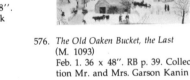

571. *The Old Checkered House in 1853* (M. 1103)
Jan. 2. 14 x 20¾". RB p. 37

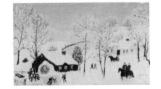

572. *Old Red Mill in Virginia*
Jan. 10 (erroneously dated on label Jan. 10, 1936). 9⅛ x 16". Collection Mr. and Mrs. George O. Cook

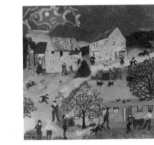

573. *Halloween Pranks*
January. 13½ x 14¾". Collection Sharon R. Curry and Carol R. Wakefield

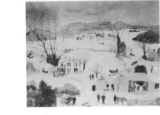

574. *The Cambridge Hospital* (M. 1091)
Feb. 1. Canvas, 36 x 48". RB p. 39 numbered 1094. Sold through Vigeveno, Los Angeles

575. *Grandma Moses's Childhood Home* (M. 1092)
Feb. 1. Canvas, 36 x 48". Collection Alfred J. Ostheimer III. *Reproduced:* Bihalji-Merin; GMSB; Hallmark; *The Washington Farmer* (Spokane), Jan. 18, 1951 (cover). (See plate 226)

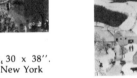

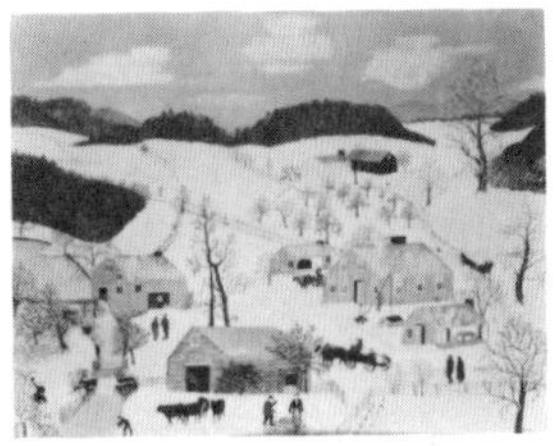

576. *The Old Oaken Bucket, the Last* (M. 1093)
Feb. 1. 36 x 48". RB p. 39. Collection Mr. and Mrs. Garson Kanin

577. *Grandma Moses Going to Big City*
Feb. 1. 36 x 48". RB p. 39 numbered 1091. Private collection. *Reproduced:* Ford; *The Four Seasons* portfolio; GMAP; *New York State Vacationlands* (cover). (See plate 225)

578. *Christmas Tree in Church* (M. 1095)
Feb. 1. 18½ x 23¼". RB p. 39. Sold through Vigeveno, Los Angeles

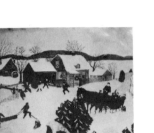

579. *Hurrah for Christmas* (M. 1096)
Feb. 1. 18½ x 23¼". RB p. 39. *Reproduced:* Parke-Bernet Sale No. 1564, Jan. 19, 1955, No. 77

580. *We Go Around by the Mill* (M. 1097)
Feb. 1. RB p. 39. Sold through Ferargil Galleries, New York

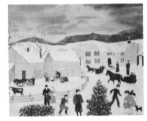

581. *Here Comes Aunt Judith* (M. 1098)
Feb. 1. 18½ x 23¼". RB p. 39. *Reproduced:* GMAP ("Bringing in the Christmas Tree"); Lipman & Winchester

582. *They Are Having Company at Job's* (M. 1099)
Feb. 1. 18½ x 23¼". RB p. 39. Sold through Vigeveno, Los Angeles

583. *Shoot, Daddy Shoot* (M. 1100)
Feb. 8. 18½ x 23¼". RB p. 39. Collection Dorothy Gould Burns

584. *Rabbit Hunting* (M. 1101)
Feb. 8. 18½ x 23¼". RB p. 39. Sold through Ferargil Galleries, New York

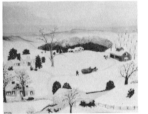

585. *Whoa There* (M. 1102)
Feb. 8. 18½ x 23½". RB p. 39. *Reproduced:* Parke-Bernet Sale No. 1576, March 9, 1955, No. 77

586. *Christmas at Home* (M. 1103)
March 26. 18 x 23". RB p. 39. Collection Mrs. F. Kallir. *Reproduced:* *American Bar Assoc. Journal*, Vol. 56, Dec. 1970 (cover); BG; Bihalji-Merin; Eliot; GMFP; Hallmark; MLH; color reproduction. (See plate 236)

587. *Rabbits, Rabbits* (M. 1104)
March 26. 18 x 23". RB p. 39. Collection Thomas Moses

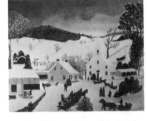

588. *Church Christmas Tree* (M. 1105)
March 26. 18 x 23". RB p. 39. Private collection. *Reproduced:* Hallmark; *House and Garden*, Dec. 1946 (cover)

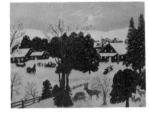

589. *Bringing in the Yule Log* (M. 1106)
March 26. 18 x 23". RB p. 39. University of California at Los Angeles

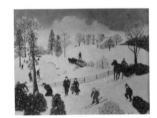

590. *Fallen the Pine Tree* (M. 1107)
March 26. 18 x 23". RB p. 39. Sold through ABAC, New York

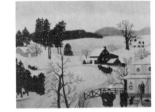

591. *Christmas Evening* (M. 1108)
March 26. 18 x 23". RB p. 39. Collection George M. Foster

592. *A Christmas Gift* (M. 1109)
March 26. 18 x 23". RB p. 39. Collection Dr. F. Norman Nagel

593. *Fredericktown, Jan. 7, 1834* (M. 1110)
March 26. c. 18 x 23". RB p. 39

594. *The Lone Traveler* (M. 1111)
March 26. 16 x 19¾". RB p. 39. Private collection. *Reproduced:* GMSB. (See plate 117)

595. *A Tramp on Christmas Day* (M. 1112)
March 26. 16 x 19⅞". RB p. 39. The Shelburne Museum, Shelburne, Vt. *Reproduced:* *The New York Times Magazine*, May 11, 1947; Oldenbourg. (See plate 118)

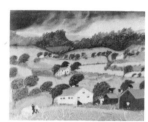

596. *How the Wind Blows* (M. 1113)
March 26. 16 x 19¾". RB p. 39.
Galerie St. Etienne, New York

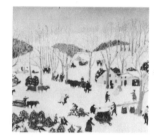

597. *Sugaring Off*
March. 20½ x 23¼". Collection
Mr. and Mrs. George O. Cook

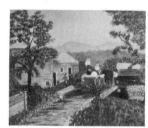

598. *Old Carpenter's Home*
March. 9 x 11". Collection Mr.
and Mrs. George O. Cook

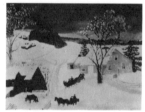

599. *Moses Homestead in 1639, N.H., in
Winter* (M. 1114)
April 16. 12½ x 16¼". RB p. 39
"Moses Homestead 1639
Portsmouth, N.H." Collection
Arthur K. Watson

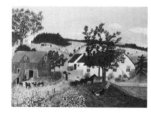

600. *Moses Homestead in 1639 in Summer*
(M. 1115)
April 16. 12½ x 16¼". RB p. 39
"Moses Homestead in Winter,
1639, N.H. and in Summer." Col-
lection Arthur K. Watson

601. *Study for Miss Helen Frick's
Residence, Bedford, N.Y.*
April. c. 5½ x 8¾". Collection
Mrs. Raymond C. Harper

602. *Miss Helen Frick's Estate: Study of
Waterfall*
April. 5½ x 8⅝"

603. *Miss Helen Frick's Residence, Bed-
ford, N.Y.* (M. 1116)
April 16. 21¼ x 25¼". RB p. 40.
Collection Miss Helen C. Frick.
(See plate 119)

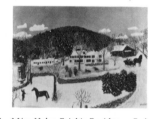

604. *Miss Helen Frick's Residence, Bedford, N.Y.* (M. 1117)
April 16. 17½ x 25". RB p. 40. Collection Miss Helen C. Frick

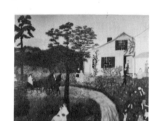

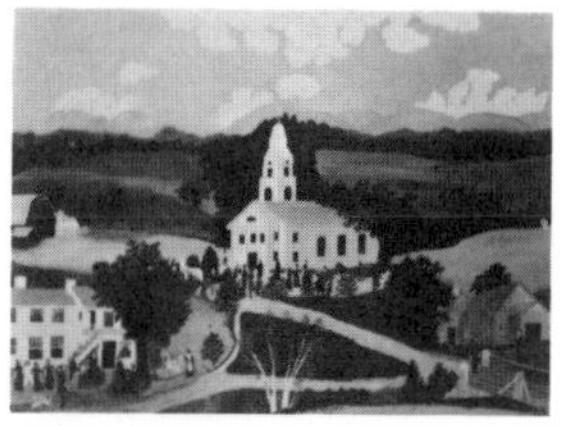

605. *Service Is Over* (M. 1117)
June 10. 25½ x 36". RB p. 40. Collection Margaret Mallory

606. *Out for Christmas Trees* (M. 1118)
June 10. 26 x 36". RB p. 40. Pri-
vate collection. *Reproduced:* Eliot;
GMSB; Hallmark; Arthur Jaffe;
Magazine of the Carnegie Institute,
Dec. 1949 (cover); NBC; *The New
York Times Magazine,* May 11,
1947. (See plate 227)

607. *The Hunter* (M. 1119)
June 10. 18 x 23". RB p. 40. Collection Margaret Mallory

608. *Sly Fox* (M. 1120)
June 10. RB p. 40. Collection Mrs.
Dwight Marvin

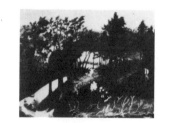

609. *An Autumn Day* (M. 1121)
June 10. 18 x 24". RB p. 40. Collection M.A. Hoffman. *Reproduced:*
Parke-Bernet Sale No. 1330, March
27, 1952, No. 177

610. *Beyond the Lake* (M. 1122)
June 10. 18 x 24". RB p. 40. Far-
mington School, Conn.

611. *Hoosick Valley (from the Window)*
(M. 1123)
June 10. 19½ x 22". RB p. 40. Collection Otto Kallir. *Reproduced: Art
in America* portfolio; MLH. (See
plate 220)

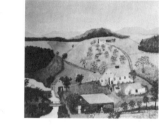

612. *Home for the Day* (M. 1124)
June 10. 18 x 24". RB p. 40. Collection Jerome Hill

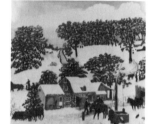

613. *The Postman* (M. 1125)
June 10. 21 x 25". RB p. 40. Collec-
tion Louis Bromfield. *Reproduced:*
Hallmark

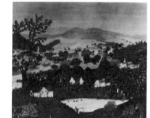

614. *Staunton, Virginia* (M. 1126)
Aug. 16. 19 x 23¼". RB p. 40. Rock
Springs High School Art Collec-
tion, Fine Arts Center, Rock
Springs, Wyo.

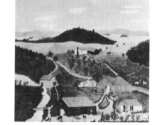

615. *The Old Oaken Bucket* (M. 1127)
Aug. 16. 24½ x 29". RB p. 40(?).
Collection Mr. and Mrs. John M.
Schiff

616. *The Old Oaken Bucket* (M. 1127)
Aug. 16. 20 x 24½". RB p. 40; also
p. 41 numbered 1156, the label for
which exists but is not attached to
the painting. Formerly collection
Helen Hayes

617. *Williamstown* (M. 1128)
Aug. 16. Canvas, 36 x 48". RB p.
40. Collection Mrs. Rockefeller
Prentice. *Reproduced: The Art
Digest,* May 15, 1947 (cover). (See
plate 218)

618. *All Is Calm* (M. 1129)
Aug. 16. 14 x 17¾". RB p. 40

619. *So Restful* (M. 1130)
Aug. 16. 10 x 14". RB p. 40

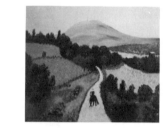

620. *Back in the Lane* (M. 1132)
Aug. 16. 10¼ x 14¼". RB p. 40
numbered 1131. Collection Charles
Sessler

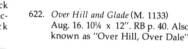

621. *The Country Road* (M. 1133)
Aug. 16. 8¾ x 10¾". RB p. 40
numbered 1132. Sold through
Vose, Boston

622. *Over Hill and Glade* (M. 1133)
Aug. 16. 10¼ x 12". RB p. 40. Also
known as "Over Hill, Over Dale"

623. *Down by the Bridge* (M. 1134)
Aug. 16. 6 x 8". RB p. 40. Sold
through Marshall Field, Chicago

624. *A Breakdown* (M. 1135)
Aug. 16. 6¾ x 9". RB p. 40

625. *He Has Fallen* (M. 1136)
Aug. 16. 5 x 8". RB p. 40. Sold
through Vigeveno, Los Angeles

626. *A Warning* (M. 1137)
Aug. 16. 11 x 18½". RB p. 40. Collection Mrs. Roger Hull

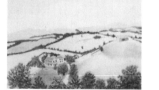

627. *The Potter Homestead* (M. 1138)
Aug. 16. 11 x 14¼". RB p. 40. Collection Hildegard Bachert

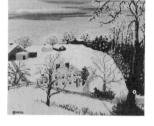

628. *The Pink House* (M. 1141)
Aug. 16. 10¼ x 12". RB p. 40. For-
merly collection Mrs. Stephen C.
Clark. Parke-Bernet Sale No. 1497,
Feb. 24, 1954, No. 61

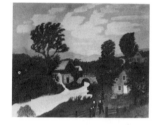

629. *Come with Me* (M. 1142)
Aug. 16. 18 x 23". RB p. 40. *Reproduced:* Christie, Manson &
Woods, London, Sale of Feb. 25,
1972, No. 196

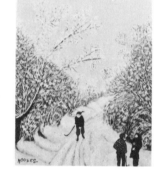

630. *Around the Bend* (M. 1142)
Sept. 12. 10 x 7¾". Collection Edward Moses

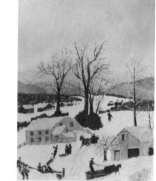

631. *Snowballing* (M. 1143)
Sept. 20. 27 x 21". RB p. 41. Col-
lection Mr. and Mrs. Walter L.
Wolf. *Reproduced:* Hallmark; *Holi-
day Magazine,* Feb. 1947 (cover);
MLH

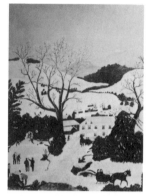

632. *No Skating for Me* (M. 1144)
Sept. 20. 27 x 21". RB p. 41. Collection Mr. and Mrs. John M.
Schiff. *Reproduced:* Parke-Bernet
Sale No. 2034, April 26, 1961, No.
55; *Tidens Kvinder* (Denmark), Dec.
1957 (cover); *Winter, New York State*
(N.Y. State Dept. of Commerce),
1947 (cover)

633. *See Them Skate* (M. 1145)
Sept. 20. 6¾ x 8¾". RB p. 41. Collection Mrs. Herbert Pratt

634. *Beyond the River* (M. 1146)
Sept. 23. 9¼ x 12¼". RB p. 41. Collection Gertrude Burnham

635. *Down by the River* (M. 1147)
Sept. 27. Small. RB p. 41

636. *Sunday Morning* (M. 1148)
Sept. 27. 10¾ x 15¾". RB p. 41.
Collection Mrs. N. Blumberg

637. *Monday Morning* (M. 1149)
Sept. 27. 7¾ x 10". RB p. 41. Collection Judson Bemis

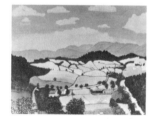

638. *Hoosick Valley* (M. 1150)
Oct. 18. 18 x 21¾". RB p. 41. Collection Mrs. Paul Mellon. Parke-
Bernet Sale No. 2336, March 18,
1965, No. 119

639. *Down in the Valley* (M. 1151)
Oct. 18. Small. RB p. 41

640. *Which Way* (M. 1152)
Oct. 18. 13½ x 10¾". RB p. 41.
Collection Mrs. N. Blumberg

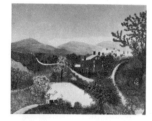

641. *The State Line House* (M. 1153)
Oct. 18. 13½ x 17¾". RB p. 41.
Collection Lowell C. Camps

642. *Taking Leg Bale for Security* (M. 1154)
Oct. 18. 27 x 20¾". RB p. 41. Collection George M. Newell. (See plate 121)

643. *Home in the Springtime* (M. 1155)
Oct. 18. 27¼ x 21½". RB p. 41. Private collection. (See plate 122)

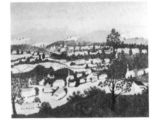

644. *In the Green Mountains*
About October 1946. 17½ x 21½"

645. *Covered Bridge with Carriage* (M. 1158)
Nov. 6. 27½ x 21½". RB p. 41 "The Black Buggy," numbered 1160. The Shelburne Museum, Shelburne, Vt. *Reproduced: Detroit Athletic Club News,* July 1949 (cover); MLH. (See plate 116)

646. *Belvedere* (M. 1157)
Nov. 16 (begun in 1944). 16¾ x 27". RB p. 41. Collection Dr. and Mrs. Max Ascoli. (See plate 8)

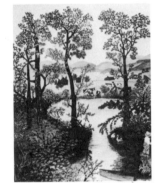

647. *Pond in Fall* (M. 1159)
Nov. 16. 27¼ x 21½". RB p. 41 "Out in the Country"

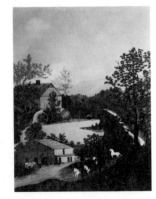

648. *The Old Mill and Stage Coach* (M. 1160)
Nov. 16. 27 x 21". RB p. 41 "White Horses," numbered 1158. Collection Mrs. Norman Bacon

649. *We Love to Skate*
About 1946. c. 8 x 10". Collection Mrs. Rodney Fiske

1947

650. *Mary and Little Lamb* (M. 1161)
Jan. 18. 24 x 34½". RB p. 41. Collection Mrs. F. Kallir. *Reproduced: Art in America* portfolio; GMSB; MLH; *The New York Times Magazine,* May 11, 1947. (See plate 124)

651. *Frosty Morn* (M. 1162)
March 20. RB p. 41. Collection Mrs. John Costello

652. *Old Hoosick Bridge* (M. 1163)
March 20. RB p. 41. Collection Mr. and Mrs. Harry Squires

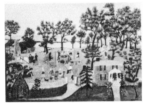

653. *Apple Butter Making* (M. 1164)
March 20. 16½ x 23⅝". RB p. 41. Collection Forrest K. Moses

654. *Apple Butter Making* (M. 1165)
March 21. 19¼ x 23¼". RB p. 41. Galerie St. Etienne, New York. *Reproduced:* color reproduction. (See plate 222)

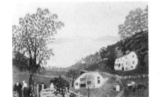

655. *On the Hudson* (M. 1166)
March 21. 22 x 31". RB p. 41. Collection Mrs. Albert D. Lasker

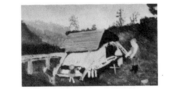

656. *The Old Bake Oven in Canada* (M. 1176)
March 21. 5 x 8". RB p. 42

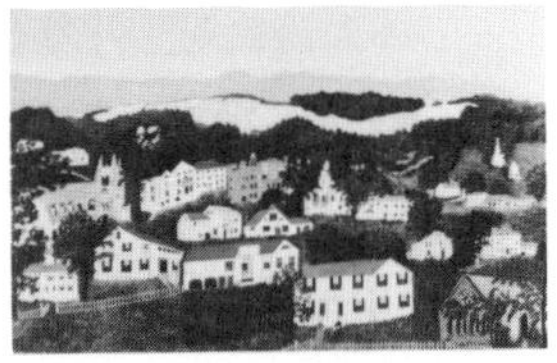

657. *Williamstown* (M. 1167)
March 21. 22 x 36". RB p. 41

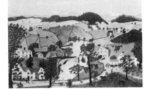

658. *Bought with a Prize* (M. 1168)
March 21. 24 x 38¼". RB p. 41. Private collection

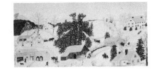

659. *Over the River to Grandma's* (M. 1169)
March 21. 19½ x 41¾". RB p. 41. Private collection. *Reproduced:* GMSB; Parke-Bernet Sale No. 1490, Feb. 3, 1954, No. 72

660. *Little Boy Blue* (M. 1170)
March 21. 20½ x 23". RB p. 41. Private collection. (See plate 125)

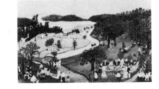

661. *The Picnic* (M. 1171)
March 21. 24¼ x 39". RB p. 41. Private collection. *Reproduced:* Parke-Bernet Sale No. 1959, March 16, 1960, No. 89

662. *A Frosty Morning* (M. 1172)
March 21. 9½ x 10⅞". RB p. 42 "A Frosty Morning, second." Collection Frank La Farge

663. *The Old Hoosick Bridge* (M. 1172)
March 21. 11¾ x 14¾". RB p. 42

664. *Little Boy Blue* (M. 1173)
March 21. 10¼ x 12". RB p. 42 "Little Boy Blue, second." Private collection

665. *Who Is Afraid* (M. 1174)
March 21. 8 x 10". RB p. 42. Collection Mrs. Charles E. Glore

666. *A Storm Is on the Waters Now* (M. 1175)
March 21. 16 x 20¼". RB p. 42. Collection Margaret Mallory. (See plate 230)

667. *All Is Calm* (M. 1177)
RB p. 42 dated March 26, 1947. Collection William H. Shanahan

668. *All Is Calm* (M. 1177)
April 26. 15 x 19". Collection Mr. and Mrs. Norman Scott

669. *The Old Oaken Bucket* (M. 1178)
Spring, 1947. 23½ x 27½". RB p. 42. Collection Mrs. Hugh W. Moses

670. *Old Hoosick Bridge* (M. 1179)
RB p. 42 dated April 30, 1947. Collection Elsie M. Toombs

671. *Breaking the Roads* (M. 1180)
April(?). 8½ x 18"

672. *Sunshine* (M. 1180)
RB p. 42 dated April 30, 1947

673. *The Lake in Summer* (M. 1181)
April 30. 12¾ x 14½". RB p. 42. Collection Mrs. A.S. Chisholm

674. *The Lake in Fall* (M. 1181)
April 30. 12¾ x 14½". RB p. 42 numbered 1182. Collection Emma Little

675. *Over the River* (M. 1183)
April 30. 20 x 30". RB p. 42

676. *A May Morning* (M. 1184)
May. 19½ x 22". RB p. 42 dated May 24, 1947. Collection Mr. and Mrs. Walter L. Wolf. (See plate 123)

677. *Away Down in the Valley* (M. 1185)
May. 9¾ x 11½". RB p. 42 dated May 24, 1947. Collection James Cook

678. *Going Out to Sea* (M. 1186)
May 24. 9½ x 13½". RB p. 42

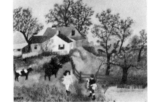

679. *A Trout* (M. 1187)
May 27. 10½ x 14½". RB p. 42 dated May 24, 1947. Collection Lillian Gish

680. *The Wood Road* (M. 1188)
May. 8¾ x 6". RB p. 42 dated May 24, 1947

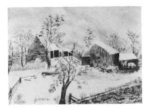

681. *Snow Scene* (M. 1190?)
May 1947(?). 8 x 12". Collection H.D. Carter

682. *Harpers Ferry* (M. 1189)
June. RB p. 42 dated June 5, 1947. Sold through ABAC, New York

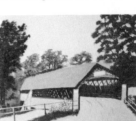

683. *The Old Hoosick Bridge* (M. 1190)
June 14. 8 x 10". RB p. 42. Collection Mrs. Howard Harrington

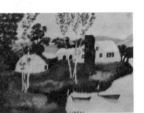

684. *By the Side of the River* (M. 1191)
June 16. 7 x 9". RB p. 42. Sold through Maxwell Galleries, San Francisco

685. *My Geese* (M. 1192)
June 16. 7¼ x 9". RB p. 42. Collection Stanley H. Hinlein

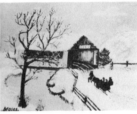

686. *A Ride in the Cutter* (M. 1193)
June 16. 7 x 9". RB p. 42. Sold through Vigeveno, Los Angeles

687. *The Old Barn in Winter* (M. 1194)
June 16. 9¾ x 11⅛". RB p. 42

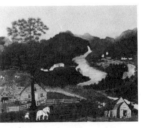

688. *Away Back* (M. 1195)
June 16. 16 x 20". RB p. 42. Formerly Collection Ala Story

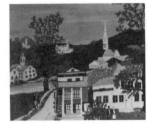

689. *As I Was Going Down the Street* (M. 1196)
June 16. 11 x 12¾". RB p. 42. Sold through Vose, Boston

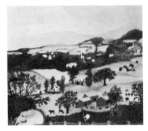

690. *East from Mt. Colefax* (M. 1197)
July 2. 21½ x 23½". RB p. 42 "Looking East from Mt. Colefax." Collection Mrs. Walter J. Kohler

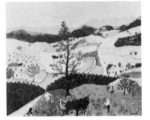

691. *West of Mt. Colefax* (M. 1198)
July 2. 16 x 20". RB p. 42 "Looking West from Mt. Colefax"

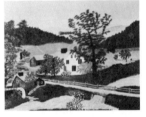

692. *The Old Mill on Sunday* (M. 1199)
July 2. 16 x 20". RB p. 42. Collection Dr. and Mrs. Max Ascoli

693. *The Old Hoosick Bridge* (M. 1200)
Autumn(?), 1947. 8 x 12"

694. *A Fire in the Woods* (M. 1201)
Sept. 2. 24 x 36¼". RB p. 43 dated Sept. 15. Private collection. (See plate 126)

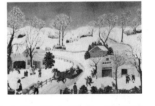

695. *A Nice Winter Morning* (M. 1202)
Sept. 2. 24 x 36½". RB p. 43 dated Sept. 15. Collection Mrs. Clifford Mallory, Sr. *Reproduced:* Hallmark

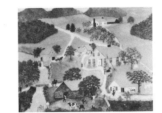

696. *Roanoke River (Over the Roanoke)*
(M. 1203)
Sept. 2. 25 x 37''. RB p. 43 dated
Sept. 15

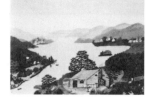

697. *On the Banks of the Hudson River*
(M. 1204)
Sept. 2. 25¼ x 37¼''. RB p. 43
dated Sept. 15. *Reproduced:* Parke-
Bernet Sale No. 1897, April 15,
1959, No. 64

698. *Obadiah's Home* (M. 1207)
Sept. 2. 9½ x 12½''. RB p. 43 dated
Sept. 15

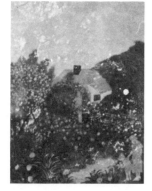

699. *The Rose Garden* (M. 1209)
Sept. 2. 9 x 7''. RB p. 43 dated
Sept. 15

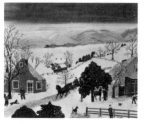

700. *Winter Sports* (M. 1205)
Sept. 14. 22½ x 28''. RB p. 43
dated Sept. 15. Formerly collection
Mrs. Stephen C. Clark

701. *The Dividing of the Ways* (M. 1206)
Sept. 15. 16 x 20''. RB p. 43. Private collection. (See plate 128)

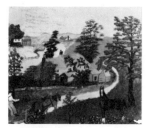

702. *The Salmon Place* (M. 1208)
September. 10 x 12''. RB p. 43.
Collection H.D. Carter

703. *[Untitled] Snow Landscape with Gray
Sky*
About September. Collection Mrs.
Dwight Marvin

704. *Under the Butternut Tree* (M. 1209)
Oct. 11. 27 x 21''. RB p. 43. Collec-
tion Mr. and Mrs. Patrick John
Nugent. (See plate 127)

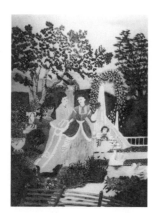

705. *A Wish of Childhood* (M. 1210)
Oct. 11. 27 x 21''. RB p. 43. Copy
of a picture which was in the artist's childhood home

706. *The Spring in Evening* (M. 1211)
Oct. 11. 27 x 21''. RB p. 43. Private
collection. *Reproduced:* Cover il-
lustration for score of *Down in the
Valley* by Kurt Weill (G. Schirmer,
N.Y., 1948); also on record album
of RCA Victor recording of same.
(See plate 120)

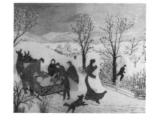

707. *Going from the Mill* (M. 1212)
Oct. 11. 27 x 21''. RB p. 43. Collection Mrs. Raymond C. Harper

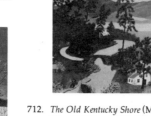

708. *Winter Sport* (M. 1213)
Nov. 5. 19 x 22¾''. RB p. 43

709. *When the Cows Come Home*
(M. 1214)
Nov. 5. 16 x 21¾''. RB p. 43. For-
merly collection Ala Story

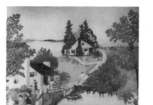

710. *Tom, Tom, the Piper's Son* (M. 1215)
Nov. 5. 16 x 19¾''. RB p. 43

711. *For This Is the Fall of the Year*
(M. 1216)
Nov. 5. 16 x 21¾''. RB p. 43. Pri-
vate collection. *Reproduced:* GMSB;
Hallmark; MLH (German and
Dutch editions); Oldenbourg. (See
plate 130)

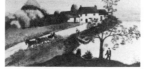

712. *The Old Kentucky Shore* (M. 1217)
Nov. 5. 16¾ x 19¾''. RB p. 43. *Reproduced:* Parke-Bernet Sale No.
2751, Oct. 24, 1968, No. 87

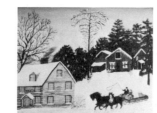

713. *The Potter Home* (M. 1218)
Nov. 5. 13 x 15½''. RB p. 43. Formerly collection Ala Story

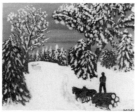

714. *The Last Load* (M. 1219)
Nov. 5. 8 x 10''. RB p. 43. Collection Mrs. Leonard Feathers

715. *What a Pal Is Mother* (M. 1220)
Nov. 5. 8 x 10'' (oval). RB p. 43

716. *Waiting* (M. 1221)
Nov. 5. 8 x 10'' (cut corners). RB
p. 43

717. *Oh for a Slide* (M. 1222)
Nov. 5. 9 x 11''. RB p. 43

718. *Jack and Jill* (M. 1224)
Nov. 10. 12½ x 19¾''. RB p. 43.
Private collection. (See plate 133)

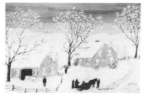

719. *Brother's Home*
Nov. 21. 8 x 16⅛''. Collection Mr.
and Mrs. George O. Cook

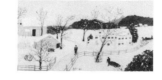

720. *Oh, Strawberries*
Nov. 21. 8 x 16⅛''. Collection Mr.
and Mrs. George O. Cook

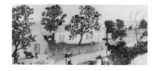

721. *No Game*
Nov. 21. 7 x 11''

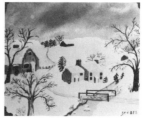

722. *Around the Lake*
Nov. 21. Small

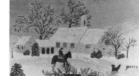

723. *Get Along Topsy*
Nov. 28. 10 x 12''. Collection
Richard Moses

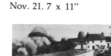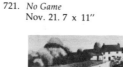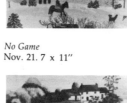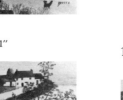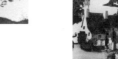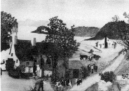

724. *Gray Buildings*
December. 10 x 16''. Collection
Mr. and Mrs. George O. Cook

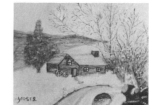

725. *Little Brown House*
About 1947. Small. Collection
Eleanor Potter

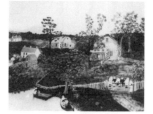

726. *Bridge, Winter*
About 1947. 8¾ x 10½''. Collection Mrs. Howard Harrington

1948

727. *In Olden Times on Hudson River*
(M. 1225)
Feb. 16. 20 x 30''. RB p. 45. Sold
through Vigeveno, Los Angeles

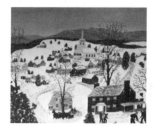

728. *Back from the Hudson River*
(M. 1226)
Feb. 16. 20 x 26''. RB p. 45

729. *The Thunderstorm* (M. 1227)
Feb. 16. 20¾ x 24¾''. RB p. 45. Pri-
vate collection. *Reproduced: Art in
America* portfolio; Jasmand and
Kallir; MLH; *Die Weltkunst*
(Munich), Feb. 1, 1955 (cover). (See
plate 134)

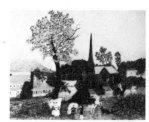

730. *We Are Swinging on the Gate*
(M. 1228)
Feb. 16. 19¼ x 23¼''. RB p. 45.
Collection Roy K. Ferguson

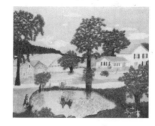

731. *Deep Snow* (M. 1229)
Feb. 16. 16 x 20''. Collection Mr.
and Mrs. Walter L. Wolf

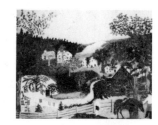

732. *Back in the Country* (M. 1230)
Feb. 16. 16 x 20''. RB p. 45. Collection Dr. and Mrs. Ben F. Feingold

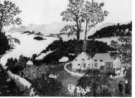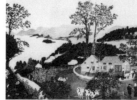

733. *The Prat Homestead* (M. 1231)
Feb. 16. 16 x 20''. RB p. 45. Private
collection

734. *Come On Old Topsy* (M. 1232)
Feb. 16. 16¼ x 20''. RB p. 45

735. *White Birches* (M. 1233)
Feb. 16. 16 x 20''. RB p. 45

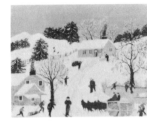

736. *The Old Snow Roller* (M. 1234)
Feb. 16. 16 x 20''. RB p. 45. Sold
through Vigeveno, Los Angeles.
Reproduced: Hallmark

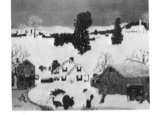

737. *A Fine Gobbler* (M. 1235)
Feb. 16. 16 x 20''. RB p. 45. *Reproduced:* Parke-Bernet Sale No.
1599, May 11, 1955, No. 79

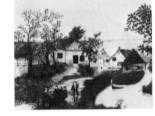

738. *The Old Automobile* (M. 1237)
Feb. 16. 16 x 20''. RB p. 45. Sold
through Vose, Boston

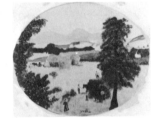

739. *The Harvest* (M. 1238)
Feb. 16. 11 x 14'' (oval). RB p. 45.
The Parrish Art Museum,
Southampton, N.Y.

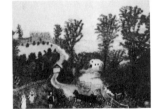

740. *The Old Shedd Bridge* (M. 1240)
Feb. 16. 16 x 20''. RB p. 45. Collection Mr. and Mrs. Myron G.
Halperin

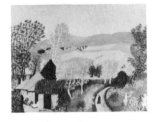

741. *Scotland* (M. 1241)
Feb. 16. 17½ x 23½''. RB p. 45

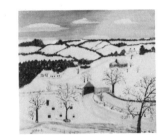

742. *September* (M. 1242)
Feb. 26. 13½ x 19½''. RB p. 45.
Sold through Maxwell, San Francisco

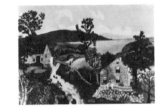

743. *Mine Own Country* (M. 1243)
Feb. 28. 24 x 30''. RB p. 45. Formerly collection Ala Story

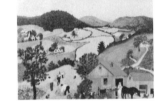

744. *There Goes the Red Sledge* (M. 1244)
April 24. 12¼ x 14''. RB p. 45.
Parke-Bernet Sale No. 1599, May
11, 1955, No. 44

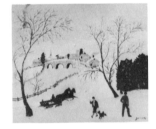

745. *The Lost Ox and Cart* (M. 1245)
April. 12¼ x 14½''. RB p. 45 dated
April 24, 1945. Parke-Bernet Sale
No. 1564, Jan. 9. 1955, No. 57

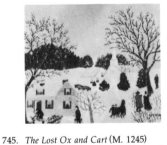

746. *Bridge over Owl Kill* (M. 1246)
April 24. 12¼ x 14''. RB p. 45. Collection A.L. Flesh

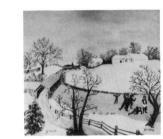

747. *John Going Home* (M. 1247)
April 24. 12¼ x 14''. RB p. 45. Sold
through California Palace of the
Legion of Honor, San Francisco

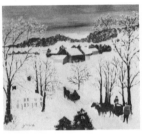

748. *The Presbyterian Sledge Ride*
(M. 1248)
April 24. 12 x 14''. RB p. 45

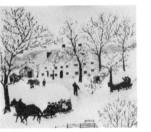

749. *The Baptist Sledge Ride* (M. 1249)
April 24. 11 x 15''. RB p. 45. Collection Robert Peterson

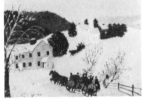

750. *We'll Be Back for Supper* (M. 1250)
April 24. 13¾ x 18½''. RB p. 45

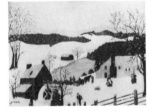

751. *High Ho! Bob Is Down* (M. 1251)
April 24. 12 x 14''. RB p. 45.
Parke-Bernet Sale No. 1576, March
9, 1955, No. 60

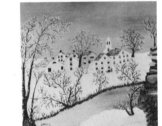

752. *Over to the Village* (M. 1252)
April 24. 12 x 14''. RB p. 45

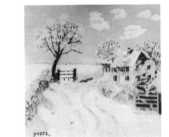

753. *Cold and Windy* (M. 1253)
April 24. 10¾ x 11½''. RB p. 45

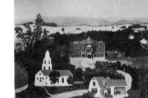

754. *The Hospital* (M. 1255)
April 30. 30 x 36''. RB p. 45. Collection Chester La Roche. *Reproduced:* United Hospital Campaign Fund Christmas card

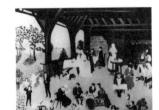

755. *The Proposal* (M. 1254)
April 30. 35 x 45¼''. RB p. 46.
Galerie St. Etienne, New York

756. *Jenny McCree's Home* (M. 1256)
April 30. 30 x 36''. RB p. 46. Collection Mr. and Mrs. James M.
Blacklidge

757. *Going Home from Church* (M. 1257)
June 11. 11½ x 10''. RB p. 46. Sold
through California Palace of the
Legion of Honor, San Francisco

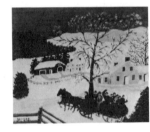

758. *So Long* (M. 1258)
June 11. 9 x 10¾''. RB p. 46. Collection G.G. Buttel. *Reproduced:*
Hallmark

759. *Williamstown in Winter* (M. 1259)
June 12. 16 x 20''. RB p. 46. Sold
through Vigeveno, Los Angeles

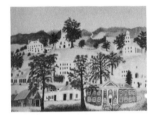

760. *Williamstown in Summer* (M. 1260)
June 12. 15¾ x 20''. RB p. 46.
Riverdale Drapery Fabrics, New
York

761. *The Night Is Coming On* (M. 1261)
June 16. 14¾ x 7½''. RB p. 46. Sold
through California Palace of the
Legion of Honor, San Francisco

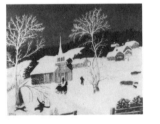

762. *Oh Help Me, Bowser* (M. 1262)
June 16. 16 x 20''. RB p. 46

763. *Goodbye All* (M. 1263)
June 16. 16 x 20''. RB p. 46. Collection L. Arnold Weissberger

764. *Will They Be Home?* (M. 1264)
June 16. 17¼ x 8''. RB p. 46. Sold
through California Palace of the
Legion of Honor, San Francisco

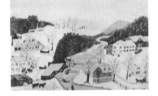

765. *Over the River to Grandma's House*
(M. 1265)
July 26. 20½ x 30¾''. RB p. 46.
Collection Mr. and Mrs. George O.
Cook

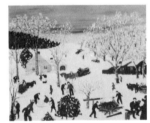

766. *Sugaring Off* (M. 1266)
July 26. 16 x 20''. RB p. 46. Collection Mrs. T. DeWitt Vandervoort.
Reproduced: Hallmark

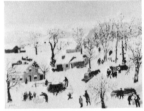

767. *Sugaring Off, Dark Sky* (M. 1267)
July 26. 16 x 20¼''. RB p. 46. Private collection

768. *The Old Mill Below the Lake*
(M. 1268)
July 26. 16 x 20¼''. RB p. 46 numbered 1269

769. *Through the Bridge by the Mill*
(M. 1269)
July 26. 20 x 30''. RB p. 46 numbered 1268. Formerly collection
Ala Story. (See plate 129)

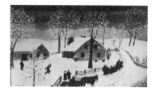

770. *Oh Wait for Me* (M. 1270) July 26. 10¼ x 16″. RB p. 46. Collection Mrs. Henry Wendt

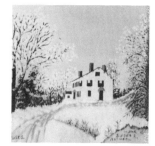

771. *Home of Susan B. Anthony* (M. 1271) July 26. 7 x 7″. RB p. 46. Collection Elwood Whitney

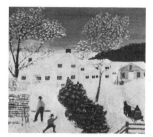

772. *I'm Coming Pop* (M. 1272) July 26. 10¾ x 12¼″. RB p. 46 numbered 1276. Sold through Vose, Boston

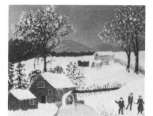

773. *I Love to Fish* (M. 1273) July 26. 7¼ x 9½″. RB p. 46. Collection Mrs. N. Salzman

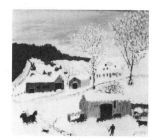

774. *Go for Him, Rover* (M. 1274) July 26. 9 x 10″. RB p. 46. *Reproduced:* Hallmark

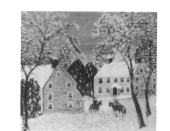

775. *I'll Meet You by the Woods* (M. 1275) July 26. 9 x 9½″. RB p. 46. Collection Mrs. I. H. Van Gelder

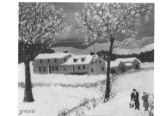

776. *We'll Go Brodyes* (M. 1276) July 26. 6 x 7¾″. RB p. 46 "We'll Go Brodys," numbered 1272. Sold through Vigeveno, Los Angeles

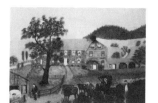

777. *The Betsey Russell Home in Summer* (M. 1277) July 26. 12 x 17″. RB p. 46. Sold through Vose, Boston

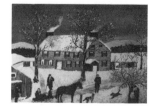

778. *The Betsey Russell Winter House* (M. 1278) July 26. 12¼ x 16″. RB p. 46

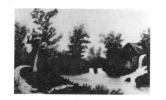

779. *All Is Calm* (M. 1279) July 26. 10 x 16″. RB p. 46. Formerly collection Ala Story

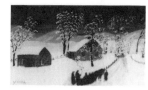

780. *The Breakdown* (M. 1280) July 26. 7¼ x 12¼″. RB p. 47 numbered 1281.

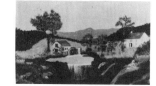

781. *The Frog Pond* (M. 1281) July 26. 7¼ x 12¼″. RB p. 47 numbered 1280. Collection Elise Strouse

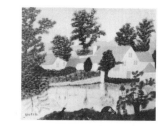

782. *The Winner* August. c. 10 x 10″. Formerly collection Linda May Nilsson

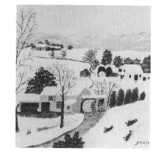

783. *Home by the Lake* (M. 1282) Sept. 6. 10 x 12″. RB p. 47. Sold through Vigeveno, Los Angeles

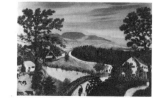

784. *We Will Go for a Walk* (M. 1283) Sept. 6. 16 x 24″. RB p. 47. Collection Jerome Sinsheimer

785. *The Hitching Post* (M. 1285) Sept. 6. 15 x 19¼″. RB p. 47 numbered 1284. Private collection. (See plate 44)

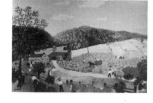

786. *Hunting for Water* (M. 1286) Sept. 6. 16 x 24″. RB p. 47 numbered 1285. National Art Gallery of New South Wales, Sydney, Australia

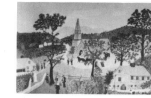

787. *A Beautiful World* (M. 1286) Sept. 6. 20 x 24″. RB p. 47. Collection F. Kallir. *Reproduced:* GMSB

788. *The Church in the Wild Wood* (M. 1286) Sept. 6. 16¼ x 20″. RB p. 47 numbered 1282. Collection Mrs. William Hayward. (See plate 131)

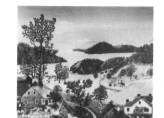

789. *The Old Ox Cart* (M. 1288) Sept. 6. 6 x 7½″. RB p. 47. The Bennington Museum, Bennington, Vt.

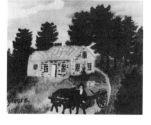

790. *The Old Grist Mill in Winter* (M. 1289) Sept. 6. 16 x 20″. RB p. 47. Formerly collection Ala Story

791. *Over the Bridge, Home* (M. 1290) Sept. 6. 10½ x 15″. RB p. 47. Collection Mrs. Anthony Farrara

792. *The Dead Tree* (M. 1291) Sept. 6. 16 x 20″. RB p. 47. Musée National d'Art Moderne, Paris. *Reproduced: Fifty American Masterpieces* (Shorewood, 1968); color reproduction. (See plate 132)

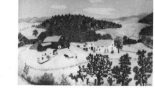

793. *Haying in Vermont* (M. 1294) Oct. 5. 16 x 24″. RB p. 47. Private collection

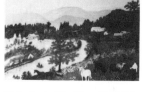

794. *Harvesting in Olden Times* (M. 1295) Oct. 5. 16 x 24″. RB p. 47. Formerly collection Ala Story

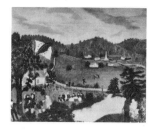

795. *At the Bend of the River* (M. 1296) Oct. 5. 16 x 24″. RB p. 47. Collection John E. Katz

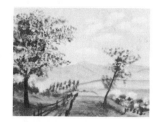

796. *Community Chest, No. 1* (M. 1297) Oct. 5. 16 x 20″. RB p. 47. Galerie St. Etienne, New York

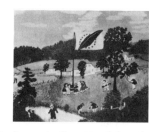

797. *Community Chest, No. 2* (M. 1298) Oct. 5. 16 x 20″. RB p. 47. Community Chests and Councils of America, Inc., New York

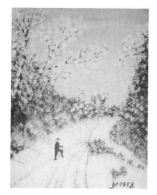

798. *Going Home* (M. 1299) Oct. 5. 7½ x 5¾″. RB p. 47. Sold through Vose, Boston

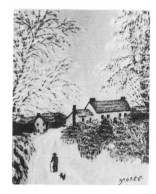

799. *Almost Home* (M. 1300) Oct. 5. 7½ x 5¾″. RB p. 47. Sold through Vigeveno, Los Angeles

800. *Spring in the Valley* (M. 1301) Oct. 5. 5¾ x 7½″. RB p. 47. Collection Glenda Harrington

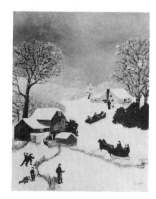

801. *Grand Skating* (M. 1301) Nov. 20. 20 x 16″. RB p. 48 numbered 1310. Collection Mr. and Mrs. Sam Brodherson

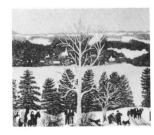

802. *Cazenovia Lake, N.Y.* (M. 1302) Nov. 20. 16 x 20″. RB p. 47. Everson Museum of Art, Syracuse, N.Y.

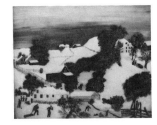

803. *Greenwich, N.Y.* (M. 1303) Nov. 20. 16 x 20″. RB p. 47. Collection Arthur Whitcomb

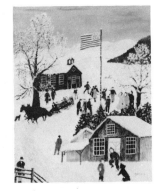

804. *The Old School* (M. 1304) Nov. 20. 20 x 16″. RB p. 47

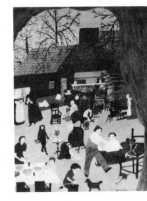

805. *The Old Kitchen* (M. 1305) Nov. 20. 20 x 16″. RB p. 47

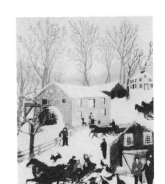

806. *The Old Grist Mill* (M. 1806; *sic)* Nov. 20. 20 x 16″. RB p. 47 numbered 1306. *Reproduced:* Hallmark

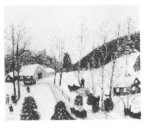

807. *Beautiful Thanksgiving Day* (M. 1307) Nov. 20. 16 x 20″. RB p. 47. Private collection. *Reproduced:* Hallmark

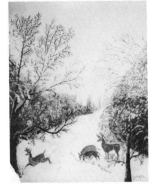

808. *On the Road to North Adams* (M. 1308) Nov. 20. 20 x 16″. RB p. 47. Galerie St. Etienne, New York. *Reproduced:* Hallmark

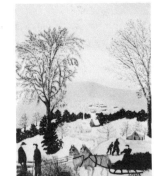

809. *I'm Milking My Cow* (M. 1309) Nov. 20. 16 x 20″. RB p. 48. Sold through Vigeveno, Los Angeles

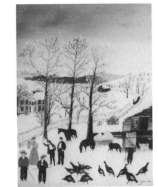

810. *The Mill by the Bridge* (M. 1311) Nov. 20. 20 x 16″. RB p. 48. Sold through Vigeveno, Los Angeles. *Reproduced:* Hallmark

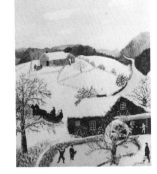

811. *In the Glen with the Deer* (M. 1312) Nov. 20. 20 x 16″. RB p. 48. Collection Mr. and Mrs. Raymond B. Chrisman

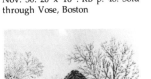
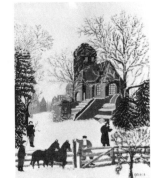

812. *Getting Ready for Thanksgiving* (M. 1313) Nov. 20. 20 x 16″. RB p. 48. Collection Mrs. I. H. Van Gelder. *Reproduced:* Hallmark

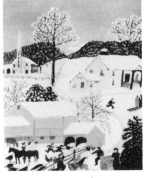
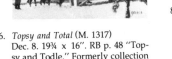
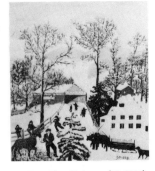

813. *The Day After Christmas* (M. 1314) Nov. 30. 20 x 16″. RB p. 48. Collection Louis Wehle

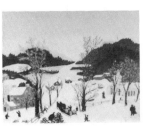

814. *Which Turkey?* (M. 1315) Nov. 30. 20 x 16″. RB p. 48. Turner Co., Cedar Rapids, Iowa

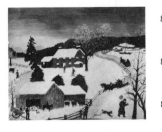

815. *The Old Home on the Hill* (M. 1316) Nov. 30. 20 x 16″. RB p. 48. Sold through Vose, Boston

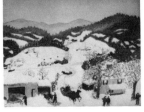

816. *Topsy and Total* (M. 1317) Dec. 8. 19¾ x 16″. RB p. 48 "Topsy and Todle." Formerly collection Ala Story

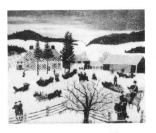

817. *Give Us a Ride* (M. 1318) March 1. 16¾ x 21½″. RB p. 48. Sold through Vose, Boston. *Reproduced:* Hallmark

818. *The Mailman Has Gone* (M. 1319) March 2. 16¾ x 21½″. RB p. 48. The Shelburne Museum, Shelburne, Vt. *Reproduced:* Hallmark; MLH (German and Dutch editions); Oldenbourg. (See plate 46)

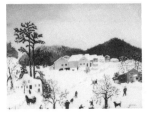

819. *The Checkered House in 1717* (M. 1320) March 3. 16¾ x 21½″. RB p. 48

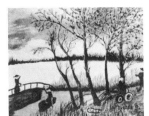

820. *Did You See Uncle John?* (M. 1321) March 4. 16¾ x 21½″. RB p. 48. Collection Mrs. Edward C. Flynn. *Reproduced:* Hallmark

821. *The Old Oaken Bucket* (M. 1322) March 5. 16¾ x 21½″. RB p. 48. Collection Dr. R. M. Schmidt. *Reproduced:* Hallmark. (See plate 135)

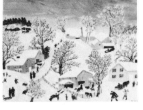

822. *The First Fall of Snow* (M. 1323) March 6. 16¾ x 21½″. RB p. 48. Collection Pamela Woolworth. *Reproduced:* Hallmark

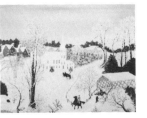

823. *Very Deep Snow* (M. 1324) March 7. 16¾ x 21½″. RB p. 48. Collection Mr. and Mrs. John P. Morgan II. *Reproduced:* Hallmark

824. *A Little Ball Game* (M. 1325) March 8. 16¾ x 21½″. RB p. 48. Collection Mrs. J. Mahlon Buck. *Reproduced:* Hallmark

824a. *Now for the Harvest* (M. 1339) March 8. 5¾ x 7½″. RB p. 51. Sold through Vigeveno, Los Angeles

825. *Home by the Brook* (M. 1340) March 8. 6¼ x 8¼″. RB p. 51. Collection Mrs. George Eckweiler

826. *Out for a Sleigh Ride* (M. 1341) March 8. 6¼ x 8¼″. RB p. 51. Collection Mrs. George Eckweiler

827. *A Winter Storm* (M. 1326) March 9. 16¾ x 21½″. RB p. 48. Formerly collection Ala Story. *Reproduced:* Hallmark

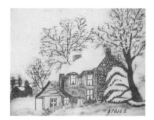

828. *Everyone Is Gone* (M. 1338)
March 9. 5¾ x 7½". Sold through Federation of Arts, Fort Dodge, Iowa

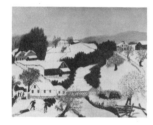

829. *We Will Celebrate* (M. 1327)
March 10. 16¾ x 21½". RB p. 48. Collection Mrs. Charles H. Dunning

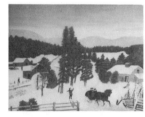

830. *Near Dorset* (M. 1337)
March 10. 5¾ x 7½". RB p. 51. Sold through Vigeveno, Los Angeles

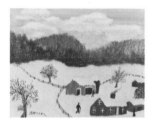

831. *Down Out of the Woods* (M. 1328)
March 11. 16¾ x 21½". RB p. 48. Collection Mrs. Clifford Mallory, Sr.

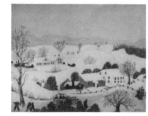

832. *A Parade* (M. 1329)
March 12. 17 x 21¾". RB p. 48. Collection Mr. Ohland

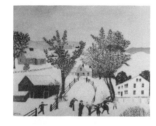

833. *Going for the Mail* (M. 1330)
March 13. 17 x 21¾". RB p. 48. *Reproduced:* Hallmark

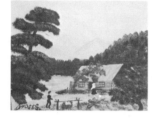

834. *We Are Camping* (M. 1342)
March 13. 5¾ x 7½". RB p. 51. Sold through Vigeveno, Los Angeles

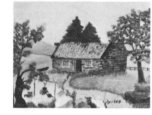

835. *At the Camp* (M. 1343)
March 13. 5¾ x 7½". RB p. 51. Sold through Vigeveno, Los Angeles

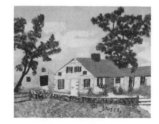

836. *The Old Home* (M. 1344)
March 13. 5¾ x 7½". RB p. 51. Sold through Vigeveno, Los Angeles

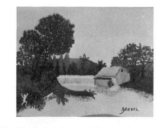

837. *The Swimming Pool* (M. 1345)
March 13. 5¾ x 7½". RB p. 51. Sold through Vigeveno, Los Angeles

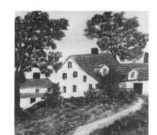

838. *The Alan House* (M. 1346)
March 13. c. 5¾ x 7½". RB p. 51. Sold through Vigeveno, Los Angeles

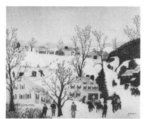

839. *A Village Store* (M. 1331)
March 14. 16¾ x 21¾". RB p. 48. Collection Gerson Hall. *Reproduced:* Hallmark

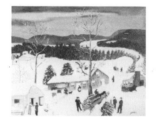

840. *The Last Load of Wood* (M. 1332)
March 15. 17 x 21½". RB p. 48. Collection Mrs. Edward C. Flynn. *Reproduced:* Hallmark

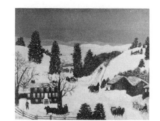

841. *The Harrington House* (M. 1333)
March 16. 16¾ x 21½". Title on label: "The Hirrington House." RB p. 48. *Reproduced:* Hallmark

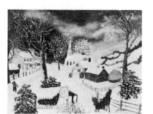

842. *A Wild Winter Day* (M. 1334)
March 17. 11¾ x 16¼". RB p. 48

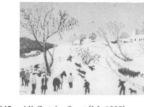

843. *All Out for Sport* (M. 1335)
March 18. 11¾ x 17". RB p. 48

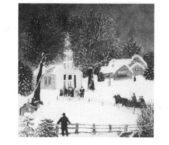

844. *We Are Coming to Church* (M. 1336)
March 19. 15¾ x 16½". RB p. 48. Formerly collection Ala Story

845. *All Is Quiet* (M. 1352)
March 23. 16 x 20". RB p. 51 numbered 1351, dated July 8, 1949. Collection Mrs. Howard Harrison

846. *Falls of Minniehaha [Minnehaha]* (M. 1353)
Formerly collection Fred E. Robertson

847. *Year 1860, Year 1940* (M. 1347–1348) April 18. 26 x 21". RB p. 51. *Reproduced: L'Amérique et les Amériques de la Préhistoire à nos jours* by Pierre Chaunu (Colin, Paris, 1964). (See plate 138)

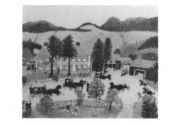

848. *The Old Checkered House* (M. 1349)
April 18. 24 x 30". RB p. 51 numbered 1348. Sold through Vigeveno, Los Angeles

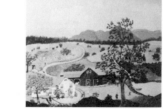

849. *Ho Well Go Sailing* (M. 1351)
April 18. 17 x 21¾". RB p. 51 numbered 1349. The picture bears two labels which are erroneously dated April 18, 1948. Russell Sage College Permanent Collection, Troy, N.Y.

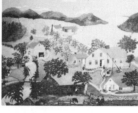

850. *The Old Oaken Bucket* (M. 1351)
July 8. 24 x 30". RB p. 51 numbered 1350. Collection Mrs. S. E. Jeliffe

851. *All Is Calm* (M. 1352)
July 8. Small. RB p. 51 "for Mary"

852. *A Winter Day* (M. 1353)
July 8. Small. RB p. 51. Collection Mrs. Elmer Hill

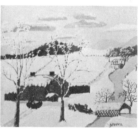

853. *A Winter's Day* (M. 1354)
July 8. 11¾ x 13½". RB p. 51

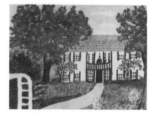

854. *Thomas Moses, Norfolk, Conn.* (M. 1355)
July 8. 5¾ x 7½". RB p. 51 numbered 1354. Collection Mr. and Mrs. L. M. Parsons

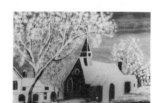

855. *So Dreary* (M. 1356)
July 8. 5¾ x 7½". RB p. 51 numbered 1355. Collection Mrs. M. Hickok

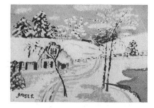

856. *Now We Can Skate* (M. 1357)
July. 5¾ x 7½". RB p. 51 numbered 1356. Formerly collection Ala Story

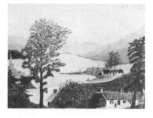

857. *Scotland* (M. 1358)
July 20. 14 x 18½". RB p. 51 numbered 1363, dated Sept. 2, 1949

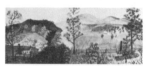

858. *Out of My Window* (M. 1359)
July 20. 6¾ x 16¼". RB p. 51 numbered 1357. Collection John Kallir

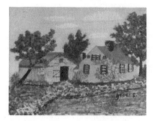

859. *The Old Home* (M. 1360)
July. 5¾ x 7½". RB p. 51 numbered 1358. Sold through Vose, Boston

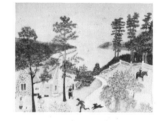

860. *Lake George* (M. 1361)
July. 14 x 18¼". RB p. 51 numbered 1359. Sold through Maxwell, San Francisco

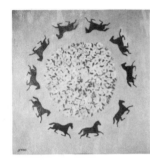

861. *Carpet Pattern*
Aug. 25. Cardboard, 18 x 18''. Similar design painted on both sides. RB p. 51 numbered 1361

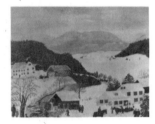

862. *Over the River* (M. 1362)
September. 22 x 28''. RB p. 51 numbered 1360, dated Aug. 25. Collection Lowell C. Camps

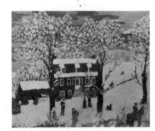

863. *The Harrington Home* (M. 1364)
13 x 16''. RB p. 51 numbered 1362, dated Sept. 2. Collection Mrs. Elmer Hill

864. *The Schoolhouse* (M. 1364)
September. 21 x 25''. RB p. 51 dated Sept. 2. Collection Mrs. Hugh W. Moses. *Reproduced:* GMSB. (See plate 219)

865. *Through the Bridge* (M. 1365)
Oct. 1949(?). 5¾ x 7½''. Collection Mrs. Anthony Farrara

866. *Bringing the Sheep Home* (M. 1366)
October. 11 x 13''. RB p. 51. Collection Mrs. Anthony Farrara

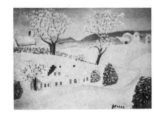

867. *Quiet Winter Day* (M. 1367)
October. 9¼ x 12''. RB p. 52 dated Nov. 5, 1949

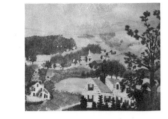

868. *Mountain Village* (M. 1368)
October. 13 x 16''. RB p. 52 dated Nov. 5, 1949. Collection Mrs. G. C. Cline

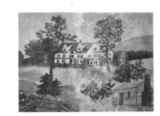

869. *Home in Manchester* (M. 1369)
October. 12 x 16''. RB p. 52 dated Nov. 5, 1949

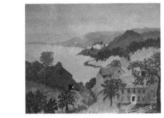

870. *On Lake George* (M. 1370)
October. 13 x 16''. RB p. 52 dated Nov. 5, 1949. Sold through Dalzell-Hatfield, Los Angeles

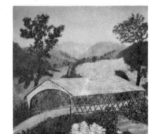

871. *Sheehy Bridge* (M. 1371)
October. 11½ x 11½''. RB p. 52 dated Nov. 5, 1949

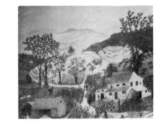

872. *The Archer* (M. 1372)
October. 21 x 25''. RB p. 52 dated Nov. 5, 1949. Sold through Maxwell, San Francisco

873. *Road Above Village*
November. Small. Collection Mrs. Ellis K. Baldwin

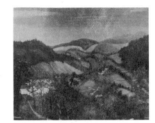

874. *Mary McClellan Hospital*
About November. Small. Private collection

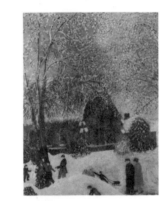

875. *Old Stone Bridge*
Dec. 15. 4 x 9''. The label on the painting is erroneously dated Dec. 15, 1939. Collection Mr. and Mrs. George O. Cook

876. *Watering the Horses*
December. 19¾ x 24''. Collection Mrs. J. B. Olstein

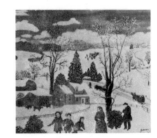

877. *The Hay Is In*
December. 20 x 24''. Collection Mrs. David Levy

878. *The Meeting House*
December. 18¾ x 26¼''. Sold through Maxwell, San Francisco. (See plate 136)

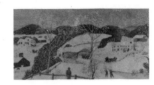

879. *Over the River to Grandma's House* (M. 1265)
Painted in 1948, revised in 1949. 16 x 30¼''. RB p. 46(?). A photograph exists of the earlier version of this picture

1950

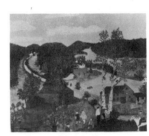

880. *From My Window* (M. 253)
Painted May 6, 1942, completely revised Jan. 1950. 16 x 20¼''. Collection Mr. and Mrs. Thomas G. Vitez

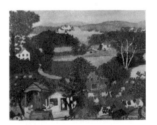

881. *Follow Me* (M. 1236)
Begun Feb. 16, 1948, finished Jan. 1950. 20 x 16''. RB p. 45. A photograph exists of this painting in an unfinished state

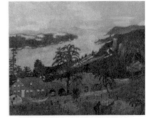

882. *Grandmother* (M. 1373)
January. 20 x 24''. RB p. 52 listed twice: numbered 1373, dated Dec. 13, 1949, and numbered 1375, dated Jan. 3, 1950. Collection Mr. and Mrs. John M. Schiff

883. *The Quilting Bee* (M. 1374)
January. 20 x 24''. RB p. 52 listed twice: numbered 1374, dated Dec. 13, 1949, and numbered 1376, dated Jan. 3, 1950. Private collection. *Reproduced:* MLH. (See plate 237)

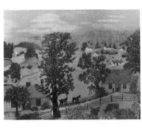

884. *The Dairy Farm* (M. 1375)
January. 20 x 24''. RB p. 52 listed twice: numbered 1375, dated Dec. 13, 1949, and numbered 1377, dated Jan. 3, 1950

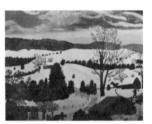

885. *The Counting of the Geese* (M. 1376)
January. 20 x 24''. RB p. 52 listed twice: numbered 1376, dated Dec. 13, 1949, and numbered 1378, dated Jan. 3, 1950. Formerly collection Ala Story

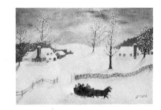

886. *At the Well* (M. 1377)
January. 20 x 24''. RB p. 52 listed twice: numbered 1373, dated Dec. 13, 1949, and numbered 1379, dated Jan. 3, 1950

887. *The Wind in Winter* (M. 1378)
January. 20 x 24''. RB p. 52 numbered 1380, dated Jan. 3, 1950. Private collection. *Reproduced:* MLH (German and Dutch editions); Oldenbourg. (See plate 139)

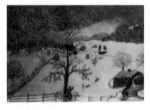

888. *On the Hudson Many Years Ago* (M. 1381)
January. 20 x 24''. RB p. 52. Formerly collection Ala Story

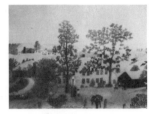

889. *One Little Hut Among the Bushes* (M. 1382)
January. 18 x 24''. RB p. 52. Collection Mrs. Richard H. Bryant

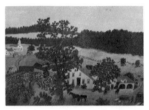

890. *Apple Blossom Time at Home* (M. 1383)
January. 18 x 24''. RB p. 52. Sold through Maxwell, San Francisco

891. *A January Thaw* (M. 1384)
January. 17¾ x 22''. RB p. 52. Collection Mrs. William Hayward

892. *Down by the Old Stone Wall* (M. 1385)
January. 11½ x 16''. RB p. 52. Collection Marjorie M. Whiteman

893. *Better Going over the Hill* (M. 1386)
January. 11¼ x 15¾''. RB p. 52

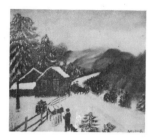

894. *The Mail Is Here* (M. 1387)
January. 10 x 12''. RB p. 52

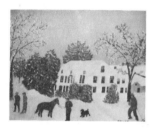

895. *The Norton Home* (M. 1388)
January. 10 x 12''. RB p. 52

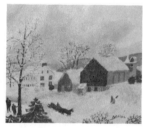

896. *The Snow So Deep* (M. 1389)
January 10 x 12''. RB p. 52. Sordoni Collection

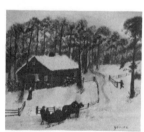

897. *We'll Go to the Woods* (M. 1390)
January. 10 x 12''. RB p. 52

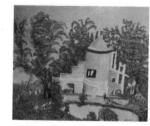

898. *The Witch's Castle* (M. 1391)
February. 14½ x 17¾''. RB p. 52 dated Feb. 10, 1950

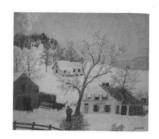

899. *I'll Mail the Letter* (M. 1392)
February. 16 x 19''. RB p. 53. Sold through Vose, Boston

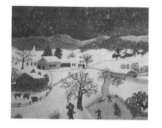

900. *Haw, Haw, Now It Snows* (M. 1393)
February. 14½ x 17½''. RB p. 53. Collection Mrs. Russel Crouse

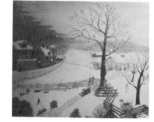

901. *Down by the Old Rail Fence* (M. 1394)
February. 16 x 19''. RB p. 53. Collection Mr. and Mrs. George Greenspan

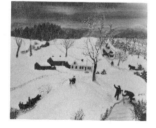

902. *The Ice Is Thick* (M. 1395)
February. 14½ x 17½''. RB p. 53 dated Feb. 10, 1950. *Reproduced:* Parke-Bernet Sale No. 2251, Jan. 29, 1964, No. 37

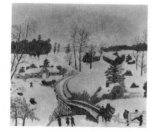

903. *Building the Fence* (M. 1396)
March. 16 x 19''. RB p. 53 dated March 6, 1950. Formerly collection Ala Story

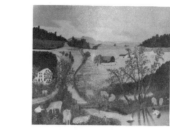

904. *On the Watch* (M. 1397)
March. 16 x 19''. RB p. 53 dated March 6, 1950. Collection Mrs. H.W. Armstrong

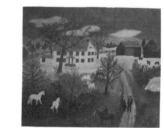

905. *Our Old Saw Mill* (M. 1398)
March. 16 x 19''. RB p. 53. Collection Eleanore Fleming

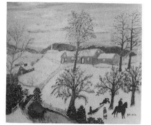

906. *The Owl Kill* (M. 1401)
March. 16 x 19''. RB p. 53. Collection Mr. and Mrs. E.E. Fogelson

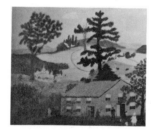

907. *The Old Plank House* (M. 1402)
April. 16 x 19''. RB p. 53 dated April 13, 1950. Formerly collection Ala Story

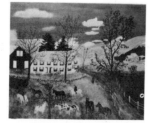

908. *The Spotted Horses* (M. 1403)
April. 16 x 19''. RB p. 53. Formerly collection Ala Story

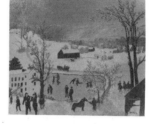

909. *A Herd of Jerseys* (M. 1405)
April. Canvas, 20 x 24''. RB p. 53 dated April 13, 1950. Formerly collection Ala Story

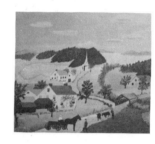

910. *When the Leaves Have Fallen* (M. 1406)
April. Canvas, 20 x 24''. RB p. 53 dated April 13, 1950

911. *A Quilting Bee* (M. 1407)
April. 20 x 24''. RB p. 53 dated April 13, 1950. Private collection. (See plate 140)

912. *The Old Oaken Bucket in Winter* (M. 1408)
April. 20 x 24''. RB p. 53 dated April 13, 1950. (See plate 48)

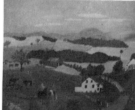

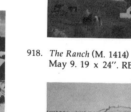

913. *The Old Checkered House (Winter)* (M. 1409)
April. 19¾ x 24''. RB p. 53 dated April 13, 1950. Collection Otto Kallir. *Reproduced:* Hallmark; MLH

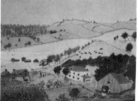

914. *Down the Road* (M. 1410)
April. 19 x 24''. RB p. 53 dated April 13, 1950. Collection Mrs. J.B. Olstein

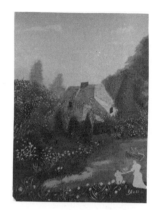

915. *Sunday Skating* (M. 1411)
May 9. Canvas, 20 x 24''. RB p. 53. Collection Mrs. A.F. Johnson

916. *Laundry Day* (M. 1412)
May 9. Canvas, 20 x 24''. RB p. 53. Collection Eleanore Fleming. (See plate 144)

917. *Dorset* (M. 1413)
May 9. Canvas, 20 x 24''. RB p. 53

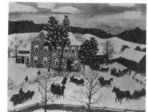

918. *The Ranch* (M. 1414)
May 9. 19 x 24''. RB p. 53

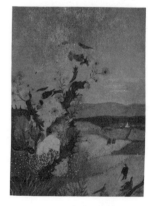

919. *Hoosick Hills* (M. 1415)
May 9. 19 x 24''. RB p. 53. Collection Mrs. J. Mahlon Buck

920. *The Barn Dance* (M. 1416)
May 9. Canvas, 35 x 45''. RB p. 53. Hammer Galleries, New York. (See plate 228)

921. *Country Fair* (M. 1417)
May 9. Canvas, 35 x 45''. RB p. 53. Collection David H. Griffin. *Reproduced: BG; The Four Seasons* portfolio; GMSB. (See plate 229)

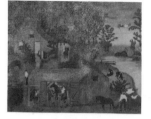

922. *The Back Yard* (M. 1418)
May 9. Canvas, 20 x 24''. RB p. 53. Private collection

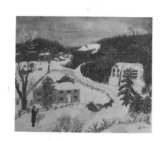

923. *In the Rose Garden* (M. 1423)
May 19. Canvas, 16 x 12''. RB p. 54. Collection Eleanore Fleming

924. *Over Land* (M. 1419)
May 30. Canvas, 20 x 24''. RB p. 53. Collection Mr. and Mrs. John S. Schulten. (See plate 145)

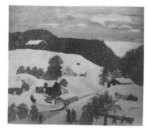

925. *The Yellow Birds* (M. 1420)
June 19. Canvas, 16 x 12''. RB p. 54

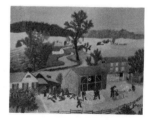

926. *The Work to Do* (M. 1421)
June 19. Canvas, 12 x 16''. RB p. 54. Formerly collection Ala Story

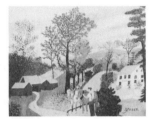

927. *In Autumn Time* (M. 1422)
June 19. Canvas, 12 x 16″. RB p. 54. Sold through Maxwell, San Francisco

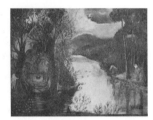

928. *In the Camp* (M. 1424)
June 19. Canvas, 12 x 16″. Collection Mr. and Mrs. Harry Gelles

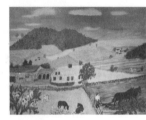

929. *The Plow Boy* (M. 1425)
June 20. 12 x 16″. RB p. 54. Sold through Dalzell-Hatfield, Los Angeles

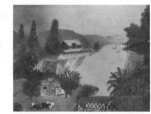

930. *A Boy with Oxen* (M. 1426)
June 20. 12 x 16″. RB p. 54. Sold through Maxwell, San Francisco

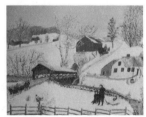

931. *Going for the Mail* (M. 1427)
June 20. 12 x 16″. RB p. 54. Collection Mrs. Gordon E. Robbins

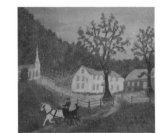

932. *Going for a Buggy Ride* (M. 1428)
June 20. 8 x 9½″. Title inscribed by the artist: "A Home of 1772." RB p. 54. Sold through Vigeveno, Los Angeles

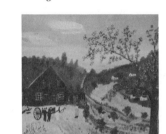

933. *In the Blacksmith Shop* (M. 1429)
June 20. 8 x 9½″. RB p. 54. Collection Mrs. Harry Chadima

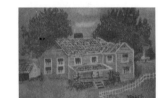

934. *Aunt Margret's* (M. 1430)
June 20. 5½ x 7″. RB p. 54. Collection Mrs. David Shelly

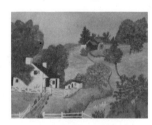

935. *The Duck Pond* (M. 1431)
June. Canvas, 12 x 16″. RB p. 54 dated June 20, 1950. Sold through Maxwell, San Francisco

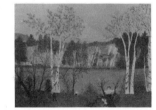

936. *On the Other Side of the River* (M. 1432)
June 30. 12 x 15¾″. RB p. 54

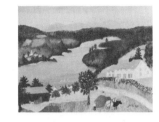

937. *Down the Hudson Many Years Ago* (M. 1433)
June 30. 12 x 15¾″. RB p. 54. Sold through Vigeveno, Los Angeles

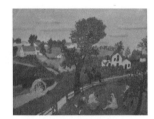

938. *Happy Days* (M. 1434)
June 30. 12 x 15¾″. RB p. 54. Sold through Dalzell-Hatfield, Los Angeles

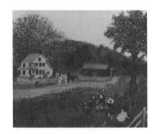

939. *See Old Topsy* (M. 1435)
June 30. 8 x 9¼″. RB p. 54. Collection J.B. de la Faille

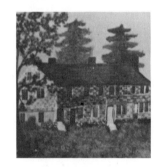

940. *The Old Checkered House of N.H., 1800* (M. 1436)
June 30. 9¼ x 9″. RB p. 54 "The Old Checkered House, Hinsdale, N.H. in 1800." Collection Mrs. H. Osborne

941. *Candle Dip Day in 1800* (M. 1437)
June 30. 9 x 9¼″. RB p. 54. Private collection. *Reproduced:* BG; GMSB. (See plate 137)

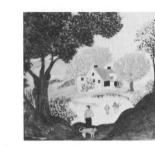

942. *That Happy Land* (M. 1438)
June 30. 9¼ x 9½″. RB p. 54

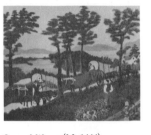

943. *Here Comes Daddy* (M. 1439)
June 30. 8 x 9¼″. RB p. 54. Collection Elise Strouse

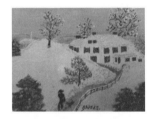

944. *The Long Cold Road* (M. 1440)
June 30. 5¾ x 7½″. RB p. 54. Sold through Vigeveno, Los Angeles

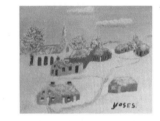

945. *The Descent* (M. 1441)
June 30. 5¾ x 7½″. RB p. 54. Sold through Vigeveno, Los Angeles

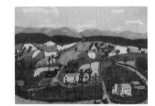

946. *Belvedere* (M. 1442)
Aug. 9. 25 x 36″. RB p. 55 "Loyed Robert Moses Birthplace," dated July 24. Sometimes called "The Eakle Place"

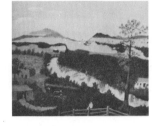

947. *Hoosick River* (M. 1443)
Aug. 30. 16½ x 19″. RB p. 55 dated July 24. Collection Morris L. Ernst

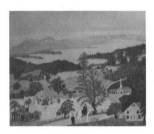

948. *Covered Wagon* (M. 1444)
Aug. 30. 16 x 19″. RB p. 55 dated July 24. Formerly collection Ala Story

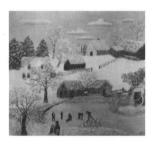

949. *The Saddle Bags* (M. 1446)
Aug. 30. 19 x 24″. RB p. 55 dated July 24. Collection Mrs. Clifford Mallory, Sr.

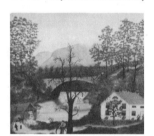

950. *Skating on the Mill Pond* (M. 1399)
Begun March 1950, finished Aug. 1950. 16 x 19″. RB p. 53 dated March 6, 1950. A photograph exists of this picture in an unfinished state. Collection Hal Wallis

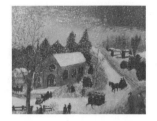

951. *The Town Hall* (M. 1400)
Begun March 1950, finished Aug. 1950. 16 x 19″. RB p. 53 dated March 6, 1950. A photograph exists of this picture in an unfinished state. Collection Mr. and Mrs. Jules Reiner

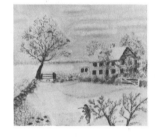

952. *Now for a Quail* (M. 1404)
Dated Apr. 13, 1950, revised in Aug. 1950. 16 x 19″. RB p. 53 "Too Little Boys." A photograph exists of the earlier version of the picture. Formerly collection Ala Story

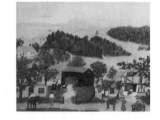

953. *Hoosick River* (M. 1447)
November. 16 x 19″. RB p. 55. Collection Mrs. Carl Moses

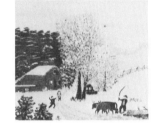

954. *Saddle Bags* (M. 1448)
November. 19 x 24″. RB p. 55. Collection Mrs. Kenneth Bullard

1950 *(cont'd)*

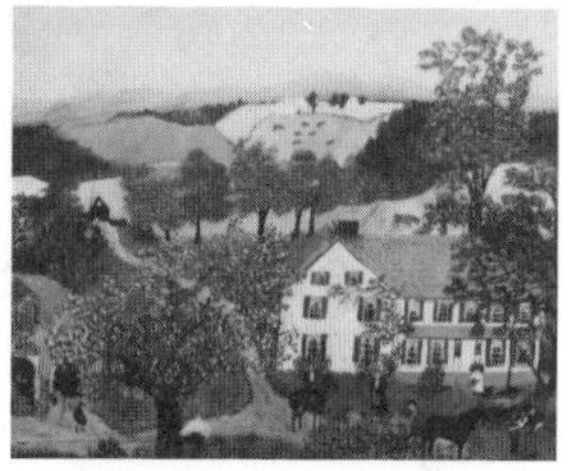

955. *Saddle Bags* (M. 1449)
November. 19 x 24″. RB p. 55. Collection Dr. Arthur Robertson

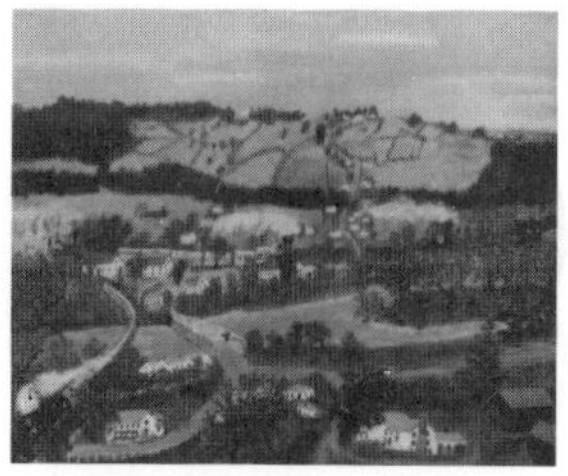

956. *Podunk* (M. 1450)
Nov. 16. 24 x 30″. RB p. 55

957. *The Doctor* (M. 1451)
Dec. 6. 20 x 24″. RB p. 55. Collection Otto Kallir. (See plate 45)

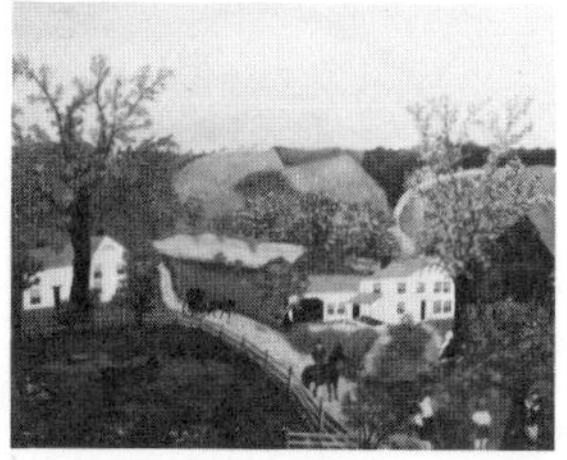

958. *The Pond* (M. 1452)
Dec. 6. 19 x 24″. RB p. 55. Collection Mrs. F. Kallir

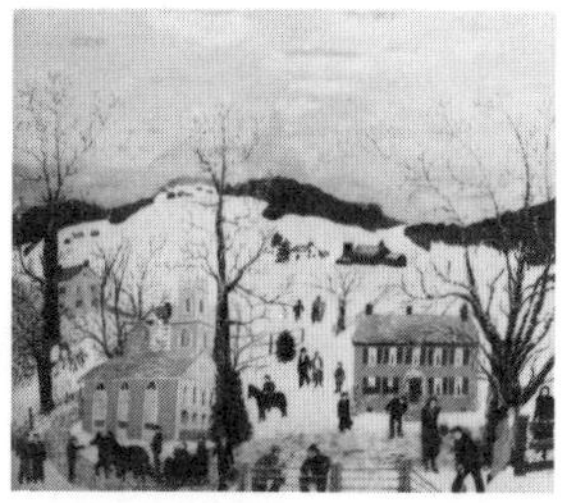

959. *In 1671* (M. 1453)
Dec. 6. 20 x 24″. RB p. 55. Collection George L. Erion

960. *[Untitled] Winter Scene*
About 1950. 6 x 7¼″. Collection Jane Comiskey

961. *[Untitled] Autumn Picture*
About 1950. 6 x 7¼″. Collection Jane Comiskey

962. *[Untitled] Sugaring Scene*
About 1950. 16 x 24″. Collection Betty McCart

1951

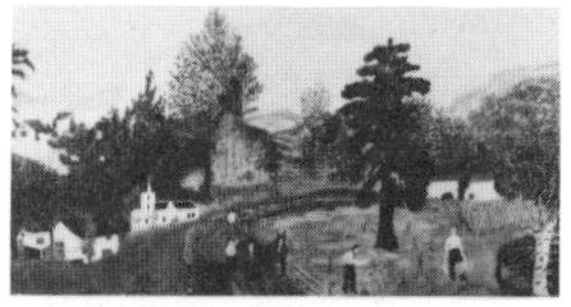

963. *Over in the Valley* (M. 1454)
Feb. 26. 14 x 26¼″. RB p. 55. Collection Mrs. A.F. Johnson

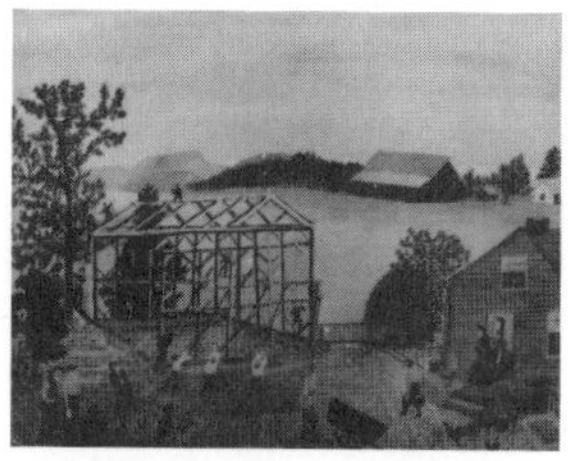

964. *Building a Barn* (M. 1455)
Feb. 26. 17 x 21¾″. RB p. 55. Collection Mrs. Mary C. Everts. *Reproduced:* Parke-Bernet Sale No. 2336, March 18, 1965, No. 118

965. *Moving Day on the Farm* (M. 1456)
Feb. 26. 17 x 22″. RB p. 55. Galerie St. Etienne, New York. *Reproduced:* MLH. (See plate 141)

966. *The Family Picnic* (M. 1457)
Feb. 26. 16¾ x 22″. RB p. 55. (See plate 142)

967. *Taking in Laundry* (M. 1458)
Feb. 26. 17 x 21¾″. RB p. 55. Private collection. *Reproduced:* GMSB; MLH; *Six of My Favorite Paintings* portfolio. (See plates 231, 232)

968. *A Country Wedding* (M. 1459)
Feb. 26. 17 x 22″. RB p. 55 "A Spring Country Wedding." Collection Mr. and Mrs. Wyatt Cooper. *Reproduced:* Hallmark. (See plate 143)

969. *The Departure* (M. 1460)
Feb. 26. 17 x 22″. RB p. 55. Private collection. *Reproduced:* Hallmark; MLH; Oldenbourg. (See plate 146)

970. *We Are Resting* (M. 1461)
Feb. 26. 24 x 30″. RB p. 55. Private collection. *Reproduced:* GMSB. (See plate 147)

971. *It Snows, Oh It Snows* (M. 1462)
Feb. 26. 24 x 30″. RB p. 55. Collection Mrs. F. Kallir. *Reproduced: Art in America* portfolio; GMSB. (See plate 151)

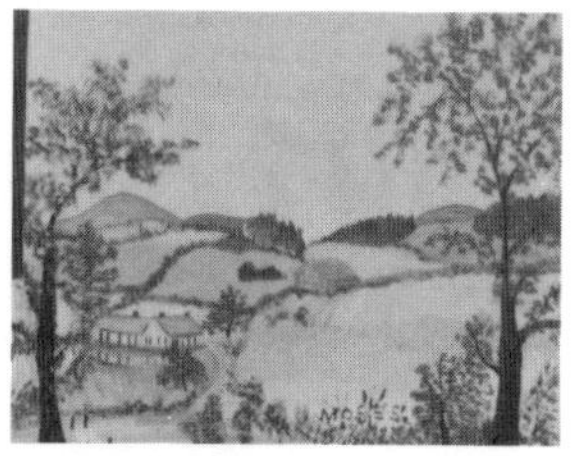

972. *Bettle Hill* (M. 1463)
April 30. 5⅝ x 7⅜″. RB p. 55

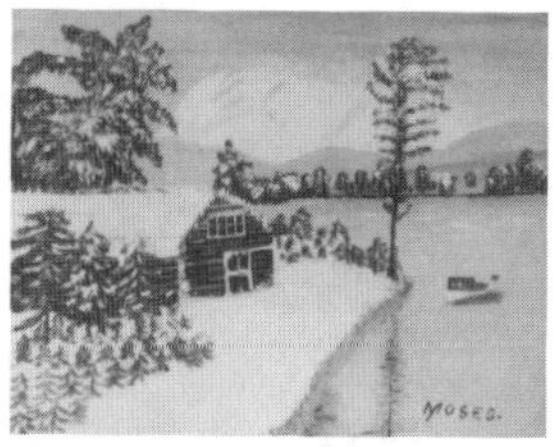

973. *The Old Shop* (M. 1464)
April 30. 5⅝ x 7⅝″. RB p. 55

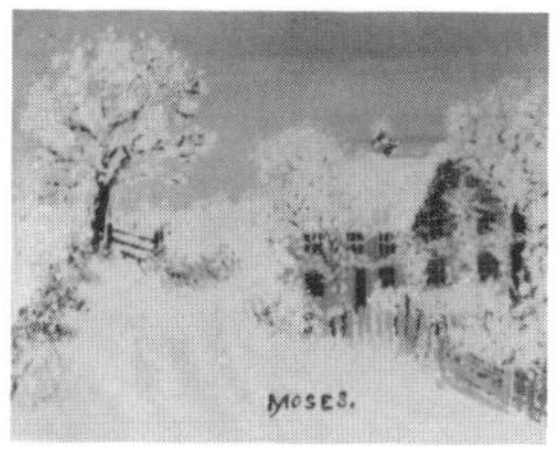

974. *A Pink House* (M. 1465)
April 30. 5⅝ x 7½″. RB p. 55. Sold through Vigeveno, Los Angeles

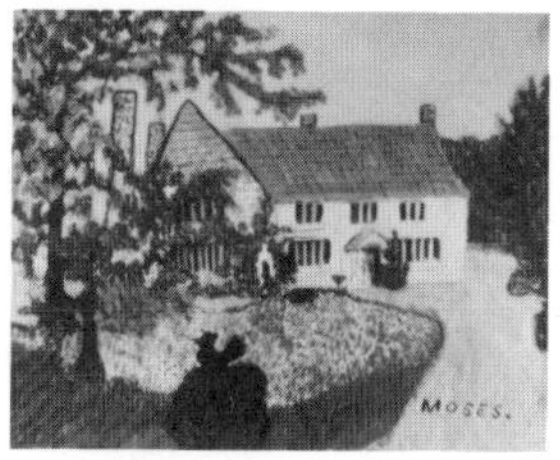

975. *England* (M. 1466)
April 30. 5¾ x 7½″. RB p. 55. Collection Mrs. Wesley Fillmon

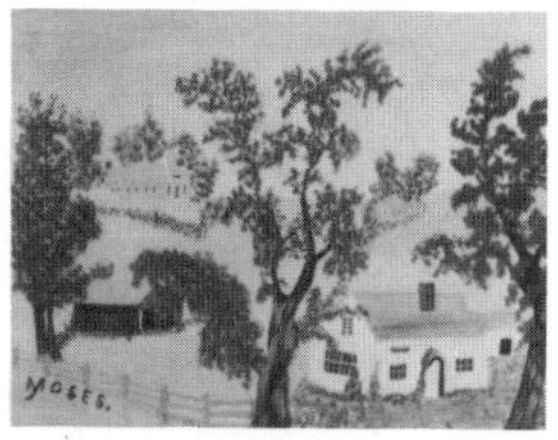

976. *A Church* (M. 1467)
April 30. 5⅝ x 7½″. RB p. 55. Collection Paul Simon

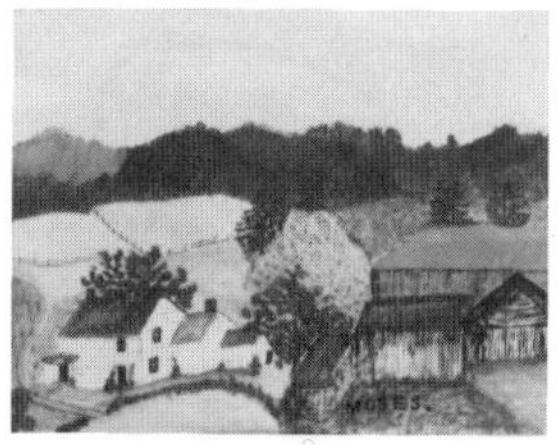

977. *Down Home* (M. 1468)
April 30. 5¾ x 7⅞″. RB p. 55. Collection Mrs. Wesley Fillmon

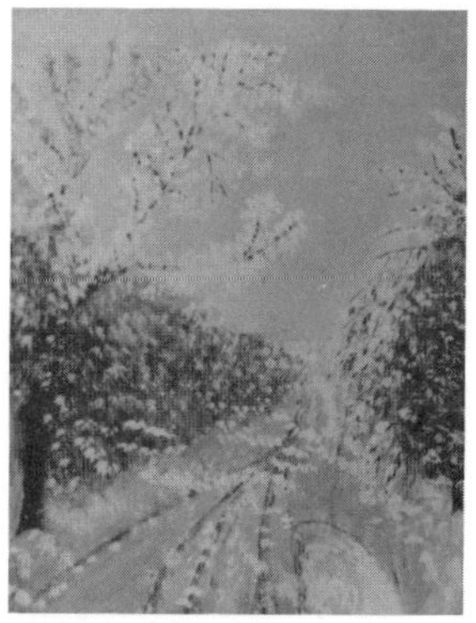

978. *A Winter Road* (M. 1469)
April 30. 7⅜ x 5⅝″. RB p. 55. Sold through Vigeveno, Los Angeles

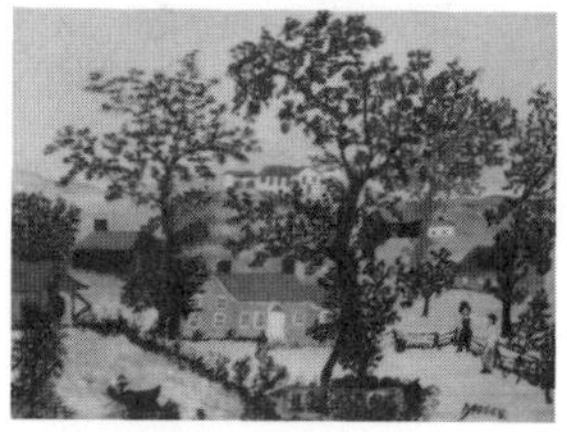

979. *On the Lake* (M. 1470)
April 30. 10 x 14″. RB p. 55. Collection Mrs. Robert L. Fasig

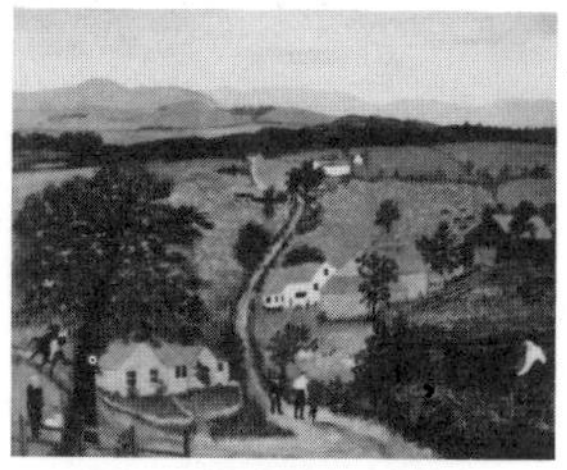

980. *Plowing in May* (M. 1471)
May 1. 18 x 24″. RB p. 56. Collection Mr. and Mrs. Raymond B. Chrisman

981. *Flying Kites* (M. 1473)
May 20. 18¼ x 24″. RB p. 56. Collection Mrs. Arthur Choate, Jr. (See plate 149)

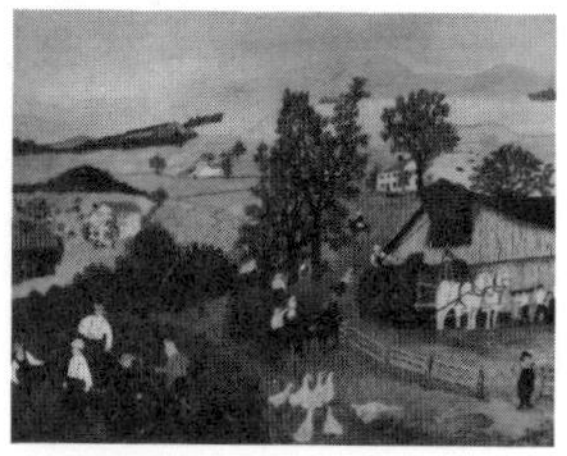

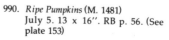

982. *Harvest Home* (M. 1476)
May 20. 18 x 24″. RB p. 56. Formerly collection Ala Story

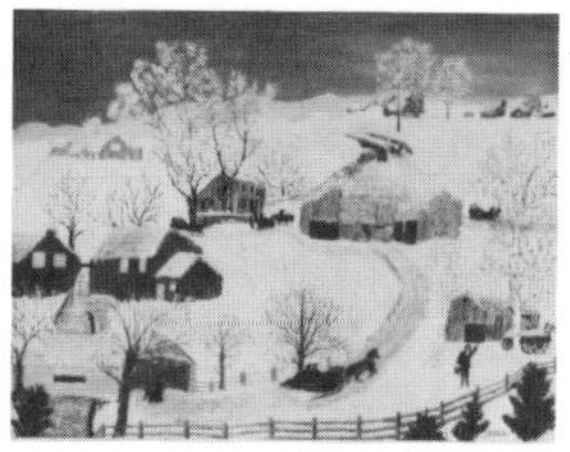

983. *The Brown Mills* (M. 1477)
May 20. 18 x 24″. RB p. 56. Collection Mrs. H. Frank Forsyth. *Reproduced:* Hallmark

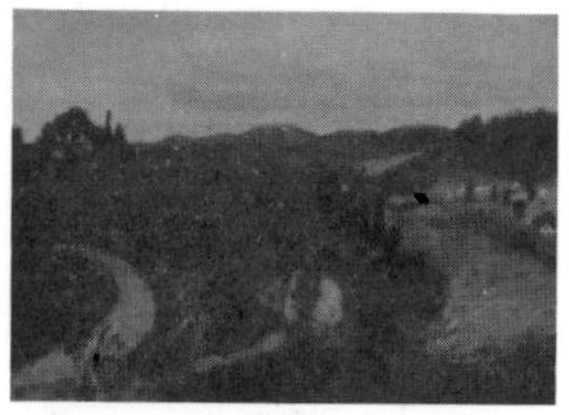

984. *The Trout Pond* (M. 1472)
May 21. 8 x 11¾″. RB p. 56 dated May 20

985. *A Frosty Day* (M. 1474)
May 21. 18 x 24″. RB p. 56 dated May 20. Private collection. *Reproduced: Art in America* portfolio; Hallmark; Oldenbourg. (See plates 248, 249)

986. *Barn Roofing* (M. 1475)
May 21. 18 x 24″. RB p. 56 dated May 20. Formerly collection Ala Story. (See plate 148)

987. *Husking Bee* (M. 1478)
July 5. 19 x 24″. RB p. 56. Hammer Galleries, New York. (See plate 152)

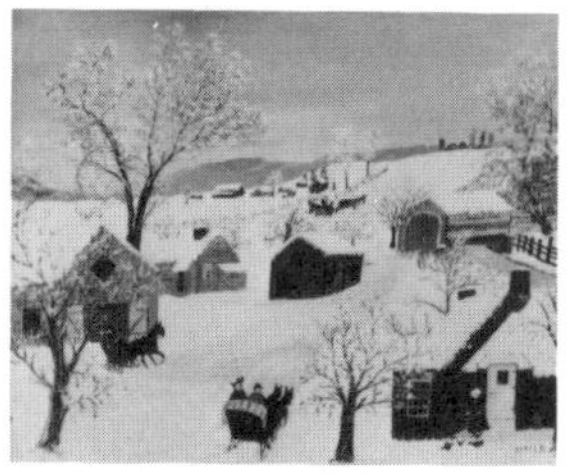

988. *Out to Vote* (M. 1479)
July 5. 16 x 20″. RB p. 56. Private collection

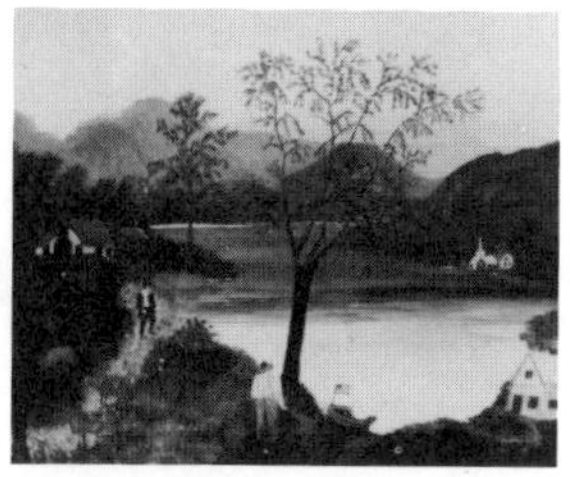

989. *Golden Sunset* (M. 1480)
July 5. 13 x 15⅞″. RB p. 56

990. *Ripe Pumpkins* (M. 1481)
July 5. 13 x 16″. RB p. 56. (See plate 153)

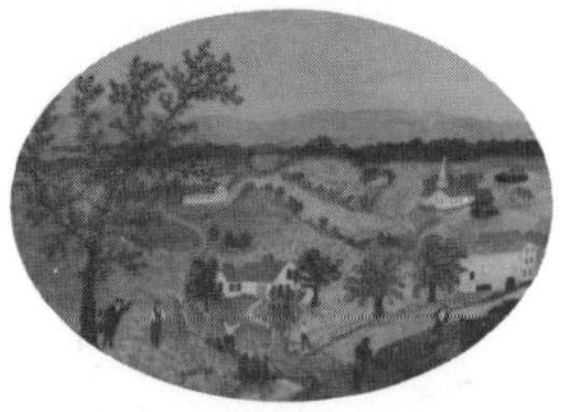

991. *Lazy Brook* (M. 1482)
July 5. 13¾ x 19½″ (oval). RB p. 56. Collection Mr. and Mrs. James Binger

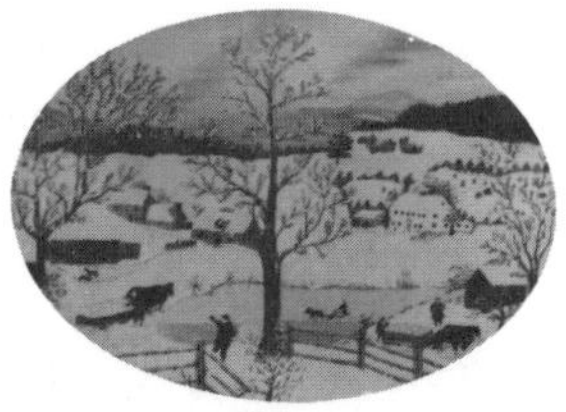

992. *Cutting Ice* (M. 1483)
July 5. 13¼ x 19¾″ (oval). RB p. 56. Collection Mr. and Mrs. James Binger

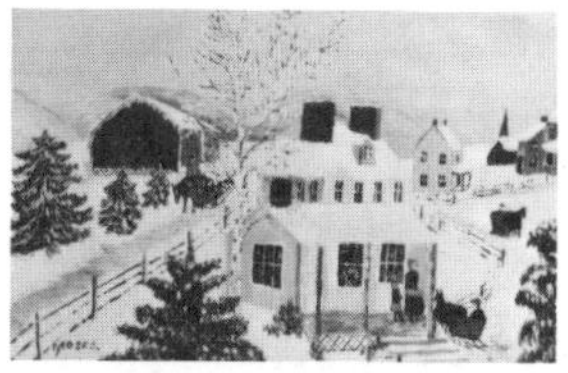

993. *Country Store* (M. 1484)
July 5. 8 x 13⅛″. RB p. 56. Collection Mrs. Thomas G. Herrick

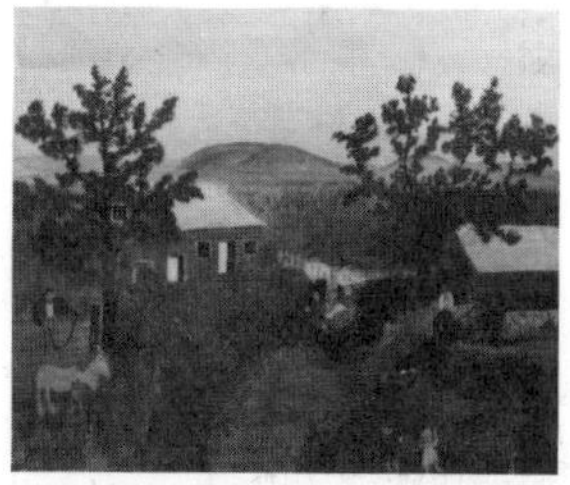

994. *The Old Carpenter Home* (M. 1485)
July 24. 13 x 16″. RB p. 56. Collection Elise Strouse

995. *Grandpa's House* (M. 1486)
July 24. 9¼ x 12″. RB p. 56. Private collection. (See plate 98)

996. *Blacksmith Shop* (M. 1487)
July 24. 16 x 28″. RB p. 56. Collection Forrest K. Moses. (See plate 158)

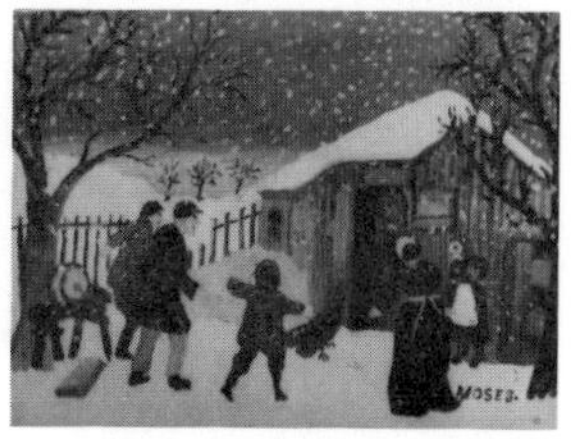

997. *Poor Turkey* (M. 1488)
July 24. 6 x 8″. RB p. 56. *Reproduced:* Hallmark

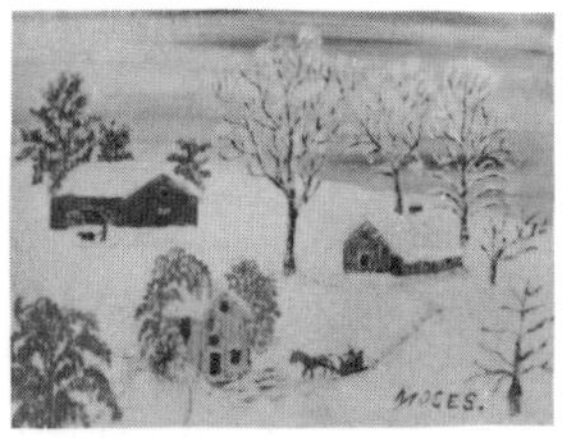

998. *The Willows* (M. 1489)
July 24. 6 x 8″. RB p. 56. Collection Dr. and Mrs. Richard C. Franklin

999. *July Fourth* (M. 1490)
Aug. 22. 23⅞ x 30″. RB p. 56. The White House, Washington, D.C. *Reproduced: Art in America* portfolio; GMSB; U.S. postage stamp, 1969. (See plate 95)

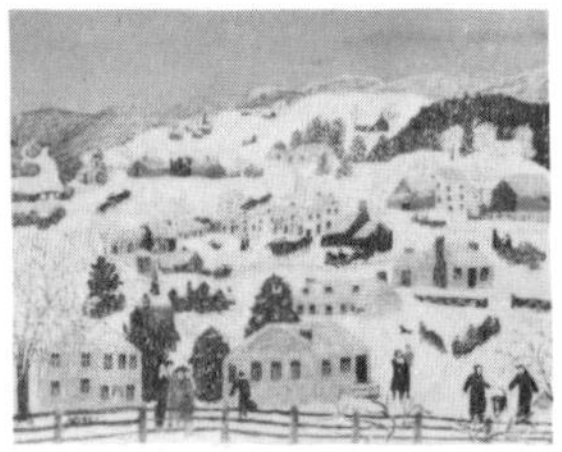

1000. *Winter Twilight* (M. 1491)
Sept. 21. 17⅞ x 23⅞″. RB p. 56. Collection Mr. and Mrs. John S. Schulten. *Reproduced: The Four Seasons* portfolio

1001. *The Village Clock* (M. 1492)
Sept. 21. 18 x 24″. RB p. 56. Collection Mrs. Thomas Morganstern. *Reproduced:* Hallmark. (See plate 150)

1002. *Early Skating* (M. 1493)
Sept. 21. 17⅞ x 23⅞″. RB p. 56. Collection R. Thornton Wilson. *Reproduced:* Hallmark (See plate 156)

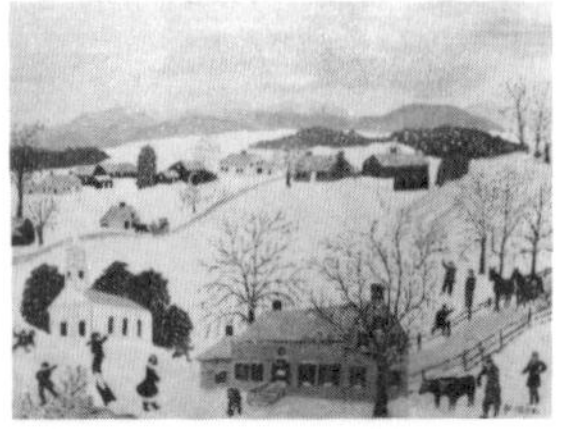

1003. *The Gray House* (M. 1494)
Sept. 21. 17⅞ x 24″. RB p. 56. Collection Mrs. Arthur McLean

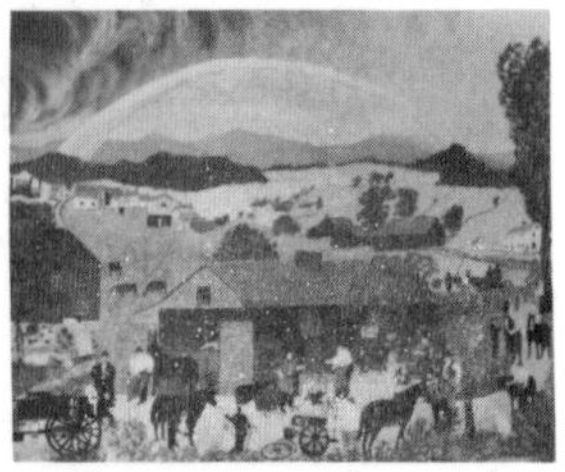

1004. *The Rainbow* (M. 1495)
Sept. 21. 19⅝ x 23⅞″. RB p. 56. Galerie St. Etienne, New York

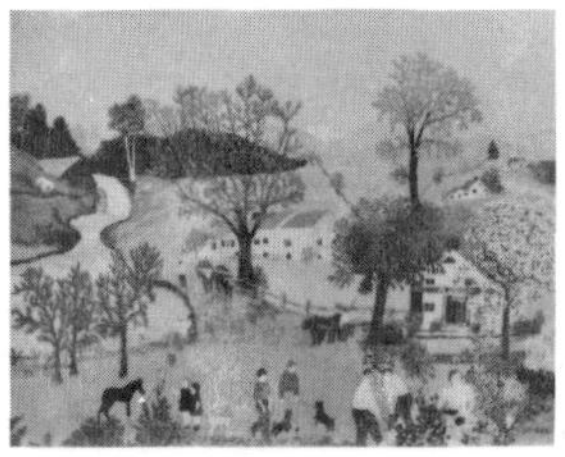

1005. *The Flower Garden* (M. 1496)
Sept. 21. 18 x 24″. RB p. 56. Formerly collection Ala Story

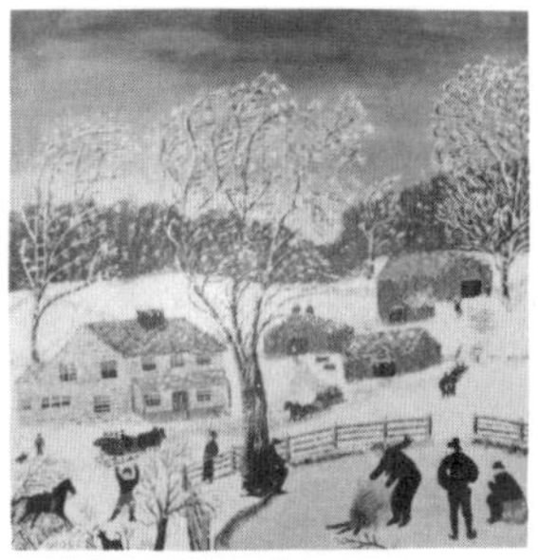

1006. *The Bonfire* (M. 1497)
Sept. 21. 16 x 16″. RB p. 56. Collection Walter K. Earle

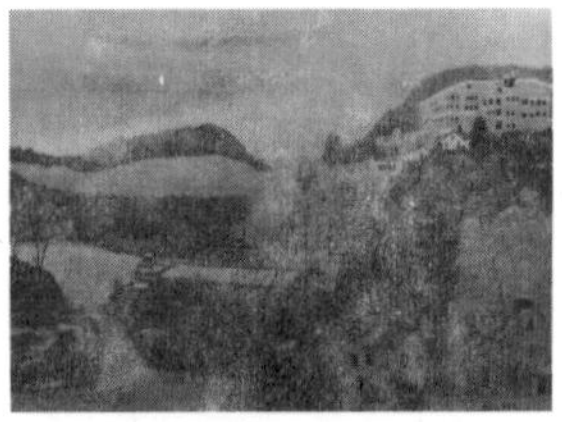

1007. *Imagination* (M. 1498)
Sept. 21. 15½ x 21⅝″. RB p. 56. Formerly collection Ala Story

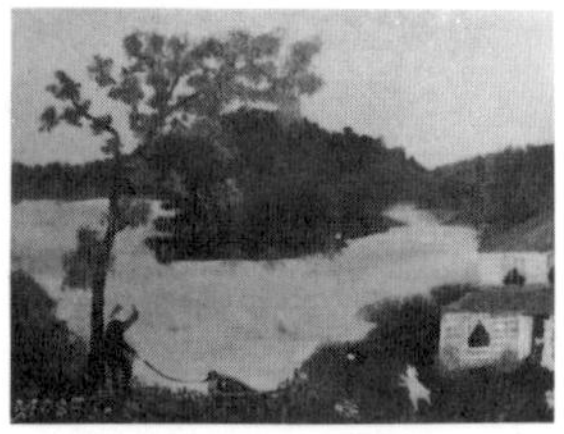

1008. *The Landing* (M. 1499)
Sept. 21. 4⅞ x 6¾″. RB p. 56. Collection Byron Harvey

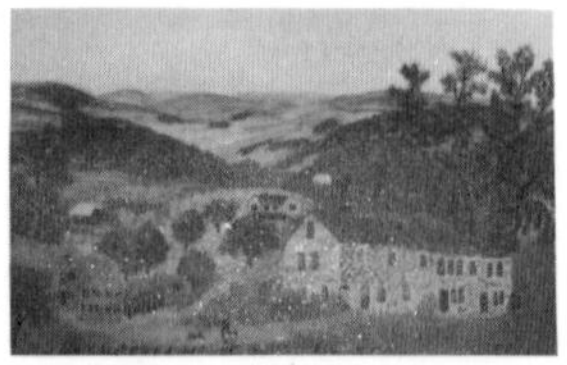

1009. *The Checkered House of N.H., 1800* (M. 1500)
Sept. 21. 7⅞ x 13″. Title inscribed by the artist: "The Old Checkered House, Built 1800, N.H." RB p. 57. Collection A. Pilicer

1010. *A Beautiful Morning* (M. 1501)
Sept. 21. 18 x 24″. RB p. 57. Private collection. (See plate 157)

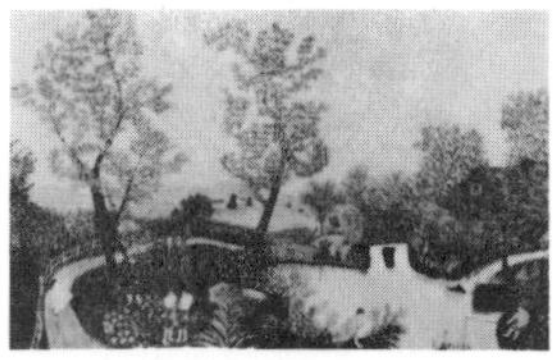

1011. *Quiet Day* (M. 1502)
Oct. 18. RB p. 57. Collection Clayton E. Shaw, Jr.

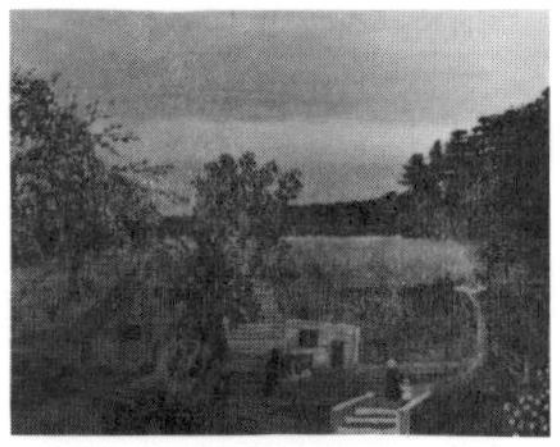

1012. *Over the Stile* (M. 1503)
Dec. 4. 10¾ x 14⅜″. RB p. 57. Parke-Bernet Sale No. 2169, Feb. 20, 1963, No. 26

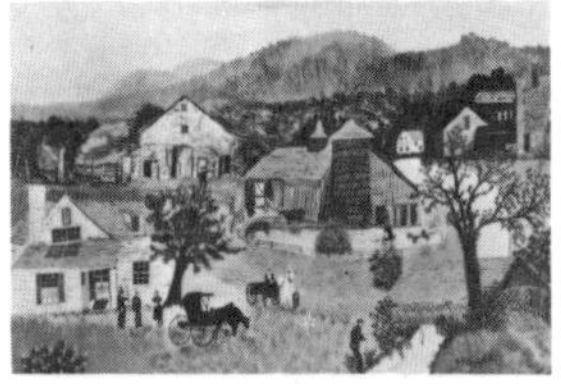

1013. *Goodbye* (M. 1504)
Dec. 4. 12 x 18″. RB p. 57

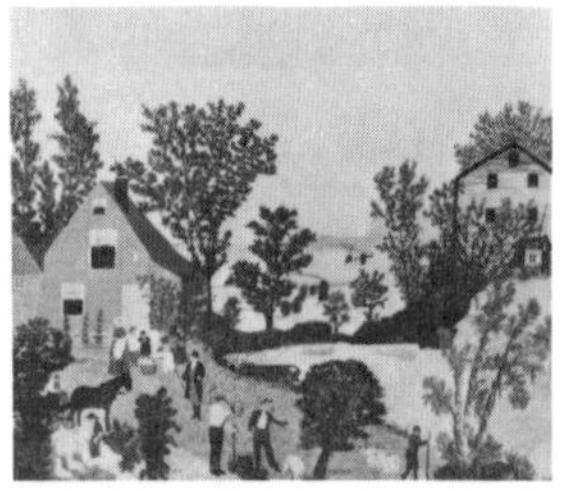

1014. *Building Fence* (M. 1505)
Dec. 4. 20 x 24″. RB p. 57. Formerly collection Ala Story

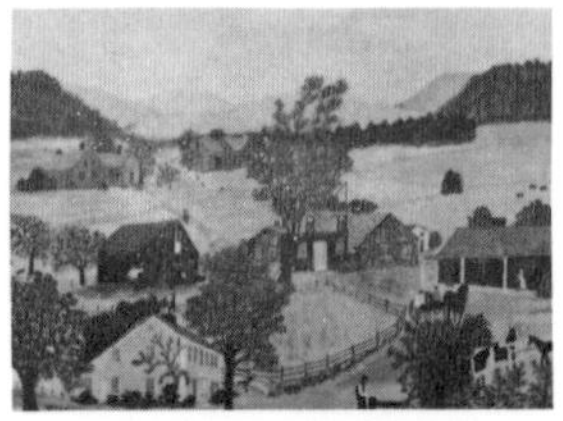

1015. *Beautiful Clouds* (M. 1506)
Dec. 4. 20 x 24″. RB p. 57. Collection Dr. Carlton Palmer

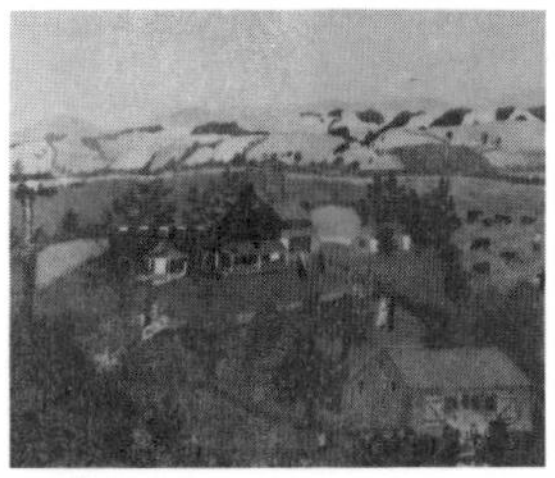

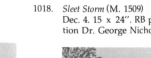

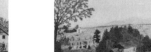

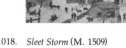

1016. *Mount Airy* (M. 1507)
Dec. 4. 20 x 24″. RB p. 57. Galerie St. Etienne, New York

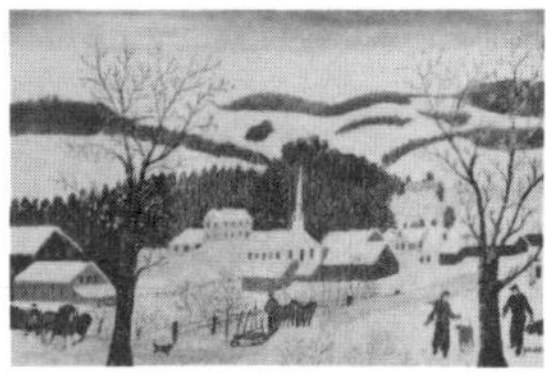

1017. *Ice Storm* (M. 1508)
Dec. 4. 14⅞ x 24″. RB p. 57. Collection Alexander Voemel

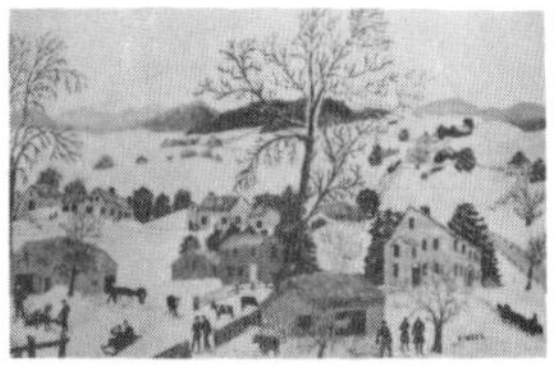

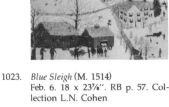

1018. *Sleet Storm* (M. 1509)
Dec. 4. 15 x 24″. RB p. 57. Collection Dr. George Nichols, Jr.

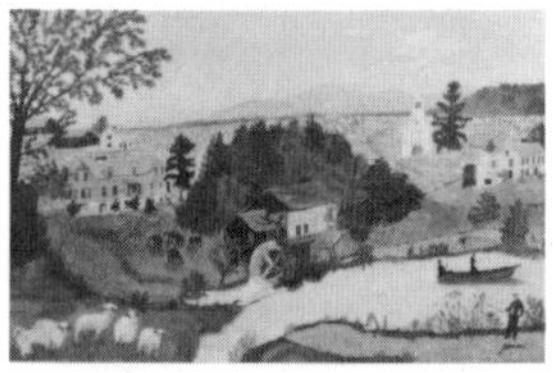

1019. *My Sheep* (M. 1510)
Dec. 4. 15 x 24″. RB p. 57. Formerly collection Ala Story

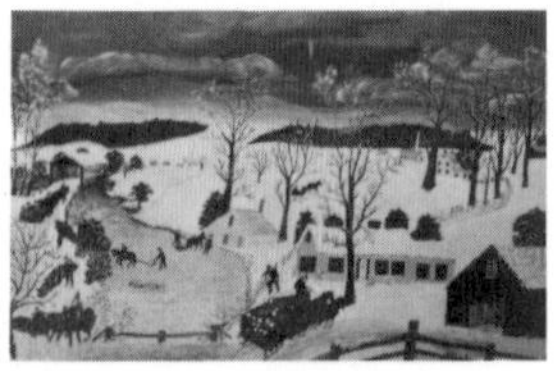

1020. *Cutting Ice* (M. 1511)
Dec. 4. 15 x 24″. RB p. 57. Collection J.C. Anderson

1952

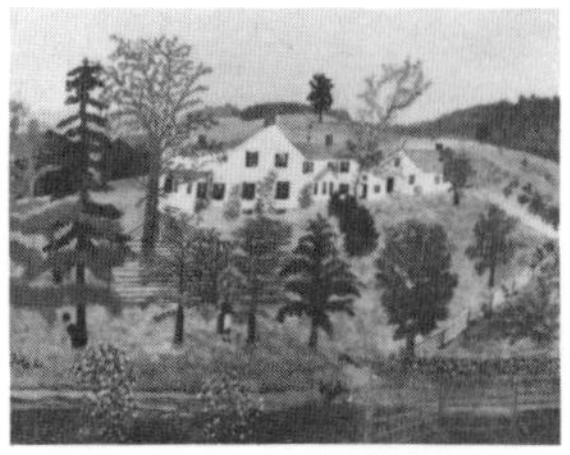

1021. *Grandma Moses's Home, 1913* (M. 1512)
Feb. 6. 18 x 24″. RB p. 57. Collection Mr. and Mrs. George O. Cook

1022. *Grandma Moses's Home, 1925* (M. 1513)
Feb. 6. 18 x 24″. RB p. 57. Private collection. (See plate 10)

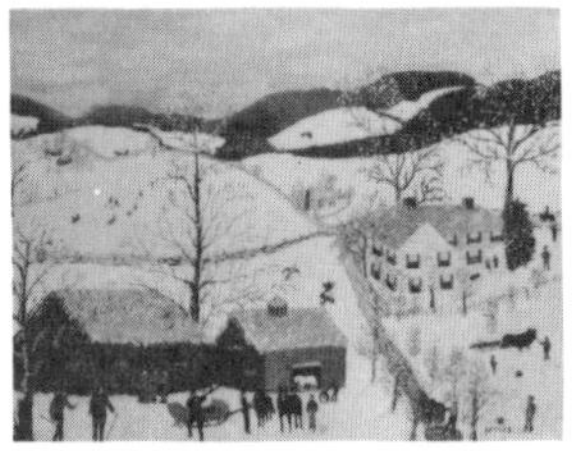

1023. *Blue Sleigh* (M. 1514)
Feb. 6. 18 x 23⅞″. RB p. 57. Collection L.N. Cohen

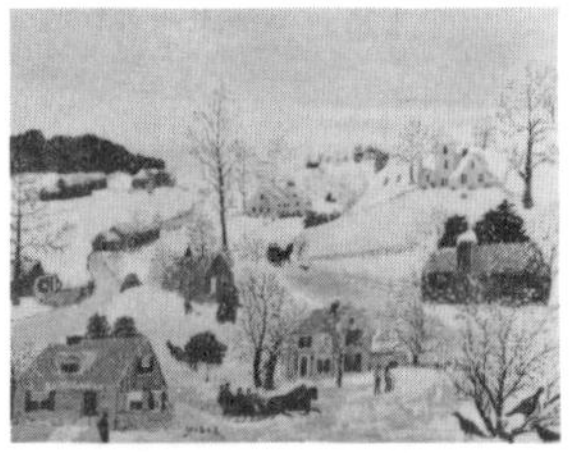

1024. *Turkey Roost* (M. 1515)
Feb. 6. 18 x 24″. RB p. 57. Collection Forrest K. Moses

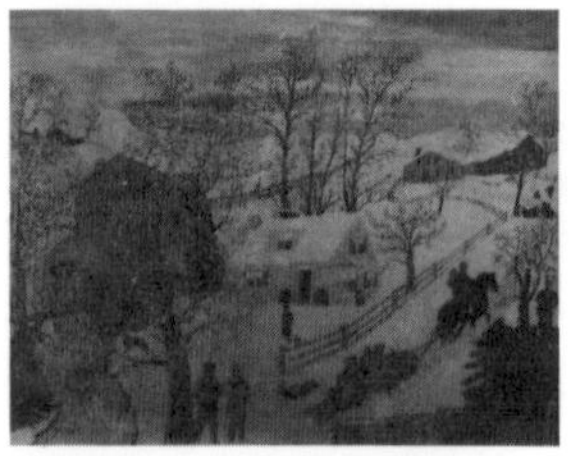

1025. *Old Water Wheel* (M. 1516)
Feb. 6. 18 x 24″. RB p. 57. Collection Dr. Carlton Palmer

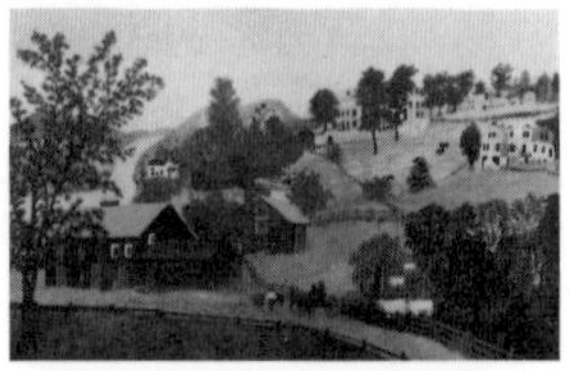

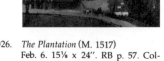

1026. *The Plantation* (M. 1517)
Feb. 6. 15⅛ x 24″. RB p. 57. Collection The Honorable and Mrs. Harry S Truman

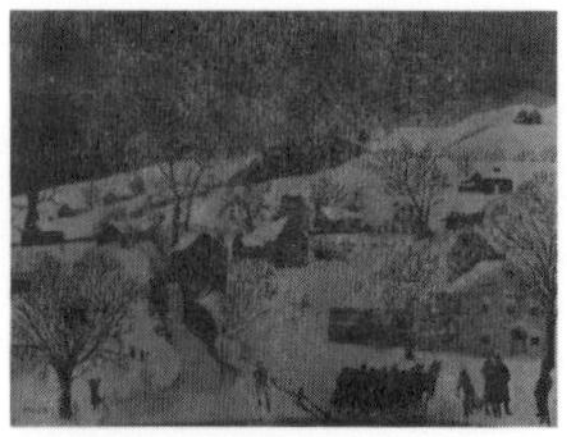

1027. *Come On* (M. 1518)
Feb. 6. 18⅛ x 24″. RB p. 57. Collection Hal Wallis

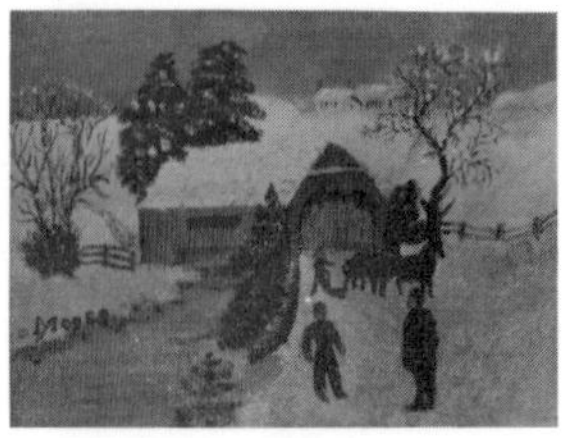

1028. *Snow Plowing* (M. 1519)
Feb. 6. 5¾ x 8″. RB p. 57. Collection Mrs. John A. Ferguson

1029. *The Old Oak* (M. 1520)
Feb. 6. Glass, 10½ x 13¾″. RB p. 57. Collection John Sherman

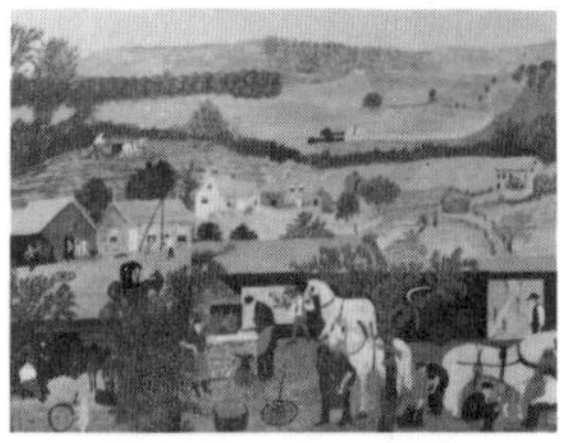

1030. *Horseshoeing* (M. 1521)
March 7. 18 x 24″. RB p. 57. Collection Mrs. Edward C. Flynn

1031. *Hoosick River, Winter* (M. 1522)
March 7. 18 x 24″. RB p. 57. Private collection. *Reproduced:* GMSB. (See plate 221)

1032. *Hoosick River, Summer* (M. 1523)
March 7. 18 x 24″. RB p. 57. Private collection. *Reproduced:* GMSB; *The Studio,* London, April 1956 (cover). (See plate 160)

1033. *Busy Day* (M. 1524)
March 7. 18 x 24″. RB p. 57. Collection Mrs. Russel Crouse. *Reproduced:* Hallmark. (See plate 155)

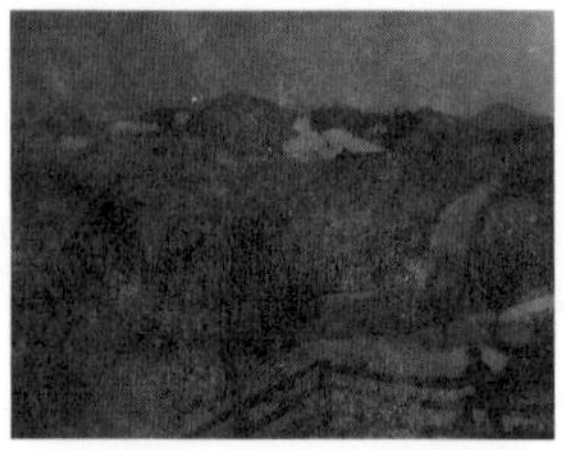

1034. *The Hoosick in March* (M. 1525)
May 2. 18 x 24″. RB p. 57. Collection W.H. Perry

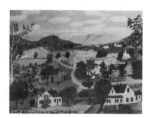

1035. *In 1800* (M. 1526)
May 2. 18 x 24''. RB p. 57.
Queensland National Art Gallery,
Brisbane, Australia

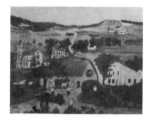

1036. *Good Fishing* (M. 1527)
May 2. 18 x 24''. RB p. 57

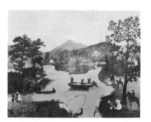

1037. *Children Haying* (M. 1528)
May 2. 18 x 24''. RB p. 57. Collection Mr. and Mrs. George O. Cook

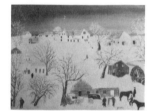

1038. *The Willow Mill* (M. 1529)
May 2. 18 x 23⅞''. RB p. 58. Collection Alfreda Rochelle Thomas

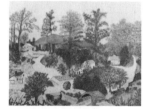

1039. *September* (M. 1530)
May 2. 18 x 24''. RB p. 58. Collection Mrs. Loyd R. Moses

1040. *Crossroads* (M. 1531)
May 2. 18 x 24''. RB p. 58. Collection M.W. Greenstein

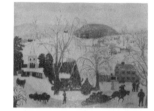

1041. *Stone Boat* (M. 1532)
May 2. 18 x 24''. RB p. 58. Private collection

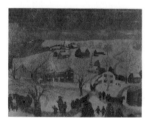

1042. *New Snow* (M. 1533)
May 13. 18 x 24''. RB p. 58. Hammer Galleries, New York

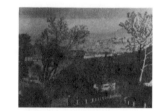

1043. *The Purple House* (M. 1535)
June 30. 18 x 24''. RB p. 58. Collection Mr. and Mrs. L.M. Parsons

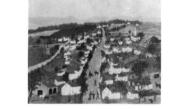

1044. *Staunton, Va.* (M. 1536)
June 30. 18 x 24⅛''. RB p. 58. Collection Ernst Kober

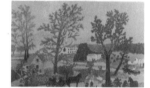

1045. *A Toll Gate* (M. 1538)
June 30. 12 x 16''. RB p. 58. Collection Mrs. Herbert Polacheck

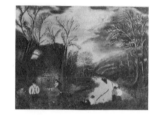

1046. *Want a Ride* (M. 1534)
July 10. 16 x 24''. RB p. 58. Collection Mr. and Mrs. Walter K. Howard

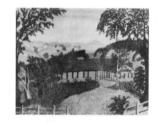

1047. *Campfire* (M. 1537)
July 10. 12 x 16''. RB p. 58. Collection Mrs. Robert Tiller

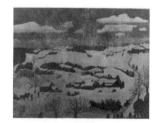

1048. *Forrest Moses's Home* (M. 1539)
July 10. 11⅞ x 16''. RB p. 58

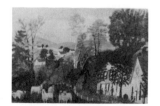

1049. *Poesenkill* (M. 1540)
July. 18 x 24''. RB p. 58. Collection Mrs. Roland Beers

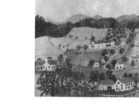

1050. *King Church* (M. 1541)
Aug. 28. 18 x 24''. RB p. 58 dated Aug. 26. Collection Mrs. William Schweitzer

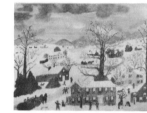

1051. *Gray Day* (M. 1542)
Aug. 28. 18 x 24''. RB p. 58. Hallmark Cards, Inc., Kansas City, Mo. *Reproduced:* Hallmark

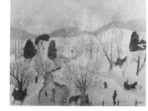

1052. *Pink Sunset* (M. 1543)
Aug. 28. 18 x 24''. RB p. 58. Collection Alexander M. Arnstein

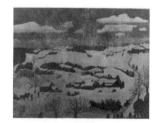

1053. *Sleigh Ride* (M. 1544)
Aug. 28. 18 x 24''. RB p. 58. Sold through Knoedler & Co., New York

1054. *Busy Street* (M. 1545)
Aug. 28. 18 x 24''. RB p. 58. Hallmark Cards, Inc., Kansas City, Mo. *Reproduced:* Hallmark; MLH (German and Dutch editions); Oldenbourg. (See plate 159)

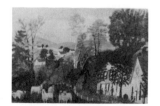

1055. *The Sheep* (M. 1546)
Aug. 28. 16 x 24''. RB p. 58. Living Arts Foundation, New York

1056. *Father's Home* (M. 1547)
Aug. 28. 18 x 24''. RB p. 58. (See plate 106)

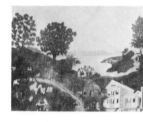

1057. *Birthday Cake* (M. 1548)
Aug. 28. 18 x 24''. RB p. 58. Collection Dr. and Mrs. William H. Saunders

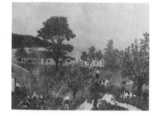

1058. *Lakeside* (M. 1549)
Oct. 6. 18 x 24''. RB p. 58. Collection Mr. and Mrs. John D. Rauh

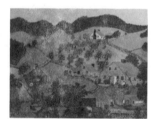

1059. *October* (M. 1550)
Oct. 6. 18 x 24''. RB p. 58. Collection Mr. and Mrs. Walter L. Wolf

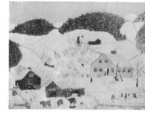

1060. *Old Oaken Bucket in Summer* (M. 1551)
Dec. 4. 18 x 24''. RB p. 58. Private collection

1061. *Old Oaken Bucket in Winter* (M. 1552)
Dec. 4. 18 x 24''. RB p. 58

1062. *Home for Thanksgiving* (M. 1553)
Dec. 4. 18 x 24''. RB p. 58. Collection Mr. and Mrs. Alan Kempner. *Reproduced: Six of My Favorite Paintings* portfolio. (See plate 154)

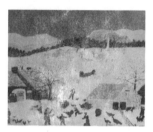

1063. *Catching the Turkey* (M. 1554)
Dec. 4. 16 x 20''. RB p. 58. Collection J. Cattier

1064. *White Creek* (M. 1555)
December. 16 x 20''. Collection Betty McCart

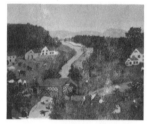

1065. *How Much Pay?* (M. 1556)
Dec. 4. 16 x 20''. RB p. 59. Sold at Sotheby's, Toronto, Oct. 1967

1953

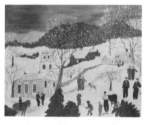

1066. *Let Me Help* (M. 1557)
Jan. 5. 16 x 20''. RB p. 59. Collection Andrew Monness

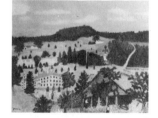

1067. *Dog Churn* (M. 1559)
Feb. 1. 16 x 20''. RB p. 59. Collection Paul Simon

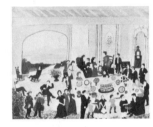

1068. *Birthday Cake* (M. 1560)
Feb. 2. 16 x 20''. RB p. 59. Collection Dr. Paul Lariviere

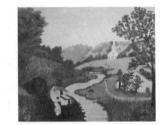

1069. *Church in Dell* (M. 1561)
Feb. 3. 16 x 20''. RB p. 59. The Fenway Press, Inc.

1070. *Bennington* (M. 1562)
Feb. 3. 18 x 24''. RB p. 59. Collection George Eisenpresser. *Reproduced:* GMSB. (See plate 189)

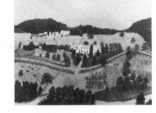

1071. *Moses* (M. 1555)
Feb. 5. 17¾ x 24''. RB p. 59

1072. *Dark Sky* (M. 1558)
Feb. 6. 18¼ x 24''. RB p. 59. Collection Mrs. Maurice Blin. (See plate 190)

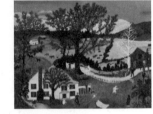

1073. *White Birch* (M. 1563)
Feb. 7. 18 x 24''. RB p. 59. Collection His Excellency E. Propper de Callejon

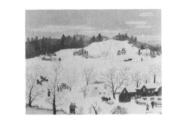

1074. *Now We Can Skate* (M. 1564)
Feb. 7. 18 x 24''. RB p. 59. *Reproduced:* Parke-Bernet Sale No. 1897, April 15, 1959, No. 73

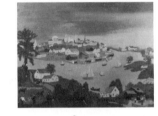

1075. *Canada* (M. 1565)
Feb. 7. 18 x 24''. RB p. 59

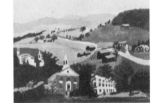

1076. *Brick Church* (M. 1566)
Feb. 11. 18¼ x 24''. RB p. 59. Collection Joseph J. Seaman

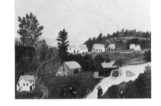

1077. *We Go for a Walk* (M. 1567)
Feb. 11. 18 x 24''. RB p. 59. Collection Mrs. Irving G. Snow

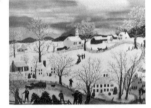

1078. *Swans* (M. 1568)
Feb. 12. 18 x 24''. RB p. 59. Collection the Reverend Francis C. Huntington

1079. *Joy Ride* (M. 1569)
Feb. 12. 18 x 24''. RB p. 59. *Reproduced: Colliers Magazine,* Dec. 23, 1955 (cover); Hallmark; Arthur Jaffe; MLH (German and Dutch editions); Oldenbourg; *Six of My Favorite Paintings* portfolio. (See plates 53, 188)

1080. *Springtime* (M. 1570)
Feb. 13. 18 x 24''. RB p. 59. Collection Dr. and Mrs. John Cinelli. *Reproduced:* Parke-Bernet Sale No. 2326, Jan. 27, 1965, No. 48. (See plate 191)

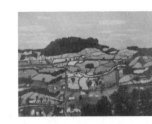

1081. *My Horse* (M. 1571)
Feb. 13. 18 x 24''. RB p. 59. Collection W.P. Hutchison

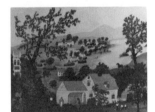

1082. *In the Woods* (M. 1572)
Feb. 14. 18 x 24''. RB p. 59

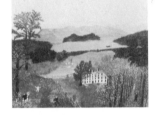

1083. *Deep Hole* (M. 1573)
March 2. 18 x 24''. RB p. 59. Collection Mrs. John H. Livens

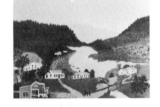

1084. *Depot* (M. 1574)
March 2. 18 x 24''. RB p. 59

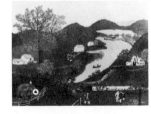

1085. *Between Seasons* (M. 1575)
March 2. 18 x 24''. RB p. 59

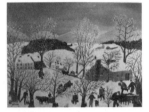

1086. *In the Valley* (M. 1576)
March 27. 18 x 24''. RB p. 59. Private collection

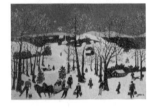

1087. *Sap Gathering* (M. 1577)
March 27. 18 x 24''. RB p. 59. Collection Mrs. Richard R. Costello

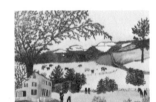

1088. *Maple Bush* (M. 1578)
March 27. 12 x 18''. RB p. 59. Formerly collection Louis J. Caldor

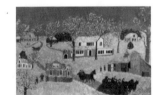

1089. *Green Pasture* (M. 1579)
March 27. 12 x 18''. RB p. 59. Collection Joseph Graf

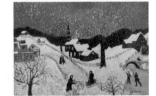

1090. *A Gay Time* (M. 1580)
March 27. 12 x 18''. RB p. 59

1091. *Oh It Snows* (M. 1581)
March 27. 12 x 18''. RB p. 59. Formerly collection Dr. Eric Berne

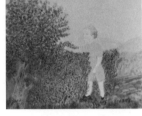

1092. *Our Son* (M. 1582)
8 x 10''. RB p. 59

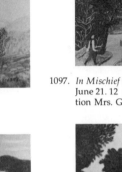

1093. *Our Son* (M. 1582)
March 27. 9 x 9''. RB p. 59. Collection Ronald Ferry

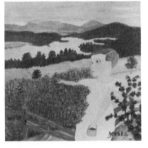

1094. *Home from School* (M. 1583)
April 6. 12 x 18''. RB p. 60. Parke-Bernet Sale No. 2034, April 26, 1961, No. 92

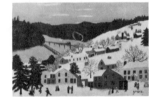

1095. *Harpers Ferry* (M. 1584)
April 6. 12 x 18''. RB p. 60. Formerly collection Louis J. Caldor

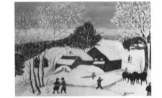

1096. *Thrashing Cane* (M. 1585)
June 21. 18 x 24''. RB p. 60

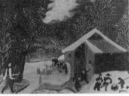

1097. *In Mischief* (M. 1587)
June 21. 12 x 18''. RB p. 60. Collection Mrs. Gordon Ritz

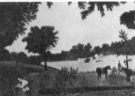

1098. *Over the Lake* (M. 1588)
June 21. 12 x 18''. RB p. 60. Collection Mr. and Mrs. A. M. Nakamura

1099. *Before the Battle of Bennington* (M. 1589)
June 21. 18 x 30''. RB p. 60. (See plate 171)

1100. *The Battle of Bennington* (M. 1590)
June 21. 18 x 30½''. RB p. 60. *Reproduced:* GMSB. (See plate 170)

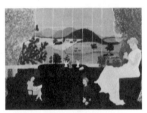

1101. *Out on the Porch* (M. 1586)
June 22. 18 x 24''. RB p. 60

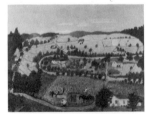

1102. *Mt. Airy* (M. 1591)
June. 5¾ x 7½''. RB p. 60. Collection Mrs. Hugh W. Moses

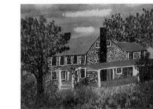

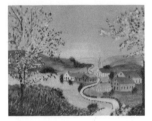

1103. *When the Apples Are in Blossom* (M. 1592)
June. 5¾ x 7½''. RB p. 60. Collection Robert Young

1954

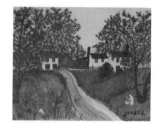

1104. *Back in the Lane* (M. 1593) June. 5¾ x 7½". RB p. 60

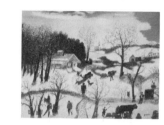

1105. *Old House* (M. 1594) June. 5½ x 7½". RB p. 60. Collection Cletas Heller

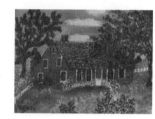

1106. *The Last Load* (M. 1595) Sept. 18. 18 x 24". RB p. 60. Rembrandt Enterprises, Inc.

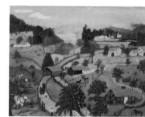

1107. *Plow Boy* (M. 1596) Sept. 18. 17½ x 23½". RB p. 60. Collection Dr. and Mrs. Richard R. Weigler

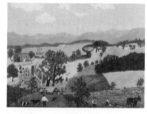

1108. *Horses Horses* (M. 1597) Sept. 18. 18 x 24". RB p. 60. *Reproduced:* Parke-Bernet Sale No. 1869, Jan. 14, 1959, No. 56

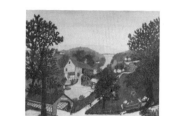

1109. *Twilight* (M. 1598) Sept. 18. 18 x 24". RB p. 60. Collection Mrs. E.J. Bellinger

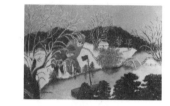

1110. *No Fish* (M. 1599) Sept. 18. 12 x 18". RB p. 60. Collection Mrs. Frederick D. Suydam

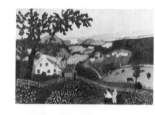

1111. *See the Kite* (M. 1600) Sept. 18. 12 x 18". RB p. 60. Collection Mr. and Mrs. Robert Guy Williams

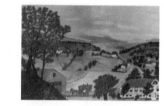

1112. *Last Load Hay* (M. 1601) Sept. 18. 12 x 18". RB p. 60. Collection Mr. and Mrs. Albert E. Firmenich

1113. *Battle of Bennington* (M. 1602) Sept. 18. 17½ x 29¾". RB p. 60. National Society, Daughters of the American Revolution, Washington, D.C. *Reproduced:* Hallmark. (See plate 172)

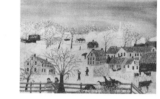

1114. *The Oaks* (M. 1603) Feb. 25. 18 x 24½". RB p. 60. Collection Mrs. Gerald Tsai

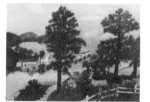

1115. *Look Ye There* (M. 1604) Feb. 25. 12 x 18". RB p. 60. *Reproduced:* Parke-Bernet Sale No. 2024, March 23, 1961, No. 81

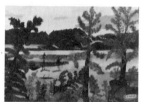

1116. *Quack, Quack* (M. 1605) Feb. 25. 12 x 18". RB p. 60. Collection Mrs. Frederick D. Suydam

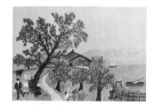

1117. *May* (M. 1606) Feb. 25. 12 x 18". RB p. 60

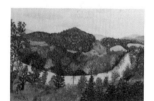

1118. *August* (M. 1607) Feb. 25. 12 x 18". RB p. 60

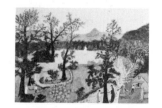

1119. *So Busy* (M. 1608) Feb. 25. 12 x 18". RB p. 60. Collection Mrs. M.T. Greene

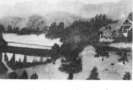

1120. *Turk, Turk* (M. 1609) Feb. 25. 12 x 18". RB p. 61. Collection Mr. and Mrs. L.M. Parsons

1121. *An Artist* (M. 1610) Feb. 25. 12 x 18". RB p. 61. Collection Philip Frank. (See plate 194)

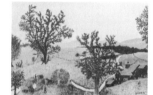

1122. *In Summertime* (M. 1611) Feb. 25. 12 x 18". RB p. 61. Collection Mrs. Richard Levi

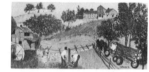

1123. *A Load of Logs* (M. 1612) Feb. 25. 9¼ x 17½". RB p. 61

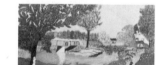

1124. *Going Home* (M. 1613) Feb. 25. 8¼ x 17⅛". RB p. 61. Collection J. Vincent Early

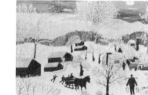

1125. *Gathering Sap* (M. 1614) Feb. 25. 12 x 17½". RB p. 61. Sold through Knoedler & Co., New York

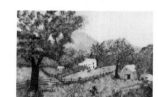

1126. *Back Country* (M. 1615) Feb. 25. 6⅜ x 10". RB p. 61

1127. *Long Bridge* (M. 1616) Feb. 25. 6¾ x 10". RB p. 61. Parke-Bernet Sale No. 3025, April 15, 1970, No. 212

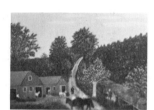

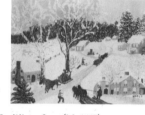

1128. *Winter Scene* (M. 1617) February. 10¾ x 14". RB p. 61. Collection James Cook

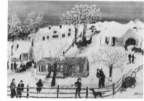

1129. *In Snow Drift* (M. 1618) June 4. 12 x 18". RB p. 61. Collection James P. Shea

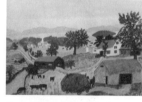

1130. *Green Pasture* (M. 1619) June 4. 12 x 18". RB p. 61. Collection Mr. and Mrs. Richard P. Limburg

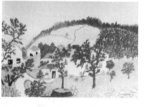

1131. *Father's Home* (M. 1620) June 4. 12⅛ x 18". RB p. 61. Collection Mr. and Mrs. George O. Cook

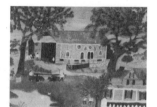

1132. *Penn Barn* (M. 1621) June 4. 11 x 15½". RB p. 61. Collection Mr. and Mrs. Jules Reiner. *Reproduced:* Parke-Bernet Sale No. 2001, Nov. 30, 1960, No. 119

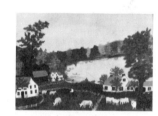

1133. *October* (M. 1622) June 4. 12⅛ x 18". RB p. 61. Collection Mr. and Mrs. Arnold Michaels

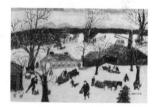

1134. *Lauderdale* (M. 1623) June 4. 12 x 18". RB p. 61. Collection Dr. George W. Slaughter

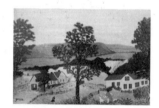

1135. *Sap Gathering* (M. 1624) June 4. 12 x 18". RB p. 61. Collection John S. Mason

1136. *My Flowers* (M. 1625) June 4. 12 x 18". RB p. 61. Collection Wanda Français

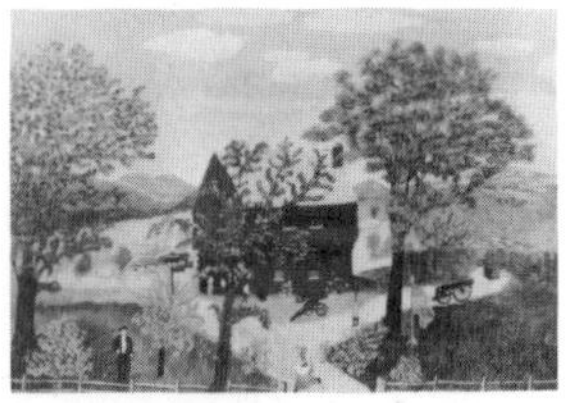

1137. *Block House* (M. 1626)
June 4. 12 x 18″. RB p. 61. Collection John E. Katz

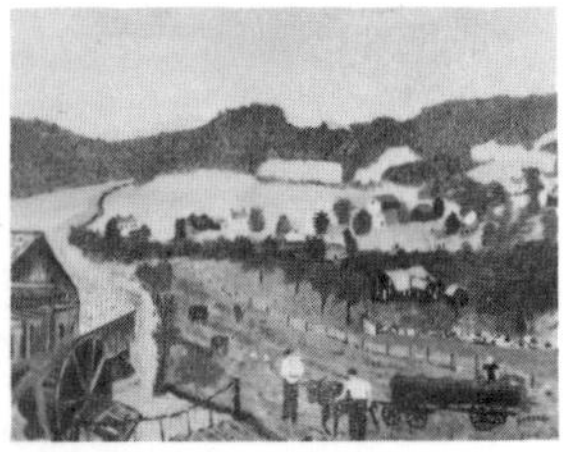

1138. *Old Water Wheel* (M. 1627)
June 4. 12 x 16″. RB p. 61. Collection Sam Shaw

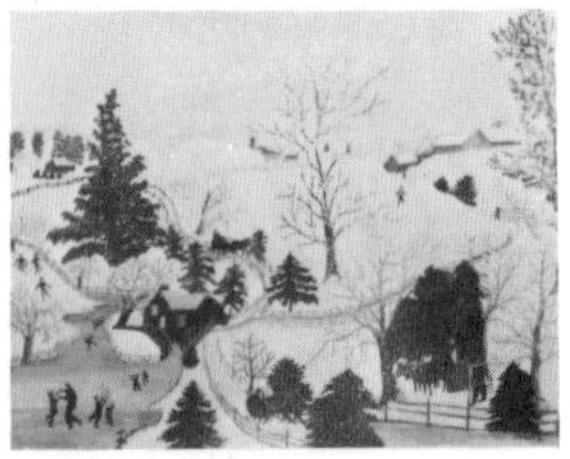

1139. *Hill Road* (M. 1628)
June 4. 18 x 23⅞″. RB p. 61. State University of New York at Albany

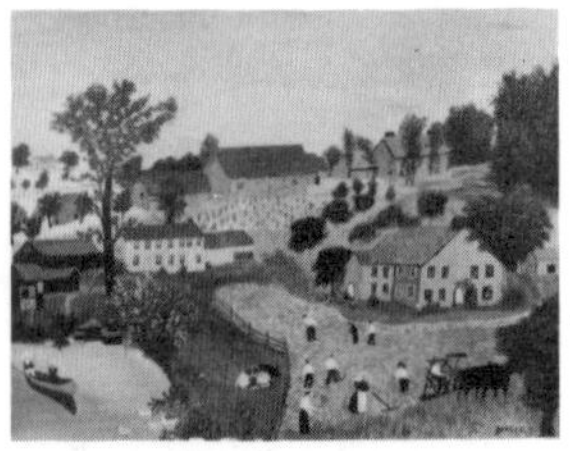

1140. *Harvest Time* (M. 1629)
June 4. 18 x 24″. RB p. 61. Collection Mr. and Mrs. George L. Schultz

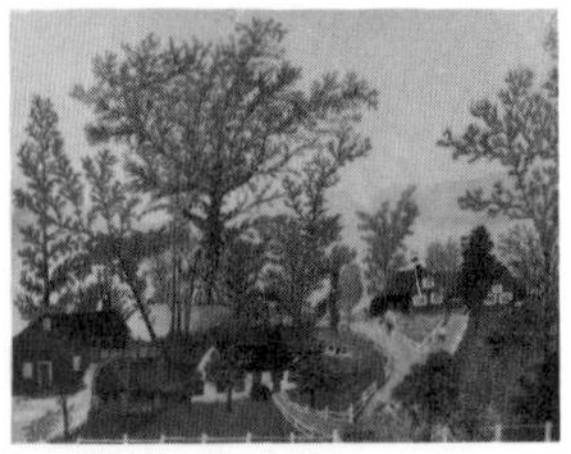

1141. *The Spillway* (M. 1630)
June 4. 18 x 24″. RB p. 61. Collection Mrs. Albert D. Lasker

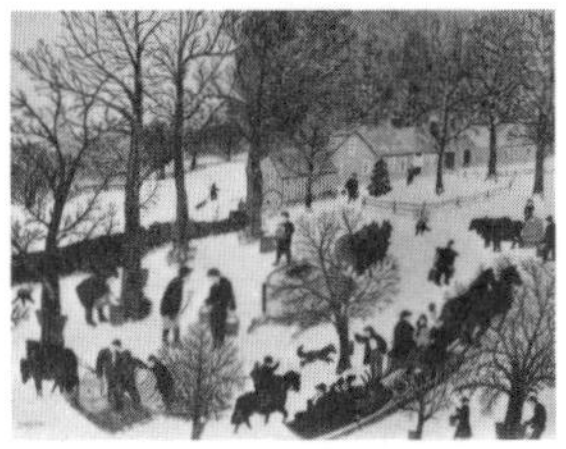

1142. *Last Run of Sap* (M. 1631)
June 4. 18⅛ x 24″. RB p. 61. Collection Mr. and Mrs. George O. Cook

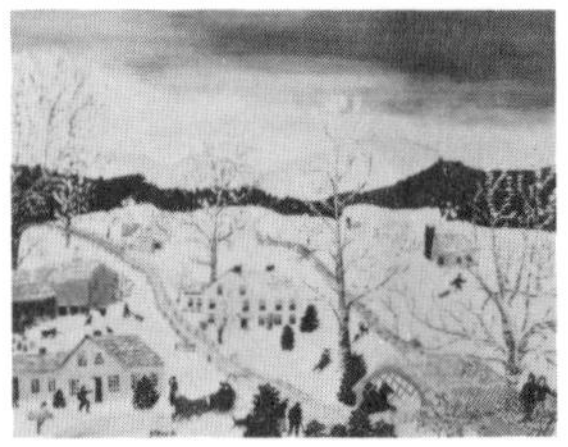

1143. *Lattice Bridge* (M. 1632)
June 4. 18 x 24″. RB p. 61. Collection Mrs. A.V. Stout

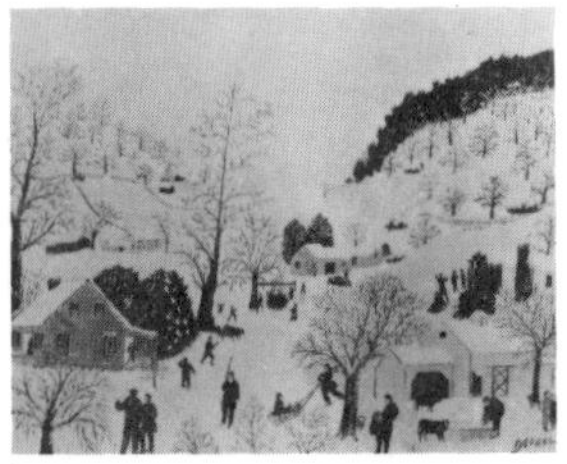

1144. *Sugaring Time* (M. 1633)
June 4. 18 x 24″. RB p. 61. Private collection

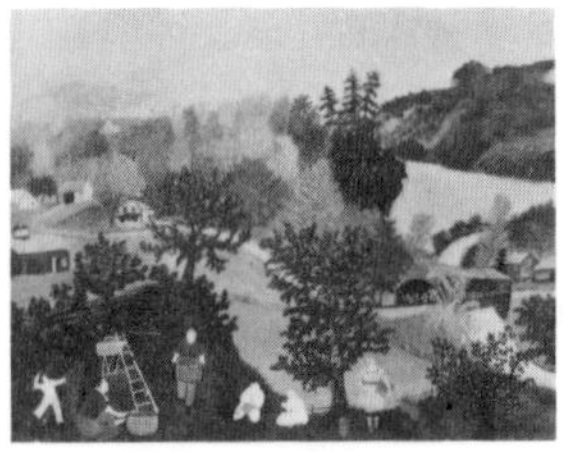

1145. *Apple Pickers* (M. 1634)
June 4. 18⅛ x 24″. RB p. 61. National Fruit Products Co.

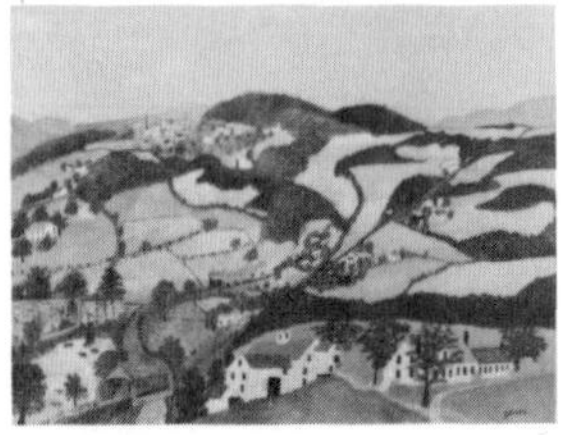

1146. *Virginia* (M. 1635)
June 4. 18 x 24″. RB p. 63. Collection Mrs. Paul Mellon

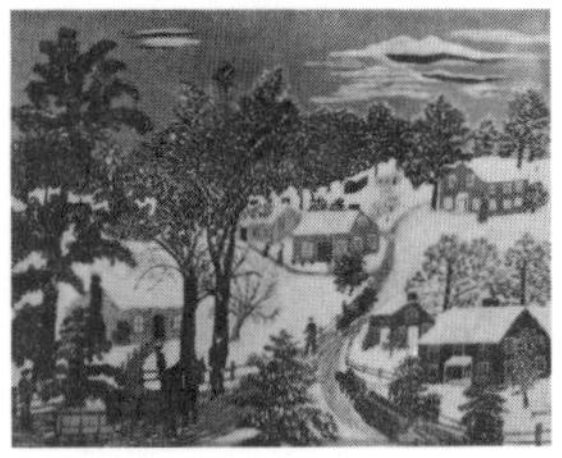

1147. *Frisky Horses* (M. 1636)
June 4. 18 x 24″. RB p. 63. Collection Mr. and Mrs. George O. Cook

1148. *The Thrashers* (M. 1637)
June 4. 18 x 24½″. RB p. 63. *Reproduced: The Four Seasons* portfolio. (See plate 193)

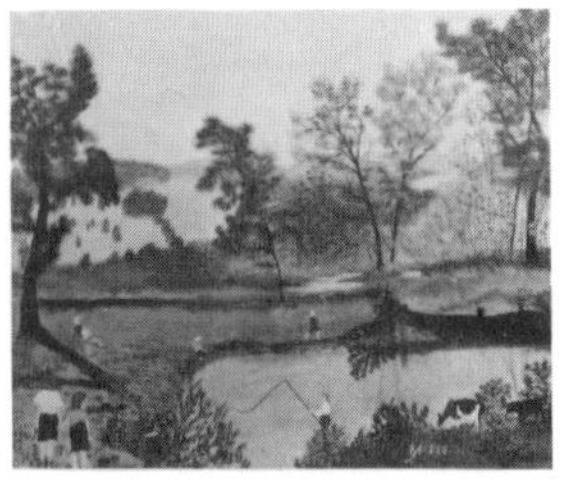

1149. *Watering Hole* (M. 1638)
June 4. 16 x 20″. RB p. 63

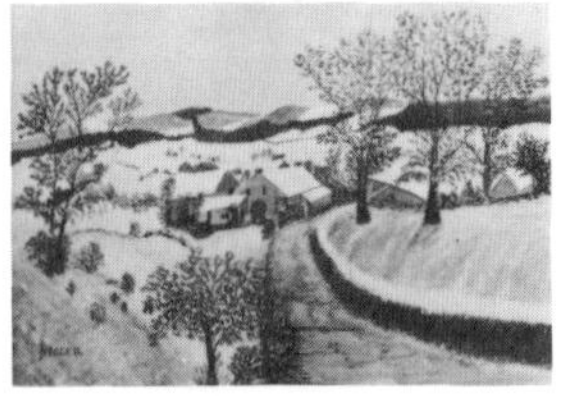

1150. *Baker Home* (M. 1639)
June 4. 12 x 18″. RB p. 63. The Bennington Museum, Bennington, Vt.

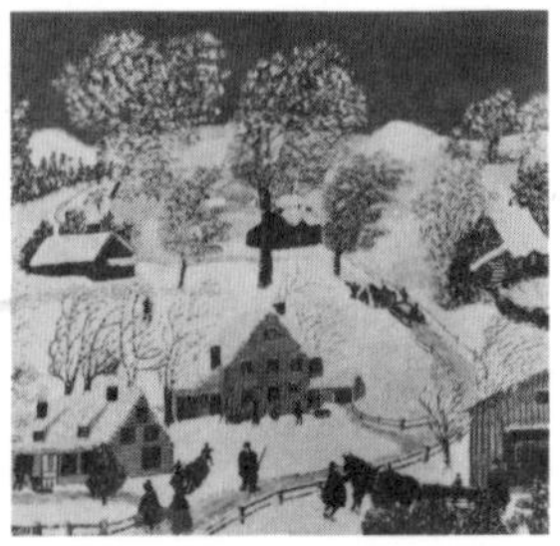

1151. *Home Again* (M. 1640)
Oct. 5. 16⅛ x 18″. RB p. 63. Collection Kenneth Hill

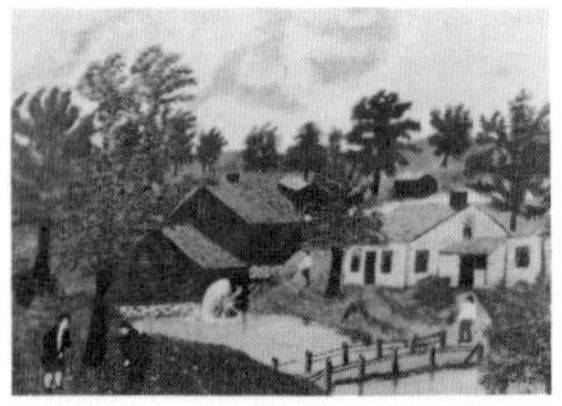

1152. *No, I Would Not* (M. 1641)
Oct. 5. 12 x 18″. RB p. 63. Collection Mr. and Mrs. Seymour D. Wolf

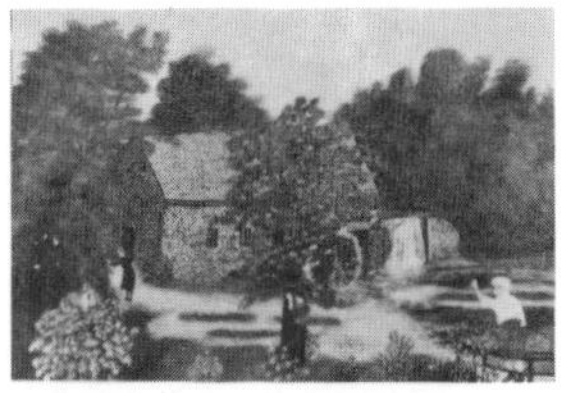

1153. *Old Stone Mill* (M. 1642)
Oct. 5. 12⅛ x 17¾″. RB p. 63

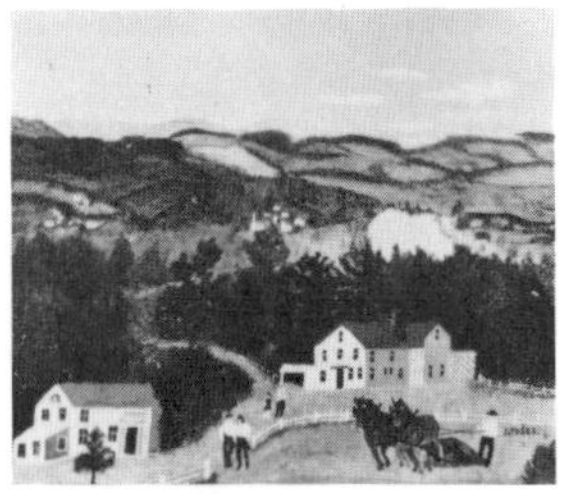

1154. *It Is Autumn* (M. 1643)
Oct. 5. Small. RB p. 63

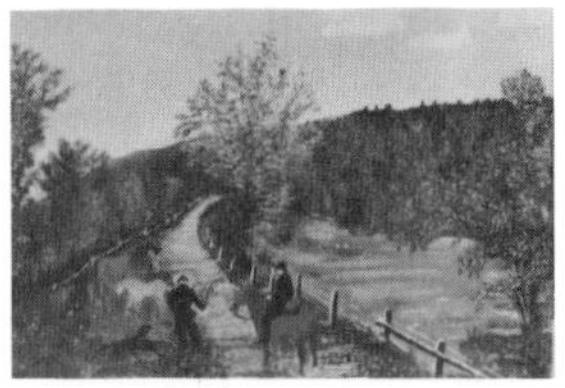

1155. *Whoa There* (M. 1644)
Oct. 5. 12 x 18″. RB p. 63. Collection Edith Evans Asbury

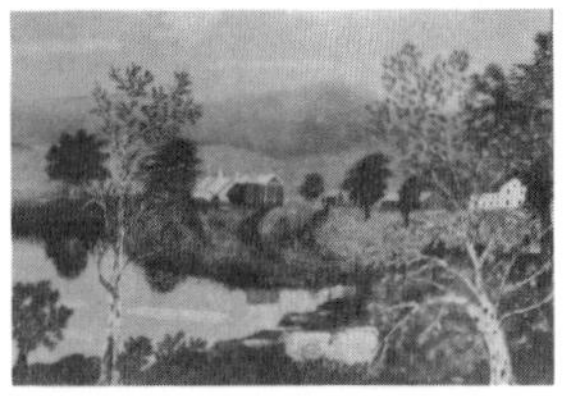

1156. *Still Waters* (M. 1645)
Oct. 5. 12 x 18″. RB p. 63

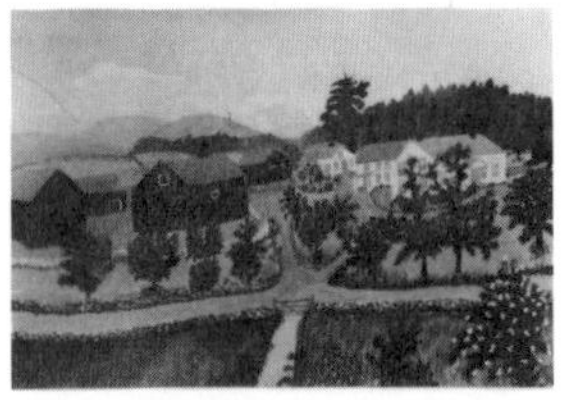

1157. *Moses* (M. 1646)
Oct. 5. 11⅞ x 18⅛″. RB p. 63. Collection Lillian Gish

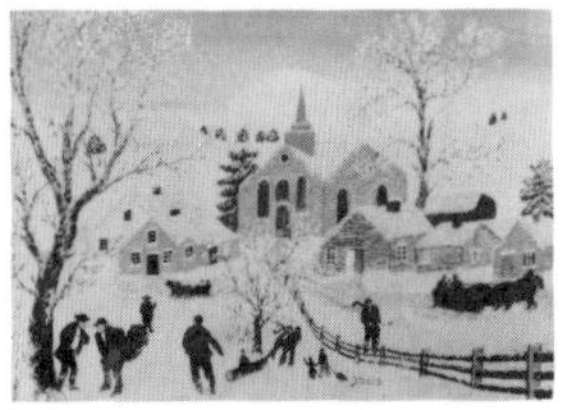

1158. *A Snowy Morn* (M. 1647)
Oct. 5. 12 x 18″. RB p. 63. Collection F. Willis

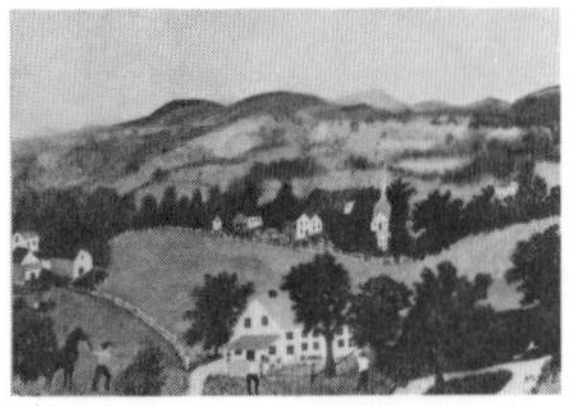

1159. *Fall in the Hills* (M. 1648)
Oct. 5. 12 x 18″. RB p. 63. Collection Raymond Weaver

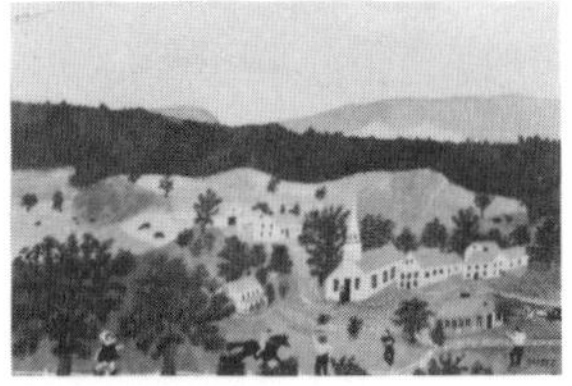

1160. *Hang On* (M. 1649)
Oct. 5. 12 x 18″. RB p. 63. Collection H.T. Rowe

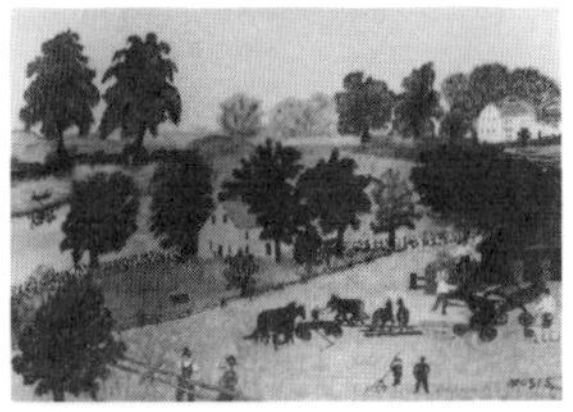

1161. *Harvest Time* (M. 1650)
Oct. 5. 9⅞ x 13⅞″. RB p. 63. Collection Mrs. Mitchell Flaum

1162. *White Christmas* (M. 1651)
Nov. 26. 23¾ x 19¾″. RB p. 63. Collection Mr. and Mrs. Irving Berlin. (See plate 192)

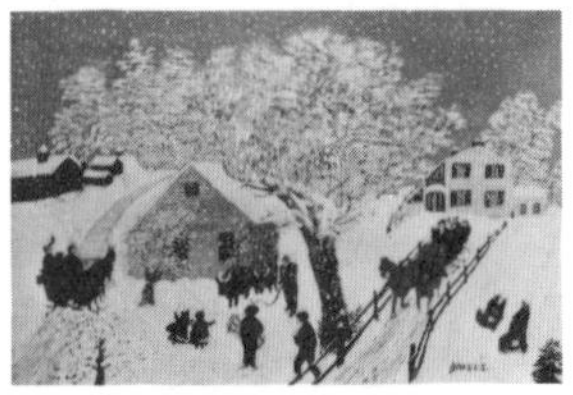

1163. *A Blizzard* (M. 1652)
Nov. 26. 11¾ x 17¾″. RB p. 63. Collection Mr. and Mrs. Albert E. Firmenich

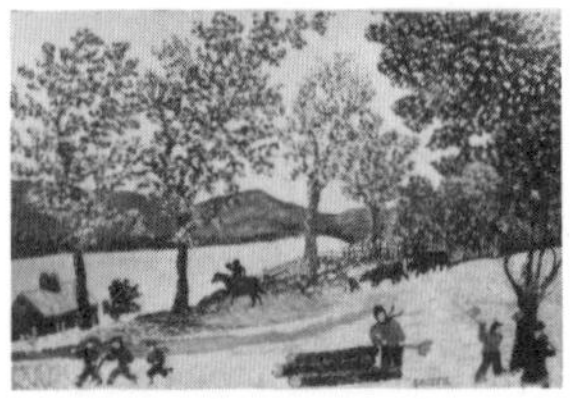

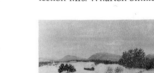

1164. *Logging* (M. 1653)
Nov. 26. 12 x 17⅞″. RB p. 63. Collection Mrs. Max Schur

1955

1165. *Checkered House* (M. 1654)
March 10. 18 x 24″. RB p. 63. *Reproduced:* GMSB. (See plate 51)

1166. *Sugaring Off* (M. 1655)
March 10. 18 x 24″. RB p. 63. (See plate 195)

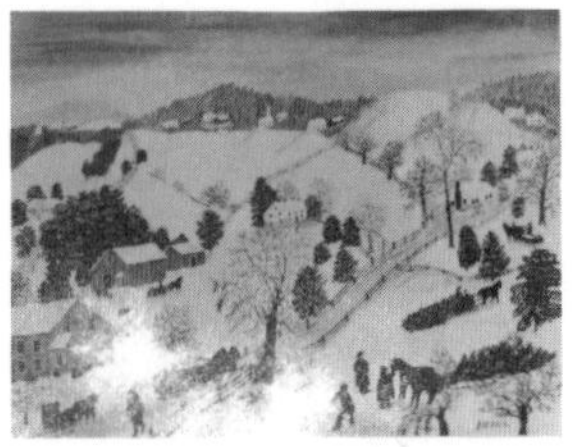

1167. *Bringing in the Christmas Tree* (M. 1656)
March 10. 18 x 24″. RB p. 63. Collection Mr. and Mrs. George O. Cook

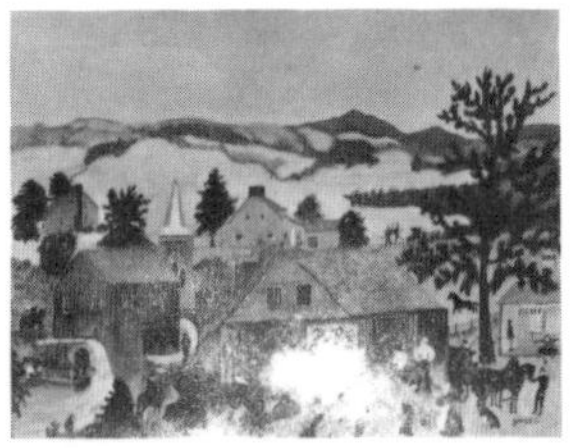

1168. *Blacksmith Shop* (M. 1657)
March 10. 18 x 24″. RB p. 63. Collection R.D. Lipp

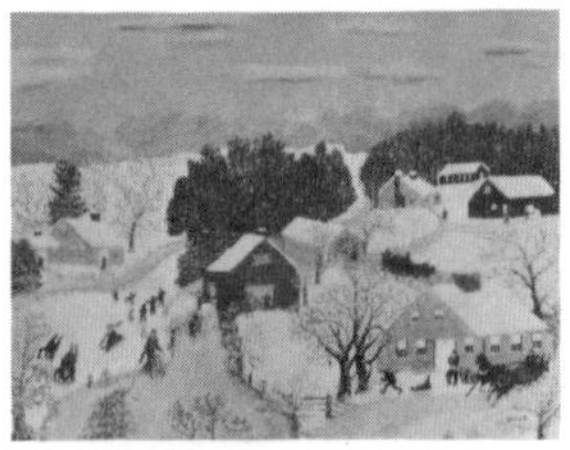

1169. *Deep Pond* (M. 1658)
March 10. 18 x 24″. RB p. 63. Collection Mrs. Wharton Sinkler

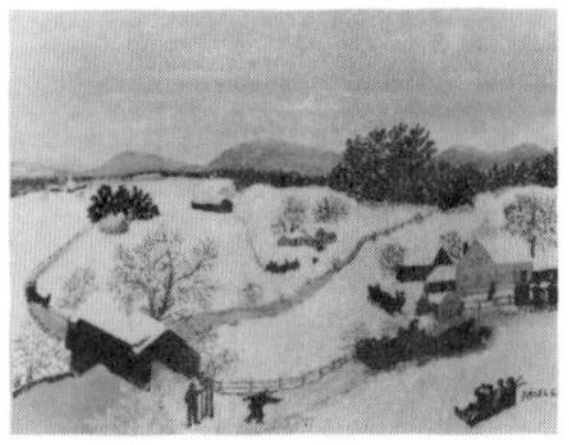

1170. *Red Bridge* (M. 1659)
March 10. 12 x 16⅛″. RB p. 63. Collection Mrs. Arthur McLean

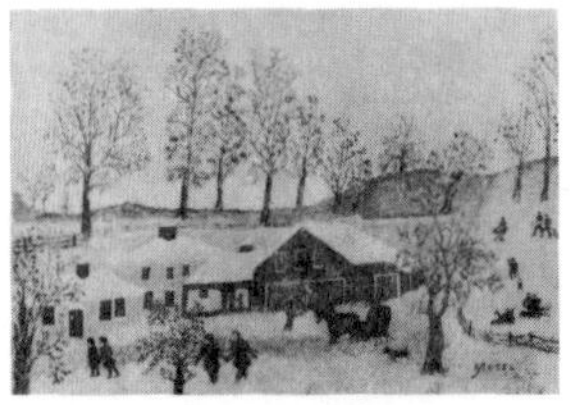

1171. *Yellow House* (M. 1660)
March 10. 12 x 17⅞″. RB p. 63. Collection John H. Hosch

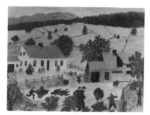

1172. *Catching the Turkey* (M. 1661)
March 10. 12 x 16". RB p. 65. Collection Lauren R. Gunn. *Reproduced: GMSB*

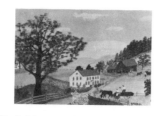

1173. *Family Party* (M. 1662)
March 10. 11⅞ x 16". RB p. 65. Collection Mrs. Morris Abrams

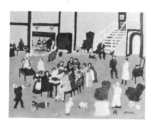

1174. *Vermont* (M. 1663)
March 10. 12¼ x 18". RB p. 65. Collection Lindsay A. Lovejoy

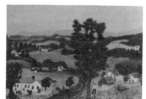

1175. *Out the Window* (M. 1664)
March 10. 12 x 16⅛". RB p. 65. Collection John Hall II

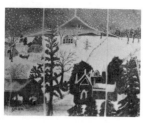

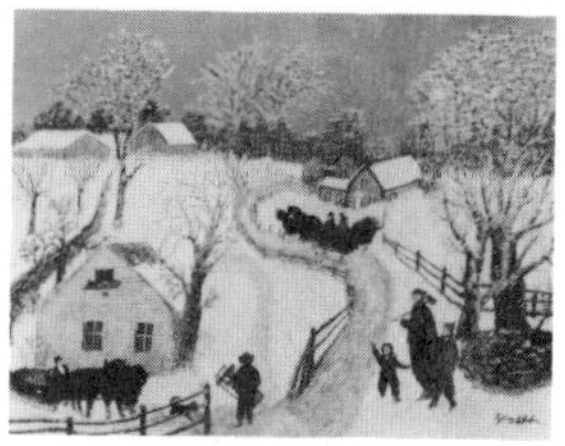

1176. *Hi There* (M. 1665)
March 10. 12⅛ x 16⅛". RB p. 65. Collection Dr. R.T. Beldegreen

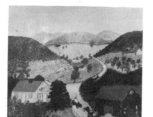

1177. *Building Fence* (M. 1666)
March 10. 11⅞ x 17⅞". RB p. 65. Collection Gertrude Stamper

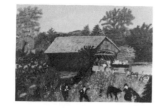

1178. *My Pets* (M. 1667)
March 10. 11⅞ x 18". RB p. 65. Collection Lillie Eigen Sornik. Parke-Bernet Sale No. 2132, Oct. 17, 1962, No. 28

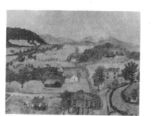

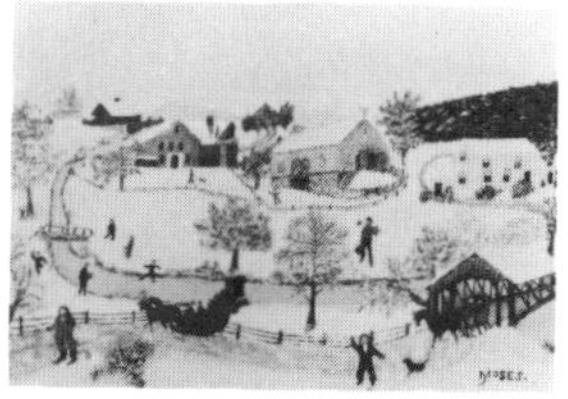

1179. *Open Bridge* (M. 1668)
March 10. 12 x 18". RB p. 65. Collection Mary Alexander

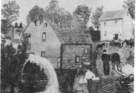

1180. *Catching the Turkey* (M. 1669)
March 10. 12 x 16". RB p. 65. Collection Mrs. Andrew D. Wolfe

1181. *Horseshoeing* (M. 1670)
March 10. 12 x 16". RB p. 65. Collection Henri Moreault. (See plate 196)

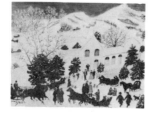

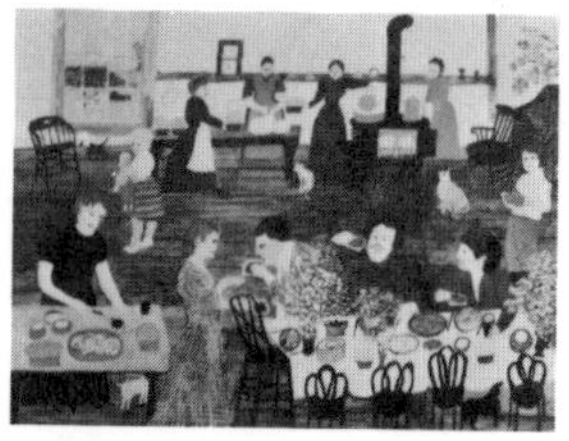

1182. *Baking Bread* (M. 1671)
March 10. 12 x 16". RB p. 65. Collection Mr. and Mrs. A.M. Nakamura

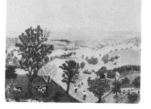

1183. *Old Automobile* (M. 1672)
April 29. 13 x 16". RB p. 65. Collection Mrs. William P. Roth

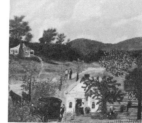

1184. *Load of Oats* (M. 1673)
April 29. 11⅞ x 16". RB p. 65. Collection Dr. and Mrs. Ernst Glaessel

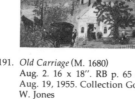

1185. *Baker Boy* (M. 1674)
April 29. 12 x 16". RB p. 65. Collection Mr. and Mrs. A.M. Nakamura

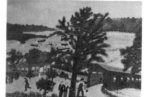

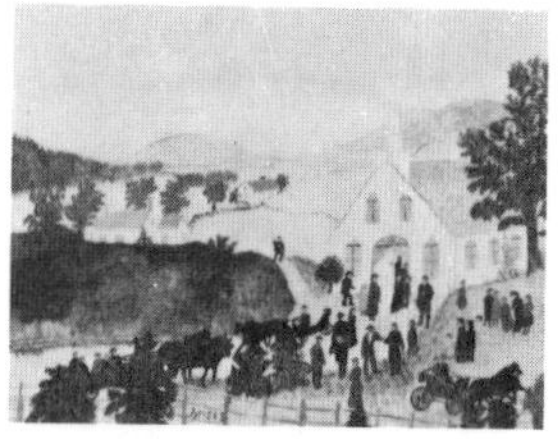

1186. *June Bride* (M. 1675)
April 29. 12 x 16". RB p. 65. Collection Mrs. Jack Currier Lewis

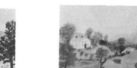

1187. *Winter Bride* (M. 1676)
April 29. 12 x 16". RB p. 65. Collection Henry Malkin

1188. *Halloween* (M. 1677)
April 29. 18 x 24". RB p. 65. *Reproduced: GMSB; Six of My Favorite Paintings* portfolio. (See plates 233, 234, 235)

1189. *Christmas Trees* (M. 1678)
April 29. 18 x 24". RB p. 65. Collection Lenore Priest Millhollen and Joyce Priest. *Reproduced:* UNICEF card. (See plate 197)

1190. *Sugaring* (M. 1679)
July 2. 11⅛ x 16". RB p 65 "C.B.S. picture." This painting was done during the artist's interview with Edward R. Murrow, June 29–July 2, 1955. (See plate 164)

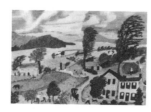

1191. *Old Carriage* (M. 1680)
Aug. 2. 16 x 18". RB p. 65 dated Aug. 19, 1955. Collection Gordon W. Jones

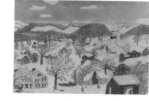

1192. *Buskirk Bridge* (M. 1681)
Aug. 2. 11⅛ x 16⅛". RB p. 65 dated Aug. 19, 1955. Collection Mr. and Mrs. C.S. Ohsner

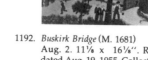

1193. *Milking* (M. 1683)
Aug. 2. 11½ x 16". RB p. 65 dated Aug. 19, 1955. Collection Mr. and Mrs. George O. Cook

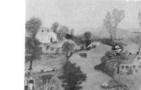

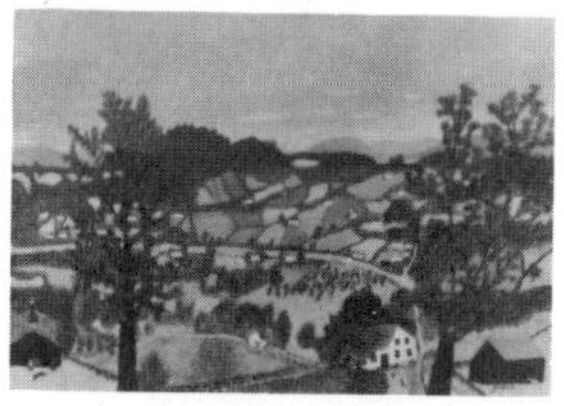

1194. *Cambridge Valley* (M. 1685)
Aug. 2. 16 x 23¾". RB p. 65 dated Aug. 19, 1955. Collection Jack S. Josey

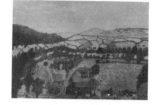

1195. *Harvest Time* (M. 1686)
Aug. 2. 18 x 24". RB p. 65 dated Aug. 19, 1955. Private collection

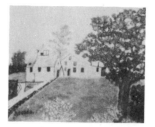

1196. *The Storm* (M. 1687)
Aug. 2. 16 x 24⅛". RB p. 65 dated Aug. 19, 1955. Collection Mr. and Mrs. Stuart B. Padnos

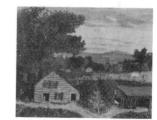

1197. *November* (M. 1688)
Aug. 2. 16 x 24". RB p. 65 dated Aug. 19, 1955. Collection Roy Moses

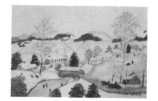

1198. *March* (M. 1689)
Aug. 2. 16 x 24". RB p. 67 dated Aug. 19, 1955. *Reproduced:* Hallmark

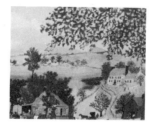

1199. *Apple Blossoms* (M. 1692)
Aug. 2. 16 x 20". RB p. 67 dated Aug. 19, 1955. Collection Hal Watters

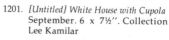

1200. *Calhoun* (M. 1693)
Aug. 2. 16¾ x 24". RB p. 67. Collection Forrest K. Moses

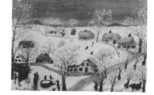

1201. *[Untitled] White House with Cupola*
September. 6 x 7½". Collection Lee Kamilar

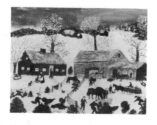

1202. *September* (M. 1695)
Oct. 12. 8 x 10½". RB p. 67. Private collection

1203. *The Oxen* (M. 1696)
Dec. 13. 12 x 18½". RB p. 67. Gift to Thomas J. Watson, 1955

1956

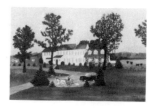

1204. *Eisenhower Home* (M. 1697)
Jan. 9. 16 x 24". RB p. 67

1205. *The Eisenhower Farm* (M. 1698)
Jan. 9. 16 x 24". RB p. 67. The Dwight D. Eisenhower Library, Abilene, Kan. (See plate 167)

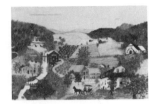

1206. *September* (M. 1699)
March 1. 16 x 24⅛". RB p. 67. Collection Mrs. Stanley Newhouse

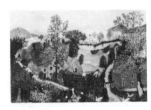

1207. *October* (M. 1700)
March 1. 16 x 24". RB p. 67. Estate of Lily McCall Davis

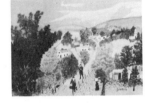

1208. *November* (M. 1701)
March 1. 15⅞ x 24⅛". RB p. 67. Collection Mr. and Mrs. Fred W. Parker, Jr.

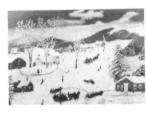

1209. *December* (M. 1702)
March 1. 16 x 24". RB p. 67. Collection Mrs. William Gilmore. *Reproduced: BG*

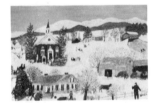

1210. *January* (M. 1703)
March 1. 15⅞ x 24⅛". RB p. 67

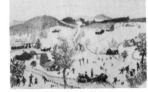

1211. *February* (M. 1704)
March 1. 15⅞ x 24⅛". RB p. 67. Private collection

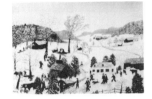

1212. *March* (M. 1705)
March 1. 16 x 24". RB p. 67

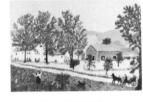

1213. *Autumn* (M. 1706)
March 1. 12 x 18". RB p. 67. Collection Mary O'Brien Perazzo

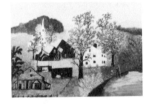

1214. *Coming Home* (M. 1707)
March 1. 11⅞ x 18". RB p. 67. Private collection

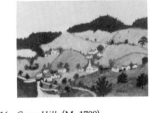

1215. *Fishing* (M. 1708)
March 1. 11⅞ x 18". RB p. 67. Collection Mary O'Brien Perazzo

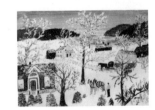

1216. *Green Hills* (M. 1709)
March 1. 11⅞ x 17⅞". RB p. 67. Collection Mary O'Brien Perazzo

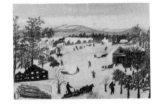

1217. *Too Cold* (M. 1710)
March 1. 12 x 18". RB p. 67. Collection Mary O'Brien Perazzo

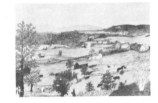

1218. *Hoosick Hills* (M. 1711)
April 16. 16 x 24". RB p. 67. The Cheney Free Public Library, Hoosick Falls, N.Y.

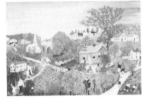

1219. *June* (M. 1712)
April 24. 16 x 24". RB p. 69. Collection Mr. and Mrs. James M. Blacklidge

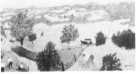

1220. *July* (M. 1713)
April 24. 16 x 24". RB p. 69. Collection Mrs. Paul Mellon

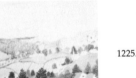

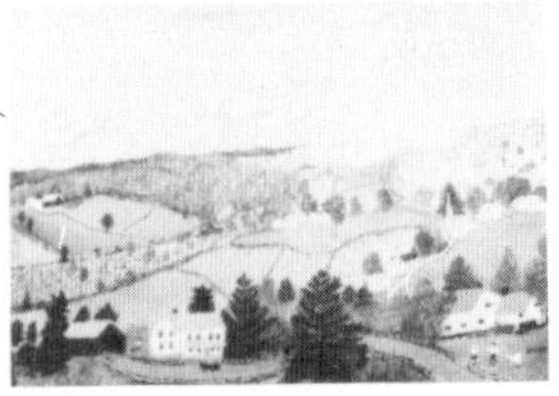

1221. *August* (M. 1714)
April 24. 14 x 22". RB p. 69. Collection Marcella M. Day

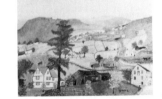

1222. *Upland* (M. 1715)
April 24. 16 x 24". RB p. 69. Collection Mrs. William P. Roth

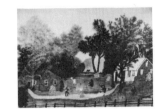

1223. *I'll Catch* (M. 1682)
Dated Aug. 2, 1955, revised April 1956. 11⅛ x 16". RB p. 69 under "Retouched." A photograph exists of an earlier version of this picture which was listed as "We Will Dance," RB p. 65. Collection Mr. and Mrs. William F. Loving

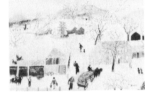

1224. *March, No. 2* (M. 1684)
Dated Aug. 2, 1955, completely revised April 1956. 16 x 24". RB p. 69 under "Retouched." A photograph exists of an earlier version of this picture, listed as "Apple Tree," RB p. 65. Collection Mrs. M. Levy

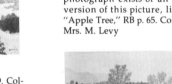

1225. *April* (M. 1690)
Dated Aug. 2, 1955, revised April 1956. 16 x 23⅞". RB p. 69 under "Retouched." A photograph exists of an earlier version of this picture, listed as "Owlkill Bridge," RB p. 67. Collection the Reverend Wesley Gallup

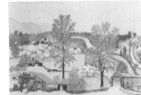

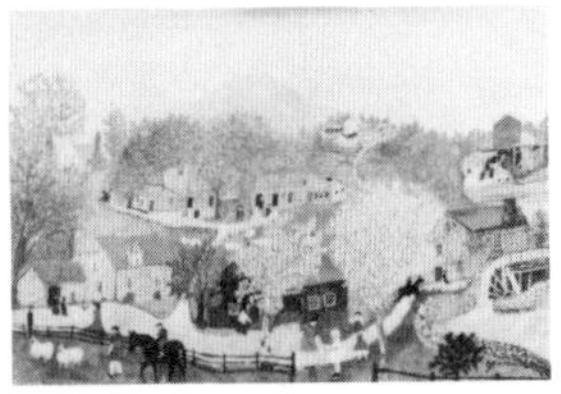

1226. *Sunshine* (M. 1691)
Painted April, erroneously dated June 30. 16 x 24". Collection Mrs. M. Levy

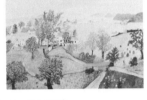

1227. *May* (M. 1691)
Painted April 1956, erroneously dated Aug. 2, 1955. 16 x 24". RB p. 69 numbered "1691? 1716"

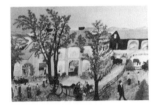

1228. *Thanksgiving* (M. 1717)
June 30. 16 x 24". RB p. 69. Collection Mrs. Skitch Henderson

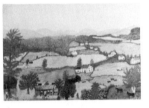

1229. *Hoosick Hills* (M. 1718)
June 30. 16 x 24". RB p. 69. Collection Mrs. James A. Beresford

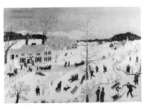

1230. *Christmas* (M. 1719)
June 30. 16 x 23⅞". RB p. 69

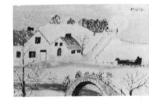

1231. *Wintery* (M. 1720)
June 30. 5¼ x 8¼". RB p. 69. Collection Jane Kallir

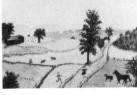

1232. *O, a Colt* (M. 1721)
June-July. Small. RB p. 69

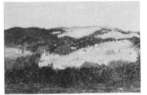

1233. *The Village* (M. 1722)
June-July. Small. RB p. 69

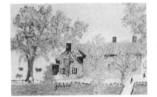

1234. *Home* (M. 1723)
June-July. Small. RB p. 69. Collection Garry Grant

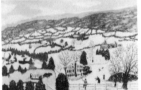

1235. *Help* (M. 1724)
July 6. 16 x 24". RB p. 69 dated June 30, 1956. Collection Arthur Oldham II

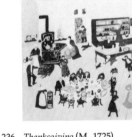

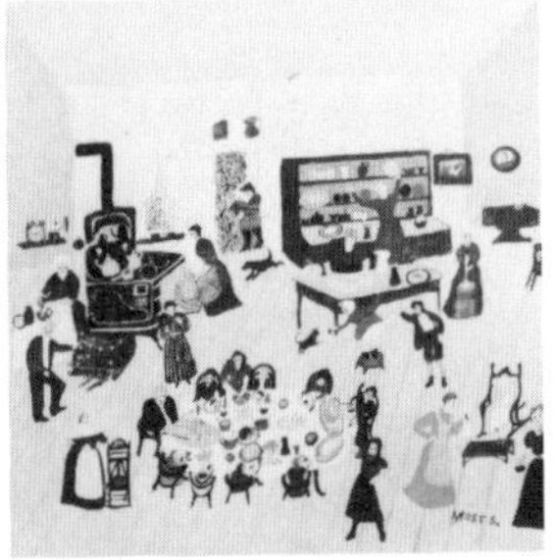

1236. *Thanksgiving* (M. 1725)
July 6. 18 x 18". RB p. 69 dated June 30, 1956. Collection Franklyn M. Moffitt

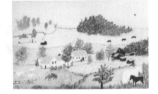

1237. *Black Colt* (M. 1726)
Sept. 20. 10 x 16". RB p. 69. Collection Robert Wortmann

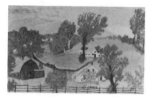

1238. *Spring* (M. 1727)
Sept. 20. 10 x 16". RB p. 69. Parke-Bernet Sale No. 2001, Nov. 30, 1960, No. 106

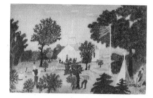

1239. *The Flag* (M. 1728)
Sept. 20. 10 x 16". RB p. 69. Private collection

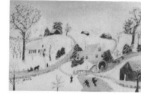

1240. *Winter* (M. 1729)
Sept. 20. 10 x 16". RB p. 69. High Museum of Art, Atlanta, Ga.

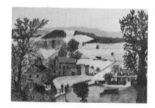

1241. *Foot Bridge* (M. 1730)
Sept. 20. 16 x 24". RB p. 69. Collection Mary Orr Denham

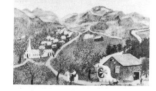

1242. *Shenandoah* (M. 1731)
Sept. 20. 16 x 24". RB p. 69. Collection Mr. and Mrs. M.A. Cancelliere

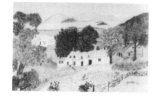

1243. *Old Fort* (M. 1732)
Sept. 20. 10 x 16". RB p. 69. Collection Kenneth F. Zehren

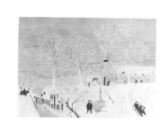

1244. *Home* (M. 1733)
Nov. 6. 11½ x 16". RB p. 71. Collection Mrs. Skitch Henderson

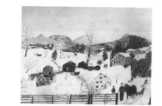

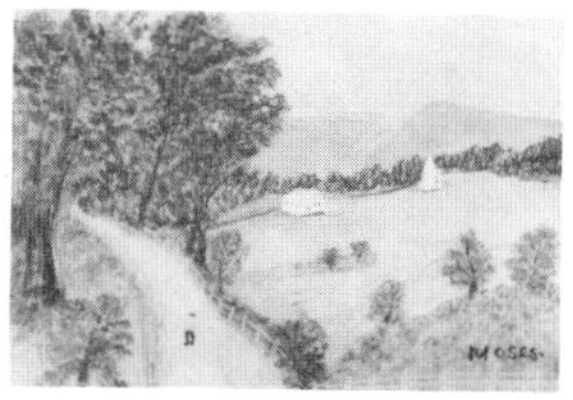

1245. *Sailing* (M. 1734)
Nov. 6. 6 x 8⅞". RB p. 71. Collection Connie Hahn

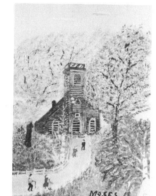

1246. *Brown Church* (M. 1735)
Nov. 6. 8¾ x 6". RB p. 71. Collection C. Coon

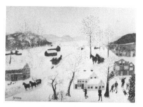

1247. *Gray House* (M. 1736)
Nov. 6. 6 x 8¾". RB p. 71. Collection G. Greaves

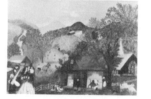

1248. *Halloween* (M. 1737)
Nov. 23. 14 x 24⅜". RB p. 71. Meri Jaye & Associates, San Francisco, Calif.

1249. *A Blizzard* (M. 1738)
Nov. 23. 15⅞ x 24". RB p. 71. Private collection. *Reproduced:* Hallmark. (See plate 198)

1250. *Wind Storm* (M. 1739)
Nov. 23. 16 x 24". RB p. 71. Private collection. (See plate 199)

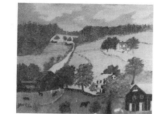

1251. *Logging* (M. 1740)
Nov. 23. 16 x 24". RB p. 71

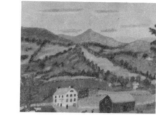

1252. *Tandem* (M. 1741)
Nov. 23. 16 x 24". RB p. 71. *Reproduced:* Hallmark

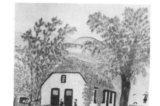

1253. *Bridge Builders* (M. 1742)
Nov. 23. 15⅞ x 24". RB p. 71. Collection Mrs. E.W. Lane, Jr.

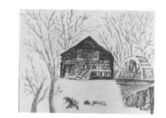

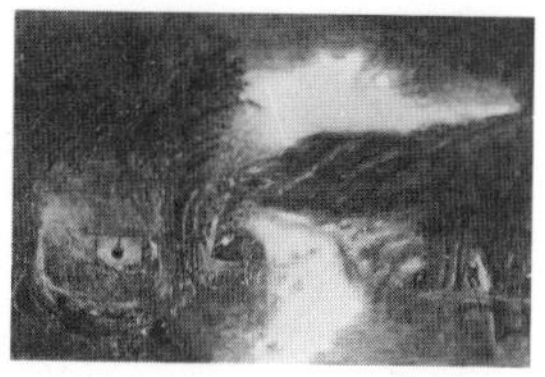

1254. *Campfire* (M. 1743)
Nov. 23. 11⅛ x 19⅛". RB p. 71

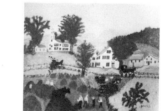

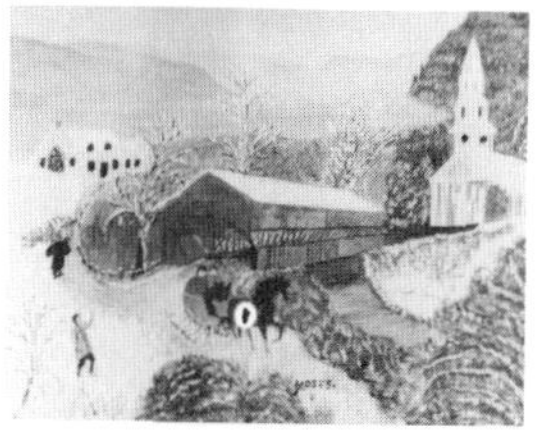

1255. *Hello* (M. 1744)
Nov. 23. Canvas, 9 x 12". RB p. 71. Parke-Bernet Sale No. 2001, Nov. 30, 1960, No. 98

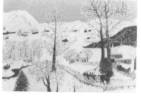

1256. *Red Barn* (M. 1745)
Nov. 23. 11 x 14⅛". RB p. 71. Collection Henry Holt

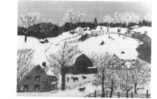

1257. *Early Fall* (M. 1746)
Nov. 23. 11 x 13⅛". RB p. 71. *Reproduced:* Parke-Bernet Sale No. 2666, March 14, 1968, No. 161

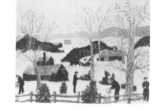

1258. *Stone Church, Va.* (M. 1747)
Nov. 23. 6⅞ x 8⅞". RB p. 71. Collection Germaine A. Grum

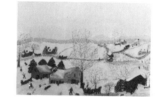

1259. *Old Mill* (M. 1748)
Nov. 23. 6⅞ x 8½". RB p. 71. Collection Ernest A. Gross

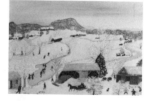

1260. *Haying* (M. 1749)
Nov. 23. 11⅞ x 15¾". RB. p. 71. The Shelburne Museum, Shelburne, Vt.

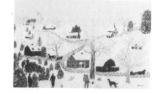

1261. *Traveling* (M. 1750)
Dec. 19. 10½ x 15⅞". RB p. 73. Collection Mr. and Mrs. Russell G. Allen

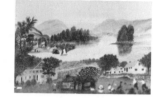

1262. *Colts* (M. 1751)
Dec. 19. 10¾ x 16". RB p. 73. Collection H.D. Carter

1263. *Sap Pouring* (M. 1752)
Dec. 19. 11⅞ x 16". RB p. 73. Collection H.D. Carter

1957

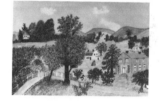

1264. *Lattice Bridge* (M. 1753)
Feb. 11. 15⅞ x 24". RB p. 73. Collection Edwin Andrews, Jr.

1265. *Logging* (M. 1754)
Feb. 11. 15⅞ x 24". RB p. 73. *Reproduced:* Hallmark

1266. *My Dog* (M. 1755)
Feb. 11. 15⅞ x 24". RB p. 73. Collection Henry Harnishfaeger

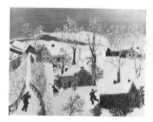

1267. *Batten Kill* (M. 1756)
Feb. 11. 16 x 24". RB p. 73. Private collection

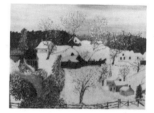

1268. *May* (M. 1757)
Feb. 11. 16 x 24". RB p. 73. Collection Dr. Joseph Armenio

1269. *Sleet Storm* (M. 1758)
Feb. 11. 11⅞ x 16". RB p. 73. Collection Mrs. Samuel S. Stratton

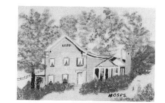

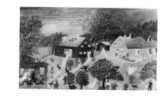

1270. *Red Sunset* (M. 1759)
Feb. 11. 11⅞ x 16". RB p. 73. Collection Mr. and Mrs. George O. Cook

317

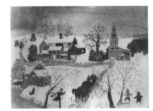

1271. *Hurry Up* (M. 1760)
Feb. 11. 12 x 16″. RB p. 73. Collection Harry R. Samuels

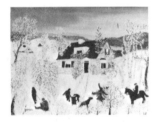

1272. *Black Horse* (M. 1761)
Feb. 11. 12 x 16″. RB p. 73. Collection Mrs. Bernard H. Ridder

1273. *Snowed In* (M. 1762)
Feb. 11. 12 x 16″. RB p. 73. (See plate 200)

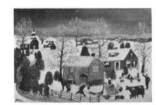

1274. *Run Pig Run* (M. 1763)
March 6. 15⅞ x 24″. RB p. 73. Collection Edwin H. Stern

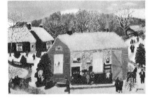

1275. *Cheerful Fire* (M. 1764)
March 6. 16 x 24″. RB p. 73. Private collection

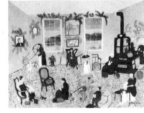

1276. *Christmas, 1860* (M. 1765)
March 6. 12 x 16″. RB p. 73. Collection Donald Stone

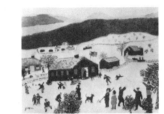

1277. *Snowballing* (M. 1766)
March 6. 12 x 16″. RB p. 73. Collection Dr. and Mrs. Ernst Glaessel. *Reproduced:* BG; GMSB

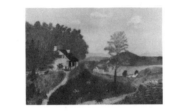

1278. *Spring* (M. 1767)
April 23. 16 x 24″. RB p. 73

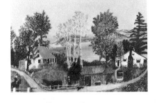

1279. *The Lake* (M. 1768)
April 23. 15⅞ x 23⅞″. RB p. 73. Collection Jean C. Taupin

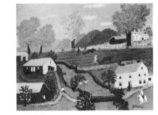

1280. *Plowing* (M. 1769)
April 23. 12 x 16″. RB p. 73. Galerie de Tours, Carmel, Calif.

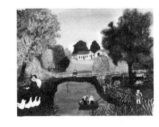

1281. *Autumn* (M. 1771)
April 23. 12 x 16″. RB p. 73. The Bennington Museum, Bennington, Vt.

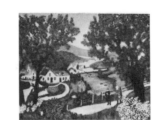

1282. *Lilacs* (M. 1772)
April 23. 11⅞ x 15⅞″. RB p. 73. Collection Mr. and Mrs. George O. Cook

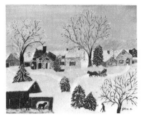

1283. *Yellow Cutter* (M. 1773)
April 23. 12 x 15⅞″. RB p. 73. Collection Myron Boyce

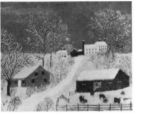

1284. *Feeding Time* (M. 1774)
April 23. 12 x 15⅞″. RB p. 73. Collection Mr. and Mrs. Raymond B. Chrisman

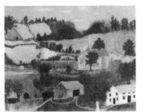

1285. *Empty Barn* (M. 1775)
July 2. 12 x 16⅛″. RB p. 75. Collection Dr. and Mrs. Richard B. Westman

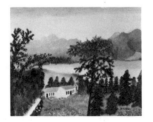

1286. *Scotland* (M. 1776)
July 2. 12 x 16″. RB p. 75. Private collection

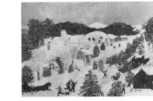

1287. *Sleigh Ride* (M. 1777)
July 2. 15⅞ x 24″. RB p. 75. Collection Mrs. H. Stillman Taylor. *Reproduced:* GMSB

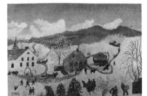

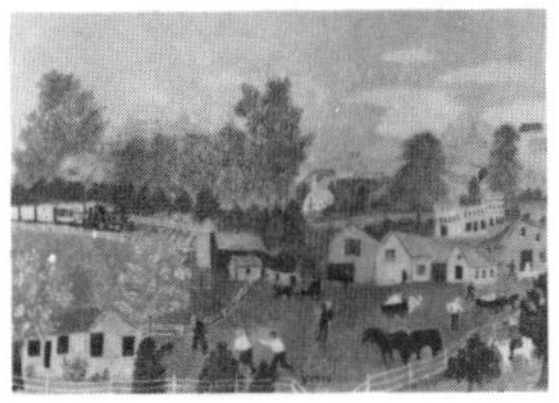

1288. *The Train* (M. 1778)
July 2. 15⅞ x 23⅞″. RB p. 75. Collection Mrs. R.B. Jenkins

1289. *Balloon* (M. 1780)
July 2. 15⅞ x 24″. RB p. 75. Collection Otto Kallir. (See plate 204)

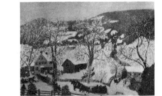

1290. *Deep Snow* (M. 1781)
July 2. 15⅞ x 24″. RB p. 75. *Reproduced:* Hallmark

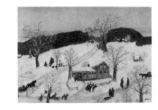

1291. *Sleigh Ride* (M. 1782)
July 2. 16 x 24″. RB p. 75

1292. *Sunset* (M. 1783)
July 2. 16 x 24″. RB p. 75

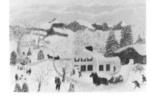

1293. *Christmas* (M. 1784)
July 2. 16 x 24″. RB p. 75. Collection Mr. and Mrs. Charles W. Fribley, Jr.

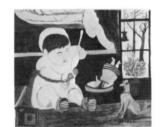

1294. *To Janie* (M. 1785)
July 2. 10 x 12″. RB p. 75. Collection Jane Kallir

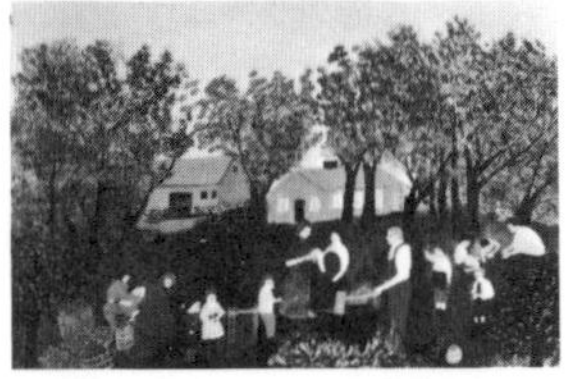

1295. *Apple Butter* (M. 1786)
Aug. 26. 16 x 24″. RB p. 75. Collection W.H. Perry

1296. *Old Times* (M. 1787)
Aug. 26. 16 x 24″. RB p. 75. (See plate 207)

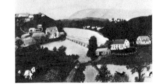

1297. *The Ferry* (M. 1788)
Aug. 26. 16 x 24″. RB p. 75. Collection Alex G. Campbell

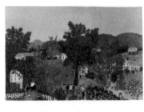

1298. *The Gate* (M. 1789)
Aug. 26. 15⅞ x 24″. RB p. 75. Collection Alfreda Rochelle Thomas

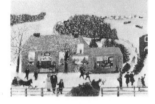

1299. *Cold Day* (M. 1790)
Aug. 26. 16⅛ x 24″. RB p. 75. Collection Dr. John E. Kyger

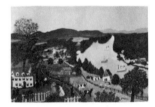

1300. *The Dam* (M. 1791)
Aug. 26. 16 x 24″. RB p. 75. Collection Mrs. Walter K. Rush

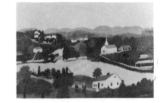

1301. *Jersey Cows* (M. 1792)
Aug. 26. 15⅞ x 24″. RB p. 75. Collection W.H. Perry

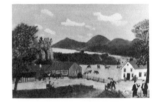

1302. *Croquet* (M. 1793)
Aug. 26. 16 x 24″. RB p. 75. Collection James Alexander

1303. *Rockabye* (M. 1794)
Aug. 26. 11⅞ x 16″. RB p. 75. Private collection. (See plate 238)

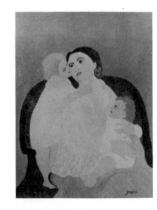

1304. *Mother* (M. 1795)
Aug. 26. c. 16 x 12″. RB p. 75

1305. *Lincoln* (M. 1796)
Aug. 26. 12 x 16⅛″. RB p. 75. Collection Shirley Futterman. *Reproduced:* BG; GMSB. (See plate 169)

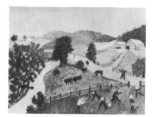

1306. *Ball Game* (M. 1797)
Aug. 26. 11⅞ x 16″. RB p. 75. Collection Mrs. Edward Babbott

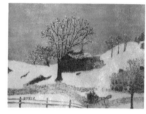

1307. *Sugar House* (M. 1798)
Aug. 26. 12 x 16⅛″. RB p. 75. Collection David H. Griffin

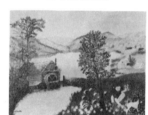

1308. *Daisies* (M. 1799)
Aug. 26. 12 x 16″. RB p. 75

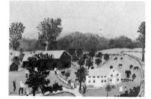

1309. *Balloon Landing in Cambridge, 1806* (M. 1800)
Oct. 7. 16 x 24″. RB p. 77

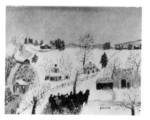

1310. *Good Fun* (M. 1801)
Oct. 7. 12 x 15⅞″. RB p. 77. Collection Arthur R. Armstrong

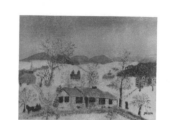

1311. *Old Home* (M. 1802)
Oct. 7. 11⅞ x 15⅞″. Inscribed: "To my dear friend / Electra Havemeyer Webb / Merry Christmas 1957. / Grandma, Moses." RB p. 77. The Shelburne Museum, Shelburne, Vt.

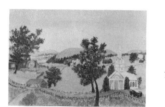

1312. *Most There* (M. 1803)
Oct. 7. 8 x 12″. RB p. 77. Collection Anna Rochlitz

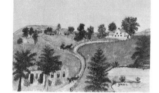

1313. *The Pond* (M. 1804)
Oct. 7. 7⅞ x 11⅞″. RB p. 77. Collection Margaret Carr and Ruth Garner

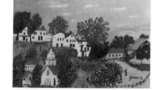

1314. *Lilacs* (M. 1805)
Oct. 7. 8 x 11⅞″. RB p. 77

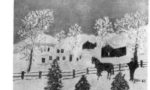

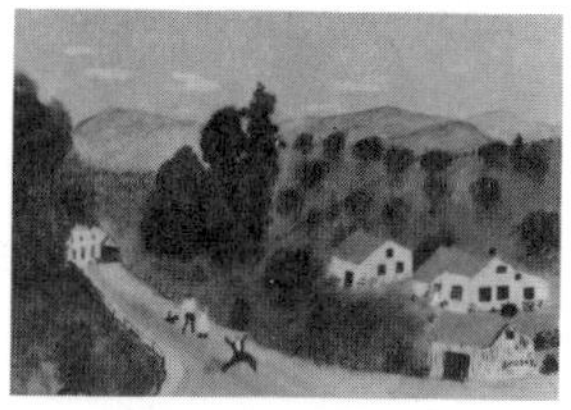

1315. *Hurry* (M. 1806)
Oct. 7. 8 x 12″. RB p. 77. Collection P. Staub

1316. *Whoa!* (M. 1807)
Oct. 7. 8 x 12″. RB p. 77. Collection Mrs. C. Robert Fine

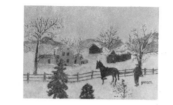

1317. *Get Along* (M. 1808)
Oct. 7. 7⅞ x 11⅞″. RB p. 77. Collection Mr. and Mrs. Jerome Speltz

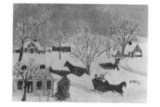

1318. *First Snow* (M. 1809)
Oct. 7. 8 x 13″. RB p. 77. Collection John D. Frisoli

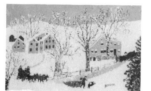

1319. *Pull Boys* (M. 1810)
Oct. 7. 7⅞ x 12⅞″. RB p. 77. Collection M. Carr

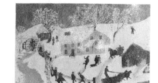

1320. *Whoa!* (M. 1811)
Nov. 20. 8 x 12″. RB p. 77. Collection R. Gipson

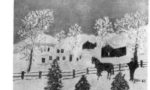

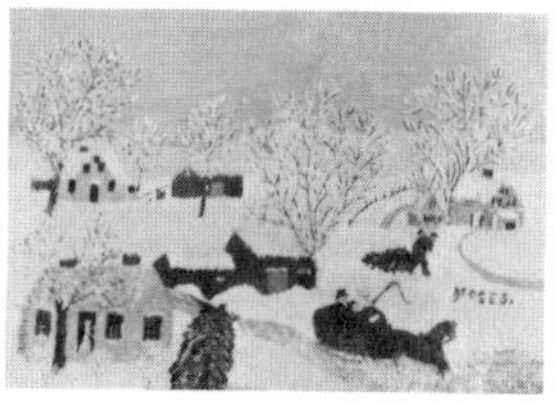

1321. *Get Along* (M. 1812)
Nov. 20. 8 x 12″. RB p. 77. The Bennington Museum, Bennington, Vt.

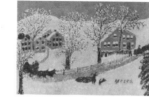

1322. *First Snow* (M. 1813)
Nov. 20. 8 x 12″. RB p. 77. The Bennington Museum, Bennington, Vt.

1958

1323. *The Deer* (M. 1814)
Jan. 9. 16 x 24″. RB p. 79. Collection Tate Brown. (See plate 201)

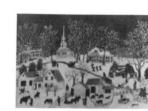

1324. *The Pump* (M. 1815)
Jan. 9. 15⅞ x 24″. RB p. 79. Private collection

1325. *Turkeys* (M. 1816)
Jan. 9. 16 x 24″. RB p. 77 "1816 replaces 1779 7/2/57 Snow Man repainted." The picture bears two labels: one, numbered 1779 and dated July 2, 1957, is titled "Snow Man"; the other, numbered 1816, is dated Jan. 9, 1958 and titled "Turkeys." (See plate 202)

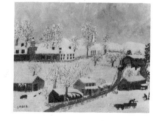

1326. *Going Fishing* (M. 1770)
Dated April 23, 1957, revised Jan. 1958. 12 x 16″. RB p. 79 "1770 Originally 'Rainbow' repainted / Now called Going Fishing." A photograph exists of the earlier version of this picture

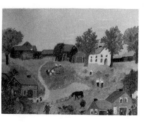

1327. *Toboggan* (M. 1817)
Jan. 9. 16 x 24″. RB p. 79. Collection Ann Scheinberg

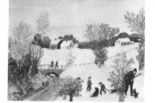

1328. *The Bridge* (M. 1818)
Jan. 9. 12 x 16″. RB p. 79. Collection Mrs. Don Belding

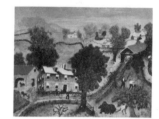

1329. *The Lake* (M. 1819)
Jan. 9. 11⅞ x 15⅞″. RB p. 79. Collection Hildegard Bachert

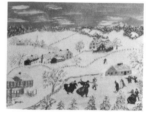

1330. *Skating* (M. 1820)
Jan. 9. 12 x 16″. RB p. 79. Collection Dr. and Mrs. Ernst Glaessel

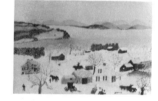

1331. *Ox Cart* (M. 1821)
Jan. 9. 12 x 16″. RB p. 79. Collection Otto Kallir

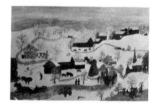

1332. *Haying* (M. 1822)
Jan. 9. 12 x 16″. RB p. 79. Collection George Cothran

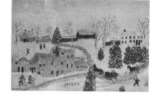

1333. *Take Us* (M. 1823)
Jan. 9. 8 x 12″. RB p. 79. Collection Mr. and Mrs. Walter K. Howard

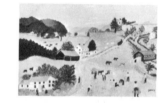

1334. *Big Tree* (M. 1824)
Jan. 9. 12 x 16″. RB p. 79. Collection Mrs. Carl Leeds

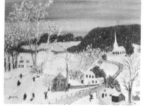

1335. *Gleaners* (M. 1825)
June 16. 15⅞ x 24″. RB p. 81. Collection Mrs. H. Stillman Taylor

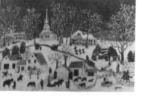

1336. *Long Lake* (M. 1826)
June 16. 15⅞ x 24″. RB p. 81

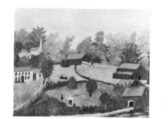

1337. *Bob Sled* (M. 1827)
June 16. 16 x 23⅞″. RB p. 81

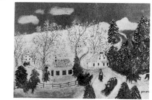

1338. *Red Barn* (M. 1828)
June 16. 16 x 23⅞″. RB p. 81 "dirty sky"

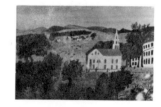

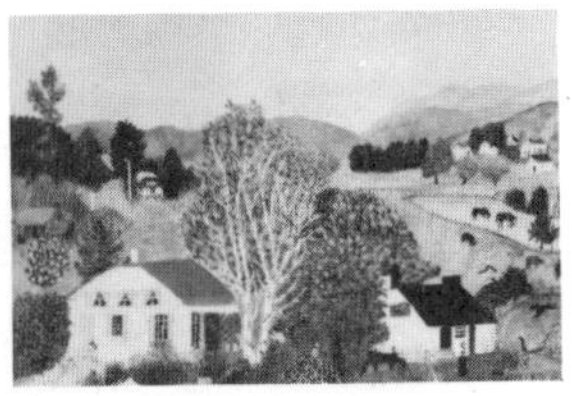

1339. *Birches* (M. 1829)
June 16. 16 x 23⅞''. RB p. 81

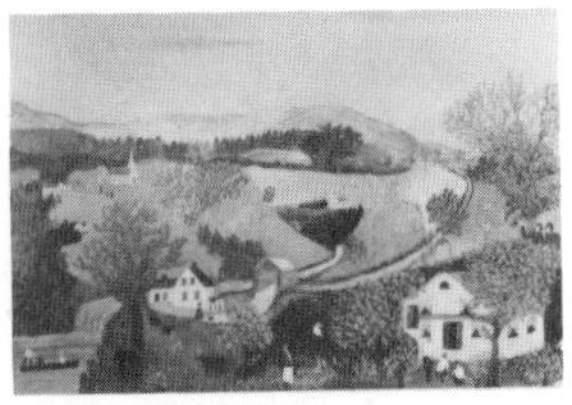

1340. *The Valley* (M. 1830)
June 16. 16 x 23⅞''. RB p. 81. Collection Mrs. J. Campanella

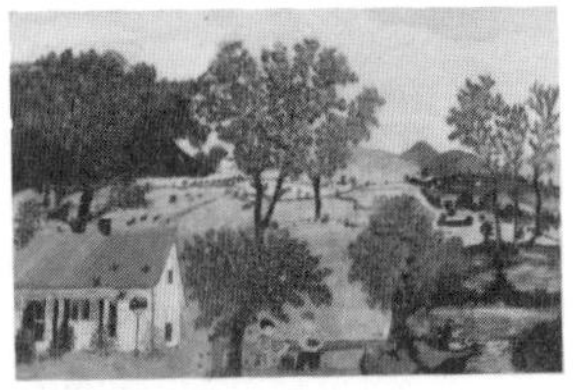

1341. *Blue Birds* (M. 1831)
June 16. 16 x 23⅞''. RB p. 81. Collection Mrs. A.V. Stout

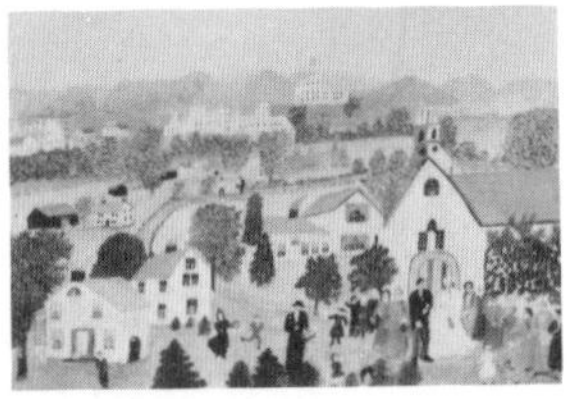

1342. *The Bride* (M. 1832)
June 16. 16 x 23⅞''. RB p. 81. Collection Walter Eisenberg

1343. *A Blizzard* (M. 1833)
June 16. 16 x 24⅛''. RB p. 81. (See plate 203)

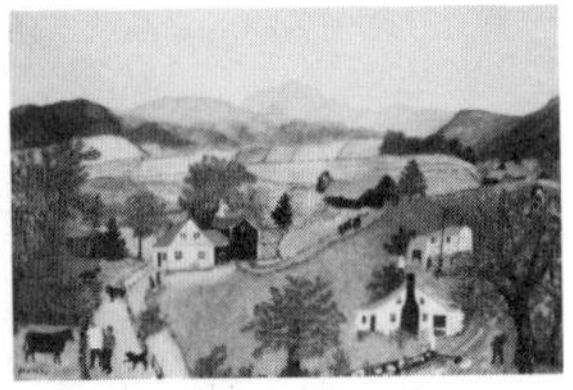

1344. *Vermont* (M. 1834)
June 16. c. 16 x 24''. RB p. 81. Collection Margaret Carr and Ruth Garner

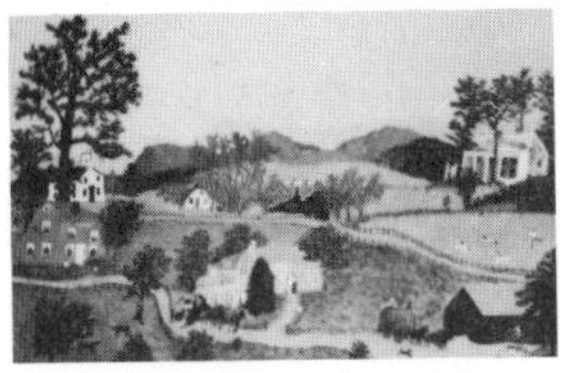

1345. *Stage Stop* (M. 1835)
June 16. c. 16 x 24''. RB p. 81. Collection Margaret Carr and Ruth Garner

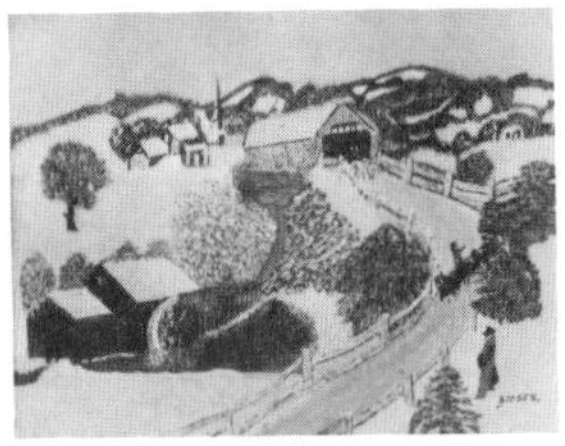

1346. *Mill Pond* (M. 1836)
July 7. 11⅞ x 16''. RB p. 82. Collection Mr. and Mrs. Robert M. Stein

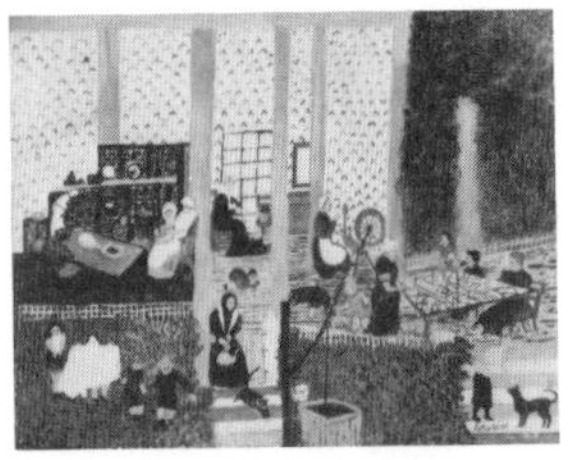

1347. *Busy Folks* (M. 1837)
July 7. 12 x 16''. RB p. 82

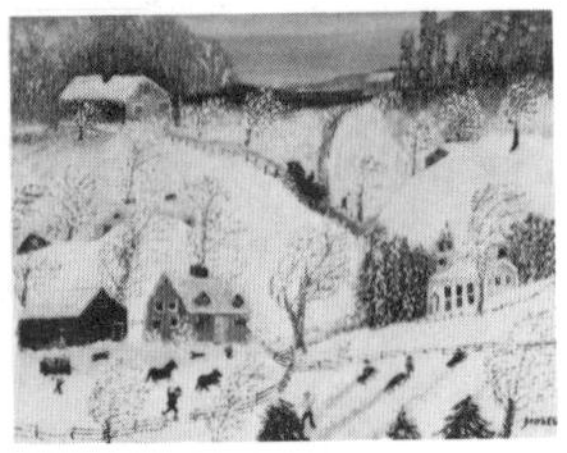

1348. *Whoa!* (M. 1838)
July 7. 12 x 16''. RB p. 82. Collection Mr. and Mrs. Sam Brodherson

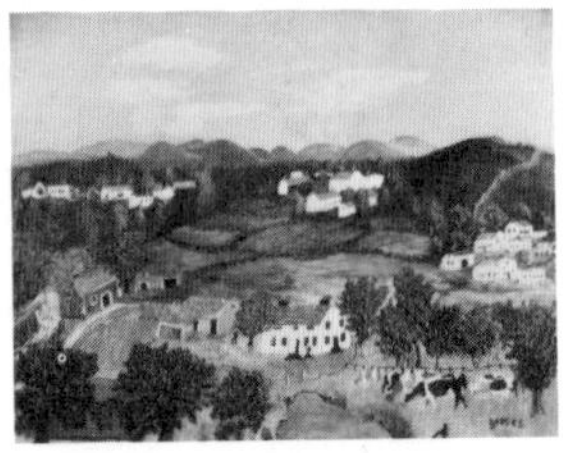

1349. *My Cows* (M. 1839)
July 7. 12 x 15⅞''. RB p. 82. Collection John B. Kirby, Jr.

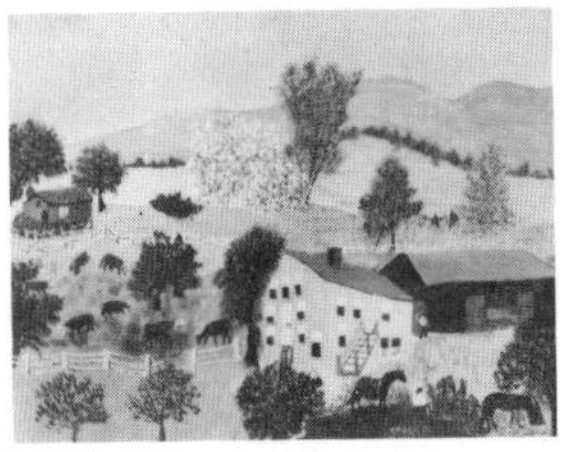

1350. *Big Rock* (M. 1840)
July 7. 12⅛ x 16''. RB p. 82

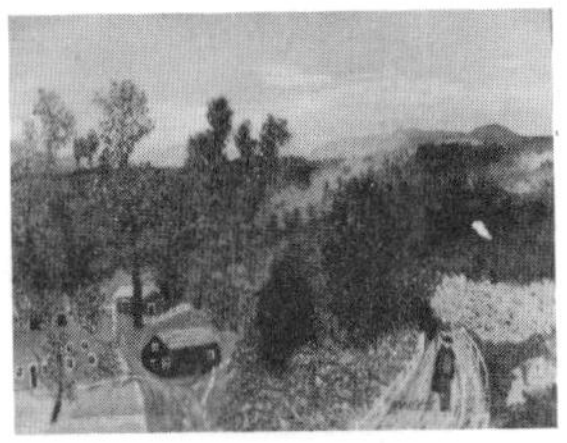

1351. *Autumn* (M. 1841)
July 7. 12⅛ x 16''. RB p. 82. Collection Betty McCart

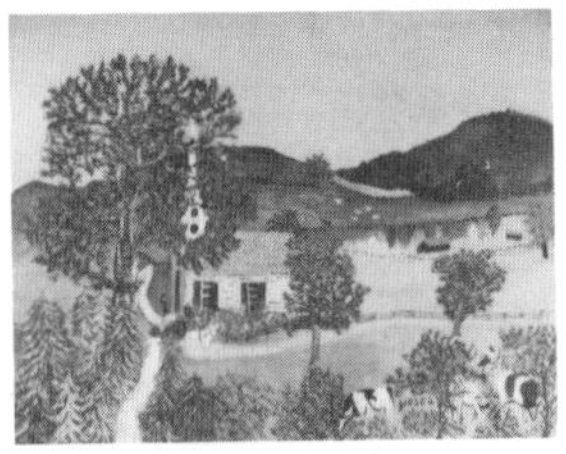

1352. *Waiting* (M. 1842)
July 7. 12 x 16''. RB p. 82. Collection Mr. and Mrs. T.D. Jones

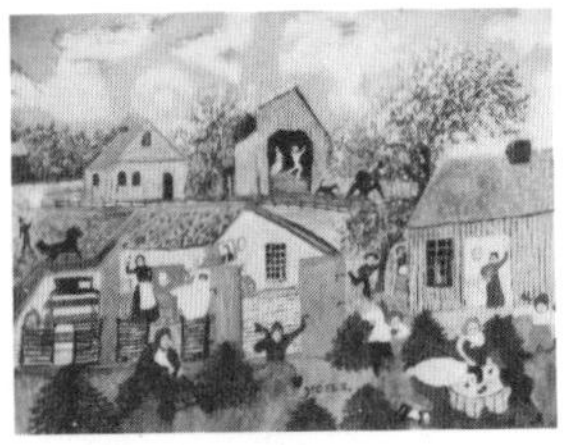

1353. *Halloween* (M. 1843)
July 7. 11⅞ x 16''. RB p. 82. Collection Mr. and Mrs. A.M. Nakamura

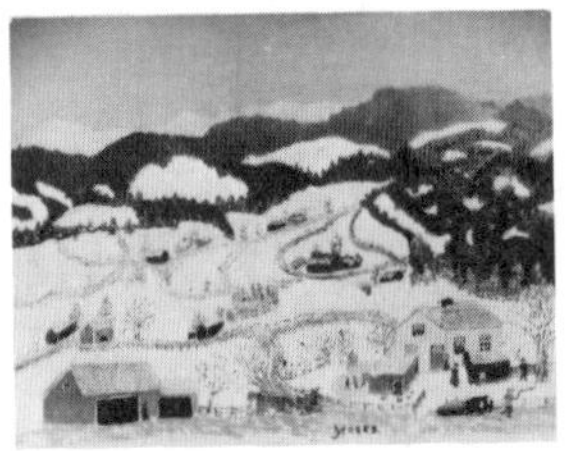

1354. *Green Hills* (M. 1844)
July 7. 12 x 16''. RB p. 82. Private collection

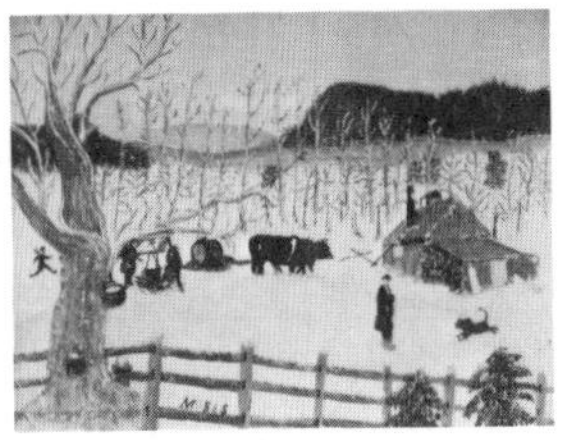

1355. *Oxen* (M. 1845)
July 7. 12⅛ x 16''. RB p. 82. Collection Mr. and Mrs. A.M. Nakamura

1356. *Fall* (M. 1846)
July 7. 16 x 24''. RB p. 82

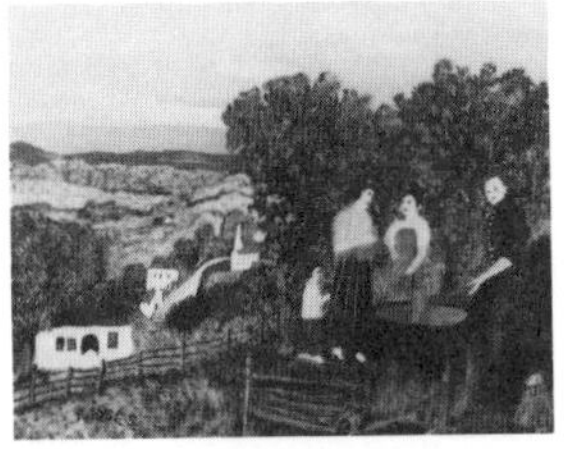

1357. *Making Apple Butter* (M. 1847)
Nov. 10. 12⅛ x 16''. RB p. 83. Collection Mrs. Ignatius Jelinsky

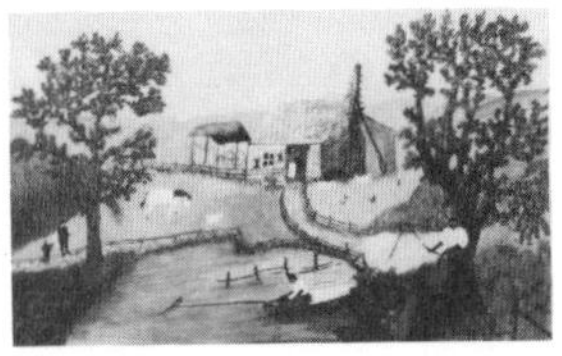

1358. *Old Darky Cabin* (M. 1848)
Nov. 10. 11¼ x 19⅛''. RB p. 83. Collection Mrs. Allen Gerye

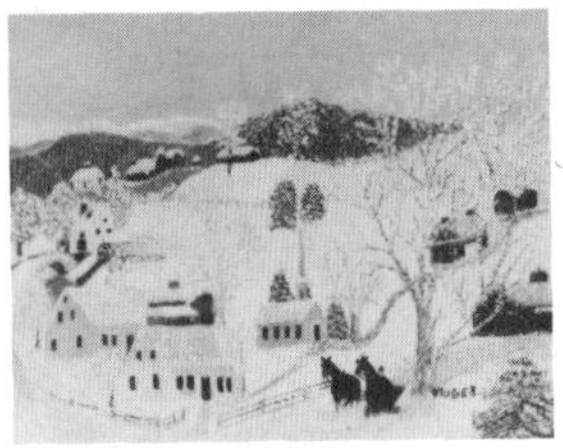

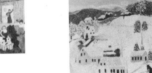

1359. *Come Up, Joe* (M. 1849)
Nov. 10. 11¾ x 16''. RB p. 83. Collection Zoeanne Koloseus

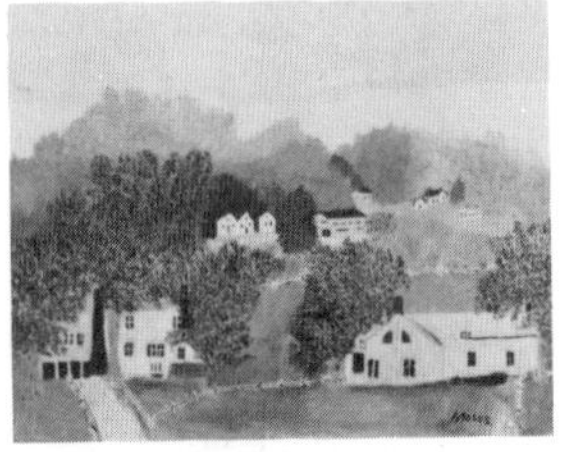

1360. *Spring* (M. 1850)
Nov. 10. 12¼ x 16¼''. RB p. 83. Collection Zoeanne Koloseus

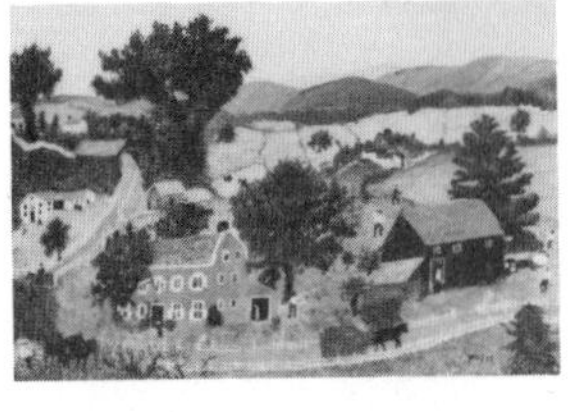

1361. *Stump Fence* (M. 1851)
Nov. 10. 16 x 24⅛''. RB p. 83. Collection Mrs. Paul Mellon

1362. *Corn* (M. 1852)
Nov. 10. 16 x 23⅞''. RB p. 83. Pushkin Museum, Moscow, U.S.S.R. *Reproduced:* BG. (See plate 183)

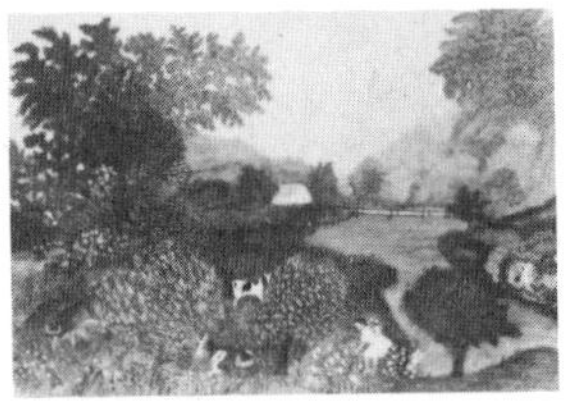

1363. *Sleepy Cow* (M. 1853)
Nov. 10. 15¾ x 24''. RB p. 83

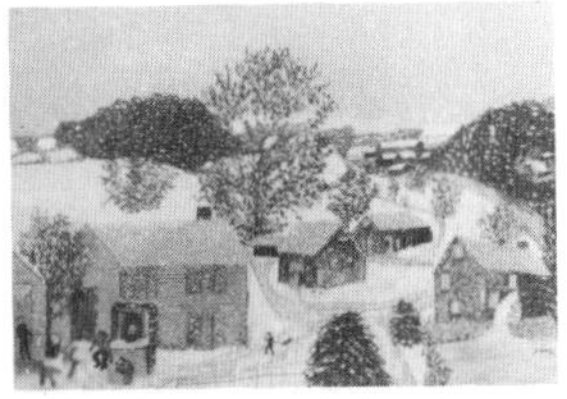

1364. *Snow Storm* (M. 1854)
Nov. 10. 16 x 24⅛''. RB p. 83. Collection Pamela Curran

1365. *Come Bossy* (M. 1855)
Nov. 10. 16⅛ x 24⅛''. RB p. 83. Collection W.B. Ford II. (See plate 205)

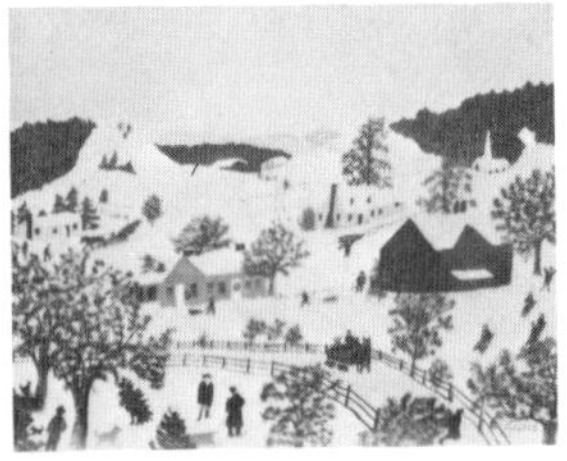

1366. *Christmas* (M. 1856)
November-December. 16⅛ x 20⅛''. RB p. 83. Collection Charles H. Brower

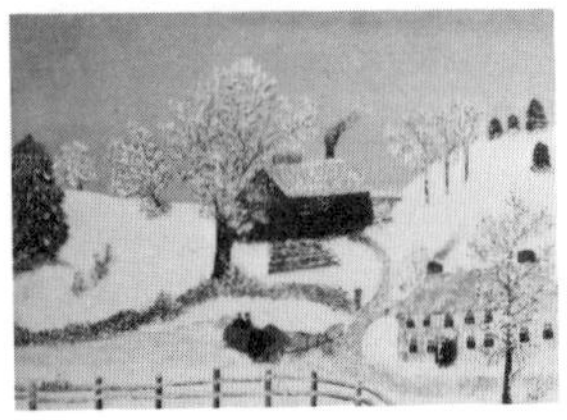

1367. *Sugar House* (M. 1857)
November-December. 9 x 14''. RB p. 83

1368. *Old Glory* (M. 1858)
Dec. 6. 12 x 16''. RB p. 83. (See plate 173)

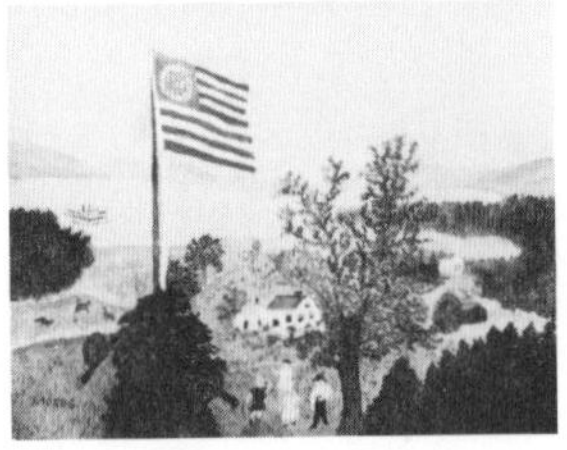

1369. *The Flag* (M. 1859)
Dec. 6. 12 x 16''. RB p. 83. *Reproduced:* GMSB

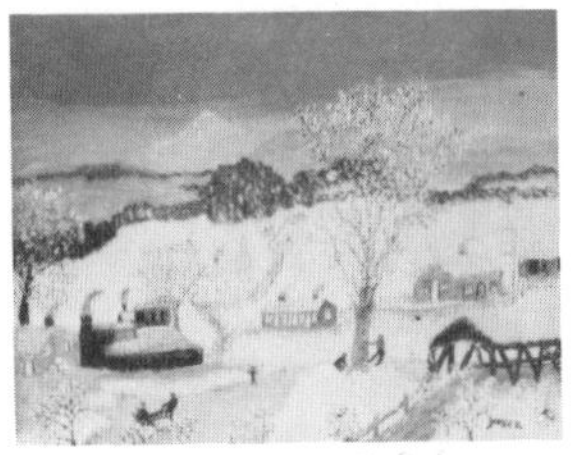

1370. *Snowball* (M. 1860)
Dec. 27. 12 x 15⅞''. RB p. 83. Collection Mr. and Mrs. William F. Loving

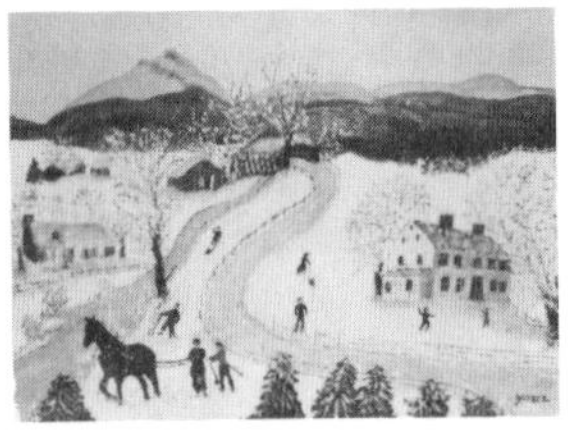

1371. *Foothills* (M. 1861)
Dec. 27. 11⅞ x 15⅞''. RB p. 83. Collection Frank Cotton

1959

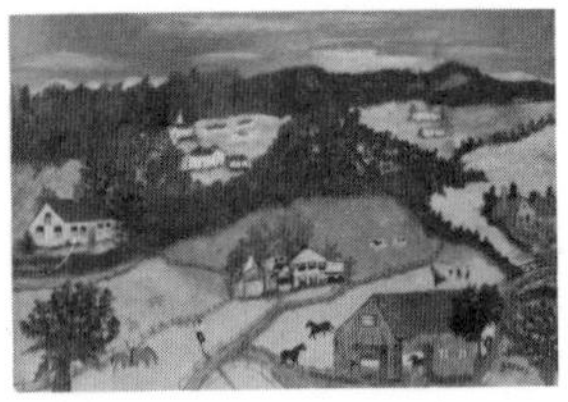

1372. *Dark Morning* (M. 1868)
January. 16 x 24''. RB p. 83. Collection W.H. Perry

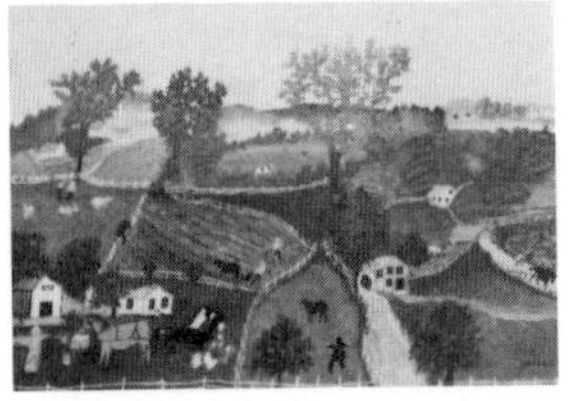

1373. *Callers* (M. 1871)
January. 16 x 24''. RB p. 83. Montclair Art Museum, N.J. Gift of The William Lightfoot Schultz Foundation

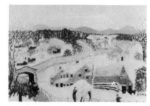

1374. *Morning* (M. 1872)
January. 16 x 24". RB p. 83. Collection Mr. and Mrs. Daniel M. Galbreath

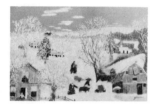

1375. *Deep Snow* (M. 1874)
January. 16 x 24". RB p. 83. Collection Frances Hough

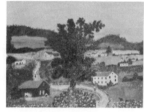

1376. *Soft Spring* (M. 1877)
January. 12⅛ x 16". RB p. 85. *Reproduced:* Parke-Bernet Sale No. 2518, Feb. 16, 1967, No. 95

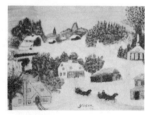

1377. *Soft Snow* (M. 1862)
Feb. 22. 12 x 16". RB p. 83. Collection Mr. and Mrs. Edward Stanby

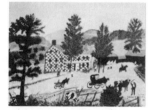

1378. *Checkered House* (M. 1863)
Feb. 22. 12 x 16⅛". Inscribed by the artist: "In the Year 1841." RB p. 83. Collection Arthur R. Armstrong

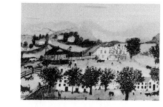

1379. *Dalton House* (M. 1865)
February. 16 x 24". RB p. 83. Collection Mrs. William P. Schweitzer

1380. *Pumpkins* (M. 1866)
February. 16 x 24". RB p. 83. *Reproduced: Six of My Favorite Paintings* portfolio. (See plate 208)

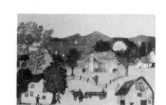

1381. *Fishermen* (M. 1867)
February. 16 x 24". RB p. 83. Collection Edwin Andrews, Jr.

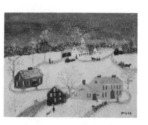

1382. *Plowing* (M. 1876)
February. 11⅞ x 15⅞". RB p. 85. Collection Mrs. Skitch Henderson

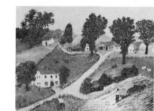

1383. *Skiing* (M. 1869)
March. 16 x 24". RB p. 83. Collection W.H. Perry

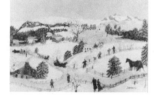

1384. *Spring* (M. 1873)
March. 16 x 24". RB p. 83. Collection Mr. and Mrs. George L. Schultz

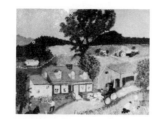

1385. *Chickens* (M. 1875)
March. 12 x 16". RB p. 85. Collection Mr. and Mrs. Frank L. Harrington

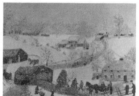

1386. *Early Snow* (M. 1878)
March. 11¾ x 16". RB p. 85. Collection Mrs. Thomas B. Appleget

1387. *Eagle Bridge Hotel* (M. 1864)
April. 16 x 24". RB p. 83. (See plate 211)

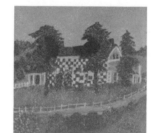

1388. *Snowballs* (M. 1870)
April. 16 x 24". RB p. 83

1389. *The Last Snow* (M. 1902)
April. 16 x 24". RB p. 87. (See plate 206)

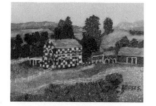

1390. *Checkered House* (M. 1879)
July 8. 6⅝ x 7¼". RB p. 85

1391. *Old Checkered House* (M. 1880)
July 8. 5⅞ x 8¼". RB p. 85

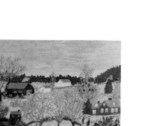

1392. *Hurrah* (M. 1881)
July 8. 8 x 12⅞". RB p. 85 "Mrs. McDill, N.H." Collection Mrs. Lou Willinger

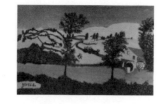

1393. *Church Time* (M. 1882)
July 8. 8⅜ x 11". RB p. 85 "Mrs. Mitchell." Collection Hazel Robertson Mitchell

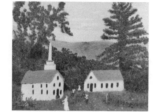

1394. *Look Out There* (M. 1883)
July 8. 12 x 16". RB p. 85. Collection George Kostas

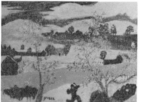

1395. *Grandma's Birthplace* (M. 1884)
July 8. 12 x 16". RB p. 85

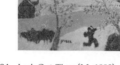
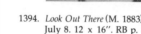

1396. *Ice Houses* (M. 1885)
July 8. 12 x 16". RB p. 85. Collection Dr. Houston Brummit

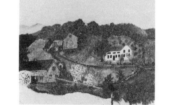

1397. *Pond* (M. 1886)
July 8. 12 x 16". RB p. 85. Collection Mrs. Paul Mellon

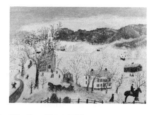

1398. *My Span* (M. 1887)
July 8. 16 x 24". RB p. 85. Private collection

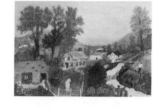

1399. *Autumn* (M. 1888)
July 8. 16 x 24". RB p. 85

1400. *The Farm* (M. 1889)
July 8. 16 x 24". RB p. 85. Collection Carl Moses

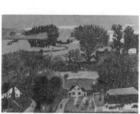

1401. *My Birthplace* (M. 1890)
July 8. 16 x 24". RB p. 85

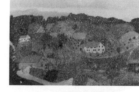

1402. *Home* (M. 1891)
July 8. 16 x 24". RB p. 85. Collection Vance Van Dine

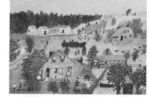

1403. *Picnic* (M. 1892)
July 8. 16 x 24". RB p. 85. Collection Mrs. Loyd R. Moses

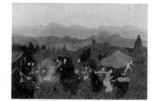

1404. *House on the Hill* (M. 1893)
July 8. 16 x 24". RB p. 85. Birmingham Museum of Art, Ala.

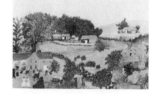

1405. *Wild Horse* (M. 1895)
July. 16 x 24". RB p. 85. Collection Ted Gopin and Hiram Plasterer

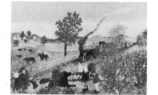

1406. *Mill Stream* (M. 1897)
July. 16 x 24". RB p. 85. Collection W.H. Perry

1407. *Great Fire* (M. 1911)
July. 12 x 16". RB p. 87. (See plate 40)

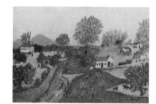

1408. *Mountains* (M. 1894)
August. 16 x 24". RB p. 85

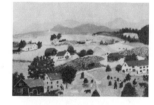

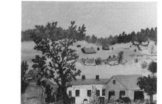

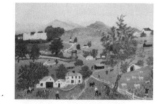

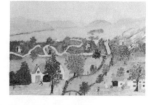

1409. *Champlain* (M. 1896)
August. 16 x 24". RB p. 85. Collection Carl Moses

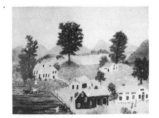

1410. *Plowing* (M. 1905)
August. 12 x 15⅞". RB p. 87

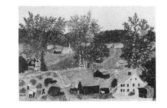

1411. *Early Settlers* (M. 1910)
August. 12 x 16". RB p. 87. Collection Mr. and Mrs. Wm. W. Willock, Jr.

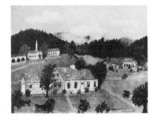

1412. *Soft Spring* (M. 1918)
August. 12 x 16". RB p. 87

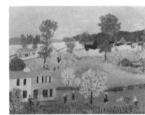

1413. *Snow Flakes* (M. 1919)
August. 12 x 16". RB p. 87. Collection Mrs. C.B. Van Bomel

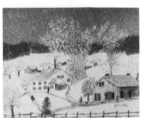

1414. *Early Summer* (M. 1921)
August. 8 x 12". RB p. 87. Collection Mrs. Herbert W. Saltford

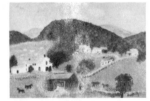

1415. *Visitors* (M. 1898)
September. 16 x 24". RB p. 85

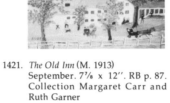

1416. *Haying Time* (M. 1899)
September. 16 x 24". RB p. 85.
Collection Arthur R. Armstrong

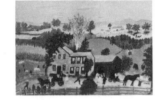

1417. *Noon Time* (M. 1900)
September. 16 x 24". RB p. 85.
Collection Mrs. C.B. Van Bomel.
Reproduced: GMSB

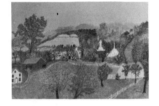

1418. *Fall* (M. 1903)
September. 16 x 24". RB p. 87.
Collection Mr. and Mrs. N. Hahn

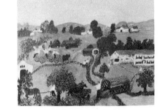

1419. *Holiday* (M. 1907)
September. 12 x 16". RB p. 87.
Collection M. Lewin

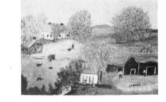

1420. *Autumn* (M. 1912)
September. 8 x 12". RB p. 87. Collection Margaret Carr and Ruth Garner

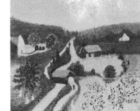

1421. *The Old Inn* (M. 1913)
September. 7⅞ x 12". RB p. 87.
Collection Margaret Carr and Ruth Garner

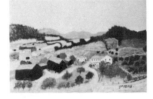

1422. *Countryside* (M. 1914)
September. 7⅞ x 12". RB p. 87.
Collection Margaret Carr and Ruth Garner

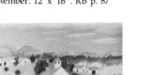

1423. *Snow Flakes* (M. 1915)
September. 8 x 12". RB p. 87. Collection Mrs. Gus Ellis

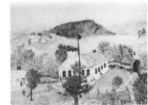

1424. *Eagle Bridge School* (M. 1916)
September. 12 x 16". RB p. 87

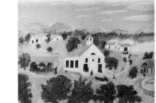

1425. *Whiteside Church* (M. 1917)
September. 12 x 16". RB p. 87

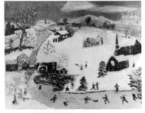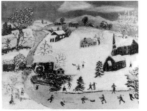

1426. *Snow Squalls* (M. 1920)
September. 12 x 16". RB p. 87.
Collection Mrs. Hugh W. Moses

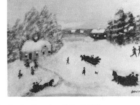

1427. *Arthur* (M. 1929)
September. 8 x 10". RB p. 87. Collection Arthur R. Armstrong

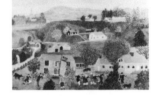

1428. *Early Fall* (M. 1901)
October. 16 x 24". RB p. 85. Collection Clayton E. Shaw, Jr.

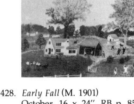

1429. *Busy Time* (M. 1904)
October. 16 x 24". RB p. 87

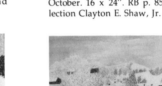

1430. *Early Morning* (M. 1906)
October. 12 x 16". RB p. 87

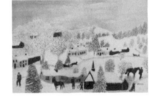

1431. *Grist Mill* (M. 1922)
October. 7⅞ x 12". RB p. 87. Collection John Seeley

1432. *Autumn Leaves* (M. 1923)
October. 16 x 24". RB p. 87. (See plate 242)

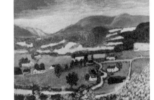

1433. *November* (M. 1908)
November. 12 x 16". RB p. 87

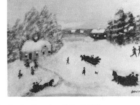

1434. *Early Evening* (M. 1909)
November. 12 x 16". RB p. 87.
Collection Frances Lynn

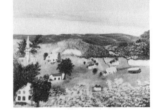

1435. *Summer Party* (M. 1924)
November. 16 x 24". RB p. 87

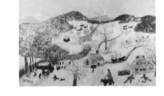

1436. *Busy Winter Day* (M. 1925)
November. 16 x 24". RB p. 87.
Delegated for placement in the future Presidential Library and Museum of Richard M. Nixon

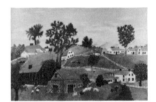

1437. *Summer Days* (M. 1926)
November. 16 x 24". RB p. 87.
Private collection

1438. *Last Snowfall* (M. 1927)
December. 16 x 24". RB p. 87. (See plate 243)

1960

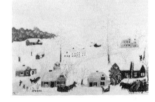

1439. *Going Fishing* (M. 1928)
January. 16 x 24". RB p. 87

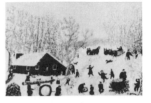

1440. *Sugar Time* (M. 1930)
January. 16 x 24". RB p. 87

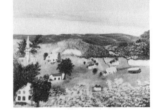

1441. *All Is Quiet* (M. 1932)
January. 16 x 24". RB p. 89. Collection Mrs. Victor B. Glindmeyer

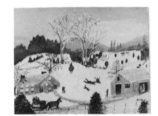

1442. *Pink Sunset* (M. 1936)
January. 12 x 16". RB p. 89. Collection Robert E. BonDurant

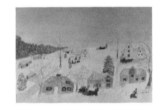

1443. *One Horse Sleigh* (M. 1941)
January. 16 x 24". RB p. 89. The Bennington Museum, Bennington, Vt.

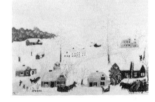

1444. *Sleigh Ride* (M. 1942)
January. 16 x 24". RB p. 89

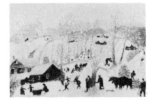

1445. *Maple Sugar* (M. 1931)
February. 16 x 24". RB p. 87

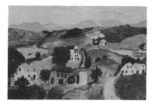

1446. *Stone Mill* (M. 1933)
February. 16 x 24". RB p. 89

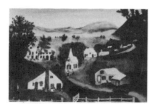

1447. *Lake Village* (M. 1934)
February. 12 x 16". RB p. 89

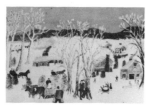

1448. *Sugaring Off* (M. 1943)
February. 16 x 24". RB p. 89. Unfinished

1449. *Green Sleigh* (M. 1944)
February. 16 x 24". RB p. 89. (See plates 250, 251)

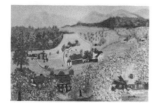

1450. *Flowering Trees* (M. 1945)
February. 16 x 24". RB p. 89. Collection Arthur R. Armstrong

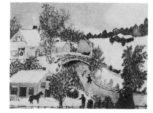

1451. *First Snowfall* (M. 1935)
March. 12 x 16". RB p. 89. Collection Mr. and Mrs. Wm. W. Willock, Jr.

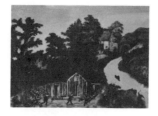

1452. *Big Fish* (M. 1937)
March. 12 x 16". RB p. 89. Collection Mrs. M.R. Shook

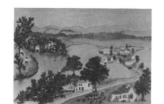

1453. *River* (M. 1946)
March. 16 x 24". RB p. 89

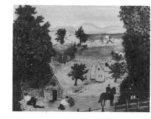

1454. *Arbor Day* (M. 1938)
April. 12 x 16". RB p. 89. Collection David G. Brodman

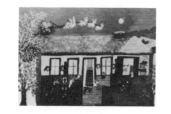

1455. *Santa Claus I* (M. 1939)
April. 16 x 24". RB p. 89. Grandma Moses Properties, Inc., New York. *Reproduced:* NBC (cover)

1456. *Santa Claus II* (M. 1940)
April. 16 x 24". RB p. 89. Grandma Moses Properties, Inc., New York. *Reproduced:* Hallmark. (See plate 177)

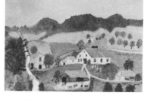

A.

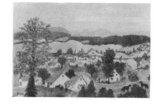

B.

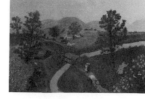

C.

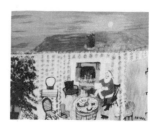

D.

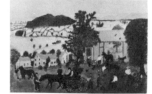

E. 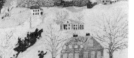 F.

1457. Sketches for *The Night Before Christmas*
About April. RB p. 89. Grandma Moses Properties, Inc., New York
A. 8 x 12". *Reproduced:* NBC
B. 8 x 12". *Reproduced:* NBC
C. 8 x 12". *Reproduced:* NBC
D. 8 x 12". *Reproduced:* NBC; GMSB
E. 9¼ x 4¾". *Reproduced:* NBC
F. 10 x 5". *Reproduced:* NBC

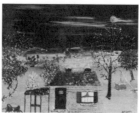

1458. *Here Comes Santa Claus* (M. 1947)
May. 12 x 16". RB p. 89. Grandma Moses Properties, Inc., New York. *Reproduced:* Hallmark; NBC

1459. *Santa Claus Is Here* (M. 1948)
May. 16 x 23¾". RB p. 89. Grandma Moses Properties, Inc., New York. *Reproduced:* Hallmark; NBC

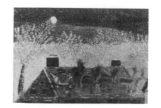

1460. *Down the Chimney He Goes* (M. 1949)
May. 16 x 23¾". RB p. 89. Grandma Moses Properties, Inc., New York

1461. *So Long till Next Year* (M. 1950)
May. 16 x 24". RB p. 89. Grandma Moses Properties, Inc., New York. (See plate 178)

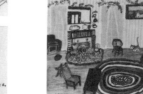

1462. *Night Before Christmas* (M. 1951)
July. 12 x 16". RB p. 89. Grandma Moses Properties, Inc., New York. *Reproduced:* NBC

1463. *Waiting for Santa Claus* (M. 1952)
July. 12 x 16". RB p. 89. Grandma Moses Properties, Inc., New York. *Reproduced:* NBC. (See plate 176)

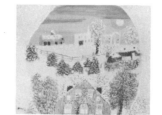

1464. *Christmas Garden* (M. 1953)
July. 12 x 16". RB p. 89. Grandma Moses Properties, Inc., New York. *Reproduced:* NBC

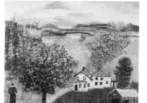

1465. *Fall Color* (M. 1956)
July. 12 x 16". RB p. 89. Collection Brenda McCart

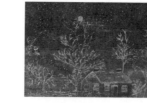

1466. *The Old Bucket* (M. 1957)
July. 16 x 24". RB p. 89. Collection Mrs. T. Warner Harrison

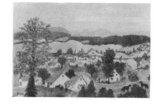

1467. *Lake Front* (M. 1967)
July. 16 x 24". RB p. 91. Private collection. Parke-Bernet Sale No. 2733, Sept. 18, 1968

1468. *Sugar Time* (M. 1958)
August. 16 x 24". RB p. 91. (See plate 212)

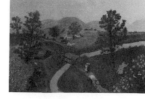

1469. *Spring Flowers* (M. 1961)
August. 16 x 24". RB p. 91

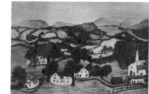

1470. *Farming Country* (M. 1966)
August. 16 x 24". RB p. 91

1471. *Horseshoeing* (M. 1960)
September. 16 x 24". RB p. 91. Collection Mrs. Loyd R. Moses. (See plate 209)

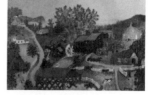

1472. *Lost Calf* (M. 1962)
September. 16 x 24". RB p. 91. Collection Harry Moses

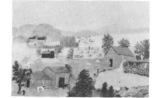

1473. *Trout Brook* (M. 1963)
September. 16 x 24". RB p. 91. Collection Gerald Moses

1474. *Get Out the Sleigh* (M. 1965)
September. 16 x 24". RB p. 91. (See plate 213)

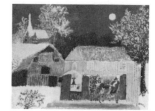

1475. *Jolly Old Santa* (M. 1954)
October. 12 x 16". RB p. 89. Grandma Moses Properties, Inc., New York. *Reproduced:* NBC

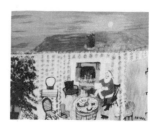

1476. *You Better Be Good* (M. 1955)
October. 12 x 16". RB p. 89. Grandma Moses Properties, Inc., New York. *Reproduced:* NBC

1477. *Witches* (M. 1959)
October. 16 x 24". RB p. 91. *Reproduced:* GMSB. (See plate 210)

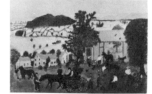

1478. *Wagon Repair Shop* (M. 1964)
October. 16 x 24". RB p. 91. The Bennington Museum, Bennington, Vt.

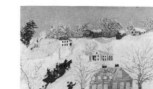

1479. *Over the Bridge* (M. 1968)
October. 16 x 24". RB p. 91. Collection Mr. and Mrs. R. Somerset

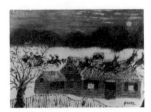

1480. *Santa Claus, No. 3* (M. 1969)
November. 8 x 12''. RB p. 91.
Grandma Moses Properties, Inc.,
New York

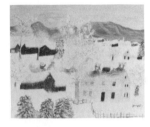

1481. *Santa Claus, No. 4* (M. 1970)
November. 11 x 14''. RB p. 91.
Grandma Moses Properties, Inc.,
New York

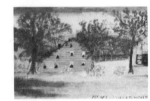

1482. *Home Sweet Home*
7¼ x 11''. Title inscribed by the
artist. Gift to Martha Eaton

1961

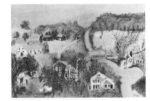

1483. *Soft Green* (M. 1971)
January. 16 x 24''. RB p. 91. The
Bennington Museum, Bennington,
Vt.

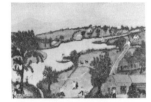

1484. *Blue Lake* (M. 1972)
January. 16 x 24''. RB p. 91

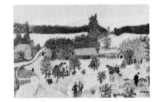

1485. *Waterfalls* (M. 1973)
January. 16 x 24''. RB p. 91. Collection Mr. and Mrs. Edwin L. Cox

1486. *The Deep Snow* (M. 1980)
January. 16 x 24''. Inscribed by
the artist: "It Snows." RB p. 91.
Collection Paul Simon. (See plate
241)

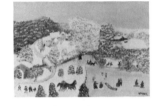

1487. *More Fun* (M. 1982)
January. 16 x 24''. RB p. 91

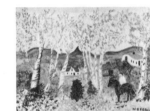

1488. *The Guard* (M. 1986)
January. 11¾ x 16''. RB p. 91

1489. *White Birches* (M. 1991)
January. 16 x 24''. RB p. 94. (See
plate 214)

1490. *Falling Leaves* (M. 1993)
January. 16 x 24''. Inscribed by
the artist: "For This is The Fall of
The Year." RB p. 93. Collection
Walter K. Rush. (See plate 240)

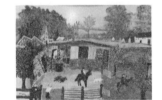

1491. *Making Horseshoes* (M. 1974)
February. 16 x 24''. RB p. 91. Collection Betty McCart

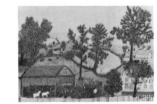

1492. *Catching Fish* (M. 1975)
February. 16 x 24''. RB p. 91

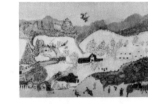

1493. *On the Move* (M. 1976)
February. 16 x 24''. RB p. 91

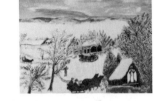

1494. *Quiet Village* (M. 1979)
February. 16 x 24''. RB p. 91. Collection Ralph H. Skinner, Jr.

1495. *Sugar Candy* (M. 1989)
February. 16 x 24''. RB p. 93. (See
plate 215)

1496. *Vermont Sugar* (M. 1990)
February. 16 x 24''. RB p. 93. (See
plate 244)

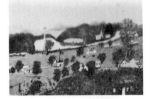

1497a. *Flax Farm* (M. 1985)
About February. 8 x 12''. RB p. 91.
Gift to the late Allen Eaton

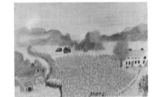

1497b. *[Untitled] Landscape*
Reverse of the above

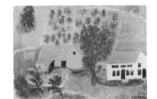

1498. *Lots of Fun* (M. 1977)
March. 16 x 24''. RB p. 91

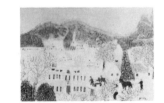

1499. *The Ice Is Good* (M. 1978)
March. 16 x 24''. RB p. 91

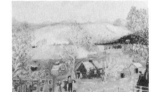

1500. *Going to Church* (M. 1981)
March. 16 x 24''. RB p. 91. Private collection

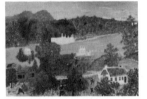

1501. *The Deep River* (M. 1983)
March. 16 x 24''. RB p. 91

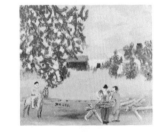

1502. *Cutting Wood* (M. 1984)
March. 9 x 11''. RB p. 91. Collection Ann Armstrong

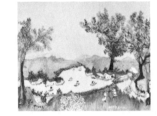

1503. *Boat Sailing* (M. 1987)
March. 12 x 16''. Inscribed by the
artist: "Hodson" [sic]. RB p. 93.
Collection Carl Moses

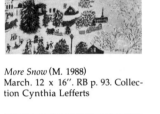

1504. *More Snow* (M. 1988)
March. 12 x 16''. RB p. 93. Collection Cynthia Lefferts

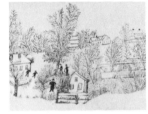

1505. *Happy Days* (M. 1992)
March. 16 x 24''. RB p. 93. Collection John Ketcham

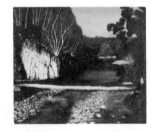

1506. *Invisible* (M. 1994)
April. 11¾ x 15⅞''. Title inscribed
by the artist. RB p. 93 "One Black
& White No Number 12 x 16 to
Kallir"

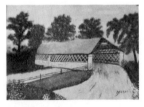

1507. *The Old Home* (M. 1996)
April. 16 x 24''. RB p. 93

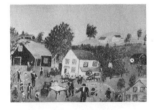

1508. *Auction, No. 2* (M. 1995)
May. 16 x 24''. RB p. 93. *Reproduced:* GMSB

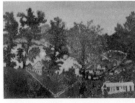

1509. *Lake* (M. 1998)
May. 16 x 24''. RB p. 93. Unfinished

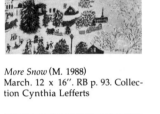

1510. *School* (M. 1999)
May. 16 x 24''. Title inscribed by
the artist. RB p. 93. Unfinished.
The Bennington Museum, Bennington, Vt.

1511. *Rainbow* (M. 1997)
June. 16 x 24''. RB p. 93. (See plate
245)

PAINTINGS WHICH COULD NOT BE RELIABLY DATED

(In alphabetical order)

1512. *All Is Calm* (M. 1090?)
Formerly collection Fred E.
Robertson

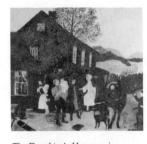

1513. *Blue Water*
Before 1945. 9¼ x 11¼''. Sidney
Janis Gallery, New York

1513a. *The Church by the Bridge*
Before 1942. 16 x 21''. Collection
Mr. and Mrs. Martin Grossman

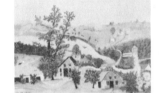

1514. *Covered Bridge*
8¼ x 12½''. Collection R.J. Popel-
man

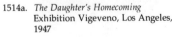

1514a. *The Daughter's Homecoming*
Exhibition Vigeveno, Los Angeles,
1947

PAINTINGS WHICH COULD NOT BE RELIABLY DATED *(cont'd)*

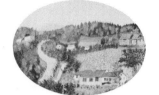

1515. *Grandpa's House*
1951 or later. 13½ x 19½" (oval)

1516. *Haying Time*
Collection J.J. Doherty

1517. *The Whispering Hills*
Collection Jay Slade. Hoosick Falls Exhibition 1962

1518. *The Old Blue Mills*
Collection Mr. and Mrs. John Burke. Hoosick Falls Exhibitions 1949, 1962

1519. *The Old Mill* (M. 563?)
Collection Mrs. Gerald Niles. Hoosick Falls Exhibitions 1949, 1962

1520. *A Frosty Morning*
Collection Mr. and Mrs. Arthur Hoffman. Hoosick Falls Exhibition 1962

1521. *The Home of Anna Mary Robertson Moses*
Collection Isabelle S. Eldridge

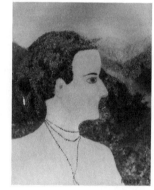

1522. *Portrait*
Oilcloth, 10 x 7¾". (Found as backing of 3-W *Cairo*.) The Bennington Museum, Bennington, Vt.

1523. *Just Roses*
Formerly collection Fred E. Robertson

1524. *Sap Time*
9 x 11". Collection Margaret McClelland

1525. *Lake Scene in Scotland*
Canvas, c. 10 x 14". There is a halftone print cut out and pasted on the canvas. Collection the Reverend W.D. Kring

1526. *Scotland*
Early 1950s(?). 14 x 19". Collection the Honorable and Mrs. Dean P. Taylor. Hoosick Falls Exhibition 1962

1527. *A Shiner*
Collection Mrs. Raymond Taber. Hoosick Falls Exhibition 1962

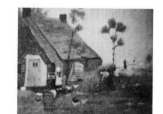

1528. *So Cold*
9 x 12". Collection Mrs. Forrest Moses

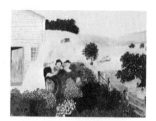

1529. *The Spirit of the Cider Barrel*
Canvas, 9 x 12¼". Collection Mr. and Mrs. M. Riklis

1530. *Small Spring* (M. 1694)
6¼ x 7". RB p. 67 "1694 old." The painting, though made earlier, was numbered only in 1955. Collection the Reverend and Mrs. Roscoe Anderson

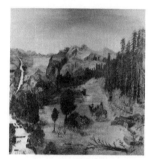

1531. *The Old Stage Coach*
18 x 22". Collection Laurance S. Rockefeller

1532. *Stone Bridge*
Collection Carl Moses. Hoosick Falls Exhibition 1962

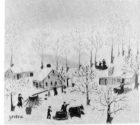

1533. *Sugaring*
7⅜ x 8½". Galerie St. Etienne, New York

1534. *Taber Homestead*
Collection Mrs. Raymond Taber. Hoosick Falls Exhibition 1962

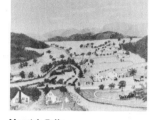

1535. *[Untitled] Cabin Backyard*
9 x 9¾". On reverse: sketch of old automobile with four people in it. Collection Bee Hoover

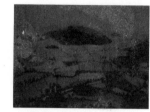

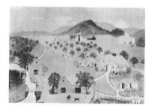

1536. *[Untitled] Indians on Horses*
20 x 20". The Bennington Museum, Bennington, Vt.

1537. *[Untitled] White Horse and Sleigh*
10 x 14". Collection Carl Moses

1538. *[Untitled] River and Log Cabin*
15 x 15". Collection Sam Wood

1538a. *[Untitled] Summer*
About 1942-43. 19½ x 23½". Collection Mr. and Mrs. I. Donald Grossman

1539. *Homestead in Wales*
1946(?). Collection Sharon R. Curry and Carol R. Wakefield

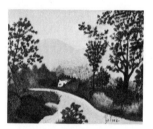

1540. *A Welcome in the Window*
Before 1945. 7½ x 15". Title inscribed by the artist. Sidney Janis Gallery, New York

1541. *Back in the Woodlands*
Collection Dr. Harry P. Harrison. Hoosick Falls Exhibition 1962

1542. *Back in the Woodlands*
Collection Jennie Hoffman. Hoosick Falls Exhibition 1962

UNIDENTIFIED PHOTOGRAPHS

The following photographs from the author's files are of paintings about which no information was available. They are listed here by subject:

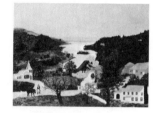

Cambridge Valley

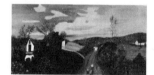

Old Oaken Bucket (Spring)

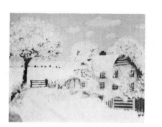

Road and Distant Village

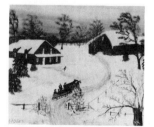

River Landscape

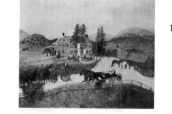

House and Barn with Sleigh

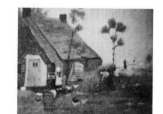

Hoosick Falls
Reproduced: Catalogue, Vigeveno, Los Angeles, Oct.-Nov. 1945

TILES

1951-1952. 6 x 6". Numbered and
titled by the artist on reverse.

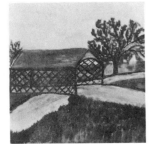

1. *Open Bridge*

2. *A House.*
   Reproduced: Hallmark.
   (See plate 110)

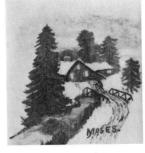

3. *A Foot Bridge*

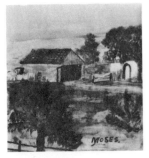

4. *A Covered Bridge*

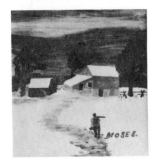

5. *The Hunter.*
   Reproduced: GMSB

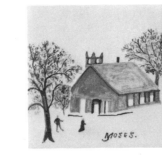

6. *The Old Button Shop*

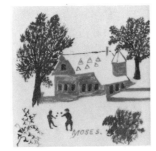

7. *The Bridge of 1800*

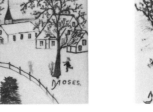

8. *Valley Bridge*

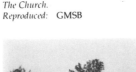

9. *Lake George*

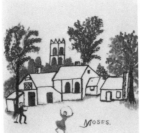

10. *The Bridge in the Woods*

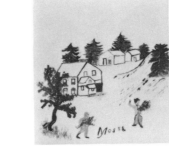

11. *Old Church*

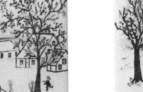

12. *Grandma Is Coming*

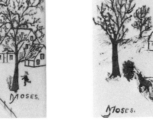

13. *The Church.*
    Reproduced: GMSB

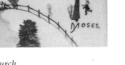

14. *All Alone.*
    Reproduced: GMSB

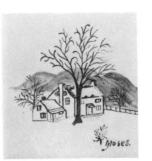

15. *Sunrise*

16. *Narrow Road*
    (See plate 111)

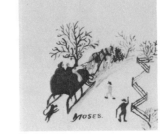

17. *I've Got Some*

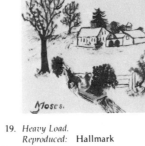

18. *By the River*

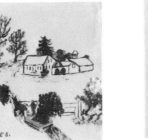

19. *Heavy Load.*
    Reproduced: Hallmark

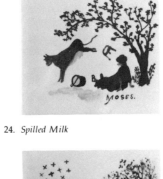

20. *On the Bridge*

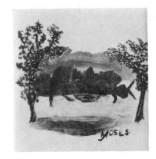

21. *Canoe*

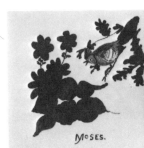

22. *Whoa*

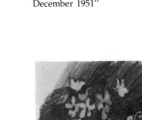

23. *Blue Jay*

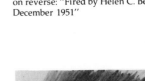

24. *Spilled Milk*

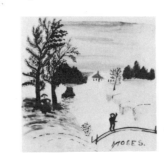

25. *Dancers*

26. *Church Goers*
    (See plate 112)

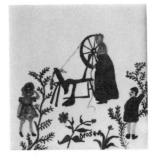

27. *Spinning*

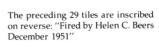

28. *A Squirrel*

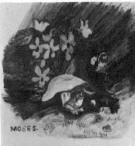

29. *Violet*

The preceding 29 tiles are inscribed
on reverse: "Fired by Helen C. Beers
December 1951"

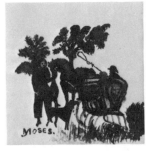

30. *Toad Stool*

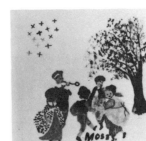

31. *Wan-a-Ride*

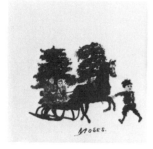

32. *Look Out*

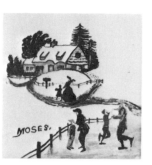

33. *We Are Skating*

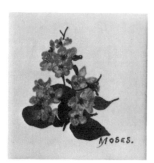

34. *Pinks*

35. *Playing*
(See plate 113)

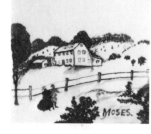

36. *Windy*

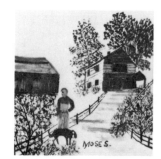

37. *Boy and Dog*

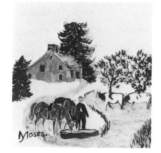

38. *Thirsty*

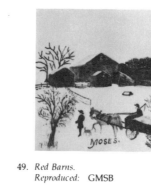

39. *Fairies*

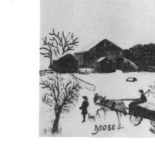

40. *Spinning*

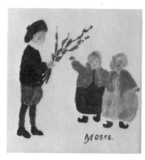

41. *The Bee*

42. *Hilltop*
(See plate 114)

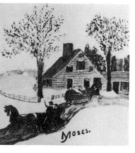

43. *Bartering.*
Reproduced: **Hallmark**

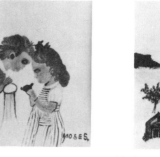

44. *Dutch Girls*

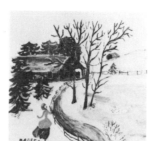

45. *Bunny*

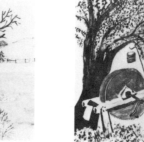

46. *Old Mill*

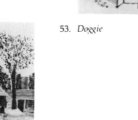

47. *Gossip.*
Reproduced: **Hallmark**

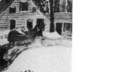

48. *Company.*
Reproduced: **Hallmark**

49. *Red Barns.*
Reproduced: GMSB

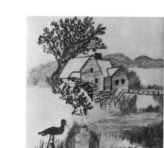

50. *The School*

51. *The Marsh*
(See plate 115)

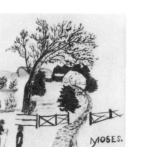

52. *The Stork*

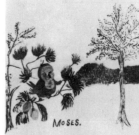

53. *Doggie*

54. *The Turtle*

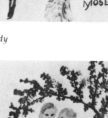
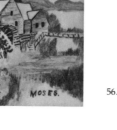
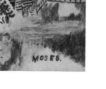

55. *Grindstone*

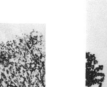

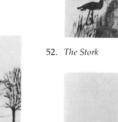
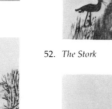
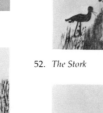

56. *Howdy*

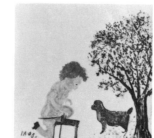
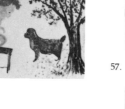
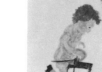

57. *Singing*

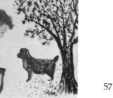

58. *Birdie*

59. *Thistle*

60. *Summer*

The preceding 31 tiles are inscribed on reverse: "Fired by Helen C. Beers January 1952"

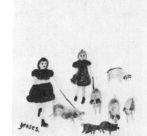
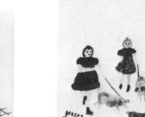
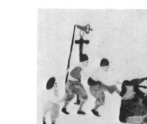
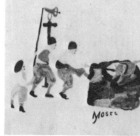
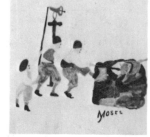

61. *This Little Pig*

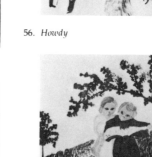

62. *Ding Dong the Bell*

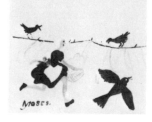

63. *The Maid Is in the Garden*

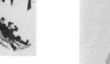
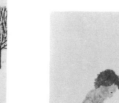

TILES *(cont'd)*

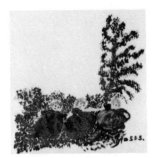

64. *Mary, Mary Quite Contrary*

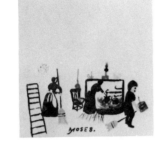

69. *Old Woman Says I*

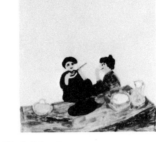

74. *Jack Spratt*

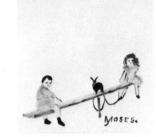

79. *Hiram Gordon*

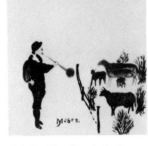

84. *Little Boy Blue; Cows in the Corn*

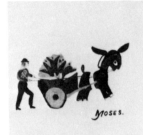

65. *John Cook*

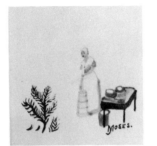

70. *Come Butter Come*

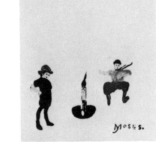

75. *Jack Be Nimble.*
Reproduced: GMSB

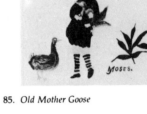

80. *Jack and Jill*

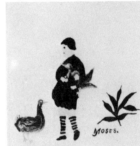

85. *Old Mother Goose*

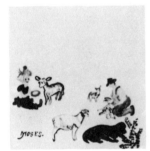

66. *Baa Baa Black Sheep*

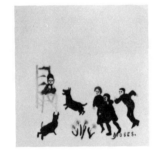

71. *Hark, Hark, the Dogs Do Bark*

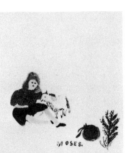

76. *Mary's Little Lamb*

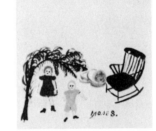

81. *Rockabye Baby*

The preceding 25 tiles are inscribed on reverse: "Fired by Helen Beers 1952"

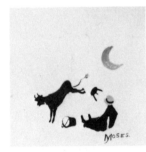

67. *Hey Diddle Diddle*

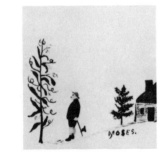

72. *Jack and the Beanstalk*

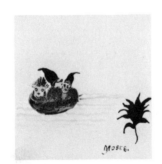

77. *Rub a Dub Dub*

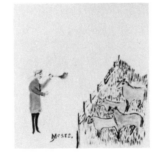

82. *Little Boy Blue*

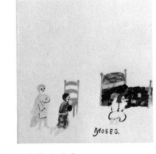

68. *Let's Go to Bed*

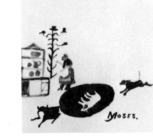

73. *Old Mother Hubbard*

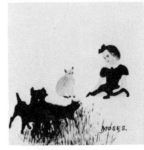

78. *Pussy Cat, Pussy Cat*

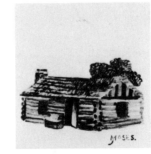

83. *The House That Jack Built.*
Reproduced: GMSB

Index to the Works

Both the titles of identified pictures and titles representing unsubstantiated listings that appear only in Grandma Moses's Record Book are given. Titles of known works are followed by their Catalogue numbers. Unsubstantiated Record Book entries through November 1941 appear as follows, for example: RB pp.6–17:3 listings. This means that the title appears three times within those pages of the Record Book. Later unsubstantiated titles are given by date, the artist's M number if any, and, in the case of a picture that is probably small, a dagger (for example: RB Nov. 1946, M. 1079†). See also the Introduction to the Catalogue of the Works.

Titles are listed both in normal index style and also, for the convenience of the researcher, by family name or place name in that order of precedence. Themes significant in Grandma Moses's work are also indexed when the theme is stated in the title. Compound nouns and phrases from songs and expressions are indexed under the first word.

337

Selected Bibliography

BOOKS WRITTEN OR ILLUSTRATED BY GRANDMA MOSES

1. *Christmas.* Facsimile edition of the handwritten manuscript. 500 copies. Galerie St. Etienne, New York, 1952.

2. *Christmas with Grandma Moses.* Phonograph record of Christmas music with commentary spoken by Grandma Moses. Paintings, photographs, and quotations from the artist's writings in the descriptive booklet bound into the record album. RCA Victor No. LOP–1009, 1958.

3. *Grandma Moses, American Primitive.* Edited by Otto Kallir. Introduction by Louis Bromfield. Comments on forty paintings and a brief autobiography by Grandma Moses. First edition: Dryden Press, New York, 1946. Second edition: Doubleday & Co., Garden City, New York, 1947.

4. *The Grandma Moses Storybook.* Stories and poems by 28 writers. Edited by Nora Kramer. Illustrated by Grandma Moses. Biographical sketch of the artist by Otto Kallir. Random House, New York, 1961.

5. *My Life's History.* Edited by Otto Kallir. Trade edition and a special autographed, numbered edition of 270 copies bound in half-leather. Harper & Row, New York, 1952. British edition: André Deutsch, London, 1952. German edition: *Meine Lebensgeschichte.* Ullstein Verlag, 1957. Dutch edition: *Het verhaal van mijn leven.* A. W. Bruna & Zoon, 1958.

6. *The Night Before Christmas.* Clement C. Moore. With pictures by Grandma Moses especially painted for this book. Random House, New York, n.d. [1962].

CHILDREN'S BOOKS

7. *Barefoot in the Grass: The Story of Grandma Moses.* William H. Armstrong. Doubleday & Co., Garden City, New York, 1971.

8. *Grandma Moses, Favorite Painter.* Charles P. Graves. Garrard Publishing Co., Champaign, Ill., 1969.

BOOKS IN WHICH GRANDMA MOSES IS MENTIONED

9. Bihalji-Merin, Oto. *Modern Primitives: Masters of Naive Painting.* Harry N. Abrams, Inc., New York, 1959.

10. Black, Mary, and Lipman, Jean. *American Folk Painting.* Clarkson N. Potter, New York, 1966.

11. Eliot, Alexander. *Three Hundred Years of American Painting.* Time, Inc., New York, 1957.

12. Ford, Alice. *Pictorial Folk Art in America, New England to California.* The Studio Publications, Inc., New York & London, 1949.

13. Janis, Sidney. *They Taught Themselves: American Primitive Painters of the 20th Century.* Dial Press, New York, 1942.

14. Jasmand, Bernhard, and Kallir, Otto. *Sonntagsmaler: Das Bild des einfältigen Herzens.* Verlag Otto Aug. Ehlers, Berlin & Darmstadt, 1956.

15. Lipman, Jean, and Winchester, Alice. *Primitive Painters in America, 1750–1950.* Dodd, Mead & Co., New York, 1950.

REPRODUCTIONS

16. *Art in America.* Portfolio of eight color reproductions, with an Appreciation by John Canaday. 1967.

17. The Brundage Company. Publishers of a series of Christmas cards. New York, 1946.

18. *The Four Seasons.* Portfolio of four color reproductions. Donald Art Company, Port Chester, N.Y., 1956, reprinted 1965.

19. The Hallmark Company. Publishers of numerous Christmas and greeting cards. Kansas City, Mo., 1947–55; 1964–69.

20. Arthur Jaffe Heliochrome Co. Printers of six color reproductions. New York, 1948–49, 1961–63, 1965.

21. R. Oldenbourg, Graphische Betriebe. Printers and publishers of a series of greeting cards. Munich, Germany, 1957.

22. *Six of My Favorite Paintings.* Portfolio of six color reproductions. Catalda Fine Arts, Inc., New York, 1959.

PERIODICALS

An extraordinary amount of material has been published about Grandma Moses in newspapers and periodicals around the world. Only some of the more significant items have been selected for inclusion here.

23. "Primitives from America—The Innocent Eye" (digest of reviews from European newspapers). *Art in America,* October 1955.

24. Fisher, Barbara E. Scott. "Go Ahead and Paint." *Christian Science Monitor Magazine,* January 5, 1946.

25. Grafly, Dorothy. "Primitive and Primitives." *American Artist,* October 1949.

26. Herbert, François. "Grandma Moses, 100 ans peintre." *Match* (Paris), December 10, 1960.

27. Kutner, Nanette. "Grandma Moses: Norman Rockwell Talks About His Neighbor." *McCall's,* October 1949.

28. Lansford, Alonzo. "Grandma Moses." *The Art Digest* (now *Arts*), May 15, 1947.

29. Lipman, Jean. "Fourth of July Art." *Cosmopolitan,* July 1956.

30. Roden, Max. "Die amerikanischen Primitiven." *Die schönen Künste* (Vienna), 1947.

31. Schoenberg, Harold C. "Grandma Moses—Portrait of the Artist at 99." *The New York Times Magazine,* September 6, 1959.

32. Seckler, Dorothy. "The Success of Mrs. Moses." *Art News,* May 1951.

33. Soby, James Thrall. "A Bucolic Past and a Giddy Jungle." *The Saturday Review of Literature,* November 4, 1950.

34. Sullivan, Frank. "An Afternoon with Grandma Moses." *The New York Times Magazine,* October 9, 1949.

35. Stahly, François. "Grandma Moses/Morris Hirshfield." *Graphis* (Zurich), Vol. 7, No. 35, 1951.

36. Thompson, Dorothy. "The World of Grandma Moses." *Ladies' Home Journal,* January 1957.

37. Waldinger, Ernst. "Die Geschichte eines amerikanischen Erfolges." *Annabelle* (Zurich), March 1947.

38. Woolf, S. J. "Grandma Moses, Who Began to Paint at 78." *The New York Times Magazine,* December 2, 1945.

List of Exhibitions

1939   October 18–November 18
Contemporary Unknown American Painters: Opening Exhibition of the Advisory Committee of the Museum of Modern Art
The Members' Rooms, The Museum of Modern Art, New York
Included 3 paintings by Grandma Moses
Catalogue: Introduction by Sidney Janis. 4 pp.

1940   October 9–31
What a Farm Wife Painted: Works by Anna Mary Moses
Galerie St. Etienne, New York
33 paintings, one worsted picture
Mimeographed list of the pictures

November 14–25
Auditorium, Gimbels, New York
50 paintings and worsted pictures

1941   January
Whyte Gallery, Washington, D.C.
One-man show of 26 paintings

May
New York State Art Show
Syracuse Museum of Fine Arts (now Everson Museum of Art)
Included 3 or more paintings by Grandma Moses
(*The Old Oaken Bucket* received the N.Y. State Prize)

June
A portion of the *New York State Art Show,* including at least one work by Grandma Moses
Grand Central Galleries, New York

1942   February 9–March 7
They Taught Themselves: American Primitive Painters of the 20th Century

Marie Harriman Gallery, New York
Included 3 paintings by Grandma Moses
Catalogue: *A Statement by André Breton.* 5 pp.

September
Munson–William Proctor Institute, Pine Camp (now Camp Drum), Watertown, New York
One-man show of 33 paintings and 7 worsted pictures

December 7–22
Anna Mary Robertson Moses: Loan Exhibition of Paintings
American British Art Center, New York
32 paintings
Catalogue: 4 pp.

1943   November
Grandma Moses
E. B. Crocker Art Gallery, Sacramento, Calif.
30 paintings

1943–44   *Self-Taught Painters*
Traveling Exhibition:
Everhart Museum, Scranton, Pa.
University of New Hampshire, Durham
Indiana University, Bloomington
Art Association of Richmond, Ind.
Smith Art Gallery, Springfield, Mass.
Included 3 paintings by Grandma Moses

1944   February
New Paintings by Grandma Moses–The Senior of the American Primitives
Galerie St. Etienne, New York
32 paintings

April 2–29
Grandma Moses–The Senior of the American Primitives

343

James Vigeveno Galleries, Los Angeles
21 paintings
Catalogue: 4 pp., illustrated

September 6–October 9
Syracuse Museum of Fine Arts (now Everson Museum of
Art)
One-man show of 23 paintings

December
Grandma Moses
Galerie St. Etienne, New York
36 paintings
4-page folder

1944–45 *Grandma Moses*
Traveling Exhibition:
Mt. Holyoke College, South Hadley, Mass.
Lawrence Art Museum, Williams College, Williamstown,
Mass.
Amherst College, Amherst, Mass.
Centennial Art Club, Nashville, Tenn.
Currier Gallery of Art, Manchester, N. H.
Whyte Gallery, Washington, D. C.
Montana State College, Dillon
20 paintings

Portrait of America
Metropolitan Museum of Art, New York
Exhibition of 150 paintings conducted by Artists-for-
Victory, Inc., presented in many leading museums in the
United States after the New York show
Included one painting by Grandma Moses

1945 May 1–31
*Grandma Moses: The Senior of American Primitives in
Her Initial San Francisco Showing*
Maxwell Galleries, San Francisco, Calif.

October 11–December 9
Painting in the United States, 1945

Carnegie Institute, Pittsburgh, Pa.
Included one painting by Grandma Moses
Catalogue

October 28–November 17
*Recent Paintings by the Senior of American Primitive
Painters: Grandma Moses*
James Vigeveno Galleries, Los Angeles, Calif.
30 paintings
Catalogue: 7 pp., illustrated

November 13–18
*Women's International Exposition: Woman's Life in
Peacetime*
Madison Square Garden, New York
One-man show

1945–46 *Grandma Moses*
Traveling Exhibition:
Utica Public Library, Utica, N.Y.
Norfolk Museum of Arts & Sciences, Norfolk, Va.
Pomona College, Claremont, Calif.
20 paintings

1946 February 25–March 23
Exhibition of Paintings by Grandma Moses
The American British Art Center, New York
44 paintings
Catalogue: 11 pp., illustrated

October 10–December 8
Painting in the United States, 1946
Carnegie Institute, Pittsburgh, Pa.
Included one painting by Grandma Moses
Illustrated catalogue

October 20–November 16
Recent Work by America's Beloved Grandma Moses
James Vigeveno Galleries, Los Angeles, Calif.
32 paintings
Catalogue: 4 pp., illustrated

1946–47 *Grandma Moses*
Traveling Exhibition:
Public Library, Manitowoc, Wis.
St. Paul Gallery and School of Art, St. Paul, Minn.
Texas Technological College Art Institute, Lubbock
Art Institute of Zanesville, Ohio
Cornell University College of Architecture, Ithaca, N.Y.
State Teachers' College, Lock Haven, Pa.
Marshall Field & Co., Chicago, Ill.
20 paintings

1947 May 17–June 14
Grandma Moses: Paintings
Galerie St. Etienne, New York
34 paintings
Catalogue: *How Do I Paint?* by Grandma Moses. 16 pp.,
illustrated

1947–48 *Grandma Moses*
Traveling Exhibition:
Rockford Art Association, Rockford, Ill.
Beloit College, Beloit, Wis.
State Art Gallery, Raleigh, N. C.
Cheltenham Township Art Center, Cheltenham, Pa.
Abilene Museum of Fine Arts, Hardin-Simmons Univer-
sity, Abilene, Tex.
Museum of Art, University of Kansas, Lawrence
Baltimore Museum of Art, Baltimore, Md.
Mattatuck Historical Society, Waterbury, Conn.
20 paintings

1948 May 25–June 12
Thirty Paintings by Grandma Moses
The American British Art Center, New York
Catalogue: Introduction by Archibald MacLeish. 8 pp.,
illustrated

September 20–through October
Grandma Moses
California Palace of the Legion of Honor, San Francisco
22 paintings

October 14–December 12
Painting in the United States, 1948
Carnegie Institute, Pittsburgh, Pa.
Included one painting by Grandma Moses
Illustrated catalogue

October 18–November 12
*Exhibition of Recent Paintings by the Senior of American
Primitive Painters, America's Beloved Grandma Moses*
James Vigeveno Galleries, Los Angeles, Calif.
34 paintings
Catalogue: 4 pp., illustrated

Thanksgiving–Christmas
Ten Years—Grandma Moses
Galerie St. Etienne, New York
42 paintings
Catalogue: *I Remember* by Grandma Moses (facsimile of
her handwritten manuscript). 16 pp., illustrated

1948–49 *Grandma Moses*
Traveling Exhibition:
Montgomery Museum of Fine Arts, Montgomery, Ala.
The Mint Museum of Art, Charlotte, N. C.
Brooks Memorial Art Gallery, Memphis, Tenn.
Monmouth College, Monmouth, Ill.
Grinnell College, Grinnell, Iowa
Charles A. Wustum Museum of Fine Arts, Racine, Wis.
20 paintings

1949 January 9–30
Art in the United States, 1949
Museum of Fine Arts of Houston, Tex.
Included 2 paintings by Grandma Moses
Catalogue: Introduction by James Chillman, Jr.

January 16–February 20
*Contemporary American Paintings: 61st Annual Exhibi-
tion*
John Herron Art Museum, Indianapolis, Ind.
Included one painting by Grandma Moses

May 8–31 (extended to June 9)
Paintings by Grandma Moses
The Phillips Gallery, Washington, D. C.
30 paintings

August 26–September 19
Exhibition of Paintings and Sculpture
Art Gallery of Toronto, Canada
Included one painting by Grandma Moses
Catalogue

October 3–22
First Boston Exhibition of Paintings by Grandma Moses
Robert C. Vose Galleries, Boston, Mass.
19 paintings

October 9–November 10
Grandma Moses: Honoring Her on Her 89th Birthday
Combined show with Camille Bombois
James Vigeveno Galleries, Los Angeles, Calif.
17 paintings
Catalogue: 8 pp., illustrated

October 13–December 11
Painting in the United States, 1949
Carnegie Institute, Pittsburgh, Pa.
Included one painting by Grandma Moses
Illustrated catalogue

November 6
St. Mark's Episcopal Church, Hoosick Falls, N.Y.
One-man show of 120 paintings and worsted pictures

1950 January 30–February 18
Selected Paintings by Grandma Moses
The American British Art Gallery, New York
20 paintings
Catalogue: Essay by Thomas Carr Howe, Jr. 4 pp.

September 7–October 15
Grandma Moses: Exhibition Arranged on the Occasion of Her 90th Birthday

Albany Institute of History and Art, Albany, N.Y.
55 paintings and additional worsted pictures
Catalogue: Foreword by Robert G. Wheeler, Introduction by Louis Bromfield. 24 pp., illustrated

October 19–December 21
Pittsburgh International Exhibition of Paintings
Carnegie Institute, Pittsburgh, Pa.
Included one painting by Grandma Moses
Illustrated catalogue

June–December
Grandma Moses: 50 Paintings
Traveling Exhibition under the auspices of the U.S. Information Service:
Neue Galerie, Vienna
Amerika Haus, Munich
Künstlerhaus, Salzburg
Kunsthalle, Berne
Gemeentemuseum, Amsterdam
United States Embassy, Paris
Illustrated catalogue published by each display center

December 10–January 15, 1951
Paintings by Grandma Moses
The Taft Museum, Cincinnati, Ohio
32 paintings
Catalogue

1951 March–April
Grandma Moses: Twenty-Five Masterpieces of Primitive Art
Galerie St. Etienne, New York
Catalogue: *My Tip-Up Table* by Grandma Moses; *About Grandma Moses* by Allen Eaton. Reviews and comments on the European Moses Exhibitions. 30 pp., illustrated

April 9–28
Grandma Moses: Sixty of Her Masterpieces
The Dayton Company, Minneapolis, Minn.
Catalogue: 12 pp., illustrated

May 6–13
An Exhibition of Paintings by Grandma Moses
Brooks Memorial Art Gallery, Memphis, Tenn.
27 paintings
Catalogue: 4 pp., illustrated

October 29–November 17
Second Boston Exhibition of Paintings by Grandma Moses
Robert C. Vose Galleries, Boston, Mass.
17 paintings
Catalogue: 4 pp., illustrated

Grandma Moses
Traveling Exhibition:
William Rockhill Nelson Gallery [now Nelson-Atkins Museum] of Art, Kansas City, Mo.
Joslyn Art Museum, Omaha, Neb.
Des Moines Art Center, Des Moines, Iowa
Philbrook Art Center, Tulsa, Okla.
26 paintings

1952 January 11–March 2
Paintings by Grandma Moses
Art Gallery of Toronto, Canada

March 5–21
Twenty Famous Paintings by Grandma Moses
The American British Art Gallery, New York
Catalogue: 3 pp.

April
A Group of Contemporary American Natural Painters
Galerie St. Etienne, New York
Included one painting by Grandma Moses
Illustrated catalogue

May–June
Grandma Moses
Syracuse Museum of Fine Arts (now Everson Museum of Art), Syracuse, N.Y.
23 paintings
Catalogue: 3 pp.

October
Grandma Moses
The Memorial Art Gallery, Rochester, N.Y.
About 30 paintings, 2 worsted pictures

1952–53 *Grandma Moses*
Traveling Exhibition:
Cedar Rapids Art Association, Cedar Rapids, Iowa
Davenport Municipal Art Gallery, Davenport, Iowa
Southwest Missouri State College, Springfield
Laguna Beach Art Association, Laguna Beach, Calif.
Saint-Gaudens Memorial, Windsor, Vt.
Wilmington Society of Fine Arts, Wilmington, Del.
Museum of Fine Arts of Houston, Tex.
The Isaac Delgado Museum of Art, New Orleans, La.
M. H. DeYoung Memorial Museum, San Francisco, Calif.
Purdue University, Lafayette, Ind.
Indiana State Teachers' College, Terre Haute
Birmingham Art Museum, Birmingham, Ala.
Florida Gulf Coast Art Center, Clearwater
Lyman Allyn Museum, New London, Conn.
24 paintings

1953 February–March
Grandma Moses
Santa Barbara Museum of Art, Santa Barbara, Calif.

March 14–22
Art Exhibition: Grandma Moses
Part of the California International Flower Show under the auspices of the Los Angeles Municipal Art Commission
Hollywood Park, Inglewood, Calif.
57 paintings

April–May
"A Grandma Moses Album": Exhibition of Recent Paintings
Galerie St. Etienne, New York
26 paintings
Catalogue: 24 pp., illustrated

December 18–early September 1954
American Painting, 1754–1954

347

Metropolitan Museum of Art, New York
Included one painting by Grandma Moses

1954 February 14–28
Grandma Moses
Buffalo Historical Society, Buffalo, N.Y.
29 paintings

May 10–June 17
Grandma Moses
James Vigeveno Galleries, Los Angeles, Calif.
Illustrated folder: 4 pp.

October 19–November 21
Man and His Years
The Baltimore Museum of Art, Baltimore, Md.
Included 2 paintings by Grandma Moses
Illustrated catalogue

1954–55 *American Primitive Paintings from the 17th Century to
the Present*
Circulated in Europe by the Smithsonian Institution for
the U.S. Information Agency:
Kunstmuseum, Lucerne, Switzerland
Oesterreichisches Museum für angewandte Kunst, Vienna
Amerika Haus, Munich
Städtisches Museum, Dortmund
Liljevalchs Konsthall, Stockholm
Kunstnernes Hus, Oslo
City Art Gallery, Manchester
Whitechapel Gallery, London
Trier Museum, Trier, Germany
Included 5 paintings by Grandma Moses
Extensive illustrated catalogue published by each display
center

American Natural Painters
Circulated by the Smithsonian Institution:
Montana State College, Bozeman
Tacoma Art League, Tacoma, Wash.
Eastern Washington State Historical Society, Spokane
Art Institute of Zanesville, Ohio
Philbrook Art Center, Tulsa, Okla.

Historical Society of Montana, Helena
Miami Beach Art Center, Miami Beach, Fla.
George Thomas Hunter Gallery of Art, Chattanooga,
Tenn.
Columbia Museum of Art, Columbia, S.C.
Bloomington Normal Art Association, Bloomington, Ill.
Currier Gallery of Art, Manchester, N.H.
Albany Institute of History and Art, Albany, N.Y.
Included 3 paintings by Grandma Moses

1954–56 *Grandma Moses*
Traveling Exhibition:
Johnson Humrickhouse Memorial Museum, Coshocton,
Ohio
Rockford Art Association, Rockford, Ill.
Davenport Municipal Art Gallery, Davenport, Iowa
Art Museum, Seattle, Wash.
Tweed Gallery, University of Minnesota, Duluth
Oakland Municipal Art Museum, Oakland, Calif.
Fine Arts Gallery of San Diego, Calif.
Rosicrucian Egyptian Oriental Museum, San Jose, Calif.
Arnot Art Gallery, Elmira, N.Y.
Kaufmann Department Stores, Pittsburgh, Pa.
Blanden Memorial Art Gallery, Fort Dodge, Iowa
St. Paul Gallery and School of Art, St. Paul, Minn.
Florida Gulf Coast Art Center, Clearwater
Greenville Art Association, Greenville, S.C.
20 paintings

1955 November 29–through December
A Tribute to Grandma Moses
Loan exhibition of paintings presented by Thomas J.
Watson and the Fine Arts Department of the International
Business Machines Corp.
IBM Gallery, New York
42 paintings
Catalogue: Tribute by Thomas J. Watson; *Work and
Happiness* and *My Tip-Up Table* by Grandma Moses
32 pp., illustrated

1955–57 *Grandma Moses*
Traveling Exhibition:
Paula-Becker-Modersohn-Haus, Bremen, Germany

Württembergischer Kunstverein, Stuttgart
Kölnischer Kunstverein, Cologne
Galerie Commeter, Hamburg
The Matthiesen Gallery, London
Kunstnernes Hus, Oslo
The Art Gallery, Aberdeen
Royal Scottish Academy Galleries, Edinburgh
The Art Gallery, Glasgow
35 paintings
Extensive illustrated catalogue published by each display center

1957   May 6–June 4
Grandma Moses: New York Showing of an Exhibition of Paintings Presented in Europe During 1955–1957
Galerie St. Etienne, New York
33 paintings
Catalogue: *Grandma Moses* by Hubertus, Prince zu Löwenstein; excerpts from European reviews. 24 pp., illustrated

August 31–October 13
Grandma Moses: A Selection of Thirty-Four Paintings from Public and Private Collections
California Palace of the Legion of Honor, San Francisco
Catalogue: 8 pp., illustrated

1958   October 4–November 2
Famous Paintings and Famous Painters
Dallas Museum of Fine Arts, Dallas, Texas
Included 5 paintings by Grandma Moses
Illustrated catalogue

1958–59   *American Primitive Paintings*
Circulated by the Smithsonian Institution:
Parrish Art Museum, Southampton, N. Y.
Centenary College of Louisiana, Shreveport
The John Herron Art Institute, Indianapolis, Ind.
G. T. Hunter Gallery of Art, Chattanooga, Tenn.
Birmingham Museum of Art, Birmingham, Ala.
Davenport Municipal Art Gallery, Davenport, Iowa
Fine Arts Gallery of San Diego, Calif.
J. B. Speed Art Museum, Louisville, Ky.

Included 12 paintings by Grandma Moses
Catalogue: Introduction by Otto Kallir. Biographical notes on 20 artists. 31 pp., illustrated

1960   July 30–August 14
Grandma Moses: 100th Birthday Loan Exhibition
Southern Vermont Art Center, Manchester
20 paintings

Fall
100th Birthday Celebration Exhibition
Webb Art Gallery, The Shelburne Museum, Shelburne, Vt.
17 paintings
Catalogue: Museum Pamphlet Series No. 5

September 12–October 6
My Life's History: A Loan Exhibition of Paintings by Grandma Moses
Assembled on the occasion of the artist's hundredth birthday
IBM Gallery of Arts and Sciences, New York
44 paintings and one worsted picture
Catalogue: Tributes by Governor Nelson A. Rockefeller, Otto Kallir, Jean Cassou. Autobiographical notes accompany the pictures. All works illustrated. 64 pp.
This exhibition, with the same catalogue, was subsequently circulated by the Smithsonian Institution, as follows:

1960–61   Marquette University, Milwaukee, Wis.
Jewish Community Center, Washington, D.C.
G. T. Hunter Gallery of Art, Chattanooga, Tenn.
Louisiana State Art Commission, Baton Rouge
Charles and Emma Frye Museum, Seattle, Wash.
Laguna Beach Art Association, Laguna Beach, Fla.
Fort Worth Art Center, Fort Worth, Tex.
Winnipeg Art Gallery, Winnipeg, Canada
McCormick Place Art Gallery, Chicago, Ill.

1961   September 7–15
Original Paintings Illustrating The Grandma Moses Story Book, *to Be Published by Random House in October 1961*
Galerie St. Etienne, New York
24 paintings

1962   April 28–29
Grandma Moses' Original Paintings
Hoosick Falls Central School, Hoosick Falls, N. Y.
95 paintings and worsted pictures

November–December
Grandma Moses: Memorial Exhibition
Galerie St. Etienne, New York
54 paintings
Catalogue: *On the Style and Technique of Grandma Moses* by Otto Kallir. 32 pp., illustrated

1962–64   *A Life's History in Paintings*
Traveling Exhibition:
Künstlerhaus, Vienna
Musée d'Art Moderne de la Ville de Paris
Paula-Becker-Modersohn-Haus, Bremen, Germany
Galerie Commeter, Hamburg
Kunstkreis, Hameln
Vonderau-Museum, Fulda
Kunsthalle, Düsseldorf
Kunstverein, Darmstadt
Städtische Kunsthalle, Mannheim
Amerika Haus, Berlin
Amerika Haus, Frankfort
Kunstnerforbundet, Oslo
Svenska Handelsbanken, Stockholm
Galerie Hoerhammer, Helsinki
Svenska Handelsbanken, Gothenburg, Sweden
Louisiana Art Museum, Copenhagen
The Pushkin Museum, Moscow
39 paintings and one worsted picture
Extensive illustrated catalogue published by each display center

1963   February
American Traditionalists of the 20th Century
Columbus Museum of Arts and Crafts, Columbus, Ga.
Included one painting by Grandma Moses
Illustrated catalogue

June 29–October 22
The Home Country of Grandma Moses: Twenty of Her Best Paintings of Local Areas and Activities
The Bennington Museum, Bennington, Vt.
Folder: 4 pp.

December 5–8
The Original Paintings of "The Night Before Christmas" by Grandma Moses
Rensselaer County Historical Society, Troy, N.Y.
10 paintings
Folder: 4 pp.

1964   July–September
Die Welt der naiven Malerei
Salzburger Residenzgalerie, Salzburg
Included 4 paintings by Grandma Moses

July–October
Le Monde des Naïfs
Museum Boymans–Van Beuningen, Rotterdam
Musée National d'Art Moderne, Paris
Included 2 paintings by Grandma Moses
Catalogue: Essays by Jean Cassou, J. C. Ebbinge Wubben, and Oto Bihalji-Merin. Biographical notes. All works illustrated. Unpaged

1964–65   December 14–January 9, 1965
My Life's History: Paintings by Grandma Moses
Forty paintings which toured seventeen European cities; in addition, 25 pictures never previously shown
Hammer Galleries, New York
Catalogue of 40 paintings, all illustrated, 64 pp.; catalogue of 25 paintings, all illustrated, 8 pp.

1965   April 2–May 16
Women Artists of America
The Newark Museum, Newark, N. J.
Included 1 painting by Grandma Moses
Catalogue: 32 pp., illustrated

June 18–October 18
Paintings by Grandma Moses: Twenty of Her Best Paintings of Local Areas and Activities
The Bennington Museum, Bennington, Vt.
Catalogue: 4 pp.

July 17–31
Grandma Moses Art Festival: A Loan Exhibition
The Buck Hill Art Association, Buck Hill Falls, Pa.
35 paintings
Catalogue: 35 pp., illustrated

December 7–24
Forty Grandma Moses Paintings Never Shown Before
Hammer Galleries, New York
Catalogue: 12 pp., illustrated

1966 July 26–October 2
1st Triennial of Insitic Art
Slovenska Národná Galéria, Bratislava, Czechoslovakia
Included 11 paintings by Grandma Moses
Extensive illustrated catalogue

December 6–24
The World of Grandma Moses
Hammer Galleries, New York
25 paintings
Catalogue: 8 pp., illustrated

1966–72 *An Exhibition of Mementos*
Grandma Moses Schoolhouse, Eagle Bridge, N.Y.
Folder: 4 pp.

1967 June 9–October 24
Paintings by Grandma Moses: Twenty-Three of Her Best Paintings of Local Areas and Activities
The Bennington Museum, Bennington, Vt.

December 5–30
Paintings by Grandma Moses
Hammer Galleries, New York
28 paintings
Catalogue: *An Appreciation* by John Canaday. 12 pp., illustrated

December 10–30
The Art of Grandma Moses
The Stamford Museum and Nature Center, Stamford, Conn.
12 paintings

1968 May 10–31
A Grandma Moses Album
Maxwell Galleries, San Francisco, Calif.
Illustrated catalogue

1968–72 May 1968–December 1972
The Grandma Moses Gallery
The Bennington Museum, Bennington, Vermont
81 paintings, the "tip-up" table, documentary material on the artist's life and career

1969 February 20–March 30
Art and Life of Grandma Moses
Paintings from American museums and private collections; in addition, *The Grandma Moses Gallery* of the Bennington Museum
The Gallery of Modern Art, New York (now New York Cultural Center)
151 paintings, the "tip-up" table, documentary material
Catalogue: Edited by Otto Kallir. Lists pictures and documentary material. Reprints previously published writings by and about Grandma Moses. 168 pp., illustrated. Published by The Gallery of Modern Art, New York; A. S. Barnes & Co., South Brunswick and New York; Thomas Yoseloff, Ltd., London

December 2–30
Grandma Moses
Hammer Galleries, New York
43 paintings
Catalogue: 8 pp., illustrated

1971 December 6–31
Grandma Moses
Hammer Galleries, New York
28 paintings
Catalogue: 12 pp., illustrated

351

1972   February 22–March 11
        Four American Primitives: Edward Hicks, John Kane,
        Anna Mary Robertson Moses, Horace Pippin
        ACA Galleries, New York
        Included 15 paintings by Grandma Moses
        Catalogue: Essays by Andrew J. Crispo, Leon Anthony
        Arkus, Otto Kallir, and Selden Rodman. 64 pp., illustrated

1972   April 21–May 7
        Paintings by Grandma Moses
        Old Capitol Museum, Jackson, Miss.
        15 paintings
        Catalogue: 4 pp.

List of Plates

*Colorplates are marked with an asterisk.**

355

Acknowledgments

Special mention should be made of those who very early recognized the unique quality of Grandma Moses's art and helped to make her known: Louis J. Caldor, the artist's "discoverer," Sidney Janis, Allen Eaton, Thomas J. Watson, and Ala Story.

My cordial thanks go to the members of Grandma Moses's family for making available over the years much documentary material, particularly records and letters which were used in the preparation of this book: Winona R. Fisher, Loyd R. Moses, Forrest K. Moses, Hugh W. Moses, Dorothy Moses, Fred E. Robertson, and Mrs. B. Russell Robertson.

Grateful acknowledgment is made to the museums which furnished photographs and data on paintings: The Phillips Collection, Washington, D.C.; The Metropolitan Museum of Art, New York; Museum of Art, Rhode Island School of Design, Providence; Memorial Art Gallery of the University of Rochester, N.Y.; New York State Historical Association, Cooperstown; The Shelburne Museum, Shelburne, Vt.; The Bennington Museum, Bennington, Vt.; The Fine Arts Gallery of San Diego, Calif.

Special appreciation is expressed to Dr. Armand Hammer, Victor Hammer, and his staff for their valuable assistance, as well as to hundreds of collectors who have supplied information on the Grandma Moses works in their possession.